SCIENCE CURRICULUM RESOURCE HANDBOOK

A Practical Guide for K-12 Science Curriculum

KRAUS INTERNATIONAL PUBLICATIONS
A Division of The Kraus Organization Limited
Millwood, New York

Consulting editors:

Dennis W. Cheek
*Coordinator, Curriculum Development, New York Science,
Technology and Society Education Project,
New York State Education Department, Albany, New York*

Robert Briggs
*Science Supervisor,
Office of Public Instruction, Helena, Montana*

Robert E. Yager
*Professor of Science Education
University of Iowa, Iowa City, Iowa*

First Printing 1992
Printed in the United States of America

Library of Congress Cataloging-in-Publication Data

Science curriculum resources handbook : a practical
  guide for K–12 science curriculum.
    p.   cm.
  Includes bibliographical references and index.
  ISBN 0-527-20806-X : $19.95
  1. Science—Study and teaching (Elementary)—United
States—Handbooks, manuals, etc. 2. Science—Study and
teaching (Secondary)—United States—Handbooks, manuals,
etc.
I. Kraus International Publications
LB1585.3.S3 1992
507.1'273—dc20   92-28471

Printed on recycled paper

CONTENTS

Publisher's Foreword v

Series Introduction 1
    P. Bruce Uhrmacher • University of Denver

PART I: CURRICULUM DEVELOPMENT IN THE SUBJECT

1 • Trends and Issues in Science Curriculum 16
    Alan J. McCormack • San Diego State University

2 • Curriculum Guides: Process and Design 42
    Jurg Jenzer • Lamoille North Supervisory Union

3 • Funding Curriculum Projects 61

4 • Topics in the Science Curriculum, Grades K-12 72
    Gary Nakagiri • San Mateo County Office of Education

5 • State-Level Curriculum Guidelines: An Analysis 91
    Mary Nalbandian • Chicago Public Schools

6 • State-Level Curriculum Guidelines: A Listing 116

PART II: CURRICULUM GUIDELINES AND SUPPLEMENTARY MATERIALS

7 • Recommended Curriculum Guides 126
    David L. Haury • Ohio State University

8 • Curriculum Guide Reprint 149

9 • Source List for Ideas and Materials 221

    by Bonnie B. Barr • State University of New York, College at Cortland

10 • Children's Trade Books in Science 239

    Antoine B. Gosioco • Detroit Public Schools

PART III: TEXTBOOKS, CLASSROOM MATERIALS, AND OTHER RESOURCES

11 • Curriculum Material Producers 255

12 • Statewide Textbook Adoption 274

13 • Index to Reviews of Educational Materials 325

14 • Kraus Curriculum Development Library Customers 363

Index 374

PUBLISHER'S FOREWORD

T HE *Science Curriculum Resource Handbook* is one of a new series of practical references for curriculum developers, education faculty, veteran teachers, and student teachers. The handbook is designed to provide basic information on the background of the science curriculum, as well as current information on publications, standards, and special materials for K-12 science. Think of this handbook as the first place to look when you are revising or developing your science curriculum—or if you need basic resource information on science any time of the year.

This handbook does not seek to prescribe any particular form of curriculum, nor does it follow any set of standards or guidelines. Instead, the book provides a general grounding in the science curriculum, so that you can use this information and then proceed in the direction best suited for your budget, your school, and your district. What this handbook gives you is a sense of the numerous *options* that are available—it is up to you to use the information to develop the appropriate curriculum or program for your situation.

How To Use This Handbook

There are various ways to use this resource handbook. If you are revising or creating a science curriculum, you should read the Introduction (for an overall sense of the different philosophies of curriculum—and how this will affect the program you develop), chapter 1 (for basic background on the trends and research in K-12 science), and chapter 2 (for a how-to guide to developing curriculum materials). With this background, you can go through the other chapters for the specific information you need—

ranging from topics to be covered at various grade levels (chapter 4), to state requirements (chapter 5), to publishers and producers (chapter 11).

If you know what type of information you need, then you should check the Table of Contents for the most appropriate chapter, or check the Index to see where this material is covered. For instance:

1. If you are looking for materials for use in science fairs, lab projects, and so on, turn to chapter 9.
2. If you are looking for a new textbook or new supplementary material (book, video, or software), turn to chapter 11.
3. If you need to contact state departments of education for curriculum documents, check the list provided in chapter 6.

What's in the Handbook

The *Introduction* provides an overview of the ideologies and philosophies that have affected American curriculum through the years. This section will acquaint you with the various ideologies, so that you can determine whether your school is following one such philosophy (or a combination), and how this might influence the development of your curriculum. The Introduction is generic by design, since these ideologies pertain to all subject areas.

Chapter 1 provides an overview of *Trends and Issues* in science curriculum. This chapter discusses the development of present-day curriculum, and looks at the directions science curriculum is taking. The major research works are cited, so that you can get more detailed information on particular topics.

Chapter 2 is a step-by-step description of *Curriculum Process and Design.* It is meant to be a practical guide to creating or revising science curriculum guides. This chapter is also somewhat generic, but includes examples specific to science.

Chapter 3 gives information on *Grants for Program Development.*

Chapter 4 outlines the *Important Topics* in K-12 Science. This is not meant to be a pattern to follow, but instead is a reflection of what most schools cover and what current research recommends.

Chapter 5 analyzes the *State Departments of Education Guidelines and Frameworks.* The curriculum materials are described, and the analysis includes the similarities among states and within regions, plus differences and gaps in coverage.

Chapter 6 supplements the previous chapter by listing *State Curriculum Publications* with addresses of state departments of education.

Chapter 7 is an annotated list of *Recommended Curriculum Guides* for science.

Chapter 8 reprints a science curriculum guide, to use as an example in creating your own curriculum materials.

Chapter 9 is a *Source List for Ideas and Materials* in science. This list provides the names and addresses of organizations that sponsor special programs, as well as publications that provide ideas for these projects.

Chapter 10 gives a sampling of *Children's Trade Books* that can be used as supplementary texts in science classrooms. This chapter also includes many of the lists and references that give more information on these books.

Chapter 11 is an annotated list of *Publishers and Producers* of textbooks, videos, software, and other materials for use in K-12 science.

Chapter 12 describes *Statewide Textbook Adoption,* with lists of the textbooks adopted by the states that have such an adoption policy.

Chapter 13 is an *Index to Reviews* of science textbooks and supplementary materials. Since these items are reviewed in a wide variety of publications, we have assembled the citations of appropriate reviews in index form (cited by title, author, publisher/distributor, subject, and grade level).

Chapter 14 provides a list of Kraus Curriculum Development Library (KCDL) subscribers; KCDL is a good source for models of curriculum guides in all K-12 subject areas.

Acknowledgements

The content of this handbook is based on numerous meetings and discussions with educators and curriculum specialists across the country. Our thanks go to the curriculum supervisors in schools across the United States; the faculty at education departments in the colleges and universities we visited; and curriculum librarians. Special thanks go to the members of the Curriculum Materials Committee (CMC) and the Problems of Access and Control of Education Materials (PACEM) committee of the Association of College and Research Libraries' Education and Behavioral Science Section (ACRL/EBSS). Our meetings with the committees during American Library Association conferences continue to provide Kraus with valuable ideas for the handbooks and for future curriculum projects.

We also acknowledge with thanks the assistance of Anne Isner, Marjorie Miller Kaplan, Carrie Lesh, Paula Martin, Barbara Meyers, Jean Russo, and the indexers at AEIOU, Inc.

Your Feedback

We have a final request of our readers. At the back of this handbook is a user survey that asks your opinions about the book, its coverage, and its contents. Once you have used this book, please fill out the questionnaire—it should only take a minute or so—and mail it back to us. If the form has already been removed, please just send us a letter with your opinions. We want to keep improving this new series of handbooks, and we can only do this with your help! Please send questionnaires or other responses to:

Kraus International Publications
358 Saw Mill River Road
Millwood, NY 10546-1035
(914) 762-2200 / (800) 223-8323
Fax: (914) 762-1195

SERIES INTRODUCTION

P. Bruce Uhrmacher

Assistant Professor of Education
School of Education, University of Denver, Denver, Colorado

WHEN I travel by airplane and desire conversation, I inform the person sitting next to me that I'm in education. Everyone has an opinion about education. I hear stories about teachers (both good and bad), subject matter ("The problem with the new math is . . ."), and tests ("I should have gotten an A on that exam in seventh grade"). Many people want to tell me about the problems with education today ("Schools aren't what they used to be"). Few people are apathetic about schooling. When I do not wish to be disturbed in flight, however, I avoid admitting I'm in education. "So, what do you do?" someone trying to draw me out asks. I reply matter-of-factly, "I'm a curriculum theorist." Unless they persist, my retort usually signals the end of the dialogue. Unlike the job titles *farmer, stockbroker,* or even *computer analyst,* for many people *curriculum theorist* conjures few images.

What do curriculum theorists do? The answer to this question depends in part on the way curriculum theorists conceive of curriculum and theory. The term *curriculum* has over 150 definitions. With so many different ways of thinking about it, no wonder many curriculum theorists see their task differently. In this introduction, I point out that curriculum theorists have a useful function to serve, despite the fact that we can't agree on what to do. In short, like economists who analyze trends and make recommendations about the economy (and, incidentally, who also

agree on very little), curriculum theorists generate a constructive dialogue about curriculum decisions and practices. Although curricularists originally fought over the word *curriculum,* trying to achieve conceptual clarity in order to eliminate the various differences, in time educators recognized that the fight over the term was unproductive (Zais 1976, 93). However, the problem was not simply an academic disagreement. Instead, curricularists focused on different aspects of the educational enterprise. At stake in the definition of curriculum was a conceptual framework that included the nature of the role of the curricularist and the relationships among students, teachers, subject matter, and educational environments. Today, most curricularists place adjectives before the term to specify what type of curriculum they're discussing. Thus, one often reads about the intended, the operational, the hidden, the explicit, the implicit, the enacted, the delivered, the experienced, the received, and the null curriculum (see glossary at the end of this chapter). Distinctions also can be made with regard to curricularist, curriculum planner, curriculum worker, and curriculum specialist. I use the terms *curricularist* and *curriculum theorist* to refer to individuals, usually at the college level, who worry about issues regarding curriculum theory. I use the other terms to refer to people who actually take part in the planning or the implementation of curriculum in schools.

In order to trace the development that has

brought the field of curriculum to its present state, I will begin with a brief overview of the progression of curriculum development in the United States. First, I examine issues facing the Committee of Ten, a group of educators who convened in 1892 to draft a major document regarding what schools should teach. Next, I focus on the perennial question of who should decide what schools teach. Curriculum was not a field of study until the 1920s. How were curriculum decisions made before there were curriculum specialists? How did curriculum become a field of study? We learn that the profession began, in part, as a scientific endeavor; whether the field should still be seen as a scientific one is a question of debate. Finally, I provide a conceptual framework that examines six curriculum "ideologies" (Eisner 1992). By understanding these ideologies, educators will discern the assumptions underlying various conceptions of curriculum. Then they should be able to decide which ideology they wish to pursue and to recognize its educational implications.

What Should Schools Teach?

In the nineteenth century, curriculum usually meant "the course of study," and what many educators worried about was what schools should teach. Under the theoretical influence of "mental discipline" (derived from the ideas of faculty psychologists), many educators believed that certain subjects strengthened the brain, much like certain exercises strengthened body muscles. Greek, Latin, and mathematics were important because they were difficult subjects and thus, presumably, exercised the brain. By the 1890s, however, with the great influx of Italian, Irish, Jewish, and Russian immigrants, and with the steady increase of students attending secondary schools, a concern grew over the relevance and value of such subjects as Greek and Latin. Why should German or French be any less worthy than Greek or Latin? In addition, students and parents raised further questions regarding the merits of vocational education. They wanted curricula that met their more practical needs.

While parents pressed for their concerns, secondary school principals worried about preparing students for college, since colleges had different entrance requirements. In 1892 the National Education Association (NEA) appointed the Committee of Ten to remedy this

problem. Headed by Charles W. Eliot, president of Harvard University, the committee debated and evaluated the extent to which a single curriculum could work for a large number of students who came from many different backgrounds with many different needs. In its final report, the committee suggested that colleges consider of equal value and accept students who attended not only the classical curriculum program, but also the Latin scientific, the modern language, and the English programs.

By eliminating the requirement of Greek for two of the programs and by reducing the number of required Latin courses, the committee broke with the traditional nineteenth-century curriculum to some degree. Yet, they were alert to the possibility that different kinds of curriculum programs taught in different ways could lead to a stratified society. Eliot had argued that the European system of classifying children into "future peasants, mechanics, trades-people, merchants, and professional people" was unacceptable in a democratic society (Tanner and Tanner 1975, 186). The committee believed all should have the opportunity for further studies under a "rational humanist" orientation to curriculum, a viewpoint that prizes the power of reason and the relevance and importance of learning about the best that Western culture has to offer.

The committee's report met with mixed reviews when it came out. One of its foremost opponents was G. Stanley Hall, a "developmentalist," who argued that the "natural order of development in the child was the most significant and scientifically defensible basis for determining what should be taught" (Kliebard 1986, 13). According to Hall, who had scientifically observed children's behavior at various stages of development, the committee did not take into account children's wide-ranging capabilities, and it promulgated a college-bound curriculum for everyone, even though many high school students would not go to college. Rather than approaching curriculum as the pursuit of a standard academic experience for all students, Hall and other developmentalists believed that knowledge of human development could contribute to creating a curriculum in harmony with the child's stage of interest and needs.

Thus far I have indicated two orientations to curriculum: the rational humanist and the developmentalist. We should understand, however, that at any given time a number of interest groups struggle for power over the curriculum. Historian Herbert Kliebard observes:

> We do not find a monolithic supremacy exercised by one interest group; rather we find different interest groups competing for dominance over the curriculum and, at different times, achieving some measure of control depending on local as well as general social conditions. Each of these interest groups, then, represents a force for a different selection of knowledge and values from the culture and hence a kind of lobby for a different curriculum. (Kliebard 1986, 8)

Who Should Decide What Schools Teach?

Thinking about curriculum dates back in Western culture to at least the ancient Greeks. Plato and Aristotle, as well as Cicero, Plutarch, and Rousseau, all thought about curriculum matters in that they debated the questions of what should be taught to whom, in what way, and for what purposes. But it wasn't until 1918 that curriculum work was placed in the professional domain with the publication of *The Curriculum* by Franklin Bobbitt, a professor at the University of Chicago. Although supervisors and administrators had written courses of study on a piecemeal basis, "Professor Bobbitt took the major step of dealing with the curriculum in all subjects and grades on a unified and comprehensive basis" (Gress 1978, 27). The term *curriculum theory* came into use in the 1920s, and the first department of curriculum was founded at Teachers College, Columbia University, in 1937. Of course, the question arises: If curricularists (a.k.a. curriculum specialists, curriculum theorists, and curriculum workers) were not making decisions about what should be taught in schools prior to the 1920s, then who was?

As we have seen, national commissions made some of the curricular decisions. The NEA appointed the Committee of Ten to address college–high school articulation in 1892 and the Committee of Fifteen to address elementary school curriculum in 1895. In the early 1900s the NEA appointed another committee to develop fundamental principles for the reorganization of secondary education. Thus, university professors, school superintendents, and teachers made some curricular decisions as they acted in the role of acknowledged authorities on national commis-

sions.

Along with commissions, forces such as tradition have shaped the curriculum. One long-time student of curriculum, Philip Jackson, observes:

> One reason why certain subjects remain in the curriculum is simply that they have been there for such a long time. Indeed, some portions of the curriculum have been in place for so long that the question of how they got there or who decided to put them there in the first place has no answer, or at least not one that anyone except a historian would be able to give. As far as most people are concerned, they have just "always" been there, or so it seems. (Jackson 1992, 22)

Jackson also notes here that subjects such as the three R's are so "obviously useful that they need no further justification"—or, at least, so it seems.

Texts and published materials have also been factors in shaping the curriculum. Whether it was the old *McGuffey Readers* or the modern text-books found in almost any classroom in the United States, these books have influenced the curriculum by virtue of their content and their widespread use. According to some estimates, text materials dominate 75 percent of the time elementary and secondary students are in class-rooms and 90 percent of their time on homework (Apple 1986, 85). Textbook writers are de facto curriculum specialists.

National Commission committees, tradition, textbooks, instructional materials, and the influence from numerous philosophers (e.g., Herbart and Dewey) were focal in deciding what schools should teach. Of course, parents, state boards of education, and teachers had their own convictions as to what should be in the curriculum. However, as the United States moved toward urbanization (30 percent of 63 million lived in cities in 1890; over 50 percent of 106 million lived in cities in 1920 [Cremin 1977, 93]), new factors influenced schooling. In particular, the industrial and scientific revolutions commingled in the minds of some to produce new ways of thinking about work. Franklin Bobbitt applied these new ideas to education. Influenced by Frederick Winslow Taylor, the father of the scientific management movement, Bobbitt assumed that the kinds of accomplishments that had been made in business and industry could be made in education. What was needed was the application of scientific principles to curriculum.

Briefly, Bobbitt believed that "educational engineers" or "curriculum-discoverers," as he called them, could make curriculum by surveying the array of life's endeavors and by grouping this broad range of human experience into major fields. Bobbitt wrote:

> The curriculum-discoverer will first be an analyst of human nature and of human affairs. . . . His first task . . . is to discover the total range of habits, skills, abilities, forms of thought . . . etc., that its members need for the effective performance of their vocational labors; likewise the total range needed for their civic activities; their health activities; their recreations, their language; their parental, religious, and general social activities. The program of analysis will be no narrow one. It will be as wide as life itself. (Bobbitt 1918, 43)

Thus, according to Bobbitt, curriculum workers would articulate educational goals by examining the array of life's activities. Next, in the same way one can analyze the tasks involved in making a tangible object and eliminate waste in producing it, Bobbitt believed one could streamline education by task analysis, by forming objectives for each task, and by teaching skills as discrete units.

Bobbitt's push for the professionalization of curriculum did not replace other factors so much as it added a new dimension. By arguing that schools needed stated objectives and that curricularists should be chosen for the task since they were trained in the science of curriculum, Bobbitt opened up a new line of work. He and his students would be of direct help to practitioners because they would know how to proceed scientifically (analyze the range of human experience, divide it into activities, create objectives) in the making of curriculum, and this knowledge gave curricularists authority and power. The world was rapidly changing in communications, in agriculture, in industry, and most of all in medicine. Who could argue with the benefits of science?

If Franklin Bobbitt created the field of professional curriculum activities, Ralph Tyler defined it. In his short monograph, *Basic Principles of Curriculum and Instruction* (1949), Tyler offered a way of viewing educational institutions. He began his book by asking four fundamental questions that he believed must be answered in developing curriculum:

1. What educational purposes should the school seek to attain?
2. What educational experiences can be provided that are likely to attain those purposes?
3. How can these educational experiences be effectively organized?
4. How can we determine whether these purposes are being attained? (Tyler 1949, 1)

Tyler devoted one chapter to each question. Unlike some curricularists, Tyler did not say what purposes a school should seek to attain. He recognized that a school in rural Idaho has different needs from an urban one in Boston. Rather, Tyler suggested that schools themselves determine their own purposes from three sources: studies of the learners themselves, studies of contemporary life, and studies from subject matter specialists.

Tyler, like Bobbitt before him, wished to bring order to the complex field of education. Although there are differences between the two men, both believed there was work to be done by professional curricularists. Both men trained students in the field of curriculum, and both believed in the liberal ideals of rationality and progress. Curricularist Decker Walker summarizes the tradition that Bobbitt and Tyler started as follows:

> Since Bobbitt's day, planning by objectives (PBO) had developed into a family of widely used approaches to curriculum improvement. As a method of curriculum materials design, PBO focuses early attention on developing precise statements of the objectives to be sought. If the process is to be fully scientific, the selection of objectives must be rationally justifiable and not arbitrary. (Walker 1990, 469)

While Bobbitt and Tyler taught students how to become professional curricularists and encouraged them to conduct research, to write, and to attain university positions, differences of opinion on what curricularists should be doing soon mounted. At issue was not only the utility of scientific curriculum making, but also the specific endeavors many curricularists pursued.

A Framework for Thinking about Curriculum

Tyler produced a seminal work that provided curriculum workers with a way of thinking about curriculum. While some elaborated on his ideas (Taba 1962), others wondered whether indeed Tyler provided the best questions for curricularists to think about. During the 1970s, numerous educators began to seek other ways of thinking about curriculum work. William Pinar, for example, asked, "Are Tyler's questions . . . no longer pertinent or possible? Are they simply cul-de-sacs?" (Pinar 1975, 397). Reconceptualizing the term *curriculum* (race course) from the verb of the Latin root, *currere* (to run a race), Pinar goes on to argue:

> The questions of *currere* are not Tyler's; they are ones like these: Why do I identify with Mrs. Dalloway and not with Mrs. Brown? What psychic dark spots does the one light, and what is the nature of "dark spots," and "light spots"? Why do I read Lessing and not Murdoch? Why do I read such works at all? Why not biology or ecology? Why are some drawn to the study of literature, some to physics, and some to law? (402)

More will be said about Pinar's work later. My point here is that curriculum theorists do not necessarily agree on how one should approach thinking about curriculum. By trying to redefine curriculum entirely, Pinar drew attention to different aspects of the educational process.

Out of this continuing discussion among curricularists, various ideologies—beliefs about what schools should teach, for what ends, and for what reasons—have developed (Eisner 1992). In this section, I present six prominent curriculum ideologies that should prove useful in thinking about developing, adapting, or implementing curriculum. While these ideologies are important, they are not the only ones. Elliot Eisner writes of religious orthodoxy and progressivism and excludes multiculturalism and developmentalism. Some authors may include constructivism rather than developmentalism.

I remind the reader that few people actually wear the labels I describe. These conceptualizations are useful in helping one better articulate a set of assumptions and core values. They help us see the implications of a particular viewpoint. They also help us understand issues and concerns that may otherwise be neglected. Sometimes ideologies are specified in mission statements or some other kind of manifesto; at other times, ideologies are embedded in educational practice but are not made explicit. Rarely does a school adhere to one curriculum ideology—though some do. More often, because public schools are made up of people who have different ideas about what schools should teach, a given school is more likely to embrace an array of curricular ideas. While some readers may resonate strongly with a particular ideology because it expresses their inclinations, some readers may appreciate particular ideas from various ideologies. In either case, it may be a good idea to examine the strengths and weaknesses of each one. Later in this chapter I argue that one does not need to be ideologically pure in order to do good curriculum work.

Rational Humanism

We have already seen, in the historical example of Charles Eliot and the Committee of Ten, an early exemplar of rational humanism. During Eliot's day, rational humanists embraced the theory of mental discipline, which provided a handy rationale for traditional studies. Why study Greek and Latin? Because these subjects exercised the mind in ways that other subjects did not. While mental discipline fell by the wayside, rational humanism did not. From the 1930s through the 1950s, Robert Maynard Hutchins and Mortimer Adler championed the rational humanistic tradition, in part by editing *The Great Books of the Western World*. Hutchins argued that the "great books" offer the best that human beings have thought and written. Thus, rather than reading textbooks on democracy, science, and math, one ought to read Jefferson, Newton, and Euclid.

Today, one may find the rational humanist ideology in some private schools and in those public schools that have adopted Adler's ideas as represented in the *Paideia Proposal* (Eisner 1992, 310). In short, the Paideia plan provides a common curriculum for all students. Except for the choosing of a foreign language, there are no electives. All students learn language, literature, fine arts, mathematics, natural science, history, geography, and social studies.

While Adler endorses lecturing and coaching as two important teaching methods, the aspect of teaching Adler found most engaging was maieutic or Socratic questioning and active participation. In essence, maieutic teaching consists of a seminar situation in which learners converse in a group. The teacher serves as a facilitator who moves the conversation along, asks leading questions, and helps students develop, examine, or refine their thinking as they espouse particular viewpoints. This process, according to Adler, "teaches participants how to analyze their own minds as well as the thought of others, which is to say it engages students in disciplined conversation about ideas and values" (Adler 1982, 30).

Another important educational feature of these seminars is that one discusses books and art but not textbooks. In a follow-up book to *The Paideia Proposal*, Adler (1984) provides a K–12 recommended reading list in which he recommends for kindergarten to fourth grade Aesop, William Blake, Shel Silverstein, Alice Walker, Jose Marie Sanchez-Silva, Langston Hughes, and Dr. Seuss, among other authors. I indicate these authors in particular because the charge that Adler's program embraces only the Western European heritage is not entirely accurate. While Adler would argue that some books are better than others, and that, in school, students should be reading the better ones, one can see that Adler includes authors who are not elitist and who are from culturally diverse backgrounds.

Developmentalism

Another approach to curriculum theory, which was discussed briefly in the historical section of this chapter, is developmentalism. Although a range of scholars falls under this heading, the basic point is that, rather than fitting the child to the curriculum, students would be better served if the curriculum were fitted to the child's stage of development. Why? One argument is that doing otherwise is inefficient or even detrimental to the child's development. It would be ridiculous to try to teach the Pythagorean theorem to a first grader, and it could be harmful (to use a fairly noncontroversial example) to teach a fourth grader to master throwing a curve ball. By understanding the range of abilities children have at various ages, one can provide a curriculum that meets the needs and interests of students. Of course, while the stage concept cannot pinpoint the development of a particular child at a given age, it serves as a general guide.

One might also pay attention to the idea of development when creating or adapting curriculum because of the issue of "readiness for learning." There are two ways of thinking about readiness. Some educators, in their interest to hurry development, believe that encouraging learners to perform approximations of desired behaviors can hasten academic skills. In this case, one tries to intervene in apparently natural development by manipulating the child's readiness at younger and younger ages. The research findings on whether one can greatly enhance one's learning processes are somewhat mixed, but, in my opinion, they favor the side that says "speed learning" is inefficient (Duckworth 1987, Good and Brophy 1986, Tietze 1987). I also think the more important question, as Piaget noted, is

"not how fast we can help intelligence grow, but how far we can help it grow" (Duckworth 1987, 38).

A different way of thinking about readiness for learning concerns not how to speed it up, but how to work with it effectively. Eleanor Duckworth, who studied with Piaget, believes the idea of readiness means placing children in developmentally appropriate problem situations where students are allowed to have their own "wonderful ideas." She believes that asking "the right question at the right time can move children to peaks in their thinking that result in significant steps forward and real intellectual excitement" (Duckworth 1987, 5). The challenges for teachers are to provide environmentally rich classrooms where students have the opportunity to "mess about" with things, and to try to understand children's thought processes. Students should have the opportunity to experiment with materials likely to afford intellectual growth, and teachers should learn how their students think. In this approach to curriculum, mistakes are not problems; they are opportunities for growth.

The developmental approach to curriculum teaches us to pay attention to the ways humans grow and learn. One basic idea underlying the various theories of human development in regard to curriculum is that the curriculum planner ought to understand children's abilities and capabilities because such knowledge enables one to provide worthwhile educational activities for students.

Reconceptualism

As noted earlier with Pinar's use of the term *currere*, during the 1970s numerous individuals criticized the technical aspects and linear progression of steps of the Tyler rationale. Loosely labelled as reconceptualists, some educators felt the following:

> What is missing from American schools . . . is a deep respect for personal purpose, lived experience, the life of imagination, and those forms of understanding that resist dissection and measurement. What is wrong with schools, among other things, is their industrialized format, their mechanistic attitudes toward students, their indifference to personal experience, and their emphasis on the instrumental and the out of reach. (Pinar 1975, 316)

Reconceptualists have focused on Dewey's observation that one learns through experience. Given this assertion, some important questions arise. For example, how can teachers, teacher educators, or educational researchers better understand the kinds of experiences individual students are having? To answer this question, reconceptualists employ ideas, concepts, and theories from psychoanalysis, philosophy, and literature.

Another question that arises when one reflects on understanding experience is, How can teachers provide worthwhile conditions for students to undergo educational experiences? Maxine Greene divides educational experiences into two types: "an education for having" and "an education for being." Education for having is utilitarian—for example, one may learn to read in order to get a job. Some students need this kind of experience. Education for being is soulful—one may learn to read for the sensual qualities it can provide. All students, she says, need the latter kind of experience. One problem is that the latter has often been neglected or, if not, often provided for the talented or gifted at the expense of others (Green, 1988a).

In their effort to reperceive education, reconceptualists such as Maxine Greene, Madeleine Grumet, and William Pinar do not usually offer specific educational ideas that are easily implemented. In part, this is because the kind of education with which they are concerned is not easy to quantify or measure. In general, reconceptualists do not believe their theories and ideas need quick utilization in schools in order to validate their worth. If in reading their writings you think more deeply about educational issues, then I think they would be satisfied.

Nevertheless, I can think of two practical challenges for education that stem from their writing. First, how could you write a rigorous and tough-minded lesson plan without using objectives? What would such a lesson plan look like? Second, if you wanted to teach students a concept such as citizenship, how would you do it? Rational humanists would have students read Thomas Jefferson or Martin Luther King, Jr. Reconceptualists, however, would wonder how teachers can place students in problematic situations (i.e., in the classroom or on the playground) where students would grapple with real issues concerning citizenship.

Critical Theory

The idea of critical theory originated at the Institute for Social Research in Frankfurt ("the Frankfurt school") in the 1920s. Today, scholars who continue to recognize the value and importance of Marxist critiques of society and culture draw from and build on ideas from critical theory. In education they reveal, among other things, that schooling comprises a value-laden enterprise where issues of power are always at play.

For instance, while many people perceive schools as neutral institutions, places that will help any hard-working student to get ahead in life, critical theorists suggest that, on the contrary, schools do not operate that way. Michael Apple points out, "Just as our dominant economic institutions are structured so that those who inherit or already have economic capital do better, so too does cultural capital act in the same way" (Apple 1986, 33). According to Apple, schools reflect the general inequities in the larger society. Rather than changing society through cultural transformation (teaching students to question or to be independent thinkers), schools actually maintain the status quo through cultural reproduction.

Unlike some curricularists who try to appear neutral in exercising judgments about curriculum matters, Apple's values are well known. He believes in John Rawls's insight that "for a society to be truly just, it must maximize the advantage of the least advantaged" (Apple 1979, 32). Apple encourages curricularists to take advocacy positions within and outside of education. While critical theory makes for a powerful theoretical tool, one question frequently asked of critical theorists is how this information can be used in the classroom. Teachers point out that they may not be able to change the school structure, the kinds of material they must cover, or the kinds of tests that must be given. Although admittedly application is difficult, one high school English educator in Boston who employs the ideas of critical theory is Ira Shor.

In an activity called "prereading," for example, Shor tells students the theme of a book they are about to read and has them generate hypothetical questions the book may answer. At first students are reluctant to respond, but after a while they do. Shor believes this kind of exercise has numerous functions. First, it provides a bridge for students to decelerate from the "rush of mass culture" into the slow medium of the printed word. Habituated to rock music and MTV, students need a slow-down time. Also, after creating a list of questions, students are curious how many will actually be addressed. Students may still reject the text, says Shor, but now it won't be a result of alienation. Perhaps most importantly, prereading demystifies the power of the written word. Rather than approaching the text as some kind of untouchable authority, "students' own thoughts and words on the reading topic are the starting points for the coordinated material. The text will be absorbed into the field of their language rather than they being ruled by it" (Shor 1987, 117).

Critical theory offers a radical way of thinking about schooling. Particularly concerned with students who are disenfranchised and who, without the critical theorists, would have no voice to speak for them, critical theory provides incisive analyses of educational problems.

Multiculturalism

In some ways, multiculturalists are in affinity with the critical theorists. Though critical theory traditionally is more concerned with class, most critical theorists have included race and gender in their analyses and discussions. Multiculturalism, however, deserves its own category as a curriculum ideology because it is rooted in the ethnic revival movements of the 1960s. Whether the purpose is to correct racist and bigoted views of the larger community, to raise children's self-esteem, to help children see themselves from other viewpoints, or to reach the child's psychological world, the multicultural ideology reminds educators that ethnicity must be dealt with by educators.

One major approach to multicultural education has been termed "multiethnic ideology" by James Banks (1988). According to Banks, Americans participate in several cultures—the mainstream along with various ethnic subcultures. Therefore, students ought to have cross-cultural competency. In addition to being able to participate in various cultures, Banks also suggests that when one learns about various cultures, one begins to see oneself from other viewpoints. The multiethnic ideology provides greater self-understanding.

When teaching from a multiethnic perspective, Banks advises that an issue not be taught from a dominant mainstream perspective with other points of view added on. This kind of teaching still suggests that one perspective is the "right one," though others also have their own points of view. Rather, one should approach the concept or theme from various viewpoints. In this case, the mainstream perspective becomes one of several ways of approaching the topic; it is not

superior or inferior to other ethnic perspectives. In addition to what takes place in the classroom, Banks also argues that a successful multiethnic school must have system-wide reform. School staff, school policy, the counseling program, assessment, and testing are all affected by the multiethnic ideology.

Cognitive Pluralism

According to Eisner, the idea of cognitive pluralism goes back at least to Aristotle; however, only in the last several decades has a conception of the plurality of knowledge and intelligence been advanced in the field of curriculum (Eisner 1992, 317). In short, cognitive pluralists expand our traditional notions of knowledge and intelligence. Whereas some scientists and educators believe that people possess a single intelligence (often called a "g factor") or that all knowledge can ultimately be written in propositional language, cognitive pluralists believe that people possess numerous intelligences and that knowledge exists in many forms of representation.

As a conception of knowledge, cognitive pluralists argue that symbol systems provide a way to encode visual, auditory, kinesthetic, olfactory, gustatory, and tactile experiences. If, for example, one wants to teach students about the Civil War, cognitive pluralists would want students not only to have knowledge about factual material (names, dates, and battles), but also to have knowledge about how people felt during the war. To know that slavery means by definition the owning of another person appears quite shallow to knowing how it feels to be powerless. Cognitive pluralists suggest students should be able to learn through a variety of forms of representation (e.g., narratives, poetry, film, pictures) and be able to express themselves through a variety of forms as well. The latter point about expression means that most tests, which rely on propositional language, are too limiting. Some students may better express themselves through painting or poetry.

One may also think about cognitive pluralism from the point of view of intelligence. As I mentioned, some scholars suggest that intelligence may be better thought of as multiple rather than singular. Howard Gardner, a leading advocate of this position (1983), argues that, according to his own research and to reviews of a wide array of studies, a theory of multiple intelligences is more viable than a theory about a "g factor." He defines intelligence as follows:

> To my mind, a human intellectual compe-
> tence must entail a set of skills of problem-
> solving—enabling the individual to resolve
> genuine problems or difficulties that he or
> she encounters and, when appropriate, to
> create an effective product—and must also
> entail the potential for finding or creating
> problems—thereby laying the groundwork for
> the acquisition of new knowledge. (Gardner
> 1983, 60–61)

Gardner argues that there are at least seven distinct kinds of human intelligence: linguistic, musical, logical–mathematical, spatial, bodily–kinesthetic, interpersonal, and intrapersonal. If schools aim to enhance cognitive development, then they ought to teach students to be knowl-edgeable of, and to practice being fluent in, numerous kinds of intelligences. To limit the kinds of knowledge or intelligences students experience indicates an institutional deficiency.

Applying Curriculum Ideologies

While some teachers or schools draw heavily on one particular curriculum ideology (e.g., Ira Shor's use of critical theory in his classroom or Mortimer Adler's ideas in Paideia schools), more often than not, a mixture of various ideologies pervade educational settings. I don't believe this is a problem. What Joseph Schwab said in the late 1960s about theory also applies to ideologies. He argued that theories are partial and incomplete, and that, as something rooted in one's mind rather than in the state of affairs, theories cannot provide a complete guide for classroom practice (1970). In other words, a theory about child development may tell you something about ten year olds in general, but not about a particular ten year old standing in front of you. Child development cannot tell you, for example, whether or how to reprimand a given child for failing to do his homework. Schwab suggested one become eclectic and deliberative when work-ing in the practical world. In simpler terms, one should know about various theories and use them when applicable. One does not need to be ideo-logically pure. One should also reflect upon one's decisions and talk about them with other people. Through deliberation one makes new decisions which lead to new actions which then cycle around again to reflection, decision, and action.

To understand this eclectic approach to using curriculum ideologies, let's take as an example the use of computers in the classroom. Imagine you are about to be given several computers for your class. How could knowledge of the various curriculum ideologies inform your use of them?

Given this particular challenge, some ideolo-gies will prove to be more useful than others. For example, the rational humanists would probably have little to contribute to this discussion be-cause, with their interests in the cultivation of reason and the seminar process of teaching, computers are not central (though one of my students noted, that, perhaps in time, rational humanists will want to create a "great software" program).

Some developmentalists would consider the issue of when it would be most appropriate to introduce computers to students. Waldorf educa-tors, who base their developmental ideas on the writings of philosopher Rudolf Steiner (1861–1925), do not believe one should teach students about computers at an early age. They would not only take into account students' cognitive devel-opment (at what age could students understand computers?), but they would also consider students' social, physical, and emotional develop-ment. At what age are students really excited about computers? When are their fingers large enough to work the keyboard? What skills and habits might children lose if they learned comput-ers at too early an age? Is there an optimum age at which one ought to learn computers? Waldorf educators would ask these kinds of developmen-tal questions.

Developmentalists following the ideas of Eleanor Duckworth may also ask the above questions, but whatever the age of the student they are working with, these educators would try to teach the computer to children through engaging interactive activities. Rather than telling students about the computer, teachers would set up activities where students can interact with them. In this orientation, teachers would con-tinue to set up challenges for students to push their thinking. Sustaining students' sense of wonder and curiosity is equally important. In addition to setting new challenges for students, teachers would also monitor student growth by trying to understand student thought processes. In short, rather than fitting the child to the curriculum, the curriculum is fitted to the child.

Reconceptualists' first impulse would be to consider the educational, social, or cultural meaning of computers before worrying about their utility. Of course, one should remember that there isn't one party line for any given ideological perspective. Some reconceptualists may be optimistic about computers and some may not. Although I don't know William Pinar's or Madeleine Grumet's thoughts on computers, I imagine they would reflect on the way computers bring information to people. Pinar observes that place plays a role in the way one sees the world (Pinar 1991). The same machine with the same software can be placed in every school room, but even if students learn the same information, their relationship to this new knowledge will vary. Thus, to understand the impact of computers one needs to know a great deal about the people who will learn from and use them. Having students write autobiographies provides one way to attain this understanding. Students could write about or dramatize their encounters with technology. After such an understanding, teachers can tailor lessons to meet student needs.

Critical theorist Michael Apple has examined the issue of computers in schools. Though he points out that many teachers are delighted with the new technology, he worries about an uncritical acceptance of it. Many teachers, he notes, do not receive substantial information about computers before they are implemented. Consequently, they must rely on a few experts or pre-packaged sets of material. The effects of this situation are serious. With their reliance on purchased material combined with the lack of time to properly review and evaluate it, teachers lose control over the curriculum development process. They become implementers of someone else's plans and procedures and become deskilled and disempowered because of that (Apple 1986, 163).

Apple also worries about the kind of thinking students learn from computers. While students concentrate on manipulating machines, they are concerned with issues of "how" more than "why." Consequently, Apple argues, computers enhance technical but not substantive thinking. Crucial political and ethical understanding atrophies while students are engaged in computer proficiency. Apple does not suggest one avoid computers because of these problems. Rather, he wants teachers and students to engage in social, political, and ethical discussions while they use the new technology.

Multiculturalists would be concerned that all students have equal access to computers. Early research on computer implementation revealed that many minority students did not have the opportunity to use computers, and when they did, their interaction with computers often consisted of computer-assisted instruction programs that exercised low-level skills (Anderson, Welch, Harris 1984). In addition to raising the issue that all students should have equal access to computers, multiculturalists would also investigate whether software programs were sending biased or racist viewpoints.

Finally, cognitive pluralists, such as Elliot Eisner, would probably focus on the kinds of knowledge made available by computers. If computers were used too narrowly so that students had the opportunity to interact only with words and numbers, Eisner would be concerned. He would point out, I believe, that students could be learning that "real" knowledge exists in two forms. If, however, computers enhance cognitive understanding by providing multiple forms of representation, then I think Eisner would approve of the use of this new technology in the classroom. For example, in the latest videodisc technology, when students look up the definition of a word, they find a written statement as well as a picture. How much more meaningful a picture of a castle is to a young child than the comment, "a fortified residence as of a noble in feudal times" (*Random House Dictionary* 1980, 142).

In addition to learning through a variety of sensory forms, Eisner would also want students to have the opportunity to express themselves in a variety of ways. Computers could be useful in allowing students to reveal their knowledge in visual and musical as well as narrative forms. Students should not be limited in the ways they can express what they know.

Each curriculum ideology offers a unique perspective by virtue of the kinds of values and theories embedded within it. By reflecting on some of the ideas from the various curriculum ideologies and applying them to an educational issue, I believe educators can have a more informed, constructive, and creative dialogue. Moreover, as I said earlier, I do not think one needs to remain ideologically pure. Teachers and curricularists would do well to borrow ideas from the various perspectives as long as they make sure they are not proposing contradictory ideas.

The following chart summarizes the major proponents, major writings, educational priorities, and philosophical beliefs of each curriculum ideology covered in this chapter. (Of course, this chart is not comprehensive. I encourage the

CURRICULUM IDEOLOGIES

Ideology	Major Proponent	Major Writings	Educational Priorities	Philosophical Beliefs	Teachers, Curriculum, or Schools Expressing Curriculum Ideology	Suggestions for Curriculum Development
Rational Humanism	R. M. Hutchins M. Adler	The Paideia Proposal (Adler 1982) Paideia Problems and Possibilities (Adler 1983) The Paideia Program (Adler 1984)	Teaching through Socratic method. The use of primary texts. No electives.	The best education for the best is the best education for all. Since time in school is short, expose students to the best of Western culture.	Paideia Schools. See Adler (1983) for a list of schools.	Teach students how to facilitate good seminars. Use secondary texts sparingly.
Developmentalism	E. Duckworth R. Steiner	Young Children Reinvent Arithmetic (Kamii 1985) "The Having of Wonderful Ideas" and Other Essays (Duckworth 1987) Rudolf Steiner Education and the Developing Child (Aeppli 1986)	Fit curriculum to child's needs and interests. Inquiry-oriented teaching.	Cognitive structures develop as naturally as walking. If the setting is right, students will raise questions to push their own thinking.	Pat Carini's Prospect School in Burlington, VT.	Allow teachers the opportunity to be surprised. Rather than writing a curriculum manual, prepare a curriculum guide.
Reconceptualism	W. Pinar M. Grumet	Bitter Milk (Grumet 1988) Curriculum Theorizing (Pinar 1975) Curriculum and Instruction (Giroux, Penna, Pinar 1981)	Use philosophy, psychology, and literature to understand the human experience. Provide an "education for having" and an "education for being."	One learns through experience. We can learn to understand experience through phenomenology, psychoanalysis, and literature.	See Oliver (1990) for a curriculum in accordance with reconceptualist thinking.	Write lesson plans without the use of objectives. Curriculum writers ought to reveal their individual subjectivities.
Critical Theory	M. Apple I. Shor P. Freire	Ideology and Curriculum (Apple 1979) Teachers and Texts (Apple 1986) Pedagogy of the Oppressed (Freire 1970) Freire for the Classroom (Shor 1987)	Equal opportunities for all students. Teaching should entail critical reflection.	A just society maximizes the advantage for the least advantages. Schools are part of the larger community and must be analyzed as such.	See Shor's edited text (1987) for a number of ideas on implementing critical theory.	Curriculum writers ought to examine their own working assumptions critically and ought to respect the integrity of teachers and students.
Multiculturalism	J. Banks E. King	Multiethnic Education (Banks 1988) Multicultural Education (Banks and Banks 1989)	Students should learn to participate in various cultures. Approach concept or theme from various viewpoints.	Students need to feel good about their ethnic identities. All people participate in various cultures and subcultures.	See King (1990) for a workbook of activities teaching ethnic and gender awareness.	Make sure that text and pictures represent a variety of cultures.
Cognitive Pluralism	E. Eisner H. Gardner	"Curriculum Ideologies" (Eisner 1992) The Educational Imagination (Eisner 1985) Frames of Mind (Gardner 1983)	Teach, and allow students to express themselves, through a variety of forms of representation. Allow students to develop numerous intelligences.	Our senses cue into and pick up different aspects of the world. Combined with our individual history and general schemata, our senses allow us to construct meaning.	The Key School in Indianapolis.	Curriculum lesson plans and units ought to be aesthetically pleasing in appearance. Curriculum ought to represent a variety of ways of knowing

reader to examine the recommended reading list for further works in each of these areas.) In the fifth column, "Teachers, Curriculum, or Schools Expressing Curriculum Ideology," I indicate places or texts where readers may learn more. One could visit a Paideia school, Carini's Prospect School, or the Key School in Indianapolis. One may read about reconceptualism, critical theory, and multiculturalism in the listed texts. Finally, in the sixth column, "Suggestions for Curriculum Development," I also include interesting points found in the literature but not necessarily contained in this chapter.

Recommended Reading

The following is a concise list of recommended reading in many of the areas discussed in this chapter. Full bibliographic citations are provided under *References.*

Some general **curriculum textbooks** that are invaluable are John D. McNeil's *Curriculum: A Comprehensive Introduction* (1990); William H. Schubert's *Curriculum: Perspective, Paradigm, and Possibility* (1986); Decker Walker's *Fundamentals of Curriculum* (1990); and Robert S. Zais's *Curriculum: Principles and Foundations* (1976). These books provide wonderful introductions to the field.

The recently published *Handbook of Research on Curriculum* (Jackson 1992) includes thirty-four articles by leading curricularists. This book is a must for anyone interested in research in curriculum.

For a discussion of **objectives** in education, Tyler (1949) is seminal. Also see Kapfer (1972) and Mager (1962). Bloom refines educational objectives into a taxonomy (1956). Eisner's (1985) critique of educational objectives and his notion of expressive outcomes will be welcomed by those who are skeptical of the objectives movement.

Good books on the **history of curriculum** include Kliebard (1986), Schubert (1980), and Tanner and Tanner (1975). Seguel (1966), who discusses the McMurry brothers, Dewey, Bobbitt, and Rugg, among others, is also very good.

Some excellent books on the **history of education** include the following: Lawrence Cremin's definitive book on progressive education, *The Transformation of the School: Progressivism in American Education, 1876–1957* (1961). David Tyack's *The One Best System* (1974) portrays the evolution of schools into their

modern formation; and Larry Cuban's *How Teachers Taught: Constancy and Change in American Classrooms, 1890–1980* (1984) examines what actually happened in classrooms during a century of reform efforts. Philip Jackson's "Conceptions of Curriculum and Curriculum Specialists" (1992) provides an excellent summary of the evolution of curriculum thought from Bobbitt and Tyler to Schwab.

For works in each of the ideologies I recommend the following:

To help one understand the **rational humanist** approach, there are Mortimer Adler's three books on the **Paideia school**: *The Paideia Proposal: An Educational Manifesto* (1982), *Paideia Problems and Possibilities* (1983), and *The Paideia Program: An Educational Syllabus* (1984). Seven critical reviews of the Paideia proposal comprise "The Paideia Proposal: A Symposium" (1983).

For works in **developmentalism** based on Piaget's ideas see Duckworth (1987, 1991) and Kamii (1985). Among Piaget's many works you may want to read *The Origins of Intelligence* (1966). If you are interested in Waldorf education see Robert McDermott's *The Essential Steiner* (1984) and P. Bruce Uhrmacher's "Waldorf Schools Marching Quietly Unheard" (1991). Willi Aeppli's *Rudolf Steiner Education and the Developing Child* (1986), Francis Edmunds's *Rudolf Steiner Education* (1982), and Marjorie Spock's *Teaching as a Lively Art* (1985) are also quite good.

A general overview of the developmental approach to curriculum can be found on pages 49–52 of Linda Darling-Hammond and Jon Snyder's "Curriculum Studies and the Traditions of Inquiry: The Scientific Tradition" (1922).

Two books are essential for examining **reconceptualist** writings: William Pinar's *Curriculum Theorizing: The Reconceptualists* (1975) and Henry Giroux, Anthony N. Penna, and William F. Pinar's *Curriculum and Instruction* (1981). Recent books in reconceptualism include William Pinar and William Reynolds's *Understanding Curriculum as Phenomenological and Deconstructed Text* (1992), and William Pinar and Joe L. Kincheloe's *Curriculum as Social Psychoanalysis: The Significance of Place* (1991).

Some excellent works in **critical theory** include Paulo Freire's *Pedagogy of the Oppressed* (1970) and *The Politics of Education* (1985). Apple's works are also excellent; see *Ideology and Curriculum* (1979) and *Teachers and Texts* (1986). For an overview of the Frankfurt School and the application of Jürgen Habermas's ideas, see Robert Young's *A Critical Theory of Education: Habermas and Our Children's Future* (1990).

For an application of critical theory to classrooms see the Ira Shor–edited book, *Freire for the Classroom* (1987) with an afterword by Paulo Freire.

In **multicultural education** I recommend James Banks's *Multiethnic Education: Theory and Practice* (1988) and Banks and Banks's *Multicultural Education: Issues and Perspectives* (1989). Also see Gibson (1984) for an account of five different approaches to multicultural education. Nicholas Appleton (1983), Saracho and Spodek (1983), and Simonson and Walker (1988) are also important. Edith King's *Teaching Ethnic and Gender Awareness: Methods and Materials for the Elementary School* (1990) provides useful ideas about multicultural education that could be used in the classroom. John Ogbu's work (1987) on comparing immigrant populations to involuntary minorities is also an important work with serious educational implications.

Important works in the field of **cognitive pluralism** include Elliot Eisner (1982, 1985, 1992) and Howard Gardner (1983, 1991). Some philosophical texts that influenced both of these men include Dewey (1934), Goodman (1978), and Langer (1976).

For $20.00, the Key School Option Program will send you an interdisciplinary theme-based curriculum report. For more information write Indianapolis Public Schools, 1401 East Tenth Street, Indianapolis, Indiana 46201.

Glossary of Some Common Usages of Curriculum

delivered curriculum: what teachers deliver in the classroom. This is opposed to Intended curriculum. Same as operational curriculum.

enacted curriculum: actual class offerings by a school, as opposed to courses listed in books or guides. *See* official curriculum.

experienced curriculum: what students actually learn. Same as received curriculum.

explicit curriculum: stated aims and goals of a classroom or school.

hidden curriculum: unintended, unwritten, tacit, or latent aspects of messages given to students by teachers, school structures, textbooks, and other school resources. For example, while students learn writing or math, they may also learn about punctuality, neatness, competition, and conformity. Concealed messages may be intended or unintended by the school or teacher.

implicit curriculum: similar to the hidden curriculum in the sense that something is implied rather than expressly stated. Whereas the hidden curriculum usually refers to something unfavorable, negative, or sinister, the implicit curriculum also takes into account unstated qualities that are positive.

intended curriculum: that which is planned by the teacher or school.

null curriculum: that which does not take place in the school or classroom. What is not offered cannot be learned. Curricular exclusion tells a great deal about a school's values.

official curriculum: courses listed in the school catalogue or course bulletin. Although these classes are listed, they may not be taught. *See* enacted curriculum.

operational curriculum: events that take place in the classroom. Same as delivered curriculum.

received curriculum: what students acquire as a result of classroom activity. Same as experienced curriculum.

References

Adler, Mortimer J. 1982. *The Paideia Proposal: An Educational Manifesto.* New York: Collier Books.

——. 1983. *Paideia Problems and Possibilities.* New York: Collier Books.

——. 1984. *The Paideia Program: An Educational Syllabus.* New York: Collier Books.

Aeppli, Willi. 1986. *Rudolf Steiner Education and the Developing Child.* Hudson, NY: Anthroposophic Press.

Anderson, Ronald E., Wayne W. Welch, and Linda J. Harris. 1984. "Inequities in Opportunities for Computer Literacy." *The Computing Teacher: The Journal of the International*

Council for Computers in Education 11(8): 10–12.

Apple, Michael W. 1979. *Ideology and Curriculum.* Boston: Routledge and Kegan Paul.

——. 1986. *Teachers and Texts: A Political Economy of Class and Gender Relations in Education.* New York: Routledge and Kegan Paul.

Appleton, Nicholas. 1983. *Cultural Pluralism in Education.* White Plains, NY: Longman.

Banks, James A. 1988. *Multiethnic Education: Theory and Practice.* 2d ed. Boston: Allyn and Bacon.

Banks, James A., and Cherry A. McGee Banks, eds. 1989. *Multicultural Education: Issues and Perspectives.* Boston: Allyn and Bacon.

Bloom, Benjamin S., ed. 1956. *Taxonomy of Educational Objectives: The Classification of Educational Goals, Handbook 1: Cognitive Domain.* New York: McKay.

Bobbitt, Franklin. 1918. *The Curriculum.* Boston: Houghton Mifflin.

Cremin, Lawrence A. 1961. *The Transformation of the School: Progressivism in American Education, 1876–1957.* New York: Vintage Books.

——. 1977. *Traditions of American Education.* New York: Basic Books.

Cuban, Larry. 1984. *How Teachers Taught: Constancy and Change in American Classrooms 1890–1980.* White Plains, NY: Longman.

Darling-Hammond, Linda, and Jon Snyder. 1992. "Curriculum Studies and the Traditions of Inquiry: The Scientific Tradition." In *Handbook of Research on Curriculum: A Project of the American Educational Research Association,* ed. Philip W. Jackson, 41–78. New York: Macmillan.

Dewey, John. 1934. *Art as Experience.* New York: Minton, Balch.

Duckworth, Eleanor. 1987. *"The Having of Wonderful Ideas" and Other Essays on Teaching and Learning.* New York: Teachers College Press.

——. 1991. "Twenty-four, Forty-two, and I Love You: Keeping It Complex. *Harvard Educational Review* 61(1): 1–24.

Edmunds, L. Francis. 1982. *Rudolf Steiner Education.* 2d ed. London: Rudolf Steiner Press.

Eisner, Elliot W. 1982. *Cognition and Curriculum: A Basis for Deciding What to Teach.* White Plains, NY: Longman.

——. 1985. *The Educational Imagination.* 2d ed. New York: Macmillan.

——. 1992. "Curriculum Ideologies." In *Handbook of Research on Curriculum: A Project of the American Educational Research Association,* ed. Philip W. Jackson, 302–26. New York: Macmillan.

Freire, Paulo. 1970. *Pedagogy of the Oppressed.* Trans. Myra Bergman Ramos. New York: Seabury Press.

——. 1985. *The Politics of Education.* Trans. Donaldo Macedo. South Hadley, MA: Bergin and Garvey.

Gardner, Howard. 1983. *Frames of Mind.* New York: Basic Books.

——. 1991. *The Unschooled Mind: How Children Think and How Schools Should Teach.* New York: Basic Books.

Gibson, Margaret Alison. 1984. "Approaches to Multicultural Education in the United States: Some Concepts and Assumptions." *Anthropology and Education Quarterly* 15: 94–119.

Giroux, Henry, Anthony N. Penna, and William F. Pinar. 1981. *Curriculum and Instruction: Alternatives in Education.* Berkeley: McCutchan.

Good, Thomas S., and Jere E. Brophy. 1986. *Educational Psychology.* 3d ed. White Plains, NY: Longman.

Goodman, Nelson. 1978. *Ways of Worldmaking.* Indianapolis: Hackett.

Greene, Maxine. 1988a. "Vocation and Care: Obsessions about Teacher Education." Panel discussion at the Annual Meeting of the American Educational Research Association, 5–9 April, New Orleans.

——. 1988b. *The Dialectic of Freedom.* New York: Teachers College Press.

Gress, James R. 1978. *Curriculum: An Introduction to the Field.* Berkeley: McCutchan.

Grumet, Madeleine R. 1988. *Bitter Milk: Women and Teaching.* Amherst: Univ. of Massachusetts Press.

Jackson, Philip W. 1992. "Conceptions of Curriculum and Curriculum Specialists." In *Handbook of Research on Curriculum: A Project of the American Educational Research Association,* ed. Philip W. Jackson, 3–40. New York: Macmillan.

Kamii, Constance Kazuko, with Georgia DeClark. 1985. *Young Children Reinvent Arithmetic: Implications of Piaget's Theory.* New York: Teachers College Press.

Kapfer, Miriam B. 1972. *Behavioral Objectives in Curriculum Development: Selected Readings and Bibliography.* Englewood Cliffs, NJ: Educational Technology.

King, Edith W. 1990. *Teaching Ethnic and Gender Awareness: Methods and Materials for the Elementary School.* Dubuque, IA: Kendall/Hunt.

Kliebard, Herbert M. 1986. *The Struggle for the American Curriculum, 1893–1958.* Boston: Routledge and Kegan Paul.

Langer, Susanne. 1976. *Problems of Art.* New York: Scribners.

McDermott, Robert A., ed. 1984. *The Essential Steiner.* San Francisco: Harper & Row.

McLaren, Peter. 1986. *Schooling as a Ritual Performance: Towards a Political Economy of Educational Symbols and Gestures.* London: Routledge and Kegan Paul.

McNeil, John D. 1990. *Curriculum: A Comprehensive Introduction.* 4th ed. Glenview, IL: Scott, Foresman/Little, Brown Higher Education.

Mager, Robert. 1962. *Preparing Instructional Objectives.* Palo Alto, CA: Fearon.

Ogbu, John. 1987. "Variability in Minority School Performance: A Problem in Search of an Explanation." *Anthropology and Education Quarterly* 18(4): 312–34.

Oliver, Donald W. 1990. "Grounded Knowing: A Postmodern Perspective on Teaching and Learning." *Educational Leadership* 48(1): 64–69.

"The Paideia Proposal: A Symposium." 1983. *Harvard Educational Review* 53 (4): 377–411.

Piaget, Jean. 1962. *Play, Dreams and Imitation in Childhood.* New York: Norton.

——. 1966. *Origins of Intelligence.* New York: Norton.

Pinar, William F., ed. 1975. *Curriculum Theorizing: The Reconceptualists.* Berkeley: McCutchan.

Pinar, William F., and Joe L. Kincheloe, eds. 1991. *Curriculum as Social Psychoanalysis: The Significance of Place.* Albany: State Univ. of New York Press.

Pinar, William F., and William M. Reynolds, eds. 1992. *Understanding Curriculum as Phenomenological and Deconstructed Text.* New York: Teachers College Press.

The Random House Dictionary. 1980. New York: Ballantine.

Saracho, Olivia N., and Bernard Spodek. 1983. *Understanding the Multicultural Experience in Early Childhood Education.* Washington, DC: National Association for the Education of Young Children.

Schubert, William H. 1980. *Curriculum Books: The First Eight Years.* Lanham, MD: Univ. Press of America.

——. 1986. *Curriculum: Perspective, Paradigm, and Possibility.* New York: Macmillan.

Schwab, Joseph J. 1970. *The Practical: A Language for Curriculum.* Washington, DC: National Education Association.

Seguel, M. L. 1966. *The Curriculum Field: Its Formative Years.* New York: Teachers College Press.

Shor, Ira, ed. 1987. *Freire for the Classroom: A Sourcebook for Liberatory Teaching.* Portsmouth, NH: Heinemann.

Simonson, Rick, and Scott Walker, eds. 1988. *The Graywolf Annual Five: Multi-Cultural Literacy.* St. Paul, MN: Graywolf Press.

Spock, Marjorie. 1985. *Teaching as a Lively Art.* Hudson, NY: Anthroposophic Press.

Taba, Hilda. 1962. *Curriculum Development: Theory and Practice.* New York: Harcourt Brace Jovanovich.

Tanner, Daniel, and Laurel N. Tanner. 1975. *Curriculum Development: Theory into Practice.* New York: Macmillan.

Tietze, Wolfgang. 1987. "A Structural Model for the Evaluation of Preschool Effects." *Early Childhood Research Quarterly* 2(2): 133–59.

Tyack, David B. 1974. *The One Best System: A History of American Urban Education.* Cambridge: Harvard Univ. Press.

Tyler, Ralph W. 1949. *Basic Principles of Curriculum and Instruction.* Chicago: Univ. of Chicago Press.

Uhrmacher, P. Bruce. 1991. "Waldorf Schools Marching Quietly Unheard." Ph.D. diss., Stanford University.

Walker, Decker. 1990. *Fundamentals of Curriculum.* New York: Harcourt Brace Jovanovich.

Young, Robert. 1990. *A Critical Theory of Education: Habermas and Our Children's Future.* New York: Teachers College Press.

Zais, Robert S. 1976. *Curriculum: Principles and Foundations.* New York: Thomas Y. Crowell.

TRENDS AND ISSUES IN SCIENCE CURRICULUM

by Alan J. McCormack
Professor of Science Education
San Diego State University, San Diego, California

SCIENCE education has been of great concern in the United States for more than one hundred years. August committees and national level panels have called repeatedly for updating the science curriculum, more "hands-on" approaches, attention to our environment, emphasis on scientific literacy and the processes of science, and other familiar reforms. Various themes become more pressing at various historical periods due to the social, economic, and political forces in place at the time. About every two decades, a reform movement sparks the public interest and promotes changes in the science classroom and in how science is taught. This sometimes results in imbalance—with overemphasis on some aspects of the science curriculum, and de-emphasis on other important dimensions. Ultimately, identification of all the important dimensions of science curricula and reasoned decision making about appropriate balance among the various dimensions would seem desirable. A brief survey of the important historical movements in science education during the past century and a half might help place today's reform movement in perspective. (For other reviews of science education in the United States, see Hurd 1982, 1983, 1984, 1992.)

The Beginnings: 1860–1920

Little that we would recognize as "science" took place in schools in the early 1800s. Emphasis on the three Rs and rote memorization was the order of the day. Of course, the era of Big Science was still in the future. "Science" itself was well established, just not well funded or collaborative in nature, so little societal pressure was brought to bear on including science as a school subject. The first inkling of activity in classrooms that might be considered similar to the science familiar in today's schools was the "object teaching" promoted by the Swiss educator Pestalozzi. "Object lessons" focused on actual objects brought into classrooms for observation and study, as opposed to the predominantly verbal and didactic teaching approaches of the day. Emphasis was placed on careful observation of objects, and, to some extent, on asking questions and making inferences about the objects. Though little attention was given to anything recognizable as scientific experimentation, students were encouraged to use their senses and to think rather than memorize. Thus, object teaching can be cited as the basis from which our current emphases on scientific processes and higher-order thinking skills eventually evolved. Historically, however, it had *no* influence on later decisions to emphasize these aspects of science.

During the late nineteenth century, the American population began a dramatic movement away from farms to cities. Our formerly agrarian society was becoming industrialized. Liberty Hyde Bailey, a professor of biology at Cornell University, became concerned that children would grow up out of contact with nature and would lack concern for natural environments. Bailey championed the Nature-Study Movement with his Cornell School Leaflets, an extensive school gardening program, and with nature-oriented in-service programs for teachers. He emphasized awareness, appreciation, and conservation of nature so successfully that classical nature study became the basic science program in many elementary schools throughout the nation from about 1890 to 1910.

During the same period, high school science was molded by two important forces: (1) College science teaching—dominated by formal lectures and deductive laboratory work—was used as the model for instruction; and (2) industrialization and the growth of cities created a need for practicality and the inclusion of technology in science courses. Thus, practice-oriented courses such as navigation and surveying were offered alongside classical courses in physics, astronomy, botany, and geology. As early as 1893, the beginning of a conflict in philosophy of secondary science education was already apparent. Universities viewed high schools as important institutions for preparing students academically to enter universities. A more egalitarian group viewed college-preparatory—type science courses as too specialized and not appropriate for the majority of students who would not go on to college. The influential Committee of Ten report (1893) marked the beginning of a curricular emphasis in American high schools on non-college-oriented vocational and general-education skills for *all* students.

These events of roughly a century ago might seem distant and irrelevant to today's "high-tech" schools, but they illustrate that many of today's trends reflect the same unresolved science education issues (DeBoer 1991). We still are challenging the value of lecture as a primary instructional mode for today's high school science classrooms. And we are still fighting the battle begun with object teaching and the Nature-Study Movement, believing that hands-on experiences with real materials are superior to memorization and recitation of facts for science lessons.

The Utilitarian/Textbook Period: 1920–1957

This was a period of prodigious economic and political growth tempered by war, a major depression, and rapid technological development. First an 8–4 pattern of elementary–high school organization was developed. This was followed by a 6–3–3 pattern-as the children of the middle years were observed to be in an emotional and physical growth period requiring a transitional schooling phase which became known as the junior high school.

At the elementary level, the science curriculum evolved into a "read about science" program organized around commercially prepared textbooks. This program resulted from the work of Gerald Craig at the Horace Mann Laboratory School at Columbia University. Craig developed a scope-and-sequence curriculum designed to provide coverage of all the major disciplines of scientific knowledge in a comprehensive, simple-to-complex organization. Yet the byword of the times was industrial efficiency, and it was believed that reading about science was the quickest, most efficient means to cover organized scientific information; thus discovery through hands-on learning was largely ignored. At the same time, the overevaluation of the industrial-production model and the emphasis on the practical, everyday uses of science led to a distorted view of science that was considered far removed from the view of science held by practicing scientists. Little attention was given to the processes and thinking skills used in establishing scientific knowledge. Much attention was delegated to the structure of practical technological devices, such as telephones and refrigerators, with insufficient emphasis given to a true understanding of the basic laws of physics underlying the functioning of these devices. Unfortunately, memorization of names and facts was reborn as a primary goal for science teaching.

At the high school level, biology became the standard course for tenth grade, with electives in chemistry and physics typically offered at the eleventh and twelfth grades. The junior high program became one year each of life, earth, and physical science, although ninth-grade science was general science in a large number of school systems.

Curricula at all levels became somewhat fossilized. Pre–World War II technologies became ingrained in textbooks, and new scientific developments typically didn't get into textbooks until ten to fifteen years after their development. Scientists began to complain that what they saw in school science textbooks didn't realistically or effectively reflect either what they knew or did as scientists. With the more materialistic orientation of the American population that exploded after World War II, it also became apparent that too few students were choosing science as a career. Then *Sputnik* slammed the collective American ego in 1957.

The First Revolution in Science Education: 1957-1978

It was unthinkable! Another country launched an artificial satellite to orbit the earth before the United States did. The "best in the world" complacency of American science was rattled, and the American public was aghast. What had happened? The usual finger-pointing in times such as these is aimed toward public education, and 1957 was no exception. Professional scientists and mathematicians were organized by professional scientific societies and commissions to examine science textbooks and teaching practices. According to Collette and Chiappetta, the science groups found that school science courses and textbooks "lacked rigor, were dogmatically taught, were content-oriented, lacked conceptual unity, were outdated, and had little bearing on what was really happening in the scientific disciplines" (1989, 41).

A huge reform movement quickly ensued, unlike anything seen before in American education. The National Science Foundation (NSF) instituted a Directorate in Science Education which funneled many millions of dollars into curriculum development and teacher training for about a decade and a half. Curriculum projects were instituted at all school levels, K-12, and many approaches to science were created and tested in schools. NSF teacher institutes were widely available during summer sessions at dozens of universities, some aimed at updating teachers' content knowledge in the sciences, others intended to prepare teachers to implement the new science programs. We know now that a disproportionate amount of money was spent on new program development as compared to what was spent on preparing teachers for program

implementation. Installing the new programs in schools required significant expenditures for material kits and equipment that many school districts were unable or unwilling to pay. Thus, although some extremely innovative course materials were developed during this period, they were never implemented in schools as widely as would have been desirable. Pockets of excellence developed around the country where well-trained teachers conducted wonderful new NSF science programs, but the majority of teachers changed their approaches and philosophies of science education very little (Kyle 1985).

The NSF curriculum projects focused on reflecting the nature of science, as seen by practicing scientists, and on learning by inquiry and discovery. "Pure" science, consisting of the basic principles and theories underlying science, was given preference over "applied" science, the technological and engineering uses of scientific principles for creation of practical devices. Learning by inquiry meant that students were to behave like scientists: observing, measuring, experimenting, and analyzing data in hands-on, laboratory situations. Learning by discovery allowed students to generalize scientific principles for themselves from data collected through their own investigations. This was very different from doing laboratory work simply to verify principles presented verbally by a science teacher or a textbook.

In all of the new NSF-sponsored programs of this era, learning through hands-on investigations became the focus of science learning and instruction. Learning from teacher lectures, demonstrations, and from books was de-emphasized to such an extent that, in some programs, no books or readings at all were made available to students.

Brief descriptions of some of the key programs of this period follow.

Elementary Level

Many new elementary programs were developed during this era, but three appear today to have been the most widely used and influential. These are the *Elementary Science Study* (ESS), the *Science Curriculum Improvement Study* (SCIS) and *Science—A Process Approach* (SAPA). These programs, or variations of them, are still in use today and have strongly influenced both textbook and hands-on programs.

ESS is composed of fifty-six independent units that encourage free or loosely guided exploration by children in the physical, life, and earth sciences. The range of units provides a "smorgasbord" from which a school district can custom design a sequence of units for each grade level. ESS is characterized by low structure and maximum flexibility. Students are cast in the role of questioners and investigators of nature, while teachers are viewed as guides to learning rather than disseminators of information.

Students are encouraged to play around with science, and cast off in directions tangential to unit topics, as their individual interests lead them. Some of the more famous and influential ESS units—"Batteries and Bulbs," "Gases and Airs," "Clay Boats," and "Behavior of Mealworms"—have been adopted and revised by some of the most current programs. They have served as some of our best models of discovery learning for both pre-service and in-service teacher training programs.

SAPA is unique in that it is focused and organized around the processes of science, and the concepts of science are introduced only as they relate to the processes. (Scientific processes are those behaviors that scientists use as they "do" science: observing, measuring, designing experiments, inferring, and interpreting data.) SAPA is organized in a highly structured hierarchy of behavioral objectives, each of which fits into the development of a scientific process. Teachers' manuals include flow charts showing precisely how behavioral objectives and supporting science activities are linked together. Of all the new elementary science programs of this era, SAPA was the most complicated, the most difficult to train teachers for, and required the largest number and most specialized of learning kits.

SCIS fills the role of a balanced program that compromises between the rigid hierarchy of SAPA and the free-swinging openness of ESS. SCIS is intended to develop "scientific literacy," which includes both the understanding of key scientific concepts and a command of the thinking and laboratory skills of the scientist. Each grade level consists of only two units, one in physical science and one in life science. These are focused on major ideas such as organisms, life cycles, energy sources, and interaction. SCIS authors believe that guided discovery should be used by teachers to help students see for themselves how each new discovery they make fits into an ever-expanding pattern of generalizations. This is accomplished by lessons based on the "Learning Cycle," and has three phases: *explora-*

tion, initial opportunities to become familiar with new materials and conduct some experiments; *invention,* in which a teacher helps children verbalize and label the concepts derivable from their experiments; and *application,* in which newly formed concepts are expanded into new experimental situations and contexts (Renner and Marek 1988).

Junior High Level

Of the many new science programs developed during the First Revolution, two stand out: *Introductory Physical Science* (IPS) and the *Earth Science Curriculum Project* (ESCP).

IPS is a totally laboratory-oriented course—no lectures, discussions, films, or transparencies are included—in which the major objective is to guide students in collecting evidence from which they derive an atomic view of matter. An inexpensive set of laboratory hardware for each student is one of the highlights of the program. With the hardware kit and the students' experimental guide in hand, a student can complete the entire year's course with only limited guidance from a teacher. The most recent edition of IPS continues this basic orientation.

ESCP was launched in 1958 by The American Geological Institute. The course does include a textbook (Mathews et al. 1989), but laboratory investigations form the core of the course. The flavor of the course is that science is exciting, forever changing, and oriented toward solving problems. The textbook is intended to focus on the big ideas and logic of science, rather than on cataloging facts. Many unique laboratory activities from ESCP have had considerable influence on subsequently developed junior high science programs.

Senior High Level

The Physical Science Study Committee (PSSC) was organized in 1956 at the Massachusetts Institute of Technology by physicists who were dissatisfied with existing high school physics courses. The group felt that the standard courses of the day really didn't reflect the nature of modern physics and were overly concerned with mechanical technology rather than with the conceptually pure ideas of physics. They were also concerned about the idea-verification approach to laboratory exercises, and found little evidence of anything like actual scientific investigation going on in secondary-level physics laboratories.

The PSSC group developed materials intended to "present physics as a unified but continuing process by which the nature of the physical world is understood; to use laboratory experimentation to encourage the spirit of inquiry" (Simpson and Anderson 1981, 351). A unique textbook, student laboratory guide, hardware store–style laboratory apparatus, films, and over forty supplemental paperback books were produced by the project. Many of these materials are no longer part of the most recent edition of the program.

A parallel development for high school chemistry was the *Chemical Education Material Study* (CHEM Study). The course focused on making the basic concepts of chemistry understandable and encouraged students to pursue careers in chemistry. Great emphasis was given to the evidence used by chemists as the basis for chemical principles and on recent research breakthroughs in the field. More attention was given to teacher training, and extensive student learning materials were developed, including a text, laboratory manual, unit tests, individualized instruction materials, twenty-six films, and a number of filmstrips. As was true in most other programs, chemistry was approached inductively: students conducted laboratory activities to collect data *before* concepts were formally introduced by the teacher or text.

The field of biology proved to be so extensive and divided in such a diversity of conceptual orientations that three different First Revolution biology courses were developed. The *Biological Science Curriculum Study* (BSCS) reform group was formed and comprised of a large group of practicing biologists and secondary school biology teachers. Joseph Schwab, of the University of Chicago, provided leadership emphasizing inquiry as a major teaching strategy for the programs.

BSCS produced three textbook programs widely known by the color of their book covers. The BSCS Yellow Version was an updated version of classical biology courses but had greater emphasis than usual on cell biology and inquiry. The Green Version approached biology from an ecological viewpoint, emphasizing organisms and their interactions with environments. The Blue Version focused on molecular and genetic biology while de-emphasizing many of the classical organismic topics.

BSCS curriculum developers were inquiry enthusiasts. They rebelled against teaching biology as an organized system of fixed truths.

Instead, they oriented laboratory activities toward helping students understand how scientific problems are posed and investigated and how data are tentatively interpreted.

In the late 1960s, environmental education became a distinct area of science teaching. While many science courses already covered earth science, energy, and related topics, the environmental education movement developed out of a heightened awareness of humankind's impact on the earth. An early impetus came in 1972, when the United Nations Conference on the Human Environment produced the Stockholm Declaration and Action Plan, which called for every nation to promote program development in environmental education. The declaration also called for the establishment of Earth Day, which soon became a focal point for environmental activities. Numerous reports called for the development of environmental education in the schools (Schafer and Disinger 1975a, 1975b; Stapp 1978; Gustafson, et al. 1983). Environmental education synthesizes such subjects as conservation, energy alternatives, the population explosion, pollution, and community involvement; it is meant to be truly thematic and interdisciplinary, integrating science, social studies, mathematics, language and fine arts, health, physical education, practical and industrial arts, career education, and values education.

Many activity packages were designed for environmental education programs, and some have been revised through the years to stay current. For example, *Project Learning Tree,* dealing with forests and land management, was first field tested in 1977; the newest edition is scheduled to be available in autumn 1993 (American Forest Council 1992). *Project WILD,* emphasizing wildlife and conservation, was founded in 1980 by the Western Regional Environment Education Council and the Western Association of Fish and Wildlife Agencies; the project has gone through several revisions (Project WILD 1991). Another popular program, the *CLASS Project,* was created in 1982 (with a revised edition in 1985), but it is no longer available (National Wildlife Federation 1982). A new program in the same spirit, *Project WET,* has been developed by Western Water Course in Montana.

Although many schools developed separate courses in environmental education during the 1970s and 1980s, many districts are now opting to integrate environmental topics into the core subjects instead. In addition, many of the tenets involved in environmental education have been incorporated into the development of the Science, Technology, and Society (STS) movement (see below).

Trends of the First Revolution Reforms

The First Revolution in Science Education was an exciting departure from the classical teacher-and-facts approach to school science (Hurd 1969). These new trends can be summarized as follows:

FROM	TO
1. The textbook as the authoritative source of information.	1. Laboratory data as a primary source of knowledge.
2. Everyday technology is presented as science.	2. "Pure" science is emphasized.
3. Many science topics studied briefly.	3. In-depth studies of fewer topics.
4. Laboratory activities used to verify concepts in textbook.	4. Laboratory activities used to collect data from which concepts are derived.
5. Deductive thinking is emphasized to arrive at "correct answers."	5. Inductive thinking is stressed in arriving at reasonable tentative answers.
6. Rote and receptive learning.	6. Discovery and inquiry learning.

The Second Revolution in Science Education: 1980–Present

The First Revolution was a reaction against ingrained classicism, rote memorization of facts, didactic teaching, and a largely outdated and irrelevant science curriculum. Its proponents aimed to install inquiry as the standard teaching strategy in science and to increase the number of students opting for scientific careers. Before long, however, critics began identifying problems and holes in the new curriculum projects. Some of the problems noted were:

1. Teachers found teaching the courses difficult. Large classes, lack of preparation time, inadequate materials, and other logistical problems prevented teachers from implementing the courses the ways they were designed to be implemented.
2. The courses were overly discipline-centered. They appealed mainly to a small percentage of college-bound students.
3. There was too much attention to theory and pure science, to the exclusion of "real-world" applications.
4. "Relevance," in terms of the social, historical, and humanistic dimensions of science, was perceived to be lacking.
5. Inquiry and discovery seemed to be foreign ideas to many science teachers. They deemed these procedures to be too time-consuming and difficult for the average student.
6. Standardized tests were not based on the new programs. The tests focused on classical scientific facts and ignored testing for the processes and inquiry dimensions of the curriculum.

Stake and Easley (1978) conducted nationwide studies of the extent of the use of inquiry in science classrooms, finding the approach barely visible. They found that students spent most of their classroom time listening to lectures, completing worksheets, and doing verification-type laboratory exercises. Other studies found that American youth were not performing well on national assessments of scientific knowledge and that students were turning away from taking science courses and from selecting science as a vocation (Helgeson, Blosser, and Howe 1977; Weiss 1978). Then, in 1983, The National Commission on Excellence in Education published *A Nation at Risk,* the first in a series of critical reports from national committees. These reports all heavily criticized American schools in general and painted a dismal picture of the effectiveness of science education.

About the same time, the NSF funded *Project Synthesis* (Harms and Yager 1982), an attempt by science educators to distill data from major studies of the professional science education literature and to make projections of what ought to be in the future. This report provided a rationale for an emerging movement that drew science education away from its "pure" discipline base to a merger with technology and the societal implications of science, a movement known as Science, Technology, and Society (STS). This approach was based on science courses that encouraged students to investigate such local and national issues as energy, soil, and water conservation. It would have students identify and solve pressing problems related to science and society. It would focus on such issues as human overpopulation, nuclear waste, and endangered species, and encourage students toward careers in science and technology. Students would become investigators of the social, economic, legal, political, and environmental ramifications of scientific issues, and would become active decision makers regarding the applications of scientific discoveries. (For additional background on STS, see Hurd 1975, 1986, 1991.)

The National Science Teachers Association (NSTA) buttressed the STS movement when its Board of Directors developed an official position statement, *Science/Technology/Society: Science Eduation for the 1980's* (1982). The statement maintains that "The goal of science education during the 1980's is to develop scientifically literate citizens who understand how science, technology, and society influence one another and who are able to use this knowledge in their everyday decision-making" (NSTA 1988, 162). The NSTA board's position comprehensively suggests application of STS principles in curricula at all levels, K–12, and in pre-service and in-service training of teachers. Further NSTA support for the STS approach is documented in two subsequent yearbooks, *Redesigning Science and Technology Education* (Bybee, Carlson, and McCormack 1984) and *Science/Technology/Society* (Bybee 1985). That the STS movement continues as a strong force in science education is evidenced in an excellent new book by Dennis Cheek (1992), *Thinking Constructively about Science, Technology and Society.*

As we move into the 1990s, several national science programs reflect an STS approach. *Chemistry in the Community* (ChemCom), now in its second edition, was produced by the American Chemical Society to help high school students learn about both chemistry and the impact of chemistry on society. *Chemical Education for Public Understanding* (CEPUP) is an innovative middle school science program that looks at science/society problems such as toxicity, household solutions, and ground water. The focus is on chemicals and their interactions with people and their environments.

In a somewhat different direction, Project 2061—sponsored by the American Association for the Advancement of Science—is a unique curriculum reform project based on concepts of scientific literacy. The first report of the project's work—*Science for All Americans* (1989)—is an

unusual report from an educational reform group in that it does not prescribe specific solutions to our science education problems. Instead, it presents its purpose to "characterize scientific literacy" in the form of basic learning goals for all children. The project takes its name from the next year Halley's Comet will visit near Earth— but the project planners expect significant changes well before that date!

Project 2061 organizers suggest that the basic dimensions of scientific literacy are:

- Being familiar with the natural world and recognizing both its diversity and its unity
- Understanding key concepts and principles of science
- Being aware of some of the important ways in which science, mathematics, and technology depend upon one another
- Knowing that science, mathematics, and technology are human enterprises and what that implies about their strengths and limitations
- Developing scientific habits of mind
- Using scientific knowledge and ways of thinking for individual and social purposes (American Association for the Advancement of Science 1989).

Project 2061 is organized into three phases: Phase I will attempt to spell out the knowledge, skills, and attitudes as targets for all science programs; Phase II will involve teams of teachers and scientists to develop several different curriculum models for use in a diversity of school districts; and Phase III will be a widespread collaborative effort, lasting for many years, in which the results of the earlier phases will be implemented on a large scale to reform science education nationally. In the 1990-91 school year, six school districts were chosen as Phase II sites, for development of curriculum models based on the recommendations compiled in Phase I (American Association for the Advancement of Science 1992); in early 1993 the results are scheduled to be published.

The latter 1980s produced another reform movement mainly fostered by the NSTA—the *Project on Scope, Sequence, and Coordination* (SS&C). This project grew from a synthesis of reports and studies indicating that U.S. schools produce a majority of students lacking a basic understanding of science, mathematics, and technology (Aldridge 1992). Proponents of SS&C charge that education's primary goal has been mastery of facts and that "Schools, teachers, and parents, educated in this tradition themselves, felt compelled to perpetuate this mind-numbing experience and to construct an education edifice of facts (NSTA 1992, 13).

The SS&C project takes aim at the organization of science programs in American secondary schools, calling it a "layer cake." For virtually all high school science programs, the bottom of the cake is biology, supporting a layer of chemistry, which in turn supports a layer of physics. The science of any one year is disconnected from what came before or what will come after. One major consequence of this arrangement is that three-quarters of American high school graduates take no science beyond biology and receive essentially no exposure at all to physical sciences.

SS&C advocates aim to dismantle the layer cake and its associated memorization of facts and unconnected trivia. They subscribe to a "less is more" philosophy and claim that if students study fewer topics in greater depth over a longer period of time, they will acquire a far deeper and more useful understanding of science. The project's supporters believe that the secondary science program should span all six secondary school years with biology, chemistry, physics, and earth/space science topics included each year (and preferably each week). Part of the rationale for this approach is from the cognitive science research on the effectiveness of "spaced learning," the discovery that repeated experiences with concepts within different contexts result in superior understanding of abstract ideas (NSTA 1992, 15).

SS&C promotes linkage and integration within and among the sciences so that students become aware of the interdependency of the sciences and their place within the larger body of human experience. Ideas about molecular structure are not confined to chemistry, for instance, but have great relevance in biology, physics, and earth/space sciences. Specific examples of how concepts may be approached in a coherent scope and integrated sequence are provided in *The Content Core: A Guide for Curriculum Designers* (NSTA 1992). (Also see chapters 2 and 4 of this handbook for summaries of the scope and sequence.)

One of the in-process science education reforms was spurred by recent developments in mathematics education. During the 1980s, disappointing cross-national assessments came to the fore, suggesting dismal comparative mathematics achievement by American students. This stimulated a response on the part of the National Council of Teachers of Mathematics: the influential statement of *Curriculum and Evaluation Standards for School Mathematics* (NCTM 1987). The NCTM standards have influenced virtually all textbook and other program development in mathematics since 1987, and have been adopted as a model by science educators who believe a similar set of standards is crucial to curricular reform in science. Thus, in 1991, the prestigious governing board of the National Research Council established a National Committee on Science Education Standards and Assessment. This committee is working in phases to consult with major professional science education organizations. Subcommittees have been established to produce three sets of standards by late fall 1993:

1. *Science Curriculum Standards*—narrative descriptions of what students should learn about science and its applications
2. *Science Teaching Standards*—criteria to be used to guide the development and assessment of teaching and learning strategies
3. *Science Education Assessment Standards*—criteria to be used for guiding the development and implementation of student assessments and program evaluations.

The standards will not be equivalent to curricula, prescriptive descriptions of the "best" way to teach, or actual assessment instruments of tests. They will be stated in a manner that encourages diversity in teaching, learning, and assessment while providing criteria by which science content and teaching procedures can be judged (Stage 1992).

The science education reform trend, as shown in the STS movement, Project 2061, and NSTA's SS&C project, continues strongly into the 1990s. The trend is buttressed by continually produced reports from professional organizations that seem to call almost uniformly for relevance in the science curriculum and the inclusion of societal issues, decision-making skills, and technology (especially computers), and the integration of topics both within the sciences and with science and other disciplines. Current philosophical trends in science education call for attention to scientific literacy, science as a way of thinking and knowing, and science as a human activity. Learning by inquiry is still widely espoused by curriculum developers, but a new trend, led by cognitive psychologists, would have students use their existing knowledge base regarding a science concept, and then have experiences from which new (and more accurate) concepts are constructed by the student. This new movement—constructivism—is really an old idea, but it is a more recent influence in U.S. science education. More will be said about this approach later in this chapter.

Science Education Today

The traditional view considered that science was knowledge of the universe that had accumulated throughout recorded history. Only recently (the last thirty-five years) has there been much attention directed to science processes, the skills that scientists use to discover new knowledge. However, it is clear today that there is much more to science education than content and processes. McCormack and Yager (1989b) developed a new "Taxonomy for Science Education" that broadens the view of science education beyond the two domains of content and process into five domains that should be considered crucial for any good science curriculum. Curriculum developers can use the taxonomy as a blueprint for direction in designing a new program. Evaluators can use the taxonomy as a yardstick against which existing programs can be assessed. The taxonomy's authors "see five domains of science education which are *all* important as we work toward helping all students attain a scientific literacy needed for living in our current society—and one needed if we are to resolve current problems thereby producing a better future" (McCormack and Yager 1989b, 47-48). The taxonomy follows, along with a sample classroom activity for each domain:

A Taxonomy for Science Education

Domain I—Knowing and Understanding (knowledge domain)
Science aims to categorize the observable universe into manageable units for study, and to describe physical and biological relationships. Ultimately, science aims to provide reasonable explanations for observed relationships. Part of any science instruction always involves learning by students of some of the information developed through science.

The *Knowing and Understanding Domain* includes:

- Facts
- Concepts
- Laws (principles)
- Existing hypotheses and theories being used by scientists
- Science and societal issues

All of this vast amount of information is usually classified into such manageable topics as matter, energy, motion, animal behavior, plant development.

Classroom Activity: Assumptions vs. Observed Facts. A teacher presents a test tube containing a red liquid. She asks the students to predict what will happen when the liquid is heated. They predict it will boil and it will make steam. The teacher heats the liquid over a flame, and it turns to a solid! A discussion ensues in which students become aware that they assumed the liquid was water or a waterlike substance in making their predictions. Understanding of the terms *assumption*, *observation*, and *fact* are clarified. Finally, it is revealed that the liquid heated was colored egg white.

Domain II—Exploring and Discovering (process of science domain)
Use of the processes of science to learn how scientists think and work. Some processes of science are:
- Observing and describing
- Classifying and organizing
- Measuring and charting
- Communicating and understanding communication of others
- Predicting and inferring
- Hypothesizing
- Hypothesis testing
- Identifying and controlling variables
- Interpreting data
- Constructing and using instruments, simple devices, and physical models

Classroom Activity: Measuring. Students are given a sugar cube (though not told what it is), a metric ruler, a balance scale, a steel pin, and a prescribed amount of water. They are challenged to make as many observations and measurements as they can of the cube, and to use as many of their senses as they can in doing so.

Domain III—Imagining and Creating (creativity domain)
Most science programs view a science program as something to be done to students to help them

learn a given body of information. Little formal attention has been given in science programs to development of students' imagination and creative thinking. Here are some of the human abilities important in this domain:

- Visualizing—producing mental images
- Combining objects and ideas in new ways
- Producing alternate or unusual uses for objects
- Solving problems and puzzles
- Fantasizing
- Pretending
- Dreaming
- Designing devices and machines
- Producing unusual ideas

Much research and development has been done on developing students' abilities in this creative domain, but little of this has been purposely incorporated into science programs.

Classroom Activity: The Water-Expanding Machine. A science teacher claims to have invented a machine that expands the volume of water by a factor of three. She points to a box that has an input funnel on top and an outlet tube at its base. She has a volunteer measure 500 mL of water and pour it into the funnel. In a short time, 1500 mL of water pours out of the outlet. Since the teacher has presented this in a tongue-in-cheek fashion, students are suspicious. She asks, "How many of you believe the water really expanded?" Very few do. "You *did* see the water *appear* to be expanded. See if you can draw an idea of what could be inside the box to create this illusion. Try to come up with an idea that no one else will think of." As kids create their models, they are thinking creatively.

Domain IV—Feeling and Valuing
(attitudinal domain)

In these times of increasingly complex social and political institutions, environmental and energy problems, and general worry about the future, scientific content, processes, and even attention to imagination are not sufficient parameters for a science program. Human feeling, values, and decision-making skills need to be addressed. This domain includes:

- Developing positive attitudes toward science in general, science in school, and science teachers
- Developing positive attitudes toward oneself (an "I can do it" attitude)
- Exploring human emotions
- Developing sensitivity to, and respect for, the feelings of other people
- Expressing personal feelings in a constructive way
- Making decisions about personal values
- Making decisions about social and environmental issues

Classroom Activity: The Od Ogg. Students are presented with a problem: A drawing of an Od Ogg is shown. It is half human and half animal. This individual is the last of its kind. Some people think it should be destroyed. Some would display it in a zoo or circus. Others say it should be used for horror films. What should be done?

Students work on this dilemma in cooperative discussion groups, considering pros and cons and the ethics of this discussion. In doing so, they become aware of some of their personal attitudes and those of classmates.

Domain V—Using and Applying
(applications and connections domain)

It seems pointless to have any science program if the program does not include some substantial amount of information, skills, and attitudes that can be transferred and used in students' everyday lives. Also, it seems inappropriate to divorce "pure" or "academic" science from technology. Students need to become sensitized to those experiences they encounter which reflect ideas they have learned in school science. Some dimensions of this domain are:

- Seeing instances of scientific concepts in everyday life experiences
- Applying learned science concepts and skills to everyday technological problems
- Understanding scientific and technological principles involved in household technological devices
- Using scientific processes in solving problems that occur in everyday life
- Understanding and evaluating mass media reports of scientific developments
- Making decisions related to personal health, nutrition, and life style based on knowledge of scientific rather than on "hear-say" or emotions
- Integrating science with other subjects

Classroom Activity: Invention Dissection. Over a period of time, students are encouraged to collect and bring to school "dead" household appliances (old toasters, electric mixers, blenders, etc.). These are in abundance in garages and attics due to industry's common policy of planned obsolescence! Students are also asked to bring in borrowed screwdrivers, wrenches, and pliers. As part of an Invention or Technology unit, they take apart the old appliances and try to learn or infer as much as they can about how they operate. Much can be learned about gears, motors, switches, and solenoids through this experience, and students gain some appreciation and respect for engineering and inventiveness.

Viewing science from any one domain may limit the opportunity for students to see the richness of science. Certainly there is no evidence that the information—that included in textbooks, curriculum guides, and state lists of science competencies—is a prerequisite for learning and experience in other domains. Without a doubt, good science lessons frequently draw simultaneously from several domains. The process of measurement, for example, might be used in timing the movement of cylinders down a ramp while learning about the concept of accelerated motion.

Cognitive Science and Constructivism

Since the 1930s, a behaviorist school of psychology has dominated American education which has assumed that the human mind is an unfathomable "black box." According to this point of view, learning could be studied only as a set of reinforceable behaviors that were affected by stimulus and reward. Teaching, therefore, was the process of building hundreds of "associations" through practice and reinforcing rewards. Behaviorist researchers eventually realized that there were many levels in the complexity of learning knowledge and skills, so they developed taxonomies of objectives and intellectual skills. The most widely known and applied of those hierarchies were those proposed by Robert Gagné (1974) and Benjamin Bloom et al. (1954). "Higher-order" levels of thinking needed for problem solving were relegated to lofty capstones at the top of hierarchies that were not reachable by many students.

The behaviorist view of learning has had its critics who proposed an opposing point of view. Jean Piaget and his energetic disciples argued that memorized knowledge was not real or useful in that it generally could not be applied by the child to genuine problems in life's experiences. Piaget maintained that knowledge, and even "intelligence," must be uncovered and con-

structed through intensely personal activity by the child. Knowledge and the development of thinking skills were phenomena that happened internally, not by administering external drill and practice. For Piaget, the child is a natural scientist who tries to understand the world and construct his own meaning or explanations. Piagetians theorized that young humans have two basic strategies for interacting with their surroundings: assimilation, where they absorb experiences into already formed but evolving cognitive structures, and accommodation, where they modify existing cognitive structures to deal with discrepant experiences (Inhelder and Piaget 1958).

The followers of Piaget believed his theories could be widely applied to science education. Since the child's spontaneous activity was a key to learning, students should be encouraged to design experiments to solve questions arising from personal experiences with materials. Overly structured or directed experiences should be avoided. Piagetian proponents also argued that students needed time to develop at their own individual rates. Children followed the same stages in a developmental sequence, they said, but at different paces.

Piaget's work has great philosophical appeal, but science educators have had some difficulty in applying a true Piagetian approach within a mainstream science program that could be assessed by achievement on standardized tests. It was no simple task to develop a program to teach both concepts and intellectual skills within the context of a philosophy that eschewed all attempts to teach directly. Hands-on laboratories and process skills became major foci for school science programs during the First Revolution, but it was found difficult to balance process emphases with concept development, and even more difficult to incorporate goals in the domains of attitudes, creativity, and applications (White 1988).

Current cognitive science offers promising solutions to what appear to be serious limitations to Piaget's tenets. New perspectives on learning offer central places for both thinking skills and knowledge and also give appropriate recognition to the domains of attitudes, creativity, and applications. Present-day cognitive scientists adopt from Piaget a constructivist view of learning, postulating that humans are not passive recipients of knowledge but active constructors of knowledge structures. Receiving information is not truly learning; the information must be placed in perspective, interpreted, and related to other existing knowledge in the brain's memory structures. Skill in mastering a scientific process requires more than just mechanically performing a procedure; you must also know when to perform it and how to modify it or adapt it to unique situations.

The essence of constructivist learning is the idea that *what is already in the student's mind matters.* The prior knowledge that students bring to each learning experience intimately affects how and what they will learn. During a constructivist learning experience, students have opportunities to become aware of their preexisting ideas—they interact with materials, observe, and then verbalize their inherent existing explanations for a phenomenon. Then they test and scrutinize their explanations, often modifying them and sometimes abandoning them.

Constructivists do not simply provide materials to children and "get out of the way" as some Piagetian proponents suggested. Constructivists offer a much more definitive direction to educators, while also incorporating into their instructional theories attention to the major questions that have always plagued teachers: how to motivate students, how to help students learn concepts, how concepts might be sequenced for learning, where to use laboratory approaches versus other learning procedures, and how to assess student learning. The key difference in constructivism, as compared to earlier theories of learning, is that instruction is not something done *to* students. Instruction is done in a way that helps the students become conscious of their own personal knowledge structures and helps them nourish, refine, modify, or replace those structures. The constructivists' goal is to help students develop their own capacity to learn.

Here are some general principles associated with a constructivist approach to teaching science (Brooks 1990; Loucks-Horsley et al. 1990):

1. Provide an invitational/interactive phase at the beginning of new learning sequences in which students identify a scientific phenomenon and verbalize their existing "theories" to account for the problem. Encourage alternative explanations and discussion.
2. Use student conceptions and thinking to drive lessons. Provide opportunities for tests of ideas (even apparently "bad" ones).
3. Alternate hands-on data-seeking with dialogue among peers and with the teacher.
4. Ask probing questions requiring students to justify, back up, or find evidence for their tentative explanations.
5. Allow ample wait time after posing questions *and* before responding to students' responses.
6. Encourage students to elaborate their explanations, but do not judge them.
7. Insist on *predictions* of outcomes before conducting a scientific test or experiment.
8. Always be on the alert for students' alternative conceptions and design lessons through which evidence collects to challenge the misconceptions.
9. Adopt the philosophy "less is more." It is impossible to cover huge numbers of scientific concepts quickly using a constructivist approach.

A good constructivist-oriented instructional model has been developed by Susan Loucks-Horsley et al. (1990). If applied in schools, this model should engender both good constructivist teaching and attention to all five domains in the previously discussed Taxonomy for Science Education. The model reflects the parallel, yet unique, qualities of science and technology. The four-stage model can be summarized in the following chart.

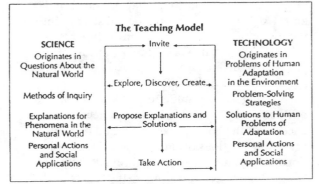

From *Elementary School Science for the '90s.*
Andover, MA: The Network, Inc.;
Alexandria, VA: Association for Supervision
and Curriculum Development.
Reproduced with permission.

In Stage 1, students are *invited* to learn. This can be done through the presentation of a discrepant event demonstration or a photograph that suggests a problem or perplexity, by a hands-on experience, or simply through teacher questions. Naturally occurring events such as earthquakes, or manmade disturbances such as the *Exxon Valdez* oil spill, can be used to focus on phenomena or problems for investigation. It is essential that adequate attention be given to the conscious expression of students' prior or existing beliefs, questions, and concerns. Curiosity should be used to advantage. At the end of this stage, students should be focused on one or more problems or questions, be excited, and feel the need to investigate.

Stage 2 challenges students to *answer their own questions* through observation, measurement, or experimentation. They compare and test their ideas and try to make "sense" out of data they collect. Not all groups of students will be working on the same question or be doing the same experimental tests.

This does not rule out guidelines from the teacher. Suggestions for "community activities" might be made by the teacher so that a common base of essential experience is provided for all students in the class. In some lessons, students explore and seek scientific understanding through experiments; in others they create or invent. For instance, students might be challenged to invent a method to remove a mini—oil spill from a bowl of water. Their inventions would fall more into the realm of technology than of science, but they would also be expanding their scientific knowledge of concepts such as density, absorption, immiscibility, and buoyancy. Expeditions into inventiveness, of course, go beyond the familiar knowledge and process domains of science into the realm of creativity. Also, since students are actively engaged in working on problems of interest to them personally, there should also be fallout into the attitudinal domain.

During Stage 3, students *propose explanations and solutions*. Since they have had new experiences with the concept being studied through preceding portions of the lesson, prior conceptions may be modified or even replaced by new ones. The teacher encourages students to verbalize the new views they have gained through observation and experimentation. They are given time to convince themselves and their peers that their conceptions coincide with what has actually been observed.

Stage 4 challenges students to find applications for, and take action on, what they have learned. If they have discovered, for example, that electrical switches operate by controlling gaps in the wires making up a circuit, they may design and construct new types of switches from simple materials, survey their own homes for switches, and propose safety guidelines that manufacturers should follow in the design of

switches for use in various electrical household devices. Or the teacher may find a newspaper clipping about someone who was accidentally electrocuted and have students analyze the causes of the accident and what precautions might have prevented it.

Cognitive Science Research Related to Constructivism

Restructuring the existing knowledge of students has become a principal educational goal for constructivists. It has been widely documented that the minds of students are not scientifically blank when they come to our classes (McDermott 1984; Driver, Guesne, and Tiberghien 1985). They have strong initial conceptions about clouds, gases, motion, living organisms, and chemical changes. All humans have a "common sense" view of natural phenomena. Unfortunately, common sense views frequently vary widely from the views held by professional scientists. Researchers have found that traditional science instruction typically does not deal with students' alternate, or commonsense, explanations, and that traditional instruction in a straight transmission mode is ineffective in changing these conceptions appreciably (Minstrell 1984; Goldberg and McDermott 1987).

Fortunately, a growing body of research indicates that if constructivist principles are applied in science lessons, students' prior conceptions may be positively altered. The most comprehensive guide to this literature in science education is that of Carmichael et al. (1990).

Misconceptions

There are many ways curriculum developers can think about the beginning state of learners in an educational sequence. One is to consider learners to be passive receivers that simply need to be exposed to the proper information. The constructivist's view is that students come to learning tasks already well supplied with their own sets of knowledge and expectations. These initial-state ideas can be called preconceptions. When preconceptions are inaccurate, they can be considered misconceptions or naive conceptions.

Science education researchers have recently been giving much attention to misconceptions found in the prior knowledge of students. Anderson and Smith (1984), for example, studied responses of fifth graders to the question, "What is food for plants?" Students mostly gave replies of "water," "soil," and "plant food that we can buy in stores." Students' common sense tells them that plant food must be analogous to people food. They lack the conception that plants make their own food through photosynthesis.

Anderson and Smith (1984) also identified misconceptions held by children about light and vision. Their data indicate that most middle school students believe that their eyes somehow actively "see" objects rather than detect reflected light. Some believe that some illusive "force" moves from their eyes to the objects, resulting in vision. These students also conceived of white light as being clear or colorless rather than as a fusion of spectral colors. Misconceptions like these need to be brought to students' conscious levels and confronted with appropriate experiences if effective learning of science is to proceed.

The Inert Knowledge Problem

It is assumed that knowledge and skills learned in school will somehow transfer for use in real-life situations experienced by students. However, students frequently learn ideas within very specific contexts, and if they are not challenged to apply new knowledge to tangential contexts, the knowledge will remain "inert" (Whitehead 1929; Perfetto, Bransford, and Franks 1983; Weisberg, DiCamillo, and Phillips 1978).

Unfortunately, researchers have found that much of what is learned from textbooks remains inert knowledge. Simply reading new information does not necessarily replace previous misconceptions. Anderson and Smith (1984) had middle school students read a textbook analogy of a rubber ball bouncing off a wall that illustrated the concept of reflection and compared this with the reflection of light. Students were subsequently asked to solve problems such as this: "When sunlight strikes a tree it helps the boy see the tree. How does it do this?" Apparently the bouncing-ball analogy remained as inert knowledge, since 80 percent of the students said nothing about reflected light in their responses to the problem.

A study of how students read science textbooks, conducted by Roth (1985), provides insights into this learning difficulty. She found that five different strategies may be used by students in reading textbooks:

1. Completely avoid thinking about the meaning of the text while reading and rely entirely on prior knowledge or guesswork in answering text-related questions.

2. Memorize facts as they are read but not relate these to real-world experiences whatsoever.
3. Search for key words in text-related questions and match them up with words in the text. Answers are merely key word–containing sentences copied from the text.
4. Distort the information in the text to conform to prior knowledge.
5. Change prior knowledge to make it conform to the text.

Only users of the fifth strategy (a small percentage of students) demonstrated significant conceptual change. It is interesting to note that the students using this strategy were somewhat aware of the conflicts between their own conceptions and those presented by the text: they complained of being confused or having trouble understanding the book. Roth's work indicates that we need to help students learn to relate what they read in science to real-world counterparts. Prereading questions or challenges might help. Better yet, more active learning by doing, rather than reading, seems to be a far superior solution.

Motivation

In traditional psychology, research on motivation was conducted quite separately from research on learning. Motivation was studied mainly by social psychologists, who were not concerned with learning. Learning was studied by behavioral or cognitive psychologists, who viewed motivation as an impetus to launch a learning or thinking episode, but not as a key part of the ongoing process.

This division of efforts now seems to be vanishing. Both social psychologists and cognitive psychologists now see motivation as a vital element in most cognitive processes. Social psychologists Dweck and Elliot (1983), for example, looked at influences of types of motivation and their effects on student studying and test-taking performances. The researchers found two groupings of students in terms of student views of intelligence:

Group A. Intelligence is thought of as a fixed, inherited talent, something that you either have or do not have. These students are motivated to perform only when the task is something they have previously mastered and can perform well. They avoid unusual situations or new challenges.

Group B. Intelligence is thought to be developmental and can be improved through effort and hard work. These students accept or even seek new challenges, which are looked upon as intelligence-building experiences.

When encountering a difficult problem, both Group A and Group B students may fail in their initial attempts to solve it. Group B students love the challenge; Group A students attempt to avoid or retreat from the situation and thus miss an opportunity to learn.

The implication of this research for curriculum developers—the idea that intelligence is a changeable, improvable entity—should pervade student learning materials, teachers' guides, and in-service programs. It has long been known in education that teacher expectations for students frequently become a self-fulfilling prophecy: if a teacher believes her students are intelligent and will learn well, they will. If students come to believe they can improve their intelligence and learning ability through educational experience, they will be more likely to want to engage in those experiences.

A constructivist approach to science learning encourages students to transform from Group A types to Group B types. Teacher respect for students' prior knowledge "theories" is something they haven't likely experienced in nonconstructivist classrooms. The feelings of success derived from testing and rethinking personally held ideas can be a boost to self-esteem and a challenge to deeply held ideas about fixed intelligence.

Psychologists have always held that there are two forms of motivation: intrinsic and extrinsic. Intrinsic motivation is exemplified by willingness to participate energetically in a task for its own sake—for instance, observing ants collecting food simply to satisfy curiosity about ant behavior. To study ant food-collecting behavior for extrinsic reasons, students might do so for a reward such as a good grade or a candy bar. Researchers have found that the most effective and lasting learning takes place when driven by intrinsic motivation (Lepper and Greene 1978).

According to Lepper and Chabay (1985), cognitive psychologists have identified three factors that affect intrinsic motivation: challenge, control, and curiosity. There appears to be an optimum level for each of these factors; higher or lower levels of each seem to decrease motivation.

Challenge consists of "bet you can't do it" teasers that promote a desire for achievement. The realm of science, fortunately, is full of possible challenges. Discrepant events, for instance, are science demonstrations that present observations that seem counter to the expecta-tions most of us have due to "common knowledge." If an ice cube is placed in a glass of water, most people expect it to float. If it sinks to the bottom of the glass, we have a discrepancy between what we actually see and what we expect. Students can be challenged to suggest explanations and do experiments to test their ideas. Many teachers use mystery boxes to challenge students' thinking. McCormack (1981) suggests other means for bringing challenge into science classrooms in his *Inventors Workshop* program. Students are challenged to construct "push-rod boxes" to operate in the same way that a teacher's box works. One push-rod box has dowels protruding through opposite sides of the box. When one rod is pushed in, the other moves out three times the distance of the first rod.

Students are also challenged to propose an explanatory model for a "water-expanding machine" that apparently changes 500 ml of water poured into its input funnel to 1500 ml of water that exits the machine's output tube. Later in the *Inventors Workshop*, students are given a list of challenges that can be solved through construction of Rube Goldberg–style contraptions. They are challenged to build a device that would automatically crush an ice cube, crack an egg, toss dice, remove the pit from an olive, or perform dozens of other challenges.

Challenge, used properly, can promote active engagement with materials and enthusiastic mental invention and analysis of ideas. The trick is for teachers to find challenges at the correct level of difficulty. Tasks that are too easy may fail to motivate because they do not provide sufficient challenge, but tasks that are too difficult or impossible can cause countermotivational frustration.

Control involves a sense of command over the environment and a feeling of self-determination. On one level, a sense of control is gained if students are actively involved in manipulating materials and designing experiments, rather than observing passively. But a more focused strategy for engendering a sense of control is to give students choices of topics to be studied, the ways to structure scientific questions or problems, and the criteria to be used for evaluation of performance.

Learning-center and contract approaches to organization have great possibilities for providing options for students, thus maximizing sense of control. A learning center organizes individual or small-group science activities from a table at one side of the classroom. A standing trifold card-board backdrop on the table has card pockets attached to it which offer multiple science tasks or activities that students can choose. Manipulative materials needed in completing the tasks are located in boxes beneath the table. Learning centers may be focused on a familiar science topic—"electricity," "animals," or "pollution"— or on science processes—"How to be a Super Observer," or "Measurement of Liquids."

Contract approaches require students to choose from a printed menu the goals and activities they need to complete in order to achieve a certain grade. They may choose, for example, to complete five experiments from a group of ten, to read and summarize three magazine articles from a library of thirty, to build a measuring device by selecting one construction blueprint out of five provided, and to solve one creative challenge from a pool of ten challenge cards. Using a contract approach, the teacher becomes an advisor and coach rather than the "sage on the stage." When students work at their own pace and on projects that they control, they tend to have high levels of intrinsic motivation.

Curiosity is the realm of naturally occurring human interest. Humans seem to have an inborn drive to explore new places, things, and ideas. Because natural curiosity is programmed into the brain, people find pleasure in experiences that are novel, bizarre, mysterious, perplexing, surprising, counter to intuition, or phenomenal. Repetitive, uniform, unvarying school tasks become boring and, hence, nonmotivational. Experiences that pique students' curiosity are those that involve departures from the everyday into the world of the oddball, fantastic, and mind-bending. Studies of children's interests for fifty years have found dinosaurs near the top of the list of items that are "interesting" and that "we would like to know more about." Why is this? Because dinosaurs are infinitely *mysterious* (no person has ever really seen one), *bizarre* (they came in unthinkable shapes and sizes), *huge* (some taller than our two-story homes), and *frightening* (they had monstrous claws and big, sharp teeth). Fortunately, we have a vast supply of similar high-interest subjects for study in science. The trick is to highlight and capitalize on the mysteriousness and bizarreness of our subject. For instance, observing a rich pond-water culture under a microscope can become an adventure in which beasts as unusual as dinosaurs can be experienced. *Amoebas* and *Paramecia* are fasci-

nating creatures, and they should be introduced with an appropriate background or challenge to take full advantage of their uncommonness.

Williams (1983) suggests the use of fantasy as a door to students' inner worlds. She suggests taking students on fantasy trips, in which students are given a set of instructions enabling them to relax and close their eyes. Then the teacher uses a soothing voice to direct their imaginations on a make-believe journey through the human blood-stream, through an electric circuit, or perhaps to a distant planet. Since time and space pose no problem to the mind, students can revisit the epoch of the dinosaurs or shrink themselves to the size of an electron. Fantasy trips are "pleasant and motivating experiences," and one can also develop "the ability to transcend physical limitations through the mind, to project oneself into something and explore it mentally or to imagine oneself become the thing, . . . an extremely important skill for problem solving and other creative endeavors" (Williams 1983, 117). In some respects, fantasy is the ultimate skill needed for constructivist-oriented learning!

Curiosity can also be tapped through the use of science-based illusions. McCormack (1990) found dramatic presentation of illusions to be highly generative of student interest and willingness to participate in science problem-solving activities. Story lines, humor, fantasy, and enthusiasm were identified as key ingredients needed by teachers in the invitation phase of lessons. In combination with unusual discrepant illusions ("invisible glue," "anti-gravity water"), these techniques were found both to provoke curiosity and to benefit attitudes.

Cooperative Learning

One of the exciting trends in science education involves a departure from the competitive, individualistic classroom organizations characteristic of American schools. Recent research suggests that immense benefits can be gained when science is taught via a cooperative learning method.

Three human interaction patterns are possible within science classrooms:

1. Individualistic: students work independently toward set criteria
2. Competitive: students work in rivalry to see who "wins" (achieves the best grade)
3. Cooperative: youngsters work together in groups toward a mutual set of goals.

The first two models have traditionally dominated American education. Students have been required to work quietly and independently and to be concerned only with their own personal learning. However, a substantial and growing body of research indicates that cooperative group learning can result in improved learning, more positive attitudes about both science and self, improved thinking and social skills, and better attitudes toward peers who are members of diverse ethnic and socioeconomic groups (Johnson and Johnson 1987b).

There are many ways to organize cooperative learning in a science classroom. For example, teachers can organize students into a number of small, heterogeneous groups of two to five students with high, medium, and low ability. These groups are trained to work cooperatively on science tasks and to "sink or swim" together (Johnson et al. 1986, 8). Students are assigned specific roles within their groups. For instance, the following roles would be appropriate for group members working on a hands-on science investigation:

1. The getter is responsible for obtaining the appropriate materials from a classroom materials distribution center.
2. The reader reads instructions or story lines related to the science activity.
3. The activity director first assembles the materials used in the activity and then makes sure that all group members take part in hands-on experimentation.
4. The recorder makes notes, data tables, or graphs of all important observations.
5. The returner is responsible for transporting materials back to their appropriate storage area and ensures that cleanup is accomplished by the group.

Once cooperative groups are in place, a teacher can spend more time teaching and less time being an administrator or manager. While groups work, the teacher is free to circulate around the room to give one-on-one assistance, build spirit and motivation, and observe and listen to group interactions. In a traditional classroom organization, the teacher is most frequently the focal point for the entire class, a questioner, taskmaster, and competition coordinator.

Research in education and psychology provides a very strong basis in favor of cooperative group approaches as follows:

Achievement

Johnson et al. (1981) conducted a meta-analysis of all research studies conducted since 1924 that compared the relative effects of competitive, cooperative, and individualistic learning management programs. This synthesis indicates that significantly higher achievement is promoted by the cooperative method. The studies encompassed all age levels and school subjects and scrutinized data regarding concept learning, verbal and spatial problem solving, memory and retention of information, and even motor performance.

Higher-Order Thinking Processes

Skon, Johnson, and Johnson (1981) studied the reasoning strategies used by students in cooperative, competitive, and individualistic classrooms. They found students learning in the cooperative mode to be superior in the use of classification strategies, in solving challenging story problems, and in spatial-reasoning tasks. The study concluded that the discussion processes inherent in cooperative groups promote significant development of higher-quality cognitive strategies and also tend to result in more metacognitive thinking (self-scrutinization of thought processes). These findings were confirmed in a subsequent study by Johnson and Johnson (1981).

Involvement in Learning

Cooperative learning stimulates more active oral involvement in learning, since the approach necessitates that students discuss the material being learned. Johnson and Ahlgren (1976) found a strong positive relationship between cooperative learning and students' willingness to express their ideas and opinions to their classmates. They also observed that students in cooperative groups were significantly more actively involved with learning activities than were students in competitive or individualistic environments.

Group Cohesion

Cooperative group members typically form strong group bonds and evidence considerable liking for each other (Johnson and Johnson 1982). Additionally, low- and medium-ability students especially benefit from the approach. High-ability students have been found to be better off academically when they cooperate with their less gifted peers than when they work independently; in the worst case, achievement scores of high-ability students are not diminished by cooperative grouping (Johnson and Johnson 1987a).

Social Interdependence and Acceptance

Evidence has been gathered indicating that cooperative learning promotes more positive attitudes toward heterogeneous peers (Gunderson and Johnson 1980; Johnson, Johnson, and Maruyama 1983). Other studies found that cooperative grouping resulted in improved positive feelings between ethnic minority and majority students (Cooper et al. 1980; Johnson et al. 1983), and among handicapped and nonhandicapped students (Smith, Johnson, and Johnson 1981).

In summary, it appears that cooperative learning can help improve science achievement, students' higher-order thinking skills, and social interaction. Cooperative skills are essential, not only in school, but as lifetime skills necessary for building successful marriages, careers, and friendships. Teamwork and cooperation are essential in most real-life situations, and appropriately organized time spent in science classrooms can be effective preparation for successful participation in our society.

Technology

Computers, television, videodiscs, and telecommunications are making inroads into science education and continue to promise a technological revolution for our schools. However, due mainly to budgetary limitations, the "revolution" has been far from generally realized.

Key questions continue to remain unresolved:

1. How can our science curricula and teaching strategies be redesigned to maximally capitalize on the new technologies?
2. What are the most effective ways to use these technologies?
3. Can new technologies be effectively used to improve learning and problem-solving skills of female and minority students?

By far the most important of the new technologies is the computer. Yet, despite the growing numbers of these wonder-machines in schools, their actual use is neither extensive enough nor always appropriate. Cole and Griffin (1987) synthesized studies of the effects of computers in our schools, finding that:

- Middle- and upper-class children are far more likely to have regular experiences with computers than are lower socioeconomic group children.

- In schools populated by lower socioeconomic group children, computers are used for rote drill and practice instead of the "cognitive enrichment" focus that characterizes use in higher socioeconomic schools.
- Irrespective of socioeconomic class, female students consistently have less involvement with computers than male students.

Education technology advocates have pushed to disseminate computers as widely as possible, but have demonstrated a degree of naivete about the complexity of learning processes that has resulted in ineffective and inappropriate uses of computers in classrooms. Unless science educators are willing to reconceptualize the deepest foundations of how learning takes place, computers have little chance of revitalizing school experiences. A number of studies (Cole and Griffin 1987; Nix 1988; Perkins and Salomon 1989) show that computers and other technologies (videodiscs and telecommunications) can be used extensively in schools without significantly changing or improving either the curriculum or the instruction. The majority of technological applications in schools seems to perpetuate learning theories and teaching practices that are themselves desperately in need of reform.

The main reason computers have not, as yet, resulted in a revitalized curriculum is that their major educational application is for computer-assisted instruction (CAI), which entails primarily low-level drill-and-practice skills. As argued in earlier portions of this chapter, this approach to learning varies dramatically with those being promoted by constructivists and their inquiry/discovery predecessors. Teachers using a CAI approach tend not to focus on higher-level thinking skills and self-constructed conceptualization.

Some Promising Uses of Technology

Science *is* problem solving. To a scientist, this means becoming curious about a phenomenon, observing, suspecting relationships, and creating models. Technology can encourage problem-solving processes while improving students' drive to learn. Excellent technological learning can involve students in problem solving, help them uncover basic concepts, and improve their attitudes toward science. Following are some promising practices:

Simulations of Laboratory and Field Experiments. Computer programs can involve students in exciting simulated experiments in which they control variables associated with roller coasters in amusement parks, gravitational forces on space-craft, or food levels in an ecosystem. In IBM's *Investigating Gravitational Force* simulation, for example, students command "sensors" that can measure the mass, density, distance, and gravitational forces of imaginary planets. Any of these variables can be modified by the press of a key, and the computer determines how the gravitational force responds. This process gives the student an early conception of the nature of gravitation and helps to develop modified conceptualizations more in line with those held by physicists.

Kracjik, Simmons, and Lunetta (1988) found that student experiences with computer simulations compared very favorably with genuine laboratory or field experiences. The simulations were found to be just as effective in having students (1) generate questions, (2) control variables, (3) design experiments, (4) interpret data, and (5) develop scientific models to explain observations.

Computer Interfacing. Computers can be coupled with probes to directly measure temperature, sound, light intensity, breathing rate, pulse, distance, and velocity. Probes are commercially available and can be linked to a microcomputer via a game port, printer port, or an integrated-circuit card. The best news is that measurements through these probes can be screen-displayed in real time as data are collected. Commonly, data can be plotted as a graph. When students can change a variable and instantly see the results on the curve of a graph, this obviates the drudgery of plotting data points.

Using computer probeware, students are more likely to see logical connections between experimental measurements and the resulting graph. Students can spend more time thinking and engaging in problem solving. Nachmias and Linn (1987) found that eighth-grade students improved their understanding of science processes through the use of probes. Krendl and Lieberman (1988) found computer interfacing to improve student motivation, experimental involvement, and self-esteem.

Interactive Information Technology. Vast resources of information can be made easily available to students through interactive information systems. These systems enable students to tap into still and motion video, audio, and textual information. These miracles are accomplished through optical, rather than electronic, storage systems (videodiscs and CD-ROM).

A standard 12-inch laser videodisc can store 108,000 single-frame pictures. These frames can also be displayed as full-motion "movies," complete with stereo sound. When the systems include a computer, the learner can be involved in an interactive dialogue in which both the learner and the system can both give and respond to commands. Even if a computer is not included, the laser disc offers teachers and students access to a huge visual database. The *Bioscience* discs developed by Video Discovery, for example, include slides detailing all groups of biological organisms plus animated sequences of abstract processes such as DNA replication and cell division. Students can use the disc to look up answers to questions as they might with a standard textbook, while teachers can program visuals from the disc to illustrate lessons.

Telecommunications. Through telephone lines attached to computers, telecommunications can link students to information available virtually anywhere in the world. Students can word-process data and send it by electronic mail to students in other schools. Weather services can be tapped for up-to-the-minute information about weather conditions anywhere in the country. And teachers can seek teaching ideas from colleagues throughout the country by using electronic bulletin boards such as PSInet of the Council of State Science Supervisors or the NSTA Bulletin Board.

Gender and Cultural Inequities in Science Education

Our world is becoming increasingly technologically oriented, and it is imperative that all people understand the importance of science in everyday living. As jobs become increasingly intermeshed with technology, individuals without skills in science and technology will be at a severe disadvantage in finding a livelihood. *All* citizens will need sufficient scientific background to make informed decisions on science/technology/society–related issues such as pollution, acid rain, tropical-rainforest deforestation, and AIDS.

Achievement tests in math and science consistently show that both females and minorities are outperformed by white males (NAEP 1984). Only about 15 percent of the Hispanic and African-American 17-year-olds assessed by the National Assessment of Educational Progress (NAEP) in 1986 demonstrated the ability to analyze experimental procedures and scientific data, compared with about 50 percent of the white students at the same age (NAEP 1988). Another national assessment conducted by the Minnesota Science Assessment and Research Project revealed that even as early as age nine, white students scored 12 percent higher than African-American and Hispanic students (Rakow and Walker 1985).

Blocks to Girls in Science

Though boys and girls enter elementary school with equal interest in science, they receive unequal science experiences throughout the elementary years. Compared with girls, boys more frequently use scientific instruments and manipulatives, read more science-oriented books, are given higher grades on science assignments, and are asked more higher-order questions during science lessons (Kahle 1991). Morse and Handley (1985) studied classroom interactions and found that boys were asked significantly more classroom questions than were girls. The number of interactions initiated by boys increased over time, while that of girls decreased. Boys also received more teacher feedback. Other researchers found that teachers challenged boys to finish scientific tasks, while directly showing girls how to do the tasks or finishing the work for them (Whyte 1986).

Blocks to Minority-Group Achievement

Not as much research has been conducted on the causes of less successful performance by underrepresented groups in science as has been on the causes of gender differences in performance. But cognitive style and locus of control have been the focus of some relevant research.

Cognitive style is the tendency to process information in an analytic ("field independent") style versus a global ("field dependent") style (Olstad et al. 1981). Children of underrepresented groups tend to be field dependent more often than white children (Ramirez and Price-Williams 1974; Kagan and Zahn 1975).

Minority group members have been characterized as tending to an external locus of control, whereas Anglo-Americans tend to have an internal locus of control. Individuals are classified as external if they believe their lives are controlled by outside events and circumstances over which they have no influence. For them, life is a dice game. People are internal in their locus of control if they believe they have control over their

environment and can influence the unfolding of their lives. For them, life is a bowling match.

These ethnic group–related differences in cognitive style and locus of control have serious implications for success in science. A positive relationship has consistently been found between school achievement and field independence (Kagan and Buriel 1977), and an internal locus of control (Trachtman 1975).

Language and cultural differences have also frequently been cited as blocks to minority-group science achievement. Llabre and Cuevas (1983) suggested that this problem could be ameliorated by testing in the native language of the learners. Sanchez (1978) found that Mexican-American students succeeded better in bilingual classroom environments. It was also found that Mexican-American pupils responded more favorably to a cooperative rather than a competitive teaching style (Sanchez 1978).

Implications of Research

The overwhelming results of research indicate that the lower achievement of girls and minority groups in science is related to environmental, rather than innate, factors. Even within schools, many factors tend to act as filters preventing girls and minorities from achieving success in science. Unconscious differential treatment of girls and minorities results in less effective experiences within science programs for these students and fewer opportunities to study science as they move through the school and career pipeline. Careers continue to be stereotyped by sex, with the preponderant image of the scientist in our society being that of a white male. School science education needs to become an agent to transform rather than transmit societal stereotypes.

Researchers have examined characteristics of teachers and classroom environments that result in girls, boys, and minorities participating and achieving equally. Galton (1981) found female secondary students to prefer teachers who emphasized student-initiated and -maintained behavior in experimental design and hypothesis testing. He interpreted that this teaching style was well received because it reduced teacher intervention and subtly acknowledged students' capacity to think for themselves. Smith and Erb (1986) found that providing women scientists as role models helped reduce the gender-stereotyped masculine image of science. Kahle (1985) identified good gender-equitable science programs as including the use of nonsexist instructional materials and the frequent use of all-participant discussions and laboratory exercises. She suggests that direct, skills-related science activities are essential for girls. Teacher training concerning differential classroom-participation problems was the most influential variable.

Clewell (1987) maintains that minorities and females will benefit most simply from good science education. Her summary of the research resulted in the following recommendations:

- Science teachers need to adopt teaching methods to accommodate varying stages of cognitive development.
- Students should seek solutions to problems through direct use of manipulatives.
- Instruction should proceed from concrete to abstract.
- Teachers need to be aware of how their expectations and stereotypes can affect students' achievement.
- Females and minorities should be thoroughly exposed to activities encouraging the exploration of mechanical apparatus, computation, and other science skills.
- Mexican-American students (and most others) benefit from the use of cooperative-learning techniques in bilingual settings with bilingual teachers.
- Instructional approaches should accommodate cognitive styles and locus-of-control orientations of learners.
- Grouping students homogeneously is less effective than grouping heterogeneously.
- Programs should recognize the diverse life experiences of students and adjust the curriculum and learning activities accordingly.

Assessment Reforms in Science Education

Assuredly, great foment characterizes current curricula and research in science education. However, the professional literature clearly indicates that assessment strategies have not kept pace with extant learning theory, instructional strategies, educational technology, and curricular advances. It is becoming increasingly obvious that scores on existing standardized and teacher-made tests reveal only a narrow and incomplete glimpse of human achievement. The ubiquitous multiple-choice testing format is nearly universally criti-cized as being too narrow in scope, not relevant to the assessment of higher-order thinking skills, and resulting in a disservice to minorities (Dowling 1988).

Testing, especially standardized testing, continues to be a driving force for science curricula and classroom instructional patterns. The idea that "teachers teach to the test" is a familiar cliche, but unfortunately it is painfully accurate. However, if trends in science education are moving toward teaching and learning within all of the Five Domains of Science Education, assessment should do likewise (Yager 1987).

The NAEP group has been conducting research in the use of performance-based assessments. Students demonstrate their problem-solving abilities using laboratory apparatus to solve actual scientific problems. Performance assessments are being tested in grades 3, 7, and 11, requiring students to use their minds *and* hands while being tested. Tasks trial-tested so far challenge students to classify, observe, infer and hypothesize, detect patterns, and design and conduct experiments (NAEP 1987). "Hands-on," authentic testing has been found to be both possible and desirable in these studies, and the researchers believe these tests will be useful for studying how students' performance varies with their backgrounds and their approaches to problem solving.

The Biological Sciences Curriculum Study (BSCS) is another national group that is directing considerable attention to authentic assessment. In *Getting Started in Science: A Blueprint for Elementary School Science Education* (1989), emphasis is given to "testing in the *service* of learning." Authentic assessment is difficult to separate from learning activities, and, in fact, advances learning. The BSCS, agreeing with NAEP, promotes performance testing, observational records of student performance, and documentation of student work via portfolio collections of their achievements. Loucks-Horsley et al. (1990) argue for pushing beyond our customary "confined image and practice of assessment" to the use of these possibilities:

Portfolios
Self-reports
Concept mapping
Drawings
Problem analysis
Research analysis
Practical laboratory tests
Games and simulations

Out-of-doors tests
Computer-based assessment
Cooperative tests
Construction projects
Journals
Observation of experimental procedures

The authors observe that the movement to create alternative means of assessment is growing, but there is still a scarcity of ready-made adoptable models.

Summary

Science education has a long history of repeated calls for reform. More than a century ago, reformers called for less attention in science programs to "facts and trivia" and more concern for problem-solving processes and applications of science to "real life." This theme repeats in numerous permutations through a textbook/utilitarian period, a post-*Sputnik* curriculum revolution, a Science/Technology/Society movement, and a current large-scale reform movement.

Current reforms are deep, widespread, and serious. Cognitive scientists have produced impressive research findings favoring constructivist learning. Science educators are working to develop learning activities to accomplish goals in all of the Five Domains of Science Education. Cooperative grouping has become a mainstay of class organization at the elementary and middle school levels. NSTA's Scope, Sequence, and Coordination Project is designed to involve all students in all scientific disciplines in an interconnected way throughout their secondary years. Technology shows promise for making learning more efficient, exciting, and empowering. And all these approaches are being tempered by a new national awareness of the need to make science accessible to all Americans, regardless of gender, cultural/ethnic background, or socioeconomic group.

References

Aldridge, B. G. 1992. "Project on Scope, Sequence, and Coordination: 1992. A New Synthesis for Improving Science Education." *Journal of Science Education and Technology* 1 (1): 13-21.

American Association for the Advancement of Science. 1989. *Science for All Americans.* Washington, DC.

American Forest Council. 1992. *Project Learning Tree.* Washington, DC: American Forest Council; cosponsored by the Council and the Western Regional Environmental Education Council.

Anderson, C. W., and E. L. Smith. 1984. "Children's Preconceptions and Content-Area Textbooks." In *Comprehension Instruction: Perspectives and Suggestions,* ed. G. Duffy, L. Roehler, and J. Mason, 126-40. White Plains, NY: Longman.

——. 1991. "Teaching Science." In *The Educator's Handbook: A Research Perspective,* ed. V. Koehler, 87-109. White Plains, NY: Longman.

Biological Sciences Curriculum Study and The Network. 1989. *Getting Started in Science: A Blueprint for Elementary School Science Education.* Washington, DC; Colorado Springs, CO.

Bloom, B. S., et al. 1954. *Taxonomy of Educational Objectives. Handbook 1: Cognitive Domain.* New York: Longmans, Green

Brooks, J. G. 1990. "Teachers and Students: Constructivists Forging New Connections." *Educational Leadership* 47 (5): 68-71.

Bybee, R. W. 1985. *Science/Technology/Society.* Washington, DC: NSTA.

Bybee, R. W., J. Carlson, and A. J. McCormack. 1984. *Redesigning Science and Technology Education.* Washington, DC: NSTA.

Carmichael, P., et al. 1990. *Research on Students' Conceptions in Science: A Bibliography.* Leeds, England: Children's Learning in Science Research Group, Univ. of Leeds.

Cheek, D. W. 1992. *Thinking Constructively about Science, Technology and Society.* Albany: State Univ. of New York Press.

Clewell, C. C. 1987. "What Works and Why: Research and Theoretical Bases of Intervention Programs in Math and Science for Minority and Female Middle School Students." In *Students and Science Learning,* ed. A. B. Champagne and L. E. Hornig, 95-135. Washington, DC: American Association for the Advancement of Science.

Cole, M., and P. Griffin. 1987. *Improving Science and Mathematics Education for Minorities and Women: Contextual Factors.* Madison, WI: National Research Council, Wisconsin Center for Educational Research.

Collette, A. T., and E. L. Chiappetta. 1989. *Science Instruction in the Middle and Secondary*

Schools. Columbus, OH: Merrill.

Cooper, L., et al. 1980. "The Effects of Cooperation, Competition, and Individualization on
Cross-Ethnic, Cross-Sex, and Cross-Ability
Friendships." *Journal of Social Psychology* 111:
243-52.

Cuevas, G. J. 1983. "Mathematics Learning in
English as a Second Language." *Journal for
Research in Mathematics Education* 14 (2): 134-
44.

DeBoer, G. 1991. *A History of Ideas in Science
Education: Implications for Practice.* New York:
Teachers College Press.

Dowling, K. W. 1988. "Science Achievement
Testing: Aligning Testing Method with Teaching Purpose." In *Students and Science Learning,*
ed. A. B. Champagne and L. E. Hornig, 137-
51. Washington, DC: American Association for
the Advancement of Science.

Driver, R., E. Guesne, and A. Tiberghien. 1985.
Children's Ideas in Science. Philadelphia: Open
Univ. Press.

Dweck, C. S., and E. S. Elliot. 1983. "Achieve-
ment Motivation." In *Socialization, Personality,
and Social Development,* ed. E. M.
Hetherington, 217-75. Handbook of Child
Psychology, ed. P. H. Mussen, vol. 4. New York:
Wiley.

Gagné, R. M. 1974. *The Conditions of Learning.*
2d ed. New York: Holt, Rinehart & Winston.

Galton, M. 1981. "Differential Treatment of Boy
and Girl Pupils During Science Lessons." In
The Missing Half: Girls and Science Education,
ed. A. Kelly, 180-91. Manchester, England:
Manchester Univ. Press.

Goldberg, F., and L. McDermott. 1987. "An
Investigation of Student Understanding of the
Real Image Formed by a Converging Lens or
Concave Mirror." *American Journal of Physics*
55: 108-19.

Gunderson, B., and D. W. Johnson. 1980. "Building Positive Attitudes By Using Cooperative
Learning Groups." *Foreign Language Annals*
13: 39-46.

Gustafson, J. A., et al. 1983. *The First National
Congress for Environmental Education Futures:
Policies and Practices.* Columbus, OH: SMEAC
Information Reference Center.

Harms, N. C., and R. E. Yager, eds. 1982. *What
Research Says to the Science Teacher.* Washington, DC: National Science Teachers Association.

Helgeson, S. L., P. E. Blosser, and R. W. Howe.
1977. *The Status of Pre-College Science, Math-*

ematics, and Social Science Education: 1955-75.
Science Education, vol. 1. Columbus, OH:
ERIC Center for Science and Mathematics
Education, Ohio State Univ.

Holmes, B. J. 1982. "Black Students' Performance
in the National Assessments of Science and
Mathematics." *Journal of Negro Education* 51
(4): 392-405.

Hurd, P. DeH. 1969. *New Directions in Teaching
Secondary School Science.* Chicago, IL: Rand
McNally.

———. 1975. "Science, Technology, and Society:
New Goals for Interdisciplinary Teaching."
Science Teacher 42 (2): 27-30.

———. 1982. "Transformation of Science Education: Challenges and Criteria." *Science Education* 66 (2): 281-85.

———. 1983. "Science Education: The Search for a
New Vision." *Educational Leadership* 41 (4):
20-22.

———. 1984. *Reforming Science Education: The
Search for a New Vision.* Occasional Paper 33.
Washington DC: Council for Basic Education
(ERIC number ED 242 515).

———. 1986. "A Rationale for a Science, Technol-
ogy and Society Theme in Science Education."
In *Science, Technology, and Society,* ed. R.
Bybee, 94-104. Washington, DC: National
Science Teachers Association.

———. 1991. "Closing the Educational Gaps
between Science, Technology, and Society."
Theory into Practice 15 (4): 251-59.

———. 1992. "NSTA—A Look Backward: A Look
Forward." Paper presented at National Science
Teachers Association National Convention.

Inhelder, B., and J. Piaget. 1958. *The Growth of
Logical Thinking from Childhood to Adoles-
cence.* New York: Basic Books.

Johnson, D. W., and A. Ahlgren. 1976. "Relation-
ship Between Students' Attitudes about
Cooperative Learning and Competition and
Attitudes Toward Schooling." *Journal of
Educational Psychology* 68: 29-102.

Johnson, D. W., and R. Johnson. 1981. "Effects of
Cooperative and Individualistic Learning
Experiences on Interethnic Interaction."
Journal of Educational Psychology 73: 454-59.

———. 1982. "Effects of Cooperative, Competitive,
and Individualistic Learning Experiences on
Cross-Ethnic Interaction and Friendships."
Journal of Social Psychology 118: 47-58.

———. 1987a. *Learning Together and Alone:
Cooperation, Competition, and Individualiza-
tion.* 2d ed. Englewood Cliffs, NJ: Prentice-
Hall.

———. 1987b. "Cooperative Learning and the Achievement and Socialization Crises in Science and Mathematics Classrooms." In *Students and Science Learning,* ed. A. B. Champagne and L. E. Horning, 67-93. Washington, DC: American Association for the Advancement of Science.

Johnson, D. W., R. Johnson, and G. Maruyama. 1983. "Interdependence and Interpersonal Attraction Among Heterogeneous and Homogeneous Individuals: A Theoretical Formulation and a Meta-Analysis of the Research." *Review of Educational Research* 53: 5-54.

Johnson, D. W., et al. 1981. "Effects of Cooperative, Competitive, and Individualistic Goal Structures on Achievement: A Meta-Analysis." *Psychological Bulletin* 89: 47-62.

Johnson, D. W., et al. 1983. "Are Low Achievers Disliked in a Cooperative Situation? A Test of Rival Theories in a Mixed-Ethnic Situation." *Contemporary Educational Psychology* 8: 189-200.

Johnson, D. W., et al. 1986. "Oral Interaction in Cooperative Learning Groups: Speaking, Listening, and the Nature of Statements Made by High-, Medium-, and Low-Achieving Students." *Journal of Psychology* 119: 303-21.

Kagan, S., and R. Buriel. 1977. "Field Dependence-Independence and Mexican-American Culture and Education." In *Chicano Psychology,* ed. J. L. Martinez, 279-328. New York: Academic Press.

Kagan, S., and G. L. Zahn. 1975. "Field Dependence and the School Achievement Gap Between Anglo-American and Mexican-American Children." *Journal of Educational Psychology* 67: 643-50.

Kahle, J. B. 1985. "Retention of Girls in Science: Case Studies of Secondary Teachers." In *Women in Science: A Report from the Field,* ed. J. B. Kahle, 49-76, 193-229. London: Falmer Press.

———. 1991. "The Underutilized Majority: The Participation of Women in Science." In *Science Education in the United States: Issues, Crises and Priorities,* ed. S. K. Majumdar et al., 483-502. Easton, PA: Pennsylvania Academy of Sciences.

Kracjik, J. S., P. E. Simmons, and V. N. Lunetta. 1988. "A Research Strategy for the Dynamic Study of Students' Concepts and Problem Solving Strategies Using Science Software." *Journal of Research in Science Teaching* 25 (2): 147-55.

Krendl, K. A., and D. A. Lieberman. 1988. "Computers and Learning: A Review of Recent Research." *Journal of Educational Computing Research* 4 (4): 367-89.

Kyle, W. C. 1985. "What Became of the Curriculum Development Projects of the 1960's?" In *Research Within Reach: Science Education,* ed. D. Holdzkum and P. B. Lutz, 3-24. Washington, DC: National Institute of Education.

Larkin, J. H., and R. W. Chabay. 1989. "Research on Teaching Scientific Thinking: Implications for Computer-Based Instruction." In *Toward the Thinking Curriculum: Current Cognitive Research,* ed. L. B. Resnick and L. E. Klopfer, 150-72. Alexandria, VA: Association for Supervision and Curriculum Development.

Lepper, M. R., and R. W. Chabay. 1985. "Intrinsic Motivation and Instruction: Conflicting Views on Motivational Processes in Computer-Based Education." *Educational Psychologist* 20: 217-30.

Lepper, M. R., and D. Greene. 1978. *The Hidden Costs of Reward: New Perspectives on the Psychology of Human Motivation.* Hillsdale, NJ: Lawrence Erlbaum Associates.

Llabre, M. M., and G. Cuevas. 1983. "The Effects of Test Language and Mathematical Skills Assessed on the Scores of Bilingual Hispanic Students." *Journal of Research in Mathematics Education* 14 (4): 318-24.

Loucks-Horsley, S., et al. 1990. *Elementary School Science for the '90's.* Andover, MA: Network.

McCormack, A. J. 1981. *Inventors Workshop.* Belmont, CA: David S. Lake.

———. 1990. *Magic and Showmanship for Teachers.* Riverview, FL: Idea Factory.

McCormack, A. J., and R. E. Yager. 1989a. "Assessing Teaching/Learning in Multiple Domains of Science and Science Education." *Science Education* 73 (1): 44-58.

———. 1989b. "A New Taxonomy for Science Education." *Science Teacher* 56 (2): 47-48.

McDermott, L. 1984. "Research on Conceptual Understanding in Mechanics." *Physics Today* 37 (July): 24-32.

Mathews, W. H., et al. 1989. *Investigating the Earth.* Dallas: Houghton Mifflin.

Minstrell, J. 1984. "Teaching for the Development of Understanding of Ideas: Focus on Moving Objects." In *Observing Science Classrooms: Observing Science Perspectives from Research and Practice. 1984 AETS Yearbook.* Columbus, Ohio: Ohio State Univ.

Morse, L. W., and H. M. Handley. 1985. "Listening to Adolescents: Gender Differences in Science Classrooms." In *Gender Influences in Classroom Interaction,* ed. L. C. Wilkerson and C. B. Mannett, 37-56. Madison, WI: Academic Press.

Nachmias, R., and M. C. Linn. 1987. "Evaluations of Science Laboratory Data: The Role of Computer-Presented Information." *Journal of Research in Science Teaching* 24 (5): 491-506.

National Association for Educational Progress. 1988. *The Science Report Card: Elements of Risk and Recovery.* Princeton, NJ: Educational Testing Service.

———. 1987. *Learning by Doing: A Manual for Teaching and Assessing Higher Order Thinking Skills in Science and Mathematics.* Princeton, NJ: Educational Testing Services.

National Commission on Excellence in Education. 1983. *A Nation at Risk: The Imperative for Education Reform.* Washington, DC: Government Printing Office.

National Council of Teachers of Mathematics. 1987. *Curriculum and Evaluation Standards for School Mathematics.* Reston, VA.

National Science Teachers Association. 1982. *Science/Technology/Society: Science Education for the 1980's.* Committee on STS Report. Washington, DC: NSTA.

———. 1988. *NSTA Handbook: 1988-89.* Washington, DC.

———. 1992. *The Content Core: A Guide for Curriculum Development.* Scope, Sequence, and Coordination of Secondary School Science, vol. 1. Washington, DC.

National Wildlife Foundation. 1982. *The CLASS Project.* Washington, DC: National Wildlife Federation, under a grant from the National Science Foundation. Revised edition 1982. No longer available.

Nix, D. 1988. "Should Computers Know What You Can Do with Them?" *Teachers College Record* 49 (3): 84-95.

Olstad, R. G., et al. 1981. *Inhibitors to Achievement in Science and Mathematics by Ethnic Minorities.* Seattle: Univ. of Washington. (ERIC Document Reproduction Service No. ED 223 404).

Osborne, R., and P. Freyberg. 1985. *Learning in Science: The Implications of Children's Science.* Portsmouth, NH: Heinemann.

Perfetto, B. A., J. D. Bransford, and J. J. Franks. 1983. "Constraints on Access in a Problem Solving Context." *Memory and Cognition* 11: 24-31.

Perkins, D. N., and G. Salomon. 1989. "Are Cognitive Skills Context-Bound?" *Educational Researcher* 18 (1): 16-25.

Project WILD. 1991. Boulder, CO: Project WILD; joint project of the Western Association of Fish and Wildlife Agencies and the Western Regional Environmental Education Council.

Rakow, S. J., and C. L. Walker. 1985. "The Status of Hispanic Students in Science: Achievement and Exposure." *Science Education* 69 (4): 557-65.

Ramirez, M., and D. R. Price-Williams. 1974. "Cognitive Styles of Children of Three Ethnic Groups in the United States." *Journal of Cross-Cultural Psychology* 5: 212-19.

Renner, J. W., and E. A. Marek. 1988. *The Learning Cycle and Elementary School Science Teaching.* Portsmouth, NH: Heinemann.

Roth, K. J. 1985. "Conceptual Change Learning and Student Processing of Science Texts." Paper presented at annual meeting of the American Educational Research Association.

Sanchez, J. L. 1978. "A Comparison of Achievement of Mexican and Mexican-American Children in the Areas of Reading and Mathematics When Taught within a Cooperative and Competitive Goal Structure." Ph.D. diss., Univ. of California, Santa Barbara. (ERIC Document Reproduction Service No. ED 204 098).

Schafer, R.J.H., and J. F. Disinger, eds. 1975a. *Environmental Education: Perspectives and Prospectives: Key Findings and Recommendations.* Columbus, OH: SMEAC Information Reference Center.

———. 1975b. *Environmental Education: Perspectives and Prospectives: Supporting Documentation.* Columbus, OH: SMEAC Information Reference Center.

Simpson, R. D., and N. D. Anderson. 1981. *Science Students and Schools: A Guide for the Middle and Secondary School Teacher.* New York: Wiley.

Skon, L., D. W. Johnson, and R. Johnson. 1981. "Cooperative Peer Interaction Versus Individual Competition and Individualistic Efforts: Effects on the Acquisition of Cognitive Reasoning Strategies." *Journal of Educational Psychology* 73: 83-92.

Smith, K., D. W. Johnson, and R. Johnson. 1981. "Can Conflict Be Constructive? Controversy Versus Concurrence Seeking in Learning Groups." *Journal of Educational Psychology* 73: 651-63.

——. 1982. "Effects of Cooperative and Individualistic Instruction on the Achievement of Handicapped, Regular, and Gifted students." *Journal of Social Psychology* 116: 277-83.

Smith, W., and L. Erb. 1986. "Effect of Women Science Career RoleModels on Early Adolescents' Attitudes toward Science and Women in Science." *Journal of Research in Science Education* 23: 667-76.

Stage, E. 1992. *Draft Time Plan for National Science Education Standards.* Washington, DC: National Research Council.

Stake, R. E., and J. A. Easley. 1978. *Case Studies in Science Education.* Urbana, IL: Univ. of Illinois Center for Instructional Research and Curriculum Evaluation.

Stapp, W. B., ed. 1978. *From Ought to Action in Environmental Education: A Report of the National Leadership Council on Environmental Education.* Columbus, OH: SMEAC Information Reference Center.

Trachtman, J. P. 1975. "Cognitive and Motivational Variables as Predictors of Academic Performance among Disadvantaged College Students." *Journal of Counseling Psychology* 22: 324-28.

Weisberg, R., M. DiCamillo, and D. Phillips. 1978. "Transferring Old Associations to New Situations: A Nonautomatic Process." *Journal of Verbal Learning and Verbal Behavior* 17: 219-28.

Weiss, I. R. 1978. *Report of the 1977 National Survey of Science, Mathematics, and Social Studies Education.* Research Triangle Park, NC: Center for Educational Research and Evaluation.

Welch, W. W. 1976. "Evaluating the Impact of National Curriculum Projects." *Science Education* 60 (4): 475-83.

——. 1979. "Twenty Years of Science Curriculum Development: A Look Back." In *Review of Research Education 7,* ed. D. C. Berliner. Washington, DC: AERA.

White, R. T. 1988. *Learning Science.* Oxford, England: Basil Blackwell.

Whitehead, A. N. 1929. *The Aims of Education.* New York: Macmillan.

Whyte, J. 1986. *Girls into Science and Technology.* London: Routledge and Kegan.

Williams, L. V. 1983. *Teaching for the Two-Sided Mind.* New York: Simon and Schuster.

Yager, R. E. 1987. "Assess All Five Domains of Science." *Science Teacher* 54: 33-37.

CURRICULUM GUIDES: PROCESS AND DESIGN

by Jurg Jenzer

Director of Curriculum, Supervision, and Instruction
Lamoille North Supervisory Union, Hyde Park, Vermont

CURRICULUM designers face complex decisions in developing a quality science program. The stakes are high, with judgments being made for years to come about what teachers should teach and what students should learn. Many factors are involved: district size, geographic location, funding capability, philosophy, state statutes, and demographic characteristics. Many are affected by these curricular decisions, and therefore, many should participate in determining a course of action.

Improving scientific literacy and worldwide competitiveness has become a national priority. The President and the Congress appear committed to turning this priority into a reality. At the forefront of this mission stand all educational institutions. Public schools, private schools, colleges, and universities bear a major responsibility in the quest to recapture this nation's leadership role in science. At a more practical level, much of this immense task rests on the shoulders of teachers. They are expected to teach more science—and better science. A science curriculum guide can coordinate the selection, organization, instruction, and evaluation of science in a school or school district. Since classroom teachers are the primary users of curriculum guides, it is important that teachers participate in developing these materials.

Textbooks still drive the curriculum in many districts, and in many cases science textbooks structure much of the teachers' knowledge regarding the curriculum. In science, textbooks offer a scope of topics, as well as the sequence in which they are to be taught and learned. Unlike teachers, textbook authors have the time and logistical support to develop and test science programs. As a result, teachers' dependency on textbooks has increased dramatically. For good or ill, textbooks are a powerful force on a curriculum developed by states or single school districts, and it is not surprising to see textbook language and design reflected in many locally developed science curricula.

Numerous critics have argued that the textbook has eroded the need to train teachers to design and evaluate curriculum (Apple 1979; Aronowitz and Giroux 1985; Giroux 1983). Designing curriculum at the district level challenges both the textbook industry and the dependency teachers have on textbooks. A curriculum process, moreover, allows teachers to discover some surprising facts. Alternatives to textbook-style scope and sequence programs in science are not only possible but can offer some interesting instructional alternatives as well.

Veteran teachers are already curriculum designers by practice. They tend to use textbooks eclectically, identifying strengths and weaknesses in each book. They pick and choose from all available resources. A formal, district-level curriculum guide fosters this development and is at odds with the adoption of any single textbook series, unless the structure of the text is copied directly into the curriculum. A locally developed curriculum raises the issue of eclecticism. It may also generate a crisis for teachers who have to face their dependency on textbooks. Some teachers are ready for this step; others are not.

For them curriculum synchronizes the learning process between grade levels and schools. Isolated from their colleagues for much of the working day, teachers rely on curriculum guides for this coordination. A guidebook to school science does not, however, guarantee quality teaching unless teachers understand the usefulness and limitations of a science curriculum. Teachers' experiences as students in public school and higher education programs are a critical force in shaping their instructional style and conceptualization of science. Teachers' assumptions about children and scientific literacy can either facilitate or block new approaches to teaching science. From this standpoint, a curriculum process takes on the characteristics of a demanding graduate course.

In curriculum implementation, teachers must be given the opportunity to experience for themselves the very transformation they are expected to accomplish in their classrooms. This chapter outlines key decisions curriculum designers and committees encounter when developing or revising elementary, middle, and/or secondary science. This model identifies key factors which should be considered in the process of making informed and responsible decisions for the future of K-12 science.

A curriculum development process with and for teachers provides insight into the decision-making process that generates both textbooks and curriculum guides. It is the process, rather than the document, which provides an exciting opportunity: time to examine one's own assumptions and practices, an environment to discuss and test new assumptions and practices, and a reasonable incentive to get involved.

Curriculum is not so much a document as it is instruction. At its best, it teaches all those involved with its development and implementation. The actual curriculum in science (or in any other subject) is the one being taught. The taught curriculum may or may not resemble the planned curriculum (textbook or curriculum guide). This point is crucial. The curriculum process organized as a challenging learning opportunity will affect instruction far more than the document alone. A local curriculum process challenges the separation of planning and implementation, an issue all too often obscured by arguments for state or national curriculum initiatives. Unless teachers understand the process and decisions that generate a curriculum guide, implementation may be in jeopardy.

In general, the total process of curriculum design and implementation can be divided into numerous steps that curriculum designers and committees may need to deal with when developing or revising elementary, middle, and/or high school science programs. These steps can be outlined as follows:

· Performing a needs assessment
· Defining the mission statement
· Choosing the participants
· Scheduling the project
· Forming a curriculum committee
· Budgeting
· Looking at standards
· Examining key science topics
· Choosing curriculum features and design options
· Population analysis (target students)
· Field testing
· Public input
· Editing, ratification, production, and dissemination
· Adoption process
· Staff development and support
· Monitoring and supervision
· Evaluation and revision

Note that the steps described here are only *typical* of the process involved. The actual steps may differ in your district—there may be more steps or fewer ones, and some steps may occur in a different order. But you will most likely encounter many of these steps at some stage in the process, and this chapter is meant to acquaint you with these steps and many of the related decisions.

Before a curriculum can be written and implemented, curriculum designers plan and organize a process.[1] Just as importantly, these designers must set realistic expectations for teachers who will ultimately be asked to turn these blueprints into meaningful experiences for children and young adults in the science classroom.

Performing a Needs Assessment

The needs assessment is an important part of curriculum planning in any subject area, in that it provides a direction for the curriculum. The assessment defines the priorities of the curriculum (under local and state standards and in view of recommendations from national organizations), the goals of curriculum development in science, and the gaps that exist in the current curriculum.

In order to get a clearer picture of the school's needs in science, curriculum planners may wish to compare their current and planned curriculum program with those of other states and other districts (for further discussion on sources of curriculum materials, see below under *Examining Key Science Topics* and *Choosing Curriculum Features and Design Options*).

Defining the Mission Statement

Closely related to the needs assessment is the creation of the school or district mission statement. While curriculum implementation may be the province of teachers and school administrators, the mission statement should be developed with members of the school board, teachers, parents, students, state education officials, the private sector, and others within the community. A widely shared understanding of the mission of the school district in curricular and programmatic terms greatly enhances the odds for successful implementation. Formulating a new curriculum is expected to do the following:

- Establish a relationship between district goals and instructional programs and methods
- Establish a relationship between local programs, state and national standards, laws, and policies
- Link curriculum and educational programs with important policy and budgetary decisions
- Inform communities about the schools' direction and programs
- Ensure a coordinated and planned educational program

Choosing the Participants

Curriculum affects a teacher's behavior and decision making. The teacher's understanding, acceptance, and implementation of a science curriculum are at once the most important and, oddly enough, the most commonly missed factor in the curriculum process.

All schools and school districts employ teachers of varying degrees of ability, from novice teachers to seasoned veterans. Their growth and development as professional educators will define their relationship with the curriculum.[2] It is critical to gain insight into the quality and dynamics of the teaching staff for whom the curriculum is written. Important questions must be asked, including the following:

- How many teachers will be charged with implementation? What are their experiences specifically with curriculum development? Have they worked with districtwide curricula before?
- What are the teachers' attitudes regarding the current curriculum? How well or to what extent are current curricula implemented?
- Can the school district support a curriculum process in which teachers have leverage over the curriculum?
- How many building administrators have experience specifically with curriculum development?

Interviewing prospective participants and reviewing appropriate records allow curriculum designers to recruit actively those teachers best suited for the task ahead.

Scheduling the Project

When developing a reasonable timetable for a curriculum process, numerous factors must be faced. The following is a list of some of the more common concerns:

- Scope of the project (e.g., K-4, 5-8, 9-12, K-12)
- Mission of the project (complete revision, partial revision, etc.)
- Number of employees and students affected by the curriculum
- How the project fits into the participants' work schedules
- Staff development time that will be required to implement the new curriculum
- Available resources (also see below, under *Budgeting*)
- Deadlines (from the state, from local education agency, from federal agency mandates)
- Meeting times (see below)

Since teachers have relatively inflexible classroom

schedules, a method must be chosen that will ensure their participation. Three of the more common methods used are *pullout projects*, *after-school projects*, and *course projects*. Each method offers significant fiscal and procedural advantages.

Pulling teachers out of the classrooms for full-day work sessions allows them to concentrate on the project. Typically, this reduces the number of meetings necessary to complete the project. On the other hand, this method requires substitute teachers, with the resulting cost. Teachers who leave their classrooms for entire days must devote considerable effort to preparing substitutes. In addition, the frequency with which teachers are pulled out of the classroom must be calculated so as to eliminate any potentially negative impact on students.

After-school projects avoid most of the negative implications of the pullout project. Some costs remain if contracts require reimbursement of personnel for extra duty. The most significant problem with this method, however, is that teachers are often tired after spending a day in the classroom; this minimizes their energy level and the quality of their work. This method also increases the number of meetings needed, because after-school meeting time is limited.

Course projects are usually planned in collaboration with institutions of higher educa-tion. The strength of this method is its scheduling flexibility. Course projects can be organized as evening courses or as intensive two- or three-week work sessions during school vacations. Graduate credits issued by the cooperating college or university can be an attractive incentive for teachers who apply credits toward graduate degrees and/or salary schedules. One well-known problem with this method lies in potential conflicts between school district personnel and higher education faculty over controlling the project, the mission, and the curriculum itself.

Forming a Curriculum Committee

Curriculum designers, whether they be adminis-trators, classroom teachers, or education profes-sors, must be able to work effectively with adults. In addition, curriculum designers must have an excellent grasp of the subject, have classroom experience, and communicate effectively in order to be accepted and respected by teachers.

In forming a curriculum committee, curricu-lum designers encounter such questions as these:

· Who wants to participate? Who should be recruited?
· Which teachers can play leadership roles? Who will chair the committee?
· Should all affected schools and grade levels be represented?
· What are the advantages of small versus large committees?
· Should elementary-level committees work separately from middle- or secondary-level committees? How will they coordinate transitions between levels?
· What types of incentives are available to recruit quality committees?
· How committed are the school board and the administration to the committee's work?
· Are department heads, administrators, program specialists, guidance counselors, parents, students, board members, and business and community representatives on the committee?

The First Committee Meeting: Checklist
The importance of the first meeting cannot be overstated. Curriculum designers should carefully plan and orchestrate this meeting in order to develop team spirit and purpose within the committee itself.

Scheduling: If the first meeting is held during the school year, check with building principals about events or meetings. If the meeting occurs after school, limit it to setting the agenda, getting to know one another, and starting a checklist of current topics and issues in science.

Committee Structure: Identify the committee's mission, meeting schedule, political conditions (e.g., level of administrative or school board support), preliminary activities (conducting needs assessment, obtaining copies of state statutes and regulations, gathering important articles or resources, etc.).

Meeting Environment: If at all possible, meet outside the schools in a comfortable room equipped with comfortable chairs, large tables, climate controls, chalkboard or overhead projec-tor, and a steady supply of coffee and juice. In all-day meetings, do not skimp on lunch.

Budgeting

Resource Checklist
There are numerous factors to be considered when deciding about resources. The budget[3] and

other logistical problems deserve careful consideration. Some of the factors are as follows:

Logistics
  · Secretarial assistance
  · Access to computers
  · Access to databases and other forms of information (i.e., ERIC, KCDL, libraries, etc.)
  · A place for the committee to meet
  · Possible collaboration with a local college or university
  · Access to production facilities (i.e., graphics, desktop publishing, printing, copying, editing, etc.)

Budgetary Considerations
  · Hiring substitutes
  · Consultant(s)
  · Computer
  · Secretarial
  · Production (layout, paper, printing, copying, distribution, binders, graphics, etc.)
  · Administrative
  · Legal (reviews for compliance with state and federal laws)
  · Other costs

Curriculum developers might want to explore the possibilities of outside funding to help support the extra costs involved in the project. Some national foundations provide grants for the development of particular curricula; these organizations often have regional restrictions or will fund only certain types of curricula. In addition, some corporations fund educational projects in their state or region. Chapter 3 provides a listing of foundations that offer grants for education projects; this list gives some idea of the types of funding available.

Looking at Standards

It is essential to consult existing standards—and to keep track of emerging ones—when designing or adopting curriculum guides. As arguments over national curriculum and testing systems fly back and forth, curriculum designers should be concerned first and foremost with understanding the upcoming changes in the teaching of science (see chapter 1 for an overview of these trends). While national standards will make a difference, major curriculum decisions still reside at the local level.

Every school district has standards that emerge from: (*a*) a multitude of community values; (*b*) the quality of the teaching force; (*c*) the successes and failures of local reform and restructuring efforts in response to pressures from state and federal agencies; and (*d*) the curriculum in use. Curriculum designers must decide on standards with these factors in mind. After all, standards for the nation's K-12 science curricula have yet to be tested.

Even the best curriculum documents will become outdated once new standards and trends emerge. Teachers in school districts that have an ongoing curriculum development process will be better equipped to adapt to new standards from any source.

State and Local Standards

Copies of all statutes, regulations, and policies regulating a curriculum development or revision project should be made available to all parties participating in, or affected by, the curriculum process.

Under the United States Constitution, each state has the ultimate responsibility for education, and state education agencies define standards and conditions under which schools operate. This is where commonality ends, however, because the degree to which states regulate curriculum process and development varies widely. In some cases, the state sets standards for science and defines acceptable instructional resources to implement that curriculum. In other cases, the curriculum process is largely controlled by local educational agencies (LEAs). Curriculum designers need to ascertain the nature and scope of these standards as well as the degree of flexibility LEAs have in interpreting and implementing these standards (for details regarding individual states, see chapter 5).

When state regulations are mostly generic, they allow for significant local variation. This opens the door to local emphases on issues such as science/technology programs, school-business partnerships, or hands-on approaches to science instruction. Such emphases often find their way into curriculum guides and school board policies.

In addition to state regulations, there are other factors that may have created de facto standards in school districts. For instance, the district may have adopted a particular way of teaching science which unifies instruction in some way (e.g., a common textbook series, adoption of activity-oriented science teaching at all grade levels, districtwide pairing of technology with science, etc.). Just as significantly, when teachers "import" new ideas, materials, or methods into the school, they act as role models for other teachers. In fact, this is the most common way in which science is transformed at the classroom level, and it is an excellent indicator of what can be termed "local standards."

National Standards

The publication—and widespread acceptance—of curriculum standards by the National Council of Teachers of Mathematics (NCTM) demonstrates the importance of a national consensus that supplies direction and focus to local curriculum efforts. National standards do not necessarily suggest a national curriculum, however, although this option is supported by some in the United States.

Following the NCTM example, the National Science Teachers Association's (NSTA) *The Content Core: A Guide for Curriculum Designers* (1992) seizes this opportunity to provide direction and specifics. Curriculum designers involved with developing or revising science curriculum cannot afford to ignore this and other attempts to shape national standards. Table 1 compares NSTA's key recommendations for restructuring science with more traditional practices.

More recently, the National Academy of Sciences has been examining the question of national science standards as well. The Academy's Coordinating Council for Education is overseeing the newly formed National Committee on Science Education, Standards, and Assessment, which will coordinate the work of three other groups: the chairman's advisory committee, the curriculum standards committee, and the assessment committee. A major task of the curriculum committee is to coordinate the final science standards with NCTM's standards for math. The committee will also examine how to incorporate the various curriculum ideas proposed by the American Association for the Advancement of Science (AAAS) and by the NSTA (see below). The national committee expects to have drafts of curriculum standards completed late in 1992, with drafts of the teaching and assessment standards completed in spring 1993. The council also plans to publish the final standards document late in 1994 (West 1992).

Examining Key Science Topics

Review of the Literature

The literature regarding elementary, middle, and high school science is rich and somewhat overwhelming, but curriculum designers cannot afford

Table 1. Comparison of NSTA's Scope, Sequence, and Coordination Guidelines with Traditional Science Teaching Concepts	
NSTA Conceptual Guidelines and Standards	**Traditional Concepts and Standards**
Application of important science concepts in multiple contexts and hands-on problem situations	Mastery of facts evidenced by performance on multiple-choice tests
Instruction based on theme-oriented, supplement-type texts emphasizing integration of mathematics, writing/ communication, and social science skills	Instruction based on fact-filled textbooks, covering the four science disciplines
Secondary science (6-12) features biology, chemistry, earth/space science, and physics at every grade level	Secondary science organized in layer-cake design: biology (9th grade), earth science (10th grade), chemistry (11th grade). Three-fourths of high school graduates never move to 11th or 12th grade science (advanced courses, physics, etc.)
Elementary science focuses on first-hand exploration, nurturing curiosity for investigation and inquiry; the content is based on broad conceptual themes which span all science disciplines	Elementary science focuses on acquisition of vocabulary, recognizing some important science phenomena; the content is based primarily in introductory biology and earth science

to ignore it (see chapter 1 for an overview of trends and the literature and chapter 4 for a discussion of topics in science teaching). How designers deal with this material is usually related to the time they have available. Should teachers be involved in reviewing and discussing this literature, or should the facilitator conduct a review and brief the participants? Such a review allows participants to gain a critical perspective on current controversies in science, as well as on their own assumptions regarding what a science curriculum is today and will be in the future.

An alternative approach is to review other school districts' curricula or current textbooks. (An annotated list of recommended, current curriculum guides in science is provided in chapter 7, and a discussion of state curriculum guides is given in chapter 5.) This review yields a great deal of practical comparisons between districts as well as a sense of security in choosing topics that are used by other educators. However, if committee members are not well versed in current trends and methods, this method could lead to the continued use of potentially obsolete curriculum design features and instructional topics.

A balanced picture of the literature can be gained through the review of three types of information: the publishing sector (textbooks), the school sector (current curricula), and the academic sector (research).

The next step could be the most difficult one in the curriculum development and design procedures. The curriculum committee must make choices regarding the organization of the guide and the relationship between strands (i.e., Should earth science be separated from space science, or should a technology strand be developed?). In addition, specific topics, themes, and issues must be chosen for each strand, grade level or grade cluster, or developmental level.

Again, _The Content Core_ (NSTA 1992) serves as an excellent starting point. NSTA recommends that biology, chemistry, earth/space science, and physics all be taught at every grade level from six to twelve. This basic outline should be contrasted against, or supplemented with, other sources of topics, issues, themes, and strands in K-12 science education. (Chapter 4 in this handbook provides more detailed information on topics in K-12 science.) The outline follows.

KEY TOPICS IN SCIENCE FOR
GRADES 6-12, AS RECOMMENDED BY
THE NATIONAL SCIENCE TEACHERS ASSOCIATION
(Topics and subtopics shown are for all grade levels (6-8, 9-10, 11-12), unless otherwise noted.)

BIOLOGY
I. Properties of living things
    A. Structures unique to life
    B. Interaction with the environment (covered in 6-8, 9-10)
    C. Reproduction
    D. Composition (covered in 6-8)
II. The living organism
    A. Systems
    B. Cycles (covered in 6-8)
III. The biological planet
    A. Components (covered in 6-8)
    B. Interactions
    C. Patterns

CHEMISTRY
I. Properties of matter
    A. Physical properties (covered in 6-8, 9-10)
    B. Chemical properties (covered in 6-8, 9-10)
    C. Properties of solutions
II. Nature of chemical change
    A. Inorganic, organic, biochemical equations
    B. Acid-base reactions
    C. Oxidation-reduction reactions
    D. Rates of chemical change
III. Structure of matter
    A. Atoms
    B. Bonding
IV. Energy and change
    A. Forms of energy
    B. Conservation of energy during phase change (covered in 6-8, 9-10)
    C. Changes associated with chemical reactions
    D. Energy alternatives
V. Models for change
    A. Particulate nature of matter

EARTH/SPACE SCIENCE
I. The physical planet
    A. Properties of Earth: materials and features
    B. Solid earth processes: Crust and interior
    C. Solid earth processes: Surfaces
    D. Biological processes
    E. Hydrological processes

F. Atmospheric processes
II. Earth in space

PHYSICS
I. Matter
    A. Kinds and characteristics (covered in 6-8, 11-12)
    B. Properties
    C. Change process
    D. Models (covered in 9-10, 11-12)
II. Motion and force
    A. Descriptors of motion (covered in 6-8, 9-10)
    B. Causes of motion
    C. Equilibrium
    D. Momentum: a conserved quantity (covered in 9-10, 11-12)
III. Energy
    A. Kinds of energy
    B. Energy transformations (covered in 9-10, 11-12)
    C. Conservation of energy
    D. Second law of thermodynamics (covered in 6-8, 11-12)
IV. Electricity and magnetism
    A. Static charge (covered in 6-8, 11-12)
    B. Moving charge and magnets
    C. Electric currents
    D. Fields (covered in 11-12)
V. Waves and light
    A. Mechanical waves (covered in 6-8, 9-10)
    B. Sound
    C. Light: characteristics and models
    D. Image formation

Source: National Science Teachers Association. *The Content Core: A Guide for Curriculum Designers* (Washington, DC: NSTA, 1992). Reproduced with permission.

An interesting contrast to the NSTA scope and sequence plan is embedded in *The Science Report Card—Trends and Achievement,* based on the 1986 National Assessment (Educational Testing Service 1988). The science content area subscales (see figure 4.1 in the report) are a good reflection of the most common science topics during the 1970s and 1980s; an outline of these areas follows.

CONTENT AREAS RECOMMENDED IN *THE SCIENCE REPORT CARD.*

LIFE SCIENCES (BIOLOGY)
    A. Cellular and molecular biology
    B. Energy transformations (photosynthesis and cellular metabolism)
    C. Structure and functions of organisms (protists, plants, animals)
    D. Diversity of organisms (classification)
    E. Genetics and development
    F. Evolution
    G. Ecology
    H. Behavior

PHYSICS
    A. Mechanics (motion, force, principles of conservation)
    B. Waves and optics
    C. Electricity and magnetism
    D. Modern physics (atomic, nuclear, relativity)
    E. Heat and kinetic theory

CHEMISTRY
    A. Structure of matter (nuclear, atomic, and molecular)
    B. Periodic classification
    C. States of matter and nature of solutions
    D. Reactions to matter (chemical transformations)
    E. Stoichiometry

EARTH AND SPACE SCIENCES
    A. The Earth's history
    B. Materials of the Earth
    C. Agents of processes of change on the Earth's surface
    D. Earth's atmosphere and weather
    E. Describing and measuring time and location
    F. The oceans
    G. The solar system

NATURE OF SCIENCE
    A. Processes of science
    B. Assumptions of science
    C. Characteristics and limitations of scientific methods
    D. Ethics in science

Source: Educational Testing Service, *The Science Report Card—Trends and Achievement* (Princeton, NJ: 1988).

Another set of recommendations was proposed by Project 2061, an initiative developed by the AAAS. In 1989, under the aegis of the AAAS, Project 2061 published the report *Science for All Americans*, which contained Project 2061's philosophy and a detailed definition of scientific literacy—that is, the knowledge and abilities students should have in science, mathematics, and technology by the time they have completed school. The following summarizes the Project 2061 recommendations. By the end of 1991, the project had selected six school districts around the United States as sites for development of curriculum models based on these recommendations (AAAS 1992).

PROJECT 2061 RECOMMENDATIONS
FOR SCIENTIFIC LITERACY

General concepts	The nature of science, mathematics, and technology, how they are similar and different.
Scientific view of the world	The physical setting, the environment, the human organism, human society, the designed world; the mathematical world
Scientific endeavor	Historical perspectives, common themes (systems, models, conservation, symmetry, chaos, evolution, etc.), habits of mind (values and attitudes, skills, social value of science/mathematics/technology, etc.)
Principles of nature	Consistent with the effective teaching of scientific inquiry, aim to counteract learning anxieties, extend beyond the school, take time

Source: American Association for the Advancement of Science, *Science for All Americans: Literacy Goals in Science, Mathematics, and Technology.* (Washington, DC: 1989).

Choosing Curriculum Features and Design Options

When considering the design and content of a curriculum and the accompanying curriculum guide(s), a designer must analyze the teachers as an audience, as well as what type of guide the teachers would find most attractive and useful. This brings designers back to an earlier step (*Choosing the Participants*) and the expansion of the user analysis begun there. In general, the larger the audience (number of future users) for your science curriculum, the more difficult the search is for appropriate design and content. The curriculum designer's own classroom experience and interaction with teachers will greatly facilitate the assessment of what teachers need and/or want.

Do some curriculum designs and content options work better than others? This depends on the audience and the intended use of the guide. Here are some factors to consider:

· Which topics should be taught at certain grade levels to secure a high degree of achievement for most learners?
· How should these topics be described in the curriculum? Should they be described as "skills" that students should master or discrete "content" areas that teachers ought to cover?
· Should a curriculum guide be much like a textbook and describe all aspects of instructional work and implement state or local goals and objectives?
· Should a curriculum guide be brief and merely outline instructional scope and sequence in "blueprint fashion," thus leaving most curriculum decision making to teachers?
· Should curriculum guides contain one feature or multiple features or types of information?
· Does the actual curriculum content or design make any difference to teachers?
· Can curriculum guides be made attractive to teachers and thus shift the incentive for implementation from top-down mandates to the inherent benefits of the document itself?
· If teachers have greatly varied professional needs and practices, should the curriculum in fact consist of multiple documents with varied content?

Different science curriculum guides offer different choices of content features, emphasizing one above others, or vary both the number and combination of features. One of the best ways to examine the different features of curriculum guides is to use actual guides as examples and models (see chapter 7 for information on recent science guides with important content or unique features).

One source for curriculum models is the Kraus Curriculum Development Library (KCDL). This annual program offers a large number of curriculum guides (commercial and noncommercial), all reproduced on microfiche. KCDL includes a "Science" section, plus one on "Environment"; science-related materials may also be found in the "Mathematics" subject area. Chapter 14 in this Handbook provides a list of current KCDL customers, whose fiche collections can be viewed.

Another good source for information on current guides is the Association for Supervision and Curriculum Development (ASCD). For many years, ASCD has organized an exhibit of noncommercial curriculum materials for display at its annual conference. Most of these displays have included curriculum guides on science and special science-related topics. In more recent years, ASCD has published a directory of the documents on display (the newer editions of this directory will be included in a CD-ROM package being planned by ASCD). Contact ASCD for information on the annual conference and for the availability of directories for the noncommercial curriculum materials display.

In addition, the Education Department of the University of California at Sacramento has begun to collect and catalogue the guides that were on display at ASCD conferences. Once the cataloguing is completed, the guides themselves will be available on interlibrary loan.

The following list describes some of the more common curriculum features:

A. Objectives/Instructional Strategies
Instructional objectives are written as specific topics that teachers must cover, described as specific knowledge areas.

B. Student Activities
Most often expressed in terms of student projects, games, or specific behaviors, this feature often translates instructional objectives into desired or proven methodologies focusing on engaging the student in the learning process as actively as possible.

C. Skills/Competencies
This feature is by far the most common type of information in curriculum guides. The national agenda for accountability in education has clearly left its mark in guides published during the past decade. The focus on outcomes of instruction sets a baseline for testing or measurement of achievement, giving the teacher the result rather than the "what" or "how." Many curriculum documents actually code skills in reference to standardized testing instruments.

D. Subject Information
This is perhaps the oldest feature found in curriculum guides. Its use dates back to the days when textbooks were the primary source for curriculum, focusing on the legitimacy and preponderance of certain areas of knowledge over others. In some cases, excerpts from textbooks are copied directly into the guide.

E. Resources
This feature is prevalant in school district guides where the state establishes the legitimacy of certain textbooks or instructional resources.

F. Evaluation/Testing
Again, this feature is commonly found in curriculum guides, often in conjunction with Skills/Concepts, which are then cross-referenced with specific testing instruments. A similar feature is the curriculum map, which places specific skills or objectives at specific age or grade levels to indicate mastery (see below).

G. Curriculum Maps
The chief purpose of curriculum maps is to give teachers information regarding where and how single units, chapters, or topics fit into the overall (i.e., K-12) program. Maps may also include cues regarding students' previous learning experiences which may be of consequence to the teacher's instructional style (e.g., introduce, reinforce, test, and evaluate).

H. Document Size and Number of Features
Some school districts wish to increase both the number of features (e.g., to meet different types of needs) and the amount of detail. On the other hand, some schools deliberately limit the number of content features (e.g., to provide emphasis or direction) as well as the size of the curriculum guides (e.g., to make the guides more manageable or to increase individual teachers' control over the curriculum).

There is little evidence, if any, suggesting that one format or combination of features works better than another. Much is based on the characteristics of the school district, the mission of the curriculum project, administrative agendas to empower teachers or increase centralized control, and other decisive factors.

While these curriculum designs clearly rule the landscape in science, there is no compelling reason to limit curriculum guides to these formats. In fact, educators and textbook publishers alike challenged this tradition, including the assumption that a curriculum guide has to be limited to one subject.

Through the years, curriculum designers have searched for alternatives to the standard features. School districts have experimented with integrated or interdisciplinary designs.[4] In doing so, they have challenged many fundamental assumptions about the nature of curriculum as well as about the nature of schooling.

The key challenge issued within all interdisciplinary designs is directed toward the very organization of school schedules. The artificial segregation of academic disciplines may have served to develop a specialized workforce rather than the current agenda of versatile and broadly educated children and young adults. For most public school graduates, the world of work does not revolve around forty-five minutes of science followed by forty-five minutes of mathematics. Their world presents problems that must be handled with knowledge and skills borrowed from science, mathematics, social studies, and other disciplines. The majority of designers using interdisciplinary models argue that the curriculum ought to reflect those realities and provide corresponding learning situations.[5]

Most alternative designs result from locally developed experiments, often in conjunction with more traditional subject-based guides. Two possible designs, the thematic curriculum and the interdisciplinary curriculum, are described below.

I. The Thematic Curriculum

An instructional unit or theme—chosen by teachers, administrators, students, parents, or a combination of these groups—serves as a focus for study and investigation for a given period of time. The theme is examined from a variety of perspectives or traditional disciplines, such as mathematics, art, science, home economics, and physical education. For example, an evolution and human development unit could be taught through the fossil record (physical science/archaeology); the Scopes trial (history); readings of creation accounts from the Bible, Native American sources, and other sources (theology/literature); studies of primitive tribes (anthropology); and investigations into ancient trading and monetary systems (economics).

J. The Interdisciplinary Curriculum

This design model can focus on discrete skills that are considered essential for the students' future work or study, such as reading, collaborative skills, problem-solving techniques, test-taking skills, numeracy, research techniques, interpreting information, and others. Subject areas such as physics, natural science, geography, or language arts serve as diverse contexts in which those skills are acquired and practiced.

Population Analysis (Target Students)

While teachers are the audience for whom curricula are written, the students are the true beneficiaries of high-quality guides. The demographic characteristics of the student population are a key factor in defining curriculum content (choosing features), scope, resource specifications, etc. For example, a curriculum developed in an affluent Los Angeles suburb may work very well there, but the same guide could fail completely when implemented in a Detroit inner-city school.

This consideration is particularly important for districts with diverse student populations and for schools in districts with diverse cultural and economic settings.

The characteristics of a given student population determine the teacher's ability to implement a curriculum. While such guides are usually formatted to outline performance expectations or specific topics for *all* ninth graders or fifth graders, such generic design assumptions about student populations may simply ignore realities teachers must deal with on a daily basis. In fact, any given grade-level classroom will include students above and below grade level in science ability. Some classes may have up to 25 percent of students on individual education programs (IEPs), requiring the teacher to make drastic adaptions to curriculum expectations. In this light, the blame for "failing to implement" may rest not with the teacher but with the designer. It also explains the surging interest in curriculum guides designed not for grade levels but for developmental levels.

Field Testing

There is no need to separate the drafting process from the field testing of a developing curriculum; indeed, such a separation may be counterproductive. Field testing at its best involves a limited number of teachers who either are participants or have been experimenting with changing their present science program (the curriculum in use); the tests should be cleared with the department chair and faculty, in order to have their cooperation.

There are numerous reasons to conduct field tests during the drafting stage. First, it allows all building-level teachers an early look at upcoming changes in the science program. If that new program, for example, builds heavily upon NSTA standards, the transition from a traditional curriculum to an NSTA-type curriculum could require some additonal staff development. Building ownership for a new mathematics program throughout the design process will greatly facilitate successful implementation.

The final stage of field testing should be conducted with a completed curriculum guide at a building or district level. One or two years of a district-level field test may be required for a gradual transition; teachers should be asked to provide feedback to the curriculum committee in order to provide practical information for final editing work. This should include, if possible, one-on-one interviews with each teacher who participated in the field test, preferably conducted by curriculum committee members. Some of the more important questions than can be posed are:
- Have you found the curriculum useful? How has it been useful?
- Do you have any reservations or concerns you would like to share?
- Are suggested activities useful for implementation?
- What do you need to implement this curriculum?
- Is there anything else you would like the curriuclum committee to know?

Public Input

Schools—and curriculum development—can benefit a great deal from collaborating with parents, community-based organizations and agencies, the private sector, and institutions of higher education. The question for the curriculum designer is, How can this be organized and what do we do with the information?

There are a number of critical factors to consider in organizing public input:
1. Should public input be sought at the very beginning of the curriculum process in order to avoid the impression that such input amounts to mere formality after educators have made all the decisions?
2. Should public input be sought after field testing in order to give the curriculum an opportunity to prove itself?
3. Should public input be conducted through an open forum (public meeting, curriculum or parent night at the school, press report, etc.), or should such input be targeted by inviting feedback from specific individuals, constituencies, or organizations which are most likely to understand science?

Public input, particularly when conducted in an open forum, can often yield contradictory opinions and requests. It is critical for the implementation process, however, to combine public input with feedback received from future users. Regardless of the nature of public feedback, or whether or not all such input translates into actual changes in the science curriculum, experienced curriculum designers (or school districts) respond for those who have answered the invitation to participate.

Editing, Ratification, Production, and Dissemination

Editing

Editing a curriculum has two major purposes. First, it should minimize jargon and technical language without eliminating the technical detail that teachers need for clarity; this is especially true for science curriculum guides, since they often include a certain amount of technical content. Whenever possible, a school district should hire an outside curriculum specialist or auditor when editing new guides or curricula in use (English 1988).

Second, the curriculum committee edits the drafted curriculum guide in order to fix weaknesses or missing parts identified in the interviews with future users (discussed above, under *Field Testing*) and the public (see above, under *Public Input*).

Ratification

Curriculum designers need to discuss ratification procedures with the administration in order to comply with state statutes, regulations, and local school board policies. Such procedures often involve local school board action. If that is the case, it is important to plan this event carefully.

School boards and communities should be informed about curriculum changes on an ongoing basis rather than being confronted with finalized documents; the school board members may choose to review the document themselves before granting final approval. When a board is ready to vote on the matter, the curriculum designer (or responsible administrator) should make a formal presentation. This gives the entire district an opportunity to celebrate its achievement, to congratulate all participants for their efforts (including award ceremonies), and to confirm the importance of curriculum and instruction matters publicly (Carr and Harris 1992). This event should include participants and citizens and be publicized in the local media.

Production

Curriculum designers should consider ways to make a new curriculum attractive as well as high quality in terms of content. A well-designed and well-printed document reveals care and commitment to the curriculum on the part of the district—and it may facilitate implementation.

Three-ring binders of various sizes offer significant advantages: (*a*) the name of the district, titles, and graphic designs can be silk-screened on binders at reasonable prices; (*b*) binders allow users to add new sections of the curriculum during revisions, remove outdated sections, or add their own instructional plans to it; (*c*) binders tend to have a longer life than cardboard covers or spiral-bound documents.

Curriculum production involves numerous decisions leading to printing and publication:

· Should the science curriculum be published in its entirety (K-12) in order to demonstrate a comprehensive approach to science?
· Should the science curriculum guide be published in sections or as separate documents (e.g., K-3, 4-6, 7-8, 9-12, etc.) to accommodate varying user needs and/or to save paper?
· Should the curriculum be prepared by a layout specialist in order to prepare an attractive document (typeface, graphics, etc.)?
· Does the district have desktop publishing capability, and can the district develop its own layout?
· Should the document be bound in book fashion (may prolong cohesion), be bound with plastic spirals (may save production costs), or be placed in three-ring binders?
· Who should be given authorship for the final document? (Note: It is recommended that the school district retain all rights; the district can issue letters or certificates to participating committee members to affirm their contribution).

Production efforts should be entirely planned and coordinated by the curriculum designer or administrative staff. Production may involve the contracted services of a printing company (unless administrative staff can handle the job). The process for purchasing binders (or an alternative) may follow a similar route.

Dissemination

The timing of dissemination should be carefully planned. Summer break and other vacations offer teachers an opportunity to read the documents and to incorporate curriculum objectives into plans for upcoming quarters or semesters. An additional concern regarding dissemination addresses district plans for staff development or in-service training. It can be helpful to disseminate new curricula during staff development time; this provides opportunities for reading and discussion among teachers or for carefully targeted workshops that address the new curriculum.

Adoption Process

By far the most challenging phase of the curriculum process is the adoption of a curriculum at the building level, along with the assurance that teachers plan instruction with the curriculum in hand. In this phase, curriculum is translated into instruction. The complexity of the curriculum, the degree to which assumptions about science are spelled out or hidden, the volume of the curriculum, and the teacher's disposition toward that guide are all factors that affect adoption.

In facing a mandatory curriculum, teachers must first decide whether or not they will work with that curriculum. This is a decision that can be mandated but not necessarily implemented. Because curriculum adoption at the classroom level is, at least in part, a personal decision, curriculum designers must take several factors into consideration which influence that decision:

· The degree to which teachers feel they "own" the curriculum
· Level of experience working with district curriculum
· The degree to which the teacher depends on the textbook
· The teacher's flexibility and willingness to change
· The administration's willingness and ability to support teachers
· Availability of necessary resources and materials
· Level of support from community, school board, state officials, etc.
· Availability and quality of staff development opportunities

Staff Development and Support

Staff development can be an effective implementation strategy; this is voiced by many writers (Fullan 1990; Joyce and Showers 1988; Goodlad 1990; Holmes Group 1990; Loucks-Horsley et al. 1987; Schon 1987). From this standpoint, the teachers charged with implementing the curriculum may require specific training. Curriculum designers often see multiple training needs. To assess those needs as accurately as possible, administrators need to examine several factors:

1. *Who are the users of the new curriculum?* This information will determine the scale of training which will have to be provided to the district (e.g., How many classroom teachers per grade level? How many specialists?).
2. *Which local, state, or national goals and standards are being adopted?* This information must be included in order to effectively train and inform staff about adopted standards or goals.
3. *Has a timetable been adopted?* This information defines the curriculum implementation timetable. Ideally, staff development targeted

to facilitate curriculum implementation should be planned over several years and linked with a clear message to teachers that adoption is a longitudinal learning process.
4. *What types of resources are needed/available?* Available resources such as trainers and staff development consultants must be identified and included in the district's staff development budget.
5. *Who has served on the curriculum committee?* Educators who have participated in the curriculum design process can be used as discussion leaders or to model implementation in their own classrooms.
6. *What are current topics in K-12 science?* Current topics, controversies, or problems in K-12 science should have been identified in the review of the literature; this information can be helpful in defining topics for staff development workshops. In addition, authors and researchers may be available to serve as trainers or lecturers.
7. *Which design format has been adopted?* If the chosen format differs significantly from previously used district curricula, some staff development may be required to instruct teachers in using the new materials.
8. *What are the results from the field test?* Teachers will often reveal staff development needs and topics when interviewed anonymously during the field testing process.

Monitoring and Supervision

Supervisors who observe teachers play a key role in supporting the implementation process. They provide opportunities for teachers to share and discuss problems and uncertainties with regard to their implementation efforts. In order for supervisors to be effective in this role, they must consider the following guidelines:

· Prove to teachers that supervision aims to support the teacher's many tasks. In order to do this, it may be necessary to separate the supervisor's two roles, and to emphasize the *supervision* role over the *evaluation* role.
· Be familiar with the curriculum and the teacher's stage of professional development; focus on issues, students, lesson plans, and instructional techniques in reference to, and appropriate for, his/her classroom.
· Provide feedback to the curriculum designer

or committee that deals with staff development plans or curriculum revision.

Evaluation and Revision

Evaluation

After all the dust has settled, all the decisions have been made, and, at long last, a new science guide has been adopted for implementation, all participants surely deserve a rest. For the curriculum designer, however, the greatest challenge still lies ahead.

Curriculum documents—for science and for most other subject areas—which are more than four or five years old require a thorough evaluation. Changes in the teaching of science, new research information, new standards, and better instructional methods appear quickly, making curricular adjustments necessary on an ongoing basis. This explains the necessity for school districts to have a curriculum process rather than a mere document. Curriculum designers should communicate this issue to all educators, to parents, and to policymakers.

Traditionally, achievement scores are held to be indicators of the quality of a science curriculum. Achievement scores, however, are only one source of curriculum evaluation data, and they are useful only insofar as the tested curriculum matches both the planned and the taught curriculum (English 1980).

Again, curriculum designers face several critical decisions:

1. What is the purpose of evaluating the curriculum? Is it a tool to evaluate teachers, students, or schools?
2. Who will participate in evaluating the curriculum? Should the same curriculum committee be used, or would a different perspective, and therefore a fresh committee, serve better?

The curriculum evaluation committee should be empowered to investigate the strengths and weaknesses of an implemented curriculum in pursuit of the truth.

Curriculum designers should clarify the evaluation process in advance. Included in this process is a clarification of the following:

· Who the evaluation committee *participants* will be
· To what degree curriculum process *goals* have been achieved

· Whether the overall *mission* of the curriculum project has been reached
· Whether curriculum *content* is appropriate in light of district characteristics and mission objectives
· Whether *instruction* is based on the curriculum
· Whether the *assessment* process measured the taught curriculum against the planned curriculum.

Table 2 provides a sampling of the goals and questions that could be addressed during evaluation of a curriculum.

The evaluation, then, will yield a *needs assessment* to clarify what types of resources, time demands, training and workshops, and supervision strategies must be in place in order for successful implementation to continue. In addition, a *revision plan* should be issued for the curriculum guide itself, giving specifics for additions or deletions.

Revision

Planning for the next generation of science programs begins now. The first step consists of educating the school board, the staff, and the community that implementation will yield a variety of positive experiences as well as numerous problems. Information of this sort must be collected and organized in view of future revisions of the curriculum. Any curriculum has room for improvement and must be dynamic enough to incorporate upcoming changes in teaching science.

Curriculum designers should, therefore, present a *curriculum development process,* if not at the outset, then certainly at the time of adoption and implementation. This will clarify the ground rules for all concerned. A development process at the district level should incorporate all curriculum areas. However, in order to remain manageable, the district should avoid revising all curricula during the same year. Revising a science curriculum can be as complex as designing it in the first place. Numerous decisions must be made, and numerous sources of information should be considered; just a few are listed here:

· Is a revision necessary in view of available information, or should the revision cycle be changed (to revise sooner or later than planned)?
· Should a committee be established to carry out the revision?
· Have conditions changed since the science curriculum was first implemented (new standards, new testing systems, new staffing

Table 2. Sample Evaluation of K-5 Science Curriculum			
Rationale	**Participants**	**Goals**	**Mission**
The evaluation will identify strengths and weaknesses in the K-5 science program.	Curriculum committee members; supervisory personnel; consultant	Quality of document (design, format, volume, type of information); effectiveness of staff development; effectiveness of supervision; quality of achievement	To what degree has the curriculum been implemented? Have adopted standards and goals been achieved? Have science achievement scores risen? Have teachers adopted the curriculum?
Content	**Needs Assessment**	**Assessment**	**Instruction**
Is the information in the document accurate, verifiable, measurable, "teachable," developmentally appropriate?	The K teachers must be involved in redesigning the life science strand. The grade 4 curriculum is too demanding, geared to advanced students. Staff development efforts for grades 4-6 teachers ineffective. Grade 3 goals do not meet intent of NSTA standards.	Does the testing program cover this curriculum? Have teachers changed their assessment tools and strategies effectively to accommodate the curriculum? Have achievement scores changed with the implementation of this curriculum?	Do teachers have sufficient time to teach the curriculum? Have teachers changed instructional methods? Have teachers used the curriculum in planning instruction? Are instructional resources (textbooks, lab equipment, software, etc.) available?

patterns, significant changes in enrollment, budget crises, etc.)?

Curriculum designers often battle the assumption that completed curriculum guides finalize the curriculum process—in reality, a curriculum guide marks the *beginning* of a curriculum. A curriculum guide that looks the same five years after it was written will most likely be outdated. Teachers tend to leave them on the shelf, and for good reason.

Each school or district must have a process in place for curriculum development and revision. Schools and districts with an ongoing curriculum revision process can best react to new standards and methods in teaching science and in all other K-12 subjects—and these are the schools that can best serve their students and prepare them for the world beyond graduation.

Notes

1. Other practical guidebooks are available to supplement this one. See Carr and Harris 1992; Frey et al. 1989; Bradley 1985; National Science Teachers Association 1992; American Association for the Advancement of Science 1988; California State Department of Education 1987; Connecticut State Board of Education 1991.

2. Among the numerous outstanding resources which discuss the issue of teachers as adult learners in detail are Thies-Sprinthall 1986; Sprinthall and Thies-Sprinthall 1983; McNergney and Carrier 1981; Oja and Ham 1987.

3. Budget models based on curricular or programmatic priorities are discussed in Wood 1986.

4. For a historical perspective on the interdisciplinary curriculum, see Vars 1991.

5. For a comprehensive review of interdisciplinary curriculum models and procedures, see Palmer 1991; Jacobs 1989; Miller, Cassie, and Drake 1990; and Drake 1991.

References

Abruscato, J. 1982. *Teaching Children Science.* 2d ed. Englewood Cliffs, NJ: Prentice-Hall.

American Association for the Advancement of Science. 1989. *Science for All Americans: Literacy Goals in Science, Mathematics, and Technology.* A Project 2061 Report. Washington, DC.

American Association for the Advancement of Science. 1988. *Science for All Americans: Literacy Goals in Science, Mathematics, and Technology.* A Project 2061 Report. Washington, DC.

American Association for the Advancement of Science. 1992. *Update: Project 2061. Education for a Changing Future.* Washington, DC.

Anderson, S. A., et al. 1987. *Curriculum Process: Yale Public Schools.* Yale, MI.

Apple, M. W. 1979. *Ideology and Curriculum.* Boston: Routledge and Kegan Paul.

Argyris, C. 1982. *Reading, Learning, and Action: Individual and Organizational.* San Francisco: Jossey-Bass.

Aronowitz, S., and H. A. Giroux. 1985. *Education under Siege.* South Hadley, MA: Bergin and Garvey.

Bradley, L. H. 1985. *Curriculum Leadership and Development Handbook.* Englewood Cliffs, NJ: Prentice Hall.

Caine, R. N., and G. Caine. 1991. *Making Connections—Teaching and the Human Brain.* Alexandria, VA: Association for Supervision and Curriculum Development.

California State Department of Education. 1987. *Science: Model Curriculum Guide—Kindergarten through Grade Eight.* Sacramento.

Campbell, M., et al. 1989. "Board Members Needn't Be Experts to Play a Vital Role in Curriculum." *American School Board Journal* 176 (Apr.): 30–32.

Carr, J. F., and D. E. Harris. 1992. *Getting It Together: A Process Workbook for Curriculum Development, Implementation, and Assessment.* Boston: Allyn & Bacon.

Connecticut State Board of Education. 1991. *Science: A Guide to Curriculum Development.* Hartford.

Connelly, F. M., and D. J. Clandinin. 1988. *Teachers as Curriculum Planners: Narratives of Experience.* New York: Teachers College Press.

Doll, R. C. 1989. *Curriculum Improvement: Decision Making and Process.* 7th ed. Boston: Allyn & Bacon.

Drake, S. M. 1991. "How Our Team Dissolved the Boundaries." *Educational Leadership* 49 (Oct.): 20–22.

Educational Testing Service. 1988. *The Science Report Card—Trends and Achievement.* Princeton, NJ.

English, F. W. 1988. *Curriculum Auditing.* Lancaster, PA: Technomic.

———. 1980. "Improving Curriculum Management in the Schools." Occasional Paper 30. Washington, DC: Council for Basic Education.

Frey, K., et al. 1989. "Do Curriculum Development Models Really Influence the Curriculum?" *Journal of Curriculum Studies* 21 (Nov.–Dec.): 553–59.

Fullan, M. G. 1990. "Staff Development, Innovation, and Institutional Development." In *ASCD Yearbook,* 3–25. Alexandria, VA: Association for Supervision and Curriculum Development.

Giroux, H. A. 1983. *Theory and Resistance in Education.* South Hadley, MA: Bergin and Garvey.

Glatthorn, A. A. 1987. *Curriculum Leadership.* Glenview, IL: Scott, Foresman.

Glickman, C. 1990. *Supervision of Instruction: A Developmental Approach.* 2d ed. Boston: Allyn & Bacon.

Goodlad, J. I. 1990. *Teachers for Our Nation's Schools.* San Francisco: Jossey-Bass.

Harris, D. E., and Jenzer, J. 1990. "The Search for Quality Curriculum Design: Four Models for School Districts." Paper presented at National Association of Supervision and Curriculum Development Conference, San Antonio, TX.

Harste, J. 1989. *New Policy Guidelines For Reading: Connecting Research and Practice.* Urbana, IL: National Council of Teachers of English.

Hickman, F. M., et al. 1987. *Science/Technology/Society: A Framework for Curriculum Reform in Secondary School Science and Social Studies.* Funded by National Science Foundation, Washington, DC. Boulder, CO: Social Science Education Consortium.

Holmes Group. 1990. *Tomorrow's Schools: Principles for the Design of Professional Development Schools.* East Lansing, MI.

Jacobs, H. H. 1989. *Interdisciplinary Curriculum—Design and Implementation.* Alexandria, VA: Association for Supervision and Curriculum Development.

Joyce, B., and B. Showers. 1988. *Student Achievement through Staff Development.* White Plains, NY: Longman.

Kanpol, B., and E. Weisz. 1990. "The Effective Principal and the Curriculum—A Focus on Leadership." *NASSP Bulletin* 74 (Apr.): 15–18.

Linn, M. C. *Science Curriculum Design: Views From a Psychological Framework.* Funded by National Science Foundation. Washington, DC.

Loucks-Horsely, S., et al. 1987. *Continuing to Learn: A Guidebook for Teacher Development.* Andover, MA: Regional Laboratory for Educational Improvement of the Northeast and the Islands.

McNeil, J. D. 1985. *Curriculum—A Comprehensive Introduction.* 3d ed. Boston: Little, Brown.

McNergney, R., and C. Carrier. 1981. *Teacher Development.* New York: Macmillan.

Miller, J., B. Cassie, and S. M. Drake. 1990. *Holistic Learning: A Teacher's Guide to Integrated Studies.* Toronto: Ontario Institute for Studies in Education.

Montana State Office of the Superintendent of Public Instruction. 1990. *The Curriculum Process Guide: Developing Curriculum in the 1990's.* Helena, MT.

National Science Resources Center. 1988. *Science For Children, Resources For Teachers.* Washington, DC: National Academy Press.

National Science Teacher Association. 1992. *The Content Core—A Guide for Curriculum Designers.* Washington, DC.

Oja, S. N., and M. Ham. 1987. *A Collaborative Approach to Leadership in Supervision.* Project funded by U.S. Department of Education (OERI). Washington, DC.

Oregon State Department of Education. 1989. "Contributions of Piaget to Science Education." Science Curriculum Concept Paper 2. Salem, OR.

Palmer, J. M. 1991. "Planning Wheels Turn Curriculum Around." *Educational Leadership* 49 (Oct.): 57–60.

Schon, D. 1987. *Educating the Reflective Practitioner.* New York: Basic Books.

Sprinthall, N. A., and L. Thies-Sprinthall. 1983. "The Teacher as an Adult Learner: A Cognitive-Developmental View." In *Eighty-second Yearbook of the National Society for the Study of Education,* 13–35. Chicago, IL: National Society for the Study of Education.

Thies-Sprinthall, L. 1986. "A Collaborative Approach to Mentor Training: A Working Model." *Journal of Teacher Education* 19 (Nov.–Dec.): 13–20.

United States Department of Education. 1983. *A Nation at Risk: The Imperative for Educational Reform.* Washington, DC.

Vars, G. F. 1991. "Integrated Curriculum in Historical Perspective." *Educational Leadership* 49 (Oct.): 14–15.

West, P. 1992. "Academy Names Members to Four Science-Standards Panel." *Education Week* 11 (37): 10.

Wood, R. C., ed. 1986. *Principles of School Business Management.* Reston, VA: Association of School Business Officials International.

Wulf, K. M., and B. Schave. 1984. *Curriculum Design.* Glenview, IL: Scott, Foresman.

Young, H. J. 1990. "Curriculum Implementation: An Organizational Perspective." *Journal of Curriculum and Supervision* 5 (Winter): 132–49.

■

FUNDING CURRICULUM PROJECTS

THE greatest challenge curriculum developers often face is locating money to finance their projects. We hear that money is available for such projects, but are at a loss as to how this resource can be obtained. Frequently, it requires as much creativity to locate financing as it does to generate the curriculum. This chapter includes information on three types of funding that are available for education projects:

1. Federal programs that provide money for special school projects
2. Foundations and organizations that have recently endowed science education projects
3. Foundations and organizations that provide funds for state education, including special projects, as a mission.

When seeking a potential funding source for a project, first review any information that is available about the organization. Specifically look at the following areas:

- Purpose: Is a mission of the foundation to provide money for education?
- Limitations: Are there specific geographic requirements? Are there some areas that are disqualified?
- Supported areas: Does the organization provide funding for special projects?
- Grants: After reviewing the education projects that have been funded, does it appear that the organizations and projects are similar to yours?

Your search will be even more useful if you keep these questions in mind:

- Has the foundation funded projects in your subject area?
- Does your location meet the geographic requirements of the organization?
- Is the amount of money you are requesting within the grant's range?
- Are there foundation policies that prohibit grants for the type of support you are requesting?
- Will the organization institute grants to cover the full cost of a project? Does it require that costs of a project be shared with other foundations or funding sources?
- What types of educational groups have been supported? Are they similar to yours?
- Are there specific application deadlines and procedures, or are proposals accepted continuously?

This information can be found in the annual report of the foundation or in *Source Book Profiles.* Many of the larger public libraries maintain current foundation directories. If yours does not, there are Foundation Center Libraries located at:

79 Fifth Avenue
New York, NY 10003-3050
(212) 620-4230

312 Sutter Street
San Francisco, CA 94180
(415) 397-0902

1001 Connecticut Avenue, NW
Suite 938
Washington, DC 20036
(202) 331-1400

1442 Hanna Building
1442 Euclid Avenue
Cleveland, OH 44115
(216) 861-1934

Identifying appropriate foundations is the first step in your quest for money. The next step is initiating contact with the foundation, either by telephone or by correspondence. It is a good idea to direct your inquiry to the person in charge of giving; otherwise, your letter could easily go astray. A phone call to the foundation will provide you with the necessary information.

Federal Programs that Provide Money for Special School Projects

Jacob B. Javits Gifted and Talented Students
Research Applications Division
Programs for the Improvement of Practice
Department of Education
555 New Jersey Avenue, NW
Washington, DC 20202-5643
(202) 219-2187
Provides grants for establishing and operating model projects to identify and educate gifted and talented students.

Technology Education Demonstration
Division of National Programs
Office of Vocational and Adult Education
Department of Education
400 Maryland Avenue, SW
Washington, DC 20202-7242
(202) 732-2428
Provides funding to establish model demonstration programs for technology education in secondary schools, vocational education centers, and community colleges.

Eisenhower National Program for Mathematics and Science Education
Department of Education
FIRST
Office of Educational Research and Improvement
Washington, DC 20208-5524
(202) 219-1496
Supports innovative projects of national significance to improve public and private elementary and secondary school mathematics and science instruction.

Aerospace Education Services Project
Elementary and Secondary Programs Branch
Code XEE
NASA Field Center
Washington, DC 20546
(202) 453-8386
Funds projects that provide information about U.S. aeronautics and space research. Goals include the development of activities and results of the activities, the enhancement of knowledge for students and teachers, motivation for them in science education and careers, enrichment of the regular curricula, and assistance with in-service teacher training.

Teacher Preparation and Enhancement
Division of Teacher Preparation and Enhancement
National Science Foundation
1800 G Street, NW
Washington, DC 20550
(202) 357-7073
Funding for projects that support networking activities to encourage talented teachers to remain in K–12 science and math careers. Restricted to areas of astronomy, atmospheric science, biological science, chemistry, computer science, earth science, engineering, information science, mathematical science, oceanography, physics, social science, and technology.

Materials Development, Research, and Informal Science Education
National Science Foundation
1800 G Street
Washington, DC 20550
(202) 357-7452
Provides funds for projects that expand knowledge and provide new and improved models, and material resources, needed to enhance the quality of pre-college educational systems in mathematics, science, and technology.

Minority Math Science Leadership Development Recognition
Department of Energy
MI, Room 5B-110
1000 Independence Avenue, SW
Washington, DC 20585
(202) 586-1593
Promotes education of minorities in the areas of science and math.

The Secretary's Fund for Innovation in Education
Department of Education
FIRST
Office of Educational Research and Improvement
Washington, DC 20208–5524
(202) 219-1496
Funding for educational programs and projects that identify innovative educational approaches.

Foundations and Organizations that Have Recently Endowed Science Education Projects

ARCO Foundation
515 South Flower Street
Los Angeles, CA 94104
(415) 421-2629
Contact: Eugene R. Wilson, President
Giving primarily in San Francisco Bay area.
· $50,000 to the American Chemical Society, Washington, DC, for chemistry curriculum development in urban schools.

The Blandin Foundation
100 Pokegama Avenue, North
Grand Rapids, MN 55744
(218) 326-0523
Contact: Paul M. Olson, President
Funding limited to Minnesota, with an emphasis on rural areas.
· $125,500 grant to Grand Rapids Independent School District #318. Rapids Quest Program, Grand Rapids, MN, to continue imaginative enrichment programs for Grand Rapids students.
· $25,000 grant to Independent School District #317, Deer River, MN, to produce Ojibwe K-12 curriculum.
· $50,000 grant to Mahnomen School District #432, Mahnomen, MN, for their Ojibwe curriculum.

Carnegie Corporation of New York
437 Madison Avenue
New York, NY 10022
(212) 371-3200
· A three-year grant of $150,000 to the Cleveland Education Fund for a new science curriculum in the Cleveland public schools.

Cray Research Foundation
1440 Northland Drive
Mendota Heights, MN 55120
(612) 683-7386
Contact: William C. Linder-Scholer, Executive Director
Giving primarily in Minnesota and Wisconsin for science and engineering education.
· $25,000 to St. Paul Public Schools, Saturn School, St. Paul, MN, for science curriculum development.

Du Pont Community Initiatives Fund
Du Pont External Affairs
Wilmington, DE 19898
(302) 774-1000
Matching-grant program for projects that encourage company sites to develop or adopt programs in their communities that will improve the quality of public education and increase public understanding of environmental matters.

W. Alton Jones Foundation, Inc.
232 East High Street
Charlottesville, VA 22901
(804) 295-2134
· $70,000 to the Episcopal School of New York City, for general school development and teacher professional development.

W. K. Kellogg Foundation
400 North Avenue
Battle Creek, MI 49017-3398
(616) 968-1611
· $2,500,000 to Battle Creek School District in Michigan for an improved science curriculum for K-12.

The Nellie Mae Fund for Education
50 Braintree Hill Park, Suite 300
Braintree, MA 02184
Contact: Edgar E. Smith, Vice President
(617) 849-1325
Generally limited to the six New England states.
· $10,000 to Volunteers in Providence Schools, Providence, RI, for after-school study centers in 11 sites throughout Providence.
· $12,000 to Winthrop School Department, Winthrop, ME, to develop "Modeling for Success" project (positive role models for at-risk middle school students).

The Medtronic Foundation
7000 Central Avenue, NE
Minneapolis, MN 55432
(612) 574-3029
Giving primarily in areas of company operations.
· $12,500 to Minneapolis Public Schools,
Minneapolis, MN to work with the community on general curriculum development.

The Reader's Digest Foundation
Pleasantville, NY 10570
· 100 mini-grants of up to $500 each to fund
innovative-teaching programs in Westchester
and Putnam counties, NY, schools.

Research Corporation
6840 East Broadway Boulevard
Tucson, AZ 85710-2815
(602) 296-6771
Contact: Brian Anderson, Science Advancement
Program
The Partners in Science program makes awards
available to college and university scientists to act
as mentors to high school science teachers, for
summer research.

The Spencer Foundation
900 North Michigan Avenue, Suite 2800
Chicago, IL 60611
Grants for various research projects related to
cultural variations, high-school teaching, mathematics, school choice, etc.

Steelcase Foundation
P.O. Box 1967
Grand Rapids, MI 49507
(616) 246-4695
Funding limited to areas of company operations.
· $20,000 to Forest Hills Education Founda-
tion, Grand Rapids, MI, for development of
science curriculum for special education
students.

The Tandy Corporation
1800 One Tandy Center
Fort Worth, TX 76102
·Tandy Educational Grants to 11 schools and
colleges/universities for "Using Microcomputers for Classroom Management to
Increase Student/Teacher Productivity."

Toyota Motor Sales, USA
c/o NSTA/TAPESTRY
1742 Connecticut Avenue, NW
Washington, DC 20009
Toyota's Appreciation Program for Excellence to
Science Teachers Reaching Youth (TAPESTRY),
administered through the National Science
Teachers Association.
· Grants of up to $10,000 and $25,000 to high
school science teachers for innovative
classroom science projects.

Foundations and Organizations that Provide Funds for Education, Including Special Projects, as a Mission

Aetna Foundation, Inc.
151 Farmington Avenue
Hartford, CT 06156-3180
(203) 273-6382
Contact: Diana Kinosh, Management Information   Supervisor

The Ahmanson Foundation
9215 Wilshire Boulevard
Beverly Hills, CA 90210
(213) 278-0770
Contact: Lee E. Walcott, Vice President and
Managing Director
Giving primarily in southern California.

Alcoa Foundation
1501 Alcoa Building
Pittsburgh, PA 15219-1850
(412) 553-2348
Contact: F. Worth Hobbs, President
Giving primarily in areas of company operation.

The Allstate Foundation
Allstate Plaza North
Northbrook, IL 60062
(708) 402-5502
Contacts: Alan Benedict, Executive Director;
Allen Goldhamer, Manager; Dawn Bougart,
Administrative Assistant

American Express Minnesota Foundation
c/o IDS Financial Services
IDS Tower Ten
Minneapolis, MN 55440
(612) 372-2643
Contacts: Sue Gethin, Manager, Public Affairs,
    IDS; Marie Tobin, Community Relations
    Specialist
Giving primarily in Minnesota.

American National Bank & Trust Company of
Chicago Foundation
33 North La Salle Street
Chicago, IL 60690
(312) 661-6115
Contact: Joan M. Klaus, Director
Giving limited to the six-county Chicago metro-
politan area.

Anderson Foundation
c/o Anderson Corporation
Bayport, MN 55003
(612) 439-5150
Contact: Lisa Carlstrom, Assistant Secretary

The Annenberg Foundation
St. Davids Center
150 Radnor-Chester Road, Suite A-200
St. Davids, PA 19087
Contact: Dr. Mary Ann Meyers, President

AON Foundation
123 North Wacker Drive
Chicago, IL 60606
(312) 701-3000
Contact: Wallace J. Buya, Vice President
Offers no support for secondary educational
institutions or vocational schools.

Atherton Family Foundation
c/o Hawaiian Trust Company, Ltd.
P.O. Box 3170
Honolulu, HI 96802
(808) 537-6333; Fax: (808) 521-6286
Contact: Charlie Medeiros
Giving limited to Hawaii.

Metropolitan Atlanta Community
    Foundation, Inc.
The Hurt Building, Suite 449
Atlanta, GA 30303
(404) 688-5525
Contact: Alicia Philipp, Executive Director
Giving limited to the city of Atlanta and its
surrounding regions.

Ball Brothers Foundation
222 South Mulberry Street
Muncie, IN 47308
(317) 741-5500
Fax: (317) 741-5518
Contact: Douglas A. Bakker, Executive Director
Giving limited to Indiana.

Baltimore Gas & Electric Foundation, Inc.
Box 1475
Baltimore, MD 21203
(301) 234-5312
Contact: Gary R. Fuhronan
Giving primarily in Maryland, with an emphasis
in Baltimore.

Bell Atlantic Charitable Foundation
1310 North Courthouse Road, 10th Floor
Arlington, VA 22201
(703) 974-5440
Contact: Ruth P. Caine, Director
Giving primarily in areas of company operations.

Benwood Foundation, Inc.
1600 American National Bank Building
736 Market Street
Chattanooga, TN 37402
(615) 267-4311
Contact: Jean R. McDaniel, Executive Director
Giving primarily in the Chattanooga area.

Robert M. Beren Foundation, Inc.
970 Fourth Financial Center
Wichita, KS 67202
Giving primarily to Jewish organizations.

The Frank Stanley Beveridge Foundation, Inc.
1515 Ringling Boulevard, Suite 340
P.O. Box 4097
Sarasota, FL 34230-4097
(813) 955-7575; (800) 356-9779
Contact: Philip Coswell, President
Giving primarily in Hampden County to organi-
zations that are not tax-supported.

F.R. Bigelow Foundation
1120 Norwest Center
St. Paul, MN 55101
(612) 224-5463
Contact: Paul A. Verret, Secretary-Treasurer
Support includes secondary education in the
greater St. Paul metropolitan area.

Borden Foundation, Inc.
180 East Broad Street, 34th Floor
Columbus, OH 43215
(614) 225-4340
Contact: Judy Barker, President
Emphasis on programs that benefit disadvantaged children in areas of company operations.

The Boston Globe Foundation II, Inc.
135 Morrissey Boulevard
Boston, MA 02107
(617) 929-3194
Contact: Suzanne Watkin, Executive Director
Giving primarily in the greater Boston area.

The J. S. Bridwell Foundation
500 City National Building
Wichita Falls, TX 76303
(817) 322-4436
Support includes secondary education in Texas.

The Buchanan Family Foundation
222 East Wisconsin Avenue
Lake Forest, IL 60045
Contact: Huntington Eldridge, Jr., Treasurer
Giving primarily in Chicago.

The Buhl Foundation
Four Gateway Center, Room 1522
Pittsburgh, PA 15222
(412) 566-2711
Contact: Dr. Doreen E. Boyce,
   Executive Director
Giving primarily in southwestern Pennsylvania, particularly in the Pittsburgh area.

Edyth Bush Charitable Foundation, Inc.
199 East Welbourne Avenue
P.O. Box 1967
Winter Park, FL 32790-1967
(407) 647-4322
Contact: H. Clifford Lee, President
Giving has specific geographic and facility limitations.

California Community Foundation
606 South Olive Street, Suite 2400
Los Angeles, CA 90014
(213) 413-4042
Contact: Jack Shakley, President
Orange County:
13252 Garden Grove Boulevard, Suite 195
Garden Grove, CA 92643
(714) 750-7794

Giving limited to Los Angeles, Orange, Riverside, San Bernadino, and Ventura Counties.

The Cargill Foundation
P.O. Box 9300
Minneapolis, MN 55440
(612) 475-6122
Contact: Audrey Tulberg, Program Director
Giving primarily in the seven-county Minneapolis metropolitan area.

H.A. & Mary K. Chapman Charitable Trust
One Warren Place, Suite 1816
6100 South Yale Street
Tulsa, OK 74136
(918) 496-7882
Contacts: Ralph L. Abercrombie, Trustee; Donne
   Pitman, Trustee
Giving primarily in Tulsa, OK.

Liz Claiborne Foundation
119 West 40th Street, 4th Floor
New York, NY 10018
(212) 536-6424
Limited to Hudson County and the metropolitan New York area.

The Coca-Cola Foundation, Inc.
P.O. Drawer 1734
Atlanta, GA 30301
(404) 676-2568

The Columbus Foundation
1234 East Broad Street
Columbus, OH 43205
(614) 251-4000
Contact: James I. Luck, President
Giving limited to central Ohio.

Cowles Media Foundation
329 Portland Avenue
Minneapolis, MN 55415
(612) 375-7051
Contact: Janet L. Schwichtenberg
Giving limited to Minneapolis area.

Dade Community Foundation
200 South Biscayne Boulevard, Suite 4770
Miami, FL 33131-2343
(305) 371-2711
Contact: Ruth Shack, President
Funding limited to Dade County.

Dewitt Families Conduit Foundation
8300 96th Avenue
Zeeland, MI 49464
Giving to Christian organizations.

Dodge Jones Foundation
P.O. Box 176
Abilene, TX 79604
(915) 673-6429
Contact: Lawrence E. Gill, Vice President,
　Grants Administrator
Giving primarily in Abilene.

Carrie Estelle Doheny Foundation
911 Wiltshire Boulevard, Suite 1750
Los Angeles, CA 90017
(213) 488-1122
Contact: Robert A. Smith III, President
Giving primarily in the Los Angeles area for non-tax supported organizations.

The Educational Foundation of America
23161 Ventura Boulevard, Suite 201
Woodland Hills, CA 91364
(818) 999-0921

The Charles Engelhard Foundation
P.O. Box 427
Far Hills, NJ 07931
(201) 766-7224
Contact: Elaine Catterall, Secretary

The William Stamps Farish Fund
1100 Louisiana, Suite 1250
Houston, TX 77002
(713) 757-7313
Contact: W. S. Farish, President
Giving primarily in Texas.

Joseph & Bessie Feinberg Foundation
5245 West Lawrence Avenue
Chicago, IL 60630
(312) 777-8600
Contact: June Blossom
Giving primarily in Illinois to Jewish organizations.

The 1525 Foundation
1525 National City Bank Building
Cleveland, OH 44114
(216) 696-4200
Contact: Bernadette Walsh, Assistant Secretary

Giving primarily in Ohio, with an emphasis on Cuyahoga County.

The Flinn Foundation
3300 North Central Avenue, Suite 2300
Phoenix, AZ 85012
(602) 274-9000
Contact: John W. Murphy, Executive Director
Giving limited to Arizona, with an emphasis on the biological sciences.

The Edward E. Ford Foundation
297 Wickenden Street
Providence, RI 02903
(401) 751-2966
Contact: Philip V. Havens, Executive Director
Funding to independent secondary schools.

George F. & Sybil H. Fuller Foundation
105 Madison Street
Worcester, MA 01610
(508) 756-5111
Contact: Russell E. Fuller, Chairman
Giving primarily in Massachusetts, with an emphasis in Worcester.

The B. C. Gamble & P. W. Skogmo Foundation
500 Foshay Tower
Minneapolis, MN 55402
(612) 339-7343
Contact: Patricia A. Cummings, Manager of
　Supporting Organizations
Giving primarily for disadvantaged youth, handicapped, and secondary educational institutions in the Minneapolis and St. Paul metropolitan areas.

The Gold Family Foundation
159 Conant Street
Hillside, NJ 07205
(908) 353-6269
Contact: Meyer Gold, Manager
Supports primarily Jewish organizations.

Golden Family Foundation
40 Wall Street, Room 4201
New York, NY 10005
(212) 425-0333
Contact: William T. Golden, President
Funding is to higher educational sciences and is limited to New York.

The George Gund Foundation
1845 Guildhall Building
45 Prospect Avenue West
Cleveland, OH 44115
(216) 241-3114; Fax: (216) 241-6560
Contact: David Bergholz, Executive Director
Giving primarily in northeastern Ohio.

The Haggar Foundation
6113 Lemmon Avenue
Dallas, TX 75209
(214) 956-0241
Contact: Rosemary Haggar Vaughan,
    Executive Director
Giving is limited to areas of company operations
in Dallas and south Texas.

Gladys & Roland Harriman Foundation
63 Wall Street, 23rd Floor
New York, NY 10005
(212) 493-8182
Contact: William F. Hibberd, Secretary

Hasbro Children's Foundation
32 West 23rd Street
New York, NY 10010
(212) 645-2400
Contact: Eve Weiss, Executive Director
Funding for children, under the age of 12, with
special needs.

The Humana Foundation, Inc.
The Humana Building
500 West Main Street
P.O. Box 1438
Louisville, KY 40201
(502) 580-3920
Contact: Jay L. Foley, Contributions Manager
Giving primarily in Kentucky.

International Paper Company Foundation
Two Manhattanville Road
Purchase, NY 10577
(914) 397-1581
Contact: Sandra Wilson, Vice President
Giving primarily in communities where there are
company plants and mills.

The Martha Holden Jennings Foundation
710 Halle Building
1228 Euclid Avenue
Cleveland, OH 44115
(216) 589-5700

Contact: Dr. Richard A. Boyd,
    Executive Director
Funding is limited to Ohio.

Walter S. Johnson Foundation
525 Middlefield Road, Suite 110
Menlo Park, CA 94025
(415) 326-0485
Contact: Donna Terman, Executive Director
Giving primarily in Alameda, Contra Costa, San
Francisco, San Mateo, and Santa Clara counties,
as well as in Washoe, Nevada. There is no
financial support of private schools.

Donald P. & Byrd M. Kelly Foundation
701 Harger Road, #150
Oak Brook, IL 60521
Contact: Laura K. McGrath, Treasurer
Giving primarily in Illinois, with an emphasis in
Chicago.

Carl B. & Florence E. King Foundation
5956 Sherry Lane, Suite 620
Dallas, TX 75225
Contact: Carl Yeckel, Vice President
Giving primarily in the Dallas area.

Thomas & Dorothy Leavey Foundation
4680 Wiltshire Boulevard
Los Angeles, CA 90010
(213) 930-4252
Contact: J. Thomas McCarthy, Trustee
Giving primarily in southern California to
Catholic organizations.

Levi Strauss Foundation
1155 Battery Street
San Francisco, CA 94111
(415) 544-2194
Contacts: Bay Area: Judy Belk, Director of
    Contributions; Mid-South Region: Myra
    Chow, Director of Contributions; Western
    Region: Mario Griffin, Director of Contribu-
    tions; Rio Grande: Elvira Chavaria, Director
    of Contributions; Eastern Region: Mary
    Ellen McLoughlin, Director of Contributions
Giving is generally limited to areas of company
operations.

Lyndhurst Foundation
Suite 701, Tallan Building
100 West Martin Luther King Boulevard
Chattanooga, TN 37402-2561
(615) 756-0767

Contact: Jack E. Murrah, President
Giving is limited to the southeastern United
States, especially Chattanooga.

McDonnell Douglas Foundation
c/o McDonnell Douglas Corporation
P.O. Box 516, Mail Code 1001440
St. Louis, MO 63166
(314) 232-8464
Contact: Walter E. Diggs, Jr., President
Giving primarily in Arizona, California, Florida,
Missouri, Oklahoma, and Texas.

Meadows Foundation, Inc.
Wilson Historic Block
2922 Swiss Avenue
Dallas, TX 75204-5928
(214) 826-9431
Contact: Dr. Sally R. Lancaster, Executive Vice
President
Giving limited to Texas.

The Milken Family Foundation
c/o Foundation of the Milken Families
15250 Ventura Boulevard, 2nd floor
Sherman Oaks, CA 91403
Contact: Dr. Jules Lesner, Executive Director
Giving limited to the Los Angeles area.

The New Hampshire Charitable Fund
One South Street
P.O. Box 1335
Concord, NH 03302-1335
(603) 225-6641
Contact: Deborah Cowan, Associate Director
Funding limited to New Hampshire.

The New Haven Foundation
70 Audubon Street
New Haven, CT 06510
(203) 777-2386
Contact: Helmer N. Ekstrom, Director
Giving primarily in greater New Haven and the
lower Naugatuck River Valley.

Dellora A. & Lester J. Norris Foundation
P.O. Box 1081
St. Charles, IL 60174
(312) 377-4111
Contact: Eugene Butler, Treasurer
Funding includes secondary education.

The Northern Trust Company Charitable Trust
c/o The Northern Trust Company
Corporate Affairs Division
50 South LaSalle Street
Chicago, IL 60675
(312) 444-3538
Contact: Marjorie W. Lundy, Vice President
Giving limited to the metropolitan Chicago area.

O'Donnell Foundation
1401 Elm Street, Suite 3388
Dallas, TX 75202
(214) 698-9915
Contact: C. R. Bacan
Giving primarily in Texas for science and engineering projects.

The Principal Financial Group Foundation, Inc.
711 High Street
Des Moines, IA 50392-0150
(515) 247-5209
Contact: Debra J. Jensen, Secretary
Funding primarily in Iowa, with an emphasis on
the Des Moines area.

Sid W. Richardson Foundation
309 Main Street
Forth Worth, TX 76102
(817) 336-0497
Contact: Valleau Wilkie, Jr., Executive Vice
President
Giving limited to Texas.

R.J.R. Nabisco Foundation
1455 Pennsylvania Avenue, North West, Suite 525
Washington, DC 20004
(202) 626-7200
Contact: Jaynie M. Grant, Executive Director

The Winthrop Rockefeller Foundation
308 East Eighth Street
Little Rock, AR 72202
(501) 376-6854
Contact: Mahlon Martin, President
Funding primarily in Arkansas for projects that
will benefit the state.

The San Francisco Foundation
685 Market Street, Suite 910
San Francisco, CA 94105-9716
(415) 495-3100

Contact: Robert M. Fisher, Director
Giving limited to the Bay Area, the counties of
Alameda, Contra Costa, Marin, San Francisco,
and San Mateo.

Community Foundation of Santa Clara County
960 West Hedding Street, Suite 220
San Jose, CA 95126-1215
(408) 241-2666
Contact: Winnie Chu, Program Officer
Giving limited to Santa Clara County.

John & Dorothy Shea Foundation
655 Brea Canyon Road
Walnut, CA 91789
Giving primarily in California.

Harold Simmons Foundation
Three Lincoln Center
5430 LBJ Freeway, Suite 1700
Dallas, TX 75240-2697
(214) 233-1700
Contact: Lisa K. Simmons, President
Giving is limited to Dallas, TX, area.

Sonart Family Foundation
15 Benders Drive
Greenwich, CT 06831
(203) 531-1474
Contact: Raymond Sonart, President

The Sosland Foundation
4800 Main Street, Suite 100
Kansas City, MO 64112
(816) 765-1000; Fax: (816) 756-0494
Contact: Debbie Sosland-Edelman, Ph.D.
Giving limited to Kansas City, Missouri and
Kansas areas.

Community Foundation for Southeastern
    Michigan
333 West Fort Street, Suite 2010
Detroit, MI 48226
(313) 961-6675
Contact: C. David Campbell, Program Vice
    President
Giving limited to southeastern Michigan.

Springs Foundation, Inc.
P.O. Drawer 460
Lancaster, SC 29720
(803) 286-2196
Contact: Charles A. Bundy, President

Giving limited to Lancaster County and the
townships of Fort Mill and Chester.

Strauss Foundation
c/o Fidelity Bank, N.A.
Broad & Walnut Streets
Philadelphia, PA 19109
(215) 985-7717
Contact: Richard Irvin, Jr.
Giving primarily in Pennsylvania.

Stuart Foundations
425 Market Street, Suite 2835
San Francisco, CA 94105
(415) 495-1144
Contact: Theodore E. Lobman, President
Funding primarily in California, but applications
from Washington will be considered.

T.L.L. Tempee Foundation
109 Tempee Boulevard
Lufkin, TX 75901
(409) 639-5197
Contact: M. F. Buddy Zeagler, Assistant
    Executive Director & Controller
Giving primarily in counties in Texas constituting
the Eastern Texas Pine Timber Belt.

Travelers Companies Foundation
One Tower Square
Hartford, CT 06183-1060
(203) 277-4079; (203) 277-4070
Funding for school programs limited to Hartford.

Turrell Fund
111 Northfield Avenue
West Orange, NJ 07052
(201) 325-5108
Contact: E. Belvin Williams, Executive Director
Giving limited to New Jersey, particularly the
northern urban areas centered in Essex County,
as well as to Vermont.

U.S. West Foundation
7800 East Orchard Road, Suite 300
Englewood, CO 80111
(303) 793-6661
Contact: Larry J. Nash, Director of
    Administration
Funding limited to states served by US WEST
calling areas. Address applications to the local
US WEST Public Relations Office or Community
Relations Team.

Philip L. Van Every Foundation
c/o Lance, Inc.
P.O. Box 32368
Charlotte, NC 28232
(704) 554-1421
Giving primarily in North and South Carolina.

Joseph B. Whitehead Foundation
1400 Peachtree Center Tower
230 Peachtree Street, NW
Atlanta, GA 30303
(404) 522-6755
Contact: Charles H. McTier, President
Giving limited to the city of Atlanta.

Winn-Dixie Stores Foundation
5050 Edgewood Court
Jacksonville, FL 32205
(904) 783-5000
Contact: Jack P. Jones, President
Giving limited to areas of company operation.

The Zellerbach Family Fund
120 Montgomery Street, Suite 2125
San Francisco, CA 94104
(415) 421-2629
Contact: Edward A. Nathan, Executive Director
Giving primarily in San Francisco Bay area.

This chapter includes a sampling of foundations that can be contacted for funding your curriculum project. By no means are these all the resources that can be tapped. Remember, think creatively! Are there any community service organizations such as the Jaycees, Lions Club, or Rotary International that can be contacted? Is there a local Community Fund that supports education projects? Ask friends and neighbors about the organizations they support. Ask if you can use their name as a reference—and be sure to get the names of the people to contact. Make many initial contacts, and don't be discouraged by rejections. The money is there for you; all you need is to be persistent!

References

Catalogue of Federal Domestic Assistance. 1991. Washington, DC: Government Printing Office.

Directory of Research Grants. 1992. Phoenix: Oryx Press.
   Information on a wide variety of funding organizations; index includes terms for Elementary Education, Secondary Education, Science Education, Teacher Education, etc.

The Foundation Grants Index. 1992. New York: Foundation Center.
   Provides funding patterns and other information about the most influential foundations in the United States.

Source Book Profiles. 1992. New York: Foundation Center.
   Information on the one thousand largest United States foundations.

TOPICS IN THE SCIENCE CURRICULUM, GRADES K-12

by Gary Nakagiri
Curriculum Coordinator, Math and Science
San Mateo County Office of Education, Redwood City, CA

ITEMIZING a list of "major" topics for K-12 science is a difficult task, since the priorities in science have changed through the years and the teaching of science has changed as well. Part of the difficulty lies in the definition of *science* itself. Science is a way of knowing, of understanding the natural world. Therefore, the process by which scientific information is obtained is as important as the information itself. This process has two key elements: First, it is a rigorous intellectual activity that evaluates knowledge as being testable, objective, and consistent. For example, experimental results must be replicable (hence the current problems with cold fusion). Second, it is a set of expectations based upon theoretical predictions. Scientists generally work from an extensive framework of preexisting information to guide further inquiry. Yet the process is also open-ended; there are no preordained conclusions.

To help students understand the nature of science, an ideal science education curriculum should consist of the following components:

1. The development of positive *attitudes* towards science. Students should feel that they are beginning to understand what science is, that they can successfully "do" science, and that they have developed an interest in learning more about the natural world.

2. The development of *rational thinking processes*. There are many thinking processes that are incorporated into "doing" science. The so-called scientific method is nothing more than a formalized system of rational thinking, much of which can be applied to non-scientific situations as well.

3. The development of *scientific process skills*. These will be elaborated upon later. Basically, they are the skills that scientists use in their work. Having students experience these skills provides a greater understanding of how scientists do their work and what science is.

4. The development of *scientific knowledge*. Unfortunately, most of the emphasis is typically placed upon this component of science education. While the knowledge and understanding of certain key concepts are important, what is becoming even more important is knowing how to access and use scientific information. Many scientific fields are truly experiencing a knowledge explosion; students should realize that even basic theories, such as the origin of the universe,

are still being modified, based upon the latest data. While there may be universal agreement that some content knowledge is important, there is much less agreement over what that core content should be and how it should be distributed within a K-12 grade level structure.

From this philosophical perspective, any list of science topics is somewhat arbitrary. Unlike a subject such as mathematics, science has no generally accepted sequence of topics that are taught at certain grade levels. In a traditional mathematics curriculum, for example, multiplication is usually introduced at the third-grade level; fractions, at the fifth-grade level. Scientists and science educators generally do not agree on what topics and concepts are important to teach or what grade level is the most appropriate time to teach them.

Yet there are some topics that seem to be found in every elementary science curriculum. Talk to any elementary teacher: dinosaurs, plants, and the weather seem to be universal topics. Unfortunately, at many elementary schools, these are the *only* topics that are consistently taught in the science program. An exemplary science curriculum should, and must, cover a broader range of topics, especially those in the physical and earth sciences.

Topic lists also reflect changes in educational philosophy. As new ideas and philosophies permeate the educational establishment, certain topics become more or less popular within the science curriculum. For example, as the high school curriculum became more academically rigorous in the 1980s, secondary science courses emphasized topics that would better prepare students for college science courses; topics that provided a more pragmatic understanding of the natural world were de-emphasized.

A more controversial view is that content is less important than the scientific process skills and the understanding of the nature of science. This philosophy was embodied in several of the innovative elementary science programs developed during the 1960s and 1970s, in response to the perceived shortcomings of science education.

Currently, there seems to be a fairly balanced approach to the content and processes of science. The processes should be integrated into the instructional strategies in terms of what students should experience. The following processes are generally considered to be essential to the development of students' understanding of how scientific knowledge is obtained:

- *Observing* includes all of the sensory possibilities by which humans sense their world. It also implies a certain degree of objectivity, reinforced by the accurate replication of previous observations.
- *Communicating* includes both verbal and non-verbal forms, such as photographs, charts, etc. It also includes both personal and formal presentations, such as writing for professional journals, newspapers, etc.
- *Comparing* builds upon the process of observing by focusing upon the perceived similarities and differences of objects or organisms. Comparing includes the measurement of objects: comparing a standard of length or mass with an object's length or mass. Comparing the unknown, such as a new star, with the known, the sun, is another possibility.
- *Ordering* is a form of organizing objects or events in some type of sequence or pattern. Seriation is one type of ordering in which objects might be placed in order along a continuum, such as from rough to smooth. Scales, such as those for measuring temperature or wind speed, originated from the seriating of objects. Sequencing usually involves events or activities. Linear sequences may include time, such as evolutionary events. Cyclical sequences generally involve recurring events, such as rain, evaporation, and condensation in the water cycle.
- *Categorizing* includes both grouping and classifying, using a rationale. Grouping leaves, for example, may be done using structural attributes, such as venation, serration, tip shape, etc. Classifying organisms or chemical elements involves multiple criteria and attributes that form a complex rationale for the development of elaborate systems, such as phylogenetic trees or the periodic table. Unknown or "new" organisms or substances can then be placed in the correct category, based upon the established criteria.
- *Relating* involves establishing the various types of relationships or interactions among organisms, events, or objects. The information about the relationships may be descriptive, as the relationship of the zebra's stripes to the lion's perception of shades of gray, or mathematical, as the interaction between the height of the starting point and the speed of a metal ball along a track.

• *Inferring* is a more sophisticated form of hypothesizing, in that the events or activities involved are usually remote, either in terms of time or distance. The inferences made usually involve some logical thinking based on evidence and certain premises. For example, inferences were made about the planet Mars before the first probe was sent. These inferences were based on telescopic observations and on knowledge of requirements for life on Earth.

• *Applying* involves the application of previously learned knowledge to new situations. These situations may be practical, such as the scientific expertise required to build a safe, efficient bridge; or they may be abstract, such as the contributions of various scientists to the theory of evolution.

Process skills may assist teachers in selecting topics and learning activities. One elementary science sourcebook, for example, organizes its activities by science process skills. If a teacher wants her students to practice classifying, the sourcebook provides a list of activities on various topics that all use that process skill.

To illustrate how the general educational philosophy of an era affects the choice of topics in science education, let's begin by looking at the science curricula of the 1940s and early 1950s.

The Traditional Period of Science Education

The philosophy of this period can best be described as one of complacency. Most students were not expected to continue their studies past high school; therefore, science was taught very traditionally, with an emphasis on the memorization of facts. The topics were descriptive, rather than conceptually or theoretically based. For example, a study of the life sciences would include a detailed study of the various animal and plant phyla, based primarily upon their external and internal features. Even at the elementary level, science was largely descriptive; students were expected to memorize information and perhaps occasionally draw pictures of leaves or other natural phenomena. Hands-on activities were rare—or entirely omitted. At the high school level, topics such as evolution or human reproduction were excluded. Information was presented in an authoritarian and dogmatic

manner. The few laboratory exercises were largely after-the-fact confirmations of what had already been learned. Dissections and collections were common laboratory and field activities.

The Science Education Reform Movement

By the mid-1950s, the first science curriculum reform committee, the Physical Science Study Committee (PSSC), was organized. Later, similar curriculum groups were organized for chemistry, biology, the earth sciences, engineering, and elementary science. The philosophy had changed to a greater concern for the academic preparation of future scientists and engineers, and to an emphasis on college-preparatory curricula. The federal government became involved in the reform; the National Science Foundation (NSF) spent millions of dollars funding various curriculum projects. Later, most of these projects were adapted by commercial publishers.

As a result of the reform movement, a staggering number of so-called "alphabet soup" curriculum projects evolved:

Elementary School Curricula
Science—A Process Approach (*SAPA*) was a project that emphasized the process skills of science. The curriculum materials were packaged in numerous boxes, consisting primarily of objects and supplies that children could manipulate. Instead of a content matrix, the curriculum was organized around eight basic processes in grades K-3: observing, classifying, measuring, communicating, inferring, predicting, using space/time relations, and using numbers. For grades 4-6, formulating hypotheses, controlling variables, interpreting data, defining operationally, and experimenting were the five integrated processes comprising the curriculum strands. A criticism of this program was its lack of content; activities were designed to explore the various processes but provided very little factual information.

Science Curriculum Improvement Study (*SCIS*) developed a separate sequence of physical and life science units. Titles in life science included *Organisms, Life Cycles, Populations, Environments, Communities,* and *Ecosystems*; titles in the physical sciences included *Material Objects, Interaction & Systems, Subsystems & Variables, Relative Position & Motion, Energy*

Sources, and *Scientific Theories.* Teachers were expected to teach one life science and one physical unit at each grade level. SCIS was both a content and a process program, in which carefully structured activities were designed to lead to conceptual understanding. A criticism of this program was its lack of any earth science activities and lessons.

Elementary Science Study (ESS) developed a varied set of units, including *Animal Activity, Clay Boats, Pattern Blocks,* and *Whistles and Strings.* Kits could also be purchased to supplement the guides although many of the units could be taught with teacher-collected material. This unstructured curriculum encouraged teachers to establish a learning environment that allowed for student exploration. A common criticism of this program was the lack of specific lessons; teachers were expected to develop their own with the many useful ideas provided in the guides.

Conceptually Oriented Program in Elementary Science (COPES) emphasized a conceptual scheme approach. For K-2, there were seven introductory concepts based on three basic ideas: descriptions of matter and energy, matter and energy interactions, and variability. For grades 3-6, the conceptual schemes were structural units of the universe, interaction and change, the conservation of energy, the degradation of energy, and the statistical view of nature. One criticism of this program was its lack of dissemination; it was one of several programs that was not picked up by a commercial publisher after its development was completed.

Middle School/Junior High Curricula

Introductory Physical Science (IPS) was developed to serve as preparation for the revised high school physics and chemistry curricula. It is heavily lab-oriented and follows a sequence beginning with the mass of objects and properties of matter and ending with the atomic model. Each student has a lab manual as a text; special equipment can be purchased from several different vendors for the special activities. One criticism of this program is the cost of the special materials required.

Time, Space, and Matter (TSM) is composed of nine interrelated investigations in the context of the themes of time, space, and matter. Content is drawn from astronomy, chemistry, geology, mathematics, and physics. Student materials consist of booklets by topics; equipment consisted of whatever was commonly found in a well-equipped junior high science classroom. A

criticism of this program is its emphasis on the physical and earth sciences, to the exclusion of the life sciences.

Interaction Science Curriculum Project was a commercially developed curriculum that had the same attributes as the federally financed projects. *Interaction of Matter and Energy (IME)* was a physical science program; *Interaction of Man and the Biosphere (IMB)* was a biology/life science program; and *Interaction of Earth and Time (IET)* was an earth sciences program. Opportunities for students to conduct investigations were the basis of these three programs. Student materials included a textbook in which the activities were integrated into the text information. One criticism of this program was the somewhat abstract nature of some of the activities.

Intermediate Science Curriculum Study (ISCS) was an innovative three-year program that allowed for individualized instruction. Students had some choice as to content, as well as how fast they proceeded through the course. Level I was organized around the theme of energy, its forms and characteristics. Level II focused on matter, its composition and behavior. Level III was a series of content modules that included topics from the earth/space sciences, physical sciences, and life sciences. All three levels emphasized process skills, with the skills becoming more sophisticated at each level. The second commercial revision of this program provided both a textbook and booklet format for student materials. Teachers could design their own scope and sequence with the booklets. A major criticism of this program was its sophisticated management system that many teachers found difficult to implement.

High School Curricula

Some innovative biology curricula were developed by the Biological Sciences Curriculum Study (BSCS). Three versions of a high school biology course were developed: the "Green" version, which stressed ecology; the "Yellow," which featured a more traditional structure/function approach; and the "Blue," which emphasized molecular biology and evolution. Listed below are the topics from the Blue version (1963):

Science as Inquiry
Variety of Living Things
Evolution: Two Conflicting Views
Origin of Living Things
Forerunners of Life
Chemical Energy for Life

Master Molecules
Biological Code
Light as Energy for Life
The Evolved Cell
The Cell Theory
The Multicellular Organism
Reproduction
Development
Patterns of Heredity
Genes and Chromosomes
Origin of New Species
The Human Species
Photosynthetic Systems
Transport Systems
Respiratory Systems
Digestive Systems
Excretory Systems
Regulatory Systems
Nervous Systems
Skeletal and Muscular Systems
Integrated Organism and Behavior
Populations
Societies
Communities

Similar curriculum reforms were made in physics (PSSC, Harvard Project Physics), chemistry (Chem Study, CBA), and the earth sciences (ESCP). Each of these programs retained the traditional textbook format for student materials, occasionally supplemented by special laboratory activities in separate lab manuals or booklets. Some special equipment was designed for use in some of these courses, especially the physics programs. The major criticism of these programs was that teachers needed to be trained through summer institutes or other forms of extensive staff development in order to teach these programs.

Back to Basics

The "back to basics" movement in education also affected science education. The movement led to an increased emphasis on traditional, whole-class teaching methods and less emphasis on inquiry, individualized learning, and process-centered instruction. There was much more focus on content, especially in the college preparatory courses at the secondary level. All of these programs, especially the elementary curricula, retained or returned to a more traditional textbook format. The major criticism leveled at these programs was the excessive number of "factoids" embedded in the texts.

Elementary Curriculum

The elementary curriculum reflected this content-centered approach. Science textbooks became predominant; teachers were expected to cover certain topics each year, usually through a spiral curriculum approach. For example, a popular K-6 science program called *Science: Understanding Your Environment* (Mallinson et al. 1981) had the following topics that spiraled through K-6:

* Biological Sciences: living world, plants, animals, human growth and development
* Earth Sciences: earth and its resources, air, water and oceanography, weather, the universe, and the solar system
* Physical Sciences: matter and energy, sound, machines and work, heat and light, magnetism and electricity

Secondary Curriculum

If the elementary curriculum was content-driven, the secondary curriculum was even more so; textbooks dominated the typical junior or high school science courses. For example, listed below are the topics from an earth science textbook from a popular junior high school series (Ramsey et al. 1982):

What Is Science?
Air
A Unique Planet
Energy and Water in Air
Plate Tectonics
Weather
Building the Crust
The Ocean
Weathering and Erosion
Water in the Ocean
Ice, Wind, and Waves
The Motions of the Sea
Earth's History
The Sun
Minerals
Satellites of the Sun
Rocks
Stars and Galaxies
Earth Resources

Similar lists of topics could be found in the physical and life sciences textbooks of the same series. Many textbook publishers believed that the junior high school science curriculum was merely a watered down version of high school science courses.

High schools, in turn, believed that their courses should help prepare students for future college courses. Therefore, their mission was to provide the necessary background so that students could do well in college science courses. Listed below are the topics from a popular biology textbook (Otto and Towle 1977):

Science of Life
Cell Growth and Reproduction
The Living Condition
Principles of Heredity
The Chemical Basis of Life
Mechanisms of Heredity
The Structural Unit of Life
Human Heredity
The Cell and Its Environment
Applied Genetics
Cell Energy, Respiration, and Photosynthesis
Nucleic Acids and Protein Synthesis
Organic Variation
The Spore Plants
Diversity of Life
The Seed Plants
Viruses
The Structure and Functions of Plants
Bacteria
The Structure and Functions of Stems
Infectious Diseases
The Structure and Functions of Leaves
Heterotrophic Protists
Flowers, Fruits, and Seeds
Autotrophic Protists
Plant Growth and Responses
The Fungi
Sponges and Coelenterates
Human History
Flatworms, Rotifers, and Roundworms
Skeletal and Muscular Systems
Mollusks and Segmented Worms
Digestive System
Arthropods
Circulatory and Excretory Systems
Insects and Echinoderms
Respiratory System
Introduction to Vertebrates
Nervous System and Sense Organs
Fishes
Endocrine System
Amphibians
Reproductive System
Reptiles
Tobacco, Alcohol, and Other Drugs
Birds
Populations

Mammals
Human Environmental Problems
Introduction to Ecology
The Ecosystem
Biotic Communities

Similarly, listed below are the topics in a popular chemistry textbook (Ramsey et al. 1981):

Matter, Change, and Energy
Scientific Measurement
Problem Solving in Chemistry
Atomic Structure
Chemical Names and Formulas
Chemical Quantities
Chemical Reactions
Stoichiometry
The States of Matter
The Behavior of Gases
Electrons in Atoms
Chemical Periodicity
Ionic Bonds
Covalent Bonds
Water and Aqueous Systems
Properties of Solutions
Reaction Rates and Equilibrium
Acids and Bases
Neutralization and Salts
Oxidation-Reduction Reactions
Electrochemistry
The Chemistry of Metals
The Chemistry of Nonmetals
Nuclear Chemistry
Hydrocarbon Compounds
Functional Groups and Organic Reactions

The Second Science Education Reform Movement

The mid-1980s and 1990s mark the advent of a second science education reform movement. It has since become part of the larger educational reform movement in public education. This movement has been characterized by schools committed to significant change, as evidenced by the emphasis on restructuring the total curriculum, especially in science.

The science education reform efforts include the following features:

1. A thematic approach that advocates the integration of important unifying concepts across different scientific disciplines. The following are

examples of themes found in some major curriculum documents:

Energy
Evolution
Patterns of Change
Scale and Structure
Stability/Constancy
Systems and Interactions
Models

2. An interdisciplinary approach that incorporates other subject areas, especially at the elementary and middle school levels. Environmental education and marine science curricula serve as important starting points, so that teachers do not feel that they have to reinvent the wheel. For example, the *California State Environmental Education Guide* (Sly 1988) for K-6 is organized into the following eight units, each of which incorporates science, mathematics, language arts, the visual arts, and history/social studies:

Grade Level	Units
K-1	Diversity of Life
1-2	Homes and Habitats
2-3	The Earth Supports Life
K-3	Caring for the Environment
3-4	Communities and Cultures
4-5	Adaptation and Variation
5-6	Energy
3-6	Fostering A Healthy Environment

The *Marine Science Project: For Sea* (Kolb 1978) curriculum uses topics from oceanography and the marine sciences to serve as integrative opportunities for students in grades 2-10. For example, the grade 6 curriculum guide has the following topics that relate to the marine environment:

Introduction to Marine Environments
Salt Water Environment
Sea Water Investigations
Physical Features of the Marine Environment
Oceanographic Instruments
Beach Environmental Conditions
The Biological Environment
Understanding Environment

These topics also provide opportunities for language arts activities, art projects, and simple mathematical applications.

3. A constructivist learning theory presumes that people learn best by actively constructing their own knowledge, by adding new information, thinking about it, and working through any discrepancies. Direct instruction is minimized; instead, students are provided with opportunities to explore, experiment, share ideas, and revise their thinking. The implications for science education are obvious: Curricula should encourage and support this philosophy by providing opportunities and materials for students to construct their understanding of various scientific concepts. For example, in the *Full-Option Science System (FOSS)* (Lowery et al. 1992), an elementary science program developed at the Lawrence Hall of Science, children are provided with opportunities to explore new materials before they have a more structured lesson.

4. Science for *all* students, not just the college-oriented or the more academically able. Science courses traditionally, especially at the high school level, have served as filters to restrict and limit the number of students who are "able" to do science. Now, science educators have realized that as demographic changes occur nationally, not just in the large urban areas, science education must serve to increase the number of students who are proficient in science.

One way to begin the process of incresing science proficiency is by providing quality science education to limited- and non-English-speaking students, at an early age. One promising program that targets Hispanic students is *Finding Out/ Descubrimiento* (De Avila and Duncan 1986). This bilingual program for grades 2-5 incorporates language arts, science, and mathematics within a cooperative learning environment. Limited-, non-, and proficient-English-speaking students may all participate in this program, within a heterogeneous class setting. The program includes the following topics:

Measurement
Estimation
Change and Measurement
Probability and Estimation
Shapes
Sound
Crystals and Powders
Water
Balance and Structures
Water Measurement
Coordinates and Measurement
Magnetism

Clocks and Pendulums
Electricity
Time and Shadows
Heat
Reflection, Refraction, and Optical Illusions

Another program, *Bilingual Science: An Integrated Approach* (Asian Bilingual Cross-Cultural Materials Development Center 1981), provides middle school Chinese and Filipino non- and limited-English speakers with a hands-on science integrated with language development, as well as some cultural material. The published volume 1 on the environment has the following topics:

Group Cooperation
Aquarium Life
Metric Measurement
Food Chains
Measuring Temperature
Garbage and Recycling
Controlling Variables
Seed Growth
Graphing Data
Water Cycle

The new science education reform movement is also characterized by new topics or courses. Science/Technology/Society (STS) curricula and courses emphasize the effects of technology and science on the environment, often raising ethical or societal issues. The *Global Science* (Christensen 1991) program provides high school students with an STS focus. Global Science is an innovative one-year program that attempts to integrate many of the important topics from all three subdisciplines. The topics include the following:

Our Unique Planet
Diminishing Reserves of Energy
The Ecosphere
Nonrenewable Resources
Geography and Life
Energy Conservation
Water for Life
Future Fuels
Energy and Matter
Solar Energy
Changes in Energy
Energy Alternatives
Mass and Energy in Systems
Earth's Water
Energy Flow
Water Management
Mathematics of Growth
Pollution of Water

Controlling Growth
Wastewater Treatment
Mineral Formation
Air Quality
Mineral Extraction
Atmospheric Pollution
Mineral Use
Land Quality
Economic and Political Issues
Problem of Waste
Soils
Economics of Resources
Food and Ecosystems
Economics of the Environment
Population Interactions
Options for the Future
Fossil Fuels
Atomic Energy
Electrical Energy

Controversial topics have also been more common, both in courses and in instructional materials. Human evolution has finally been accepted in the science curricula of many states, notably Texas. Topics such as animal rights/research, genetic engineering/biotechnology, and AIDS/family life education have been incorporated in many science curricula throughout the country.

Elementary Topics

Fresno Unified School District, in California, has recently revised its K-6 curriculum guide. The guide provides a good example of a modern K-6 districtwide scope and sequence (see figure 1).

The Biological Sciences Curriculum Study (BSCS) has developed a K-6 program called *Science for Life and Living* (1991), which incorporates both a thematic and a topical approach. The program is based on the following scope and sequence:

Grade Level	Theme/Topics
K	Awareness of Myself and My World
1	Order and Organization/ Objects and Properties, Materials and Structures, Safety and Security
2	Change and Measurement/Comparison and Evidence, Tools and Machines, Wellness and Personal Care
3	Patterns and Prediction/

Grade	Units
	Records and Data, Construction and Testing, Nutrition and Dental Care
4	Systems and Analysis/Interactions and Variables, Problems and Solutions, Self and Substance
5	Energy and Investigation/Energy Chains and Food Chains, Design and Efficiency, Fitness and Protection
6	Balance and Decisions/Ecosystems and Resources, Constraints and Trade-offs, Communication and Conflict

Another program, the *Full-Option Science System (FOSS)* (Lowery et al. 1992) has developed a set of units that may be selected for each grade level. So far, the following units have been developed for grades 3-6.

Grade Levels	Units
3-4	Measurement, Structures of Life, Physics of Sound, Earth Materials, Human Body, Magnetism and Electricity, Water, Ideas and Inventions
5-6	Variables, Models and Designs, Environments, Levers and Pulleys, Landforms, Food and Nutrition, Mixtures and Solutions, Solar Energy

A third program, *Science and Technology for Children* (National Science Resources Center 1991-92), features the following series of units for grades 1-6:

Grade Level	Units
1	Organisms, Weather and Me, Comparing and Measuring, Observing and Classifying
2	Life Cycle of Butterflies, Soils, Balancing and Weighing, Changes
3	Plant Growth and Development, Rocks, Chemical Tests, Sounds
4	Ourselves, Animal Behavior, Floating and Sinking, Electric Circuits
5	Microworlds, Ecosystems, Food Chemistry, Structures
6	Experiments with Plants, It's about Time, Machines and Inventions, Magnets and Motors

A fourth program, *Macmillan/McGraw-Hill Science K-8*, has a series of forty-two units that emphasize a major theme and also have related themes. It contains the following units:

Grade Span	Units
Primary	The World around You
	Looking at Earth
	Living and Growing
	Earth and Sky
	Matter and Magnets
	Life around You
	Life Then and Now
	Energy and You
	Our Big, Wet World
Intermediate	Living Things Grow and Change
	A System in the Sky
	Earth beneath Your Feet
	Pushes and Pulls
	Relationships of Living Things
	Earth's Oceans
	Properties of Matter
	Plants and Animals
	Electrical Energy
	Oceans of Air
	Forms and Uses of Energy
	Exploring Space
	Sound and Light
	Changing Earth
	Structures of Life
Intermediate/ Middle School	Forces at Work
	The Animal Kingdom
	Air, Weather, and Climate
	Electricity and Magnetism
	Earth's Riches
	The Plant Kingdom
Middle School	Simple Organisms and Viruses
	Changes in Matter
	Wave Energy
	Oceans in Motion
	Earth's Solid Crust

Earth's Ecosystems
Earth and Beyond
Changes in Ecosystems
Forces and Machines
Earth Changes through
Time
Life Changes through
Time
Using Energy

These examples serve to show the variety of possible topics for an elementary science curriculum; there are very few traditional topics. The selection of appropriate topics should be done by districts in a rational process that considers the academic needs of students and the preferences of teachers. Consideration should also be given to the concept of "less is more": fewer topics and units should be taught, but they should be taught in greater depth.

Equally important is the support for elementary science provided by the school or school district. The Mesa, Arizona, school district was highlighted several years ago in a national weekly news magazine for having one of the outstanding elementary science programs in the country. Using various kit-based science units developed by district science resource specialists and field-tested by district teachers, Mesa requires that each elementary teacher teach at least four science units per year. The maintenance, delivery, and staff development related to these kits are all provided by a district resource center. The kit includes the following core unit topics:

Grade Level	Core Unit Titles
K	Beginning Senses, My Environment, My Body
1	Animals in My World, Light and Shadows, Measurement
2	Changes, Introduction to Energy, Living in the Desert
3	Clayboats, Fin and Feather, Introduction to Ecology
4	Relative Position, Arthropods, Due to the Weather
5	Mystery Powders, Flight and Space Exploration, Animal Classification
6	Oceanography, Small Things, Electricity

Middle School/Junior High Topics

The middle school/junior high science curriculum is moving away from the traditional watered down versions of high school science courses. Concern about the learning styles and interests of students at this stage of intellectual development have resulted in some promising new programs.

Chemistry Education for Public Understanding (CEPUP) (Thier 1992), integrates some basic chemistry concepts with societal/ethical issues. The following modules have been developed:

Definition of a Chemical
Toxic Wastes
Mixtures and Solutions
Ions, Electrolytes, and Nonelectrolytes
Dilute and Concentrated Solutions
Successive Dilutions and Parts per Million
Acids and Bases
Waste Treatment and Reduction
Acid/Base Titrations/Neutralizations
Metal Replacement Reactions
Groundwater Factors
Precipitation Reactions
Pesticide Contamination
Solidification and Fixation
Methods of Treating Soil and Groundwater
Contamination

The *Foundational Approaches in Science Teaching (FAST)* project (1986) is a three-year integrated science curriculum that can be used in grades 6-12. It features the following topics:

Properties of Matter
Force, Work, and Energy
Buoyancy and Density
Mountain Building
Melting and Boiling
Weathering and Erosion
Gases and Liquids
Geologic Time
Temperature and Heat
General Motion in the Universe
Plant Growth
Models of the Universe—Past and Present
Soil and Water
Characteristics of Life
Water and the Environment
Origin and Changes in Life Forms
Animal Care
Continental Drift and Plate Tectonics
Field Ecology
Limits to Organism and Population Growth
Air Pollution
Variation and Adaptation
Light and Heat

Population Effects on the Environment
Evidence for an Atomic Theory
Energy on Earth
A Model of Matter
Human Use of Energy and Environment
Plants and Light
Decisions for the Future
Energy Storage
Respiration and the Consumer Model
Chemical Transformations
Trophic Relationships
Ecosystems
Decomposition
World Food Production
Bioenergetics

The CLASS Project (Winn 1988) is a middle school environmental program that integrates science, language arts, and mathematics. It includes the following topics:

Measuring and Using Energy
Topographic Maps
Energy Alternatives
Wetlands
Toxic Wastes
Marshlands
Environmental Considerations
Forest Management
Wildlife Management
Forests and Other Plant Communities
Endangered Species
Acid Rain and Other Issues

High School Science Topics

Several innovative programs have become popular with high school teachers in the traditional subjects of biology, chemistry, and physics. In biology, the BSCS Green version, *Biological Science, An Ecological Approach* (1990) has the following topics:

Web of Life
Human Animal: Food and Energy
Populations
Human Animal: Maintenance of Internal
  Environment
Communities and Ecosystems
Human Animal: Coordination
Matter and Energy
Flowering Plant: Form and Function
Continuity in Cells
Flowering Plant: Maintenance and
  Coordination
Continuity through Reproduction
Selection and Survival
Continuity through Development

Ecosystems of the Past
Continuity through Heredity
Biomes around the World
Continuity through Evolution
Aquatic Ecosystems
Ordering Life in the Biosphere
Human-Shaped Ecosystems
Prokaryotes and Viruses
Humankind in the Future
Eukaryotes: Protists and Fungi
Eukaryotes: Plants
Eukaryotes: Animals

In chemistry, the *Chemistry in the Community (ChemCom)* (American Chemical Society 1990) program has attracted teachers to its environmentally related and personally relevant issues through its innovative laboratory activities and role play/simulations that go beyond the traditional topics and lab exercises. It features the following topics:

Quality of Our Water
Energy and Atoms
Water and Its Contaminants
Radioactive Decay
Cause of Fish Kills
Nuclear Energy
Water Purification and Treatment
Living with Benefits and Risks
Use of Resources
Life in a Sea of Air
Why We Use What We Do
Investigating the Atmosphere
Conservation in Nature
Atmosphere and Climate
Metals: Sources and Replacements
Human Impact on the Air
Petroleum in Our Lives
Chemistry inside Your Body
Petroleum: What Is It?
Chemistry at the Body's Surface
Petroleum as a Source of Energy
Chemical Control: Drugs and Toxins
Making Useful Materials
New Industry for Riverwood
Foods: To Build or Burn?
Overview of the Chemical Industry
Food as Energy
Nitrogen Products and Their Chemistry
Foods: The Builder Molecues
Chemical Energy/Electrical Energy
Substances Present in Foods in Small Amounts

Conceptual Physics (Hewitt 1987) provides a nonmathematical approach to basic physics concepts. Some high schools have started a ninth-grade course using this program as its foundation. Others have used it to supplement their mathematically oriented physics programs. It includes the following general topics:

About Science
Temperature and Heat
Motion and Newton's Laws
Thermal Expansion
Vectors
Heat Transmission
Momentum
Change of State
Energy
Vibrations and Waves
Gravity
Sound
Motion
Light
Special Relativity
Color
Atomic Nature of Matter
Reflection and Refraction
Solids
Lenses
Liquids
Diffraction and Interference
Gases
Electrostatics
Quantum Theory
Electric Fields, Potential, Current, Circuits
Atomic Nucleus and Radioactivity
Magnetism
Nuclear Fission and Fusion
Electromagnetic Induction

Constructivism and Curriculum

One of the more popular philosophies in science teaching today is constructivism. Chapter 1 provides a detailed description of constructivism and how it affects the way in which science is taught. This philosophy can also affect the topics taught. Under constructivism, students can be given more "control" over decisions related to their learning; if this is done, then the curriculum should be structured so that students can exercise that control. For example, there might be more options of topics to be learned, or a variety of learning activities that relate to a particular topic.

There must be opportunities for students to ascertain what they already know and don't know about a particular topic. For example, students might be surveyed about, or asked to describe, what they already know about light. If an overwhelming majority of students already know almost all the important concepts about light that the teacher was planning to teach, then the wise teacher would need to modify the lesson plan. What is equally important is what students *don't* know; teachers will need better strategies for this type of assessment, and be more flexible in providing appropriate learning activities to take advantage of these "teachable" moments. Therefore, the curriculum or choice of topics would need to be equally flexible.

Since the teacher is the facilitator of learning (with the students doing the bulk of the work), the teacher must be able to provide topics and activities that are of interest and relevance to students. Merely rationalizing the learning of certain topics by "it's needed for the next course or for college" will no longer be sufficient. The selection of potential topics for a certain grade level or secondary course should be influenced by how students will respond to them or how relevant they are. The process of topic selection may become shared; teachers and students may both have input.

Scope, Sequence, and Coordination Project

In 1988 Bill Aldridge, the Executive Director of NSTA, published an article in the NSTA newspaper entitled "Essential Changes in Secondary School Science: Scope, Sequence and Coordination." He proposed that schools restructure the traditional "layer-cake" sequence of life, physical, and earth sciences at the middle/junior high school level and biology, chemistry, and physics for high school college-bound students. Aldridge argued that a more coordinated, integrated curriculum, such as those used by the former Soviet Union and China, would provide a more rational and successful approach, enabling *all* students to take more science. His article triggered a national curriculum project called *Scope, Sequence and Coordination*, with curriculum development centers in North Carolina, Texas, and California working to develop alternative courses for middle and high school science.

Recently, NSTA (1992) released a document called *The Content Core, A Guide for Curriculum Designers*. This document is meant to serve only as a guide for the design and construction of science curricula; it is not intended to be a ready-made curriculum. It is organized by the major subdisciplines (biology, chemistry, earth/space sciences, and physics) for grades 6-12. The guide is based on the following assumptions:

• A truly coherent science curriculum should

span all six or seven secondary school years and be appropriate for all students. Fewer topics taught in greater depth should replace the superficial topic coverage of many secondary textbooks.

• Topics should be carefully sequenced, based upon how students learn. As students experience the natural world, they will become adept at understanding more abstract concepts, using the appropriate terms, symbols, and equations. Fundamental concepts should be taught over years, not weeks or days, taking advantage of spaced-learning research.

• The major subdisciplines of science are connected by overarching ideas or themes. Coordinating and integrating the teaching of these subdisciplines will make students aware of these important connections and the interrelationships of topics within the subdisciplines. Tables 1-4 show some of the proposed topics, arranged by the traditional subdisciplines, to show how they could be organized and arranged over a seven-year period.

Figures 2 and 3 are examples of high school courses of study that are based upon the SSC model. Both examples represent experiments in restructuring the high school science program. They are evolving as more teachers and students become involved in the implementation process. It is hoped that the ultimate outcome will be a more relevant science curriculum to meet the needs of all students.

A Science Curriculum for the Twenty-First Century

For the future, I believe that the science education curriculum throughout the country will become more homogeneous as a result of the establishment of national standards. These standards for science education are being developed by committees of science educators, scientists, and others, under the auspices of the National Research Council, the operational arm of the National Academy of Sciences. They are scheduled to be implemented by 1996 and will be modeled after the national standards in mathematics produced in 1989 by the National Council of Teachers of Mathematics.

These standards are not a curriculum, nor will they specify what should be taught at each grade level. However, they will serve as a basis for curriculum decisions that will be made at the state, district, and school levels. The standards will also encourage more schools and districts to consider science as a "basic" subject—as important as mathematics or language arts, especially at the elementary level. Therefore, students in the future may have more science incorporated into their K-12 education.

There will also be more cutting-edge science topics incorporated into both traditional and restructured curricula. Such topics as biotechnology, environmental chemistry, and laser physics will become as common as cell biology, stoichiometry, and mechanics to the student taking science in the twenty-first century.

Another trend will be towards a more integrated, interdisciplinary approach to teaching all subjects. California, for example, has been developing plans for producing an integrated-subjects curriculum framework to complement the frameworks in each subject area. Pilot projects in various subject areas are field-testing curriculum units that provide an integrated approach and innovative materials for both traditional and restructured classes and courses.

References

Aldridge, Bill. 1988. "Essential Changes in Secondary School Science: Scope, Sequence and Coordination." *NSTA Reports!* 1 (Jan.): 4-5.

American Association for the Advancement of Science (AAAS). 1989. *Science for All Americans*. A Project 2061 Report. Washington, DC.

American Chemical Society (ACS). 1990. *Chemistry in the Community (ChemCom)*. Dubuque, IA: Kendall/Hunt.

Asian Bilingual Cross-Cultural Materials Development Center. 1981. *Bilingual Science: An Integrated Approach*. Los Angeles: California State Univ.

Begley, Sharon. 1990. "Scratch 'n' Sniff Science." Special Education Issue. *Newsweek* (Fall): n.p.

Biological Sciences Curriculum Study (BSCS). 1963. *Biological Science: Molecules to Man (Blue Version)*. Boston: Houghton Mifflin.

Biological Sciences Curriculum Study (BSCS). 1990. *Biological Science: An Ecological Approach (Green Version)*. 7th ed. Dubuque, IA: Kendall/Hunt.

Biological Sciences Curriculum Study (BSCS). 1991. *Science for Life and Living.* Dubuque, IA: Kendall/Hunt.

Christensen, John. 1991. *Global Science.* 3d ed. Dubuque, IA: Kendall/Hunt.

De Avila, Edward, and Sharon Duncan. 1986. *Finding Out/Descubrimiento.* Northvale, NJ: Santillana.

Foundational Approaches in Science Teaching (FAST) Project. 1986. *The Local Environment, The Flow of Matter and Energy through the Biosphere, Change over Time.* Honolulu: Univ. of Hawaii.

Harbeck, Mary B., ed. 1976. *Second Sourcebook for Science Supervisors.* Washington, DC: National Science Teachers Association.

Hewitt, Paul. 1987. *Conceptual Physics.* Menlo Park, CA: Addison Wesley.

Kolb, James. 1978. *Marine Science Project: For Sea.* Poulsbo, WA: Marine Science Center.

Lowery, Lawrence. 1985. *The Everyday Science Sourcebook: Ideas for Teaching in the Elementary and Middle School.* Palo Alto, CA: Dale Seymour.

Lowery, Lawrence, et al. 1992. *Full Option Science System (FOSS).* Chicago: Encyclopaedia Britannica.

Mallinson, George, et al. 1981. *Science: Understanding Your Environment.* Morristown, NJ: Silver Burdett.

Motz, LaMoine, and Gerry Madrazo, eds. 1988. *Third Sourcebook for Science Supervisors.* Washington, DC: National Science Teachers Association.

National Science Resources Center (NSRC). 1988. *Science for Children, Resources for Teachers.* Washington, DC: National Academy Press.

——. 1991-92. *Science and Technology for Children.* Burlington, NC: Carolina Biological Supply.

National Science Teachers Association (NSTA). 1992. *The Content Core, A Guide for Curriculum Designers.* The Scope, Sequence, and Coordination of Secondary School Science, vol. 1. Washington, DC: NSTA.

Otto, James H., and Albert Towle. 1977. *Modern Biology.* New York: Holt, Rinehart and Winston.

Penick, John, ed. 1983. *Focus on Excellence: Elementary Science.* Washington, DC: NSTA.

Ramsey, William, et al. 1981. *Chemistry.* Menlo Park, CA: Addison Wesley.

——. 1982. *Earth Science.* New York: Holt, Rinehart and Winston.

Science Curriculum Framework and Criteria Committee. 1990. *Science Framework for California Public Schools, K-12.* Sacramento: California Department of Education.

Sly, Carolie, coord. 1988. *The California State Environmental Education Guide, A Curriculum Guide for Kindergarten through Sixth Grade.* Hayward, CA: Alameda County Office of Education.

Thier, Herb. 1992. *Chemical Education for Public Understanding Project (CEPUP).* Menlo Park, CA: Addison Wesley.

Winn, Nina, ed. 1988. *The CLASS Project.* California ed. Costa Mesa, CA: Orange County Superintendent of Schools Office.

FIGURE 1. SAMPLE K-6 DISTRICTWIDE SCOPE AND SEQUENCE.

SCIENCE CORE CURRICULUM K-6

DRAFT 3-5-91

Grade Theme(s)	Life Science	Physical Science	Earth Science
Unifying Concepts K-6	All life forms are interrelated, interdependent, and constantly changing.	The forces of the universe cause matter to undergo changes in energy.	The earth as part of the universe undergoes changes.
Grade-level concepts/titles			
K — Patterns of Change	Living things change. *Our World: Living Things*	Matter can be observed and classified using the five senses. *Our World: Exploring Matter*	There are observable changes in the weather and seasons. *Our World: Weather and Seasons*
1 — Patterns of Change; Systems and Interactions	Living things have needs that must be met in order to survive in their environment. *Living Things on Earth*	Matter is subject to the forces of the universe. *Forces of the Earth*	Features of the earth can change. *Features of the Earth*
2 — Evolution (Change through time); Energy	All living things have both diverse and similar characteristics and are interdependent within their environment. *Groups of Living Things*	Matter undergoes changes in energy. *Energies of the Earth: Light, Heat and Sound*	Oceans and atmosphere interact to affect life. *Oceans of Air and Water*
3 — Energy; Patterns of Change; Scale and Structure	All living things interact with each other and with their physical environment. *Ecosystems*	Matter exists in the world around us and can be measured and changed. *Matter*	There are observable patterns of change in the universe. *Sun, Moon, Stars, and Planets*
4 — Scale and Structure; Systems and Interactions; Evolution (change through time)	All living things adapt to their environment. *Adapting to the World*	Forces affect objects; machines can modify the effect. *Machines do Work*	Changes occur in the structures of the earth. *Our Changing Earth*
5 — Stability; Energy; Systems and Interactions	Living things are classified according to cells, systems, and structures. *Classification of Living Things*	Electrical and magnetic forces act upon matter to change its energy. Light is a form of electromagnetic energy; heating and cooling indicate a change in energy. *Energy*	The oceans strongly influence climate, weather, and life on earth. *Oceanography*
6 — Systems and Interactions; Stability; Scale and Structure; Patterns of Change	Humans are composed of structures and systems that function interdependently. *Human Body Systems*	Physical and chemical changes in the properties of matter can be observed. *Chemistry*	The universe is composed of diverse objects and systems that exhibit predictable patterns of change. *Space Science*

FRESNO UNIFIED SCHOOL DISTRICT

Source: *Fresno Unified School District Core Curriculum Concepts K-6* (Fresno, CA: Fresno Unified School District, 1991). Reproduced with permission.

FIGURE 2. SAMPLE COURSE OF STUDY BASED ON THE SSC MODEL

LONG BEACH UNIFIED SCHOOL DISTRICT
Robert A. Mullikan High School

SSC LABORATARY SCIENCE
3-YEAR BLOCK PLAN

YEAR 1: 9th GRADE
First Semester:
Evolution of the Planet Earth
Origin and Structure of Matter
Structure and Function of Cells
Matter and Its Properties
Characteristics of Life

Second Semester:
Energy Sources and Transformations
Food Requirements
Nutrient and Waste Transport
Force and Motion
Support Systems
Movement

YEAR 2: 10th GRADE
First Semester:
Evolution of the Planet Earth
The Changing Weather
Heredity and Change
Reproduction and Population Dynamics
Matter and Its Properties
Earth's Natural Resources
Energy Sources and Transformations: Light and
Sound

Second Semester:
Forces and Motion
The Nature of Magnetism and Electricity
Gas Use and Energy Release
Removal of Wastes
Stimulus-Response Mechanisms and Hormonal
Effects

YEAR 3: 11th GRADE
First Semester:
The Evolution of Matter
Structure of Matter
Inorganic and Organic Matter
Nature of Solutions
Matter and Its Properties
Force and Motion

Second Semester:
Force and Motion
Energy Sources and Transformations
Genetics and Reproduction
Animal Organ Systems
Structures and Interactions of Ecosystems
The Taxonomy of Living Things

Source: *SSC Laboratory Science 3 Year Block Plan, Year 1/9 Grade*
(Long Beach, CA: Long Beach Unified School District, 1991). Reproduced with permission.

FIGURE 3. SAMPLE COURSE OF STUDY BASED ON THE SSC MODEL

BRAWLEY UNIFIED SCHOOL DISTRICT
BRAWLEY HIGH SCHOOL

Introduction: This is a two-year integrated science program designed at a non-college preparatory level. Focus will be on a "me and my world" problem-solving approach to world issues. Students will spend eight to ten weeks studying a topic in science, using information and techniques from the physical, chemical, and life sciences.

Year 1: Earth and the Environment

Quarter 1: Introduction to Science and the Universe
Students will be introduced by way of labs to various disciplines in science (physiology, zoology, physics-mechanics, organic chemistry and biochemistry, entomology, etc.), ending with a focus on astronomy and the universe—What is in it? How did it get there? Where is it going?

Quarter 2: Earth
Students will explore the earth's changing structure and the means by which change occurs. The effects of these changes on the biosphere and on organisms will also be a focus of study.

Quarter 3: Water
Students will explore the water cycle, drought, water ecosystems, water chemistry, water-dwelling organisms, the effects of pollution on water, and water reclamation.

Quarter 4: Atmosphere
Students will explore components of our atmosphere, weather, climate, ozone depletion, and the greenhouse effect. Emphasis will be placed on how individuals and industry affect our atmosphere and how our atmosphere affects us.

Year 2: Environment and the Human

Quarter 5: Food
Students will explore issues concerning and related to food, such as agriculture, botany, chemical and biological control of pests, and the economics of food.

Quarter 6: Energy: How It Flows
Students will explore energy in all its forms, and they will discover the role of energy in all aspects of our environment.

Quarter 7: Physiology and Health
Students will explore human anatomy, physiology, and the effects of environmental conditions and personal choices on growth and health.

Quarter 8: Our Future
Students will explore ecology and planning for the future. Emphasis will be seeing the Earth as a balanced, integrated, interdependent system.

Throughout this program, students will be exploring local issues that coincide with the themes. We will emphasize laboratory exploration, cooperative problem solving, and consensus-building techniques.

Source: *Integrated Science Curriculum for Grades 9 and 10*
(Brawley, CA: Brawley Unified High School District, 1992). Reproduced with permission.

Table 1. Biology Sequence, Grades 6-12			
Subtopics	Grades 6-8	Grades 9-10	Grades 11-12
The Biological Planet			
Patterns	Patterns of matter	Patterns of energy flow	Patterns of evolution
Patterns of Living Things			
Reproduction	Life cycles Patterns of reproduction: asexual and sexual	Reproduction of cells: mitosis and cell division	Molecular genetics

Table 2. Chemistry Sequence, Grades 6-12			
Subtopics	Grades 6-8	Grades 9-10	Grades 11-12
Properties of Matter			
Properties of solution	Conductivity, acid/base nature, color, relative solubility	Solubility, precipitation, concentration	Solubility and solubility equilibrium
Nature of Chemical Change			
Acid-base reaction	Nature of acid and base solutions	Reacting acid and base solutions	Bronsted acids and bases
Structure of Matter			
Atoms	Rationale for particle model	Atomic structure, periodic table	Quantum model

Table 3. Earth/Space Science Sequence, Grades 6-12			
Subtopics	Grades 6-8	Grades 9-10	Grades 11-12
The Physical Planet			
Properties of Earth: materials and features	Size and shape, geologic time, minerals and rocks, sedimentary rocks	Minerals, igneous rocks, metamorphic rocks, soils	Earth's interior, magnetism, dating methods, nonrenewable resources
Solid earth processes: crust and interior	Continental drift, plates	Volcanism, earthquakes, mountain building, metamorphism	Convection currents, formation of ocean basins, continental drift, plate tectonics, rock cycle
Geological processes	Fossilization and fossils	Fossil record, human use of resources	Evolution, life in the universe

Table 4. Physics Sequence, Grades 6-12			
Subtopics	**Grades 6-8**	**Grades 9-10**	**Grades 11-12**
Motion and Force			
Causes of motion	Newton's first and second laws (and friction)	Newton's second law (in one dimension), velocities and forces as directed quantities, Newton's second law (in two dimensions but qualitative), circular motion	Vector addition, Newton's second law
Energy			
Kinds of energy	Kinetic energy, thermal energy, work	Potential energy in springs and magnets, energy of batteries	Radiant energy
Conservation of energy	Simple machines	Specific heats	Quantized energy levels, conservation of mechanical energy, mechanical equivalent of heat, first law of thermodynamics
Electricity and Magnetism			
Static charge	Attraction, repulsion, neutralization, conservation of charge		Coulomb's law
Moving charge and magnets	Sparks and lightning, conductors and non-conductors, compasses, magnets, and currents	Ammeters and voltmeters, Faraday induction	Magnetic forces on moving charges, magnetic forces on currents
Electric circuits	Complete circuits, series circuits	Ohm's law, Power law	Parallel circuits

Source: *The Content Core, a Guide for Curriculum Designers* (Washington, DC: National Science Teachers Association, 1992). Reproduced with permission

STATE-LEVEL CURRICULUM GUIDELINES: AN ANALYSIS

by Mary Nalbandian
Director of Science
Chicago Public Schools, Chicago, Illinois

A new round of criticism of science education in the 1970s started a plethora of reports on the state of science education in the United States that to this date is unabated. The reports, usually comprising two or more volumes, entail everything from special reports on the science achievements of women and minorities, to the question "Who will do science?," to the involvement of corporate America in science education. As has happened so often in the past, responses to these concerns were voiced by many people both inside and outside the educational field, as well as at the national and local level.

In many states the departments of education looked at what they required in the area of science instruction and started revising or, in some instances, preparing new materials. Some states have very limited control over what is taught in public classrooms, while others have a very strong central control over both the curriculum and the textbooks that may be used.

Most recently, the federal government released the America 2000 plan, which lays out the hope of making the United States first in the world in science and mathematics by the year 2000. The American Association for the Advancement of Science (AAAS) published *Project 2061*, and the National Science Teachers Associa-

tion (NSTA) released the content core for the *Scope, Sequence, and Coordination of Secondary Science* project.

These are just a few of the efforts to undergird the science programs in the approximately 16,000 school districts in America. Many state departments of education have utilized the information in these reports to prepare their own state curricula, frameworks, or guidelines, which in turn are used by local districts and schools to build their individual programs.

A review of selected materials on science education guidelines from thirty-four states and the District of Columbia shows a wide diversity. The information ranges from the general to the specific. Although the words used to describe the goals, objectives, and what students should learn differ from state to state, the final meanings are the same. Many statements of the educational philosophy stress a need for science literacy and for students to be instructed in scientific, technological, and societal issues. More attention in recent years has focused on grades K–6. In most states the emphasis is on process skills and hands-on activities, and the content takes its lead from the skill and/or activity.

The science content for grades K–6 does not vary much from state to state, as it is taken from the three main areas of science: life, physical, and earth/space. For grades 7 and 8, most states have a life science emphasis followed by physical science or earth science. The basic high school sequence in science in the majority of the states is biology, chemistry, and physics, with additional elective courses offered. In a few states, the ninth-grade course may be life science, earth science, or physical science.

Alabama

The *Alabama Course of Study—Science* (1988) is a 244-page outline of concepts and skills which should be taught at elementary grades K–6 and for science courses at the 7-12 grade level. The document is to be used by local schools in planning their science curriculum and should be a helpful guide for teaching the process skills of science. A scope and sequence chart for the thirty-six-week school year is provided, showing the topics and the number of weeks for each topic to be taught at grades K-6. There is also a course outline for each grade. This outline includes the three main strands of life science, earth science, and physical science. Not only is the subject content given, but in a three-week time period teachers are expected to teach the contributions of science and scientists, and the types of science careers that are available.

Also, this outline is followed by a chart listing the concepts to be taught, the objectives for each concept, and the process skills appropriate for each objective. Hands-on science at each grade is emphasized, and in the sixth grade a new section called "Experimental and Laboratory Skills" is added, since students at this age are considered ready to handle more sophisticated laboratory equipment and science experimentation, and to develop abstract thinking skills.

The program for secondary students, grades 7-12, is a continuation of the science introduced in the elementary grades. A course outline is given with suggested time allotments for each topic, followed by a chart listing specific objectives for each course, similar to the K-6 program. The life science course for the seventh grade starts with the study of the scientific method and the basic tools of investigation, such as the metric system, interpreting data, and laboratory equipment. This is followed by units on the organization of living things, modifications of living things, human biology, and ecology and the environment.

The earth and space science course for the

eighth-grade program includes an overview of the universe, followed by units on the stars, solar system, and space investigation. The study of Earth includes its lithosphere, hydrosphere, atmosphere, meteorology, natural resources, and spatial location. The year ends with current trends in earth and space science. As in seventh grade, students are instructed in the tools of scientific investigation and career opportunities.

Physical science, a two-semester survey course offered at grades 9-12, can be used to fulfill the physical-science requirement for graduation. (Two units of science, one unit for physical and another for life science, are required for a standard Alabama high school diploma.) The concepts are an expansion of the physical science taught at the elementary grades, and emphasis is placed on matter, mechanics, heat, energy, light, magnetism, electricity, and chemistry. A course outline and instructional objectives are given.

Biology, chemistry, and physics outlines are provided, with a separate outline for college-preparatory biology. The content for these courses is traditional, with emphasis given to laboratory work.

In addition to the standard diploma, students may earn an advanced diploma that requires three units of science in the physical and life sciences. To accommodate this requirement, schools may offer advanced biology, aerospace science, botany, Chemistry II, ecology, genetics, human anatomy and physiology, marine science, microbiology, research and design, and zoology. Brief topic outlines are provided for each of these courses.

The course of study concludes with information about advanced-placement courses, career education, and instruction in ethics, moral values, and citizenship in science. A few pages are also devoted to science for the special-education student. A set of nine *Science Curriculum Guides*, one for each grade K–8, is also available. These provide hands-on student activities, subject-specific backround for teachers, lists of materials needed to conduct the labs, and procedural notes.

Grade K
Animals
Plants
Air
Solar energy
Weather and seasonal changes
Matter

Machines
Magnets
Contributions of science and scientists
Careers

Grade 1

Animals
Plants
Space
Seasons and weather
Matter
Energy and machines
Magnets
Contributions/careers

Grade 2

Animals
Plants
Air
Weather and oceanography
Weather
Heat and light
Magnets
Matter and energy
Contributions/careers

Grade 3

Animals
Plants
Fungi and microorganisms
Solar System
Earth resources
Machines
Matter and energy
Sound
Contributions/careers

Grade 4

Living things
Groups of organisms and interrelationships
Senses
Weather
Earth resources
Aerospace
Energy
Machines
Contributions/careers

Grade 5

Organisms
Growth and maintenance
Weather
Oceanography
Land resources

Space
Matter and energy
Sound and energy
Energy production/consumption
Contributions/careers

Grade 6

Basic structure of life
Organisms
Human body
Atmosphere
Weather
Space
Matter and energy
Energy production/consumption
Contributions/careers
Experimentation and laboratory skills

Grade 7

Life science:
Basic skills for studying life science
Introduction to living things
Organization of living things
Modifications in living things
Human biology
Ecology and the environment

Grade 8

Earth and space science:
Introduction
Universe overview
Stars
Solar System
Space investigation
Earth
Current trends in earth and space science

Alaska

Alaska's two publications for science are *Alaska: Kindergarten-Alaska Curriculum Guide* (1985) and *Alaska Model Curriculum Guide 1-12 Science* (1990). The thirty-three-page kindergarten publication is for all of the content areas and is organized in a chart format giving the topic/concept, learning outcome, and sample learning objective. The science to be taught includes the processes of observing, classifying, using numbers, communicating, measuring, predicting, interpreting data, defining operationally, and designing experiments. This is followed by the specific content study of living things, of physical properties, and of the Sun, Moon, stars, and weather.

The 257-page book for grades 1-12 is organized in much the same format as described above but with grade divisions for the elementary levels 1-3 and 4-6. In addition to a learning outcome, objectives and sample learning activities are given. Scope and sequence charts for grades 1-12 are provided for process skills, attitudes and values of science, and concepts. The content for each grade level grouping encompasses the disciplines of biology/life science; physical science-physics; chemistry; and earth/space science/geology. The conceptual schemes of change/ cycle/evolution, interaction/interrelationships/cause-effect, energy–matter/entropy, organization/order/organism/system, diversity/variation, and science careers and life are also included.

At each grade level specific outcomes/ objectives are listed along with enough sample activities so that the teacher can select the one appropriate for the grade. At grades 1-3, the topic/concept emphasis is placed on the study of the science process skills.

At grades 4-6, the topic/concept emphasis is on both content and process. Students are to be instructed in the major content areas as described previously and also in the higher-order process skills of inference, selection and control of variables, hypothesis, and model formulation. Ultimately, the student should be routinely able to apply problem-solving skills to the study of science.

For grades 7-12, the same format is used for the courses of general science (grades 7-12), life science (grades 7-12), biology (grades 10-12), earth science (grades 8-10), geology (grades 10-12), physical science (grades 7-12), chemistry (grades 10-12), and physics (grades 10-12).

Finally, this publication provides briefings on scientific and societal issues keyed to Alaska, which can be integrated into existing science courses.

Grade K
Characteristics of living things
Classifying by physical properties
Differences between Sun and Moon
Stars
Weather
Care for environment

Grades 1–8
Change/cycle/evolution
Energy--matter/entropy

Diversity/variation
Science careers and life

Grades 4–8
Interaction/interrelationships/cause-effect
Organization/order/organism/system

Arizona

The state publication for Arizona is the *Arizona Science Essential Skills Framework* (1990). For its content and organization, it relies heavily on both *Project 2061* and the *NCISE Elementary Science Framework* document. The purpose of this forty-nine-page document is to provide a framework for school districts to use in the development of their K-12 science curriculum. Four aspects of science education are addressed:

· Part I summarizes the importance of teaching science.
· Part II defines eight specific goals in scientific and technological literacy for Arizona students. The eight goals which comprise the content to be taught are attitudes/habits of mind; nature of science and technology; science content through eight organizing concepts; history of science; reasoning/ thinking skills; personal use of science and technology; societal impact of science and technology; and laboratory investigation/ hands-on learning.
· Part III provides substance for each of the eight goals in Part II by supplying "Student Outcomes and Examples of Indicators for Primary (K–3), Middle Grades (4–8), and Secondary (9–12)."
· Part IV gives suggestions for implementing the essential science skills.

These eight goals are listed in chart form along with the student outcomes and examples of indicators for the grade levels listed in Part III. This section is very general in nature. The last part of this booklet provides guidance for school districts in preparing their science curricula by giving specific characteristics of an effective curriculum and science instruction, and by discussing necessary support structures for adequate science-education implementation.

Grades K–8
Organization
Cause and effect

Systems
Models
Change
Structure and function
Diversity
Interactions

Arkansas

Arkansas has two course-content guides, *Science—Kindergarten-8* and *Science—Grades 9-12* (1990–91), which offer a curriculum framework that can be used by local schools. There is a K-12 general scope and sequence chart which lists the major topics of life and physical sciences and the specific strands which comprise each of them. In life science these strands include process skills, the cell, heredity, variation and adaptation, environment, taxonomy, and the human body. The physical science strands are process skills, force and motion, heat and pressure, sound and light, electricity and magnetism, matter, atoms, bonding, chemical reactions, geological processes, geological history, earth materials, meteorology, environment, oceanography, and astronomy. A simple coding in this scope and sequence chart tells the teacher at what grade level a specific strand is to be introduced, emphasized, or reinforced.

In addition to the scope and sequence chart, an outline of specific process skills and content is given for each grade. This outline also includes the appropriate science vocabulary that will be used during instruction of the topic, the developmental skills required by the students, the teaching strategies that can be employed, and a list of basic equipment and supplies for each grade. The course content for grades 1-6 encompasses life, earth, and the physical sciences. Starting at grade seven the content becomes specific to one area. Life science is the content for grade 7, with earth science as the content for grade 8. For grades 9-12, outlines for courses in physical science, biology, chemistry, physics, and general science are given following the same format found in the K-8 manual. Schools are expected to provide adequate laboratories and to follow safety methods and procedures in conducting laboratory activities.

Grade K

Taxonomy
Human body

Grade 1

Variation and adaptation
Taxonomy
Human body
Heat and pressure
Sound and light
Meteorology
Astronomy

Grade 2

Process skills
Cell
Environment
Taxonomy
Human body
Force and motion
Sound and light
Electricity and magnetism
Earth materials
Meteorology
Astronomy

Grade 3

Process skills
Cell
Environment
Taxonomy
Force and motion
Sound and light
Electricity and magnetism
Matter
Earth materials
Meteorology
Environment
Astronomy

Grade 4

Process skills
Cell
Heredity
Environment
Taxonomy
Human body
Force and motion
Heat and pressure
Sound and light
Electricity and magnetism
Matter
Geological processes
Earth materials
Meteorology
Environment
Astronomy

Grade 5

Process skills
Cell
Heredity
Environment
Taxonomy
Human body
Force and motion
Heat and pressure
Electricity and magnetism
Matter
Atoms
Chemical reactions
Geological processes
Earth materials
Meteorology
Environment
Astronomy

Grade 6

Process skills
Cell
Heredity
Variation and adaptation
Environment
Taxonomy
Human body
Sound and light
Electricity and magnetism
Matter
Atoms
Chemical reactions
Geological processes
Earth materials
Meteorology
Environment
Astronomy

Grade 7

Process skills
Cell
Heredity
Variation and adaptation
Environment
Taxonomy
Human body

Grade 8

Process skills
Geological processes
Geological history
Earth materials
Meteorology
Environment

Oceanography
Astronomy

California

The *Science Framework for California Public Schools—Kindergarten through Grade Twelve* (1990) is a 220-page publication that gives the state's position on "a new dynamic in science learning" and reads very much like a textbook. This framework discusses the nature of science and the need for teachers to model the attributes of scientific investigation. The theme of connections is stressed so that classroom instructors can show the interdependence of all disciplines. Three chapters in the book deal with the content of science in a thematic approach and assist teachers in relating six suggested themes to the three main branches of science—life, physical, and earth. Specific recommendations are given for the restructuring of science at all grade levels to reflect current thinking and educational research and to attract students from traditionally underrepresented groups into the science class. The book ends with some ideas about staff development, assessment, and guidelines for the selection of instructional materials.

The content is to be delivered through the six broad themes of energy, evolution, patterns of change, scale and structure, stability, and systems and interactions. Using a thematic approach, the instructor can cut across specific content matter and help students appreciate the interrelationship of all knowledge. Teaching samples are provided, and they give both process skills and content for grades K–12.

Themes K–8

Energy
Evolution
Patterns of change
Scale and structure
Stability
Systems and interactions

Content K–8

Matter
Reactions and interactions
Force and motion
Energy sources and transformations
Heat, electricity and magnetism, light, sound
Astronomy

Geology and natural resources
Oceanography
Meteorology
Living things
Cells, genetics, and evolution
Ecosystems

Connecticut

A Guide to Curriculum Development in Science
(1991) is Connecticut's most recent curriculum
publication. The intent of this guide is for local
schools to implement it into their science classes.
This 126-page book has a wide range of information to help schools plan their science curricula. It
includes the development of a science guide along
with ideas about structuring a philosophy and
stating goals and objectives. Chapters on science
for students with special needs, science facilities,
safety, instructional materials and technology,
science and the community, evaluation, and
professional development are also included.

Connecticut has a common core of learning
which includes attributes and attitudes, skills and
competencies, and understandings and applications. More specific objectives are listed for
science dealing with basic knowledge in earth and
space science, life science, and physical science.
Additionally, students are to study the limitations
of our natural resources, ecology, and the need
for conservation. They should also be able to
conduct science research using the skills and
processes necessary for such a task, as well as
understand the implications of technology.

Specific objectives are listed for life, earth/
space, and physical science for students completing grades 3, 6, 8, and 12. These objectives are in
outline form and cover content, skills, and
attitudes. Additionally, a chart gives the major
concept(s) for each of the three science areas at
each of the above stated grades. This publication
has been designed to assist schools and teachers
in implementing a science curriculum that can
take students into the next century.

Grades K–8
Characteristics of life
Plants
Animals
Humans
Environment
Matter
Energy

Sun, Earth, and Moon
Meteorology
Geology
Oceanology

Delaware

The science guidelines for Delaware are part of
the document *Content Standards for Delaware
Public Schools* (1985). The content standards for
science include forty pages of standards for
grades K–12.

At the kindergarten level these standards
include using the process skills of observing,
identifying, and classifying for the study of plants,
animals, light, seasons, properties of objects, and
some characteristics of matter.

For grades 1-3, the standards are based on
the application of process skills; life science
concepts and their application; physical science
concepts and their application, and Earth/space
science concepts and their application. The use of
appropriate scientific materials, equipment, and
techniques, and the use of scientific methods and
information are two more standards in which
students are to be given instruction.

For grades 4-6, the standards are the same as
those for grades 1-3, with the addition of problem-solving skills and the implications and
practicality of the interactions between science,
technology, and society.

The seventh-grade standards are related to
the life science areas, incorporating the characteristics of life, processes of life, the cell, classification, continuity of life, and environmental study.

The area of study for the eighth grade is
earth science, with an emphasis on meteorology,
physical and historical geology, astronomy,
oceanography, and environmental science.

The high school standards entail courses in
physical science, biology, chemistry, and physics.

In addition to the basic content areas of these
courses, standards are also listed for laboratory
safety procedures, proper technique and use of
equipment, use of the metric system, and problem-solving skills.

Grade K
Observation
Identification
Classification
Plants
Animals

Weather
Seasons
Solids and liquids
Sink and float

Grades 1–3

Apply process skills
Characteristics of living and nonliving things
Plant and animal adaptations
Life cycles
Food chains
Physical and chemical changes
Properties of matter
Simple machines
Magnets
Sound
Rotation and revolution
Earth materials
Conservation

Grades 4–6

Measurement
Human body tissues
Human cells
Plant and animal classification
Microorganisms
Photosynthesis
Matter
Forms of energy
Space
Geological processes
Meteorology

Grade 7

Life processes
Cell
Classification
Continuity of life
Environment

Grade 8

Meteorology
Physical geology
Historical geology
Astronomy
Oceanography
Environmental science

District of Columbia

The District of Columbia has listings of objectives for grades K–12 on separate sheets. For the K–6 program, the integrated science objectives for

life, physical, and earth science are correlated with the process skills of observation, measurement, use of space/time relationships, inference/prediction, communication, and classification. For grades 7 and 8, the same science topics are correlated with the process skills of communication, formulation of hypotheses, identification of variables, interpretation of data, classification, and measurement. At the high school level, the objectives for earth science are simply listed in terms of behavioral objectives with no correlation with process skills. The same format is given for biology, chemistry, and physics.

Florida

The Florida Department of Education has two curriculum frameworks for science and health: *Science and Health for Grades 6-8—Basic Programs* (1990) and *Volume VII: Science and Health for Grades 9-12 Basic and Adult Secondary Programs* (1990). These booklets give one-page descriptions of science courses, listing the major concepts/content and intended outcomes for each. This framework is intended to assist teachers in developing their own specific instruction.

The twenty-one descriptions for grades 6-8 include courses on life science, earth/space science, physical science, general science, and comprehensive science. The courses are further delineated as basic or advanced.

Descriptions for the many science courses for grades 9-12 include biology, botany, anatomy and physiology, ecology, limnology, marine biology, zoology, earth/space science, environmental science, astronomy, oceanography, general science, science and technology, space technology and engineering, integrated science, physical science, chemistry, physics, and principles of technology. Separate descriptions are given for advanced placement, honors, and international baccalaureate levels of some of the courses.

Georgia

The *Georgia Quality Core Curriculum (QCC)* has a K-8 and a 9-12 science section. At each grade level from K–6, there are four major topic strands for physical science; life science; earth science; and environment, science, technology, and society (ESTS). Each of the grade levels, in outline form, has topic areas to be taught with a stated objective and one or more associated process skill(s). Also, a statement, called a *descriptor*, is provided to clarify the objective in terms of what should be expected from the learner. The objective for the ESTS strand gives a reference objective that can be used in an interdisciplinary fashion.

At grades 7 and 8, life and earth science are taught respectively and are shown in the same format as the K-6 outlines.

Criterion-referenced tests for writing, reading, mathematics, and the Quality Basic Eduction Act (QBE) competencies have all been correlated with the science QCC objectives. The science K-8 QCC objectives are hands-on and activity-based, and teachers are urged to integrate the skills learned in science into the total instructional program.

At the secondary levels, Georgia has developed QCC objectives for two tracks: the college preparatory/general curriculum/vocational and the elective. In the first grouping, outlines are provided for biology, Chemistry I, physics, and physical science. The elective grouping includes outlines for botany, astronomy, earth science, ecology, entomology, geology, human anatomy and physiology, meteorology, microbiology, oceanography, and science, technology, and society. Like the K–8 objectives, the *Basic Skills Tests Objectives* for writing, reading, mathematics, and the QBE competencies have been correlated with the secondary QCC objectives, so that teachers can teach the science objectives in conjunction with other subjects.

Grades K–6

Sound
Magnetism/electricity
Machines and forces
Matter
Light/color
Living things
Plants
Animals
Human body
Senses
Ecology
Earth materials
Weather and climate
Earth processes
Earth history
Space

Idaho

Idaho Elementary Science Course of Study and Curriculum Guide (1989) is a seventy-six-page publication to assist teachers of grades K-6 to better plan their science activities. This booklet defines the four components of science as "Problem Solving;" "Science Knowledge;" "The Nature of Science;" and "Science, Technology, and Society." "Problem Solving" encompasses the basic processes of science. "Science Knowledge" includes the study of diversity, change, continuity, interaction, organization, and limitation. "The Nature of Science" deals with the history and philosophy of science and the actions and interactions of scientists. "Science, Technology, and Society" shows the interactions between these three constituencies.

An outline of the four science components is provided for grades K–6, and focuses on specific topics from the life, physical, and earth sciences. Also included are expected student outcomes.

Idaho prepared separate courses of study in 1985 for secondary earth science and secondary biology. These courses of study provide the goals and student objectives for each of these subjects.

Grade K

Body animals
Seeds
Senses
Push and pull
Weather
Hot and cold
Sink and float
Sky
Shadows

Grade 1

Plant parts
Kinds of animals
Insects and spiders
Rocks and soil
Air, water, and land
Sound
Movement and force

Grade 2

Plant growth and change
Endangered and extinct animals
Magnets
Light and shadows
Changes in matter
Weather and air
Moon and Earth

Grade 3

Plant life cycles
Animal life cycles
Plant and animal cells
Plant and animal habitats
Skeletons and muscles
Physical properties of matter
Simple and compound machines
Weather

Grade 4

Food chains
Digestion
Electricity and magnetism
Light
Space
Rocks, minerals, and soil
Volcanoes and earthquakes

Grade 5

Plant structures and processes
Circulatory system
Respiratory system
Excretory system
Energy sources
Forms of energy
Heat and water
Structure of matter
Environment
Oceans

Grade 6

Cells
Heredity
Endocrine system
Nervous system
Electricity
Structure and changes of matter

Illinois

The State Goals for Learning and Sample Learning Objectives-Biological and Physical Sciences (1985) is a fifty-four-page document which is to be used by local schools and school districts in preparing their own local objectives. Its four specific goals state that students will have a working knowledge of the following:

· The concepts and basic vocabulary of the biological, physical, and environmental sciences
· The social and environmental implications and limitations of technological development
· The principles of scientific research and their application in simple research projects
· The processes, techniques, methods, equipment, and available technology of science

This booklet provides general knowledge and skills statements related to each of the four goals. It presents sample learning objectives that students should attain by the completion of grades 3, 6, 8, and 10. The state tests all students in public schools at these grades.

Indiana

The *Key Elements of the Science Proficiency Guide* (1991) was distributed as a draft copy. Its fifty pages state the mission of science education for students in Indiana and list the science proficiencies, proficiency indicators, and science content themes for local schools to incorporate when preparing their science programs. In chart form the eleven science proficiencies or process skills state specific proficiency indicators for the kindergarten/primary, upper elementary, middle/junior high, and high school grades. Following this, another chart lists the thirty science themes for the physical setting, the living environment, the human organism, the designed world, and historical perspectives. In addition, theme indicators are given for these grades.

Grades K–8

Universe
Earth
Earth forces
Structure of matter
Transformation of matter
Motion
Forces of nature
Diversity of life
Heredity
Cells
Interdependence of life
Flow of matter and energy
Evolution of life
Human identity
Life cycles
Basic functions
Physical and mental health
Human presence
Agriculture
Earth's materials

Manufacturing
Energy sources
Energy use
Communications
Health technology
Science and history

Iowa

A Guide to Curriculum Development in Science (1991) is a seventy-eight-page publication. Like many state documents, this guide is not a state-mandated curriculum, but is designed to assist local school districts develop their own science curricula. This report provides an outline of the knowledge and skills that should be included in a science program for students in grades K–12. Scope and sequence charts are given for life science, earth science, and physical science, with indications of what is to be taught at grades K–3, 4–6, 7–8, and 9–12. These charts list the basic knowledge topics for each of the three broad science areas. They also indicate the emphasis that should be applied at the grade level, including a coding system of 1-incidental; 2-awareness; 3-comprehension; 4-application; 5-analysis and evaluation; and NA-not appropriate for grade. Tables are also given, listing the process skills that students should use as they study specific science topics. Sample lesson plans show teachers how to design a program whereby student outcomes can be assessed. The necessity of a proper evaluation of the quality of the science program, as well as the progress of the student, are also mentioned.

Grades K–3

Animal groups
Plant groups
Conservation
Human reproductive system
Human excretory system
Human integumentary system
Human respiratory system
Health/hygiene
Disease
Safety
Earth materials
Earth processes
Atmosphere
Weather
Sun, Moon, planets
Environment
Energy

Forces and motion
Work
Heat
Sound
Light
Electricity/magnetism
Properties of matter
Solutions

Grades 4–6

Animal groups
Animal structure, function, and behavior
Plant groups
Plant structure
Genetics
Life cycles
Populations
Community/ecosystems
Interaction among organisms
Human body systems
Societal interaction
Biotechnology/ethics
Safety
Earth's interior
Mineral, rocks, and soil
Weathering/erosion/deposition
Mountain building
Glaciers
Earth history
Atmosphere
Weather
Climate
Astronomy
Solar System
Stars
Water
Environmental issues
Measurement
Energy
Force and motion
Work
Heat
Sound
Light
Optics
Electricity and magnetism
Properties of matter
Compounds and mixtures
Solutions
Acids, bases, salts

Grades 7–8

Animal groups, structure, function, and behavior
Plant groups, structure, function, and behavior

Microbe groups, structure, function, and behavior
Genetics and natural selection
Life cycles
Populations
Community/ecosystems
Interaction among organisms
Conservation
Human body systems
Societal interaction
Disease
Health/hygiene
Biotechnology/ethics
Safety
Earth's materials
Earth processes
Earth history
Atmosphere
Weather
Climate
Astronomy
Water
Environmental issues
Measurement
Energy
Force and motion
Work
Heat
Thermodynamics
Fluids
Wave properties
Sound
Light and optics
Electricity and magnetism
Properties of matter
Atomic structure
Compounds and mixtures
Bonding
Formulas of compounds
Periodic table
Reactions and equations
Properties of gases
Solutions
Acids, bases, salts

Louisiana

The following publications are available from the state of Louisiana: *Countdown 2000 K–5 Science Curriculum Guide, Bulletin 1613* (1991); *Countdown 2000 Physical Science Middle School: Grade 6, Bulletin 1873* (1991); *Life Science Curriculum Guide, Bulletin 1614* (1984); *Earth Science Curriculum Guide, Bulletin 1643* (1984); *Physical Science Curriculum Guide, Bulletin 1644* (1984); and *General Science Curriculum Guide, Bulletin 1645* (1984).

In the K–5 guide, the topics of matter, energy, earth, astronomy, and living things and the environment should be taught along with the integration of the section dealing with the process skills of science. In a chart format, specific concepts for each of the topics are stated, with appropriate performance objectives for grade levels K–1, 2–3, and 4–5.

The physical science guide for grade 6 is formatted in a similar fashion to the K–5 guide, with three columns including concept, performance objective, and activities/notes.

The life science guide contains an outline of the basic topics common to such a course. It also lays out this outline in a columnar format including competency/performance objective, concept, process skills, and suggested activities.

The guides for earth science, physical science, and general science are similar in format to the life science guide.

Grades K–5
Matter is anything that has mass and volume
Matter is particulate
Matter is classified by its properties
Matter exists as solids, liquids, and gases
Matter can change
Energy is the ability to do work
Work is the result of moving an object through a distance
Characteristics of machines
Changes in motion are due to the effects of force
Sound, light, and heat energy
Magnetism and electricity
Conservation of natural resources
Characteristics of Earth
The changing Earth
Atmosphere
Weather and climate
The Earth's water
The universe
Space exploration
Processes of living things
Interaction in an ecosystem

Grade 6
Matter
Energy
Forces and motion
Simple machines
Sound

Light
Heat
Electricity and magnetism
Nuclear energy
Alternate sources of energy
Ecology

Grade 7

Organization of life
Protists
Simple plants
Plants
Animals
Human biology
Reproduction
Heredity and genetics
Ecology

Grade 8

Atomic structure
Physical geology
Historical geology
Oceanography
Meteorology
Astronomy

Maryland

Science: A Maryland Curricular Framework is a thirty-eight-page document to assist local schools in planning, developing, and implementing their K–12 science programs. It provides the framework upon which districts can build their individual programs. The five goals for science for Maryland schools are:

- to develop positive attitudes toward science and its relevance to the individual, society, and the environment
- to develop and apply, through science experiences, rational and creative thinking processes for problem solving
- to employ the language, instruments, and materials of science for collecting, organizing, and communicating information
- to acquire and apply scientific knowledge—its concepts, theories, principles, and laws—to interpret the natural world
- to utilize science experiences in the planning and fulfillment of personal aspirations and career decisions

These goals are further divided into subgoals, for which learner behaviors are given. The goals are used to present a scope and sequence of explicit topics for grades K–9. The content of grades 10–12 is biology, chemistry, and physics, respectively.

Grade K

Colors
Exploring the body
Likenesses and differences
Sounds
Weather and seasons
Measuring
Plants and pets

Grade 1

Using the senses
Animals
Matter and its properties
Plants
Mood and mood modifiers

Grade 2

Water
Air
Weather
You and plants and animals
Magnetism and electricity
Heat and light

Grade 3

The changing Earth
Plants
Health
Machines
Matter
Living communities

Grade 4

Sound
Light
Air and water
The changing Earth
Environments
Animal behavior

Grade 5

Man and Earth
Hidden likenesses
Light and color
Human body
Adaptation to changing environment
Family life

Grade 6

Learning
Natural resources

Harnessing muscle
Harnessing electrons
Probing the starts
Mood and mood modifiers

Grade 7

The living world
Protists, plants, animals
Human body
Family life and human development
Ecology

Grade 8

Matter and energy
Atoms and atomic bombs
Chemicals and chemical things
Electricity and magnetism
Motion and waves

Michigan

Model Core Curriculum Outcomes (1991) is a working document which serves as the basis for building a school curriculum. The recommended topics of study that schools should incorporate into their programs are:

· constructing new knowledge: learning and doing science, using scientific knowledge in life, earth, and physical science
· reflecting on scientific knowledge: the nature of science

Specific outcomes are listed for each of these topics for the elementary, middle/junior high, and high school student.

Minnesota

Model Learner Outcomes for Science Education (1991) is a 123-page book listing the learner goals for students in Minnesota which must be incorporated into the science goals of each school's curriculum. The general concepts constituting the first group of learner outcomes are cause and effect, change, cycles, energy/matter, equilibrium and homeostasis, interaction, fundamental entities, probability, patterns and symmetry, and systems. The second group of outcomes are the process skills of observation, inference, categorization, measurement, use of scientific and mathematical symbols, use of time/space relationships, interpretation of data, prediction, commu-

nication, formulation of hypotheses, identification and control of variables, scientific model building and use, and experimentation. Parts three, four, and five of the outcomes are based on personal needs which include: attitudes toward science, science/technology/society, and reading and writing in science.

Charts of developmental stages of learning are provided, and the importance of appropriate laboratory activities is stressed. The booklet concludes with information about multicultural/ gender-fair/disability-sensitive science education in the form of a checklist.

Mississippi

Mississippi Curriculum Structure-Science (1986) is a thirty-page report that states the philosophy, goals, skills, and concepts that local schools and districts should incorporate into their own curriculum as it is being developed. The goals for science are grouped for grades K–3, 4–6, and 7–12. In addition, specific skills are listed for life science, physical science, and earth/space science in a scope and sequence chart for grades K–6.

The programs for grades 7 and 8 are earth science and physical science, respectively. The scope and sequence grid also includes these two grades.

The program for high school consists of the traditional biology/chemistry/physics sequence, along with special courses in consumer science and applied life science. Brief course descriptions are provided for science in grades 7–12.

Missouri

Core Competencies and Key Skills for Missouri Schools (1991), a series of publications for grades 2–6, and *Core Competencies and Key Skills for Missouri Schools—Science Grades 7 through 10*, are the documents that define the science program for Missouri students.

Each of the publications for grades 2–6 outlines the major topics of life and living things, matter/energy, the Earth and the universe, along with specific learner outcomes. The documents also provide a brief analysis of the particular concept and process skills to be taught. Assessment strategies are given for each key skill.

The publication for grades 7-10 follows the

same format as found in the book for grades 2–6, covering the three major science topics cited above.

Grade 2
Living and nonliving things
Classification of plants and animals
Habitats
Senses
Plant parts
Seasonal changes
Plant and animal growth
Properties of matter
Sound
Magnets
Force and motion
Rocks
Water
Light and shadows
Weather

Grade 3
Habitats
Plant populations
Animal reproduction
Ecology/ecosystems
Electricity
Heat
Properties of matter
Force and motion
Solar System
Rocks and soil
Light and shadows

Grade 4
Plant and animal cells
Human body
Monocots and dicots
Plant reproduction
Sun and energy
Pollution
Food chains
Simple machines
Magnetism and electricity
Potential and kinetic energy
Fossils

Grade 5
Classification of plants and animals
Structure of flowering plants
Potential and kinetic energy
Heat
Weather
Lunar cycle
Eclipses

Grade 6
Structure and function of plants
Photosynthesis
Endangered species
Acids, bases
Chemical and physical changes
Machines
Electricity and magnets
Potential and kinetic energy
Rocks and minerals
Fossils

Grade 7
Plant and animal reproduction
Producers, consumers, and decomposers
Biomes and their flora and fauna
Elements
Atoms
Optics
Sound
Water cycle
Seasons
Solar System components
Earthquakes and volcanoes

Grade 8
Vertebrates
Plant and animal cells
Human body systems
Pollution
Energy sources
Conduction, convection, and radiation
Atoms, elements, molecules, compounds, and
    mixtures
Characteristics of waves
Kinetic and potential energy
Periodic table
Weather
Climate

Nevada

The science component for the state of Nevada is found in the publications *Elementary Course of Study* (1984) and *Nevada Secondary Course of Study, Volume I: Academic Subjects* (1987). In the seven pages devoted to science in the first publication are the skills and attitudes for major topics in life, physical, earth, and environmental science which students are to acquire at the completion of kindergarten and grades 3, 6, and 8. These brief outlines list the main concepts and objectives for each science area. Career awareness objectives are also listed for grades6 and 8.

At the secondary level, a short list of objectives are given for the courses of life science, earth science, physical science, and environmental science.

Grade K

Living things respire, need nourishment and water, and reproduce

Physical world consists of matter and energy interacting

Principles of conservation of natural resources and preservation and protection of environment

By the end of grades 3 and 6

Living things respire, need nourishment and water, and reproduce

Physical world consists of matter and energy interacting

Universe is constantly changing

Principles of conservation of natural resources and preservation and protection of environment

By the end of grade 8

Living organisms carry on life functions

Living organisms and their environment are interdependent and are constantly interacting

Living things change

Physical world consists of the interactions of matter and energy

Earth and Solar System undergo changes involving cycles

Principles of conservation of natural resources and preservation and protection of environment

New Mexico

Specific science competencies for grades 1–8 are stated in *An Elementary Competency Guide for Grades 1–8* (1990). The ten pages devoted to science list the competencies based on process skills, and range from the skills of observation and classification through inference and experimentation, and finally to the use of quantitative applications and recognizing impacts. The competencies are shown in a grade 1–8 scope and sequence chart with expected student outcomes.

New York

The state of New York has a large number of science publications. For elementary students ages 4–11, there is the *Elementary Science Syllabus* (1991). This sixty-page syllabus lays out a mechanism for developing a local science program and defines goals for problem solving, skills, science attitudes, and content. It also presents recommendations and criteria for school science curricula.

The content portion is listed by age groupings: 4–7, 7–9, and 9-11. Specific program goals addressing science attitudes, problem-solving abilities, and skills are stated and models are given. Science content is presented which builds hierarchically through the age ranges, covering life science, physical science, and culminating in the study of ecosystems.

Separate supplements to the syllabus, *Elementary Science Supplement to the Syllabus, Level 1* (grades K–2), and *Elementary Science Supplement to the Syllabus, Level II* (grades 3–4), are also available to provide information not found in the general syllabus. The final level (grades 5–6) is completed but not yet published.

For the middle and junior high school classes, the publications of blocks A-I comprise the total middle-level science syllabus. As they were produced over a period of time, it should be noted that the publication dates given are actually dates of reprintings. The individual blocks are:

A. *Living Systems: Organisms*
B. *Human Systems* (1988)
C. *Living Systems: Micro-Organisms* (1991)
D. *The Earth's Changing Surface* (1988)
E. *Weather and Climate* (1988)
F. *Astronomy and Aerospace Science* (1990)
G. *Energy and Motion* (1990)
H. *The Chemistry of Matter* (1988)
I. *Energy: Sources and Issues* (1991)
J. *Science, Technology, and Society* (1988)

Each of these booklets contains a complete course of study for a designated area, presenting both the concepts and specific questions and activities that teachers can use in their classrooms.

For grades 9–12, New York produces Regents science course syllabi and syllabi for general chemistry, general biology, and unified science. The Regents syllabi, with publication or reprint dates, are:

· *Regents Biology Syllabus* (1990)
· *Regents Chemistry Syllabus* (1989)

· *Regents Earth Science Syllabus* (1970)
· *Regents Physics Syllabus* (1989)
A new earth science syllabus is undergoing statewide field testing. Its format will be similar to the *Regents Physics Syllabus.* These publications provide a total program for teachers to follow in teaching the subject. The content outline is given with the understandings and concepts which are to be taught. Conceptual or perceptual discrepancies, practical applications, and activities to coincide with the content are also provided. In addition, supplementary information for the teacher is given to clarify specific points.

Level I (Ages 4–7)
Needs of plants and animals
Properties of plants
Animal parts and function
Plant and animal dependency
Properties of objects
Interaction of objects

Level II (Ages 7–9)
Reproduction of plants and animals
Dependency and community of plants and
    animals
Energy and matter
Interactions of energy systems

Level III (Ages 9-11)
Living things' effect on environment
Populations and community
Sources of energy
Energy transfer
Heat flow
Interactions in systems
Ecosystems

North Carolina

The state of North Carolina has two books that address the K–12 science curriculum. The *North Carolina Standard Course of Study and Introduction to the Competency-Based Curriculum* (1985) is a 526-page document containing the general curriculum for all the subject areas for grades K–12. In the science section, there is an outline of concepts for biological, physical, and earth/space sciences with the corresponding learning outcomes. There is also a listing of science attitudes to be fostered, and the process skills used in science. A specific content outline for each of the grades K–8 follows. The content for each grade has course material from the three major science areas. Content outlines for high school are for courses in physical science, biology, earth science, chemistry, and physics.

The second book, entitled *Teacher Handbook—Science K–12* (1985), is a 334-page publication detailing the presentation of science grade-by-grade. The curriculum for each grade is outlined as in the *Standard Course of Study,* and a chart lists the competency goals and the objectives and measures for each goal.

There are two secondary science-course outlines for each subject. One defines the goals, objectives, and measures for an academic (college-prep) course approach, and the second deals with an applied/technical course approach. The academic courses demand competence in communication and mathematical skills. The applied/technical approach is for the student who is interested in the practical and applied aspects of science. The use of mathematics is minimal and is limited to basic functions.

Grade K
Plants and animals
Human body
Senses
Properties of matter
Position of objects
Quantity of objects
Change in environment
Air
Soil
Water
Weather

Grade 1
How animals are alike and different
Needs of animals
Care of animals
How plants are alike and different
Needs of plants
Properties of matter
Sources of energy
Chemical changes in matter
Heat sources
Wave energy
Mechanical energy
Electrical energy
Rocks
Earth
Air and water properties

Grade 2

Animals around us
Animals in their environment
Plants around us
How people use plants and animals
Matter
Forms of energy
Chemical energy
Measuring heat energy
Wave energy
Mechanical energy
Electrical energy
Weather
Water
Ancient ancestors
Solar System
Universe/stars

Grade 3

Helpful and harmful plants and animals
Defense mechanisms
Plant and animal reproduction
Interdependence of animals and plants
Differences between living and nonliving things
Matter
Forms of energy
Chemical and physical change
Heat energy
Wave energy
Mechanical energy
Electrical energy
History of the Earth
Rock types
Soil
Water cycle
Forces changing Earth
Time
Moon
Space

Grade 4

What is science?
Animals
Matter and energy
Earth/atmosphere
Space

Grade 5

What is science?
Plants
Energy
Earth science
Environment

Grade 6

What is science
Humans
Matter and energy
Space exploration
Ecology

Grade 7

Nature of science
Scope of life science
Human growth and development
Organization and variety of living things
Plant and animal communities
Scope of earth science
Earth forms and natural phenomena
Meteorology and climatology
Astronomy and space exploration
Scope of physical science
Chemical phenomena
Physical phenomena

Grade 8

Science and its relationships to human endeavor
Adaptation
Ecology
Land and sea
Space exploration and the universe
Nuclear energy
Chemical phenomena
Physical phenomena

North Dakota

The *Elementary Science Curriculum Guide K–6* (1988) is a seventy-four-page publication that lists the goals and objectives for elementary school science for students in North Dakota. The five goals are:

· to encourage systematic and organized thinking through problem-solving
· to encourage open-minded and positive attitudes toward science and its impact on society and the student
· to relate other subject areas to the science program
· to understand the natural world by using knowledge obtained through investigation, study, and instruction of science
· to enable a student to apply science skills to everyday experiences

Each of these goals has four or five objectives described in behavioral terms. The objectives are not all-inclusive, but are suggested models for schools to use. Also included is a scope and sequence of content for grades K–6. The major areas of study are plants, animals, the Earth, ecology, health, matter, energy, weather, and space. These topics are listed along with specific student objectives for each grade.

A resource section in the document for teachers lists periodicals, supply sources, science information specific to North Dakota, and books for science experiments. Another section discusses safety, equipment, field trips, science fairs/projects/clubs, science career education, staff development, and the use of computers in science education.

Grade K

Types and needs of plants and animals
Movement and covering of animals
Rocks and soils
Earth's light and heat
Living and nonliving things
Habitats
Human body parts
Hygiene, nutrition, safety
Colors
Sounds
Seasons and weather
Planets, Sun, Moon
Night and day
Rockets and astronauts

Grade 1

Parts of plants
How plants grow
How animals are born
Where animals live
Composition of earth
Air
Local plants and animals
Interdependence of plants and animals
Pollution
Dental hygiene, food, rest
Primary colors
Simple machines
Light
Seasons
Wind
Sun's light and heat
Stars and Moon
Constellations
Space travel

Grade 2

Plant parts
Characteristics of plants

Parts of seeds
Major animal groups
Animal uses
Rocks and soil
Water cycle
Pollution
Habitats
Endangered and extinct animals and plants
Senses
Food groups
States of matter
Heat and light
Magnets
Sound transmission
Seasons
Compare stars
Planets

Grade 3

Importance of plants and animals
Animal adaptations
Life cycle of some animals
Changing Earth
Food cycle
Environments
Balanced diet
Bones and muscles
Importance of sleep
Properties and states of matter
Physical and chemical changes
Force and motion
Simple machines
Water cycle
Temperature
Rotation and revolution
Milky Way
Moon phases
History of space travel

Grade 4

Seedless plants
Monocots and dicots
Types of trees
Molds
Food chain
Life cycle of frog and insect
Types of rocks
Formation of fossils
Minerals
Interdependence in the environment
Bones, joints, muscles
Digestion
Atoms and molecules
Heat energy

Fossil fuels
Friction
Simple and compound machines
Weather instruments
Precipitation
Planets
Moon phases
Space technology

Grade 5

Plant reproduction
Photosynthesis
Annuals and biennials
Respiration and transpiration in plants
Classification of vertebrates and invertebrates
Erosion
Oceans
Habitats, niches, ecosystems
Predator-prey relationships
Skeletal, muscular, and nervous systems
Structure of digestive system
Effect of drugs on human body
Structure, properties, and states of matter
Physical and chemical change
Energy sources
Electricity
Air pressure and weather
Clouds
Constellations
Life cycle of stars
Meteors, asteroids, and comets
Tides
Benefits of space technology

Grade 6

Classification of plants by structure
Plant adaptations
Herbivores, carnivores, and omnivores
Plant and animal cells
Mitosis
Protists
Earth's natural resources
Recycling
Earthquakes and volcanoes
Plate tectonics
Human body systems
Drug use and abuse
Elements and compounds
Atoms and molecules
Structure of atoms
Mass and weight
Acids, bases, and salts
Reflection and refraction of light
Magnetic fields

Weather and climate
Interpretation of weather map
Weather instruments
Astronomy
Gravity, inertia, and friction in space
Space exploration

Oklahoma

Science outcomes for the students in Oklahoma are contained in the publication *Learner Outcomes—Oklahoma State Competencies* (1990). There are separate books for grades 1–5 and for 6–12. The competencies listed should be considered minimum outcomes for students and should be used by districts and schools as a core for developing a complete science curriculum to meet the needs of their students.

The goal of the science program is to develop scientifically literate citizens and to meet the challenge of making Oklahoma schools "First by the 21st" century. Students become science literate through the mastery of the following seven outcomes:

1. Students will accurately and objectively **observe** and **measure** objects, organisms, and events in their environment.
2. Students will **classify** objects, organisms, and events based on similarities, differences, and interrelationships.
3. Students will solve problems by **experimenting** in a sequential method.
4. Students will **interpret** collected data to develop conclusions.
5. Students will **communicate** information learned through scientific investigations.
6. Students will **develop models** from data, patterns, or relationships.
7. Students will **practice safety** procedures in all science activities.

For each grade the bold-faced terms are used as the basis for the outcomes for the specific science content, which is arranged around the topics of life, physical, and earth science. The behavioral objective that states the outcome is followed by a descriptive statement to further clarify the objective.

The science *Learner Outcomes* for grades 6–8 uses the same seven outcomes cited above and the same topics of life, physical, and earth science. In grades 9–12 the outcomes are used for biology, chemistry, and physics, but there is no distinct differentiation among the courses.

Oregon

Science-Comprehensive Curriculum Goals, A Model for Local Curriculum Development (1989) is a 115-page publication that describes the comprehensive goals and outcomes for the K–12 science program for Oregon schools. The goals have been organized into seven strands: concepts, processes, manipulative skills, interests, values, interactions, and characteristics. Outcomes are given for each of these strands, and a further delineation of student objectives is listed for every grade from K–12 in a scope and sequence format. This document is to be used by local districts and schools as the framework for their science curricula.

South Dakota

South Dakota Framework for Science Curriculum Development Kindergarten-Twelve (1980) is a 143-page report that sets forth and defines the essential ingredients, structure, and process of developing a science program for students in grades K–12. It lays out in flow-chart form the steps in the production of an effective science curriculum. Performing a needs assessment, determining a philosophy, deriving goals and objectives, determining optimum learning conditions, and revising and implementing the curriculum are steps that are all interrelated, and evaluation is continuous throughout the entire process.

The major concepts of diversity, change, continuity, interaction, organization, and limitation are given for biological, physical, and earth science. These concepts are then further described for each science area in terms of content variants for grades 1–10.

Tennessee

Tennessee has a draft of *Secondary Science—Curriculum Framework* available. This forty-three-page document has an outline description of each of the following secondary science courses:

Biology I and II
Chemistry I and II
Earth Science
Ecology and the Conservation of Natural
   Resources

Geology
Life Science
Physical Science
Physics
Physiology

Each course is described with a course goal and concepts with terminal objectives. In some cases a course prerequisite is given.

Texas

The publication for Texas is entitled *Science Framework—Kindergarten-Grade 12* (1987). This 155-page document is designed to aid schools in implementing the science-education program for students in the Texas public schools. After the general goals of the science program are presented, the publication defines the eleven essential elements of the science continuum on skills from grades K–12. These elements are:

· manipulative laboratory skills
· use of skills in acquiring data through the senses
· use of classification skills in ordering and sequencing data
· experience in oral and written communication of data in appropriate form
· experience in concepts and skills of measurement using relationships to standards
· use of skills in drawing logical inferences, predicting outcomes, and forming generalized statements
· experience in skills of relating objects and events to other objects and events
· experience in applying defined terms based on observations
· experience in identifying and manipulating the conditions of investigations
· application of science in daily life
· health concepts and skills

These essential elements are then listed along with subelements for each grade K–6, and the content is a balance of life, earth, and physical sciences.

For grades 7 and 8, course descriptions are given for life science and earth science, the two courses for these grades. Once again, these descriptions include the essential elements and subelements, and a brief course outline is given. The same format is followed for the science courses offered for grades 9–12. The courses are:

Introductory Biology and Biology I and II
Anatomy and Physiology

Environmental Science
Marine Science
Introductory Physical Science and Physical
  Science
Chemistry I and II
Physics I and II
Aerospace-Aviation Education I and II
Geology
Meteorology
Astronomy
Laboratory Management

There is a special section dealing with science for special students, alternative types of assessment, and suggested science equipment lists for the various grade levels.

Utah

The publications for Utah are *Science Core Curriculum, Grades K–6* (1990) and *Science Core Curriculum: Grades 7–12* (1990). The thirty-four-page K–6 document describes the scope and sequence of the science core for each grade. In grades K–3 the students are to be provided instruction in the life, earth/space, and physical sciences in a spiral format. Six to eight core standards for each grade define the content which is centered around concrete experiences. By the end of grade 3, students should be able to demonstrate the ability to use the basic process skills of observation, classification, inference, recognition and control of variables, prediction and interpretation of data, experimentation, and communication.

In grades 4–6, the content draws equally from the areas of living things, matter and energy, and Earth and the universe. The process skills reinforce the skills learned in grades K–3 and add the skills of defining operationally and formulating hypotheses and models.

In grades 7–8, the basic core of science education includes one-semester courses of physical science, earth science, and life science which have nine to eleven standards. Physical science students use the process skills to investigate the properties of matter; elements, compounds, and mixtures; physical and chemical changes; forces and work; heat; light; sound; and electricity. In earth science, the process skills are used to investigate observable properties of rocks and minerals; forces of erosion; soil; landforms; weather; and astronomy. The life science course consists of investigating observable properties of living things and their interrelationships; how

they reproduce; and why they live as they do.

In the seventeen standards for biology, students develop the background necessary to react responsibly to problems associated with:
· the ecological interaction of the Earth's living and nonliving environments
· the impact on these environments from different lifestyles and technology
· population dynamics
· the field of biological engineering and its impact on society
· cellular and evolutionary adaptations

The course on plant and soil science and technology has twenty-one standards related to a pragmatic approach to the scientific principles of plants and soils. This course is for the student in the vocational-education track.

The twelve standards for the course in human biology focus on the human organism with emphasis on the complementary nature of structure and function, homeostasis, metabolic processes, pathological disorders, and the evolution of body systems.

Physical-earth science is a course with nine standards which focus on the interrelationships between science principles, technological innovations, and societal impact.

The ten standards for chemistry include the study of the behavior of matter, atomic structure, chemical and physical properties, chemical bonding, use of the periodic table, chemical equations and reactions, solutions, and the basic structure of organic compounds.

Physics has ten standards including mechanics, heat and thermodynamics, waves, electricity, magnetism, and modern physics.

Principles of Technology is an applied physical-science course with eight standards for the study of mechanical, fluid, thermal, and electrical systems.

Grade K

Senses
Animal similarities and differences
Plant variations
Magnets
Weather
Seasonal changes

Grade 1

Senses
Animal characteristics and needs
Plant parts and seeds
States of matter

Characteristics and uses of water
Characteristics and uses of air
Energy sources
Weather
Seasons

Grade 2

Animal life stages
Light and shadows
Sound production and transmission
Properties and uses of magnets
Properties of heat
Rock classification
Water cycle
Moon

Grade 3

Animal habitats
Plant groups
Natural resources
States of matter
Static electricity
Landforms
Earth's motions
Simple machines

Grade 4

Grouping and classification of animals
Components of ecosystems
Sound and noise
Circuits
Identification and grouping of rocks
Soils
Clouds and precipitation
Solar System components

Grade 5

Animal adaptations
Characteristics of plant parts
States and forms of energy
Magnets and electricity
Atoms, elements, compounds, mixtures
Characteristics of light, mirrors, lenses
Movements of Earth, Sun, and Moon
Natural resources, conservation, and pollution

Grade 6

One-celled organisms
Classification of plants
Arthropods
Heat and temperature
Weather
Principles of jets, rockets, and satellites
Earth layers
Rocks and minerals

Vermont

The plan for science in Vermont is a fold-out chart entitled "Framework for the Development of a Science Scope and Sequence." On the left vertical axis are the grades K–3, 4–6, 7–8, and 9–12. On the horizontal axis are the terms "Processes," "Life Science," "Physical Science," "Earth and Space Science," and "Environmental Science." In the box where these intersect is listed the content to be taught for the specified grades. For high school, there is an additional listing of "Biology," "Chemistry," and "Physics" along the horizontal axis.

Grades K–3

Needs of plants and animals
Classification of plants by characteristics
Human body systems
Classification of animals
Change of states of matter
Light, color, shadow
Heat and expansion of metals
Sound, pitch
Magnets
Solar System
Sun and stars and heat and light
Water cycle
Daily and seasonal cycles of Earth
Classification of rocks
Minerals
Fossils
Pollution
Habitats and ecosystems

Grades 4–6

Differences between plant and animal cells
Cell division
Function of genes
Reproduction of plants and animals
Extinction of plants and animals
Vertebrates and invertebrates
Human body systems
Photosynthesis and respiration
Energy changes
Classification of different states of matter
Molecular models
Physical and chemical changes
Simple machines
Compounds, mixtures, solutions
Electrical circuits
Magnetism and electricity
Kinetic and potential energy
Composition of atmosphere

Weather instruments
Weather and climate
Movements of Solar System
Geologic structures
Identification and classification of rocks and minerals
Fossils
Principles of flight
Principles of jets, rockets, and satellites
Space environment
Food webs
Interaction of ecosystems
Greenhouse effect
Air, land, and water pollution

Grades 7–8
Function of cells
Comparison and contrast of plant and animal cells
Organs and systems of the human body
Use of classification keys
Diseases of humans
Physical and chemical change
Elements, compounds, and mixtures
Force and work
Kinetic and potential energy
Conservation of matter
Molecular structure
Periodic table
Properties of sound and light
Application of electricity and magnetism
Molecular formulas
Acids, bases, and salts
Relationship between Earth and Moon
Solar System
Weather phenomena
Physical properties of rocks and minerals
Identification of rocks and minerals
Composition of earth
Describption of parts of ecosystem
Renewable and nonrenewable energy sources

Virginia

Standards of Learning Objectives for Virginia Public Schools– Science (1988) is a forty-five-page booklet which names the four program goals for science and the program objectives for each of these goals. Standards of learning objectives that the student is to achieve, along with a descriptive statement for each objective, are given for each grade. At grades 7 and 8, the content is life science and physical science, and the content for

students in grades 9–12 is earth science, biology, chemistry, and physics, respectively.

Washington

Guidelines for Science Curriculum in Washington Schools (1985) is the eighty-eight-page document from the state of Washington outlining the information that local districts and schools can use in planning and implementing their science curriculum. The information is organized into a framework made up of goals and objectives, and is followed by statements of learner outputs arranged in four grade bands: primary (K–3), intermediate (4–6), junior high/middle school (6–9), and senior high school (9–12). The four program goals operationally describe science education in the most general terms. They are:
· to develop and apply knowledge of observational facts, concepts, principles, theories, and processes of science
· to develop skills in manipulating materials and equipment, and in gathering and communicating scientific information
· to develop and apply rational, creative, and critical-thinking skills
· to develop values, aspirations, and attitudes that promote personal involvement of the individual with the environment and society
Each of these goals has four to six general objectives. Learner outcomes describe the student as learning after instruction and are matched with one or more instructional implications. These implications are listed for the three main areas of science-physical, life, and earth/space-for grades K–3 and 4–6. For grades 6–9 and 9–12, the science areas are physics, chemistry, life, and earth/space.

Wisconsin

A Guide to Curriculum Planning in Science (1986) is a 183-page document which provides a comprehensive guide to curriculum planning. It deals with the basis of science education and the characteristics of effective science teaching. It then proceeds to an overview of the science program for grades K–2, 3–6, middle/junior high school, and senior high school. This overview is based on the four science-education objectives of problem solving, science knowledge, nature of science, and science, technology, and society. Chapters on a process for developing a science curriculum, evaluating students and programs, and current and future issues in science education provide pertinent background information for local districts and schools to use in implementing a viable science program.

The final sections of this publication describe the specific curriculum for grades K–2, 3–6, middle/junior high, and senior high school. This curriculum is based on the broad areas of problem-solving, science knowledge, the nature of science, and science, technology, and society. Each of these topics is further delineated with objectives and subobjectives and sample activities.

6

STATE-LEVEL CURRICULUM GUIDELINES: A LISTING

THIS chapter provides bibliographic information on the state curriculum documents discussed in chapter 5. The publications are organized by state; for each state, we have provided the full address for that state's department of education, including the office to contact regarding curriculum publications (if such an office has been specified by the state department). The phone number shown is the best number to use for ordering the publications or for getting further information on the publications. We have also provided the addresses and phone numbers for states whose departments of education do not publish statewide curriculum frameworks. These states may produce curriculum materials on specific topics in science and in other disciplines, but they are not statewide guides as described in chapter 5.

For each publication, the listing provides the full title, document number and/or ISBN (if available), number of pages, year of publication (or reprinting), and price. Pricing is given on those publications for which Kraus had information; note that the prices shown are taken from the department's order form. Shipping and handling are often extra, and some states offer discounts for purchases of multiple copies. If a document is listed in ERIC, its ED number is shown as well.

Alabama

State Department of Education
Gordon Persons Office Building
50 North Ripley Street
Montgomery, AL 36130-3901

Division of Student Instructional Services
Coordinator, Curriculum Development/Courses
of Study
(205) 242-8059

Alabama Course of Study: Science
Bulletin 1988, No. 35, 244p., 1988. $6.00.

Alaska

State Department of Education
Goldbelt Building
P.O. Box F
Juneau, AK 99811

Division of Education Program Support
Administrator, Office of Basic Education
(907) 465-2841, Fax (907) 463-5279

Alaska Model Curriculum Guide: 1-12 Science
2d ed., 260p., 1990. $6.00 in-state, $10.00 out-of-state.

Arizona

State Department of Education
1535 West Jefferson
Phoenix, AZ 85007

Education Services
Instructional Technology
(602) 542-2147

Arizona Essential Skills: Science
GAA572-5/90, 100p., 1990. $1.53. ED 325 363.

Arkansas

Department of Education
Four State Capitol Mall
Room 304 A
Little Rock, AR 72201-1071

Instructional Services
Coordinator, Curriculum and Assessment
(501) 682-4558

Science 1990-91, Kindergarten-8. Arkansas Public School Course Content Guide
36p., 1990.

Science 1990-91, Grades 9-12. Arkansas Public School Course Content Guide
15p., 1990.

California

State Department of Education
P.O. Box 944272
721 Capitol Mall
Sacramento, CA 95814

California Department of Education
Bureau of Publications
(916) 445-1260

Science Framework for California Public Schools: Kindergarten through Grade Twelve
ISBN 0-8011-0870-5, 220p., 1990. $6.50. ED 325 324.

Colorado

State Department of Education
201 East Colfax Avenue
Denver, CO 80203-1705

The Colorado State Department of Education does not produce statewide frameworks for K-12 science.

Connecticut

State Department of Education
P.O. Box 2219
165 Capitol Avenue
State Office Building
Hartford, CT 06106-1630

Program and Support Services
Division of Curriculum and Professional Development
(203) 566-8113

A Guide to Curriculum Development: Science
126p., 1991.

A Guide to Curriculum Development: Purpose, Practices and Procedures
72p., 1981.

Delaware

State Department of Public Information
P.O. Box 1402
Townsend Building, #279
Dover, DE 19903

Instructional Services Branch
State Director, Instruction Division
(302) 739-4647

Content Standards for Delaware Public Schools
233p., 1986. Includes content standards for science and for computer literacy.

Florida

State Department of Education
Capitol Building, Room PL 116
Tallahassee, FL 32301

Curriculum Support Services
Bureau of Elementary and Secondary Education
(904) 488-6547

Curriculum Frameworks for Grades 6-8 Basic Programs. Volume VII: Science and Health
53p., 1990.

Curriculum Frameworks for Grades 9-12 Basic and Adult Secondary Programs. Volume VII: Science and Health
118p., 1990.

Georgia

State Department of Education
2066 Twin Towers East
205 Butler Street
Atlanta, GA 30334

Office of Instructional Programs
Director, General Instruction Division
(404) 656-2412

Note: The Georgia State Department of Education issues its statewide frameworks only on diskette.

Georgia's Quality Core Curriculum (K-12)
25-diskette set AppleWorks version ($100.00), 17-diskette set IBM WordStar version ($68.00), 1989. Includes 271 pages for science curriculum.

Hawaii

Department of Education
1390 Miller Street, #307
Honolulu, HI 96813

Office of Instructional Services
Director, General Education Branch
(808) 396-2502, Fax (808) 548-5390

The Hawaii Department of Education is currently revising its statewide frameworks; the new publications are scheduled to be available in 1993.

Idaho

State Department of Education
Len B. Jordan Office Building
650 West State Street
Boise, ID 83720

Chief, Bureau of Instruction/School Effectiveness
(208) 334-2165

Elementary Science: Course of Study and Curriculum Guide
76p., 1989.

A Guide to Science Curriculum Development
52p., 1980.

Secondary Biology: Course of Study
20p., n.d.

Secondary Earth Science: Course of Study
20p., n.d.

Illinois

State Board of Education
100 North First Street
Springfield, IL 62777

School Improvement Services, Curriculum Improvement
(217) 782-2826, Fax (217) 524-6125

State Goals for Learning and Sample Learning Objectives. Biological and Physical Sciences: Grades 3, 6, 8, 10, 12
4M 7-475B-26 No. 238, 51p., 1986. ED 275 531.

Indiana

State Department of Education
Room 229, State House
100 North Capitol Street
Indianapolis, IN 46024-2798

Center for School Improvement and Performance
Manager, Office of Program Development
(317) 232-9157

Key Elements of "The Science Proficiency Guide."
50p., 1991 (draft).

Iowa

State Department of Education
Grimes State Office Building
East 14th and Grand Streets
Des Moines, IA 50319-0146

Division of Instructional Services
Bureau Chief, Instruction and Curriculum
(515) 281-8141

*A Guide to Curriculum Development in Science.
Curriculum Coordinating Committee Report*
78p., 1986, rev. ed. 1991.

Kansas

State Department of Education
120 East Tenth Street
Topeka, KS 66612-1182

The Kansas State Department of Education does
not produce statewide frameworks.

Kentucky

State Department of Education
Capitol Plaza Tower
500 Mero Street
Frankfort, KY 40601

Office of Learning Programs Development
Division of Curriculum Development
(502) 564-2106

*A List of Valued Outcomes for Kentucky's Six
Learning Goals. Council on School Performance
Standards*
6p., n.d.

The Kentucky State Department of Education
does not produce other statewide frameworks.

Louisiana

State Department of Education
P.O. Box 94064
626 North 4th Street, 12th Floor
Baton Rouge, LA 70804-9064

Office of Academic Programs
Elementary Education (504) 342-3366
Secondary Education (504) 342-3404

K-5 Science Curriculum Guide
Bulletin 1613, 45p., 1991. $5.50.

Physical Science. Middle School: Grade 6
Bulletin 1873, 32p., 1991. $2.25.

Computer Science Curriculum Guide
Bulletin 1610, 23p., rev. ed. 1983. $2.75.

Computer Literacy Curriculum Guide
Bulletin 1739, 67p., 1985. $2.75

General Science Curriculum Guide
Bulletin 1645, 16p., 1984. $2.25.

Physical Science Curriculum Guide
Bulletin 1644, 70p., 1984. $2.25. ED 261 865.

Earth Science Curriculum Guide
Bulletin 1643, 95p., 1984. $2.50. ED 261 861.

Life Science Curriculum Guide
Bulletin 1614, 81p., 1984. $2.25. ED 261 863.

Maine

State Department of Education
State House Station No. 23
Augusta, ME 04333

Bureau of Instruction
Director, Division of Curriculum
(207) 289-5928

The Maine State Department of Education does
not produce statewide frameworks for K-12
science.

Maryland

State Department of Education
200 West Baltimore Street
Baltimore, MD 21201

Bureau of Educational Development
Division of Instruction, Branch Chief, Arts and
Sciences
(410) 333-2307

Science. A Maryland Curricular Framework
38p., 1983. ED 256 625.

Massachusetts

State Department of Education
Quincy Center Plaza
1385 Hancock Street
Quincy, MA 02169

School Programs Division
(617) 770-7540

The Massachusetts State Department of Education does not produce statewide frameworks.

Michigan

State Board of Education
P.O. Box 30008
608 West Allegan Street
Lansing, MI 48909

Instructional Specialists Program
(517) 373-7248

Model Core Curriculum Outcomes
73p., 1991 (working document). Contains educational outcomes for K-12 subjects, including outcomes for mathematics and science combined, plus outcomes for technology.

Minnesota

State Department of Education
712 Capitol Square Building
550 Cedar Street
St. Paul, MN 55101

Minnesota Curriculum Services Center
(612) 483-4442

Model Learner Outcomes for Science Education
E723, 123p., 1991. $5.50. ED 332 872.

Mississippi

State Department of Education
P.O. Box 771
550 High Street, Room 501
Jackson, MS 39205-0771

Bureau of Instructional Services
(601) 359-3778

Mississippi Curriculum Structure: Science
30p., 1986 (fifth printing 1991).

Missouri

Department of Elementary and Secondary
Education
P.O. Box 480
205 Jefferson Street, 6th Floor
Jefferson City, MO 65102

Center for Educational Assessment (University of
Missouri--Columbia)
(314) 882-4694

*Core Competencies and Key Skills for Missouri
Schools. Grade 2: Science*
25p., 1991. $10.00 for grade 2 guide, all subjects.

*Core Competencies and Key Skills for Missouri
Schools. Grade 3: Science*
40p., 1991. $10.00 for grade 3 guide, all subjects.

*Core Competencies and Key Skills for Missouri
Schools. Grade 4: Science*
40p., 1991. $10.00 for grade 4 guide, all subjects.

*Core Competencies and Key Skills for Missouri
Schools. Grade 5: Science*
40p., 1991. $10.00 for grade 5 guide, all subjects.

*Core Competencies and Key Skills for Missouri
Schools. Grade 6: Science*
54p., 1991. $10.00 for grade 6 guide, all subjects.

*Core Competencies and Key Skills for Missouri
Schools. Grades 7 through 10: Science*
250p., 1990. $10.00.

Montana

Office of Public Instruction
106 State Capitol
Helena, MT 59620

Department of Accreditation and Curriculum
Services
Curriculum Assistance and Instructional Alternatives
(406) 444-5541

*Montana School Accreditation: Standards and
Procedures Manual*
34p., 1989.

*Science Can Make a World of Difference. Tool Kit
for Science Curriculum Development*
153p., 1991.

Nebraska

State Department of Education
301 Centennial Mall, South
P.O. Box 94987
Lincoln, NE 68509

The Nebraska State Department of Education
does not produce statewide frameworks.

Nevada

State Department of Education
Capitol Complex
400 West King Street
Carson City, NV 89710

Instructional Services Division
Director, Basic Education Branch
(702) 687-3136

Elementary Course of Study
65p., 1984. Includes scope and sequence for
science. ED 278 511.

*Nevada Secondary Course of Study. Volume 1:
Academic Subjects*
0-5282, 72p., n.d. Includes information on
required courses in science.

New Hampshire

State Department of Education
101 Pleasant Street
State Office Park South
Concord, NH 03301

Division of Instructional Services
General Instructional Services Administrator
(603) 271-2632

*Minimum Standards for New Hampshire Public
Elementary School Approval, Kindergarten-Grade
8: Working Together*
36p., 1987. Includes elementary school curriculum, K-8.

*Standards & Guidelines for Middle/Junior High
Schools*
101p., 1978. Includes information on science
education.

*Standards for Approval of New Hampshire Public
High Schools, Grades 9-12*
53p., 1984.

New Jersey

Department of Education
225 West State Street, CN 500
Trenton, NJ 08625-0500

Division of General Academic Education
(609) 984-1971

New Jersey High School Graduation Requirements
1p., 1988.

The New Jersey Department of Education does
not produce statewide frameworks.

New Mexico

State Department of Education
Education Building
300 Don Gaspar
Santa Fe, NM 87501-2786

Learning Services Division
Instructional Materials
(505) 827-6504

An Elementary Competency Guide for Grades 1-8
88p., 1987, rev. ed. 1990. Provides "competencies by subject area," including science.

Graduation Requirements
SBE Regulation No. 90-2, section A.4.3, 12p., 1990. High school graduation requirements.

New York

State Education Department
111 Education Building
Washington Avenue
Albany, NY 12234

The State University of New York
The State Education Department
Publications Sales Desk
(518) 474-3806

Handbook on Requirements for Elementary and Secondary Schools. Education Law, Rules of the Board of Regents, and Regulations of the Commissioner of Education
140p., 2d ed. 1989.

Earth Science Syllabus
50p., 1970, reprinted 1990. $1.50. ED 046 749.

Regents Physics Syllabus: A Syllabus for Secondary Schools
120p., 1967, rev. ed. 1987. $1.50. ED 296 896.

Regents Chemistry Syllabus
84p., 1984, rev. ed. 1986. $1.50.

Elementary Science Syllabus
60p., 1985, reprinted 1991. $1.50. ED 256 611.

Elementary Science. Supplement to the Syllabus. Level I (Ages 4 through 7)
103p., 1986, reprinted 1991. $2.00. ED 275 553.

Elementary Science. Supplement to the Syllabus. Level II (Ages 7 through 9)
119p., 1988, reprinted 1991. $2.00. ED 296 909.

North Carolina

Department of Public Instruction
Education Building
116 West Edenton Street
Raleigh, NC 27603-1712

Publications Sales Desk
(919) 733-4258

North Carolina Standard Course of Study and Introduction to the Competency-Based Curriculum
530p., 1985. $7.50. ED 264 640.

Teacher Handbook: Science, Grades K-12. North Carolina Competency-Based Curriculum
340p., 1985. $12.00.

North Dakota

State Department of Public Instruction
State Capitol Building, 11th Floor
600 Boulevard Avenue East
Bismarck, ND 58505-0440

Office of Instruction, Supplies
(701) 224-2272

North Dakota Elementary Science Curriculum Guide, K-6
74p., 1988. ED 292 685.

Ohio

State Department of Education
65 South Front Street, Room 808
Columbus, OH 43266-0308

Division of Curriculum, Instruction, and Professional Development
(614) 466-2761

At present, the Ohio State Department of Education does not produce statewide frameworks for K-12 science.

Oklahoma

Department of Education
Hodge Education Building
2500 North Lincoln Boulevard
Oklahoma City, OK 73105-4599

School Improvement Division
Instructional Programs
(405) 521-3361

Learner Outcomes. Oklahoma State Competencies, Grade 1
100p., 1992. Includes learner outcomes for science and for computer education.

Learner Outcomes. Oklahoma State Competencies, Grade 2
95p., 1992. Includes learner outcomes for science and for computer education.

Learner Outcomes. Oklahoma State Competencies, Grades 6-12
347p., 1992. Includes learner outcomes for science and for computer education.

Oregon

State Department of Education
700 Pringle Parkway, S.E.
Salem, OR 97310

Publications Sales Clerk
(503) 378-3589

Science: Comprehensive Curriculum Goals. A Model for Local Curriculum Development
115p., 1989. $3.50. ED 309 089.

Pennsylvania

Department of Education
333 Market Street, 10th Floor
Harrisburg, PA 17126-0333

Office of Elementary/Secondary Education
Bureau of Curriculum Academic Services
(717) 787-3785

Chapter 5 Curriculum Regulations of the Pennsylvania State Board of Education. Guidelines for Interpretation and Implementation
32p., 1990.

The Pennsylvania Department of Education does not produce statewide frameworks for K-12 science.

Rhode Island

Department of Education
22 Hayes Street
Providence, RI 02908

Division of School and Teacher Accreditation
(401) 277-2617

The Rhode Island Department of Education does not produce statewide frameworks for K-12 science.

South Carolina

State Department of Education
1006 Rutledge Building
1429 Senate Street
Columbia, SC 29201

The South Carolina State Department of Education is revising its statewide frameworks; the revised publications will be issued in 1993.

South Dakota

Department of Education and Cultural Affairs
435 South Chapelle
Pierre, SD 57501

Division of Elementary and Secondary Education
Office of Curriculum and Instruction
(605) 773-3261 and (605) 773-4670

South Dakota Framework for Science Curriculum Development, Kindergarten-Twelve
145p., 1980. $2.00.

Tennessee

State Department of Education
100 Cordell Hull Building
Nashville, TN 37219

Curriculum and Instruction
(615) 741-0878

Tennessee K-8 Curriculum Frameworks
10p., 1991. Includes frameworks for technology.

Texas

Texas Education Agency
William B. Travis Building
1701 North Congress Avenue
Austin, TX 78701-1494

Publications Distribution Office
(512) 463-9744

Science Framework, Kindergarten-Grade 12
CU637007, 156p., 1987. $4.00. ED 287 743.

Utah

State Office of Education
250 East 500 South
Salt Lake City, UT 84111

Division of Instructional Services
Coordinator, Curriculum
(801) 538-7774

Elementary Core Curriculum Standards. Levels K-6. Science
40p., 1990. $2.75.
Secondary Core Curriculum Standards. Levels 7-12. Science
90p., 1992. $3.75.

Vermont

State Department of Education
120 State Street
Montpelier, VT 05602-2703

Basic Education
Curriculum and Instruction Unit
(802) 828-3111

Framework for the Development of a Science Scope and Sequence
17 in. x 22 in. folded sheet, 1986.

Virginia

Department of Education
P.O. Box 6-Q, James Monroe Building
Fourteenth and Franklin Streets
Richmond, VA 23216-2060

Instruction and Personnel
Administrative Director of General Education
(804) 225-2730

Standards of Learning Objectives for Virginia Public Schools: Science
45p., rev. ed. 1988.

Washington

Superintendent of Public Instruction
P.O. Box 47200
Old Capitol Building
Washington and Legion
Olympia, WA 98504-7200

Curriculum/Student Services and Technology Service
Curriculum Support
(206) 753-6727, Fax (206) 586-0247

Guidelines for Science Curriculum in Washington Schools
IPS-648-88, 88p., 1985, reprinted 1988.

West Virginia

State Department of Education
1900 Kanawha Boulevard, East
Building 6, Room B-358
Charleston, WV 25305

Division of Instructional and Student Services
Instructional Services
(304) 348-2702

Science Program of Study (Learning Outcomes)
19p., 1989. Now under revision.

Educational Program Improvement: Criteria of Excellence. Science Education
8p., 1989.

Wisconsin

State Department of Public Instruction
General Executive Facility 3
125 South Webster Street
P.O. Box 7841
Madison, WI 53707-7841

Publication Sales
(608) 266-2188

A Guide to Curriculum Planning in Science
Bulletin No. 6270, 184p., 1986, reprinted 1990.
$20.00.

Wyoming

State Department of Education
2300 Capitol Avenue, 2nd Floor
Hathaway Building
Cheyenne, WY 82002-0050

School Improvement Unit
(307) 777-6808

School Accreditation
6p., n.d.

The Wyoming State Department of Education does not produce other statewide frameworks.

RECOMMENDED CURRICULUM GUIDES

by David L. Haury
Associate Professor of Science Education
Ohio State University, Columbus, Ohio

THERE are many possible pathways of science program improvement or curriculum development, and no single pathway best serves all classrooms, schools, or districts. The crucial issues in selecting a pathway relate to who is leading the way, what destinations are sought, what processes are being used, and what material resources are available. In considering what materials to recommend, I have tried to keep in mind the various pathways of program improvement and the various modes of science instruction, identifying materials that represent a broad range of practices. The emphasis, however, is on materials that facilitate and complement local curriculum development efforts, rather than program adoptions. Consequently, most of the materials presented here are curriculum guides or frameworks, rather than textbook-centered programs, with some attention given to supplementary curriculum materials and useful reference materials. State guidelines and trade books are not included in the listing since they are discussed in other chapters of this sourcebook.

Criteria Used in Selecting Materials to Recommend

In selecting material resources to recommend, I have assumed that readers are interested prima-

rily in emerging trends and practices. Therefore, most materials presented here have been produced or updated within the past three years and reflect current thinking about the appropriate dimensions of science curriculum design. Some older materials are included, however, because they offer enduring ideas.

Guidelines used in selecting materials reflect current concerns about science teaching and learning, including the desire to (*a*) foster scientific literacy among all students, (*b*) develop skills and habits of mind associated with inquiry, (*c*) promote understanding of science and technology in a societal context, and (*d*) focus attention on environmental and global conditions that are in need of responsible human attention. The first guideline was to seek materials designed with the needs of all students in mind or designed to address the particular needs of those who have traditionally experienced difficulties with standard programs. As a result, the list does not necessarily include all the *best* science curriculum materials in terms of design standards. Instead, the list represents the variety of approaches that individuals and groups have taken in trying to address the diverse needs of science students.

Without attempting to define the term *scientific literacy* (see Rutherford and Ahlgren 1990, for a thorough discussion of the topic), I have assumed that true literacy is acquired and expressed through a variety of modalities. Given this assumption and the differing instructional strategies generally employed to promote skill development and knowledge acquisition, I sought materials that accommodate a variety of teaching and learning styles. Some preference has been given, though, to resource materials that support activity-based approaches to instruction, in keeping with current trends. By *activity-based* I mean that instruction tends to be organized around activities other than reading. It is important that this point is made clear. All of the materials listed here either engage students in reading or facilitate reading, but most of them also accommodate an instructional approach in which active student involvement provides the experiential foundation on which learning is based.

From a developmental point of view, the materials listed here support instruction that is tailored to current views of learning. Without aligning strongly with any particular theoretical orientations, I have selected materials that incorporate or accommodate some degree of active learning, an approach that encourages students to construct understanding from classroom experiences, incorporate prior knowledge, and develop personal explanations of natural events (for a brief overview of a constructivist learning model, see Yager 1991). Many of the listed materials also accommodate some form of cooperative learning and emphasize depth of learning at an appropriate level of abstraction, rather than broad coverage of topics and concepts.

In terms of content coverage, most of the listed materials attempt to present an accurate image of the nature of science and of the social context in which the scientific enterprise functions. In accordance with the recommendations of the American Association for the Advancement of Science (1989), most of the listed materials present a view of inquiry that begins with questions or problems and engages students in finding answers or solutions by collecting and interpreting information or data. In many cases, the societal context is also considered, with findings being applied to real-world issues, problems, or decisions. The essence of teaching science through inquiry is to engage students in a quest for knowledge in a social context in response to authentic questions, issues, or problems.

Special attention has been given to materials that focus attention on environmental and global concerns of particular relevance to young citizens. Students who graduate from school in the future will be confronted with increasing threats to the health of the planet and with society's growing dependencies on natural resources, technical expertise, technologies, and information. It is becoming increasingly important for students to acquire knowledge and skills that will enable them to take informed action as adults in this emerging new world. Many of the materials presented here address this need by organizing content around issues or problems and integrating the traditional subject areas.

In general, listed materials tend to be organized on some thematic basis, rather than in accordance with conventional disciplinary structures. This method of organization is in keeping with emerging priorities (NSTA 1992; AAAS 1989), and also facilitates interdisciplinary, school-based curriculum development. As individual schools or districts develop frameworks around specific topics or themes, the list can be used as a source of ideas, examples, or components to be incorporated into the local vision. Most of the materials presented here are in modular form and are designed to be components of a comprehensive program, so they can be readily tailored to new settings.

Though many of the listed materials do not conform to conventional disciplinary structures, they do conform to accepted curriculum design standards. Instructional units tend to be appropriately articulated and sequenced; the scope of content tends to be well defined and appropriate; and there is the desired balance in terms of knowledge domains and the major aims. Stated goals tend to reflect attention to affects, cognitions, and skills.

Finally, there has been a deliberate attempt to identify materials that include or call for the use of microcomputers and other new forms of information technology to enhance instruction. Materials have not been separated in the list on the basis of media type, but nonprint media and materials incorporating newer forms of technology are well represented among the materials for each grade range.

Types of Materials Listed

Just as there are competing definitions of *curriculum*, there is also a diversity of opinions as to what counts as curriculum material. In an attempt to bring some order to the following list of materials while also allowing a broad definition of *curriculum,* I have separated the materials into four categories: curriculum guides, supplementary materials, program frameworks, and curriculum development resources.

Curriculum Guides typically present detailed content and procedural specifications for individual grades, units, or courses. Guides generally include goals, content outlines, concepts, central ideas, activities, evaluation guidelines, and resources for implementing a discrete portion of an overall program.

Supplementary Materials are used to enrich an existing or evolving program, course, or unit. Supplementary materials include sets of activities that can be embedded within more comprehensive plans, nonprint media that serve to enhance instruction, or discrete modules designed to extend learning into new domains, often focusing on current issues or problems relating to standard units of study.

Program Frameworks bring direction and coherence to multilevel strands or courses of study that span a series of grades or discrete courses. They generally provide the conceptual structure for a program, rather than detailed specifications for particular units, activities, or lessons. A framework is often used to guide development or the search for individual units, modules, or courses that eventually make up a program or course of study.

Curriculum Development Resources point to additional sources of information that will aid individuals and groups in locating materials or formulating school-based plans. Some resources provide guidelines for developing programs and frameworks, while others provide reviews of materials not listed here.

Recommended Materials

The list is divided into sections corresponding to the four types of documents described: curriculum guides, supplementary materials, program frameworks, and curriculum development resources. Within the first two sections, materials are separated by grade level, and the science content focus is indicated for each item. Special features that have been identified by developers and reviewers of the listed materials are indicated by numerals, in accordance with the following coding scheme:

1 Activity-based design
2 Student-centered design
3 Inquiry-oriented approach
4 Laboratory activities included or suggested
5 Problem-solving activities included
6 Critical thinking promoted
7 Decision-making activities included
8 Cooperative-learning strategies included
9 Mastery-learning approach
10 Tests or evaluation material included
11 Homework activities or guidelines included
12 Career awareness promoted
13 Global issues addressed
14 Field trip guidelines, suggestions, or plans included
15 Environmental education component included
16 Outdoor education component included
17 Personal health issues addressed
18 Student investigations or projects described or included
19 Demonstrations described or suggested
20 Basic learning skills promoted
21 Computer-assisted instruction included
22 Science, technology, and society or real-world issues addressed
23 Lesson plans for teacher use are included
24 Use of the materials requires special training
25 Worksheet masters or student handouts are included
26 Science integrated with other subjects (subjects listed)
27 Nonprint media are included with the materials (formats listed)

Materials in the final two sections are presented in standard bibliographic form, with annotations providing descriptive information. Materials are listed alphabetically, but in some cases several titles by the same author or publisher are listed as a group. Unless otherwise indicated, materials are available from the indicated developer or publisher.

Thanks to Peter Rillero and Cynthia Sponseller, who compiled most of the information included on this list of recommended materials. Theirs was a tedious task, but they performed it graciously.

An ED number is included in the citation for most of the items in this bibliography, which indicates that these documents can be found in the database of the Educational Resources Information Center (ERIC). ERIC is an information system sponsored by the Office of Educational Research and Improvement, within the U.S. Department of Education. These ERIC documents are available in microfiche and paper copies from the ERIC Document Reproduction Service (EDRS). For information about prices, contact EDRS, 7420 Fullerton Road, Suite 110, Springfield, VA 22153-2852; telephone numbers are 703-440-1400 and 800-443-3742. Use the ED numbers in this bibliography to identify and order documents from the EDRS. Overnight delivery and fax services are provided by EDRS for customers who need to obtain ERIC documents quickly. The annotation for each item in the ERIC database is quoted from *Resources in Education*, a monthly publication of the U.S. Department of Education.

Curriculum Guides

Elementary grades (K-6)

Bio Sci II Elementary

Grades: 3-6   Science content: biology

This visual database for elementary students offers 64 hands-on activities and includes bar-coded lessons and teacher plans. It covers essential themes and concepts of the life sciences. The videodisc (which is narrated in English and Spanish) includes hundreds of still images, film sequences, computer graphics, animation, and diagrams.

Features: 1, 2, 3, 5, 6, 7, 8, 18, 19, 20, 23, 25, 27-laser disc

Cost: $395

Contact: Videodiscovery

1700 Westlake Avenue North, Suite 600

Seattle, WA 98109-3012

Completing the Cycle—It's Up to Me

Grades: K-3   Science content: all

This book addresses the problem of vanishing or depleting resources. It has been prepared to enlighten the school children of Indiana to the need for all Americans to become cognizant of environmental issues.

Features: 1, 2, 3, 6, 7, 14, 15, 16, 18, 22, 23, 26-language arts, social studies, mathematics, and fine arts

Cost: Free

Contact: Indiana Department of Education

Center for School Improvement and Performance

Room 229, State House

Indianapolis, IN 46204-2798

Conservation for Children

Grades: 1-6   Science content: biology

This program teaches students about the interdependence of plants and animals, the requirements of life, energy sources and energy use, pollution problems, recycling, and other conservation concepts based on scientific principles. Teachers can use the materials as a primary resource for teaching basic skills, as supplementary materials to a core program, as enrichment activities, as skill review, or as independent units of study. Evaluation data confirm that students using the materials for a minimum of half an hour per week master 80 percent of the learning objectives. In addition, 75 percent of the parents of 2,000 students in the evaluation study responded that they observed their children implementing the newly learned conservation practices at home.

Features: 1, 2, 15, 20, 23, 24, 25, 26-language arts, mathematics, social studies

Cost: $25 per grade level or $165 for the complete program

Contact: Sopris West, Inc.

1140 Boston Avenue

Longmont, CO 80501

DASH (Developmental Approaches in Science and Health)

Grades: K-6   Science content: biology, chemistry, earth science, and physics

Still in development, this is a comprehensive K-6 program that integrates content from the sciences, health, and technology. Draft versions of modules for grades K–2 are completed, but materials for the upper grade levels are in various stages of design and field testing. The project is innovative in facilitating the use of the skills and knowledge of science, health, and technology in both personal and social contexts. DASH connects school studies to daily life, commerce, communications, transportation, medicine, and ongoing research.

Features: 1, 2, 3, 4, 5, 6, 7, 8, 9, 10, 11, 15, 16, 17, 18, 19, 20, 21, 22, 23, 24, 25, 26-language arts, mathematics, social studies, art, music, physical education

Cost: Varies by grade level

Contact: Dr. Donald B. Young

University of Hawaii—CRDG

1776 University Avenue

Honolulu, HI 96822

FOSS (Full Option Science System)
Grades: 3-6   Science content: all
FOSS provides a fresh approach to science instruction and assessment for students in grades 3–6. As the name implies, FOSS is more than a collection of activities; it is a carefully planned and coordinated science curriculum. Its modular design provides versatility, so that FOSS can be used in many different ways in any number of school settings. FOSS springs from the philosophy of the Lawrence Hall of Science that has guided science curriculum for more than twenty-five years. FOSS provides flexibility for teachers and curriculum planners, making its system adaptable to just about every science framework, guide, and program.
> Features: 1, 2, 5, 6, 8, 10, 15, 20, 22, 23, 25, 27-videotape
> Cost: Modules range from $175–$445 (grades 3-4) to $210–$445 (grades 5-6). Videos are $129
> Contact: Meg Boffey
> 310 South Michigan Avenue
> Chicago, IL 60604
> (800) 554-9862

GrowLab: Activities for Growing Minds [curriculum guide] and GrowLab: A Complete Guide to Gardening in the Classroom [companion horticultural guide]
Grades: K–8   Science content: biology
Funded in part by the National Science Foundation, GrowLab is an indoor, inquiry-based science program using "living garden laboratories." The curriculum guide and horticultural guide help teachers implement creative, student-centered investigations with classroom plants and gardens. The GrowLab program also includes instructional posters, teacher training videos, and national "partner" networks. All GrowLab resource users receive free (three times each year) the *Growing Ideas* newsletter, which provides classroom-tested projects ideas, instructional features, and a forum for the exchange of ideas among teachers using plants to stimulate learning.
> Features: 1, 2, 3, 5, 6, 7, 13, 15, 18, 22, 23, 25, 26-math, language arts
> Cost: curriculum guide: $19.95, plus shipping; horticultural guide: $14.95
> Contact: National Gardening Association
> 180 Flynn Avenue
> Burlington, VT 05401

Hands-On Nature
Grades: K-6   Science content: biology
The goals of this book are to spark children's curiosity about the natural world, to increase their awareness of the many interrelationships within nature, and to foster a positive attitude toward it.
> Features: 1, 3, 14, 15, 16, 23, 25
> Cost: $22.45, including shipping
> Contact: Vermont Institute of Natural Science
> P.O. Box 86
> Woodstock, VT 05091

Life Lab Science
Grades: K-3   Science content: biology, earth science
This is a complete garden–based, four-year curriculum for the elementary level. It includes a videodisc, comprehensive lessons, teacher materials, experiments, and everything needed for elementary science education. The multimedia videodisc includes still images, movies, computer graphics, music, storytelling, and animation. It is narrated in both Spanish and English. Broad topics include plants, animals, life cycles, habitats, climate, water, food chains, and others.
> Features: 1, 2, 3, 4, 5, 6, 7, 8, 9, 11, 12, 13, 14, 15, 16, 17, 18, 19, 20, 22, 23, 25, 26-music, art, storytelling, 27
> Cost: $975 per grade, $3,500 for complete set (grades K-3)
> Contact: Videodiscovery
> 1700 Westlake Avenue North, Suite 600
> Seattle, WA 98109-3012

Living in Water: An Aquatic Science Curriculum for Grades 4-6, 2d ed.
Grades: 4-6   Science content: biology, environmental education
Developed by the National Aquarium in Baltimore, this curriculum treats life and conditions in both marine and freshwater habitats. Each of the five sections addresses a question about water, which is then answered through inquiry. Each section also includes background information for teachers, and extension activities provide students the opportunity to pursue related topics according to interests. Procedural information is provided for teachers, and worksheets and informational sheets are provided for students.
> Features: 1, 2, 3, 4, 6, 15, 18, 19, 22, 23, 25
> Cost: $10 east of Rockies, $12 west of Rockies

Contact: National Aquarium in Baltimore
Education Department, Pier 3
501 East Pratt Street
Baltimore, MD 21202
ERIC Document Reproduction Service
(request ED number 309 071)

Living with Insects In the Big City: Urban Insect Ecology and Safe Pest Management

Grades: K-3   Science content: biology

This program has 10 units, each to be taught in 40–50-minute periods. Each unit includes a statement of purpose, concepts to be taught, a listing of necessary materials, preparation requirements, and graphics. Recommendations for follow-up activities are also included. A general introduction to insects can be found at the beginning of the curriculum. Detailed information on nontoxic pest control for some common pests has been included in the appendices. Topics include urban insects, live insects, the chain of life, pesticides, the media and insects, biting insects, kitchen insects, and pest management. Although the units have been developed to follow a sequence of concepts dealing primarily with nontoxic pest control, they can also be used separately as parts of any environmental or natural science curriculum.

    Features: 1, 3, 15, 17, 19, 23, 25
    Cost: Contact supplier
    Contact: ERIC Document Reproduction
      Service
    7420 Fullerton Road, Suite 110
    Springfield, VA 22153-2852
    (800) 443-ERIC (request ED number 306 121)

OEAGLets—Oceanic Education Activities for Great Lakes Schools for Younger Students

Grades: 1-3   Science content: biology, earth science

The package includes 3 activities related to Lake Erie that may be applied to all primary subject areas. Included are "Lake Erie—Take a Bow," a 69-page unit on the geography of the Great Lakes and their importance to people; "Build a Fish to Scale," a unit on the external characteristics of fish; and "A Day in the Life of a Fish," a unit on fish behaviors, functions of body parts, and adaptations for survival.

    Features: 1, 2, 12, 15, 20, 23, 25, 26-all
    Cost: $5 per unit (3 units), includes shipping
    Contact: Ohio Sea Grant
    1541 Research Center
    1314 Kinnear Road
    Columbus, OH 43212

Pablo Python Looks at Animals

Grades: K-3   Science content: biology, life science

This is an introductory life-science curriculum for children of all ability levels in grades K-3. It combines hands-on, multidisci-plinary classroom activities and the scientific resources of zoos to teach fundamental science concepts and observation skills. This program utilizes a multimedia approach that encourages young children to explore the world, using all their senses. It is organized around basic concepts such as size, shape, texture, pattern, color, sounds, locomotion, feeding, and animal survival. The program can be used as a whole life science curriculum or as a flexible, instructional supplement.

    Features: 1, 2, 3, 4-suggested zoo visits, 5, 6, 7,
      8, 10, 11, 14, 15, 16, 18, 20, 23, 24, 25, 26--
      language arts, mathematics, music
    Cost: $80 per basic kit, plus 15 percent ship
      ping and handling
    Contact: New York Zoological Society
    Bronx Zoo, Education Department
    185th Street and Southern Boulevard
    Bronx, NY 10460

Project SMILE

Grades: K-5   Science content: chemistry, physics

Project SMILE (Science Manipulatives in the Learning Environment) is a national project supported by the U.S. Department of Education. It is based on research identifying a critical need to improve the educational content of these sciences for elementary students. Project SMILE utilizes video-assisted packets facilitated by elementary teachers or other personnel with classroom experience. The video-assisted materials have been effective in test workshops held during the summer of 1991.

    Features: 1, 3, 4, 5, 6, 7, 8, 19, 24, 25
    Cost: Contact supplier
    Contact: Dakota State University
    c/o Project SMILE
    Madison, SD 57042-1799

Project STARWALK

Grades: 2–5   Science content: earth science

Using a process approach in observing, graphing, and predicting, students receive a series of classroom lessons structured around a planetarium laboratory lesson. These classroom lessons are designed to prepare students for their planetarium laboratory activities and to consolidate concepts in class through a specific laboratory activity, as well as to teach students how to use a seasonal star map or a star finder.

> Features: 1, 3, 5, 8, 10, 14, 16, 19, 20, 21, 22, 23, 24, 25
> Cost: $35 each
> Contact: Project STARWALK
> Southwest Math/Science Magnet High School
> 6512 Wornall Road
> Kansas City, MO 64113

Rockets: A Teaching Guide for an Elementary Science Unit on Rocketry

Grades: 5-6   Science content: physical and space sciences

This resource guide provides background information and activities for teachers to use in preparing a unit on basic concepts and principles associated with rocketry. It is suggested that this unit be used as an introduction to building and launching commercial model rockets. The activities make use of simple, inexpensive materials and do not require the use of solid-propellant model rockets. The guide includes informative diagrams, complete instructions for activities, and sources of additional information.

> Features: 1, 2, 3, 18, 19, 22, 23
> Cost: Free
> Contact: National Aeronautics and Space Administration (NASA)
> NASA Educational Affairs Division
> NASA Headquarters
> 400 Maryland Avenue, Southwest
> Washington, DC 20277-2028

Science Curriculum Guide: Kendall Demonstration Elementary School, 2d ed.

Grades: K-8   Science content: earth science, life science, physical science

This curriculum guide was developed to serve hearing-impaired children and is based on learning objectives that are organized by school year as well as by content area. The instructional plan for each objective includes teaching strategies, student activities, and suggested resources in a variety of educational media. The curriculum is organized around 7 major concepts: space, time, change, adaptation, variety, interrelationships, and equilibrium. Knowledge objectives are divided into 3 major content categories (physical science, earth science, and life science) and 10 subcategories (e.g., energy, geology, sound, and hearing). In addition, the curriculum develops the following 8 skills: observing, communicating, ex-

perimenting, formulating and testing hypotheses, classifying, measuring, inferring, and predicting.

> Features: 1, 2, 3, 10, 23, 25
> Cost: $17.95
> Contact: Outreach
> Pre-College Programs
> KDES 3400
> Gallaudet College
> Washington, DC 20002

Science for Life and Living: Integrating Science, Technology and Health (BSCS)

Grades: K-6   Science content: biology, earth science, health

Science for Life and Living is a comprehensive, yearlong program at each grade level, K-6. The curriculum is designed around major concepts and skills that integrate the disciplines of science, technology, and health. Concepts such as order, change, patterns, systems, energy, and balance broadly define the content at each grade level. Each unit of the program develops those concepts in a science, technology, or health context, using topics that relate to students' everday lives.

> Features: 1, 2, 3, 4, 5, 6, 7, 8, 9, 10, 11, 12, 13, 14, 15, 16, 17, 18, 19, 20, 22, 23, 24, 25
> Cost: Kits: $52.50–$525, goggles: $29.50–$245
> Contact: Jill McDermott
> Kendall/Hunt Publishing
> 2460 Kerper Boulevard
> Dubuque, IA 52001

Supplemental Curriculum Activities to Accompany Holling's Paddle to the Sea

Grades: 3-6   Science content: biology, earth science

Contains 168 pages of activities, at least 2 for every chapter of Holling's book. Follows the path of a carved wooden canoe through the Great Lakes to the sea.

> Features: 1, 2, 4, 13, 15, 19, 22, 23, 25, 26-art, language arts, social studies
> Cost: $10, including shipping
> Contact: Ohio Sea Grant
> 1541 Research Center
> 1314 Kinnear Road
> Columbus, OH 43212
> ERIC Document Reproduction Service (request ED number 300 248)

Turn on Units: English as a Second Language Content Area Curriculum in Math, Science, and Computer Science for Grades K–6

Grades: K-6   Science content: general

This guide is designed to be used with limited-English-proficient (LEP) children. It is intended to serve as both a ready-to-use guide and a model for developing units for LEP students. The thematic units of this guide address topics of high interest to students: robots, using computers, plants, building terrariums, architecture, and cooking. The units are designed to engage students through games, role playing, movement activities, constructions, creative arts, and field trips. The guide includes objectives, key concepts, outlines of activities, lists of materials, detailed procedures, and suggestions for evaluations and extensions.

> Features: 1, 2, 3, 8, 10, 14, 23, 25, 26-mathematics, language arts, art
> Cost: Contact supplier
> Contact: ERIC Document Reproduction Service
> 7420 Fullerton Road, Suite 110
> Springfield, VA 22153-2852
> (800) 443-ERIC
> (ED number not yet assigned)

Middle School Grades (5-8)

Bags, Beakers, and Barrels: An Action Curriculum Toward Resolving Hazardous Materials Issues
Grades: 7-12   Science content: biology, chemistry, environmental science
This interdisciplinary curriculum is organized around hazardous- materials issues at the local, state, national, and global levels. The aim of the curriculum is to promote awareness of issues, develop lifelong learning skills, and foster awareness of attitudes, values, and behaviors. Units focus on connections; hazardous materials in the home, school, and community; and community action projects. Each unit includes activities, listings of objectives, preparation suggestions, follow-up activities, and handouts. For more information refer to ERIC document number ED 313 216.

> Features: 1, 2, 3, 5, 6, 7, 8, 10, 13, 14, 15, 17, 18, 20, 22, 23, 25, 26-health, social studies, language arts
> Cost: Contact supplier
> Contact: Industrial States Policy Center
> 1406 West 6th Street
> Cleveland, OH 44113

CEPUP (Chemical Education for Public Understanding Program)
Grades: 5-12   Science content: chemistry, environmental science
This modular program is being developed at the Lawrence Hall of Science, with funding provided by the National Science Foundation and private foundations. CEPUP presents chemistry in a societal context, engaging students in chemical surveys, risk assessment, water testing, examination of plastics, study of food additives, and experiments with household chemicals. Teacher's guides provide conceptual overviews, guidelines for activities, test banks, and technical instructions. Kits of materials are available from various suppliers.

> Features: 1, 2, 3, 4, 5, 6, 7, 8, 10, 13, 15, 17, 18, 19, 22, 23, 25
> Cost: Printed material only: $19.95 per module, complete module: $20.50–$240
> Contact: Addison-Wesley Publishing Company
> Order Processing Department
> Route 128
> Reading, MA 01867

CHEM—Chemicals, Health, Environment, and Me
Grades: 5-6   Science content: chemistry, biology
CHEM is a series of 10 units designed to provide experiences to fifth grade students to help accomplish an understanding of (*a*) the nature of chemicals and how they interact with the environment; (*b*) how to collect, process, and analyze data; (*c*) how to use scientific evidence as a basis for lifestyle-oriented decisions; and (*d*) how studying science and mathematics can be a productive and relevant part of their lives.

> Features: 1, 3, 5, 7, 15, 17, 22, 23, 25, 26-mathematics, social studies, language arts
> Cost: Contact supplier
> Contact: CEPUP
> Lawrence Hall of Science
> University of California
> Berkeley, CA 94720

Earth's Mysterious Atmosphere
Grades: 5-8   Science content: chemistry, physics, earth science, and biology
Filled with activities that focus on changes occurring in the environment, the guide is organized around issues related to global warming and the thinning ozone layer and treats them as mysteries to be investigated and explained. The guide also provides background and procedural information, as well as questions to discuss,

suggestions for integration with other subjects, and home activities.

> Features: 1, 2, 3, 11, 13, 15, 18, 19, 22, 23, 25, 26
> Cost: Free
> Contact: National Aeronautics and Space Administration (NASA) NASA Educational Affairs Division
> NASA Headquarters
> 400 Maryland Avenue, Southwest
> Washington, DC 20277-2028

Earth: The Water Planet
Grades: 5-9   Science content: earth science
This book explains how to use readily available materials and a variety of instructional methods to investigate how water shapes our planet and daily lives. Included are hands-on experiments challenging students to purify swamp water, conservation-oriented activities showing how much water is wasted by a dripping faucet, and a role-playing activity in which students present opposing views at a town meeting.

> Features: 1, 2, 4, 15, 16, 18, 22, 23, 25, 27-videotape, films
> Cost: $16.50
> Contact: National Science Teachers Association
> 3140 North Washington Boulevard
> Arlington, VA 22201
> (Attn: Shirley Watt Ireton)

FAST (Foundational Approaches in Science Teaching)
Grades: 6-9   Science content: biology, chemistry, earth science, physics, environmental education
This is a full-year course that involves students in laboratory and field-oriented investigations in the context of three curricular strands: physical science, ecology, and relational study. The physical science and ecology strands introduce a typical array of concepts. The relational study strand introduces students to matters such as resource management, environmental use, world food production, and conservation. The curricular package includes teacher's guides, a student text, a student record book, a classroom library of reference booklets, and an evaluation guide. FAST has been recognized as an exemplary science program by the Search for Excellence in Science Education project of the National Science Teachers Association and by the National Diffusion Network.

> Features: 1, 2, 3, 4, 5, 6, 7, 8, 9, 10, 11, 13, 15, 18, 20, 22, 23, 24, 25
> Cost: Varies by grade level
> Contact: Dr. Donald B. Young
> University of Hawaii—CRDG
> 1776 University Avenue
> Honolulu, HI 96822

Jeffco Life Science Program
Grades: 7-8   Science content: biology
This program is a yearlong life sciences course that replaces the curriculum currently being used in general science or life science. It can also be used in an integrated science and health course. Learner materials consist of a text that integrates laboratory activities and readings. Topics include body structure, foods and digestion, body basics, body changes, cells and genetics, body controls, and ecosystems and ecology. Students use these concepts in an application activity or discussion.

> Features: 1, 2, 3, 4, 5, 7, 8, 11, 15, 17, 18, 23, 24, 25
> Cost: Student text: $26.90, teacher's guide: $39.90, teacher's resource book: $69.90
> Contact: Middle School Life Science Office
> Jefferson County Public Schools
> 1829 Denver West Drive #27
> Golden, CO 80401

Methods of Motion, Revised Edition
Grades: 5-9   Science content: physics
This manual is designed to help introduce Newtonian mechanics to students in the middle grades. The 27 teacher-created activities—including marble races, a tractor-pull using toy cars, fettuccine, carpentry, film container cannons, and others—use readily available materials to give students visual, aural, and tactile evidence to combat their misconceptions.

> Features: 1, 2, 4, 18, 23, 25, 27-videotape
> Cost: $16.50
> Contact: National Science Teachers Association
> 3140 North Washington Boulevard
> Arlington, VA 22201
> (Attn: Shirley Watt Ireton)

National Geographic Society Kids Network
Grades: 4-6   Science content: biology, earth science
With *NGS Kids Network*, students don't just study science, they take an active part in it. This innovative program—available now for Apple IIGS and IBM computers, and soon for Macin-

tosh—is highly motivational. Students conduct original research on acid rain, water pollution, weather, solar energy, and trash. They also collect data and share their findings with "research teammates" via modem. A free preview is available upon request.

> Features: 1, 2, 3, 4, 5, 6, 7, 8, 12, 13, 15, 17, 18, 22, 23, 25, 26-geography, social studies, 27-telecommunications/software
>
> Cost: *Hello!* kit, *Too Much Trash?* kit: $325 each; *Acid Rain* kit, *Weather In Action* kit, *What's In Our Water?* kit, *What Are We Eating?* kit, *Solar Energy* kit: $375 each; tuition and telecommunications: $97.50
>
> Contact: National Geographic Society Education Services, Box 98018 Washington, DC 20090
>
> (For further information, request ERIC document number ED 403 017)

Our Only Earth Series: A Global Issues Curriculum
Grades: 4-12   Science content: interdisciplinary
This series features 6 guides that target world problems: tropical deforestation; air pollution; poverty, hunger and overpopulation; war; endangered species; and oceans. The 8 lessons in each book focus on both content information and various skills, including cooperative learning, critical and creative thinking, research skills, problem solving, and communication skills. This curriculum was developed with over 2,000 Soviet and United States students involved in International Youth Summits.

> Features: 2, 5, 6, 7, 8, 10, 13, 18, 22, 25, 26-language arts, social studies
>
> Cost: $16.95 per guide
>
> Contact: Zephyr Press
> P.O. Box 13448-W
> Tucson, AZ 85732-3448

Physics at the Indy 500
Grades: 6-9   Science content: physics
Basic physics principles are taught using examples drawn from Indy 500 auto racing. The package includes a videodisc, teacher's manual, and student lessons. It covers the following 5 major principles: the Bernoulli effect, centripetal force, conservation of energy, the Doppler effect, and Newton's third law. Interactive computer software for Macintosh or IBM/DOS is also available.

> Features: 1, 2, 3, 6, 10, 11, 18, 19, 20, 22, 23, 25, 27-laser disc

Cost: $275
Contact: Videodiscovery
1700 Westlake Avenue North, Suite 600
Seattle, WA 98109-3012

The Pillbug Project
Grades: 3-7   Science content: biology
Woven through days of exploration is the story of Patricia Pillbug. Her adventures spawn creative activities and exercise the imagination. Pillbugs, also known as sowbugs and isopods, are ideal science classroom pets as they allow students to learn directly from the environment. The concepts of cooperative learning, a variety of assessment techniques, and reproducible pages that can be used to form individual student logbooks give this volume a solid pedagogical framework.

> Features: 1, 2, 4, 15, 16, 18, 20, 23, 25
>
> Cost: $14.50
>
> Contact: National Science Teachers Association
> 3140 North Washington Boulevard
> Arlington, VA 22201
> (Attn: Shirley Watt Ireton)

Project Earth Science: Astronomy
Grades: 5-9   Science content: physics, earth science
Hands-on, teacher-tested activities bring the concepts of astronomy down to Earth. The guiding theme of this book is Earth's uniqueness among the planets of the Solar System.

> Features: 1, 2, 4, 16, 18, 23, 25
>
> Cost: $16.50
>
> Contact: National Science Teachers Association
> 3140 North Washington Boulevard
> Arlington, VA 22201
> (Attn: Shirley Watt Ireton)

PROJECT W.I.Z.E. (Wildlife Inquiry through Zoo Education): Survival Strategies
Grades: 7-10   Science content: biology, physics, environmental studies
Project WIZE, a comprehensive environmental-science curriculum project for grades 7-10, enables teachers to combine hands-on and traditional classroom activities with those conducted in the field. The field components can utilize local zoos, aquariums, nature centers, or parks.

> Features: 1, 2, 3, 4-field, 5, 6, 7, 8, 10, 11, 12, 13, 14, 15, 16, 18, 22, 23, 24-optional, 25, 26-mathematics, social studies, 27-videotape,

audiotape
Cost: $325 per curriculum set
Contact: New York Zoological Society
Bronx Zoo, Education Department
185th Street and Southern Boulevard
Bronx, NY 10460

Science CAP

Grades: 5-8   Science content: all
Science CAP for Macintosh computers helps
teachers prepare great classroom science activities and can save hundreds of hours of preparation time. It is a collection of more than 500 files
containing science-related activities, diagrams,
worksheets, overheads, teaching forms, and tests
and answer sheets. The files cover topics ranging
from astronomy to consumer product testing, to
science fairs. Each file is easy to use, to modify,
and to customize. This system provides an
excellent resource database and a framework for
cataloging, enhancing, and refining lessons.

 Features: 1, 3, 4, 5, 6, 7, 8, 10, 11, 12, 14, 18,
 19, 20, 21, 22, 24, 25, 26-mathematics,
 language arts, 27-computer
 Cost: individual license: $499, building-site
 license: $995
 Contact: DEMCO
 P.O. Box 7488
 Madison, WI 53791-9955

Science Discovery: Science Sleuths and *Image and Activity Bank*

Grades: 6-9   Science content: biology, earth
science
Image and Activity Bank (disc 1) is a visual
database of photographs, movies, computer
graphics, animation, and diagrams—all integrating major concepts in the earth, life, and physical
sciences. The multimedia videodisc is narrated in
English and Spanish and includes 24 student
lessons. *Science Sleuths* (disc 2) consists of 24
science-oriented mysteries, and all the clues, data,
and resources needed to solve them. It is very
interactive and student-centered. The science
mysteries are cross-disciplinary, integrating the
major science disciplines, and include also
teacher and student materials.

 Features: 1, 2, 3, 4, 5, 6, 7, 8, 10, 11, 12, 13, 15,
 17, 18, 19, 20, 21, 23, 27-laser disc
 Cost: $597
 Contact: Videodiscovery
 1700 Westlake Avenue North
 Suite 600
 Seattle, WA 98109-3012

Science Essentials

Grades: 4-8   Science content: various
The *Science Essentials* video program is intended
to stimulate viewers to actively explore scientific
phenomena, and learn by doing. The program
consists of 12 series, each of which contains 4
episodes (on 4 VHS videotapes or 1 CAV videodisc). Each series focuses on a single topic:
animals, ecosystems, electricity and magnetism,
geology, heat, the human body, light, matter,
plants, simple machines and motion, sound, and
weather.

 Features: 1, 2, 4, 5, 6, 7, 10, 15, 19, 20, 21, 22,
 23, 24, 25, 27-laser disc, videotape
 Cost: $249 per series
 Contact: Meg Boffey
 310 South Michigan Avenue
 Chicago, IL 60604
 (800) 554-9862

Stones and Bones

Grades: 7–12   Science content: biology, earth
science
A biological approach to the study of humankind
provides activity-based, interdisciplinary laboratory investigations. The instructional format is
designed to meet the needs of students at all
ability levels, from unmotivated and non-college-
oriented students, to highly academic college-
bound students. Each instructional pathway
includes student laboratory explorations, student
data worksheets, a teacher's guide, and other
supplementary instructional materials, as well as
replicated casts of fossil specimens.

 Features: 1, 2, 3, 4, 5, 6, 7, 8, 9, 10, 13, 14, 15,
 18, 20, 23, 24, 25, 26, 27-audiotape, film
 Cost: $12.50 per unit when ordering 100 units.
 Prices vary
 Contact: Physical Anthropology Center
 6625 Physical Anthropology Center
 Van Nuys, CA 91406

SWOOPE Radiation and Radon Unit

Grades: K-12   Science content: biology, chemistry, physics, earth science
SWOOPE (Students Watching Over Our Planet
Earth) engages students in a study of environmental science problems important to society.
Using hands-on classroom activities written by
teachers, students learn about various aspects of
environmental science, taking measurements on
those aspects using real instruments. For example, students examine backround ionizing
radiation and measure radon levels in their

homes and schools by hand-held Geiger counters. Some of the data are sent to a national database, where they can be analyzed and used by scientists. The students receive discussions of what the data reveal.

> Features: 1, 2, 3, 4, 5, 6, 7, 8, 9, 12, 13, 14, 15, 16, 17, 18, 20, 22, 23, 24, 25, 26-language arts, social studies, art, mathematics
> Cost: $25–$1,000, depending on level of involvement
> Contact: Dianne Hyer/Roger Eckhardt
> Los Alamos National Laboratory
> MS D447
> Los Alamos, NM 87545

SWOOPE Water Quality Unit

In this unit, students examine such areas as the earth's surface; ground and city water for temperature; pH; turbidity; hardness; and the concentration of nitrates, coliform bacteria, and chlorine.

> Features: 1, 2, 3, 4, 5, 6, 7, 8, 9, 12, 13, 14, 15, 16, 17, 18, 20, 22, 23, 24, 25, 26-language arts, social studies, art, mathematics
> Cost: $25–$1,000, depending on level of involvement
> Contact: Dianne Hyer/Roger Eckhardt
> Los Alamos National Laboratory
> MS D447
> Los Alamos, NM 87545

TOPS Modules: Open-Ended Task Cards and Structured Worksheets from TOPS Learning Systems

Grades: 4-12   Science content: all major topic areas

TOPS offers 32 modules in science and mathematics covering a wide array of topics including heat light, sound, electricity, magnetism, machines, plants, animals, rocks and minerals, probability, metrics, solutions, and oxidation. Each module contains comprehensive teaching notes in the front of the book, plus reproducible student task cards or worksheets in the back. Teachers gather their own simple materials, and the modules are ready to teach. Clear directions and quality illustrations lead students into independent hands-on explorations that are educational and fun. Learning is focused on student activity, rather than on discussion or lecture.

> Features: 1, 2, 3, 4, 5, 8, 10, 18, 20, 23, 25, 26-mathematics
> Cost: $7 to $15 per module

Contact: TOPS Learning Systems
10970 South Mulino Road
Canby, OR 97013

Wet and Wild Water

Grades: not indicated   Science content: biology, physical science, earth science

As indicated by the title, this guide integrates subject matter around the topic of water. Individual modules focus on properties of water, fish and economics, water sports and animals, explorers, legends and strange occurrences, and global responsibility. Topic pages indicate core knowledge, activities, water experiments, and additional resources.

> Features: 1, 2, 3, 4, 5, 6, 7, 8, 12, 13, 15, 18, 22, 23, 25, 26-language arts, social studies, fine arts, mathematics, music
> Cost: contact supplier
> Contact: Indiana Department of Education
> Center for School Improvement and Performance
> Room 229, State House
> Indianapolis, IN 46204-2798
> ERIC Document Reproduction Service
>   (request ED number 338 478)

Wetlands Are Wonderlands

Grades: 6-8   Science content: chemistry, biology, environmental education

These 4-H marine education guides, intended for students in grades 6-8 and their teachers or leaders, stress the importance of conserving wetlands. New information has been incorporated to update the guides. Projects include taking field trips to wetland locations, investigating the various life-forms in wetland soils, making model wetlands, and showing the ways humans have destroyed wetlands. The guides provide topics for discussion, questions, and activities, as well as a vocabulary and reference list.

> Features: 1, 2, 3, 4, 5, 6, 8, 9, 10, 14, 15, 16, 18, 19, 20, 22, 23
> Cost: leader guide: $3.50, member guide: $3
> 10 percent discount on orders of 10-49
> 20 percent discount on orders of 50 or more
> Contact: Illinois-Indiana Sea Grant Program
> University of Illinois at Urbana-Champaign
> 65 Mumford Hall
> 1301 West Gregory Drive
> Urbana, IL 61801

WOW (Windows on Wildlife)
Grades: 3-6   Science content: biology, envi-
                ronmental education
This environmental science program in the
greater New York area focuses on endangered
species and their habitats, but also incorporates
social studies, mathematics, and language skills
into the framework of a wildlife studies curriculum. Teachers attend an orientation workshop,
prior to their first visit. Curriculum materials
include six booklets: *Rain Forests, Deciduous
Forests, Wetlands, Desert, Endangered Species,* and
Grasslands.
> Features: 1, 2, 3, 4, 5, 6, 13, 14, 15, 22, 25, 26-
>   social studies, mathematics, language skills
> Cost: $1.25 each title
> Contact: New York Zoological Society
> Bronx Zoo, Education Department
> 185th Street and Southern Boulevard
> Bronx, NY 10460

High School Grades (9-12)

Biological Science: An Ecological Approach, 7th ed.
Grades: 9-12   Science content: biology, earth
                 science
Using an inquiry approach to learning, this program leads students from step-by-step discussions
of observable phenomena such as cell theory and
genetics, to abstract concepts. It arms students
with the information they need to make intelligent decisions in our science-oriented world. The
program's materials are more thoroughly tested
than any other high school biology materials.
> Features: 1, 2, 3, 4, 5, 6, 7, 8, 9, 10, 11, 13, 14,
>   15, 16, 17, 18, 19, 20, 22, 23, 24
> Cost: not given
> Contact: Jill McDermott
> Kendall/Hunt Publishing
> 2460 Kerper Boulevard
> Dubuque, IA 52001

ChemCom: Chemistry in the Community, 2d ed.
Grades: 10-12   Science content: chemistry,
                  physics
This program combines core concepts of chemistry with a unique societal slant that grabs students' attention and piques their interest. Activities show students how they are surrounded by
chemistry. Once students make such connections,
they can comprehend and appreciate chemistry.
> Features: 1, 2, 3, 4, 5, 6, 7, 8, 9, 10, 11, 12, 13,
>   14, 15, 16, 17, 18, 19, 20, 22, 23, 24
> Cost: contact supplier

> Contact: Jill McDermott
> Kendall/Hunt Publishing
> 2460 Kerper Boulevard
> Dubuque, IA 52001

Death Trap: The Biology of Carnivorous Plants
Grades: 9-12   Science content: biology
The videodisc explains the detailed working of
several kinds of carnivorous plants, including
their physiology, ecology, distribution, and
evolution. Film segments include time-lapse,
close-up, high-speed photography, and animation
techniques. This format provides an excellent way
to introduce scientific questioning and hypothesizing skills. The teacher's guide provides
complete narration, along with study questions,
suggestions for classroom use, and textbook
correlations for secondary science texts.
> Features: 5, 6, 7, 8, 19, 27-laser disc
> Cost: $99
> Contact: Videodiscovery
> 1700 Westlake Avenue North
> Suite 600
> Seattle, WA 98109-3012

Evolution: Inquiries into Biology and Earth Science
Grades: 8-12   Science content: biology, earth
                 science
This curriculum-based program integrates biology
and earth science, using evolution as a unifying
theme. It includes lessons, hands-on activities,
teacher materials, and a CAV videodisc. The
program was developed in cooperation with
BSCS.
> Features: 1, 2, 3, 4, 5, 6, 7, 8, 11, 13, 23, 25, 27-
>   laser disc
> Cost: $495
> Contact: Videodiscovery
> 1700 Westlake Avenue North
> Suite 600
> Seattle, WA 98109-3012

**The Fluid Earth: Physical Science and Technology of
    the Marine Environment**
Grades: 9-12   Science content: physical ocean-
                 ography, earth science, physical
                 science, environmental educa-
tion
This is a one-semester course that explores the
physics, chemistry, and geology of the oceans, as
well as the technologies used to study them. Units
include "Earth and Ocean Basins," "Waves and
Beaches," "Physical Oceanography," "Chemical
Oceanography," and "Transportation." Materials

also include topics on satellite oceanography, ocean-mapping technologies, submersible exploration of the seafloor, and seabed mining. Current issues explored are water pollution, acid rain, the water cycle, the greenhouse effect, and exclusive economic zones.

> Features: 1, 2, 3, 4, 5, 6, 7, 8, 9, 10, 11, 12, 13, 14, 15, 16, 18, 19, 20, 22, 23, 24, 25, 26-social studies
> Cost: hardcover student text: $18.95, teacher's guide: $40, workbook masters: $12
> Contact: Dr. E. Barbara Klemm
> HMSS Project
> 1776 University Avenue
> Honolulu, HI 96822

Global Science: Energy, Resources, Environment

Grades: 9-12   Science content: all major topic areas

This book teaches students to view our world as "spaceship earth," a self-supporting environment where they will spend the rest of their lives.

> Features: 1, 2, 3, 4, 5, 6, 7, 8, 9, 10, 11, 13, 14, 15, 17, 18, 20, 22, 23, 25, 26-health.
> Cost: contact supplier
> Contact: Jill McDermott
> Kendall/Hunt Publishing
> 2460 Kerper Boulevard
> Dubuque, IA 52001

GTV: Planetary Manager

Grades: 5-12, adult   Science content: earth science

Planetary Manager explores major themes such as global warming, deforestation, and water pollution, using video technology. Specific issues are tackled, and the positive actions we can take are presented. Each show provides a springboard for further study and debate. Students use *Planetary Manager*'s computer software and large visual database to investigate environmental problems and solutions. The program helps instill a sense of responsibility for our planet.

> Features: 2, 3, 6, 7, 8, 13, 15, 22, 23, 26-social studies, geography, 27-laser disc
> Cost: Before 12/1/92: $595; after 12/1/92: $650
> Contact: National Geographic Society
> Education Services, Box 98018
> Washington, DC 20090

Informal Science Study

Grades: 5-12   Science content: physics

Informal Science Study is a supplementary and complementary physical science curriculum package with components. The materials capitalize on experiences that learners have in nonclassroom settings, such as amusement parks, athletic events, and playgrounds. The package is designed to assist students in the acquisition and application of science concepts in real-world situations.

> Features: 1, 2, 5, 19, 21, 23
> Cost: $50
> Contact: Howard Jones
> The University of Houston
> 112 Farish Hall
> Houston, TX 77004

One-Minute Readings: Issues in Science, Technology, and Society

Grades: 7-12   Science content: all major subject areas

One-Minute Readings presents opportunities for students to consider relevant, real-world problems. The readings enhance topics in conventional science courses by highlighting their connection to society and the natural world. The issues span the social and ethical aspects of topics in chemistry, physics, and biology, including medicine, environmental science, bioethics, space science, and computers. The teacher's manual contains teaching ideas and suggests related student projects.

> Features: 2, 3, 6, 7, 8, 11, 13, 15, 17, 18, 22, 23, 26-history, politics
> Cost: *One-Minute Readings*: $7.95, teacher's manual: $5.95
> Contact: Addison-Wesley Publishing Company
> Order Processing Department
> Route 128
> Reading, MA 01867

Preparing for Tomorrow's World

Grades: 7-12   Science content: all

Each module contains all the materials necessary to implement the program. Contained in a three-ring binder format, the teacher's guide presents objectives, activities, discussion questions, and other instructional aids. Where appropriate, the modules have reproducible student guides that include all necessary background information. Some of the units include a filmstrip with audiotapes to present additional background information. The modules are *Coastal Decisions, Space Encounters, Beacon City: An Urban Land-Use Simulation, and Decisions.*

> Features: 1, 2, 3, 5, 6, 7, 11, 13, 15, 17, 19, 22,

23, 24, 25, 26-social studies, technology, 27-films, audiotape
Cost: $45 to $90 per unit
Contact: Sopris West, Inc.
1140 Boston Avenue
Longmont, CO 80501

Technology Education: Mathematics and Science Interface Project
Grades: 6-12   Science content: physical sciences
This curriculum, which developed through a cooperative effort by educators in Maryland, integrates mathematics and science in the context of technology education. The materials are recommended for use as either an instructional resource collection or as a materials resource guide for creating similar units of instruction. The collection includes units on manufacturing, transportation, communication, construction, and power and energy. Each unit includes listings of concepts, transparency masters, diagrams and graphics, and informational sheets.
   Features: 4, 12, 19, 21, 22, 25, 26-mathematics, technology
   Cost: contact supplier
   Contact: ERIC Document Reproduction Service
7420 Fullerton Road, Suite 110
Springfield, VA 22153-2852
(800) 443-ERIC
(ED number not yet assigned)

Supplementary Materials

Elementary Grades (K-6)
The Great Lakes in My World
Grades: 1-8   Science content: biology, chemistry, earth science, environmental education
The activities are designed to fit into regular curriculum units in science, social studies, mathematics, and language arts, rather than stand alone as extracurricular environmental education activities crammed in at the edges of an already crowded school day. Some of the activities discuss natural processes in the Great Lakes, and some focus on pollution issues that require innovative problem solving.
   Features: 1, 2, 3, 4, 5, 6, 7, 15, 19, 22, 23, 25, 26-social studies, mathematics, language arts
   Cost: Free

Contact: Lake Michigan Federation
59 East Van Buren Street, Suite 2215
Chicago, IL 60605

Middle School Grades (5-8)
Bottle Biology Introductory Packet   *good stuff*
Grades: 1-12   Science content: biology, life sciences
Bottle Biology is a classroom-tested approach to hands-on biology. It allows students on all levels to become engaged in the actual process of science and scientific inquiry: asking questions, creating experiments, testing hypotheses, and generating "answers." Teachers and students working with this program reuse disposable containers to explore many areas of the life sciences, leading to a better understanding of ecosystems, local environments, and biotic interactions. The activities give teachers, students, and scientists a low-cost and accessible scientific world, which includes microbes, plants, insects, and environmental interactions as the ground from which to pose questions and launch investigations.
   Features: 1, 3, 6, 8, 15, 18, 22
   Cost: Free
   Contact: Bottle Biology Project
University of Wisconsin-Madison
Plant Pathology Department
1630 Linden Drive
Madison, WI 53706

CD-ROM Mammals
Grades: 4-12, adult   Science content: biology
Except for a trip to the zoo, there are few better ways to teach kids about animals than with this acclaimed CD-ROM. With the click of a mouse, students can watch mammals leap, dive, burrow, and fly—even hear them roar, bray, and howl. Featuring the most up-to-date research on mammals, this visual encyclopedia includes entries on more than 200 different animals; 155 animal vocalizations; printing capability for essays, captions, and screens; and 700 full-screen color photographs in MCGA format. There is enough information on this CD-ROM to keep a class involved for the entire school year.
   Features: 2, 6, 7, 8, 21, 26-geography, 27-CD-ROM
   Cost: $99
   Contact: National Geographic Society
Education Services, Box 98018
Washington, DC 20090

EARTHWATCHING III: An Environmental Reader
Grades: K-12   Science content: biology, physics
This reader complements classroom materials on scientific and environmental topics. It contains 200 stories originally written for "Earthwatch/ Radio." Stories are grouped under nine headings: "The Atmosphere," "The Biosphere," "The Land," "The World of Water," "Energy," "Environmental Quality," "Health and Nutrition," "People and Society," and "Around the Globe."
> Features: 6, 13, 15, 22, 23, 25
> Cost: $3.50
> Contact: EARTHWATCHING III
> Institute for Environmental Studies
> University of Wisconsin-Madison
> 550 North Park Street, 15 Science Hall
> Madison, WI 53706
> ERIC Document Reproduction Service
> (request ED number 323 094)

OEAGLS- Oceanic Education Activities for Great Lakes Schools
Grades: 5-9   Science content: biology, earth science
OEAGLS (pronounced "eagles") materials are designed to be easily integrated into existing curricula. Investigations are characterized by subject matter compatibility with existing curriculum topics, short activities lasting from one to three class periods, minimal preparation time, minimal equipment needs, standard page size for easy duplication, student workbook plus teacher's guide, and suggested extension activities for further information or creative expression. The teachability of the materials has been demonstrated in middle school classrooms, and content accuracy has been assured by critical reviewers.
> Features: 1, 2, 3, 4, 5, 6, 7, 10, 13, 15, 19, 20, 21, 22, 23, 25, 26-art, language arts, social studies
> Cost: $3 per topic (30 topics), includes workbook, teacher's guide, and shipping
> Contact: Ohio Sea Grant
> 1541 Research Center
> 1314 Kinnear Road
> Columbus, OH 43212

The Outdoor Classroom
Grades: 1-12   Science content: biology, earth science
The outdoor lessons, concepts, and experiences in this program are designed to encourage teachers to use school sites, communities, parks, forests, rivers, ponds, wildlife areas, watersheds, and nature centers to design an in-depth outdoor education teaching plan to enrich the school curriculum.
> Features: 1, 2, 6, 7, 14, 15, 16, 18, 22, 23, 26-art, health, social studies, language arts
> Cost: Free
> Contact: Indiana Department of Education
> Center for School Improvement and Performance
> Room 229, State House
> Indianapolis, IN 46204-2798
> ERIC Document Reproduction Service
> (request ED number 338 508)

Physics at Work
Grades: 9-12   Science content: physics
This is a comprehensive visual database to support secondary physics curricula. It includes thousands of still images, computer graphics, diagrams, calculus problems, animations, and demonstrations. Optional interactive computer software and lessons for IBM or Macintosh computers are also available.
> Features: 3, 5, 6, 9, 12, 13, 18, 19, 20, 22, 27-laser disc
> Contact: Videodiscovery
> 1700 Westlake Avenue North
> Suite 600
> Seattle, WA 98109-3012

Project Learning Tree
Grades: K–12   Science content: environment
This activity program is designed to help students develop an awareness of their presence in the environment, their impact upon it, and their responsibility for it; develop the skills and knowledge to make informed decisions regarding the use and management of the environment; to gain the confidence to take action on their decisions. The program contains more than 175 interdisciplinary activities for students, as well as workshops and in-service programs for teachers. Many activities are conducted outdoors. First field tested in 1977, PLT has undergone several revisions; the newest revision is expected to be available in autumn 1993. Cosponsored by the American Forest Council and the Western Regional Environmental Education Council.
> Features: 1, 2, 3, 5, 6, 7, 15, 16, 18, 22, 26
> Cost: Available free of charge by attending a six-hour workshop
> Contact: Project Learning Tree State Coordinator
> Project Learning Tree

1250 Connecticut Avenue, Northwest
Washington, DC 20036

Project WILD
Grades K–12   Science content: environment
Project WILD is a supplementary conservation
and environmental education program with an
emphasis on wildlife. Its purpose is to develop an
informed and ecologically literate citizenry who
will take responsible actions to benefit people,
wildlife, and the environment. Co-founded in
1980 by the Western Regional Environmental
Education Council and the Western Association
of Fish and Wildlife Agencies, the project is now
available in a new edition, with two activity
books: *Project WILD Activity Guide* and *Project
WILD Aquatic Activity Guide.*
  Features: 1, 2, 3, 5, 6, 7, 13, 14, 15, 16, 18, 19,
    22, 26
  Cost: Available free of charge to educators
    attending Project WILD workshops
  Contact: Project WILD State Coordinator
  Project WILD
  P.O. Box 18060
  Boulder, CO 80308-8060

*ScienceVision: An Inquiry-Based Videodisc Science
    Curriculum*
Grades: 6-8   Science content: multidisci-
                plinary
A product of the Interactive Media Science
(IMS) Project at Florida State University, this
program provides students with numerous
opportunities to become involved in activities
that would be impossible for them in the normal
classroom setting. Using the *ScienceVision*
program, students are able to conduct experiments, visit locations, listen to experts, make
decisions, collect data, and solve the problems
posed on the videodisc. The fundamental assumption of the program is that science education
should be multidisciplinary and provide a general
science background for all students. Its goals are
twofold: to provide students with a valid understanding of science as a human enterprise and to
present science as a search for knowledge based
upon the interpretation of data.
  Features: 1, 2, 3, 4, 5, 6, 7, 15, 19, 21, 22, 24,
    27-laser disc, microcomputer
  Cost: contact supplier
  Contact: ERIC Document Reproduction
    Service
  7420 Fullerton Road, Suite 110
  Springfield, VA 22153-2852

(800) 443-ERIC
(request ED number 336 257)

STV: Rain Forest
Grades: 5-12   Science content: biology, physics
STV lets you customize your lessons with the best
of the National Geographic Society's creative and
educational resources, from video clips to book
excerpts. The richness of a fragile ecosystem
comes to life in this unique multimedia resource.
Based on the TV special *Rain Forest*, this unit
provides a close-up view of a spectacular environ-
ment and the forces that endanger it.
  Features: 2, 3, 13, 15, 22, 26-geography, 27-
    laser disc
  Cost: $285
  Contact: National Geographic Society
  Education Services, Box 98018
  Washington, DC 20090

STV: Restless Earth
Grades: 5-12   Science content: earth science
Based on the TV special *Born of Fire*, this unit
covers plate tectonics, spreading, subduction, and
more. Viewers travel from Iceland to the Philip-
pines and learn about the forces that continually
change the earth.
  Features: 2, 3, 6, 7, 8, 13, 15, 22, 26-geography,
    27-laser disc
  Cost: $285
  Contact: National Geographic Society
  Education Services, Box 98018
  Washington, DC 20090

STV: Solar System
Grades: 5-12   Science content: earth science
Take your students on a fascinating tour of
Earth's nearest neighbors. Expanding on informa-
tion in the film *Exploring Our Solar System*, this
new study unit provides a complete, up-to-date
look at the planets. Resources include full-motion
footage transmitted from space, computer-
enhanced imagery and animations, a rich library
of images, and informative text.
  Features: 2, 3, 6, 7, 8, 13, 26-geography, 27-
    laser disc
  Cost: $285
  Contact: National Geographic Society
  Education Services, Box 98018
  Washington, DC 20090

Tracks Magazine
Grades: 4-6   Science content: biology, envi-
                ronmental education, outdoor

education

This is a monthly magazine, published from September through May of each year. Each month, *Tracks* features articles about the natural history of various species. It also provides special issues occasionally, highlighting a specific ecology concern such as groundwater or wetlands. The magazine's circulation is more than 80,000, and it is sent to schools in approximately 25 states.

Features: 1, 2, 13, 15, 16, 20, 22, 23
Cost: $1.50 per student per year for 9 issues
Contact: Michigan United Conservation Clubs
P.O. Box 3023S
Lansing, MI 48909

High School Grades (9-12)

After the Warming

Grades: 7-12   Science content: earth science
This teacher's guide is designed to supplement the *After the Warming* PBS television special written and hosted by James Burke. The major goal of the guide is to provide teachers with ready-to-use lessons. It has been created as a ready-to-use mini- unit, with reproducible pages of active involvement activities suitable for social studies, geography, environmental education, and general science classes. The guide also contains background notes, a program synopsis, references relevant to teacher resources, and bibliographies for the teacher and students.

Features: 1, 2, 3, 5, 6, 7, 8, 13, 15, 22, 23, 25, 26-social studies
Cost: $10
Contact: Iris Wingert
Maryland Instructional Technology
11767 Owings Mills Boulevard
Owings Mills, MD 21117

Atoms to Anatomy: A Multimedia View of Human Systems

Grades: 9-12   Science content: chemistry, biology
This is a visual database for teaching human anatomy and physiology. It includes outstanding three-dimensional images, computer graphics, and animation of human structure, drawn from state-of-the-art medical scanning technologies (MRI, ultrasound, PET scans, etc.). Major areas covered are respiration, circulation, cardiology, nervous system, hearing, vision, balance, the skeletal system, and musculature. Computer software allows the user to rotate and tilt images for maximum comprehension. This program

includes software for either IBM or Macintosh computers.

Features: 3, 17, 27-laser disc
Cost: $695 (videodisc and software)
Contact: Videodiscovery
1700 Westlake Avenue North
Suite 600
Seattle, WA 98109-3012

Bio Sci II

Grades: 7-12   Science content: biology
Bio Sci II is a visual database for the life sciences that includes over 8,000 still images, film sequences, computer graphics and 3-D animations that support standard biology and life science texts at the secondary level. It contains 9 dissections, with excellent visual specimens under ideal laboratory conditions (frog, fetal pig, earthworm, mussel, squid, crayfish, seastar, perch, and cat muscles). Also included are all topics of life science, plus animal behavior movies, representations of all five kingdoms, progressive diagrams, life cycles, and microscopic organisms. The videodisc is narrated in English and Spanish and includes a bar-coded print directory. Level III is an interactive computer software package available for Macintosh, IBM/DOS, and Apple II computers. This software contains a complete indexed database, "slide show" utility, a bar code creator, and 12 interactive lessons.

Features: 2, 3, 8, 18, 19, 27-laser disc
Cost: $549
Contact: Videodiscovery
1700 Westlake Avenue North
Suite 600
Seattle, WA 98109-3012

Cell Biology

Grades: 10-college   Science content: biology
This visual database, designed for teaching cell biology at the secondary level, contains 85 film sequences and 200 still images. It explores cell types, cell constituents, mitosis, cytokinesis, fission, and cell motility. Live footage includes cell processes from all five kingdoms, motion segments of animal cells, plant cells, budding multiple fission, protoplasmic streaming, migration of organelles, and more. It also includes a bar code print directory, indexed by cell process, structure, scientific name, and concept. Narrated in English and Spanish. Optional Level III computer software and lessons are available for Macintosh computers.

Features: 3, 27-laser disc

Cost: $549
Contact: Videodiscovery
1700 Westlake Avenue North
Suite 600
Seattle, WA 98109-3012

Chemistry at Work
Grades: 10-12   Science content: chemistry
This videodisc contains still pictures, computer
graphic designs, three-dimensional animations,
and many films. It includes a bar-coded user's
manual cross-referenced by name, chemical
formula, instructional concept, and frame number. Narrated in English and Spanish. Interactive
computer software is available for Level III.
   Features: 3, 4, 5, 6, 19, 20, 27-laser disc
   Cost: $549
   Contact: Videodiscovery
   1700 Westlake Avenue North
   Suite 600
   Seattle, WA 98109-3012

Great Lakes Pursuit
Grades: 8-12, adult   Science content: biology,
                                   earth science
A board game in a trivia-question format with
60–80 questions per topic, including history,
natural history, culture, economics, geography,
and environment.
   Features: 9, 13, 15, 22, 26-social studies
   Cost: $15 for educators, $24 for non-educators
   Contact: Ohio Sea Grant
   1541 Research Center
   1314 Kinnear Road
   Columbus, OH 43212

Landscape Plants: Woody Landscape Plants of the Temperate United States
Grades: 7-12   Science content: biology
This synoptic assemblage of photos represents the
most complete pictorial description of cultivated
woody plants available in any medium. The disc
shows over 7,400 views of over 900 species or
varieties. In addition to the main collection, there
are two special presentations. "Plant Environments" is a selection of pictures showing the
diversity of plants and the environmental moods
they can create. "How to Select a Plant," a
suitable tutorial for landscape students, is a
narrated overview of some of the factors involved
in selecting the right plant for an application.
This encyclopedia of landscape plants comes with
a printed directory that identifies every image,
provides a copy of the narratives, and a offers a

common-name quick reference. Optional com-
puter software is available.
   Features: 3, 27-laser disc
   Cost: $395
   Contact: Videodiscovery
   1700 Westlake Avenue North
   Suite 600
   Seattle, WA 98109-3012

Life Cycles: Oxford Scientific Film Collection on Reproductive Biology
Grades: 6-12   Science content: biology
The videodisc features nearly 4,000 color images,
graphics illustrations, and footage from 16 films.
The material has been carefully selected and
organized to support standard text material and
lecture plans on the subject of reproductive
biology. The disc is fully indexed in an accompa-
nying directory. Interactive software is available
for Macintosh or IBM computers.
   Features: 3, 20, 27-laser disc
   Cost: $395
   Contact: Videodiscovery
   1700 Westlake Avenue North
   Suite 600
   Seattle, WA 98109-3012

NOVA Teacher's Guide
Grades: 9-12   Science content: various
The *NOVA Teacher's Guide* accompanies each
new season of *NOVA* in the fall and spring. The
80-page guide includes lessons designed to supplement each program with background information, viewing goals, discussion questions, and
activities. In addition, it includes reproducible
student activity pages and a 32-page student
magazine.
   Features: 1, 5, 6, 7, 8, 12, 13, 15, 17, 18, 20, 22,
      25, 26-social sciences
   Cost: $4.50 (one-time fee, then added to
      mailing list)
   Contact: Educational Print and Outreach
   WGBH
   125 Western Avenue
   Boston, MA 02134

Physics of Sports
Grades: 8-12   Science content: physics
This detailed record of over 20 athletic events
provides visual data from which quantitative data
may be collected by biomechanics, kinesiology,
and physics students. It includes a bar-coded
student handbook and teacher's guide, directory
of the images, formulas, and step-by-step instruc-

tions. Optional Level III software lessons are available for Macintosh computers.

> Features: 2, 3, 5, 6, 8, 20, 23, 27-laser disc
> Cost: $275
> Contact: Videodiscovery
> 1700 Westlake Avenue North, Suite 600
> Seattle, WA 98109-3012

Pollination Biology

Grades: 6-12   Science content: biology
This videodisc deals with all facets of flower pollination. Topics include the reasons for sexual reproduction, flower anatomy, kinds of pollinators, and flower adaptations. Side A is a CAV study version containing a shortened edition of the entire movie, with full freeze-frame control. Side B is an extended play, CLV version of the original movie in its entirety. It is accompanied by a popular British soundtrack. The teacher's guide includes a complete narrative, study questions, textbook correlations, and suggestions for classroom presentations and activities.

> Features: 3, 27-laser disc
> Cost: $275
> Contact: Videodiscovery
> 1700 Westlake Avenue North, Suite 600
> Seattle, WA 98109-3012

Sci-Math: Proportional Problem Solving in Math and Science

Grades: 7-12   Science content: chemistry, physics
Sci-Math is a supplement to the science or mathematics curriculum. It teaches students to use labeled rates as the key techniques for organizing their approach to word problems. The system is designed to give students the fundamental problem-solving skills they need for dealing confidently and effectively with the kinds of problems (proportional comparisons, percents, etc.) they will encounter in mathematics and science courses as well in everyday life. *Sci-Math* is the answer for science teachers whose students say they like science but hate the mathematics involved, and for mathematics teachers whose students say they would like mathematics if it weren't for the "story problems." The program includes materials, training, and follow-up services.

> Features: 1, 4, 5, 7, 8, 10, 18, 23, 24, 25
> Cost: $16 per teacher
> Contact: Sci-Math
> 4655-25th Street
> San Francisco, CA 94114

Starfinder

Grades: 7-12   Science content: physics, astronomy
Starfinder brings the discoveries of the Hubble Space Telescope into the classroom in a context that supports the study of earth science and physics. Each program consists of three parts: "Data Stream" highlights an important finding made possible by the telescope. "Science Links" correlates one specific earth science or physics concept with the working of the universe. "The People Behind HST" profiles the jobs of people associated with the telescope and tells how their career paths evolved. 30 programs; 15 minutes each.

> Features: 1, 2, 4, 5, 12, 19, 22, 23, 25, 27-videotape
> Cost: video: $100, print: $60
> Contact: Iris Wingert
> Maryland Instructional Technology
> 11767 Owings Mills Boulevard
> Owings Mills, MD 21117

ZEST (Zoos for Effective Teaching)

Grades: 7-12   Science content: biology
ZEST provides 12 full-day sessions for teachers in middle schools and high schools, including teacher conferences, peer dissemination, and the production of a teacher's manual. The emphasis is on how to use a zoological collection within the required biological science curricula, as well as enrichment for instruction in the physical sciences.

> Features: 1, 3, 4, 5, 6, 7, 8, 9, 11, 13, 14, 15, 16, 18, 19, 22, 23, 25
> Cost: $10 to offset shipping and handling
> Contact: New York Zoological Society
> Bronx Zoo, Education Department
> 185th Street and Southern Boulevard
> Bronx, NY 10460

Program Frameworks

National Council on Science and Technology Education. 1989. *Science for All Americans.* Washington, DC: American Association for the Advancement of Science.
This document is not written in the form of a curriculum framework, but it functions as such by virtue of its message and authors. It summarizes the first phase of a long-term project (Project 2061) to identify the knowledge, skills, and attitudes that all K–12 students should acquire during their experiences in science. A strong case is made for reducing the amount of factual

material traditionally presented and placing more emphasis on active inquiry. The report is strongly influencing science reform efforts throughout the United States. The second phase of Project 2061 is to engage teams of educators and scientists in the process of developing alternative curriculum models for use in schools. Any school or district engaged in science reform efforts should become familiar with this document. The report is available from: AAAS Books, Dept. 2061, P.O. Box 753, Waldorf, MD 20604.

National Science Teachers Association. 1992. *The Content Core: A Guide for Curriculum Designers.* Scope, Sequence and Coordination of Secondary School Science, vol. 1. Washington, DC.

This guide was developed specifically as an aid to designers of science curricula (grades 6-12) and was published by the nation's largest association of science teachers. The first section of the book presents principles and strategies of curricular coordination, and the second section presents detailed recommendations for scopes and sequences for courses in biology, chemistry, earth and space sciences, and physics. The recommended content core (framework) is presented through a combination of tables and narratives. For more information, contact: Scope, Sequence, and Coordination, The Common Core, National Science Teachers Association, 1742 Connecticut Avenue, NW, Washington, DC 20009-1171.

Mayer, V. J., et al. 1992. "The Role of Planet Earth in the New Science Curriculum." *Journal of Geological Education* 40: 66-73.

Though not a curriculum framework by conventional definitions, this succinct article provides an overview of a major curriculum reform effort to place the study of planet earth at the center of K–12 science curriculum development. The article provides a strong rationale for rethinking the K–12 curriculum, presents a *Framework for Earth Systems Education*, and describes implementation efforts. This is a good example of how a robust reconceptualization of the curricular core can be concisely communicated in clear terms. Indeed, the framework alone can be presented on just one page (see V. J. Mayer 1991, "Framework for Earth Systems Education," *Science Activities* 28(1): 8-9). It is an approach to be emulated.

National Center for Earth Science Education. 1991. *Earth Science Content Guidelines Grades K–12.* Alexandria, VA: American Geological Institute.

This framework represents what can be accomplished by writing teams made up of teachers, science educators, and scientists when consensus-building deliberation occurs. The framework is based on four broad goals for students that relate to literacy in science and earth science. The framework organizes content around essential questions that relate to six content areas: solid earth, water, air, ice, life, and earth in space. The essential questions are distributed across grade levels, and for each essential question the framework provides key ideas and ways of engaging students in the ideas. Finally, some curriculum materials and resources are identified for each of the six content areas. For further information, contact: AGI Publications Center, P.O. Box 2010, Annapolis Junction, MD 20701.

National Center for Improving Science Education. 1989. *Getting Started in Science: A Blueprint for Elementary School Science Education.* Andover, MA: The Network.

Though this report treats instruction, assessment, and teacher education in addition to curriculum development, one chapter presents a vision of elementary school science in the form of a general curriculum framework that accommodates a broad range of topics and goals. The framework is organized according to broad concepts that relate to both science and technology. Some attitudes associated with scientific enterprise are also presented. For further information, contact: Susan Loucks-Horsley, Associate Director, 290 South Main Street, Andover, MA 01810.

National Center for Improving Science Education. 1991. *The High Stakes of High School Science.* Andover, MA: The Network.

This report incorporates the results of more than 300 nationwide studies aimed at improving high school science education. This blueprint for action touches on four crucial aspects of science education: curriculum and instruction, assessment, teacher education, and organizational development. The proposed framework involves restructuring the high school program into core studies and alternative pathways. For ordering information, contact: Publications Department, 300 Brickstone Square, Suite 900, Andover, MA 01810.

National Center for Improving Science Education. 1990. *Science and Technology Education for the Middle Years: Frameworks for Curriculum and Instruction.* Andover, MA: The Network. This book describes organizing principles that incorporate a suggested science content, as well as a learning sequence that illustrates how more "hands-on, minds-on" science can become more prevalent in schools serving middle-grade students. Frameworks are based on the special needs of young adolescents, including the kinds of school settings where science learning can flourish. For ordering information, contact: Publications Department, 300 Brickstone Square, Suite 900, Andover, MA 01810.

State of Connecticut Board of Education. 1991. *A Guide to Curriculum Development—SCIENCE.* Connecticut State Department of Education. This curriculum guide is designed to help districts develop their own state-of-the-art learning programs and opportunities in science. The guide describes what can and should happpen in quality K–12 science settings. It helps planners view the student as the beneficiary of the curriculum.

Curriculum Development Resources

American Ground Water Trust. 1990. *Ground Water Education in America's Schools.* Dublin, OH. Given increasing concerns regarding the quality and supply of ground water, it seems appropriate that resource materials be developed to infuse the topic into existing curricula. This catalog of resource materials for elementary and secondary educators is timely and useful in identifying scarce materials. The document is available from: The American Ground Water Trust, 6375 Riverside Drive, Dublin, OH 43017.

Dubeck, L. W., S. E. Moshier, and J. E. Boss. 1988. *Science in Cinema: Teaching Science Fact through Science Fiction Films.* New York: Teachers College Press. This is a unique resource that provides plot summaries, scientific commentary, literary commentary, discussion topics, and classroom activities for specific science fiction films that are readily available through libraries and video outlets. The authors suggest that teachers use the material to enrich standard science courses. Strategies for incorporating films into the curriculum are offered, and an extensive bibliography is provided.

Dunn, G. A. 1990. *Buggy Books: A Guide to Juvenile and Popular Books on Insects and Their Relatives.* Lansing, MI: Young Entomologists' Society. This unique compilation of 736 resources includes references to several teacher's guides and instructional aids. If you are seeking background material for units on insects, you cannot find a more comprehensive or functional listing. Books are organized by title, age-appropriateness, subject, and author. For more information, contact: Young Entomologists' Society, Inc., 1915 Peggy Place, Lansing, MI 48910-2553.

Galda, L., et al. 1990. "Exploration and Discovery: Books for a Science Curriculum (Children's Books)." *Reading Teacher* 44:316–25. This article reviews 92 children's books that would enhance many topics in a science curriculum. A good source of titles to complement unit activities or textbook information.

Helgeson, S. L., R. W. Howe, and P. E. Blosser. 1990. *Promising and Exemplary Programs and Materials in Elementary and Secondary Schools—Science.* Columbus, OH: ERIC Clearinghouse for Science, Mathematics, and Environmental Education. This document describes 36 programs or sets of materials that have been identified as exemplary in some way. Nominations were solicited from state and local coordinators, science curriculum specialists, and federal program staff members. The entry for each program or set of materials includes a program description, evaluative data or comments, specific materials available, and an address for more information. The publication is available from ERIC/CSMEE Publications, Room 310, 1200 Chambers Road, Columbus, OH 43212.

International Joint Commission. 1992. *The Directory of Great Lakes Educational Material.* Detroit, MI. This book is the result of a survey of several hundred educators to determine what materials are most useful in teaching others about the Great Lakes. It includes lists of audiovisual materials, books, booklets, instructional materials, newsletters, special reports, and sources. Available free of charge, it serves as a useful starting point for studies at the elementary and secondary level. This book is available from: International Joint Commission, Great Lakes Regional Office, P.O. Box 32869, Detroit, MI 48232.

National Research Council. 1990. *Fulfilling the Promise: Biology Education in the Nation's Schools.* Washington, DC: National Academy Press.
This report focuses on restructuring education in biology, including a historical perspective, obstacles to change, and strategies for leadership. The place of laboratories is discussed, and a case is made for reducing the amount of content typically covered in biology courses.

National Science Resources Center. 1988. *Science for Children: Resources for Teachers.* Washington, DC: National Academy Press.
A valuable compendium of curriculum materials, supplementary resources, and informational sources, with abstracts and price information. A copy of this book has been sent to every school superintendent in the nation and should be in the hands of anyone attempting to use existing materials to update programs. All the materials presented in this guide have been shown to be effective in activity-based, inquiry-oriented programs. For more information, contact: National Science Resources Center, Arts and Industries Building, Room 1201, Smithsonian Institution, Washington, DC 20560.

Office of Educational Research and Improvement. 1989. *Science Education Programs that Work: A Collection of Proven Exemplary Educational Programs and Practices in the National Diffusion Network.* Washington, DC: U.S. Department of Education.
A compendium of 16 program descriptions prepared through the efforts of the National Diffusion Network (NDN). The NDN Program Effectiveness Panel reviews programs reported to be effective, and then disseminates information and materials from those programs that it finds to be exemplary. All programs reported by the NDN are supported by evaluative data.

O'Connell, S. M., V. J. Montenegro, and K. Wolff, eds. 1988. *The Best Science Books and A-V Materials for Children.* Washington, DC: American Association for the Advancement of Science.
A listing of over 800 books and 400 media items that are recommended for use with children in grades K–9. The annotations are based on reviews published in *Science Books and Films*, a periodical produced by the American Association for the Advancement of Science.

O'Neill, John. 1991. *Raising Our Sights: Improving U.S. Achievement in Mathematics and Science.* Alexandria, VA: Association for Supervision and Curriculum Development.
A brief but thorough discussion by a member of the ASCD panel.

Paulu, N. 1991. *Helping Your Child Learn Science.* Washington, DC: Office of Educational Research and Improvement, U.S. Department of Education.
Though designed for parents, this document provides many good examples of simple science activities for children (ages 3 to 10 years) to do in their homes or communities. A useful listing of science books and resources is also included. This document is available from the ERIC Document Reproduction Service (ask for ED number 330 584).

References

American Association for the Advancement of Science. 1989. *Science for All Americans: Summary.* Washington, DC.

Rutherford, F. J., and A. Ahlgren. 1990. *Science for All Americans.* New York: Oxford University Press.

Yager, R. E. 1991. "The Constructivist Learning Model." *The Science Teacher* (Sept.): 52–57.

CURRICULUM GUIDE REPRINT

URRICULUM developers can often find ideas and models through the study of curriculum guides from state departments of education and school districts. In this chapter, we have reprinted the following material:

Living in Water: An Aquatic Science Curriculum. 1989. Baltimore: National Aquarium in Baltimore. Reproduced with permission.

The introductory matter and Section I have been reprinted here. The introductory matter contains a user questionnaire and a narrative section on research. Section I contains ten activities centered around main themes such as water-soluble substances and weather changes. Each activity specifies the skills to be acquired, the main concepts covered, a choice of objectives, the list of materials needed, lesson plans, conclusions, and ideas on how to extend the activity further.

While we are not reprinting the guide in its entirety, the table of contents is provided so that readers can see the entire scope of the guide, with the reprinted sections indicated. The entire 315-page curriculum may be purchased for $10 ($12 west of the Rockies and Canada) from the National Aquarium in Baltimore, Pier 3, 501 E. Pratt St., Baltimore, MD 21202-3194.

LIVING IN WATER

an aquatic science curriculum for grades 4-6
National Aquarium in Baltimore

NATIONAL AQUARIUM IN BALTIMORE

Developed under National Science Foundation grant no. MDR-8470190
2nd Edition, 1989

TEACHER EVALUATION FOR LIVING IN WATER

Please remove and complete this form. Your comments will help us with future projects. Return it to the address below.

State in which you teach _____ date _____

Grade level _____ Subjects _____

Circle all answers that apply.

My school is: **urban   suburban   rural.**

My students are: **at grade level   below grade level   gifted.**

My students are economically: **advantaged   disadvantaged   average.**

Did you receive this curriculum through a workshop? If yes, who did the workshop? _____ Please indicate how you felt about the workshop and about this mode of dissemination.

If no, how did you receive your copy of **Living in Water?**

Have you used this curriculum in class yet? If no, do you plan to use it and how?

If yes, please tell us how it was used and what was most successful.

Please tell us what you like best about **Living in Water.**

Please tell us what you like least, and how to make it better.

Please mail this form and any additional comments to: **Dr. Valerie Chase, Department of Education and Interpretation, National Aquarium in Baltimore, Pier 3, 501 E. Pratt St., Baltimore, MD 21202**

NATIONAL AQUARIUM IN BALTIMORE

Dr. Valerie Chase / Department of Education and Interpretation

Pier 3 / 501 East Pratt Street

Baltimore, Maryland 21202

THANK YOU
FOR
PAYING
POSTAGE

TABLE OF CONTENTS

✓ = included in reprint

✓ **INTRODUCTION** 5

✓ **PROCESS-ORIENTED SCIENCE IN THE CLASSROOM**
The Hands-on Approach: What Research Says 7
Science process skills used in this curriculum 10
Teaching hands-on science 10

✓ **SECTION I:** *SUBSTANCES THAT DISSOLVE IN WATER* 11
Do substances dissolve in water? If so, how do they affect the plants and animals in aquatic habitats?

✓   **SALTS**

        Activity 1 • *The disappearing act* 15
        What happens when different substances are added to water? Experiments that test the conditions that affect rates at which salts and other substances dissolve.
        Activity 2 • *Water, water everywhere* 21
        A classification exercise that defines water environments by saltiness (salinity) as it teaches the use of keys and the characteristics of common water habitats.
        Activity 3 • *Salty or fresh?* 31
        Which is heavier, fresh water or salt water? Experiments which ask questions about the relationship of salinity and heaviness (density) of water.
        Activity 4 • *The layered look* 35
        A demonstration of the distribution of fresh and salt water where fresh- and saltwater environments meet in estuaries.
        Activity 5 • *Some like it salty — some do not!* 39
        A demonstration of how salinity affects the distribution of some aquatic animals, relating salinity to animal distribution within estuaries.
        Activity 6 • *The great salinity contest!* 43
        A contest in which students test their understanding of salinity using experimental techniques to find the winners.

✓   **OXYGEN**

        Activity 7 • *Oxygen for life* 47
        What is the source of the oxygen that is dissolved in water?

✓   **MINERALS**

        Activity 8 • *Soil in water* 51
        What happens when soil erodes from the land and enters aquatic habitats? A long-term experiment.

✓   **POLLUTANTS**

        Activity 9: • *What's in the water?* 55
        What is water pollution? What are the effects of several kinds of pollution on aquatic habitats? A long-term experiment.

✓ **SECTION II:** *TEMPERATURE CHANGES IN AQUATIC HABITATS* 59
What are the characteristics of water with regard to temperature changes? What are the consequences of temperature changes for the plants and animals living in aquatic habitats?

✓   **RATES OF CHANGE**
        Activity 10 • *A change in the weather?* 63
        Which changes temperature faster: water or air? Does the volume of water make a difference in how fast the temperature changes?

TEMPERATURE AND RESPIRATION
Activity 11 • *Plants use oxygen?* 69
Do the plants and animals that live in water use oxygen?
Activity 12 • *When the heat's on* 75
What is the effect of temperature on the rate at which "cold-blooded" organisms that
live in water use oxygen?

TEMPERATURE AND DISSOLVED OXYGEN
Activity 13 • *When the oxygen goes* 81
What happens to the dissolved oxygen when water temperature increases?
Activity 14 • *When the oxygen is gone* 85
How do animals respond to low oxygen environments?

TEMPERATURE AND SEASONAL CHANGES
Activity 15 • *In hot water?* 89
Which weighs more: hot or cold water?
Activity 16 • *The great anadromous fish game* 93
What are some of the factors that determine the reproductive success of fish during
the seasonal migrations of river-spawning, ocean-living species? A life cycle game.
Activity 17 • *A change in the weather* 97
Predicting on seasonal changes in aquatic habitats.

SECTION III: *MOVING OR STAYING PUT: MAINTAINING POSITION WITHIN
AQUATIC HABITATS*.. 101
What are the physical characteristics of water that determine the
kinds of places that aquatic plants and animals live?

PLACES TO LIVE
Activity 18 • *To each its home* 105
Where do animals and plants live and what makes them suited to their homes? A
classification activity that introduces different parts of aquatic habitats.

SINKING OR FLOATING
Activity 19 • *Keeping your head above water* 113
Do things that float or sink behave differently in salt and fresh water? What lets
them float? Why do they sink?
Activity 20 • *Sinking slowly* 117
How do plants, which need light, maintain their position in the water column
if they are heavier than water? How do tiny drifting animals keep from sinking to
the bottom? A contest to design an organism that sinks slowest.
Activity 21 • *Sink or swim* 121
What are some of the special structures that allow fish to stay up in and move
through the water? A fish dissection.
Activity 22 • *Grace under pressure* 127
Does water pressure vary with depth?

LIVING ON SURFACE TENSION
Activity 23 • *Life at the surface* 133
What is the surface of the water like? How can animals take advantage of the water
surface as a place to live? a contest to design a model organism that rides on surface
tension.

MOVING THROUGH WATER
Activity 24 • *At the races!* 139
How do fish swim? What are the correlations between body shape, swimming
technique and speed? To be done on a trip to a public aquarium or science center
which displays fish.

SECTION IV: *LIGHT AND WATER* 143
What happens to light in water, and what are the consequences for plants and animals that live there?

LIGHT AND WATER
Activity 25 • *Light to sea by* 145
What happens to light when it shines through water?
Activity 26 • *Hide and seek* 149
What does it look like under water? What do animals see? Is camouflage the same below water as above?

LIGHT AND PLANTS
Activity 27 • *A light snack* 153
What is the relationship between light availability and photosynthesis in aquatic plants?

AQUATIC FOOD CHAINS
Activity 28: • *Competing for food* 157
What is the relationship of food availability to the number of herbivores an area can support? A simulation game.
Activity 29 • *Eating and being eaten* 163
What are the feeding relationships among the plants and animals that live in a pond? A simulation of carrying capacity and predator-prey relationships.
Activity 30 • *Getting caught* 169
Do some human activities change the feeding relationships, and thus the ecological balance, of a food web? A simulation.

SECTION V: *EXPLORATION, RESEARCH AND COMMUNICATION* 173

EXPLORATION AND RESEARCH
Activity 31 • *Getting to the bottom of things* 175
Can scientists map the bottom of a lake or ocean when they cannot see it? Mapping and sampling a model ocean.
Activity 32 • *Underwater exploration* 181
How is modern technology being used to study the physical, geological, chemical and biological nature of the oceans? Research project on technology and its applications.
Activity 33 • *Getting wet!* 185
An aquatic field investigation.

COMMUNICATION
Activity 34 • *Aquatic language arts* 189
Individual language arts projects with an aquatic theme.
Activity 35 • *Habitat detectives* 191
A group project in library research and communication.
Activity 36 • *Aquatic science symposium* 193
An aquatic conference for parents or other students.

GLOSSARY 195

RECIPES AND RESOURCES
Master list for all materials used in this curriculum 199
Teacher's outline: classroom note cards for each activity 202
Sample questions 219
Salts and solutions 224
Making water with low and high dissolved oxygen 224
Moving water and taking samples 225
Dissolved oxygen test kits 225
LaMotte dissolved oxygen test kit instructions 227

Thermometers 228
Balances 228
Spring scales 228
Measuring time 228
Measuring volume 229
Making graphs 229
Collecting and looking at zooplankton 229
Dissection 230
The classroom aquarium 231
Making water without chlorine or how to age tap water 235
Pond water 236
Elodea 236
Goldfish and guppies 236
Brine shrimp 236
Sources of equipment and animals 237
Sources for curriculum ideas and software 238

STUDENT PAGES FOR DUPLICATION
Graph paper 239
Activity 1 *worksheet* 241
Activity 2 *cards and keys* 243
Activity 3 *worksheet* 250
Activity 4 *worksheet* 251
Activity 5 *worksheet* 252
Activity 6 *worksheet* 253
Activity 7 *worksheet* 254
Activity 8 *worksheet* 255
Activity 9 *worksheet* 256
Activity 10 *worksheet* 257
Activity 11 *worksheet* 259
Activity 12 *worksheet* 261
Activity 13 *worksheet* 263
Activity 14 *worksheet* 264
Activity 15 *worksheet* 265
Activity 16 *game board, cards and rules* 266
Activity 16 *worksheet* 285
Activity 17 *worksheet* 285
Activity 18 *cards and keys* 286
Activity 19 *worksheet* 295
Activity 20 *worksheet* 296
Activity 21 *worksheet* 297
Activity 22 *worksheet* 302
Activity 23 *worksheet* 304
Activity 24 *information pages* 306
Activity 24 *worksheet* 308
Activity 27 *worksheet* 309
Activity 28 *worksheet* 310
Activity 29 and 30 *worksheet* 313
Activity 31 *worksheet* 314

INTRODUCTION

"Living in Water" is a scientific study of water, aquatic environments and the plants and animals that live in water. It was written for grades four through six, but many activities may also be of interest for use with older students. This curriculum covers both marine and freshwater habitats. Each of five sections addresses a question about water which is then answered by a variety of activities using an experimental, science process approach to enable the students themselves to arrive at answers. Each section is preceded by teachers' information with science content related to the activities written for the teacher. The emphasis for the students is not on content, but on process.

While a teacher may pick and choose from among these activities, the curriculum is organized in a way that builds a body of experience in a logical sequence. Teachers may also find ideas for science fair projects or learning centers among these activities.

In addition to experiments and classification activities, several exercises test the application of basic principles through the development of models. Following each exercise, extension activities enable students to pursue a variety of related topics. Some allow students to apply the results of their experiments to specific environmental problems. Other extensions include art and language arts projects. Math is integrated into many of the activities as are graphing skills. There are also suggestions for using a classroom aquarium to further enhance the curriculum.

Supporting materials offer how-to information on preparation of materials and sources of supplies. Worksheets and student information sheets may be used directly or may be replaced by materials prepared by the teacher. The review of what science education research says about the "hands-on" approach to teaching elementary science will help teachers understand why the emphasis in this curriculum is on process. A glossary of terms used is provided for teachers who lack extensive science background.

SUPPORT FOR PROJECT

"Living in Water" was developed by the Department of Education and Interpretation of the National Aquarium in Baltimore under National Science Foundation grant no. MDR-8470190. The LaMotte Chemical Co., the White Rose Paper Co. and the National Aquarium in Baltimore provided additional support.

REPRODUCTION PERMISSION

The National Aquarium in Baltimore retains rights to the curriculum. Worksheets and student materials may be freely duplicated. These materials may not be reproduced for profit. Permission to reproduce them for educational purposes may be obtained by writing the authors.

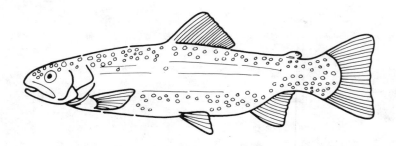

PROJECT PARTICIPANTS AND SEQUENCE

The project started with a three day meeting in July, 1985, of the authors, eight consulting teachers from the Mid-Atlantic states and a science educator. The consulting teachers were: Bonnie Bracey (Washington, DC), Cindy Dean (Delaware), Sarah Duff (Maryland), Margaret Gregory (Virginia), Jean McBean (Maryland), Jo Anne Moore (Maryland), Martin Tillett (Maryland) and Harold Wolf (Pennsylvania). Dr. Leon Ukens, Department of Physics, Towson State University, served as science education consultant. During the following school year, the authors produced first and second drafts of thirty-six activities. In July, 1986, sixteen children tested the activities during a two week class at the Aquarium. Following revision, third drafts went to the consulting teachers, who tested them in their own classes during fall of 1986 and reviewed each activity. The third drafts were read for science education and science content by Dr. Leon Ukens and Gary Heath, environmental education specialist for the Maryland State Department of Education. Dr. Thomas Malone, a biological oceanographer at the University of Maryland Horn Point Environmental Laboratories, and Dr. William S. Johnson, a marine ecologist at Goucher College, read the text for scientific content. During spring of 1987 the activities were rewritten, using comments from the above persons. First distribution was accomplished through two graduate courses for master teachers taught by the authors at Goucher College during July, 1987.

Activities 4, 5 and 24 were written by Karen Aspinwall, education specialist, NAIB. Activities 21, 22 and 23 were done by Lee Anne Campbell, education specialist, NAIB. Activity 18 was written jointly by Lee Anne and Martha Nichols, education specialist trainee, NAIB. Activity 16 was contributed by consulting teacher, Martin Tillett, Howard B. Owens Science Center. All other activities were the work of Dr. Valerie Chase, staff biologist, NAIB, who also served as editor and project director. Martha Nichols proofed final drafts and typeset copy for the entire curriculum. Layout, design and illustration are the work of Cindy Belcher, illustrator, NAIB.

The design, production and dissemination of this material is based upon work supported by the National Science Foundation under grant no. MDR 8470190. However, any opinions, findings, conclusions and recommendations expressed in this publication are those of the authors and do not necessarily reflect the views of the National Science Foundation.

Valerie Chase, Ph. D.
Department of Education and Interpretation
National Aquarium in Baltimore
Pier 3, 501 East Pratt Street
Baltimore, Maryland 21202

May, 1987

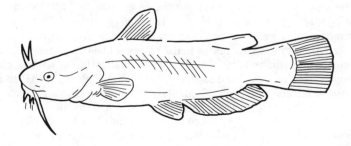

THE "HANDS-ON" APPROACH: WHAT THE RESEARCH SAYS

by
Leon Ukens
Towson State University

The activities in this book are based on a philosophy of science education in the elementary school that has children involved in doing and thinking about science instead of memorizing a lot of factual information. In short, it is a "hands-on" approach. The choice for using this approach is based on years of research evidence on the effectiveness this approach has in helping children learn science. As pointed out by Thier, children need to think about what they are doing. In other words, "hands-on" science needs to be coupled with "heads-on" science (Thier, 1986).

Unfortunately for most children, the "hands-on" approach is seldom used. Instead, in most classes, the textbook has become the sole basis for instruction. Even if the textbook has activities, there is little evidence of children being taught science through firsthand experiences (Stake and Easley, 1978). Secretary of Education Bennett has also noted this in his remarks on elementary education. About science, he said, "We need a revolution in elementary school science. There is probably no other subject whose teaching is so at odds with its true nature. We have come to think of science as a grab-bag of esoteric facts and stunts . . . we have also given students the impression that science is a dry and arcane matter gleaned solely from the pages of a textbook" (Bennett, 1986).

"Hands-on" elementary school science is not new. You probably know about the activity-oriented science curricula developed in the 60's and 70's. Perhaps you even taught, or are teaching, one. The three most widely known of these curricula were the Elementary Science Study (ESS), the Science Curriculum Improvement Study (SCIS), and Science, A Process Approach (SAPA). How effective were they? Did they get children to use higher level thought processes? Many research studies have been conducted in the years since their development to attempt to answer questions such as these. An analysis of analyses (termed a meta-analysis) of these numerous independent research studies comparing the above mentioned projects and other "hands-on" curricula to textbook approaches has been done. Shymansky, Kyle, and Alport (1982) surveyed research studies comparing the performance of children in the above three curriculum projects plus other innovative curricula with the more commonly used textbook approach. In an analysis of 105 experimental studies over the past 25 years involving over 45,000 students, they found that children in the "hands-on" approach out-performed children in textbook programs on every criterion measured. These criteria included academic achievement, attitudes, process skill development, creativity, intellectual development, and performance in related school subjects. As a result of their study, Shymansky and his colleagues concluded that children in "hands-on" science programs "achieved more, liked science more, and improved their skills more than did students in traditional, textbook-based classrooms."

Bredderman (1982) also investigated the effects of the activity-oriented curriculum with textbooks in an analysis involving the experiences of 13,000 students in over 1,000 classrooms in sixty studies over the past 15 years. His findings state: "with the use of activity-based science programs, teachers can expect substantially improved performance in science process and creativity; modestly increased performance on tests of perception, logic, language development, science content, and math; modestly improved attitudes toward science and science class; and pronounced benefits for disadvantaged students." Beane (1985) and Rowe (1975) also point out the positive effects "hands-on" elementary science can have on the disadvantaged child.

Wise and Okey (1983), also using meta-analysis, looked at how various teaching strategies affected achievement in science. They concluded that in an effective classroom, "students get opportunities to physically interact with instructional materials and engage in varied kinds of

---

7

activities." They go on to say that "the effective science classroom reflects considerable teacher planning. The plans, however, are not of a 'cookbook' nature. Students have some responsibility for defining tasks."

Renner (1973) did several research studies involving the effectiveness of SCIS. In one done with fifth graders comparing a "hands-on" approach to one that was not, he concluded that not only were the science processes of manipulating data and interpreting graphs and tables better for the "hands-on" group, but also that the content areas of reading, mathematics and social studies were being enhanced. There seems to be a basic skills development that "hands-on" science does quite well.

In summarizing several research studies, Blosser (1985) concluded that "teachers can help students learn to think scientifically . . . the indirect approach to instruction does appear of value when a teacher's goal is to help students think at a higher level than factual recall.

As a result of the research, Mechling and Oliver (1983) have summarized six important reasons for teaching science from a "hands-on" approach.

1. Students in activity-based science programs outperform students in non-activity programs. The research studies mentioned previously point this out time and time again. The performance is in content areas as well as in the processes of science.
2. Students who have "hands-on" experiences develop thinking skills. The thinking skills include classifying, inferring, hypothesizing, collection and analysis of data, and designing investigations.
3. "Hands-on" activities help students take responsibility for their own learning. The ignited curiosity about things helps to motivate the child to continue questioning and learning in and out of school situations.
4. "Hands-on" activities reinforce what we know about how youngsters learn. From a Piagetian perspective, children learn best by manipulating concrete objects. Language and concepts are learned best by providing the experience first, then the concepts.
5. "Hands-on" activities can reinforce learning in other curricular areas. Wellman (1978) after synthesizing research evidence, concluded that:
   a. Active experience with science helps language and logic development.
   b. Science instruction appears especially helpful for children who are considered physically or culturally different.
   c. Science activities provide a strong stimulus and a shared framework for converting experience into language.
   d. Reading skill development stems from language and logic development, which comes after concepts are formed from repeated encounters with objects and events through science activities.
6. "Hands-on" activities help us avoid the "mindless" curriculum. The mindless curriculum is one that forces children to memorize a lot of factual information without regard to how it all fits together. As an example, probably the most saluted man in America is a man named Richard Stans. Each day numerous children rise and "pledge allegiance to the flag of the United States of America, and to the Republic for Richard Stans . . ."

The challenge you face is to involve your students with this curriculum through a "hands-on" approach. There is much evidence to support this method of teaching if you are interested in bringing science content as well as the methods of science to your students. Challenge them!!

REFERENCES

Beane, DeAnna Banks. 1985. *Mathematics and Science: Critical Filters for the Future of Minority Students.* The Mid-Atlantic Center for Race Equity, The American University, Washington, DC.

Bennett, William J. 1986. *First Lessons, A Report on Elementary Education in America.* Washington, DC: U.S. Department of Education, ED 395.

Blosser, Patricia E. 1985. Meta-analysis research on science instruction. *ERIC/SMEAC Science Education Digest No. 1.*

Bredderman, Ted. 1982. Activity science — the evidence shows it matters. *Science and Children,* Vol. 20. No. 1: 39-41.

Mechling, Kenneth R. and Oliver, Donna L. 1983. *What Research Says About Elementary School Science.* Washington, DC: National Science Teachers Association.

Renner, John W., et. al. 1973. An evaluation of the science curriculum improvement study. *School Science and Mathematics,* Vol. 73, No. 4: 291-318.

Rowe, Mary Budd. 1975. Help is denied to those in need. *Science and Children,* Vol. 12, No. 6: 23-25.

Shymansky, James, Kyle, William Jr., and Alport, Jennifer. 1982. How effective were the hands-on science programs of yesterday? *Science and Children,* Vol. 20, No. 3: 1415.

Stake, Robert E. and Easley, Jack, 1978. *Case Studies in Science Education. Volume 1. The Case Reports.* Washington, DC: U.S. Government Printing Office.

Thier, Herbert. 1986. *Heads on Elementary Science: The Challenge for the Nineties.* Monograph and Occasional Paper Series #1. Council for Elementary Science International.

Wellman, Ruth T. 1978. Science: a basic for language and reading development in *What Research Says to Science Teachers,* Vol. 1. Washington, DC: National Science Teachers Association.

Wise, Kevin C. and Okey, James. 1983. A meta-analysis of the effects of various science teaching strategies on achievement. *Journal of Research in Science Teaching,* Vol. 20, No. 5: 419-435.

SCIENCE PROCESS SKILLS USED IN THIS CURRICULUM

These are science skills that are used in the activities in this curriculum. They are skills that are within the abilities of most children in grades 4-6. The last two are border line for children in this age group and may require special instruction.

Observing: using all five senses; taste is ruled out in many cases as children should not be encouraged to taste unknown substances.

Classifying: identifying like and unlike, and grouping into sets.

Measuring: using numbers to describe size, weight, quantity, volume or time.

Organizing: analyzing and interpreting data, including the use of graphs, charts and tables.

Inferring: drawing conclusions from facts.

Communicating: verbal, written, drawn or other forms of informing others about results.

Predicting: forming hypotheses based on past observations and results.

Experimenting: identifying and controlling variables in testing hypotheses.

TEACHING HANDS-ON SCIENCE

Principals and Parents: Will they understand why your classroom is wet and noisy? Educate your principal and parents by telling them what you plan to do and giving them a copy of Dr. Ukens' article from the preceding pages to help them understand the value of hands-on science.

Materials: Collecting and storing materials can be a pain. We hope the master materials list and addresses of suppliers will help. The entire set of materials other than the classroom aquarium will fit in 6 to 8 copier paper boxes for storage.

Motivation: The best motivation for this curriculum is a good classroom aquarium. Instructions for setting up and maintaining a classroom aquarium are included in the Recipes and Resources section.

Worksheets and Instructions: The "canned" instructions and worksheets are provided for teachers who are short of time or experience in teaching science experiments. If you have the time and teaching experience, please be more creative in having the children work with you to design the activity and the worksheet for reporting their findings. Graph paper that can be copied is provided.

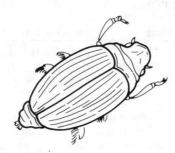

SECTION I.
SUBSTANCES THAT DISSOLVE IN WATER

TEACHER'S INFORMATION

Many substances DISSOLVE (go into SOLUTION) in water. Solids such as salts or sugar, liquids such as alcohol or acetone, and gases from the air all dissolve in water. Water is frequently called the "universal solvent" because so many different kinds of things dissolve in it. Some things do not dissolve in water. The saying that "oil and water do not mix" is based on fact.

Substances that are in solution in the water of a pond, stream, lake or ocean have a direct effect on the plants and animals that live there. Each environment is unique because of these substances. This section discusses the most common things that are in solution in water and the ways that these substances affect plants and animals.

SALTS

SALTS are special compounds that go into solution in water easily. They consist of IONS which are atoms or molecules that have a charge. Positive ions are missing one or more electrons. An example is the sodium ion written Na^+. Negative ions have one or more extra electrons. Negative chloride ions, Cl^-, join with positive sodium ions, Na^+, in a loose lattice in which the positive and negative charges are balanced and the ratio of sodium to chloride is 1:1. The combination is called sodium chloride or NaCl, also known as table salt. There are many different kinds of salts besides table salt. If salts are put into water, they dissolve very rapidly because the ions . are not firmly bound to each other and are attracted to the water molecules.

Because salts dissolve so easily, rain water or melting snow pick them up from the soil as the water runs off to streams or percolates into the ground. Eventually these weak solutions of salts and water reach the ocean or a lake such as the Great Salt Lake which has no outlet. Here the water EVAPORATES into the air, is carried aloft, CONDENSES into rain or snow and falls again on the land where it picks up more salts. Each time the salts remain behind. This water cycle constantly carries more salts to the sea. Over millions of years the oceans have become quite salty. Ocean water is called SALT WATER because of this saltiness. If 1000 g of ocean water is evaporated, 35 g of salts are left behind. This means that 35/1000ths of the weight of sea water is salts. The percent by weight that is salts is calculated by dividing 1000 into 35, which equals 0.035, and then multiplying by 100 to get the percentage. Thus sea water is 3.5% salts by weight. This is also expressed as 35 parts per thousand (ppt). The world's oceans are fairly uniformly 35 ppt salts. In lagoons where evaporation is high, it may be saltier. Salt lakes may also be saltier than the sea. Where a river runs into the sea, the saltiness is lower and is referred to as BRACKISH. The area of brackish water at the river mouth is an estuary.

Not all of the saltiness of the ocean is caused by table salt, NaCl. If you try to keep sea creatures in a solution of table salt, they will die because they require the whole range of kinds of salts in the sea. There are many kinds of things in solution in salt water. The major ions found dissolved in sea water are:

positive ions	ppt	negative ions	ppt
sodium (Na^+)	10.6	chloride (Cl^-)	17.3
magnesium (Mg^{+2})	1.3	sulfate (SO_4^{-2})	2.7
calcium (Ca^{+2})	0.4	bicarbonate (HCO_3^-)	0.7
potassium (K^+)	0.4		

Water that has little dissolved salts is called FRESH WATER. Fresh water is not absolutely pure, however. Even rain picks up things as it falls, hence problems like acid rain. Different bodies of fresh water have different compositions of things in solution, depending on the characteristics of the rock and soil of the region, the plant material that enters the water and the human activities that influence the system.

By definition fresh water is less than 0.5 ppt dissolved salts. This may not seem like much, but fresh water that has a good deal of calcium leaves a white residue behind in tea kettles and coffee makers and requires extra soap in the washing machine. It is often called "hard" water. By comparison "soft" water has little calcium. The differences from one freshwater system to another can directly influence the kinds of plants and animals found there.

OXYGEN

The gases found in air are also in solution in water. The most important to things that live in water is oxygen. In surface waters oxygen is present in the same proportions as in air. Under certain circumstances the amount of oxygen varies in different parts of a body of water. Biological activity, incomplete circulation and the slow DIFFUSION or movement of gases through water contribute to this unequal distribution of oxygen. In a shallow pond rich with plants and animals, the oxygen level may be higher than expected during the day when the plants are producing oxygen during PHOTOSYNTHESIS in excess of the use of oxygen by both plants and animals in RESPIRATION. At night the oxygen falls rapidly as the plants and animals use it during respiration. In the oceans and lakes there are areas where oxygen is low, and mixing and diffusion do not replace it as fast as it is used.

MINERALS

Many other ions and elements are also found dissolved in sea water, including the two MINERALS that are the most essential nutrients for plant growth: PHOSPHORUS as phosphate (PO_4^{-3}) and NITROGEN as ammonium (NH_4^+) or nitrate (NO_3^{-2}).

POLLUTANTS

All sorts of other things end up in solution in water. Many of them are natural products, although human actions may cause levels of these that are higher than would occur naturally. Mercury or nitrates are examples. Others are products which we have manufactured that are entirely new such as pesticides and herbicides and other organic chemicals. Run off may carry farm chemicals into streams and rivers. Factories and cities dump their sewage into SURFACE WATERS (rivers, bays and oceans). Water that percolates down into the soil to the GROUND WATER can carry chemicals from farms or waste disposal sites. Pollution of ground water is a major problem because over half the people in the United States get their drinking water from wells.

Water pollution constitutes a direct health hazard. It also may destroy the plants and animals that live in water environments or may disrupt the relationships between them in such a way that the community structure is changed.

One way of classifying pollution is to separate materials which come from an identifiable source (POINT SOURCE POLLUTION) from those that enter water all along its course (NON-POINT SOURCE POLLUTION). In the past most attention was focused on point source pollution because it was easier to see and identify. Regulators were able to write laws that specified how much pollution came out of a factory or sewage treatment plant. As point source pollution is beginning to come under some degree of control, attention is turning to non-point source pollution. It is important, but hard to define and regulate.

This table shows the basic kinds of water pollution, the sources and forms of discharge or entry to the water. Some of these are under reasonably good control. Others are just beginning to be studied.

kinds of pollution	point source pollution	non-point source pollution
disease organisms	human wastes from sewage treatment plants	some problems where people camp or backpack
man-made and naturally occuring organic compounds	chemical manufacturing plants and disposal; oil spills	agricultural run-off from pesticides, herbicides, and fertilizer
inorganic or mineral compounds; plant nutrients	mining and manufacturing electric power generation; sewage	agricultural run off of fertilizer
radioactive material	mining, manufacturing, accidental, discharge and disposal	airborne following testing or an accident
biological wastes that use oxygen in decomposition	human sewage, animal wastes, agricultural wastes, paper and food processing	some run-off manure
sediment	storm water from drains carrying eroded soil	erosion from fields and developments
heated water	primarily from electrical generating plants; also some from manufacturing	

A problem common in many bodies of water is pollution that results in oxygen use or low DISSOLVED OXYGEN (DO). Oxygen is used faster than it diffuses into the water. It is used by DECOMPOSING organisms which are acting upon such pollutants as sewage or animal wastes. The decomposing organisms may also be feeding on the remains of plants that grew in over-abundance due to excessive fertilization of the water with plant nutrients from human sewage or farm fertilizer. Environments that are very low in oxygen are said to be ANOXIC and are difficult places for most animals to survive. Bodies of water with very low dissolved oxygen may experience major fish kills, especially in summer. Warm water holds less oxygen but at the same time fosters faster decomposition.

As you can see, all sorts of human activities lead to problems of water quality. Different areas have different problems. Depending on where you live, you may want to discuss in some detail certain of these problems. For example, if you are in the northeastern U.S., acid rain may be the biggest current threat to water quality for wildlife. If you are living along the Chesapeake Bay, sediment, human waste and agricultural run-off may be of the greatest concern. In the arid western U.S. agricultural run-off carries inorganic salts that make the run-off salty and may even be toxic to wildlife. If you lived in Russia near the Chernobyl power plant, radioactive waste in the water would be of concern. For many of us downstream from Three Mile Island, it was also a very real concern as the entire Chesapeake could have been contaminated with radioactive materials. Along Lake Superior asbestos particles from mining waste was a problem. Love Canal was ground water contamination in an extreme form. As we learn more, we find new issues to address and new problems to solve.

If you find all this discouraging, do not! We have made progress in some areas. Fish are swimming in some rivers that used to be empty. Lake Erie, once a death trap for fish, seems to be recovering from its abuse. Progress can be made. Public education is a very important part of that progress, because we learn to treat our environment more carefully when we understand the consequences of our actions.

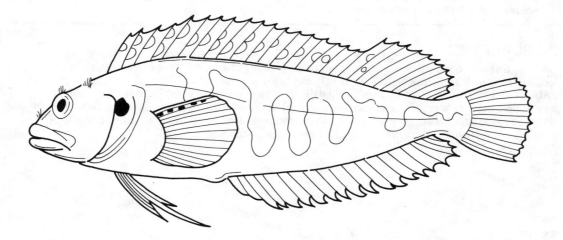

ACTIVITY
1

THE DISAPPEARING ACT

WHAT HAPPENS WHEN DIFFERENT SUBSTANCES ARE ADDED TO WATER?

SCIENCE SKILLS:

- observing
- measuring
- organizing
- inferring
- predicting
- experimenting
- communicating

CONCEPTS:

- Many substances form a solution when mixed with water; some do not.
- Some substances go into solution faster than others.

MATH AND MECHANICAL SKILLS PRACTICED:

- bar graphing
- measuring volumes of fluids and powders

SAMPLE OBJECTIVES:
- Students will design and conduct an experiment to compare rates at which different substances dissolve in water.
- Students will compare different factors which affect rates at which some substances dissolve.
- Students will display data collected in a bar graph.

INTRODUCTION:

In this set of activities, students begin to explore the characteristics of water which relate to forming solutions and suspensions. Table salt and sugar are both among the substances which form a SOLUTION with water: that is, they DISSOLVE, mixing completely with the water and staying mixed. Some substances appear to mix completely, but do not go into solution. When they are allowed to sit undisturbed, they settle out. These compounds are said to form a SUSPENSION. Corn starch is a household compound that forms a suspension with water.

MATERIALS:

FOR CLASS:
- water
- table salt (use canning or kosher salt; see Recipes for discussion)
- granulated table sugar
- corn starch
- large clear glass jar
- package of a dark flavor of unsweetened Kool-aid

FOR EACH GROUP OF STUDENTS:
- 3 clear plastic glasses
- 3 plastic straws or stirrers
- a plastic teaspoon
- 3 pieces of tape or sticky labels
- a graduated measuring cup
- data sheets
- crayons or colored pencils

LESSON PLAN:

BEFORE CLASS:
Read the lesson and gather the materials.

DURING CLASS:
METHODS: As a demonstration, show the students a large clear glass jar of water and a package of unsweetened Kool-aid. Ask them to predict what will happen if you pour the Kool-aid into the water. Do they all agree? Pour the Kool-aid in and see what happens. It should sink and then begin to dissolve and spread (diffuse) through the water. Can the students suggest a way to speed up the process of dissolving? Stirring is one approach. A second would be to use hot water. Introduce the word SOLUTION for the mixture and the word DISSOLVE for the process of mixing completely.

What other things can the students name which they would find around the house that dissolve in water? List them. Show the students the table salt, sugar and corn starch. Ask them to predict whether each will go into solution. If they predict that these substances go into solution, could they design a test of their prediction? Secondly, could the students design a test to discover which dissolves fastest?

Here is a test they might try. Each group should label one clear plastic cup each as salt, sugar and corn starch. Fill each of three plastic cups with about the same volume of water at room temperature. Leave about 1 in of space at the top. Add the equal amounts of salt, sugar and corn starch to the cup of water labelled with that substance. For example, 2 heaping teaspoons to each. Observe what happens for two minutes. Then stir each cup by making a circle around the edge of the cup with the stirrer ten times. Was there a change? Repeat stirring ten times in each until one has completely disappeared or dissolved. Record how many time it was stirred. Continue stirring and observing the other two to find out which dissolves next fastest. Last?

In order for this to be a "fair test" each cup has to be treated exactly the same way. The only thing that can be different is the substance added to each. This is referred to as controlling variables. How you discuss this concept depends on the age of your children.

RESULTS:

Each group should have three numbers which are the number of times each substance was stirred before it dissolved. How do you display such information? A bar graph would be a good way to compare three different things. Make the bar graph of the results. Now compare the results with the predictions. Were there any surprises? Sugar or salt may be faster depending on the size of the crystals in the particular brand you buy. What happened to the corn starch can be the subject of heated debate. Some will say it is in solution and others may not.

Do not throw all the solutions away when students clean up. Save two sets of solutions and place them in a safe place over night. When you check them a day later, you will have proof that the sugar and salt are completely mixed and are in solution while the corn starch was in suspension and has settled out.

CONCLUSIONS:

What conclusions can your students draw from their results? They should be able to state that not all substances go into solution. Corn starch forms a suspension which settles out. They should also be able to observe that some things dissolve faster than others.

EXTENSIONS:

1. Can your students design an experiment to test whether things go into solution faster in hot water? They should be able to state the question, design an experiment in which there is a test (hot water) and a CONTROL for comparison (room temperature water) and carry out their test.

2. Since you have some corn starch around, you might have fun with this demonstration of the fact that corn starch will mix with water when stirred to form a suspension but settles out when allowed to sit. Mix a quarter of a cup of corn starch with just enough water to form a ball. As long as you work it in your hand, it will remain a ball. Let it sit and it collapses into mush.

3. Children enjoy growing crystals, a way of demonstrating how to get subtances out of solution by EVAPORATION of the water. Use very hot water to make a very concentrated solution of salt or sugar. Put the cooled solution in a jar and suspend a nail or nut tied to a string from the surface to the bottom. Put the solutions in a warm, dry spot and check them daily. For details see *Science Scope,* February-March, 1987, pages 8-9.

ACTIVITY 1
THE DISAPPEARING ACT!

Name <u>*Possible answers*</u>

You are going to add table salt, sugar and corn starch to cups of water. What do you guess (predict) will happen to the substance in each cup?

Salt: <u>salt will go away so you can't see it</u>

Sugar: <u>sugar will make the water taste sweet</u>

Corn starch: <u>this looks like it will make lumps</u>

Fill three clear plastic cups with about the same amount of water. Leave about an inch at the top so you can stir. Label each so you know which gets salt, sugar and corn starch.

How many teaspoons will you add to each cup? Circle   1   ②   or   3. Each gets the same number.

After adding the substances, sit and observe for two minutes. What can you see happening?

<u>Both the salt and the sugar fell to the bottom and</u>
<u>spread out. The corn starch made lumps. Some</u>
<u>floated, and some sank. The corn starch water started</u>
<u>looking milky.</u>

Stir each cup 10 times using the same technique. Did any dissolve?

Repeat stirring each 10 times and then observing all of them. Mark out the number of times stirred before a substance dissapeared if it did so.

Salt:
~~10~~ ~~20~~ ~~30~~ ~~40~~ ~~50~~ ~~60~~ 70 80 90 100 110 120 130 140 150 160 170 180 190 200

Sugar:
~~10~~ ~~20~~ ~~30~~ ~~40~~ ~~50~~ ~~60~~ 70 80 90 100 110 120 130 140 150 160 170 180 190 200

Corn starch:
~~10~~ ~~20~~ 30 40 50 60 70 80 90 100 110 120 130 140 150 160 170 180 190 200

Make a bar graph of these results:

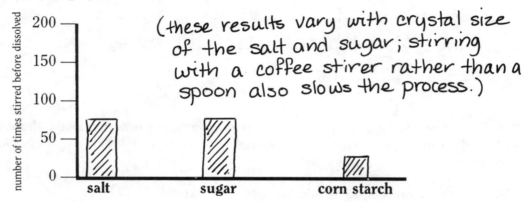

(these results vary with crystal size of the salt and sugar; stirring with a coffee stirer rather than a spoon also slows the process.)

Did each dissolve? _yes, it looked like they did. Then I let the corn starch sit, and it settled out so it didn't really._

Which dissolved fastest? _Salt and sugar tied (varies with crystal size)_

Write a complete sentence that is one conclusion that you could make based on the results of your experiment.

In my experiment salt and sugar both went into solution, but corn starch did not. Salt and sugar dissolved at the same rate.

Note: Compare results from different groups. Why weren't they all the same? Variables were controlled within each group but not between groups. Some used different amounts of H_2O and substances.

19

ACTIVITY
2

WATER, WATER EVERYWHERE
CLASSIFYING DIFFERENT KINDS OF AQUATIC HABITATS

SCIENCE SKILLS:
• classifying

CONCEPTS:
• Characteristics observed about a thing allow you to find its name and to place it in a system that groups similar things.
• An introduction to aquatic habitats.

MATH AND MECHANICAL SKILLS PRACTICED:
• following a flow chart
• using a key

SAMPLE OBJECTIVES:
• Students will be able to classify different kinds of aquatic habitats.
• Students will use a flow chart and/or a scientific key.

INTRODUCTION:

This activity introduces students to classification of habitats using their physical characteristics. Students use a FLOW CHART to visualize the process of classification. At each step they must choose between two characters in order to proceed to the next step. They may also use a scientific KEY to identify aquatic habitats. Students will learn about these habitats as they do the exercise.

MATERIALS:

• blow-up of habitat flow chart on blackboard or bulletin board
• duplicates of habitat cards (1 per student) (may use line drawings or may add photographs of appropriate aquatic habitats from magazines
• copies of flow charts and keys for students

OPTIONAL:

• salt water made with 35 gm (3 tbsp) table salt per liter (quart) water
• tap water for fresh water
• mix of tap water and salt water for brackish water
• small disposable paper cups for each child

INFORMATION:

When humans name things, they are CLASSIFYING them. Things that are classified are first named and then placed in larger groups of things that share similar characteristics. For example, many kinds of tables are lumped under the term "table" as are many kinds of chairs under "chairs." Both tables and chairs belong to a larger category, furniture. The inclusion in ever larger groups results in a hierarchical organization.

21

Why bother with classifying things? Classification requires that we look for relationships among things which enhance our understanding of their functions and characters. Also, knowing that something belongs to a certain group means that you know something about it if you are familiar with the characteristics of the group.

LESSON PLAN
BEFORE CLASS:

Read the exercise and plan which parts you will do. Make habitat cards. You may just duplicate the cards at the end of this section. For nicer cards, glue them to one side of stiff paper and add pictures of the same habitat to the reverse side. Ask parents to donate magazines like *National Geographic.* Aides or students may cut out pictures. Laminate the cards to last for years. You might not find pictures of all of the habitats — it's okay to leave some out. Make duplicates of the most common ones. Duplicate the flow chart and key.

DURING CLASS:

METHODS: Begin by asking if the students know what the word HABITAT means. It is the place where a plant or animal normally lives and is usually characterized by a dominant plant or a set of physical characters. Can they name any AQUATIC places (water habitats) where plants and animals live? Write their suggestions on the board. Can they tell you what kind of water each has? Make sure that they know the terms SALT WATER, FRESH WATER and BRACKISH WATER. Salt water has the salinity of the oceans, fresh water has little or no salt (you cannot taste any) and brackish water is a mix of salty ocean water and fresh water so it tastes less salty than the ocean. If you would like, you can have your students taste samples of each. A sip of salty water made with table salt will not hurt though it does taste bad. To make your point about brackish water, mix the fresh water with the salt water while they watch.

Now each student is going to become a mystery aquatic habitat. Each will discover what he/she is by following a CLASSIFICATION system that divides habitats up by their CHARACTERISTICS. Students will know what their characteristics or traits are from cards that tell them what they are like.

Explain that when identifying things using a system of classification, one starts with the biggest category and begins to work down to small groups. Here the first category is aquatic habitats, and the characteristic they have in common is that they all are in water. Use the flow chart on the board and have a student read one card aloud to demonstrate that at each stage, they must make a choice between two things until they come to a group in which all the things have the same characters and cannot be divided further. This is their aquatic habitat.

Pass out the cards and give all time to read them. Would they like to make a guess about what kind of habitat they are? Have them write their guess. Distribute flow charts and let them work until they have identified themselves. Trade cards for more practice.

The key is harder to use. With younger children you may delete it. With older children you may repeat the same process of one demonstration followed by independent work that you used for the flow chart.

RESULTS:

Check results of following the flow chart or keying habitats out by comparing answers with the teacher's answers provided.

CONCLUSIONS:

Have the class make a list of the important characteristics used in this exercise to classify aquatic environments. These are some of them:
- salt or fresh water
- flowing or still water
- tides or currents or waves
- shallow or deep
- sandy, rocky or muddy bottom
- plants submerged or sticking out of the water
- near shore or away from land

USING YOUR CLASSROOM AQUARIUM:

Discuss with your students the following questions:
- Which aquatic habitat most resembles your classroom aquarium?
- Does it have fresh or salt water?
- What kind of bottom does it have?
- Does the water flow or stand still?

Try keying it out. The gravel on the bottom may be a problem.

EXTENSIONS:

1. One way for students to test their own knowledge of aquatic habitats following this activity is to have the pictures of water habitats mounted on cards with a string long enough to hang them around the students' necks. The name of the habitat should be written on the back of each card. Students must find out what kind of water habitat they are by asking other students yes/no questions about themselves.

2. Have each student write several paragraphs about how it would feel to be an animal that lived in his/her aquatic habitat. Include a discussion of some of the problems each would face in making a living. Make sure the student has a picture of the habitat to help with writing.

3. On a map of your state, help your students locate the aquatic habitats they may have seen locally. While landlocked states are limited to freshwater habitats or salt lakes, states like Florida have almost everything but kelp forests. A U.S. map with markings for depth in the ocean would help you locate the saltwater habitats.

4. Research naming in other societies. Different cultures use different degrees of refinement when they create categories of names. This degree of detail in naming is frequently based on the importance of the items in their culture. For example: the South American cowboys, gauchos, have some two hundred different words or names for horse colors, but divide all plants into only four categories depending on their use in ranching.

5. Compare common names and their local origins with scientific names. Scientists use a formal classification system in giving names to plants and animals which gives each kind of plant or animal a name consisting of two words which is unique to that species. An animal's scientific name is the same anywhere in the world. Since the scientific name is based on Latin and Greek words, most people give plants and animals a common name in their own language. Because these are arrived at informally, they vary from place to place and can be very confusing because the same animal may have several different common names.

6. To test student understanding of the principles governing classification and the construction of keys, have students classify groups of other things and make their own key. Creative choices of things might include keys to different groups of adventure toys, model collections or rock groups. Let them trade keys to test the quality of their work. There should be at least ten items in each key.

AQUATIC HABITAT CARDS:

Your rocky shore is covered with seaweeds that live attached to the rocks. When the salt water is at low tide, the sun or snow or rain falls on your seaweeds and animals. Waves crash into you, so animals and plants have ways of clinging tightly to your rocks.
YOU ARE _a rocky intertidal_

Salt water mixes with fresh water from a river in your wide shallow waters. You have lots of food for fish and crabs in your open waters above your muddy bottom. You are a nursery for many ocean animals.
YOU ARE _an estuary_

You have salt water and are a big body of water. When the wind blows, waves roll over your surface. During storms the waves get huge. Things on you are far from land.
YOU ARE _an ocean_

You have cold, salt water. You are found near rocky shores. Your plants and animals are always covered by your cold water. You have forests of seaweeds called kelp which hide hundreds of kinds of animals.
YOU ARE _a kelp forest_

AQUATIC HABITAT CARDS:

Your fresh water flows over a wide, muddy bottom. Big catfish lurk in your murky waters. Cities were located on you because in the old days you were the easiest place to travel. Barges are towed up and down you in many states even today.
YOU ARE _a river_ .

Grasses grow out of your still, fresh waters. Red-winged blackbirds build nests in the grasses. The air is filled with the calls of the male blackbirds.
YOU ARE _freshwater marsh_

Your brackish water is full of nutrients for the tall grasses that emerge along your shore. In the winter these grasses die, but each spring they come back from their strong roots. The decaying grass particles are food for crabs and oysters. The grasses protect the shore from storms.
YOU ARE _a salt marsh_

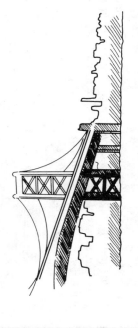

Your quiet, fresh waters are home to many fish which hide deep beneath your surface. Storms may make waves on your wide surface. Where winters are very cold, you may be covered with ice.
YOU ARE _a lake_

AQUATIC HABITAT CARDS:

You have salt water that rises and falls with the tides. Sometimes the waves roll way up on your sand while at other times much of your sand is not covered with water. Children play on you. When a storm comes, your sand is moved all around.
YOU ARE a sandy beach

Your warm, salt water and rocky bottom provide the perfect place for animals called corals to grow. Their skeletons make a great place for fish to live. Because you are in a place that is warm all year-round, you are a tropical habitat. Tourists swim out from the beach to visit you.
YOU ARE a coral reef

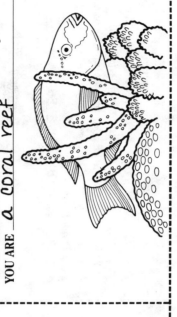

Bushes and mosses grow in your shallow, still water. Patches of very wet ground are home to pitcher plants which get their nutrients from the insects they catch in their leaves. Your water is fresh, but very acid.
YOU ARE a bog

Your sandy or muddy bottom is under salt water. In some places the water is deep, but you are along the shore. Animals burrow in your sand or mud. Your water is rich in tiny plants which provide food for many animals. Fishermen harvest your animals.
YOU ARE the continental shelf

AQUATIC HABITAT CARDS:

Short trees line the shores of your brackish or salt water. Their big roots hold the trees in the mud, even when hurricanes disturb your constant warm days. Many animals and plants find a home on your tree roots or in your waters. Because it is warm all year-round, you are said to be a tropical habitat.

YOU ARE ___a mangrove swamp___

Sun shines through your shallow, open, fresh water, allowing underwater plants to grow on the bottom. Still and small, you may freeze solid where winters are cold. In the summer turtles bask on your shore and deer drink from you.

YOU ARE ___a pond___

Underwater fields of plants grow in your shallow, brackish water or salt water. Many animals find food and shelter among the plants. The plants protect the nearby shore from erosion because they break the force of the waves.

YOU ARE ___a sea grass bed___

Your fresh water tumbles down over rocks and through small pools where fish and crayfish hide. Your water comes from rain that runs off the land and from springs that bring underground water to the surface.

YOU ARE ___a stream or creek___

AQUATIC HABITAT CARDS:

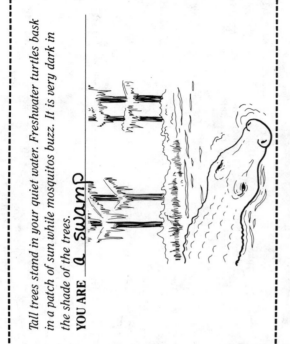

Tall trees stand in your quiet water. Freshwater turtles bask in a patch of sun while mosquitos buzz. It is very dark in the shade of the trees.

YOU ARE ___a swamp___

Your water is very salty, saltier than the sea. Water flows into you, but there is no way for it to leave except by evaporation in the hot sun. You form in low areas in deserts.

YOU ARE ___a salt lake___

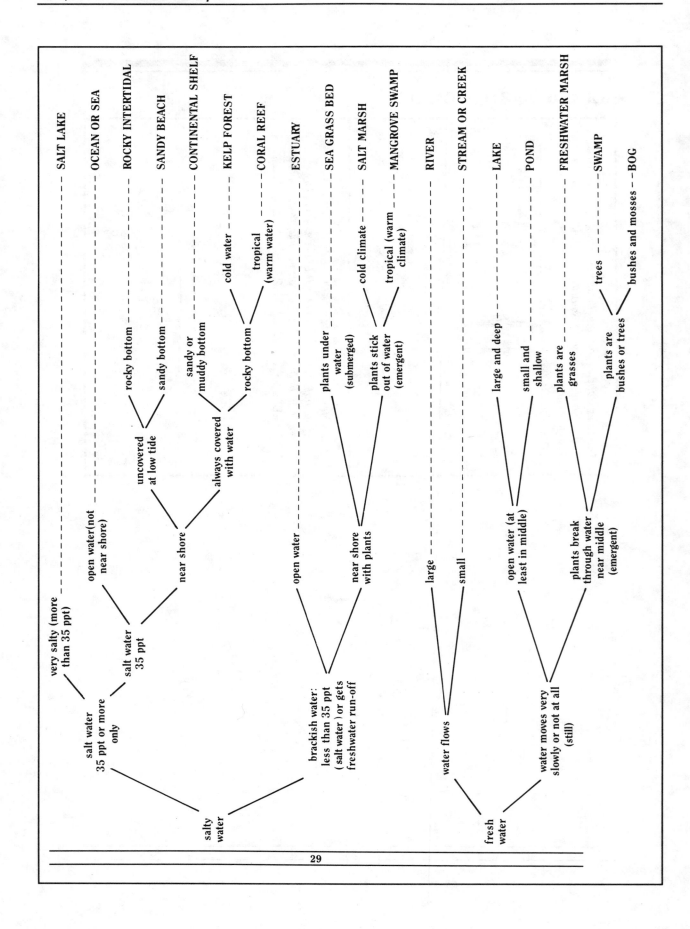

WATER HABITATS

1. Water is salty 2
1. Water is fresh 12
2. Water is salt water (sea water) or saltier than sea water only 3
2. Water is brackish, less salty than the sea or salt water 9
3. Water is saltier than sea water .... **SALT LAKE**
3. Water is salt water, 35 ppt* 4
4. Open water, not near shore .... **OCEAN OR SEA**
4. Near shore 5
5. Part uncovered at low tide 6
5. Always covered with water 7
6. Sandy .... **SANDY BEACH**
6. Rocky .... **ROCKY INTERTIDAL**
7. Bottom of sand or mud .... **CONTINENTAL SHELF**
7. Bottom hard and rocky 8
8. Cold water and cold winters (temperate) .... **KELP FOREST**
8. Warm waters and warm climate year-round (tropical) .... **CORAL REEF**
9. Open water .... **ESTUARY**
9. Near or at shore with green, rooted plants 10
10. Plants are entirely under the water (submerged) .... **SEA GRASS BED**
10. Plants grow out of the water (emergent) 11
11. Climate is cold during winter (temperate) .... **SALT MARSH**
11. Climate stays warm all year (tropical) .... **MANGROVE SWAMP**
12. Water flows in a definite bed 13
12. Water appears not to move at all unless windy (still) 14
13. Large, flowing over muddy bottom .... **RIVER**
13. Small, flowing over sandy or rocky bottom .... **STREAM OR CREEK**
14. Has open water although shores with plants are around it 15
14. Plants grow out of the water all over (emergent) 16
15. Large and deep; plants grow under water only near shore .... **LAKE**
15. Small and shallow; plants grow under water everywhere .... **POND**
16. Plants are grasses .... **FRESHWATER MARSH**
16. Plants have woody branches; they are trees or bushes 17
17. Plants are trees with definite trunk .... **SWAMP**
17. Plants are bushes; moss grows on ground .... **BOG**

*35 ppt is a way of expressing how salty the water is in the ocean or other saltwater habitats; if you had one kilogram of sea water, 35 grams of the weight would be salt.

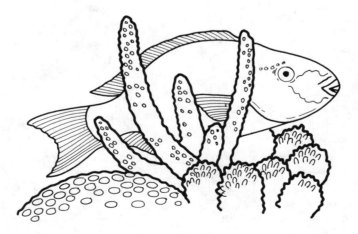

ACTIVITY
3

SALTY OR FRESH?
WHICH IS HEAVIER, FRESH WATER OR SALT WATER?

SCIENCE SKILLS:
- observing
- measuring
- predicting
- experimenting
- inferring
- communicating

CONCEPTS:
- If temperatures are the same, salt water is heavier than fresh water.
- Fresh water floats on salt water because it is lighter (less dense).

MATH AND MECHANICAL SKILLS PRACTICED:
- use of spring scale, simple balance or triple beam balance

SAMPLE OBJECTIVES:
- Students will be able to state experimental evidence proving that salt water is heavier than fresh water.
- Students will learn to control variables.
- Students will be able to compare relative weights.

INTRODUCTION:
This exercise examines the relationship of salinity to weight (density) of solutions. Subsequent studies show how these relationships determine the distribution of fresh and salt water where a river enters the ocean and forms an ESTUARY.

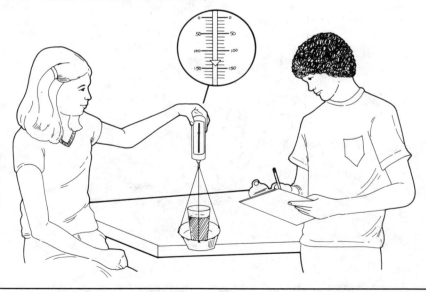

MATERIALS:

FOR EACH GROUP:
- tape or marking pen
- food coloring in dropper bottle
- 4 clear plastic cups
- plastic teaspoon

FOR CLASS:
- measuring cups or plastic graduated cylinders
- simple balances (if you use triple beam balances instead, have a training session on use)
- simple 250 gm spring scales if available
- one gallon of salt water (1 cup salt per gallon) at room temperature
- one gallon of tap water (fresh water) at room temperature
- a heavy coffee mug or cup

LESSON PLAN:
BEFORE CLASS:
Assemble the materials and read the entire lesson. If you use triple beam balances, you will have to train students to use them ahead of time. Simple balances that compare two items at once may require some testing by students before they believe that the heavier item pulls its side down and lifts the other up. Simple spring scales may require a bit of practice with reading the scale. If the spring scales lack pans, make them from small aluminum or plastic pans (frozen meat pies) and three pieces of string.

DURING CLASS:
Ask the class how they would determine which was heavier: salt water or fresh water? They will probably suggest weighing the solutions. Use a balance and two clear plastic cups of water, one with twice as much water as the other to demonstrate. Ask them if this is a "fair test". Why not? The students should be able to tell you that you must use the same amount or volume of water to tell which is heavier. Then demonstrate with a plastic glass and a heavy ceramic coffee cup filled with equal volumes of water. Is this a "fair test"? Again, they should say no and identify the difference in weight of the two containers as the problem. What rule would they have to follow for this to be a "fair test"? There can be only one difference between the two items tested, in this case, the amount of salt in the water.

Can your students do a "fair test" to answer the question you first asked: which is heavier, salt water or fresh water? Let individual groups try without telling them exactly what to do. Let them make mistakes and discuss these mistakes among themselves. They may compare equal volumes of salt and fresh water on a simple balance or they may weigh equal volumes with a scale or triple beam balance.

After most groups have answered the question, have everyone settle down and state his/her results. Salt water is heavier. Now can the students predict what would happen when fresh water meets salt water? This happens where a river flows into the sea. Have them state their predictions. Now how can they test their predictions using clear plastic glasses, salt and fresh water, food coloring and a teaspoon? Give them these materials and let them experiment. Do not tell them what to do right away.

They may add food coloring to the salt water as a marker and see what happens when a little salt water is carefully laid on top of a cup of fresh water with the teaspoon. (See the illustration for technique.) The salt water should sink to the bottom, indicating that it is heavier. Try the reverse with colored fresh water and plain salt water to prove that the food coloring is not causing the result.

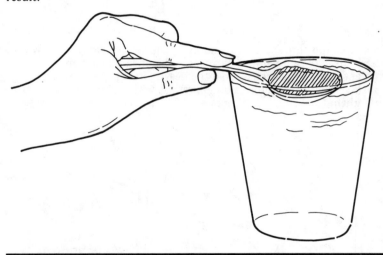

RESULTS:

If equal volumes of salt and fresh water are compared in containers that are identical, the salt water weighs more than the fresh water. When salt water is gently placed on the surface of fresh water, it can be seen to sink. Fresh water gently placed on the surface of salt water floats at the surface.

CONCLUSIONS:

Salt water is heavier than fresh water when both solutions are the same temperature. (Temperature as a variable will come in a later activity.) When two things of equal volume are compared, the heavier is said to be more DENSE.

USING YOUR CLASSROOM AQUARIUM:

Is your classroom aquarium fresh water or salt water? How could your students test the water to find out? It could be compared with fresh and salt water in the same tests done above.

ACTIVITY 3
SALTY OR FRESH?

Name __Possible answers__

Which is heavier: salt water or fresh water? __Salt water__

How did you compare salt and fresh water to reach your conclusion? _____

__I used a spring scale to compare equal volumes of__
__salt and fresh water. Salt water weighed more.__
__Then I layered salt water onto fresh water.__

What happened when salt water and fresh water were very gently layered on each other? Draw and label your results.

fresh water
salt water

when I layered fresh water onto salt water, the fresh water floated.

fresh water
salt water

When I layered salt water onto fresh water, the salt water sank.

Predict what might happen to the distribution of salt and fresh water in the mouth of a river where it meets the sea.

__I think the salt and fresh water might__
__form layers the way the water in my__
__glass did.__

34

ACTIVITY
4

THE LAYERED LOOK
A DEMONSTRATION OF THE DISTRIBUTION OF FRESH AND SALT WATER IN AREAS WHERE FRESH AND SALT WATER MEET IN ESTUARIES.

SCIENCE SKILLS:
- observing
- predicting
- communicating

CONCEPTS:
- Stratification occurs in estuaries where fresh water meets salt water.
- Fresh water will tend to flow above the saltwater layer.
- Some mixing occurs where the two layers meet.

SAMPLE OBJECTIVE:
- Students will be able to describe and explain the distribution of salt and fresh water in an estuary.

INTRODUCTION:
An ESTUARY is defined as a semi-enclosed body of water where incoming seawater is diluted with fresh water coming from the land. Because of the differences in weight (density) between fresh and salt water, salt water will move upstream in the estuary along the bottom, while fresh water will flow downstream along the surface. This causes a layered condition. Some mixing occurs at the interface where fresh and salt water meet. The layered condition is said to be STRATIFED. This teacher-led demonstration illustrates the stratification that may occur in estuaries. You can go directly from this activity to Activity 5 as this is the set-up for the next demonstration. *The thin separator tank from Concepts of Science for the fifth grade may be used in this activity.*

MATERIALS:

- colored markers or crayons
- 2 clear plastic containers such as sweater boxes or small aquaria; may use clear glass 1 gallon jars or large glass or plastic bowls
- 2 siphons — clear plastic tubing (see Recipes)
- 1 gallon of clear aged fresh water
- 1 gallon of aged fresh water with 8 drops of green food coloring
- 1 gallon of clear aged salt water (1 cup salt per gallon)
- 1 gallon of aged salt water (1 cup salt per gallon) with 8 drops of green food coloring

LESSON PLAN:
BEFORE CLASS:
Gather all materials. Make up the saltwater solutions and label bottles. This exercise works best as a teacher-led demonstration so plan a spot where all the children have a clear view on a solid surface that they cannot move as they crowd around. Aged water which has been sitting open at least overnight insures that the next activity will not hurt the animals.

DURING CLASS:

METHODS: Start by asking the students what happens when salt water meets fresh water. They may remember from Activity 2 that salt water and fresh water mixed give BRACKISH water. After Activity 3, they may also suggest that the heavier salt water will settle near the bottom, while the fresh water floats near the top.

Let's see what happens when a large body of salt water meets fresh water in a model ESTUARY. Have the students place themselves so that they can see without bumping the demonstration.

Fill one container 1/3 full with clear aged fresh water. Then slowly siphon in the colored salt-water solution, keeping the siphon tube near, but not on, the bottom of the container. A colored salt solution layer will form on the bottom of the container. Have a student hold this siphon while you do the reverse with clear salt water and colored fresh water in another container. You should end up with two stratified systems with the color on top in one and on the bottom in the other. The best way to see this is to look from the side, not the top.

RESULTS:

Ask the students to observe the containers of water. Questions to get a discussion going might include: How many layers formed? Two. Which layer is salty? Bottom. Which layer is fresh? Top. Are they completely separate? No. Is something happening at the interface between the two layers? Yes. What? Mixing is occurring. What would happen if one measured the salinity at differing depths from surface to bottom in an estuary? Salinity would increase with depth.

Why did we do this twice? The food coloring added a second variable. When it was used in the reverse order in the second experiment, you proved it was not the cause of the results.

Have the students record the results on their data sheets, using crayons or markers to indicate the location of the colored water layer. Have them label each layer of water in each container, and then fill out the rest of the data sheet.

CONCLUSIONS:

Because salty water is more dense than fresh water, it sinks below fresh water when the two come into contact. While there is some mixing at the boundary, a stratified system with regard to salinity is formed. The distribution of salinities in an estuary reflects this relationship.

USING YOUR CLASSROOM AQUARIUM:

If you do this exercise before you set up your classroom aquarium, use the tank for one model estuary.

EXTENSIONS:

1. Challenge the students to decide how they could more clearly see the mixing. Try using two different food colors in the fresh and salt water solutions which when combined produce a third where mixing takes place (for example, yellow and blue to make green).

2. Draw the distribution of salt and fresh water on the board in a cross section of a typical estuary as shown here. Include the directions of water flow. Have the students consider how the animals in an estuary might use these currents. Can they think of what animals could do with these currents of water in an estuary? Travel or MIGRATE. Animals that cannot actively swim, like ZOOPLANKTON, but that can go up and down in the water, could travel up and down the estuary by staying near the top or the bottom.

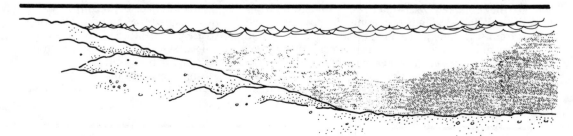

ACTIVITY 4:
THE LAYERED LOOK

Name Possible answers

State the question you are trying to answer by observing this demonstration.

What happens when salt water and fresh
water are gently added to each other?
What might happen where a river meets
the sea?

Draw the results of the demonstration here:

First tank or jar   second tank or jar

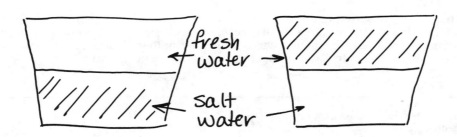

Based on the results of this demonstration, where would you expect to find the saltiest water if you were studying the mouth of a river where it formed an estuary as it meets the ocean? The top of the water or the bottom?

I would expect the salt water to be on the
bottom. If the water were mixed, maybe
by the wind, the two kinds of water might
mix as it did when John kept bumping
the table.

ACTIVITY
5

SOME LIKE IT SALTY—SOME DO NOT!
A TEACHER-LED DEMONSTRATION THAT SHOWS HOW SALINITY MAY AFFECT THE DISTRIBUTION OF SOME AQUATIC ANIMALS.

SCIENCE SKILLS:

- observing
- inferring
- predicting
- experimenting
- communicating

CONCEPTS:

- Salinity is one factor which helps determine where animals and plants live in an estuary.
- Animals can sense the salinity and move to the best location.

SAMPLE OBJECTIVE:
- Students will be able to explain how adaptation to a particular salinity may affect where an aquatic animal lives.

INTRODUCTION:

This demonstration uses the two stratified systems made in Activity 4. It shows that animals may select a position in the water based on the distribution of salinities. Do this as a demonstration and do not substitute species of fish. The species suggested are tolerant to salt and will not be harmed by short exposure. If you cannot find adult brine shrimp, skip that part of the activity.

MATERIALS:

- both demonstration jars or tanks from Activity 4
- small dip net
- 2 or more small goldfish or tropical guppies (see Recipes)
- several dozen adult brine shrimp (see Recipes)

INFORMATION:

Salinity is an important factor in determining the distribution of living things in an estuary. Marine organisms inhabit the mouth of the estuary, where high salinity occurs. Travelling up the estuary along decreasing salinity gradients, marine populations decline and are replaced by organisms that can TOLERATE different ranges of salinities. Freshwater species are found at the mouths of tributaries leading into the estuary and in upper estuarine waters. In part, due to this wide range of salinities, there are many different habitats in an estuary.

Some species of animals and plants can TOLERATE wide ranges of salinities while others have NARROW requirements. In both cases, they will seek the water with salinities within their range of tolerance. In the case of plants and those animals like oysters which live attached as adults, their location is determined by salinities present when the seeds germinated or the animal larvae settled. Animals that can swim may move to remain in the OPTIMAL or best salinity. Other factors that influence habitat selection include temperature, food supply, predators and oxygen levels.

LESSON PLAN:
BEFORE CLASS:
Order brine shrimp and fish. If brine shrimp are not available from a pet store or supply catalog, skip them. Do not use newly hatched brine shrimp as they are too small to see. Do not use fish other than goldfish or guppies. Feed the fish well.

DURING CLASS:
METHODS: Begin by asking the students what would happen if animals were introduced to the estuarine model you have created. The amount of salt in the water might influence where the animals stay in the container. How might the stratification of salt/fresh water influence their behavior? Animals that live in fresh water normally might migrate to the top and stay there. Those that live in salt water might stay near the bottom.

Introduce the guppies or goldfish and adult brine shrimp. Have the students predict which part of the model estuary each might prefer. Since guppies/goldfish are freshwater animals, they might prefer fresh while the name brine shrimp might imply that these residents of salt lakes would do best in salt water. Using the net, gently transfer fish into each container and let the students observe their swimming pattern. The students must remain quiet and not scare the fish. Questions to get a discussion going might include: How many times does each animal swim the entire depth of the container? Where does it end up swimming most of the time? You may get numerical data by assigning students to record how many fish are in each layer every minute for 5 minutes.

Next drop adult brine shrimp into each container. Observe the behavior exhibited for several minutes, and ask the same questions. Did the addition of brine shrimp alter the fishes' behavior? They may try to eat the brine shrimp, indicating that food also influences distribution.

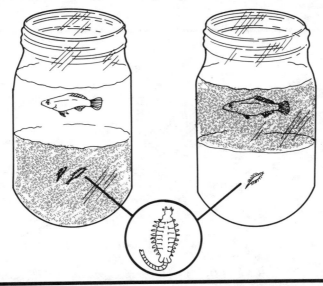

RESULTS:
Record results. Ask the students in what water habitats they might look for these fish and brine shrimp in nature, based on their observations. Goldfish and guppies prefer fresh water while brine shrimp live in salt lakes and can tolerate very high salinity.

Why did you use two tanks, one with colored fresh water and the other with colored salt water? Coloring might have affected distribution. If you use too much food coloring, the guppies may try to avoid it.

CONCLUSIONS:

Aquatic animals that can swim choose the place where they live based on many factors, one of which is salinity. In a stratified system some species might always be at the surface while others are always at the bottom. Even though they are at the same spot on a map, in three dimensions they may be vertically separated and will not come in contact with each other. When possible, aquatic animals will avoid water in which the salinity is outside their range of TOLERANCE and will seek OPTIMUM situations.

USING YOUR CLASSROOM AQUARIUM:

The fish from this exercise may come from your aquarium and may return there when done. The brine shrimp will make welcome food for your tank's inhabitants.

EXTENSIONS:

1. What are the effects of too much salt or too little salt on an organism? You could study this by immersing plant tissue (potato) in very salty and in fresh water. Generally, tissue loses water (weight) in salt water and gains it in fresh. The causes of this are somewhat difficult to adequately discuss at the elementary level and require an understanding of the diffusion of water through membranes. The what is easy to see, but the why is not. You might also put leaves from an aquatic plant in both fresh and salt water if you have microscopes to study the results. Draw the before and after of each.

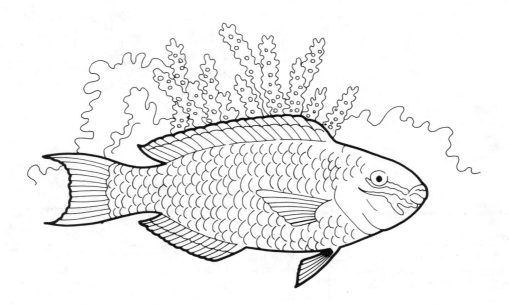

ACTIVITY 5
SOME LIKE IT SALTY — SOME DO NOT!

Name _Possible answers_

Predict which layer(s) the animals will prefer. _Since my goldfish at home like water out of the tap, I think they will like the fresh water at the top. I don't know what the brine shrimp will like._

Draw the two tanks. Label the salty and fresh water. Draw the animals in the locations they prefer.

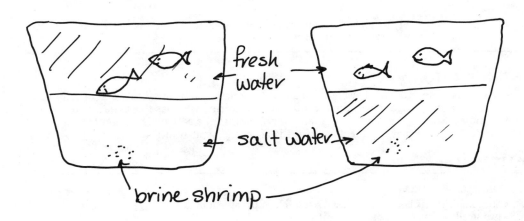

Did the animals always stay in the same kind of water? If not, describe their behavior.

No. The goldfish tried swimming in the salt water but they went back up to the fresh water.

ACTIVITY
6

THE GREAT SALINITY CONTEST!
OR WHO HAS THE SALTIEST AND THE FRESHEST WATER?

SCIENCE SKILLS:
• observing
• measuring

CONCEPTS:
• Water containing dissolved salts is heavier (more dense) than fresh water.

MATH AND MECHANICAL SKILLS PRACTICED:
• measuring volume
• weighing
• use of balance

SAMPLE OBJECTIVE:
• Students will be able to apply their knowledge about weight (density) of salt and fresh water to determine the relative salinity of unknown solutions.

INTRODUCTION:

Now that your students have learned about the relationships of salinity and density, have them put their knowledge to work in a contest by discovering who has the saltiest and the freshest water samples. Students receive the samples at random, so the activity is a lottery of sorts. The prizes to the winners may be objects or rewards of special opportunities.

MATERIALS:

FOR EACH STUDENT:
• one sample jar of about a pint (plastic soft drink bottle, peanut butter jar, large paper cup)
• two small clear plastic cups
• a plastic spoon

SHARED BY CLASS:
• volume measuring devices such as measuring cups or plastic graduated cylinders
• scales and/or balances
• food coloring in dropper bottles
• water samples of three different salinities: fresh water, water with salt at 1/4 cup per quart and water at 1/2 cup salt per quart (use kosher or canning salt, not table salt; see Recipes)
• prizes for the contest: stickers, a puzzle or maze, pencils, free time, anything that is small, but fun to win

LESSON PLAN:
BEFORE CLASS:

Collect the containers for each student. (Students may have brought them from home.) Put a number on each jar. Fill each jar with one of the three solutions. Fill a few jars with fresh water. Most get the slightly salty solution. Fill one with the very salty water. Record which jars got which solutions so you know which wins. The saltiest wins the grand prize. The freshwater jars win second prizes. The rest lost in the lottery.

DURING CLASS:

METHODS: Explain that now is the time to put what the students have learned about salinity and density or heaviness to work. Show them the jars. Each jar contains an unknown solution. Some hold fresh water, some slightly salty water, and one very salty water. Have them pick randomly among the jars. The students who picked the jars with fresh water get a prize. The person who picked the jar with the saltiest water wins the grand prize. It is like a lottery. But how do they know what they have? To discover who won, they have to test the solutions in the jars. Can they tell by looking? No. Then how?

There is one thing they cannot do: DO NOT TASTE THEM! Make sure students know that they should NEVER taste unknown solutions. Some kinds of salts are very toxic. They are not all like table salt. For example, epsom salts can cause unpleasant diarrhea. Students should plan how to test the solutions, using knowledge gained in previous exercises. Show them the array of equipment available to spark ideas. Have students fill out the worksheet with their plan before they begin.

RESULTS:

How are they going to find out who won? They can do any physical test which will get at the relationship of density or heaviness to salinity. They can check with you to find out if their results are accurate since you recorded which solution was in which sample bottle. Award the prizes when they have correctly found the fresh water and the saltiest water.

CONCLUSIONS:

Have a brief class discussion of techniques used for testing. Which was best? Which was fastest?

EXTENSIONS:

1. How about asking the question: which is saltiest, the Dead Sea (276 gm of salt per kg of water) or the Great Salt Lake (266 gm salt per kg of water)? This can be solved in a number of ways. Everyone could compete to see who can dig the answer out of the library fastest. Or you could mix up two samples representing each using the information above and have the students test them. Locate each on the map.

2. How do salt lakes form? Water flowing over the ground dissolves salts which are carried to a low spot from which there is no way for water to flow out. As the water evaporates, the salt is left behind.

3. Do salt lakes always stay the same? No! For the last several years the Great Salt Lake has had more water flowing in than has evaporated out. In 1986 the lake was rising fast. To prevent homes, roads and businesses from disappearing under water, Utah is talking about pumping water out of the valley where it is and into another desert valley.

4. Can the students think of another habitat where salinity gets high? Tide pools can get very salty on a hot day during low tide! So do the pools of water in a salt marsh during low tide on a summer day.

ACTIVITY 6
THE GREAT SALINITY CONTEST!

Name _Possible answers_

My sample number is __14__

These are the steps I will take to determine if I have fresh water, slightly salty water or the very salty sample:

I think I will try weighing my water and see if it is heavier or lighter than some one else has. I might also use food coloring and compare it to other students' samples. I can also get fresh water from the tap for comparison.

I think my sample is
__ fresh water **X** slightly salty __ very salty.

This is the evidence for my conclusion:

I lost. My water sank in tap water and floated on Linda's sample. When I weighed my sample, it weighed in between the heaviest and the lightest which were the fresh water and the very salty water.

45

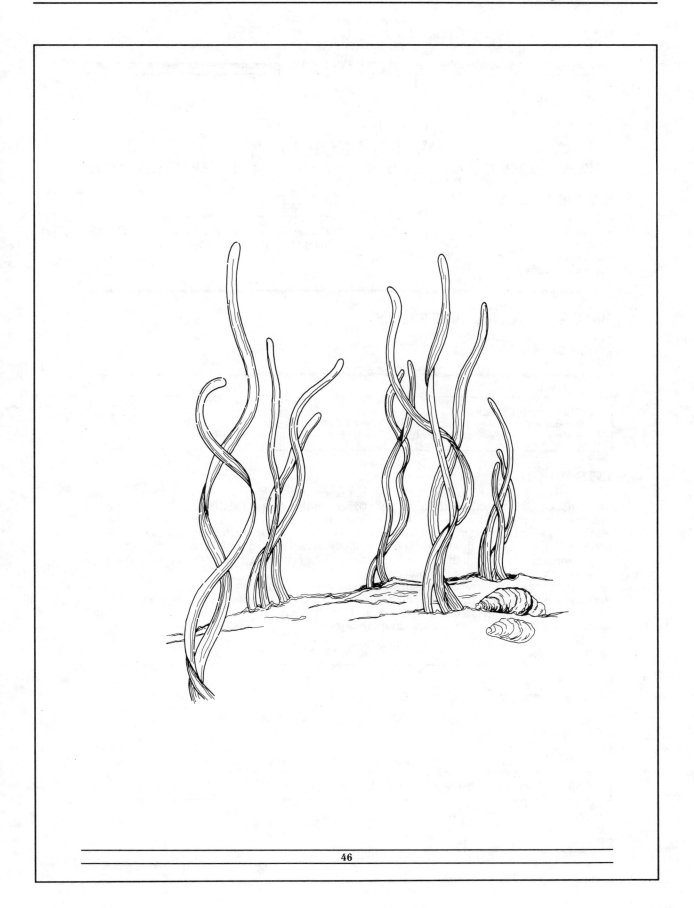

ACTIVITY 7

OXYGEN FOR LIFE
WHERE DOES THE OXYGEN THAT IS DISSOLVED IN WATER COME FROM?

SCIENCE SKILLS:
- observing
- measuring
- organizing
- inferring
- communicating

CONCEPTS:
- The oxygen that is in water comes from air.
- The oxygen dissolved in water may vary depending on the conditions of the sample.

MATH AND MECHANICAL SKILLS:
- use of dissolved oxygen test kits
- computing averages

SAMPLE OBJECTIVES:
- Students will be able to follow instructions to test for dissolved oxygen.
- Students will be able to explain why experimental results from different sources vary.

INTRODUCTION:
Measuring dissolved oxygen is difficult, but rewarding. Oxygen is as important to the animals living in water as it is to those living on land. Oxygen in the water is DISSOLVED OXYGEN, not the oxygen atom in the water molecule. Plants may add dissolved oxygen when they photosynthesize. Much of it, however, comes from the air and enters the water at the surface. Oxygen DIFFUSES slowly in the water, more slowly than it does in air. Dissolved oxygen amounts may vary significantly from one place to another in aquatic habitats. In this exercise students will prove that oxygen from air does enter or dissolve in water.

Dissolved oxygen may be measured in several different ways. One way is in parts per million (ppm) which is based on the weight of the oxygen versus the weight of the water. Oxygen in natural environments can range from no oxygen (0 ppm) which is very bad to 6-10 ppm which is sufficient for most animals to more than 15 ppm in some cases.

MATERIALS:

FOR EACH GROUP:
- a clear plastic cup
- cold water
- sealed canning jar full to the top with boiled water(see Recipes)
- goggles for each child

SHARED:
- dissolved oxygen test kits (see Recipes)
- kitchen baster or large syringe to transfer water sample

LESSON PLAN:

BEFORE CLASS:

This and all other dissolved oxygen exercises use the LaMotte Chemical Company dissolved oxygen test kit. This brand was chosen for two reasons: the results are numerical, and the kits are the kind most commonly available to teachers. The test for dissolved oxygen in these kits is the Winkler method, an old and very accurate one. Neither you nor the students need to understand the chemical transformations in this kit. You do need to understand what the results mean in terms of the natural world. The Recipes section gives you simplified directions for use of this kit. Make the modifications suggested.

After reading the exercise and assembling the materials, practice the oxygen test yourself. Then spend one science class having the students learn the techniques with tap water. Have the entire class work together under strict supervision for this first experience.

Boil and "can" water for this exercise at home. Allow the sealed jars to cool.

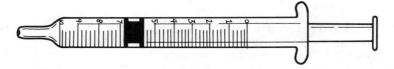

DURING CLASS:

Have the students fill a transparent plastic cup with cold water early in the day and let it sit on their desks. Observe it occasionally. If you have short periods, do this half an hour before class.

When it comes time for the science lesson, ask the students what they observed as their cup of water sat on the desk. Some of the students should have noticed that tiny bubbles formed on the sides of the cup. What do they think the bubbles are? Air. Where did it come from? It was DISSOLVED in the water. What do animals need that is in air? OXYGEN. The air is 21% oxygen.

How can we prove that oxygen dissolves in water from the air? Distribute the sealed jars. Tell them that you have treated the water in the jar to remove most of the air. But they do not have to trust you. They can test the water for DISSOLVED OXYGEN themselves using a test kit. Make sure they understand that the color changes are INDICATORS of things that cannot be seen themselves but which cause the color changes.

Have the students working in groups take turns using the test kits following the instructions provided. Record their results. If students made serious errors that you can identify, you may choose to delete their data from the final chart. Make sure they understand that you are not just making sure that things come out right. Explain the nature of their error so that they can be careful to correct it.

Pour half the water out, put the lid on and shake the jar hard. Uncap and recap and shake several times. This speeds both diffusion and mixing. Now test the water for dissolved oxygen again.

RESULTS:

Compare the first oxygen measurements with the second. Make a table on the board or an overhead projector. Did everyone get the same results? No. Anytime a group of folks do a test, there is variation in the way they do it and the way they read it. That is one of the reasons that scientific tests must be repeated many times. Average the results for low oxygen and high oxygen.

CONCLUSION:

Where did the dissolved oxygen come from? From the air. Gases from the air dissolve in water.

USING YOUR AQUARIUM:

Have your students observe the movement of water in your classroom aquarium. The air lift columns create a current that causes the water to circulate, exposing all of the water to the air and mixing the oxygen. What would happen if there were no circulation? Oxygen would be lower at the bottom if it were being used by some of the tank's inhabitants.

EXTENSIONS:

1. Oxygen normally enters at the surface of the water. Decomposers use oxygen and are frequently located at the bottom of a body of water. Oxygen must enter the water at the surface and diffuse downward. Diffusion in water is slower than diffusion in air. How long does it take for oxygen to get to the bottom of a lake? Try seeing how fast it travels in a fruit jar.

Uncap a quart fruit jar of boiled water and let it sit for 30 min. First sample the water from right at the surface and then the water from the very bottom. Do this very carefully so that the water is not stirred.

You should get a differential, even over the shallow distance in a fruit jar. What does this mean in the real world? If the wind or a current is not stirring up the water in a lake or pond, there will be a good deal more oxygen in the surface water than in the water at the bottom if bottom-dwelling organisms are actively using oxygen.

ACTIVITY 7
OXYGEN FOR LIFE

Name *Possible answers*

What did you observe happen as the plastic cup of cold water warmed to room temperature?

Little bubbles appeared on the sides of the cup.

Record the results of your group's dissolved oxygen test here.
Amount of dissolved oxygen in the water when the jar was first opened:
__2.2__ ppm (parts per million)
Amount of dissolved oxygen in the water after it was exposed to the air:
__5.6__ ppm
How much change in dissolved oxygen did you measure in your water sample?

5.6 − 2.2 ppm = 3.4 ppm dissolved oxygen; an increase.

Record the results for the class on this table:

	group number						
	1	2	3	4	5	6	average
dissolved oxygen in newly opened jar in ppm	2.2	1.8	2.4	2.0	1.6		2
dissolved oxygen in water exposed to air in ppm	5.6	4.8	5.4	5.2	5.8		5.3

average difference __3.3__ ppm

How can you explain the difference in dissolved oxygen in the two samples?

When we shook the jar, oxygen from the air must have gotten into the water.

Side calculations:
2.2, 1.8, 2.4, 2.0, 1.6 → 10.0; 5⟌10 = 2
5.6, 4.8, 5.4, 5.2, 5.8 → 26.8; 5⟌26.8 = 5.3
5.3 − 2 = 3.3

ACTIVITY 8

DIRTY WATER

WHAT HAPPENS WHEN SOIL WASHES FROM THE LAND AND ENTERS AQUATIC HABITATS?

SCIENCE SKILLS:

- observing
- inferring
- experimenting
- communicating

CONCEPTS:

- Plant nutrients from soil dissolve in water.
- Plant nutrients increase the growth of algae in aquatic habitats.

MATH AND MECHANICAL SKILLS PRACTICED:

- use of a camera

SAMPLE OBJECTIVES:
- Students will be able to compare the results of soil erosion and nutrient enrichment on aquatic systems.
- Students will be able to describe the effects of soil erosion on aquatic habitats.

INTRODUCTION:

This activity will take several weeks to complete. Model "ponds" in clear jars reveal what happens when soil ERODES from land and washes into an aquatic habitat. The NUTRIENTS from the soil over-fertilize the pond, causing abnormal growth of ALGAE. Data collection is difficult due to subjective evaluation. The use of a camera to record changes simplifies this problem. To be scientifically correct, each test should be done twice to insure that the results can be repeated. If possible, double the materials and do two replicates of each treatment group.

MATERIALS:

- five clear containers one quart or more (plastic soft drink bottles or canning jars)
- water with algae from a freshwater classroom aquarium or a pond; may also be purchased pond water from a biological supply company
- soil from a yard or flower bed or garden, or potting soil
- cloth to filter soil from water; old sheeting is okay
- plant fertilizer such as Peters or other well-balanced mix (some have green dye that goes away when exposed to light) .
- aged tap water
- good light source, either indirect sun light or strong artifical light
- camera and roll of 12 exposure print film (35mm or Polaroid best)

LESSON PLAN:
BEFORE CLASS:

After reading this exercise, consider starting this exercise and Activity 9 at the same time if you have sufficient containers. Otherwise, start Activity 9 after completing this one if the same containers must be used again.

Do these preparations before class. Mix two cups of soil with a quart of water and shake vigorously. Let the mix sit until the dirt settles and then strain the water through cloth into another container. Collect the algae-pond water sample or order a sample. In northern climates you will have trouble finding good natural samples during cold months.

DURING CLASS:

METHODS: Ask if the students have ever seen a creek, pond or river after a very hard rain. Is the water a different color? Why? The rain running over the surface of the soil has picked up soil particles and carried them into the water. Can the students identify human activities that increase this process called EROSION? Housing developments, newly logged forests, plowed fields, and tire tracks from recreational vehicles all destroy vegetation and leave soil vulnerable to erosion. Plants help hold the soil in place.

What is the immediate effect of erosion? Have students help you with these preparations. Add soil to water in one of the jars and shake. The water becomes TURBID as the soil particles become suspended. What are the short term consequences of soil erosion? Would animals and plants be affected by sediment in the water? Plants would have light blocked. Animals might have their gills clogged. Put this jar aside for future observation.

What does the soil do to the bodies of water it enters? How would we do a test to find out? Label the remaining four jars tap water (your control), 1 tsp fertilizer, 1 tbsp fertilizer and soil. Fill three jars with aged tap water and the fourth (soil) with the water you prepared at home. (Explain that this water was prepared in the same manner as the shaken soil and water demonstration.) Add the correct plant fertilizer to two jars. Now add aquarium water with algae or pond water with algae to each jar. Use equal amounts up to one cup in each. Why did one jar just get tap water? It is the CONTROL against which the other jars are measured. The control gets no treatment and differs by just one VARIABLE from each of the tests. Set all four jars where there is good light. Do not place them in a location that gets very cold. Observe them over the next several weeks to a month, recording changes two to three times each week by photographing the jars side-by-side in good light from close-up. Write the date on a piece of paper that shows in the photograph and make sure the labels show. Keep the plants in the same place in each picture.

RESULTS:

What happened? The exact results will vary depending on your algal source and growing conditions. Arrange the photographs in order. Over the weeks, the jars with soil water and fertilizer should show a much more luxurious growth of algae than the plain tap water. Why? Plant growth was facilitated by something that stayed in the water as the soil particles settled out: PLANT NUTRIENTS which DISSOLVED in the water. Plant nutrients are chemicals that are in SOLUTION in the water. Was there a difference in the amount of growth with the two dosages of fertilizer? Compare all with the control.

CONCLUSIONS:

Soil erosion can cause serious problems in aquatic environments. What are some long term results that you observed? The plant growth in the container with soil was greater. It should have resembled that of the fertilized water. A little plant growth is good. Plant nutrients in natural systems come from the surrounding land. Too much plant growth can cause serious problems, however. Under over-fertilized conditions, the kinds of algae that grow may change to undesirable toxic or foul-smelling species. Also, when the algae die, the bacteria and fungi that feed on them may use up much of the oxygen in the system during decomposition.

USING YOUR CLASSROOM AQUARIUM:

Compare your classroom aquarium with these small environments. How are they the same? Different? Where do the nutrients that support algal growth on the walls of your aquarium come from? The waste products from fish urine and feces. Think about what is used as fertilizer in organic gardens. Animal manures. Where did the animals get the nutrients in the wastes. From the food they ate which directly or indirectly came from plants. Nutrients CYCLE between plants and animals.

EXTENSIONS:

1. Study the label of the plant fertilizer container to discover what some plant nutrients are. Students should find compounds containing nitrogen, phosphate and potassium, three primary plant nutrients. Many brands have a number of other chemicals as well.

2. Can you identify a problem with soil erosion in your area that affects aquatic environments? If you cannot, you might call your local soil conservation district and ask about a local problem that your class might study. Sediment from farms and development contributes to the problems of the Chesapeake Bay. Erosion from logging smothers fish eggs in Pacific Northwest streams. Midwest farms are losing soil at an alarming rate.

3. *Conserving Soil* is an excellent book with classroom activities ready for duplication.
   To inquire about getting a copy, contact:
   National Association of Conservation Districts
   P.O. Box 8855
   League City, TX 77573
It was first published by the U.S. Department of Agriculture, which cares because soil that stays on farms keeps the farms fertile.

ACTIVITY 8
DIRTY WATER

Name _Possible answers_

Arrange all the pictures in order from the first date to the last. Study the changes you can observe with over time in each. Describe them here:

Tap water: _The algae grew a little bit and got greener. There really was not very much change._

One teaspoon of fertilizer: _At first this got greener than the control (tap water), but then it stayed the same._

One tablespoon of fertilizer: _This just kept getting greener as the algae grew._

Water from soil: _This grew best, but there must have been special things in the soil because it had some algae we didn't see in the others._

Which grew the most algae? _one tablespoon (answers vary)_

Which grew the least algae? _tap water_

One tablespoon is three times as much as one teaspoon. What was the result of one jar having three times as much fertilizer as another?

More fertilizer grows more plants. (If you used very strong fertitizer, the heavier dose may be toxic.)

Why did one jar get only tap water? _It was the control. We had to have something to compare the others to.)_

ACTIVITY
9

WHAT'S IN THE WATER?

WHAT IS WATER POLLUTION? WHAT ARE THE EFFECTS OF SEVERAL KINDS OF WATER POLLUTION ON SOME AQUATIC ORGANISMS?

SCIENCE SKILLS:

- classifying
- observing
- inferring
- predicting
- experimenting
- communicating

CONCEPTS:

- There are many different forms of water pollution.
- Human activities are a primary cause of water pollution.
- Some forms of pollution have a definite point at which they enter the water, while others do not.
- Water pollution can affect plants and animals and humans.

MATH AND MECHANICAL SKILLS PRACTICED:

- use of a camera

SAMPLE OBJECTIVES:
- Students will be able to test the effects of several common household chemicals that frequently find their way into aquatic environments.
- Students will be able to classify pollution sources.

INTRODUCTION:

This exercise, like Activity 8, is spread out over about one month. It takes a simplistic look at the effects water pollution has on aquatic systems. Use several household chemicals that are safe and that students pour down the drain without thinking. The results vary with your choice of materials. Students enjoy checking daily for changes. Like Activity 8, to be scientifically correct you should do two of each test if you possibly can which would double the number of jars needed.

MATERIALS:

TWO WEEKS BEFORE CLASS:

- four clear containers one quart or more (plastic soft drink bottles or canning jars)
- water with algae from a freshwater classroom aquarium or a pond, or purchased pond water from a biological supply company
- plant fertilizer such as Peters or other well-balanced mix (the dye in most of these will fade when exposed to light)
- aged tap water
- good light source, either indirect sunlight or strong artificial light

FOR CLASS:

- "pollutants" of choice by students; the safest to handle might include detergent (not green), motor oil, vinegar
- camera and roll of 12 exposure print film (35mm or Polaroid best)

INFORMATION:

Detailed information on water pollution is in the Information for Teachers section.

LESSON PLAN:

BEFORE CLASS:

Set up the bottles or jars at least two weeks before the experiment begins. Fill the jars with aged tap water. Add one teaspoon of plant fertilizer to each jar and stir it thoroughly. The plants need some nutrients to grow. Nutrients are found in all natural systems. (Add to as much pond water as you can.) Try a bit of soil from the bottom of a pond or gravel from your aquarium tank along with the water. Put the jars near a window where they will get good indirect light or give them strong incandescent or fluorescent light. Do not place them in a location that gets very cold.

When pollutants are selected, be careful to consider safety. Animal products of any kind could grow dangerous bacteria. Do not cover jars tightly as you might grow some undesirable bacteria this way. Regular household items should do fine. Vinegar is an acid which acts as acid rain or an acid discharge such as the "pickling liquor" from steel production or the run-off of acid from strip mines. Detergent is a common component of human sewage. Motor oil is commonly poured down storm drains. Regardless of what you use, make all your observations without coming into contact with the water and dispose of the material carefully after the experiment is over.

DURING THE LESSON:

METHODS: Start with a classification exercise on the blackboard, explaining that you want the students to see if they can organize what they already know about water pollution. Explain that some water pollution comes from specific sources such as outfalls (and is called POINT SOURCE pollution) while other kinds come from many widespread sources (called NON-POINT SOURCE pollution). Write those words at the head of two columns and have the students begin to suggest things that pollute water. Put them in the general categories found in the chart given in the Information for Teachers section. Students will not name everything in the list.

Explain that they are going to test some pollutants on model water environments. Would it be acceptable to test them by dumping them in a natural environment? No. Models are used for tests to avoid damaging the natural world. Show the students the jars with algae growing in them. Now what does the class choose to test for its effect on an artifical water environment? Let them decide with guidance. For example, if a child wants to test the effect of a dangerous compound, try to discuss why that might not be safe in the classroom environment. Settle on three pollutants. The fourth set of jars are CONTROLS.

When the class has decided what to test, you may have to wait until the following day to add the material, since it might have to come from home. Add a reasonable amount: two tablespoons of a strong detergent; enough motor oil to just cover the surface; 1/4-1/2 cup of vinegar. Leave the jars or tanks in the light as before. Have the children write their predictions for what will happen to each test container. Two or three times each week for several weeks photograph the jars with labels and a date showing.

RESULTS:

These depend on what you used. A few kinds of pollutants favor plant growth and will cause an algal population explosion. This is not healthy as it disrupts the balance of organisms. When the algae die, the oxygen is used as they decompose. Other pollutants, such as acids, will cause very clear water because they kill everything in it. Needless to say, they are not good for natural systems either. The sample with an oil spill may do better than you expect. If the algae have enough sunlight, they may make enough oxygen to keep things alive below the oxygen impervious oil layer.

CONCLUSIONS:

Human activities which result in water pollution can affect water environments in ways that are very bad for natural communities.

USING YOUR CLASSROOM AQUARIUM:

Does your classroom aquarium grow lots of algae? If you feed fish, they will produce waste products which are very much like fertilizer. Have your students discuss the procedures you use to avoid water pollution in your classroom aquarium. You are careful not to overfeed the fish, you remove algae from the sides of the tank and do water changes which reduce the level of waste products.

EXTENSIONS:

1. There are a number of social studies activities related to this experiment. Who regulates water pollution in your city, county or state? What are the federal regulations on water quality? What is the impact of these regulations on industries? What are the greatest water quality problems in your local area? How do they affect the jobs and health of people living in your area? The natural environment in your area? Have students research these topics.

2. Can any of the polluted systems be reversed and improved?

a. Countries such as Sweden have added lime to their acid lakes in an attempt to correct the acidic condition. Your students could use baking soda to turn their acid test back into a neutral environment. Use litmus paper to test for neutrality. Add new algae and see what happens.

b. Oil spills may be mopped up with straw, feathers or cotton. Can they skim the oil off of their samples and let the oxygen get through again?

3. If you live in the Chesapeake Bay region, write these folks for booklets that tell what ordinary people can do to reduce water pollution in the Bay:

Alliance for the Chesapeake
6600 York Road
Baltimore, Maryland 21212

ACTIVITY 9
WHAT'S IN THE WATER?

Name _Possible answers_

Arrange all the pictures in order from the first date to the last. Study the changes you can observe over time in each. Write in the pollutant used in each and describe the changes:

Tap water: _This jar grew more green, but not very much. It changed just a little bit. The green was algae._

Vinegar (acid) ____: _Everything in this jar died right away, and the water became very clear. It looked clean, but nothing could grow in it._

Dish detergent ____: _I thought this would kill everything but instead the algae grew a little bit. Another group used more, and their pond water died._

Salad oil _____: _The pond water stayed green which was a big surprise. How can they live without air?_

Which pollutant had the greatest effect? _Vinegar - acid like acid rain_

Which pollutant had the least effect? _Salad oil_

Were you surprised at the results? How did they compare with your predictions?
Salad oil did not kill everything. Another group used motor oil, and it did kill the pond water plants and animals.

Why did one jar get only tap water? _It was the control against which the others could be compared._

SECTION II
TEMPERATURE CHANGES IN AQUATIC HABITATS

TEACHER'S INFORMATION

Different substances change temperatures at different RATES even when they are placed in the same conditions because different materials have different SPECIFIC HEATS. The *same* amount of heat added to different substances with the same initial temperature will result in different final temperatures. Water has a very high specific heat. It absorbs a great deal of heat before its temperature rises much. Likewise, water cools very slowly and gives off a great deal of heat when it cools. Consequently, aquatic environments do not change temperature very fast and they change much slower than land habitats. Water is a stable place to live with regard to temperature. The larger the body of water, the more stable.

One consequence of the high specific heat of water is that land masses next to large bodies of water have more moderate climates than those at the same latitude and altitude farther away from water. The water gives off heat during periods when the land is colder and absorbs heat when the land mass is warmer, thus buffering the temperature of the land. You can see this effect by looking up the planting diagram for trees and shrubs given in seed catalogs or in garden books. There are warm bands that extend up both coasts, especially the east coast with its Gulf Stream current that carries warm water up from the tropics to the northern Atlantic Ocean.

Temperature affects the density of water. Differences in density may result in thermal STRATIFICATION in many bodies of water, with warmer surface waters floating on more dense, colder bottom water. The area of the water where cold and warm water meet is called the THERMOCLINE. It is the region at which the temperature changes rapidly. When stratification is caused by salinity differences, the point at which the saltier water meets the fresh water floating on it is called the HALOCLINE.

Fresh water is most dense, or heaviest, at 4°C (39°F). Water colder or warmer than 4°C floats on the 4°C water. Because of this, ice forms at the surface of a lake or pond which may remain unfrozen at the bottom during winter, providing a place for animals to live. The ice may prevent oxygen from entering the water, however.

These density differences also affect the distribution of nutrients and oxygen in water environments. Cold bottom water is frequently nutrient-rich because things that die sink to the bottom and are decomposed there, releasing nutrients like nitrogen and phosphate to the water. The act of decomposition may also deplete bottom water of oxygen. Wind and currents or upwellings may help to mix bottom water with surface water. Bottom water may also reach the surface as surface water cools in fall and its density becomes greater than that of the bottom water. When this happens, surface water sinks and displaces bottom water in a process called TURNOVER. Turnover is often followed by a rapid increase in algal growth as the needed nutrients have been delivered to the surface where algae are doing PHOTOSYNTHESIS.

Water temperature has a direct effect on the plants and animals living there. Plants and most animals are said to be cold-blooded or ECTOTHERMIC, meaning that their temperature is determined by the environment. Their respiration rates may change with temperature. Thus, their rates of oxygen usage are dependent on their temperature. They use less oxygen when it is cold and more when it is warm because respiration, which is a chemical reaction, goes faster at a warm temperature than a cold one. The increased rates of respiration in warm weather may allow greater activity. Most aquatic organisms are ectothermic.

Birds, mammals and special members of some other groups are said to be warm-blooded or ENDOTHERMIC. They maintain a constant internal temperature or at least maintain an internal temperature above that of the environment in a cold environment. This constant, warm temperature means that respiration can take place in their cells at the same rate whether it is warm or cold outside. In this case, their oxygen use is greatest in very cold or very hot environments in which they have to do increased respiration to regulate their temperature.

Many ectothermic plants and animals can change their respiration rates over time to be most efficient at the temperature at which they are held. They ACCLIMATE to a specific temperature. The plants you use may be acclimated at a high or low temperature. This will not negate your results, but may account for high respiration rates at low temperatures if your plants have been living in the cold for a long time and are acclimated to the cold.

Animals that live in deep water in the ocean or near the poles experience such constant water temperatures that they are ADAPTED to these temperatures completely and may be killed by a rise of a very few degrees. On the other hand, plants and animals living in smaller bodies of water or in shallow water near shore in larger ones where greater temperature changes are common are generally adapted to seasonal changes in temperature.

RESPIRATION generally requires oxygen. Some kinds of animals are well adapted to low oxygen environments such as mud. Worms that live in mud or turtles that bury themselves in the mud over the winter have special ways of dealing with low oxygen. The worms have blood pigments (like hemoglobin in humans) that are very efficient at picking up what oxygen is available. The turtles go into a special state in which they use very little oxygen. They may even make cellular energy without using oxygen, a process referred to as ANAEROBIC RESPIRATION.

Most water animals, however, depend on a good supply of oxygen from their environment. When it is not available, they may have several options. They may increase the rate at which water passes over their gills. This is like breathing faster when you run because you are using oxygen faster. It is called increased VENTILATION. Another tactic is to move to a better location. In really low oxygen situations, animals like crabs and eels will even crawl out of the water.

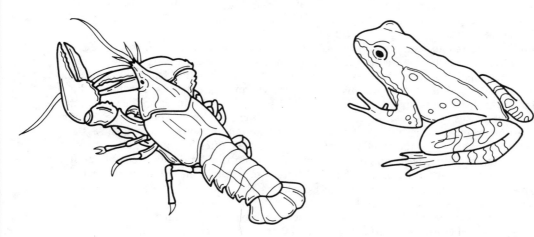

Under natural circumstances, animals generally are not exposed to great oxygen stress to which they are not adapted. Occasionally, unusual environmental conditions like prolonged high temperatures may cause abnormally low oxygen in some water habitats. A small pond on a very hot day or night might have low oxygen levels due to heated water and high biological activity (respiration). Frequently, low oxygen levels are caused by human activities. Heating water (thermal pollution) lowers the oxygen it holds. Humans also cause low oxygen in aquatic environments by adding material to the water which will be decayed or decomposed by bacteria. Sewage, plant and animal waste products from food processing plants, animal wastes from farms or feed lots, and organic waste from factories can all serve as food for bacteria living in the water. These bacteria use a great deal of oxygen in respiration as they decompose the wastes. When the problem is compounded by hot water due to climate or thermal pollution, animals that live in the water may die.

Temperature changes are a result of seasonal changes. Another seasonal phenomenon is the migration of many species for reproduction or feeding which is keyed to these temperature changes. Humpback whales migrate from warm tropical waters where they calve in the winter to colder temperate waters where food is abundant during the spring, summer and fall.

Many fish species migrate seasonally for the purpose of SPAWNING (laying eggs which get fertilized). Most are fish that live as adults in the oceans, but enter estuaries and spawn in the estuary or in its rivers. These fish are called ANADROMOUS (from the Greek for running upward). Familiar anadromous fish include salmon, herring, shad, and striped bass. There are some fish species which do the reverse. They live in fresh water and migrate to salt water to reproduce. The American and European eels are the best known members of this group called CATADROMOUS fish. Migrations are timed to take advantage of specific seasonal changes in water flow, salinity, water temperature and food availability.

As with all species, the total possible number of offspring is much greater than the actual number in each generation because of predation, competition, variations in physical characteristics such as temperature or rain fall and other causes. In the case of some species, the difference between possible and actual is huge.

In the simulation game about seasonal migration in this section, herring are used as an example of an anadromous fish. Herring occur throughout the northern hemisphere. The herring family includes members which use a complete variety of reproductive strategies. Some species live and spawn at sea. Others may spawn at sea and mature and feed in estuaries (menhaden of eastern U. S. coast) or spawn in freshwater tributaries and migrate to the ocean as adults. It is these last, the anadromous herring of the eastern United States which are used in the game. Blueback herring are also called glut herring for the huge numbers which once glutted the streams each spring. Prior to the coming of Europeans, these fish existed in incredible numbers. They have been greatly reduced by human actions.

Another anadromous fish, the striped bass, is one of the most prized sportfish on the East Coast. Adult bass in the Chesapeake Bay region spend their winters in deep water in the mid or lower Bay. Since this is a stratified estuary, the deeper water is saltier. It also has more constant temperatures. Larger adults migrate out into the Atlantic Ocean as far north as Nova Scotia during the winter and early spring. Come late spring (April–June) the adult fish move up the Chesapeake Bay into its tributaries to tidal freshwater areas or only slightly brackish waters to spawn. Strong river flow is important to keep the eggs afloat. During the summer season, some striped bass remain in the tributaries, but many move great distances to feed. After the eggs hatch, the larvae migrate downstream as they feed and grow. By winter they join the older fish in deeper water. It appears that these fish, like other anadromous fish, return to spawn in the tributary in which they were born each year. If all the fish from one river are killed, that tributary will not have striped bass again.

For reasons that are subject to debate and that include barriers to migration, water pollution, lack of larval food, acid rain, and overfishing among others, the striped bass populations of the Chesapeake Bay are in serious decline. Maryland has a ban on catching them and is trying to discover the reasons for and solutions to this decrease in numbers.

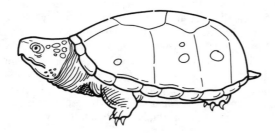

ACTIVITY
10

A CHANGE IN THE WEATHER?

WHICH CHANGES TEMPERATURE FASTER: WATER OR AIR? DOES VOLUME MAKE A DIFFERENCE IN HOW FAST A BODY OF WATER CHANGES TEMPERATURE?

SCIENCE SKILLS:

- measuring
- organizing
- inferring
- experimenting
- communicating

CONCEPTS:

- Under the same conditions, water changes temperature more slowly than air.
- In terms of temperature, aquatic habitats are more stable than land habitats.
- The larger the volume of water, the slower it changes temperature.

MATH AND MECHANICAL SKILLS PRACTICED:

- reading thermometers
- averaging numbers
- graphing data

SAMPLE OBJECTIVES:
- Students will be able to read a thermometer.
- Students will be able to compare temperature changes in water and air.
- Students will be able to graphically display results.

INTRODUCTION:

This exercise ties into earth science in that much weather is dependent on the fact that water absorbs more heat than air for each degree of temperature change. Bodies of water therefore change temperature more slowly and have more stable temperatures than land. Lakes and oceans warm adjacent land in winter and cool it in summer.

This activity depends on having access to a cold place: a refrigerator, ice chest or outside on a winter day. If you teach several sections of science, one class may start and others continue this project. Data analysis can be done on the following day. During test teaching, students reported liking to share a project with other classes.

Data manipulation will take several class periods if the students have not done averaging and graphing before. This is a good project to practice these skills because they will generate lots of numbers.

MATERIALS:

FOR CLASS:

• a cold (33-40° F) place—a refrigerator or ice chest

FOR EACH GROUP:

• 3 clear containers (two of same size and one four times as big) of the same material such as two pint bottles and a 2 liter plastic soft drink bottle or fruit jars
• lids or aluminum foil to cover tops of containers
• 3 safe, breakproof thermometers (see Recipes for sources)
• water

LESSON PLAN:
BEFORE CLASS:

In selecting containers, you may have to cheat and mix glass and plastic. Children should not try to handle large glass containers of water. In the interest of safety, you may have to accept a variable that is not controlled. Use containers that allow data collection without opening the jars. Modify the top of plastic containers to accept the thermometers. The thermometers need to fit inside, but may stick out through holes in the lids if necessary. Use cheap, small thermometers that are hard to break, not the long "scientific" glass ones. They should not break if dropped, nor should they contain mercury.

Have the students practice reading the thermometers the day before the experiment. Use tap water of several temperatures for practice.

Fill one of the smaller containers and the larger container with room temperature water, leaving a space at the top in case it freezes. Leave the third container filled with air. Add thermometers to each and record the time and temperature for each. Put lids on loosely or cover top with foil. Put them in a cold location: a refrigerator, outside on a cold day, in an ice chest. Leave in cold place overnight or until temperature near freezing is reached.

DURING CLASS:

METHODS: Introduce the exercise by asking the students which they think would be warmer on a hot day, a fish living in a big lake or a turtle sitting on a log next to the lake? How about in the dead of winter when snow is piled up, would it be colder to be under the ice in the pond or sitting on its shore? Generally, the temperature is more moderate in water than on land. Have they ever thought about why the climate is more moderate under water? Try a test to find out.

Remove the jars of cold water and air and place on desks where students can read the thermometers. Periodically record time and temperature in each (about every 5-10 minutes).

Students can calculate rates of change for each sample by:
• total temp. change (difference from start to finish) divided by
• total elapsed time (minutes or hours the experiment ran)

RESULTS:

The large body of water should change more slowly than the smaller one. Water should change more slowly than air. If you used small jars with lots of surface area, the water may not seem much different from air.

CONCLUSIONS:

What would this mean for you if you lived in water? In air? Generally, animals and plants living in water are subjected to temperature changes that are not as radical as those that land-living organisms face.

If an animal needs to stay at nearly the same temperature all year, would it prefer to spend the winter and the summer in a big body of water or a little pond? The bigger the body of water, the smaller the changes with season. Can you make any generalizations about the relative seasonal temperature changes likely to be found in a pond, a lake, the ocean. Small ponds show greater changes in temperature with the seasons. Lakes show less, and oceans even less. But even oceans, at least at the surface, have temperature changes.

USING YOUR CLASSROOM AQUARIUM:

If your classroom experiences temperature changes during the night or over the weekend and you do not have a heater in your aquarium, have your students keep a log of the temperature changes that occur in the aquarium during the day from the time they arrive until they leave. Does it change temperature much during the day? If you have a maximum/minimum thermometer, leave it out at night or over the weekend to see how cold the room gets then. Does the room's temperature change? Record these temperatures also. Graph the temperature changes of both room and aquarium on the same chart. Is the amplitude of the change greater in the aquarium or the room? How does this compare with your findings in this activity?

EXTENSION:

1. Repeat the experiment using an incandescent light as a heat source. Make sure the jars are not sealed so that the air has room to expand as it warms.

ACTIVITY 10
A CHANGE IN THE WEATHER?

Name *Possible answers*

What is the question that this experiment will answer?

Actually, we can answer two questions: which changes temperature faster - air or water and which changes temperature faster - a big body of water or a small one?

Record the TEMPERATURES for your group here:

container						time in minutes since starting					
	start	5	10	15	20	25	30	35	40	45	50
air	10°	14.5°	18°	22°	25°						
small water	10°	13°	15°	18°	20°						
large water	10°	11°	12°	14°	16°						

These temperature readings are in Farenheit _____

Centigrade ___✓___

Calculate the average temperature for all groups and record here:

container						time in minutes since starting					
	start	5	10	15	20	25	30	35	40	45	50
air	9.8	14.7	18.3	22.4	24.9						
small water	10.1	12.9	14.8	18.1	20.2						
large water	9.9	11.1	12.2	14.1	15.4						

These temperature readings are in Farenheit _____

Centigrade ___✓___

Graph the temperature changes with a line graph here for Farenheit scale:

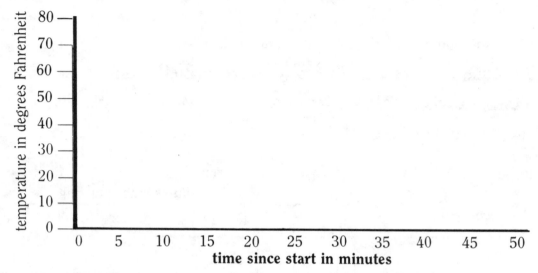

Or graph here in Centigrade or Celsius scale:

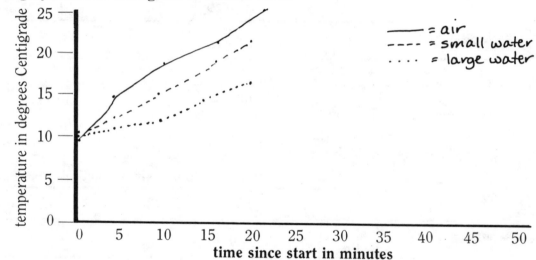

Which container changed temperature fastest? <u>The container of air</u> <u>changed temperature fastest.</u>

Which changed most slowly? <u>The large water jar changed slowest</u>

Based on your experiment, which of these would change temperatures through the seasons least? Most? Middle?

ocean <u>least</u>   pond <u>most</u>   lake <u>middle</u>

9

SOURCE LIST
FOR IDEAS AND MATERIALS

by Bonnie B. Barr
Professor of Education
State University of New York, College at Cortland, Cortland, New York

THE resources listed below are not intended to be a definitive collection of all available publications. They were selected to support curriculum development efforts that foster conceptual change, inquiry skill development and problem solving, wholistic learning, and real-world application of science concepts.

Activity Sourcebooks
for Elementary Teachers

General Science

CESI Science Sourcebooks, by The Council for Elementary Science International (Columbus, OH: ERIC Clearinghouse for Science, Mathematics, and Environmental Education).
Sourcebooks feature activities submitted by classroom teachers. Each activity includes a further challenge section that involves students in independent research. Sourcebook titles include *Using Outdoor Areas as Learning Laboratories; Expanding Children's Thinking through Science; Understanding the Healthy Body; Science Activities for Preschoolers; Physical Science Activities for Elementary and Middle School;* and *Water, Stones, and Fossil Bones.*

Creative Hands-On Science Cards and Activities, by Jerry DeBruin (Carthage, IL: Good Apple, 1990).
Cards feature step-by-step instructions for activities featuring famous scientists, library reports, career education, and science safety. Useful in individualizing instruction.

Creative Sciencing, Grades K-6, by Alfred De Vito and Gerald H. Krockover (Boston: Little, Brown, 1991).
A multitude of activities to involve the young learner in hands-on, minds-on science. Many activities are suitable for homebound science experiences.

Early Start Series, by Roy Richards (New York: Simon & Schuster, 1991).
Titles in series include *An Early Start to Science, An Early Start to Technology from Science,* and *An Early Start to the Environment.* Publications utilize a pictorial format to describe a wealth of fresh ideas and activities in elementary science. The wholistic nature of the investigations makes them good starting points for thematic units.

Earth: The Water Planet, by Jack E. Gartrell, Jr., Jane Crowder, and Jeffrey C. Callister (Washington, DC: National Science Teachers Association, 1989).

Twenty-nine classroom investigations on the themes of groundwater, reshaping the earth's surface, raindrops and erosion, limits, and physical properties of water. Two modules include a section based on a segment of the *Eureka!* video series produced by TV Ontario. Includes 18 teacher background readings.

Earthquakes, by the National Science Teachers Association (Washington, DC: 1989). Three-hole-punched manual includes a unit of activities for students in grades K-2, 3-4, and 5-6. Lessons are designed to integrate all subject areas. Teacher background information provided.

The Everyday Science Sourcebook, by Lawrence F. Lowery (Palo Alto, CA: Dale Seymour Publications, 1985). A compilation of elementary science activities coded for developmental levels. Activities are grouped under the following content categories: inorganic matter, organic matter, energy, inference models, technology, instructional apparatus, materials, and systems.

The Idea Factory's Super Science Sourcebook, by Ellyn Smith, Marilyn Blackmer, and Sandi Schlichting (Riverview, FL: Idea Factory, 1987). Over 100 elementary science activities that use everyday things. Content background, step-by-step directions, and suggestions for curricular integration accompany each lesson.

An Invitation to Science Inquiry, by Tik Liem (Chino Hills, CA: Science Inquiry Enterprises, 1990). An extensive collection of discrepant events in all science disciplines. Activities serve as sets to motivate students' conceptual learning in science.

Learning Center Activity Cards, by Addison-Wesley (Menlo Park, CA: n.d.). A set of laminated 8 1/2" x 11" activity cards is published for each grade level. Each card presents a student-centered problem, a challenge for the student, directions for meeting the challenge, and directions for reporting results. Cards are designed to be used independently by students. A teacher's guide with activity extensions accompanies each set of cards.

Mudpies to Magnets, by Robert A. Williams, Robert E. Rockwell, and Elizabeth A.

Sherwood (Mt. Rainier, MD: Gryphon House, 1987). A collection of developmentally appropriate science experiences for preschoolers. Activities involve young children in making observations and looking for patterns. Many activities are also suitable for school-age children.

Naturescope, by the National Wildlife Federation (Washington, DC: n.d.). Seventeen wholistic modules dealing with environmental topics. Each module includes student activities, copycat pages, stories, and teacher background. Titles include *Incredible Insects; Digging into Dinosaurs; Wild about Weather; Birds, Birds, Birds!; Discovering Deserts; Trees Are Terrific; Astronomy Adventures; Amazing Mammals I; Amazing Mammals II; Wading into Wetlands; Geology: The Active Earth; Endangered Species; Reptiles and Amphibians; Discovery Pac; Diving into Oceans; Wild and Crafty; Rain Forests; and Pollution.*

North Polar Constellations, by D. Louis and Mary Jane Finsand (n.p., 1991). Publication includes lesson plans keyed to the learning cycle. Reproducible masters of worksheets, sky maps, and overheads are included.

Physics for Kids: 49 Easy Experiments with Optics, by Robert W. Wood (Blue Ridge Summit, PA: TAB Books, 1990). Forty-nine graphically illustrated investigations develop understanding of optics. Content background is provided. Along with activities that investigate reflection, refraction, and color are directions for constructing solar stills, periscopes, kaleidoscopes, ice lenses, and refracting telescopes. Ideas for science fair projects are included.

Safe and Simple Electrical Experiments, by Rudolf F. Graf (New York: Dover, 1973). Well-illustrated, hands-on activities include 38 static electricity investigations, 32 investigations on magnetism, and 32 investigations on current electricity and electromagnetism. Teacher background provided.

Schoolground Science: Activities for Elementary and Middle Schools, by Charles E. Roth, Cleti Cervoni, Thomas Wellnitz, and Elizabeth Arms (Lincoln, MA: The Massachusetts Audubon

Society, 1988).
Thirty-five field-based investigations dealing with life, earth, and physical science are described. Students are involved in individual or group data collection. Directions for preparing field data sheets are provided.

School Yard—Backyard Cycles of Science, by Jerry DeBruin (Carthage, IL: Good Apple, 1989).
Hands-on experiences allow teacher and student or parent and child to work together to examine cycles of the universe, the seasons, soil nutrients, and water.

Science Activities for Children, by George C. Lorbeer and Leslie W. Nelson (Dubuque, IA: William C. Brown, 1991).
An extensive resource book of student activities and teacher demonstrations. Text includes sections on classic science topics such as matter, magnetism, electricity, heat, sound, light, plants, animals, health, ecology, earth/space/aviation, and space travel.

Science on a Shoestring, by Herb Strongin (Menlo Park, CA: Addison-Wesley, 1976).
Publication includes numerous simple content demonstrations and activities on the scientific method, change and energy, and fields and forces. Many activities are suitable for take-home science tasks.

Teaching Children about Science: Ideas and Activities Every Teacher and Parent Can Use, by Elaine Levenson (Englewood Cliffs, NJ: Prentice Hall, 1987).
A host of models, demonstrations, and simple activities useful in developing basic science concepts. Chapter titles include "Five Senses," "Magnetism," "Static Electricity," Sound," "Light," "Air and Water," "Weather," "Volcanoes/Rocks/Erosion," "Animals," "All about Plants," and "Ecology." Content background for the teacher is provided.

Teaching the Fun of Physics, by Janice Pratt Van Cleave (Englewood Cliffs, NJ: Prentice Hall, 1985).
A hundred and one models, demonstrations, and discrepant events dealing with buoyancy, liquids and gases, light, magnets/electricity, and force and motion. Text includes a chapter on "Toys that Teach Physics."

Teaching Science to Children: An Integrated Approach, by Alfred E. Friedl (New York: Random House, 1986).
Twenty hands-on elementary science units are developed utilizing the learning cycle approach. Extensive teacher background is provided.

Teaching Science with Everyday Things, by Victor E. Schmidt and Verne N. Rockcastle (New York: McGraw-Hill, 1982).
Each chapter focuses on a different content area, from air and weather, to magnetism and electricity. One chapter develops life science understandings. The numerous activities in each chapter involve students in innovative, quantitative investigations.

Think about It! Science Problems of the Day, by Anthony D. Fredericks (Oak Lawn, IL: Creative Publications, 1988).
Includes 180 daily problems and 36 weekly challenges to stimulate group investigation and library research on science problems.

Water, Stones and Fossil Bones, by Karen K. Lind (Washington, DC: Council for Elementary Science International: National Science Teachers Association, 1991).
Fifty-one innovative models, demonstrations, and activities for elementary/middle level earth science studies. Section headings include "Space," "Land," "Water," "Air," and "The Earth's Past."

Workjobs, by Mary Baratta Lorton (Menlo Park, CA: Addison-Wesley, 1972).
A wealth of sensory activities for the very young student. Skills developed through hands-on tasks include matching, classification, sets, sequence, combining and separating groups, and relationships.

Life and Environmental Science
Beyond the Classroom: Exploration of Schoolground and Backyard, by the Massachusetts Audubon Society (Lincoln, MA: 1988).
Publication includes 33 activities which involve students in real-world science with living things, weather, light, forces, and motion.

Bugplay: Activities with Insects for Young Children, Marlene Nachbar Hapai and Leon H. Burton (Menlo Park, CA: Addison-Wesley, 1990).

Publication presents a wholistic approach to the investigations of insects—from silverfish, dragonflies, and crickets to bugs, beetles, and honey bees. 26 insects are explored through hands-on investigation, poetry, art, and music. An audiotape of music included in text comes with the publication.

Consider the Earth, by Julie M. Gates
(Englewood, CO: Teacher Ideas Press, 1989).
Over 100 innovative, often quantitative, investigations for 4–8th graders. Activities presented in 8 chapters: "Soil," "Plants," "Water," "Wildlife," "Sensory Awareness," "Ecosystems," "Weather," and "Environmental Problems." Precise illustrations and the inclusion of data tables enhances useability. Vocabulary definitions are included in each chapter.

Creative Food Experiences for Children, by Mary T.
Goodwin and Gerry Pollen (Washington, DC: Center for Science in the Public Interest, 1980).
Book provides a wholistic approach to the study of nutrition. Origins of foods and a historical focus for foods are presented. Activities range from selecting foods for purchase, preparing food, and mixing ingredients for sensory delights involving taste and smell. A large bibliography of related books for children is included.

The Growing Classroom, by Roberta Jaffe and
Gary Appel (Menlo Park, CA: Addison-Wesley, 1985).
480 pages of activities and experiences related to gardening and food. Chapters focus on cooperative group problem-solving tasks, activities that develop critical thinking/process skills, investigations on soils, germination/growing, cycles/changes, interdependence, ecology, climate, and nutrition. Publication presents a wholistic approach to the study of life science.

Grow Lab: Activities for Growing Minds, by Joy
Cohen and Eve Pranis (Burlington, VT: National Gardening Association, 1990).
A collection of gardening activities that foster inquiry and encourage innovative student investigation.

*Hands-On-Nature: Information and Activities for
Exploring the Environment with Children*, by Jenepher Lengelbach, ed. (Woodstock, VT: Institute of Natural Science, 1986).
Hands-on activities are grouped into three

categories: adaptations, habitats, and cycles. Each of the 24 lessons include teacher background, activities, a puppet play, and suggested reading for children.

*Keepers of the Earth: Native American Stories and
Environmental Activities for Children*, by Michael J. Caduto and Joseph Bruchac (Golden, CO: Fulcrum, 1989).
Stories and activities help students develop insights into the relationship between people and the environment. Two audiotapes contain 25 of the Native American stories included in the book. Teacher's guide available.

*Keepers of the Animals: Native American Stories
and Wildlife Activities for Children*, by Michael J. Caduto and Joseph Bruchac (Golden, CO: Fulcrum, 1991).
The 27 stories of Native American culture and the related activities encourage responsible stewardship of all the Earth's creatures.

Life Science for Elementary Teachers, by Patricia
R. Simpson and John C. Coulter (Dubuque, IA: Kendall/Hunt, 1991).
The title of this book is misleading. The book contains 49 beautifully detailed life science investigations suitable for use with elementary students. Investigations on animals focus on bugs, worms, fairy shrimp, and crickets. Other chapters deal with plants, the environment, and the diversity of living things.

Nature Activities for Early Childhood, by Janet
Nickelsburg (Menlo Park, CA: Addison-Wesley, 1976).
Forty-four hands-on outdoor science learning experiences for young children. Activities are intended to help children become better observers of nature.

Naturewatch, by Adrienne Katz (Menlo Park, CA:
Addison-Wesley, 1986).
Publication includes over 50 projects for exploring natural environments. Section on nature crafts is included.

The Pillbug Project: A Guide to Investigation, by
Robin Burnett (Washington, DC: National Science Teachers Association, 1992).
An eight-day inquiry module on pillbugs (isopods). Central to the student investigations is a read-aloud story about Patricia Pillbug. Text provides

excellent content background for the teacher.

Protecting Our Planet, by Ava Deutsch Drutman and Susan Klam Zuckerman (Carthage, IL: Good Apple, 1991).
Three publications designed for grades Preschool–1, 1–3, and 4–8 include activities and experiences to promote understanding of global warming, waste pollution, air pollution, water pollution, ozone layer depletion, and hazardous waste.

Sharing Nature with Children, by Joseph Bharat Cornell (Nevada City, CA: Dawn Publications, 1979).
A collection of outdoor nature games that promote an emotional appreciation of nature, as well as content understanding. Activities are ideal for language arts extensions.

Teaching Kids to Love the Earth, by Marina Lachecki Herman, Joseph F. Passineau, Ann L. Schimpf, and Paul Treuer (Duluth, MN: Pfeifer-Hamilton, 1991).
Preceded by a story, each of the 186 outdoor activities included in this publication involves students with the wonder of the earth. Some activities encourage awareness and action on environmental issues.

Waste Away, by Bonnie L. Ross (Woodstock: Vermont Institute of Natural Science, 1989).
Each of the book's four sections includes activities and information for investigating trash problems and sample solutions for their remedy.

Ten-Minute Field Trips, by Helen Ross Russell (Chicago: J. G. Ferguson (Doubleday), 1991).
Text describes over 200 close-to-home field trips that trigger curiosity and stimulate investigation. A cross-referenced list of field trips on hard-topped school grounds is included for urban areas.

Activity Sourcebooks for Elementary-/Middle-Level Students

Adventures with Atoms and Molecules: Chemistry Experiments for Young People, by Robert C. Mebane and Thomas R. Rybolt (Hillside, NJ: Enslow, 1985).
Each of the 30 investigations starts with a question. From the investigations, students gain an appreciation for the behavior of molecules at different temperatures and how they interact with different liquids. Background information is provided.

Adventures with Atoms and Molecules, Book II, by Robert C. Mebane and Thomas R. Rybolt (Hillside, NJ: Enslow, 1987).
Students investigate household chemistry to learn how water acts like glue, how certain molecules can trap odors, and how others cause food to spoil. Background information is provided.

At Home with Science Series, by Eve and Albert Stevertka (Westwood, NJ: Silver, Burdett, 1992).
Drip Drop: Water's Journey and *A Chilling Story: How Things Cool Down.* Includes simple experiments about everyday science in the home.

Bet You Can! and *Bet You Can't!* by Vicki Cobb (New York: William Morrow, 1980, 1982).
Both books present numerous discrepant events which are used to stimulate thinking about basic science concepts in the physical sciences.

Brown Paper School Book series, by Linda Allison (Boston: Little, Brown, n.d.).
The Reasons for Seasons (1975). Although directions for projects are given, students are encouraged to investigate such topics as solar collectors, garbage gardens, worm farms, and crystals on their own.
Blood and Guts: A Working Guide to Your Own Insides (1976). Seventy investigations to acquaint students with the way their bodies work. Each activity is accompanied with background information and amazing facts.
Gee Whiz! (1983). An imaginative collection of experiences with exploding colors, fantastic elastic, capillary action, surface tension, magnification, and balancing. Each activity portrays science as a way of thinking.

Children's Museum Activity Books, by Bernie Zubrowski (Boston: Little, Brown, n.d.).
Bubbles (1979). Activities challenge students to be inventive in creating bubbles of different sizes, shapes, and durability. Book makes learning fun.
Messing Around with Baking Chemistry (1981). Adult supervision is necessary as students vary recipes, experiment with yeast dough, and assemble gas generators. Text helps students see science in everyday things.

Messing Around with Water Pumps and Siphons
(1981). Activities help students focus on the
similarities in the operation of pumps, from
the human heart to the toothpaste pump.
Raceways: Having Fun with Balls and Tracks
(1985). Innovative explorations of energy,
acceleration, and momentum.
*Wheels at Work: Building and Experimenting
with Models of Machines* (1986). Using
everyday things, students are shown how to
build pulleys, windlasses, gears, water wheels,
bubble-blowing devices, windmills, and
paddle wheels.

Ontario Science Centre Elementary Science
series (Menlo Park, CA: Addison-Wesley, n.d.).
Ontario Science Centre produces a series of
activity/project books for children. The content of
each book is clearly developed. Graphic illustrations enhance the readability. Books are a good
resource for teachers as well as for students.
Titles in the series include the following:
Sciencework. Sixty-five physical science activities that feature discrepant events, measuring
activities, and construction projects.
Sportworks. Fifty activities that explore the
science involved in sports and staying fit.
Science Express. Fifty discrepant events that
stimulate thinking about basic science concepts.
Foodworks. Over 100 science activities that
explore the production, processing, preservation, and preparation of foods.

*175 Science Experiments to Amuse and Amaze
Your Friends and More Science Experiments to
Amuse and Amaze Your Friends,* by Brenda
Walpole (New York: Random House, 1990).
A collection of discrepant events that should
ignite further investigation into basic science
concepts.

Science Experiments You Can Eat (1972) and *More
Science Experiments You Can Eat* (1979), by
Vicki Cobb (New York: J. B. Lippincott).
Both books develop open-ended investigations
focusing on food: composition, processing,
preservation, and chemical changes resulting
from cooking.

Science Fun series, by Rose Wyler (New York:
Julian Messner, n.d.).
Science Fun with Drums, Bells, and Whistles
(1987). Clear directions and graphic illustrations help children construct a variety of

musical instruments. Some traditional ethnic
musical instruments are described.
Science Fun with Mud and Dirt (1986). Students explore the many uses both people and
animals make of mud and dirt.
Science Fun with Toy Cars and Trucks (1987).
Early understandings of motion, friction,
inertia, momentum, and acceleration are
introduced through hands-on activities. Value
of seat belts is demonstrated.
Science Fun with a Homemade Chemistry Set
(1987). Interactions of simple household
chemicals are investigated.

Titles in the series of elementary science activity
books for children published by the
Smithsonian Institution include the following:
Science Activity Book. 20 hands-on activities
engage students in exploring topics such as
home movies, crystal gardens, bubbles, and
foods. The use of everyday things makes the
activities suitable for home science projects.
More Science Activities. 20 hands-on activities
in which students explore making ginger ale,
creating marbleized paper, and performing
magic tricks.
Still More Science Activities. Twenty hands-on
activities that involve students in making
solar cookers, paper from grass clippings, and
scientific food.

Supplemental Elementary/Middle Level Science Programs

Any thing free

Elementary Science Study (ESS) (Hudson, NH:
Delta Education, n.d.).
A series of single-topic instructional modules for
teachers. Each module provides numerous open-
ended ideas that stimulate student investigation
into real-world science. Inventive problem solving
is encouraged. The teacher is provided with
exploratory questions. Photographs and diagrams
give graphic descriptions of procedures children
have used to solve problems. Titles include
Crayfish, Pendulums, The Bone Book, Optics,
Peas and Particles, Tangrams, Mirror Cards, and
Whistles and Strings.

Great Explorations in Math and Science (GEMS)
(Berkeley: Lawrence Hall of Science, University of California, n.d.).
Over 14 single-focus teacher manuals describe
innovative process science investigations for

elementary children. Instructional emphasis is on the acquisition of inquiry skills. Titles include *Animal Defenses, Bubbles, Oobleck, Liquid Explorations, Involving Dissolving, Crime Lab Chemistry, Of Cabbages and Chemistry,* and *Color Analyzers.* Focus of investigations is on problem solving.

Anything free

Project AIMS (Fresno, CA: AIMS Education Foundation, n.d.).
A series of over 20 books provides hands-on activities to help elementary children integrate mathematics and science. Each investigation includes a teacher direction page, student activity sheets, and student data tables. Titles include *Fall into Math and Science, Seasoning Math and Science, Popping with Power, Overhead and Underfoot, Fun with Foods, Floaters and Sinkers, The Sky's the Limit, Down to Earth,* and *Our Wonderful World.*

Freebies

Science 5/13, by Sheila Parker (London: MacDonald Educational, n.d.). Available in the United States from Teacher's Laboratory, Brattleboro, VT.
Each book in the series provides extensive teacher background in both text and illustration for guiding elementary children in open-ended scientific investigations of real-world phenomena. Each book takes a wholistic approach to the subject matter. Titles include *Using the Environment; Working with Wood; Structures and Forces; Science from Toys; Minibeasts; Holes, Gaps, and Cavities; Change Stages; Coloured Things; Trees; Science Models and Toys;* and *Children and Plastics.*

Freebies

TOPS Learning Systems, by Ron Marson (Canby, OR: n.d.).
Titles in series include *Balancing, Electricity, Magnetism, Pendulums, Metric Measuring, More Metrics, Animal Survival, Green Thumbs,* and others. Each module includes student task cards and content background for the teacher. Emphasis is on the use of simple things to involve students in hands-on science.

Resources on Thematic Integrated Science Instruction

Interdisciplinary Methods: A Thematic Approach, by Alan H. Humphreys, Thomas R. Post, and

Arthur K. Ellis (Santa Monica: Goodyear Publishing, 1981).
The link between thematic units and problem solving is developed. Techniques for developing and managing thematic units and for assessing learning are presented. Fourteen sampler thematic units are included. Titles of units include "Flight," "Consumerism," "Parkland," "Sailboats," "Environments," "Growing and Using Plants," "Patterns and Changes," "Inventions," and "Go Fly a Kite!"

Purchase if possible

Science Experiences: Cooperative Learning and the Teaching of Science, by Jack Hassard (Menlo Park, CA: Addison-Wesley, 1990).
Includes wholistic learning experiences for units on the web of life, wholistic health, astronomy and oceanography, geology, density, the future, energy, and environmental science. Units focus on phenomena rather than specific content. Problem solving through cooperative learning is emphasized (4–9th grade).

Purchase if possible

Science through Children's Literature, by Carol M. Butzow and John W. Butzow (Englewood, CO: Libraries Unlimited, 1989).
Publication summarizes 33 children's trade books, develops science concepts, and describes activities to explore science. Concept-mapping strategies are used to show relationships among content understandings.

Story Stretchers, by Shirley C. Raines and Robert J. Canady (Mt. Ranier, MD: Gryphon House, 1989).
Ninety elementary science trade books are described. Ways to extend the understandings developed in each trade book into each of the curricular areas are presented. All stories have a science component.

Resources in Science and Technology for the Elementary-/Middle-Level Teacher

Connections: A Curriculum in Appropriate Technology for 5th and 6th Grades, by Joan Melcher (Butte, MT: National Center for Appropriate Technology, 1980).
Problems presented in each of the ten chapters are introduced with a historical perspective. The emphasis of each chapter is on appropriate

technology. Each chapter contains many student investigations dealing with topics such as conservation, transportation, waste, recycling, renewable resources, making solar models, and the food we eat.

Design and Technology 5-12, by Pat Williams and David Jinks (London: Falmer Press, 1989). Students develop problem-solving skills through the construction of three-dimensional objects. In the design of their object, students must make accurate drawings to scale, determine the materials from which the objects should be constructed, and make other construction decisions. Excellent four-color pictures of constructions and of students at work highlight the volume. Design case studies include levers and ducks, windmills, Roman chariot, car design, and Abbeydale industrial hamlet.

Design Technology: Children's Engineering, by Susan Dunn and Rob Larson (London: Falmer Press, 1990). Children use rolls of newspaper, plastic bottles, wood blocks, and corrugated cardboard to create imaginative structures with moveable parts. Book describes strategies for implementing design technology in the classroom. Examples of student work are used to demonstrate each stage, from exploration to celebration. The use of the learning logs as a tool for reflection is described. Excellent illustrations of constructions.

Design and Technology in Primary School Classrooms, by Les Tickle, ed. (London: Falmer Press, 1990). Seven United Kingdom elementary teachers describe the construction projects done by students in their classrooms. Student logs, designs, and constructions are included. Strategies for nurturing both problem posing and problem solving are described. Mathematics becomes an essential skill as students draw scale diagrams and build constructions from blueprints.

Design and Technology through Problem Solving, by Robert Johnsey (New York: Simon & Schuster, 1991). Problems of an open-ended nature are described. Design technology becomes an important consideration as children explore problems involving balancing models, obstacle games, paddle boats, wheels and levers, propeller-driven vehicles, electrical switches, and folding chairs.

Inventioneering: Nurturing Intellectual Talent in the Classroom, by Bob Stanish and Carol Singletary (Carthage, IL: Good Apple, 1987). Techniques for stimulating divergent thinking through brainstorming are described. Basic concepts in physical science that are useful in inventioneering are discussed. Challenge problems related to the following topics are described: "New Uses for Coat Hangers," "Spaghetti-Eating Utensil," "The Pecan Contraption," and the "The Bedroom Picker-Upper." A list of suggested readings on inventions is included.

Inventors Workshop, by Alan J. McCormack (Belmont, CA: David S. Lake, 1981). Twenty-five imaginative projects that capture the spirit of invention. Extensions that challenge student inventiveness accompany most projects. Graphics enhance the book's appeal and clarity.

Problem Solving in School Science, by Robert Johnsey (London: MacDonald Educational, 1986). Available in the United States from Teachers Laboratory, Brattleboro, VT. Students design equipment to solve problems. All investigations are open-ended. Although many ideas are provided, students are encouraged to explore original ideas when investigating topics such as elastic energy, seeds on the move, time, wheels, and paper structures.

Special Topics
The Assessment of Hands-On Elementary Science Programs, by George Hein, Ed. (Grand Forks, ND: Center for Teaching and Learning, University of North Dakota, 1990). A 300-page monograph of papers delivered by noted science educators and researchers at a national conference on assessment. Papers are grouped under four headings: "Lessons from the Assessment of Reading and Writing," "Assessment Theory," "Large-Scale Assessments," and "Assessment in Science Education Research and Development."

Junior High and High School Level Science Resources

General Science Activity Sourcebooks
Field Manual for Water Quality Monitoring, An Environmental Education Program for Schools, by Mark Mitchell and William Stapp (Dexter, MI: Thomson-Stone, 1991).

An Invitation to Science Inquiry by Tik Liem
(Chino Hills, CA: Science Inquiry Enterprises, 1991).
An extensive collection of discrepant events in all of the science disciplines. Activities serve as sets to motivate student conceptual learning in science.

Middle School Science: Demonstrations, Activities, and Labs by Salvatore Michael Trento
(Dubuque, IA: Kendall/Hunt, 1990).
Twenty-two innovative laboratory experiences designed specifically for the middle-level student. Lab topics range from "Dental Alginate Mold Activity" and "Index Card Architecture" to the "Spitball Lab." One chapter deals with the logistics of developing a research project and with soliciting family and community support for student research. Text includes a unit on "Using an Archaeological Dig" in a middle school science course.

Science Laboratory Techniques, by Rolland B. Bartholomew and Frank E. Crawley (Menlo Park, CA: Addison-Wesley, 1980).
A compilation of basic laboratory and demonstration techniques used in biological, physical, and earth sciences.

700 Science Experiments for Everyone, by UNESCO (New York: Doubleday, 1962).
A compilation of classic demonstrations to reinforce the understanding of basic science concepts. Activities range from elementary through junior high level.

SPACES: Solving Problems of Access to Careers in Engineering and Science, by Sherry Fraser (Palo Alto, CA: Dale Seymour Publications, n.d.).
A collection of activities designed to stimulate students' thinking about scientific careers, develop problem-solving skills, promote positive attitudes toward the study of mathematics, increase interest and knowledge about scientific work, and strengthen spatial visualization skills.

Super Science Activities, by Diane Bredt, Rob Beattie, Jean Lyford, Tom Weght, Steven Oshita, and Jacinta Martinez (Palo Alto, CA: Dale Seymour, 1988).
Six hands-on science units, written by classroom teachers, for junior high students. Titles include "Plate Tectonics," "Earthquakes," "Natural Selection," "Ecosystems," "Electric Circuits," and "Chromatography."

The Tapwater Tour (Chestertown, MD: LaMotte, 1991).
Activities involve the use of safe, simple chemical tests to analyze tapwater. Student data tables and chemical indicators (tablets) are included in three-ring binder format. Tablets are the same as those used by professional water analysts.

Sourcebooks of Life Science/Biology Activities
Animal Care from Protozoa to Small Mammals, by F. Barbara Orlans (Menlo Park, CA: Addison-Wesley, 1977).
Includes detailed directions for the humanistic care of animals from protozoa to mammals. Activities and investigations to learn more about each animal are provided. An excellent resource for all teachers who aspire to help children learn to appreciate animals.

Animals in the Classroom, by David C. Kramer (Menlo Park, CA: Addison-Wesley, 1989).
Detailed directions for the humane care of animals reflect the author's regard for living things. Each chapter contains a wealth of ideas for humane, experimental animal studies. An excellent resource for students contemplating animal research.

Carolina Biology Readers (Burlington, NC: Carolina Biological Supply, n.d.).
Short monographs by leading scientists on a wide range of biological topics ranging from standard high school biology topics to news-making issues.

Cycles of Nature: An Introduction to Biological Rhythms, by Andrew Ahlgren and Franz Halberg (Washington DC: National Science Teachers Association, 1990).
The latest research on biological rhythms is presented in a manner that motivates students in grades 6–12 to measure common cycles such as heart rate, body temperature, chemical reactions, plant growth, and animal sleep cycles.

Food for the Health of It, by Anne Kapitan and Carol Wintle, Project Outside/Inside (Somerville, MA: Somerville Public Schools, 1980).
Text provides a wealth of information on diet and health, additives and preservatives, and the effect of advertising on food intake.

Microcosmos: The Microcosmos Curriculum Guide to Exploring Microbial Space, by Douglas Zook

and the Microcosmos Team (Dubuque, IA: Kendall/Hunt, 1992).
A complete treatment of the microbial world, from collecting microbes to examining symbiotic partnerships in fermentation. Activities are presented in an intriguing problem-solving format. Some sections use cartoons effectively to teach understandings. Other sections use every-day things such as soap bubbles to study membranes. All investigations stress the importance of observation.

Nature Puzzlers, by Laurence E. Hillman (Englewood, CO: Libraries Unlimited, 1989).
Using 50 nature puzzles, students solve research questions in environmental education. Puzzles help students develop skill in critical thinking, as well as insights into unique environmental research.

Openers for Biology Classes, by Robert Gridley (n.p., 1990).
Two hundred short 'sets' for biology understandings. Activities to develop the understandings are included.

*Outdoor Biology Instructional Strategies*OBIS, Lawrence Hall of Science (Hudson, NH: Delta Education, n.d.).
Ninety separate activities about the environment are grouped into 27 modules. Each activity is printed in a file folder format. Module titles include "Adaptations," "Animal Behavior," "Lawns and Fields," "Ponds and Lakes," "Outdoor Study Techniques," and "Wintertime."

Save Our Planet, by Diane MacEachern (Washington, DC: National Wildlife Federation, 1990).
Provides background information and 750 actions for demonstrating environmental stewardship at school, the office, at home, or in the community.

A Sourcebook for the Biological Sciences, by Evelyn Morholt and Paul Brandwein (New York: Harcourt Brace Jovanovich, 1986).
A definitive collection of standard techniques, procedures, and demonstrations in the life sciences. Content background provided.

Teaching Science with Garbage, by Albert Schatz and Vivian Schatz (Emmaus, PA: Rodale Press, 1971).
Thirty investigations of decay, decomposition, biodegradability, and composting.

Winter Environmental Studies, by Lester A. Picker (Dubuque, IA: Kendall/Hunt, 1988).
A unique set of investigations about an often maligned season. Investigations range from galls, snowflakes, and twig studies to winter survival and using snow as an indicator of pollution. Both winter forest and pond ecosystems are explored. Interesting facts tucked into page margins contribute to the user's enjoyment.

Wisconsin Fast Plants, by Paul Williams (Burlington, NC: North Carolina Biological Supply, 1989).
A collection of classroom investigations using the rapid-cycling *Brassica rapa*. Investigations explore the following topics: germination, plant responses to light and gravity, the effects of gibberellic acid, plant nutrition, Mendelian genetics, non-Mendelian genetics, the effects of salt on germination and growth, and the effects of acid precipitation.

Sourcebooks of Physical/ Earth Science Activities

Astronomy Activity Book, by Dennis Schatz (New York: Little, Simon & Schuster, 1991).
Publication includes student activities and explanatory material that integrate mathematics and language arts. Star finder included.

Astronomy Projects for Young Scientists, by Necia H. Apfel (New York: Arco, 1984).
Describes a variety of experiences in astronomy, including making a telescope, building a planetarium, measuring the circumference of the earth, and detecting cosmic rays.

Chemistry around You: Experiments and Projects with Everyday Products by Salvatori Tocci (New York: Arco, 1985).
One hundred experiments involving household chemicals. Topics for independent study included.

Earth: The Water Planet, by Jack E. Gartrell, Jr., Jane Crowder, and Jeffrey C. Callister (Washington, DC: National Science Teachers Association, 1992).

Evidence of Energy: An Introduction to Mechanics, Book Two, by Jack E. Gartrell, Jr., and Larry E. Schafer (Washington, DC: National Science Teachers Association, 1990).
Publication includes hands-on, teacher-tested

activities that help combat common misconceptions about projectiles, motion, work energy, machines, torque, and center of gravity. Supplementary readings and suggestions for extended study are included in the text.

Experiments in Basic Chemistry, by Stephen Murov and Brian Stedjie (Sommerset, NJ: Wiley, 1989).
Laboratories in chemistry designed for low environmental impact.

The Exploratorium Science Snackbook (Exploratorium Teacher Institute: 1991).
Instructions on how to build 100 interactive science exhibits. Exhibits supplement labs or make excellent student projects. A supplemental teacher's guide is available.

I'm Madly in Love with Electricity and Other Comments about Their Work by Women in Science and Engineering, by Nancy Kreinberg, EQUALS (Berkeley, CA: Lawrence Hall of Science, University of California, n.d.).

Introduction to the Oceans: A Laboratory Manual, by Christina M. Emerick (Dubuque, IA: Kendall/Hunt, 1991).
The first 5 sets of investigations deal with physical oceanography: geology, density and circulation, and wind-driven ocean circulation. Additional chapters include investigations dealing with coastal ecology, communities, and ecosystems. Form and function lab involves students in observations of, and inferences about, the adaptations of marine organisms.

Methods of Motion: An Introduction to Mechanics, by Jack E. Gartrell, Jr. (Washington, DC: The National Science Teachers Association, 1992).
Text includes 27 student investigations that deal with describing and measuring forces and motion. A student activity worksheet and a data table are included with each investigation. Some investigations feature segments from the *Eureka!* video series produced by TV Ontario. 14 student readings reinforce basic concepts.

Polymer Chemistry (Washington, DC: National Science Teachers Association, 1989).
Divided into two sections, the publication provides information on both natural (wool, silk, cellulose) and synthetic polymers, as well as student laboratory activities, demonstrations, and polymer games.

Problem-Solving Exercises in Physics, by Jennifer Bond Hechman (Menlo Park, CA: Addison-Wesley, 1992).
An excellent collection of paper and pencil problem-solving tasks focusing on the standard topics developed in high school physics. Problems tie science into real-world situations. Space is provided in the text for student calculations.

Project Earth Science: Astronomy (Washington, DC: National Science Teachers Association, 1992).
Hands-on, teacher-tested activities that help students develop an appreciation for the uniqueness of Earth among the planets of the Solar System. Teacher background information, supplementary readings, and suggestions for student projects are included in the text.

The Thomas Edison Book of Easy and Incredible Experiments (New York: Wiley, 1988).
Sixty-four energy-related activities ranging from electrochemistry to nuclear experiments. Valuable source of science projects for the junior high student. Includes an extensive bibliography of science resource books for the teacher.

Weather Study under a Newspaper Umbrella by H. Michael Mogil (n.p., 1989).
Directions on using the newspaper to study weather, weather safety, environmental issues, energy, economics, and earth sciences. Three-ring binder format. Appendices include numerous tracking charts and tables.

Wind, Water, Fire, and Earth: Energy Lessons for Physical Sciences (Washington, DC: National Science Teachers Association, 1986).
Student activities designed to infuse themes related to energy, the environment, and economic issues into the science curriculum. Investigations explore topics from thermodynamics to the greenhouse effect.

Supplemental Programs

Chemical Education for Public Understanding Program (CEPUP) (Berkeley, CA: Lawrence Hall of Science, University of California, n.d.).
Eight modules that engage students in real-world science and technology problems. Titles include *Risk Comparison, Determining Threshold Limits,*

Investigating Groundwater: The Fruitvale Story, Toxic Waste: A Teaching Simulation, Plastics in Our Lives, Investigating Chemical Processes: Your Island Factory, and *Chemicals in Food: Additives.* Each module is accompanied by all equipment and supplies needed to conduct the investigation.

COMETS Profiles, by Ruth Noyce, ed. (1982) and COMETS Science: *Career Oriented Modules to Explore Topics in Science* (vol. 2), by Walter L. Smith, Loretta L. Molitor, Bess J. Nelson, and Catherine L. Matthews (Washington, DC: National Science Teachers Association, 1984). Teaching background activities, career information, and biographies related to career sketches of 24 women scientists. Scientists are selected from all branches of science.

Foundations and Challenges to Encourage Technology-Based Science (FACETS) (Washington, DC: American Chemical Society, n.d.). A hands-on program in which students are involved in real-world problem solving and decision making. Investigations explore science in the cities, marketplace, farmlands, shorelines, and within ourselves. Includes such topics as air quality, food additives, exercise, handling communication, artificial fabrics, pest control, and aging.

Great Exploration in Math and Science (GEMS) (Berkeley, CA: Lawrence Hall of Science, University of California, n.d.). Student investigations are presented in fifteen single-focus booklets. Titles include *Mapping Animal Movements, Convection, A Current Event, More Than Magnifiers, Chemical Reactions, Earthworms, Global Warming,* and *The Greenhouse Effect.*

Informal Science Study, by Howard Jones (Longmont, CO: National Training Network, n.d.). Five mini-units in physical science based on popular amusement park rides, sports, and playground experiences. Mini-units include *Physics of Fun and Play, The Informal Science Safari and Toy Workshop, Spaceflight Forces and Fears, Mechanics of Motion,* and *The Discovery Field Experience.*

New York Science, Technology, and Society Education Project (NYSTEP) (Albany, NY: n.d.). When completed, the science-related social issues curriculum will include twelve action-taking modules for use in middle-level science classrooms. Each module is designed for approximately a six-week period of time. Modules are open-ended, allowing students and teachers to initiate their own action on local problems. The following two modules are now ready for use: *Solid Waste Management: Is There a Solution?* Six activities in the module address solid waste problems and issues which give the students a grasp of the dimensions of the problem. Additional activities focus on waste management, and students are encouraged to improve existing plans if warranted by their research. *Using Earth's Resources: What Are the Trade-Offs?* Initial activities in the module focus on land use in the local area and the human activities that impact on its use. A three-part simulation is introduced where students must make trade-offs when determining in which of the six communities they wish to live. Later, the simulation is extended by adding information on drainage and river patterns. Given cost constraints, the students are asked to design the path of an interstate highway. Following several activities on soils, students are involved in action-taking experiences to prevent soil erosion in a local area.

Physics—Teach to Learn, by Leni Posner (Los Angeles: Los Angeles Unified School District, n.d.). Program utilizes computer simulations that require the learner to make judgements about physical events. The teacher-controlled simulations make it possible to lead a student through a step-by-step exploration, development, and application procedure individually designed to correct a student's misconceptions.

PRISMS: Physics Resources and Instructional Strategies for Motivating Students, by Roy D. Unruh (Cedar Falls, IA: Physics Department, University of Northern Iowa, n.d.). Utilizes the learning cycle approach to teach basic concepts of physics. Exploration activities encourage students to observe relationships, identify variables, and develop tentative explanations of phenomena. High-interest activities involving cars, bicycles, balloon rockets, dart guns, and sailboats, are used to teach the major concepts in physics.

Integrated Science

Science for All Americans, by F. James Rutherford and Andrew Ahlgren (New York: Oxford University Press, 1990).
Presents the rationale and need for a more interdisciplinary science curriculum to create a scientifically literate society.

Stones and Bones: A Laboratory Approach to the Study of Biology, Modern Science, and Anthropology, by Sid Sitkoff (Los Angeles: Los Angeles Unified School District, n.d.).
Program is designed to motivate non–college-oriented students. More than 30 laboratory explorations offer students the opportunity to investigate topics such as geologic time, measuring radioactivity, mapping, behavior of primates, replica casts of fossil hominids, continental drift, and interpreting archaeological records.

Science/Technology/Society Sourcebooks

The Art of Construction, by Mario Salvadori (Chicago, IL: Chicago Review Press, 1990).
Projects and principles for beginning engineers and architects. Excellent teacher background on the relationships between structure and function and the forces involved. Innovative student activities are well illustrated.

Biomedical Technology, by Mary McConnell (Dubuque, IA: Biological Sciences Curriculum Study: Kendall/Hunt, 1984).
Activities and experiences that help students appreciate the advances and apprehensions resulting from modern technology. Activities focus on public understanding of biomedical science, genetic screening, in vitro fertilization and embryo transfer, prenatal diagnosis, and recombinant DNA.

Cases in Bioethics, by Carol Levine and Robert M. Veatch, eds. (Hastings-on-Hudson, NY: Hastings Center, 1982).
An overview and commentaries from two perspectives are presented for a variety of case studies on issues in reproduction, patient-physician relationships, mental health and medical interventions, death and dying, human subjects research, allocation of scarce resources, and public policy.

Genes and Surroundings (Dubuque, IA: Biological Sciences Curriculum Study:Kendall/Hunt, 1983).
Activities explore human genetics from the perspective of variability and diversity. Students are asked to observe, record, and interpret the variability that surrounds them. They are asked to consider its biological roots and its ultimate expression in the myriad human environments that constitute modern society.

Immunology and Human Health (Scarborough, ME: Biological Sciences Curriculum Study: Foundation for Blood Research, 1986).
A collection of activities and experiences that encourage students to reflect on contemporary questions associated with AIDS and other immune system diseases. 12 activities involve students in learning about the biology of immune systems and reflecting on the social and ethical issues that confront society when coping with AIDS.

Inquiring and Problem Solving in the Physical Sciences: A Sourcebook, by Vincent N. Lunetta and Shemshon Novick (Dubuque, IA: Kendall/Hunt, 1982).
Detailed directions are given for conducting real-world science investigations on mechanics, electricity, wave motion, matter, heat, chemical reactions, dynamics, and molecular structure. Consumer investigations reinforce the science/technology/society component of science.

Investigating the Human Environment: Land Use (Dubuque, IA: Biological Sciences Curriculum Study, Kendall/Hunt, 1984).
Activities are designed to prepare students to assume leadership roles in land management decisions. Activities focus on public opinion, looking at land use, factors influencing land use, and selecting, organizing, conducting, and evaluating a land use action.

New York Science, Technology, and Society Education Project (Albany: State Education Department).
Eleven modules for middle-level science and an accompanying teacher's guide are under development. 2 modules are currently available for national use.

One-Minute Readings: Issues in Science, Technology, and Society, by Richard F. Brinckerhoff

(Menlo Park, CA: Addison-Wesley, 1992). Seventy-four issues from all science disciplines are presented. A scenario of each issue is presented, followed by a "Think about This" section. This section requires students to consider the human and economic implications of technology and its use. Issues deal with topics as diverse as solar energy, the medfly problem, and the tobacco lobby.

Product Testing Activities (Englewood Cliffs, NJ: Consumer Reports: Prentice Hall, 1992). Student activity book contains detailed challenges, investigations, and data tables for investigating products from popcorn, bandages, and lip balms to disposable cups, jeans, and yogurts. Teacher's guide available.

Question of the Week, by Catherine Valentino (Palo Alto, CA: Dale Seymour, 1985). Students are challenged by real-world problems to develop critical and innovative thinking skills. Each question is accompanied by a brief explanation, points to consider, and alternative questions. Student challenge sheets accompany each question.

Real Science, Real Decisions: A Collection of Thinking Activities from The Science Teacher (Washington, DC: The National Science Teachers Association, 1990). Publication features articles that explore modern scientific advances and the difficult ethical decisions they require. Questions for student discussion accompany each article.

Science and Technology in Fact and Fiction: A Guide to Young Adult Books, by Ann M. Kennedy, Stella S. Spangler, and Mary Ann Vanderwerf (New York: R.R. Bowker, 1990). A review of nearly 400 fiction and nonfiction trade books dealing with science and technology. Trade books selected for review deal with the physical and earth science disciplines. Each review includes a summary and evaluation. Trade books, as adjuncts to classroom instruction, provide students with an opportunity to explore a specific subject in depth.

Science in Cinema "Teaching Science Fact through Science Fiction Films," by Leroy W. Dubeck, Suzanne E. Moshier, and Judith E. Boss (New York: Teachers College Press, 1988). Resource book features 10 science fiction films

and provides a brief analysis of 24 additional films. Following a plot summary, the scientific principles related to each film are introduced. Classroom activities to extend student learning are included. Each film is reviewed from a wholistic perspective, including a literary commentary.

Science in the Marketplace, by Florence G. Korchin (Red Bank, NJ: Tiger Publications, 1983). A wealth of investigations intended to help students recognize the value of an understanding of science to the consumer. Biology investigations focus on nutrition, food preservation, labeling, and advertising. Home radiation, electrical appliances, fuels, and heat energy are among the physical science topics explored. The chemistry investigations deal with cosmetics, drugs, and pain relievers. One chapter deals with consumerism.

Science—Technology—Society: Investigating and Evaluating STS Issues and Solutions, by Harold R. Hungerford, Trudi L. Volk, and John. M. Ramsey (Champaign, IL: Stipes, 1990). Activities involve students in strategies to collect and analyze data associated with STS issues. Emphasis is on real-world involvement in which students identify a local STS problem; determine public opinion on the issue; and then develop, conduct, and evaluate an action plan which addresses the issue.

Science-Technology-Society: Preparing for Tomorrow's World, Longmont, CO: Sopris West, n.d.). A set of 12 independent curriculum modules are designed to teach higher-level thinking and social reasoning skills in the context of science, technology, and society. Modules have been used to complement courses such as English, science, reading, social studies, and biology. Topics covered include energy use and conservation, coastal issues, technological change, transportation, communications, medical technology, urban land development, cultural impact, and space travel.

Will You Help Me Create the Future Today? by John R. Eggers, (Buffalo, NY: D.O.K., 1981). 45 futuristic student activities reflect on how technology has impacted and will continue to impact the human enterprise. Activities are designed to help students develop the process skills needed to address the STS issues of the future.

Competitions and Fairs

The Complete Handbook of Science Fair Projects, by Julianne Blair Bochinski.
Publication contains 50 actual award-winning science fair projects and suggestions for 500 additional projects.

How to Do a Science Fair Project, by Salvatori Tocci (New York: Watts, 1986).
Provides pointers on selecting, researching, and presenting a science project.

Ideas for Science Projects, by Robert Gardner (New York: Watts, 1986).
Over 100 ideas for science projects in astronomy, botany, chemistry, physics, physiology, and zoology.

Invent America! (Alexandria, VA: United States Patent and Trademark Office, 1989).
Competition encourages innovative thinking to solve real-world problems. The Invent America! headquarters produces materials designed to help both teachers and students become involved in inventing. Publications include a student handbook, a teacher classroom guide, and an administrative support guide.

Nuts and Bolts: A Matter of Fact Guide to Science Fair Projects, by Barry Van Deman and Ed McDonald (Harwood Heights, IL: Science Man, 1982).
Clarifies each of the steps of experimental design. Provides experiences to help students select independent and dependent variables. Provides guidelines on communicating data and presenting results in a graphic manner.

Projects for Young Scientists Series, by David McKay and Bruce Smith (n.p., n.d.).
Titles include *Biology Projects, Energy Projects, Engineering Projects, Space Science Projects*. Background information is provided, followed by a wide range of project information.

Science and Math Events: Connecting and Competing (1990).
Publication provides directions on how to organize successful clubs and fairs. Information about 21 national and international competitions is included. 89 prize-winning scientists describe their experiences in student math and science competitions.

Science Fairs and Projects, Grades K–8, 1988 and *Science Fairs and Projects, Grades 7–12* (Washington, DC: National Science Teachers Association, 1988).
Publications describe how to initiate, organize, manage, and judge a science fair. Profiles of successful science fairs and alternatives to the traditional science fair are included.

Science Fairs with Style: A Comprehensive Step-by-Step Guide to Running a Successful Science Fair Project, by Jerry De Bruin, (Carthage, IL: Good Apple, 1991).
A step-by-step guide to encourage excellence in researching and presenting a science project.

Science Olympiad Officials Manual, by Sharon Putz (Rochester, MI: Science Olympiad, n.d.).
Provides detailed directions for planning, managing, and evaluating a Science Olympiad.

Science Projects for the Intermediate Grades, by Maxine Springer Schneider (Belmont, CA: David S. Lake Publishers, 1971).
Text describes how to construct science tools such as galvanometers, lung models, cloud chambers, sound makers, and steam turbines.

Students and Research: Practical Strategies for Science Classrooms and Competitions, by Julia H. Cothron, Ronald N. Giese, and Richard J. Rezba (Dubuque, IA: Kendall/Hunt, 1989).
Experiences are provided to help students generate research problems, design and conduct experiments, and communicate and interpret data. Checklists for each stage of a science project are included.

Resources on Science Clubs and Family/Community Science Events

Guide to Kids' Gardening, by Lynn Ocone and Eve Pranis (New York: National Gardening Association: Wiley, 1990).
Publication provides directions for establishing and maintaining a community youth garden. Text includes 70 activities.

Putting Together a Family Science Festival
   (Rockville, MD: Hands-On-Science, 1987).
Publication includes descriptions of all aspects of
conducting a community science festival. Numerous family projects are included.

Science for the Fun of It, Marvin Druger, ed.
   (Washington, DC: National Science Teachers
   Association, 1988).
Publication describes ways to extend science
learning through informal science education
experiences. Text includes articles by zoo and
museum curators, producers of TV programs,
organizers of major science competitions and
directors of family learning projects.

The Young Astronaut Program (Washington, DC:
   The Young Astronaut Council, 1984).
Thousands of chapters across the United States
involve students in innovative science explorations. Each chapter is headed by a teacher or
community leader. Educational space-related
materials are provided to the chapters. Every
chapter is eligible to participate in writing, art,
math, and science contests, with prizes that
include trips to space camp. Another feature of
the program is *Astronet*, a computer network that
links chapters across the nation.

Suppliers of Resource Books

Addison-Wesley Publishing Company
1 Jacob Way
Reading, MA 01867
Produces science resource books for teachers, K-
12. Supplies a variety of hands-on activity books
for the K-8 student.

AIMS Education Foundation
P.O. Box 7766
Fresno, CA 93747
Produces activity books that integrate mathemat-
ics and science (K-9).

Creative Learning Press
P.O. Box 320
Mansfield Center, CT 06250
Carries science materials aimed at developing
critical thinking and problem-solving skills.

Creative Learning Systems, Inc.
9889 Hilbret Street, Suite E
San Diego, CA 92132

Carries activity books and equipment related to
science and technology.

Cuisenaire Co. of America, Inc.
P.O. Box 5026
White Plains, NY 10602-5026
Carries a large collection of science activity books
for both teacher and student (K-9).

Dale Seymour Publications
P.O. Box 10888
Palo Alto, CA 94303-0879
Activity books, student trade books, kits, and
manipulative materials for K–8.

Delta Education, Inc.
P.O. Box 915
Hudson, NH 03051
Suppliers for Science Curriculum Improvement
Study (SCIS III), Outdoor Biology Instructional
Strategies (OBIS), Health Activities (HAPS), and
the Elementary Science Studies (ESS) modules.
Additional teacher and student resource books
are also available.

Denoyer-Geppert Science Company
5711 North Ravenswood Avenue
Chicago, IL 60646
Carries materials for life science, including charts
and anatomical models.

Energy Learning Center
Edison Electric Institute
1111 19th Street, NW
Washington, DC 20036
Supplies general information on energy sources
as well as kits, films, and posters.

Good Apple
1204 Buchanan Street
P.O. Box 299
Carthage, IL 62321-0299
Carries a large number of student trade books to
enhance concept development in science. Teacher
resource books and family science activities are
also available.

Idea Factory, Inc.
10710 Dixon Drive
Riverview, FL 33569
Produces and carries hands-on science activity
manuals for elementary teachers.

Lawrence Hall of Science
University of California
Berkeley, CA 94720
Produces teacher resource books that promote hands-on, inquiry-oriented science. Produces materials for GEMS, CEPUP, and SAVI/SELPH.

Learning Things, Inc.
68A Broadway
P.O. Box 436
Arlington, MA 02174
Carries books and manipulatives for science investigations.

Junior Engineering Technical (JETS)
1420 King Street, #405
Alexandria, VA 22314
Carries teacher and student resources and program dealing with design technology for middle school and high school.

National Geographic Society
17th and M Streets, NW
Washington, DC 20036
Produces student books on a variety of science topics. One series involves pop-out pictures. Also produces filmstrips, videos, software, and multi-media kits.

National Science Teachers Association
1742 Connecticut Avenue, NW
Washington, DC 20009
Produces teacher activity books on K-12 science topics. Carries a large selection of resource books for teachers. Publishes four journals for science teachers: *Science and Children, Science Scope, The Science Teacher,* and *The College Science Teacher.*

National Wildlife Federation
8925 Leesburg Pike
Vienna, VA 22180
Produces posters, audiovisual programs, and teaching guides on environmental science. Publishes *NatureScope*, a series of activity books for teachers.

Right Before Your Eyes
136 Ellis Hollow Creek Road
Ithaca, NY 14850
Produces a series of natural history posters with teacher activity guides for elementary and middle grades.

The Science Man
P.O. Box 56036
Harwood Heights, IL 60656
Carries a supply of K-12 science resource books.

The Teachers' Laboratory, Inc.
104 Canal Street
P.O. Box 6480
Brattleboro, VT 05302-6480
Carries a large collection of science resource books that focus on problem solving and conceptual development. Includes resource books on developmentally appropriate instruction. Carries *Science 5/13* and *Learning through Science* series from Great Britain.

TOPS Learning Systems
10978 South Mulino Road
Canby, OR 97013
Produces science activity manuals that feature inexpensive materials.

Suppliers of Equipment, Kits, and Prepackaged Modules

American Science and Surplus
601 Linden Place
Evanston, IL 60202
Supplies surplus items that can often be put to use in the science classroom.

Carolina Biological Supply Company
2700 York Road
Burlington, NC 27216-9988
Supplies all types of science equipment and materials, including live organisms. Also carries science kits, games, and publications.

Connecticut Valley Biological Supply Company
Valley Road
P.O. Box 326
Southhampton, MA 01073
Supplies a large variety of science materials, including live organisms.

Creative Dimensions
P.O. Box 1393
Bellingham, WA 98227
Supplies kits dealing with owl pellets, fossils, rocks, and seismograms.

Delta Education, Inc.
P.O. Box 915
Hudson, NH 03051
Supplies kits for ESS, SCIS, SAPA, OBIS, ISIS, and HAP modules.

Echo, Inc.
P.O. Box 87
2755 Columbus Avenue
Springfield, OH 45503
Supplier of thermometers including the inexpensive plastic-backed thermometers suitable for use in the elementary grades.

Estes Industries/Hi-Flier
1296 H. Street
Penrose, CO 81240
Supplier of kites, model-rocket kits, engines, and other accessories.

Frey Scientific
905 Hickory Lane
Mansfield, OH 44905
Supplier of a wide variety of science teaching materials and equipment.

Hubbard Scientific Company
P.O. Box 104
Northbrook, IL 60065
Suppliers of materials for life and earth sciences. Carries human systems activity kits.

Ideal School Supply Company
11000 South Lavergne Avenue
Oak Lawn, IL 60453
Suppliers of manipulatives and kits appropriate for grades K-6.

Lego Dacta Systems, Inc.
555 Taylor Road
Enfield, CT 06082
Suppliers of materials for design technology constructions. Producers of kits to teach physical science concepts. Carries materials for Lego-Logo program.

Ward's Natural Science Establishment, Inc.
5100 West Henrietta Road
P.O. Box 92912
Rochester, NY 14692-9012
Suppliers of life science materials and equipment, including specimens.

CHILDREN'S TRADE BOOKS IN SCIENCE

by Antoine B. Gosioco
Science Consultant and Instructional Specialist
Detroit Public Schools, Detroit, Michigan

THIS chapter provides a sampling of trade books appropriate for use in science classes, arranged according to subject areas. Teachers and curriculum designers find that science trade books can be valuable tools in teaching science in the classroom. Even though the "hands-on" approach is often the best way to teach science, supplementing lessons with informal texts gives students the opportunity to enrich their knowledge of the particular topics they are learning.

Science trade books offer a wealth of information. Students who are doing an experiment on crystals will find it more enjoyable and beneficial if they have read a trade book on crystals; the book helps to increase the students' understanding, while they see the information first-hand through their experiments. Learning the anatomy of insects and insect behavior through "hands-on" activities is enhanced if students can read about insects as well.

In addition, there are certain subject areas in science that are difficult to study because it may not be possible to conduct a direct observation. For example, direct study of volcanoes, stars, and pulsars requires sophisticated instruments and methods. Trade books about volcanoes, stars, and pulsars will supplement what direct observations and investigations could not provide in the classroom.

Science trade books also help students verify the information that they are investigating. Different authors who write about whales or sharks have unique approaches in presenting the information. Students are given the opportunity to read a variety of writing styles. Also, students will be able to assess various types of information on a topic when the information has been written by a number of different authors. For example, a child who is interested in the many theories about the extinction of dinosaurs will be able to collect varying information from different authors.

In addition, science trade books help students develop their skills in scientific research. Although students can conduct investigations and experiments in a laboratory or with some other "hands-on" approach, these experiments should be supported by what scientists have written about the subject. It is important that students learn to consult many sources of information, including science trade books.

Trade books can also help students develop a science vocabulary. Through these books students are exposed to scientific terminology and views that necessitate scientific literacy. Reading a wide variety of subjects will better prepare students to deal with the rapidly changing scientific and technological world around us. For example, research findings about global warming, AIDS, cancer, earthquakes, and bioengineering are found in science trade books. Students will be able to update their knowledge with the latest findings and information provided by these trade books.

Sources and Books that Offer a List of Science Trade Books

Appraisal: Science Books for Young People, by The Children's Science Book Review (Boston, MA: n.d.).
This is a quarterly publication of science trade books published within the year. The books are reviewed by librarians and authorities in science such as science teachers and science practitioners.

The Best Science Books and AV Materials for Children, by AAAS.
This resource book contains lists of science trade books arranged by topic area. The entries are annotated.

Eyeopeners! by Beverly Kobrin (New York: Viking, 1988), 317p.
This book presents a list of informational books written for children. In an interesting introduction the author explains why students should be exposed to these books. This book can act as a guide for parents in choosing books for their children. A wide variety of topics is covered, including science topics.

The Kobrin Letter, by Beverly Kobrin (Palo Alto, CA: n.d.).
This publication is a supplement and update to *Eyeopeners!*. It includes informational books reviewed by the author; the entries are arranged by subject areas. This is a good source for the newest trade books that have been published.

The Museum of Science and Industry Basic List of Children's Science Books, by the American Library Association (Chicago, IL: n.d.).
This yearly publication contains a wealth of information about science trade books. Entries on trade books are arranged by subject area and are annotated. The entries also give the appropriate grade levels of these books.

Science and Children, by the National Science Teachers Association (Washington, DC: n.d.).
This monthly publication contains a section on

science trade books. The books have been reviewed by a committee. Every year the March issue contains a list of the "Most Outstanding Science Trade Books" that have been selected by a panel of experts.

Science Fare; An Illustrated Guide and Catalog of Toys, Books, and Activities for Kids, by Wendy Saul and Alan R. Newman, eds. (New York: Harper and Row, 1986).
One chapter in this book provides an annotated list of science trade books. This is a good source of information on older trade publications. The selection is based on what children enjoy reading.

Science Scope, by the National Science Teachers Association (Washington, DC: n.d.).
This monthly publication comes out eight times a year; it contains an annotated list of recommended science trade books. These books are geared towards the middle school level.

Science through Children's Literature, by Carol M. Butzow and John W. Butzow (n.p.: 1989).
This publication summarizes 33 children's trade books, develops science concepts, and describes activities to explore science. Concept-mapping strategies are used to show relationships among content understandings.

Story Stretchers, by Shirley C. Raines and Robert J. Canady (Mt. Rainier, MD: Gryphon House, 1989).
90 elementary science trade books are described. Ways to extend the understandings developed in each trade book into each of the curricular areas are presented. All stories have a science component.

Life Science

African Elephants, Giants of the Land, by Dorothy Hinshaw Patent (New York: Holiday House, 1991), 40p.
Grades 4-8. Color photographs by Oria Douglas-Hamilton. The main focus of this book is that the African elephant is now becoming endangered. Poachers slaughter the elephants for their tusks. The book also includes topics such as the physical characteristics, family relationships, growth, search for food and water, and mating of these animals.

Amazing Poisonous Animals, by Alexandra Parsons (New York: Alfred A. Knopf, 1990), 32p.
Grades 1–5. Photographs by Jerry Young. This book, geared toward young readers, features ten venomous snakes.

Animal Amazing, by Judith Herbst (New York: Atheneum, 1991), 182p.
Grades 4-8. This book features animal behavior such as hibernation, regeneration of body parts, migration, and other complex behavioral patterns.

Animal Architecture, by Jennifer Owings Dewey (New York: Orchard Books, 1991), 72p.
Grades 3–6. Illustrations in black-and-white by the author. This book describes various kinds of animals who use materials in their surroundings to build their homes.

Animal Camouflage: A Closer Look, by Joyce Powzyck (New York: Bradbury, 1990), 40p.
Grades 3-8. Colorful illustrations of animals show how concealing coloration, disruptive coloration, disguise, mimicry, and masking are used by animals as protective, self-defense mechanisms.

Animals in Winter, by Susanne Riha (Minneapolis: Carolrhoda, 1989), 32p.
Grades 2–6. Illustrations and text explain why twelve European animals hibernate in the winter. An appendix compares and contrasts the European animals with their American counterparts.

Batman, by Laurence Pringle (New York: Charles Scribner & Sons, 1991), 42p.
Grades 4–6. Photos by Merlin D. Tuttle. *Batman* is the biography of Merlin Tuttle and shows how Tuttle, as the founder of Bat Conservation International, has dedicated his life to a study of bats.

Big Friend, Little Friend: A Book about Symbiosis, by Susan Sussman and Robert James (Boston: Houghton Mifflin, 1989), 32p.
Grades 4–7. Illustrated with full-color photographs. This book is a good introduction to symbiosis, describing twelve pairs of symbiotic animals that live together in mutual dependence.

The Big Tree, by Bruce Hiscock (New York: Atheneum, 1991), 34p.
Grades K–3. A sugar maple tree started as a single seedling and grew into a big tree, providing shelter to various animals. The book also describes how the maple tree has survived and withstood snowstorms throughout the years.

Book of Animals, by Martin Walters (New York: Simon & Schuster, 1991), 192p.
Grades 5-8. This book is a comprehensive guide to the world of animals, starting with invertebrates and following with the vertebrates. Much information about the phyla, classes, orders, families, genera, and species is given. The animals are identified by illustrations.

Chameleons, by Claudia Schnieper (Minneapolis: Carolrhoda, 1989), 48p.
Grades 2–5. Illustrations of various chameleons in their natural habitats make this book attractive to young readers. The author discusses the characteristics and habits of lizards that are known to change appearances to blend with the color of their surroundings.

The Chimpanzee Family Book, by Jane Goodall (Saxonville, MA: Picture Book Studio, 1989), 64p.
Grades 3–6. Illustrations by Michael Neugebauer. This photographic essay explains the habits, daily activities, and family life of a group of African chimpanzees. The author narrates her experiences in observing these animals in the African jungles.

Cows in the Parlor: A Visit to a Dairy Farm, by Cynthia McFarland (New York: Atheneum, 1990), 32p.
Grades 1–3. Color photographs by the author. This book shows the young reader the work of dairy farmers in milking, feeding, and calving the cows. It presents an idea of the seasonal nature of busy farmers' work.

Creatures That Glow, by Joanne Barkan (New York: Doubleday, 1991), 32p.
Grades 2–5. Illustrated with color photographs. This is a book about bioluminescent animals. It should be read in bright light first, and can then be examined in the dark with a flashlight.

Dolphin Adventure: A True Story, by Wayne Grover (New York: Greenwillow, 1990), 48p.
Grades 3–5. Illustrated in black-and-white by Jim Fowler. This book describes dolphin behavior and deep-sea diving.

The Dolphins and Me, by Don C. Reed (Boston: Sierra Club, 1989), 144p.
Grades 5-8. Illustrated by Pamela Carroll and Walter Carroll. The author, who has been working with dolphins for fifteen years, describes their behavior and life cycle.

Flowers, Fruits, Seeds, by Jerome Wexler (New York: Simon & Schuster, 1991), 32p.
Grades 3–5. Flowers, fruits, and seeds are briefly described and illustrated. The book includes descriptions of house plants, garden plants, grasses, vines, shrubs, and common trees.

From Seed to Plant, by Gail Gibbons (New York: Holiday House, 1991), 32p.
Grades K–3. The life cycle of plants is briefly described, from seeds to full-grown plants. The book touches on the concepts of pollination and germination, and suggests hands-on activities about plants that young readers can engage in.

The Great Butterfly Hunt: The Mystery of the Migrating Monarchs, by Ethan Herberman (New York: Simon & Schuster, 1990), 48p.
Grades 5-8. Photographs of monarch butterflies are featured in this book. The author explains their life cycle and migration. He also includes the significant contributions of scientists and volunteers who track the migratory patterns of these butterflies.

Great Northern Diver: The Loon, by Barbara Juster Esbensen (Boston: Little, Brown, 1990), 32p.
Grades 1–4. Illustrated in color by Mary Barrett Brown. The book describes the life and habitat of the loon, one of the most primitive bird species in the United States.

Heads, by Ron Goor and Nancy Goor (New York: Atheneum, 1988), 64p.
Grades 1–6. Illustrated by Ron Goor. This book examines similarities and differences among vertebrate heads. Detailed photographic illustrations of eyes, ears, noses, and mouths emphasize how the structure of body parts, such as animals' heads, is designed for animal survival.

Living Monsters, the World's Most Dangerous Animals, by Howard Tomb (New York: Simon & Schuster, 1990), 48p.
Grades 3–6. This book features animals such as the sea wasp, octopus, army and fire ants, killer bee, scorpion, black widow spider, stonefish, king cobra, rattlesnake, vampire bat, and man. It shows the protective and poisonous mechanisms that these animals use to fight their predators.

101 Questions and Answers about Pets and People, by Ann Squire (New York: Macmillan, 1988), 96p.
Grades 3–6. Illustrated by G. Brian Karas. This book contains interesting questions often asked by children about animals and people. It includes information about dogs, cats, fish, birds, horses, mice, hamsters, gerbils, ferrets, snakes, lizards, turtles, and rabbits.

Plants: Extinction or Survival? by Howard Facklam and Margery Facklam (Hillside, NJ: Enslow, 1990), 96p.
Grades 6-8. This informative text discusses the importance of plants as a source of food, medicine, and other products. It also includes the contributions made by scientists regarding plant uses.

Polar Bear Cubs, by Downs Matthews (New York: Simon & Schuster, 1989), 24p.
Grades 2–5. Illustrated with photographs by Dan Guravich. This book describes how a mother polar bear and her two cubs live by hunting seals. The cubs imitate their mother's skill in hunting, and the author describes their maturation process.

Predator! by Bruce Books (New York: Farrar, Straus & Giroux, 1991), 80p.
Grades 5-8. Illustrated with color photographs. The author presents the clever means and strategies animals use to hunt for food. The book also describes human predation and how humans are linked with the food chain.

Roses Red, Violets Blue: Why Flowers Have Colors, by Sylvia Johnson (Minneapolis: Lerner, 1991), 64p.
Grades 3–6. Photographs by Yuko Sato. This book explains the reason why flowers have colors. It provides illustrations of the structure of flowers and describes pollination and fertilization.

Scaly Babies: Reptiles Growing Up, by Ginny Johnston and Judy Cutchings (New York: Morrow Junior Books, 1988), 48p.
Grades 3–6. Illustrated with photographs. This book describes the life cycle of representative reptiles. Emphasis is on how reptilian babies are hatched, their first encounter with the environ-

ment, and their means of survival as babies.

Tomato, by Barrie Watts (Morristown, NJ: Silver Burdett, 1990), 24p.
Grades K–3. Illustrated with color photographs and black-and-white drawings. Illustrations show the life cycle of a tomato plant. The book includes hands-on activities and a picture-quiz review.

Whales, by Seymour Simon (New York: Thomas Y. Crowell, 1989), 40p.
Grades 2–5. Illustrated with full-color photographs. The physiology and characteristics of various types of whales are discussed.

Where Food Comes From, by Dorothy Hinshaw Patent (New York: Holiday House, 1991), 40p.
Grades 2–4. Dr. Patent explains where food comes from and gives the reader an idea of the essential nutrients that the four major food groups provide. At the end of the book she poses a question: the next time you eat, why not try figuring out where your food comes from?

Wild Animals of America ABC, by Hope Ryden (New York: Lodestar, 1988), 32p.
Grades pre-K–2. Illustrations by the author. Full-color photographs of wild animals typically found in America are presented in alphabetical order. The final pages contain information about each animal.

Young Lions, by Toshi Yoshida (New York: Philomel, 1989), 32p.
Grades K–3. Illustrated by the author. Three young lions attempt to hunt for food, and in the process they encounter various African plains animals. The young cubs are not successful with their hunting, and they go back to their mother. The animals are depicted in panoramic illustrations.

Environmental Science

Air Pollution, by Kathleen Gay (New York: Franklin Watts, 1991), 144p.
Grades 4-8. This book treats the problems of air pollution seriously. It also covers the issues of acid rain, the greenhouse effect, and toxic pollutants in our atmosphere. The book includes black-and-white photographs, charts, and illustrations.

Antarctica, by Helen Cowcher (New York: Farrar, Straus & Giroux, 1990), 32p.
Grades K–3. Illustrations by the author. The book describes how the environment in the Antarctic region provides a suitable habitat for the emperor penguins, Weddell seals, Adélie penguins, leopard seals, and skuas.

Cartons, Cans, and Orange Peels: Where Does Your Garbage Go?, by Joanna Foster (New York: Clarion, 1991), 64p.
Grades 3–6. Illustrated with photographs. This book describes how our garbage is becoming an issue. Solutions to the growing problems of landfills and hazardous wastes are offered. The book also describes how garbage can be a source of energy and how recycling works.

City Kid's Field Guide, by Ethan Herberman (New York: Simon & Schuster, 1989), 48p.
Grades 5-8. A wide variety of plants and animals can be found in the city. Such places as vacant lots, parks, street sides, and city homes are filled with living creatures.

Dawn to Dusk in the Galapagos, by Rita Golden Gelman (Boston: Little, Brown, 1991), 48p.
Grades 3-8. Illustrated with photographs by Tui De Roy. The book covers a twelve-hour span on the Galapagos Islands, describing various wild animals in their natural habitats.

Dying Planet: The Extinction of a Species, by John Erikson (New York: McGraw-Hill, 1991), 190p.
Grades 5 and up. This book begins with the origin of the Earth and the evolution of species of living organisms. It then explains global warming.

The Empty Lot, by Dale H. Fife (Boston: Sierra Club, 1991), 28p.
Grades K–4. Illustrated by Jim Arnosky. The book describes the preservation of a small patch of land.

Exploring Solar Energy, by Allan Kaufman (Ann Arbor, MI: Prakken, 1989), 98p.
Grades 5 and up. This book explores the possibilities of generating energy from the sun. Numerous projects and experiments are included for the reader to try. Solar collectors are shown with diagrams for the reader to follow. This book also describes how solar energy can solve some of our environmental problems.

Exploring Spring, by Sandra Markle (New York: Atheneum, 1990), 122p.
Grades 3–5. This book is a collection of ideas, activities, and projects for children to do in the spring.

Follow the Water from the Brook to Ocean, by Arthur Dorros (New York: HarperCollins, 1991), 32p.
Grades 1–3. The book explains and traces the path of flowing water from its possible sources to the ocean. Along the path, the reader discovers various plants and animals that inhabit these areas. The book also illustrates the process of changes in the water, from a liquid when it rains, to a solid in the form of snow.

Global Warming, by Laurence Pringle (Boston: Arcade, 1990), 48p.
Grades 4-8. Illustrated with color photographs, maps, and charts. The author discusses the greenhouse effect and its threat to living things.

The Great Trash Bash, by Loreen Leedy (New York: Holiday House, 1991), 32p.
Grades pre-K–2. The author narrates and illustrates the story of the town of Beaston, which has lovely houses and parks, fine restaurants and stores, but also has a very serious problem of too much trash.

How Green Are You?, by David Bellamy (New York: Clarkson N. Potter, 1991), 32p.
Grades pre-K–2. Illustrated by Penny Dann. This picture book introduces the reader to the environment and pollution. It also covers human environmental needs such as energy, water, and air, and the need for growing green plants.

Hurricane Watch, by Franklyn M. Branley (New York: Harper & Row, 1985), 32p.
Grades K–4. Illustrations by Giulio Maestro. The author gives a clear, simple explanation of how hurricanes are formed, and he provides guidelines for safety when a hurricane occurs.

The Illustrated World of Oceans, by Susan Wells (New York: Simon & Schuster, 1991), 66p.
Grades 4-8. This book explains why oceans are responsible for our climate, how they provide us with many essential products, and that they are where life originated. A special section deals with the exploration and exploitation of the ocean's rich natural resources.

Journey through a Tropical Jungle, by Adrian Forsyth (New York: Simon & Schuster, 1989), 80p.
Grades 4-8. Illustrated with photographs and prints. A biologist recounts his travels in the Monteverde Cloud Forest Reserve in Costa Rica. He discusses the importance of preserving rain forests.

Living Treasure: Saving Earth's Threatened Biodiversity, by Laurence Pringle (New York: Morrow Junior Books, 1991), 64p.
Grades 4 and up. Illustrated with black-and-white drawings by Irene Brady. The author describes the diversity of life on our planet. Natural selection, genetic variation, and the evolution of species are also explained.

Natural Wonders of America, by David M. Brownstone and Irene M. Franck (New York: Atheneum, 1989), 64p.
Grades 4-8. This book describes 42 wonders of nature in the United States and Canada. Readers will understand the need to preserve these places.

Nature Walk, by Douglas Florian (New York: Greenwillow, 1989), 32p.
Grades pre-K–2. Illustrations by the author. This book is just like going on a trail walk. The reader can enjoy the illustrations, which are accompanied by rhyming text.

A Night and Day in the Desert, by Jennifer Owings Dewey (Boston: Little, Brown, 1991), 32p.
Grades 3–5. Jennifer Dewey's book is written in poetic language, describing how animals in the desert survive the harsh environment. It stresses the interrelationships of various animals, as well as their relationships with scarce plants found in the desert.

Night Reef: Dusk to Dawn on a Coral Reef, by William Sargent (New York: Franklin Watts, 1991), 40p.
Grades 5-8. A rare collection of photographs of coral reefs in their natural setting provides the reader with a look at life and activity under water. Coral reefs glowing at night are captured in these photographs.

Rain: Causes and Effects, by Phillip Steele (New York: Franklin Watts, 1991), 32p.
Grades 4–6. This book thoroughly covers the effects of rain on our planet. The pictures add

interest to the subject of weather.

Recycling Glass, by Judith Condon (New York: Franklin Watts, 1991), 32p.
Grades 5-8. The author takes the reader through the history of glassmaking, and then describes new technology in glass recycling.

Saving Our Wildlife, by Laurence Pringle (Hillside, NJ: Enslow, 1990), 64p.
Grades 5-8. Illustrated with black-and-white photographs. The author points out the relationship between animals and their environment and the effort being made in North America to preserve and protect wildlife.

Silent Killers: Radon and Other Hazards, by Kathlyn Gay (New York: Franklin Watts, 1988), 128p.
Grades 6-8. Illustrated with photographs. This book explains the problems caused by hazardous materials, including dioxin, asbestos, carbon monoxide, radon, mercury, lead, nitrates, herbicides, pesticides, and radioactive wastes. Cleanup and preventive measures are also discussed.

Simple Weather Experiments with Everyday Materials, by Muriel Mandell (New York: Sterling, 1991), 128p.
Grades 3–5. Illustrations by Frances Zweifel. Several weather-related experiments for young children focus on Bernoulli's Law, Beaufort's scales, and Ballot's Law. Although the book is intended for young children, the experiments could be done by and are appropriate for middle school students.

Small Energy Sources: Choices That Work, by Augusta Goldin (Orlando, FL: Harcourt Brace Jovanovich, 1988), 200p.
Grades 7 and up. Illustrated with photographs, diagrams, and maps. This book offers solutions to the problem of our diminishing sources of fossil fuel energy, and discusses how we can utilize solar, wind, and water power to produce energy.

Spill! The Story of the Exxon Valdez, by Terry Carr (New York: Franklin Watts, 1991), 64p.
Grades 5-8. Dramatic photographs explain the Exxon Valdez oil spill and its consequences for living things in Alaska.

Spring, by Ron Hirschi (New York: Cobblehill, 1990), 30p.

Grades K–3. Photographs by Thomas Mangelsen. This photo-essay book is written in poetic text and shows the reader the scenery of high forest regions. It also includes animals frequently seen in the springtime.

Summer of Fire: Yellowstone 1988, by Patricia Lauber (New York: Orchard Books, 1991), 64p.
Grades 4-8. Illustrated with prints and photographs. Despite the destructive nature of forest fires, the author explains the positive ecological contributions made as a result of the 1988 fires in Yellowstone National Park. Since the fires, the flora and fauna of the locality have been examined. The book also offers questions about how people can affect the natural world.

Sunshine Makes the Seasons, by Franklyn M. Branley (New York: Harper & Row, 1985), 32p.
Grades K–4. Illustrations by Giulio Maestro. This book explains the causes of changes in seasons. It provides a good demonstration of the tilt of the earth on its axis and the angle of the sun's rays on the earth's surface.

Under the Sea from A to Z, by Anne Doubilet (New York: Random House, 1991), 32p.
Grades 1–5. Photographs by David Doubilet. This alphabet book explores the inhabitants of the sea, both the common and the unusual. The final pages give an explanation of where sea flora and fauna are found.

Volcanoes, by Seymour Simon (New York: Morrow Junior Books, 1988), 32p.
Grades 1–5. Illustrated with photographs. This photo-essay book allows the reader a look at a variety of natural occurrences, including the eruptions of Mount St. Helens and volcanoes near Iceland and Hawaii, as well as those in other parts of the world.

Weather Forecasting: A Young Meteorologist's Guide, by Dan Ramsey (Blue Ridge Summit, PA: TAB, 1990), 146p.
Grades 5-8. This book explains weather in detail. It gives instructions on how to make one's own weather forecasting implements. It shows how to keep a weather log, how to interpret data from weather instruments, and how to look for weather reports. The book offers many hands-on activities that students can do throughout the year.

Weatherwatch, by Valerie Wyatt (Reading, MA: Addison-Wesley, 1990), 93p.
Grades 1–5. Illustrations by Pat Cupples. The book uses cartoonlike illustrations to show the various factors affecting weather changes. It explains the process of the water cycle: evaporation, condensation, and precipitation. Interesting hands-on activities such as making clouds, rainbows, and wind vanes are included.

Will We Miss Them?: Endangered Species, by Alexandra Wright (Watertown, MA: Charlesbridge, 1991), 36p.
Grades 1–5. Illustrations by Marshall Peck. This book calls for help for the most endangered species. The author explains that these fast-vanishing species are threatened due to the destruction of their natural habitats.

Wintertime, by Ann Schweninger (New York: Viking, 1990), 32p.
Grades pre-K–2. This book about the winter season includes an explanation of why seasons change, and it describes typical animals seen in the wintertime, as well as animals that hibernate and migrate.

Young Naturalist, by Andrew Mitchell (Tulsa, OK: EDC, 1982), 32p.
Grades 4–7. Illustrations by Ian Jackson, et al. This is a good introductory book for the young amateur naturalist. It includes simple experiments, projects to build, tools to use for field studies, and methods of collecting and recording specimens.

Archeology, Anthropology, and Paleontology

Before the Sun Dies: The Story of Evolution, by Roy A. Gallant (New York: Macmillan, 1989), 228p.
Grades 7 and up. This comprehensive book about human evolution traces the origin of life from the big bang theory to the most current cultural evolution. The text also presents ideas concerning future evolution in space.

Dinosaur Mountain: Graveyard of the Past, by Caroline Arnold (New York: Clarion, 1989), 48p.
Grades 4–6. Photographs by Richard Hewett.

Caroline Arnold tells the story of paleontologist Earl Douglas, who in 1909 discovered the fossilized tail bones of an Apatosaurus in Utah. Eventually, more dinosaur bones were unearthed, and the burial site of these dinosaurs became the greatest fossil discovery of the century.

Discovering Dinosaur Babies, by Miriam Schlein (New York: Four Winds, 1991), 40p.
Grades 1–5. Illustrations by Margaret Colbert. The author employs modern techniques to study how dinosaurs cared for their babies. The reader can learn how scientific methods may be used to study and gather information about these extinct creatures.

The Evolution Book, by Sara Stein (New York: Workman, 1986), 390p.
Grades 5-8. Sara Stein's hands-on book explores the different theories supporting evolution. Activities for students accompany the explanations.

The Fossil Factory: A Kid's Guide to Digging up Dinosaurs, Exploring Evolution, and Finding Fossils, by Niles, Gregory, and Douglas Eldredge (Reading, MA: Addison-Wesley, 1989), 111p.
Grades 1–5. Illustrations by True Kelley and Steve Lindblom. A scientist and his teenage sons collaborated in writing this book, which is filled with activities for students interested in archeology, paleontology, and evolution. The book also uncovers many puzzling questions about the past.

Fossils Tell of Long Ago, by Aliki (New York: Harper & Row, 1990), 32p.
Grades K–4. Aliki, also the illustrator, describes how fossils have been formed. Through illustrations, the reader sees the value of fossils and how they can tell us about the earth as it was millions of years ago.

Hominids: A Look Back at Our Ancestors, by Helen Roney Sattler (New York: Lothrop, Lee & Shepard, 1988), 128p.
Grades 5 and up. Illustrated by Christopher Santoro. The author traces the evolution of man. She discusses various theories supporting evolution and cites research, archeological diggings, and findings that support these theories.

How Life Began, by Melvin Berger (New York: Doubleday, 1990), 45p.
Grades 4–6. Illustrations by Jerry Lofaro. The

author discusses the theories of the origin of the earth, starting with the big bang theory, then goes on to the formation of small and simple microorganisms that have evolved and developed into more complex organisms.

Living with Dinosaurs, by Patricia Lauber (New York: Bradbury, 1991), 48p.
Grades 1–5. Illustrations by Douglas Henderson. The setting of dinosaur land is prehistoric Montana. Lauber recreates the setting and environment as the dinosaurs lived in it 75 million years ago.

The Lost Wreck of the Isis, by Robert D. Ballard (New York: Scholastic, 1990), 64p.
Grades 4 and up. Illustrations by Wesley Lowe and Ken Marschall. Scientific exploration, archeology, and history are interwoven in an entertaining and skillful recounting of the Mediterranean expedition to study the Jason Project.

The Monsters Who Died: A Mystery about Dinosaurs, by Vicki Cobb (New York: Coward-McCann, 1983), 63p.
Grades 3–6. Illustrated by Greg Wenzel. The author offers scientifically accepted theories about why the dinosaurs became extinct.

The Secret of Vesuvius: Exploring the Mysteries of an Ancient Buried City, by Sara C. Bisel (New York: Scholastic, 1991), 64p.
Grades 3–7. Illustrated with color prints and photographs. The reader is brought back to an ancient civilization through an account of Bisel's excavations in the ancient town of Herculaneum. The modern research method of studying archeology is applied in this book.

Traces of Life: The Origins of Humankind, by Kathryn Lasky (New York: Morrow Junior Books, 1990), 144p.
Grades 5-8. Illustrations by Whitney Powell. The author traces the history of hominid research and presents the work of scientists involved in this study.

Medical and Health Sciences

America's 25 Top Killers, by Ernest Abel (Hillside, NJ: Enslow, 1991), 144p.
Grades 6 and up. A discussion of the top killers in the United States includes overviews of the diseases, their symptoms, diagnoses, treatments, and references for further information. The book provides many answers to questions that both children and adults may have concerning the leading causes of death.

Asking about Sex and Growing Up: A Question-and-Answer Book for Boys and Girls, by Joanna Cole (New York: Beech Tree, 1988), 96p.
Grades 4-8. Illustrations by Alan Tiegreen. Facts about the physiology of young boys and girls are discussed, along with topics such as masturbation, intercourse, unwanted pregnancy, birth control, homosexuality, sexual abuse, and sexually transmitted diseases.

Asthma, by Mona Kerby (New York: Franklin Watts, 1989), 96p.
Grades 6-8. Illustrated with photographs and diagrams. This book deals with the various forms and control of asthma.

Babies, by Dorothy Hinshaw Patent (New York: Holiday House, 1988), 32p.
Grades K–4. Illustrated with photographs. This photo-essay book focuses on the newborn baby and traces a child's first year of sleeping, eating, touching, crying, crawling, standing, and talking. It shows how a baby is dependent on others and the manner in which a growing infant learns about the outside world.

Be Smart about Sex: Facts for Young People, by Jean Fiedler and Hal Fiedler (Hillside, NJ: Enslow, 1990), 128p.
Grades 6 and up. Illustrations in black-and-white. This book offers young readers an informative and up-to-date guide about maturation, birth control, sex, sexually transmitted diseases, and AIDS. It also includes a listing of service organization telephone hotlines.

The Brain: What It Is, What It Does, by Ruth Dowling Bruun and Bertel Bruun (New York: Greenwillow, 1989), 64p.
Grades 3–5. Illustrated by Peter Bruun. A neurologist and a psychiatrist explain the structure of the human brain and compare and contrast its structure and function with the brains of other animals. The book explains how the brain controls the way people think, act, and respond to stimuli.

Drugs and You, by Arnold Madison (Englewood Cliffs, NJ: Julian Messner, 1990), 128p.
Grades 4-8. This book gives the reader information about various types of drugs and drug abuse. In the latter part of the book, the idea that drug abuse can also exist by overmedicating is discussed.

Getting Your Period: A Book about Menstruation, by Jean Marzollo (New York: Dial Books for Young Readers, 1989), 112p.
Grades 4-8. Illustrations by Kent Williams. In a matter-of-fact way, the author discusses feelings, fears, worries, and signs of menstruation.

Glasses and Contact Lenses: Your Guide to Eyes, Eyewear, and Eye Care, by Alvin and Virginia Silverstein (Philadelphia: J. B. Lippincott, 1989), 144p.
Grades 6-8. The authors explain the structure of the human eye and how it works. They also explain how eyeglasses and contact lenses correct vision problems and how certain eye problems can be treated with surgical procedures.

The Impact of AIDS, by Ewan Armstrong (New York: Franklin Watts, 1990), 64p.
Grades 5 and up. The author makes a clear distinction between HIV infection and AIDS. Practicing safe sex and other ways of avoiding becoming infected are thoroughly discussed.

Medical Dilemmas, by Margaret O. Hyde and Elizabeth H. Forsyth (New York: Putnam Publishing Group, 1990), 112p.
Grades 7 and up. The authors give up-to-date information on animal research, gene therapy, transplants, AIDS, and the right to die. Moral questions and bioethical issues prevalent in our society today are discussed.

My Feet, by Aliki (New York: HarperCollins, 1990), 32p.
Grades pre-K–2. Illustrations invite the reader to explore different sizes of feet and their parts and functions. The book also describes footwear for various seasons and tells how crutches supplement feet for the handicapped.

Overcoming Acne: The How and Why of Healthy Skin Care, by Alvin and Virginia Silverstein (New York: Morrow Junior Books, 1990), 112p.
Grades 6-8. Illustrations in black-and-white by Frank Schwartz. The causes of pimples and acne

and their positive treatment and care are discussed.

Taking My Cat to the Vet, by Susan Kuklin (New York: Bradbury, 1988), 32p.
Grades K–3. Illustrated with photographs. This book describes how Ben takes his cat to the veterinarian. The pictures show how the step-by-step examination by the veterinarian gives security to Ben and relieves his concerns about his pet.

Your Immune System, by Alan E. Nourse (New York: Franklin Watts, 1989), 96p.
Grades 7-8. The author discusses AIDS, allergies, and the physiology of the immune system. He also describes treatments of these diseases.

Physical Science and Technology

Adventures with Atoms and Molecules: Chemistry Experiments for Young People, Book III, by Robert Mebane and Thomas Rybolt (Hillside, NJ: Enslow, 1991), 96p.
Grades 5-8. This book contains thirty hands-on activities using simple and common household items. The activities are fun to do and demonstrate chemical reactions, physical changes, chemical and physical properties of matter, and structures of molecules.

Balloon Science, by Etta Kaner (Reading, MA: Addison-Wesley, 1989), 96p.
Grades 4–6. Illustrations by Louise Phillips. This book offers more than fifty easy balloon experiments and hands-on activities. The balloon experiments cover subjects such as air pressure, air power, and static electricity.

Balloons: Building and Experimenting with Inflatable Toys, by Bernie Zubrowski (New York: Beech Tree, 1990), 80p.
Grades 4–6. Illustrations by Roy Doty. This book introduces the reader to the physical properties of gases and the scientific concepts of force and pressure, using balloons and other inflatable toys as hands-on materials for demonstrations.

Blinkers and Buzzers: Building and Experimenting with Electricity and Magnetism, by Bernie Zubrowski (New York: Beech Tree, 1991), 112p.
Grades 3–5. Illustrations by Roy Doty. This activity-filled book provides the student with numerous projects and gives step-by-step instruc-

tions for building electrical devices, experimenting with materials, and applying the scientific method. A section is included that challenges students to do more research and to conduct experiments beyond those in the book.

Bridges, by Ken Robbins (New York: Dial Books for Young Readers, 1991), 32p.
Grades K–6. This book provides the reader with information about various vehicular and pedestrian bridges, describing their unique structures.

Cameras, by Ian Graham (New York: Franklin Watts, 1991), 32p.
Grades 1–3. This book explains how cameras work and provides ideas for practice in photography. The "Taking a Photo" section is a good hands-on activity in which students can use their cameras.

Chemistry for Every Kid, by Janice Pratt Van Cleave (New York: John Wiley & Sons, 1989), 232p.
Grades 3–6. This is a collection of hands-on activities in chemistry for young students. Step-by-step procedures and materials needed are listed for each experiment.

Color Dance, by Ann Jonas (New York: Greenwillow, 1989), 32p.
Grades pre-K–2. This book explores the mixing of primary colors and secondary colors through a dance tapestry.

The Computer Story, by Irving E. Fang (St. Paul, MN: Rada Press, 1988), 104p.
Grades 3 and up. The author discusses the development of the computer. This book is a good reference guide for students who use the computer.

Dry or Wet? by Bruce McMillan (New York: Lothrop, Lee & Shepard, 1988), 28p.
Grades pre-K–2. This wordless picture book introduces the reader to the concept of what is dry and what is wet.

Experimenting with Light, by Robert Gardner (New York: Franklin Watts, 1991), 144p.
Grades 6 and up. The main approach in this book is observation through experimentation. Black-and-white drawings, along with some photographs, illustrate the experiments. The hands-on activities are simple but interesting.

Get Ready for Robots! by Patricia Lauber (New York: Thomas Y. Crowell, 1987), 32p.
Grades 1–3. Illustrations by True Kelley. This book introduces the young reader to the concept of robots and their ability to do simple work. It also includes descriptions of robots at home and in industries.

Homemade Holograms, by John Iovine (Blue Ridge Summit, PA: TAB, 1990), 230p.
Grades 6-8. This book is full of suggestions on how to build your own holograms and assemble them for a science-fair project. It also describes the development of lasers and their use in technology.

Homemade Lightning: Creative Experiments in Electricity, by R. A. Ford (Blue Ridge Summit, PA: TAB, 1991), 198p.
Grades 6 and up. The book is a great source of projects and models on electricity. It is helpful to students doing science projects.

How Did We Find Out about Lasers?, by Isaac Asimov (New York: Walker, 1990), 64p.
Grades 5-8. Illustrations by Erika Kors. This book explains the current uses of lasers and masers. It also traces the history of the scientific investigation of electromagnetic radiation.

How to Make a Chemical Volcano and Other Mysterious Experiments, by Alan Kramer (New York: Franklin Watts, 1989), 109p.
Grades 3–6. This book offers many hands-on activities about chemical reactions.

Machines at Work, by Byron Barton (New York: Thomas Y. Crowell, 1987), 32p.
Grades K–2. This book shows the reader the various machines used by construction workers.

Magic Tricks, Science Facts, by Bob Friedhoffer (New York: Franklin Watts, 1990), 160p.
Grades 5-8. This activity-based book exposes the young reader to various concepts of physics, math, physiology, and chemistry. It not only entertains, but also arouses children's curiosity.

Nuclear Energy: Troubled Past, Uncertain Future, by Laurence Pringle (New York: Macmillan, 1989), 128p.
Grades 6-8. This book describes the study of nuclear energy in industries, with emphasis on new developments and safety problems. Mr.

Pringle cites the Three Mile Island and Chernobyl disasters to express his concern about the risks of nuclear energy and the consequences of its misuse.

Paper Science Toys, by Richard E. Churchill (New York: Sterling, 1990), 128p.
Grades 3–6. Illustrations by James Michaels. This is an interesting book on using paper to create scientific toys. The toys illustrate various physics principles.

Power Magic, by Alison Alexander and Susie Bower (New York: Simon & Schuster, 1991), 32p.
Grades 1–3. Although the title is just a catchy phrase, the book offers fifteen hands-on activities to demonstrate various aspects of energy and power.

Radical Robots, by George Harrar (New York: Simon & Schuster, 1989), 48p.
Grades 3–5. Harrar explains what robots can and cannot do. He also discusses the potential to program robots to think, sense, and decide anything beyond the programmed artificial intelligence.

The Random House Book of How Things Work, by Steve Parker (New York: Random House, 1991), 158p.
Grades 4 and up. This illustrated book explains how common devices and processes work. It is divided into sections describing the home, factory and industry, entertainment, and textiles.

Robots, by Gloria Skurzynski (New York: Bradbury, 1990), 64p.
Grades 4 and up. The reader is exposed to the world of robotics through photographs of robots, from rudimentary mechanical playthings to prototype astrobots.

Samuel Todd's Book of Great Inventions, by E. L. Konigsburg (New York: Atheneum, 1991), 32p.
Grades pre-K–2. Illustrated with paintings. A boy named Samuel Todd points out some of the overlooked inventions that we see every day, such as the belt loop and the thermos. This is a simple book about the wonder of inventions.

The Science of Music, by Melvin Berger (New York: Thomas Y. Crowell, 1989), 160p.
Grades 4-8. Illustrations by Yvonne Buchanan. This book is an excellent resource for studying pitch, loudness, and tone, and how the human body creates and interprets sound. There is also a discussion of various musical instruments and how they are related to everyday items that can make similar sounds. The final section of the book discusses methods of recording and replaying sound.

Size: The Measure of Things, by Eric Laithwaite (New York: Franklin Watts, 1988), 32p.
Grades 4–7. Illustrated with photographs and diagrams. This book introduces the young reader to the significance of size in natural and man-made phenomena. It includes hands-on activities that youngsters can do to apply the concepts.

Sounds Interesting, by David Darling (Minneapolis: Dillon, 1991), 60p.
Grades 3 and up. This book introduces the reader to the science of sound. Activities follow the scientific method of observation, formulating a hypothesis, experimenting, and drawing conclusions.

Superconductivity: From Discovery to Breakthrough, by Charlene W. Billings (New York: Cobblehill, 1991), 63p.
Grades 4 and up. In a simple way, this book describes present and future applications of superconductors in transportation, energy storage, industry, improved computers, and research. It traces the development of superconductors, from the breakthrough when Bednorz and Muller unveiled the results of their high-temperature superconductivity experiment, to modern applications and development.

Superstuff!: Materials That Have Changed Our Lives, by Alfred Bortz (New York: Franklin Watts, 1990), 96p.
Grades 6 and up. The author discusses various materials that we see every day—plastics, synthetic fabrics, miracle alloys, special kinds of glass for fiber optics, superadhesives, and other superstuff including semiconductors and superconductors. The author discusses how technology has progressed from the Stone Age to the Modern Age.

Switch On, Switch Off, by Melvin Berger (New York: Thomas Y. Crowell, 1989), 32p.
Grades K–3. Illustrations by Carolyn Croll. Using fine illustrations, this book describes how electrical current flows to the light switch in a child's room. The book also includes a simple diagram of a generator.

Telecommunications: From Telegraphs to Modems, by Christopher Lampton (New York: Franklin Watts, 1991), 96p.
Grades 6 and up. This book is divided into two main sections: analog telecommunications and digital communications. Students will find this book a good source for research.

Tops: Building and Experimenting with Spinning Toys, by Bernie Zubrowski (New York: Beech Tree, 1989), 96p.
Grades 4-8. Illustrations by Roy Doty. This hands-on activity book describes the concept of motion. A guide to the construction of yo-yos, strobes, tops, and dancing dolls, this book will spark the reader's interest in the dynamics of physics.

The Way Things Work, by David Macaulay (Boston: Houghton Mifflin, 1988), 384p.
Grades 4 and up. The author's illustrations explain the technology that surrounds us.

Wheels at Work: Building and Experimenting with Models of Machines, by Bernie Zubrowski (New York: Beech Tree, 1987), 64p.
Grades 3–6. Illustrations by Roy Doty. The author describes and provides instructions on how to build model machines such as pulleys, water wheels, and windlasses.

The Wright Brothers: How They Invented the Airplane, by Russell Freedman (New York: Holiday House, 1991), 128p.
Grades 5 and up. The author thoroughly researched how the Wright brothers invented the airplane. Photographs and black-and-white drawings bring the reader back to the historic era when the Wright brothers and their contemporaries were busy with inventions.

Space Science and Astronomy

Airborne: The Search for the Secret of Flight, by Richard Maurer (New York: Simon & Schuster, 1990), 48p.
Grades 4-8. Illustrations by Brian Lies. The author and illustrator vividly describe the development of flight from balloons and gliders to helcopters and airplanes. The text is accompanied by activities that simulate the principles of flight.

Astronomy Activity Book, by Dennis Schatz (New York: Simon & Schuster, 1991), 48p.
Grades 3–5. Drawings by Roy Doty. The book is divided into sections on the moon, sun, stars, planets, and meteors. For each section hands-on activities are suggested.

The Big Dipper and You, by E. C. Krupp (New York: Morrow Junior Books, 1989), 48p.
Grades 3–5. Illustrations by Robin Rector Krupp. This book describes the movement of the earth and the stars. It explains the constituents of the Big Dipper constellation, and refers to the North Star as a guide to locate the constellation.

The Christmas Sky, by Franklyn M. Branley (New York: HarperCollins, 1990), 48p.
Grades 3–7. Illustrations by Stephen Fieser. This book describes scientific explanations about the stellar and planetary configurations in the sky at the time of Jesus' birth.

Distance Flights, by Don Berliner (Minneapolis: Lerner, 1990), 72p.
Grades 5-8. The author traces the historical development of flight from Louis Bleriot, the first person to fly across the English Channel, in 1909, to Dick Rutan and Jeanna Yeager, who in 1986 flew nonstop around the world without refueling.

Galaxies, by Seymour Simon (New York: Morrow Junior Books, 1988), 32p.
Grades 3–6. Illustrations with photographs. The author describes the origin and existence of spiral and elliptical galaxies that whirl through a space so vast, their light travels millions of years before it reaches our eyes.

The Glow-in-the-Dark Night Sky Book, by Clint Hatchett (New York: Random, 1988), 20p.
Grades 2–5. Illustrations by Stephen Marchesi. Information about star groups is presented, along with glow-in-the-dark illustrations depicting the people and animals that have given these constellations their names.

I Want to Be an Astronaut, by Byron Barton (New York: Thomas Y. Crowell, 1988), 32p.
Grades pre-K–1. Told in the first person, the reader takes the role of the speaker who might go on a space mission.

The Illustrated World of Space, by Ian Nicolson (New York: Simon & Schuster, 1991), 64p.
Grades 3 and up. This book covers the history of astronomy, from ancient astronomy including Stonehenge and the pyramids, to current information about the solar system such as black holes and life beyond Earth.

Mars, by James A. Corrick (New York: Franklin Watts, 1991), 128p.
Grades 8 and up. Corrick's book sums up all the information gathered from the *Viking* missions of the 1970s and the *Mariner* missions of the late 1960s. It also includes recent findings about Mars and contrasts these findings with some fictionalized information about Mars.

Neptune, by Seymour Simon (New York: Morrow Junior Books, 1991), 32p.
Grades K–5. Illustrated with color photographs. The text describes new discoveries about Neptune as *Voyager 2* passed through its orbit.

The Origin and Evolution of Our Own Particular Universe, by David E. Fisher (New York: Atheneum, 1988), 192p.
Grades 8 and up. Scientific theories and investigations on the origin of the universe are presented. Principles of physics that clarify the origin of the universe are explained.

Paper Airplane Book, by Seymour Simon (New York: Puffin, 1976), 48p.
Grades 1 and up. Simon describes the principles of flight through the use of paper airplanes. The author also gives directions on how to fold paper to make different models of airplanes.

Seeing the Sky: 100 Projects, Activities and Explorations in Astronomy, by Fred Schaff (New York: Wiley, 1990), 212p.
Grades 4 and up. These hands-on activities and science-fair projects are related to astronomy. The book offers ideas on how to set up experiments and design projects about the planets, stars, and constellations. It provides good illustrations on how to use telescopes, binoculars, and other tools of astronomy.

Small Worlds: Exploring the 60 Moons of Our Solar System, by Joseph W. Kelch (New York: Julian Messner, 1990), 160p.
Grades 6-8. The author describes the origin, characteristics, and discovery of the sixty moons

in our solar system, along with the latest data collected by *Voyager* space probes.

Space and Astronomy, by Robert L. Bonnet and G. David Keen (Blue Ridge Summit, PA: TAB, 1992), 144p.
Grades 5-8. Forty-nine science fair projects related to space and astronomy are proposed in this book. The projects include creating analogies to help people better understand astronomical figures, such as the 93 million mile distance between the Earth and the sun, and making three-dimensional models of planets from two-dimensional photographs.

Space Camp, by Anne Baird (New York: Morrow Junior Books, 1992), 48p.
Grades 3 and up. The author describes the excitement and adventure in store for young children who want to attend the Huntsville Space Camp in Alabama. Illustrations and photographs invite the reader to attend these camp sessions.

The Space Shuttle, by George Ficher (New York: Franklin Watts, 1990), 64p.
Grades 2–5. The author examines the history and technology of the space shuttle. The book also includes the shuttle disaster of 1986. The final chapter is devoted to a discussion of the future space program.

Star and Planet Spotting: A Field Guide to the Night Sky, by Peter Lancaster Brown (New York: Sterling, 1990), 144p.
Grades 6-8. This book guides the reader on how to identify stars in the night sky. It tells the best time to view and what to bring when out in the field at night.

Stars, by Seymour Simon (New York: Morrow Junior Books, 1986), 32p.
Grades 3–6. From the birth of a star to the death of a supernova, this book describes with clarity the composition and life cycle of stars.

Stars and Planets, by Christopher Lampton (New York: Doubleday, 1988), 40p.
Grades 2–4. Illustrated by Ron Miller. The author describes the nature of meteors, black holes, galaxies, and space explorations, and talks about the possibility of extraterrestrial life.

Voyager to the Planets, by Necia H. Apfel (New York: Clarion, 1991), 48p.

Grades 3 and up. This book describes the photographs made by *Voyager* as it passed the outer planets, Jupiter, Saturn, Neptune, and Uranus. These photographs were collected by NASA.

Voyagers from Space: Meteors and meteorites, by Patricia Lauber (New York: Thomas Y. Crowell, 1989), 80p.
Grades 5-8. Drawings by Mike Eagle. The author describes asteroids, comets, and meteorites, how they are formed and where they come from. Theories on the origins of the solar system are also discussed.

What's Out in Space? by Susan Mayes (Tulsa, OK: EDC, 1990), 24p.
Grades 1–3. The author enables very young readers to understand basic facts about the solar system and other celestial bodies. She also describes space explorations.

Young Astronomer's Guide to the Night Sky, by Michael R. Porcellino (Blue Ridge Summit, PA: TAB, 1991), 160p.
Grades 5 and up. This book is a good reference for young astronomers. It gives the reader a guide to locate constellations, identify stars, know when to look for meteor showers, and observe the changing phases of the moon. It also tells the readers how to join amateur astronomy clubs throughout the country.

Biography

Arctic Explorer: The Story of Matthew Henson, by Jeri Ferris (Minneapolis: First Avenue Editions, 1989), 80p.
Grades 3–6. Matthew Henson, a black explorer, accompanied Robert Peary on six expeditions to the North Pole. His strong determination, courage, and adaptability are inspiring to budding scientists.

At the Controls: Women in Aviation, by Carole S. Briggs (Minneapolis: Lerner, 1991), 72p.
Grades 5-8. This book includes biographies of aviators such as Jerrie Cobb, Bonnie Tiburzi and others. The author also traces the history of modern aviation through the achievements of these female aviators.

Bearman: Exploring the World of Black Bears, by Laurence Pringle (New York: Charles

Scribner's Sons, 1989), 48p.
Grades 4–7. Photographs by Lynn Rogers. Wildlife biologist Lynn Rogers has spent twenty years studying the American black bear.

Charles Darwin and the Theory of Natural Selection, by Renee Skelton (Hauppauge, NY: Barron's Educational Series, 1987), 119p.
Grades 5 and up. This biography of Darwin includes a comprehensive view of his theory of evolution and his studies in the Galapagos Islands.

Charles Richard Drew, by Rinna Evelyn Wolfe (New York: Franklin Watts, 1991), 64p.
Grades 4 and up. This is a comprehensive biography of an African American who became assistant director of the Red Cross blood bank program and yet was denied a blood transfusion because he was black.

Christa McAuliffe: Teacher in Space, by Corinne J. Naden and Rose Blue (Boston: Millbrook, 1991), 48p.
Grades 1–5. This well-written biography is about the first teacher in space. The story includes her training and ends with the disaster of the *Challenger* in space.

Chuck Yeager: The Man Who Broke the Sound Barrier, by Nancy Smiler Levinson (New York: Walker, 1988), 133p.
Grades 5 and up. Chuck Yeager was a test pilot for many years and had many experiences in the military. He later became a captain in the Air Force and was famous for breaking the sound barrier.

Florence Sabin: Medical Researcher, by Janet Kronstadt (New York: Chelsea House, 1990), 112p.
Grades 5–8. This is the story of the first woman professor at Johns Hopkins University (1903), the first woman to become the president of the American Society of Anatomists and be elected to the National Academy of Sciences.

From Sorceress to Scientist: Biographies of Women Physical Scientists, by Kevin Allison Neis (Mission Hills, CA: California Video Institute, 1990), 93p.
Grades 5 and up. This book includes biographies of women from ancient times to modern day. With a multicultural approach, this is an espe-

cially inspiring book for young girls who like science.

George Washington Carver, by James Marion Gray (Morristown, NJ: Silver Burdett, 1991), 144p.
Grades 4–8. This is the story of a man who rose from slavery to become a world-renowned scientist. It discusses his achievements, such as improved peanut and sweet potato crops.

Julia Morgan, Architect of Dreams, by Ginger Wadsworth (Minneapolis: Lerner, 1990), 128p.
Grades 5–8. This is a story of one of the very few women who work and excel in the field of architecture. Her designs have become famous, including the Hearst Castle in San Simeon, California. Her story is an inspiration to young girls who would like to pursue architecture as a profession.

Lewis Howard Latimer, by Glennette Tilley Turner (Morristown, NJ: Silver Burdett, 1991), 132p.
Grades 5–8. Latimer discovered a method of producing long-lasting and inexpensive carbon filaments for the incandescent light bulb. This made electric lighting practical and affordable.

Ryan White: My Own Story, by Ryan White and Ann Marie Cunningham (New York: Dial Books for Young Readers, 1991), 144p.
Grades 5 and up. The story of Ryan White narrates how he contracted AIDS, how he survived the controversy in his hometown, and how he became a spokesman and an international celebrity. This book helps young readers to understand more about AIDS.

Stephen Hawking: Unlocking the Universe, by Sheridan Simon (Minneapolis: Dillon, 1991), 112p.
Grades 5 and up. This is the biography of one of the most renowned theoretical physicists of this century. Hawking unlocked some of the greatest secrets of the universe through his application of theoretical physics and mathematics to cosmology.

The Triumph of Discovery: Women Scientists Who Won the Nobel Prize, by Joan Dash (New York: Dial Books for Young Readers, 1991), 160p.
Grades 8 and up. Illustrations by Julian Messner. This book presents the story of four Nobel laureates: Maria Geoppert-Mayer, Rosalyn Yalow, Barbara McClintock, and Rita Levi-Montalcini. Each story depicts the early struggles of these women until they finally made their breakthrough discoveries.

CURRICULUM MATERIAL PRODUCERS

THIS chapter provides information on publishers and producers of science curriculum materials, textbooks, supplementary materials, software, and other items. For some of the larger publishers, we have provided a listing of science series and book titles. For other companies, we provide a description of products. Much of the information in this chapter is based on the publishers' catalogues; for more details, you should contact the publishers and producers directly. The addresses and phone numbers given are for the offices that will supply catalogues and other promotion material; note that these phone numbers are not for the editorial offices.

Addison-Wesley Publishing Company

Jacob Way
Reading, MA 01867
800-447-2226

Biology

Biology
Grades 10–12 (advanced placement). Textbook, instructor's manual, supplementary materials including software

Biology: A Systems Approach
Grades 9–10. Textbook, teacher's edition, laboratory manual, test packet

Environmental Science: A Framework for Decision Making
Grades 11–12. Textbook, teacher's manual, supplementary materials

Marine Biology: Environment, Diversity, and Ecology
Grades 10–12. Textbook, teacher's edition

Chemistry

Addison-Wesley Chemistry
Grades 10–12. Textbook, teacher's edition, teacher's support package, supplementary materials including software, videodisc

Chemistry
High school (advanced placement). Textbook, instructor guide, supplementary materials including test bank software

Earth Science

Earth Science
Grades 7–9. Textbook, teacher's edition, teacher's resource book, supplementary materials including software, videocassettes

General Science

Addison-Wesley Science Basal Program (series)
Grades K–6. Textbooks, teacher's editions, teacher's support package

Addison-Wesley Science Components
Workbooks, blackline masters, professional

information bulletins, idea maps, test scoring cards, test pads, skills guides for teachers, activity report pads, unit posters, science fair guide for teachers, outdoor education guide for teachers, transparencies, health and safety supplement, kits, videocassettes, learning centers

Connecting Science and Language, Levels 3–6 (series)
Student workbooks, teacher's editions

Science Big Books (series)
Big books, teacher's editions, teacher's support packages

Life Science

Life Science
Grades 7–9. Textbook, teacher's edition, teacher's resource book, supplementary materials including software, videocassettes

Physical Science

Introduction to Physical Science
Grades 7–9. Textbook, teacher's edition, teacher's resource book, supplementary materials including software, videocassettes

Physical Science
Grades 7–9. Textbook, teacher's edition, teacher's resource book, supplementary materials including software, videocassettes

Physics

College Physics
High school (advanced placement). Textbook, instructor's manual, supplementary materials including testing software

Conceptual Physics
Grades 9–12. Textbook, teacher's edition, teacher's resources, supplementary materials including testing software, videocassettes

Contemporary College Physics
High school (advanced placement). Textbook, instructor's manual, supplementary materials including testing software

Physics
High school (advanced placement). Textbook, instructor's manual, supplementary materials including testing software

Problem-Solving Exercises in Physics
Workbook, solutions manual

Skill Drills: Math Review for Physics
Grades 11–12 (advanced placement). Workbook

University Physics
High school (advanced placement). Textbook, supplementary materials including testing software

Physiology

The A & P Coloring Workbook

Essentials of Human Anatomy and Physiology
Softcover text, instructor's guide

Human Anatomy and Physiology
Textbook, instructor's guide, supplementary materials including test bank software

Human Anatomy and Physiology Laboratory Manuals (series)

Science, Technology, and Society

CEPUP (Chemical Education for Public Understanding) (series)
Grades 7–9. Kits, teacher's manuals. Topics include "Chemical Survey & Solutions and Pollution," "Toxic Waste: A Teaching Simulation," and "Risk Comparison"

One-Minute Readings: Issues in Science, Technology, and Society
Grades 7–12. Book and teacher's guide

AIMS Education Foundation
P.O. Box 8120
Fresno, CA 93747-8120
209-255-4094

Grades K–9. Activity and investigation books on botany, the enivronment, seasons, energy sources, weather, basic physical science, magnetism, electricity

American Chemical Society
1155 16th Street, N.W.
Room 810
Washington, DC 20036
202-872-6165

Grades K–6. Monthly publication, *WonderScience Magazine*, with physical science activities for elementary school science

American Coal Foundation
1130 17th Street, N.W.
Washington, DC 20036

Grades K–12. Curriculum materials relating to coal, electricity, land reclamation

American Institute of Mining, Metallurgical, and Petroleum Engineers
Transformations
P.O. Box 1205
Boston, MA 02130
800-433-AIME

Grades 5–8. Collection of videocassettes and teacher's guide for life science, physical science, and earth science; discussions of issues relating to mines, oil wells, steel mills, computer companies

American Institute of Physics
Marketing and Sales Division
335 East 45th Street
New York, NY 10017-3483
212-661-9404

Teaching materials and software for high school physics

American Nuclear Society
555 North Kensington Avenue
La Grange Park, IL 60525
312-352-6611

Grades K–12. Curriculum guides and information booklets on nuclear energy, nuclear waste, energy alternatives; also audiovisual lending library

Amsco School Publications, Inc.
315 Hudson Street
New York, NY 10013-1085
212-675-7000

Biology

Biology Investigations

Contemporary Biology

Fundamental Concepts of Modern Biology
Softcover text

Preparing for the College Board Achievement Test in Biology

Review Text in Biology

Reviewing Biology with Sample Examinations

Chemistry

Contemporary Chemistry

Experimental Chemistry
Textbook, workbook

Fundamental Concepts of Modern Chemistry
Softcover text

Laboratory Manual in Chemistry

Review Text in Chemistry

Reviewing Chemistry with Sample Examinations

Workbook and Laboratory Manual in Chemistry

Earth Science

Contemporary Earth Science

Earth Science, Intermediate Level
Review text, workbook

Earth Science Investigations

Reviewing Earth Science with Sample Examinations

General Science

Contemporary Science Series

General Science

Mastering Basic Skills in Science
Laboratory skills workbook

Life Science

Life Science, Intermediate Level
Review text, workbook, teacher's edition, unit tests

Life Science Series
Includes "The Meaning of Life," "The Support of Life," and "The Continuation of Life"

Understanding Life Science
Textbook, teacher's manual, unit tests

Physical Science

Physical Science, Intermediate Level
Review text, workbook

Physics

Fundamental Concepts of Modern Physics

Laboratory Manual in Physics
Student edition, teacher's edition

Physics Investigations

Preparing for the College Board Achievement Test in Physics

Review Text in Physics

Reviewing Physics with Sample Examinations

Workbook and Laboratory Manual in Physics

William K. Bradford
310 School Street
Acton, MA 01720
800-421-2009

Grades K–12. Software for Macintosh, Apple II, and MS-DOS systems. For science, programs include physical science simulation software; biology, chemistry, and astronomy software; life and earth science simulation software; weather forecasting software

Broderbund
500 Redwood Boulevard
Novato, CA 94948-6121
800-521-6263

Grades 4–12. "Science Toolkit Plus" software (for Apple II or IBM/Tandy): speed and motion, earthquake lab, body lab; "SimEarth" software (for Macintosh or IBM/Tandy): geology, evolution, technology; physics

Carolina Biological Supply
2700 York Road
Burlington, NC 27215
800-334-5551

Grades K–12. Equipment, apparatus, models, chemistry kits, rock and mineral collections, other teaching aids for science classes

Charlesbridge Publishing
85 Main Street
Watertown, MA 02172
800-225-3214
617-926-0329

Alphabet Books (series)

Big Book Programs (series)
Grades K–2. Teacher's guides

Young Discovery Library (series)
Grades 3–6. Pocket-sized encyclopedias

Children's Television Workshop
School Services Group
1 Lincoln Plaza, Dept. PBR02
New York, NY 10023
212-875-6630

Grades 4–6. Special school edition of "3-2-1 Classroom Contact," with videocassettes of programs, teacher's guide, and hands-on science kit (science kit available from Delta Education). Covers basic topics in earth science, life science, physical science, and scientific investigation

Connecticut Valley Biological
82 Valley Road, P.O. Box 326
Southampton, MA 01073
800-628-7748

Science products: books, models, charts, filmstrips, slides, videocassettes, eggs, cocoons, larvae, games, software, equipment, apparatus, records, tapes

Coronet/MTI Film & Video
108 Wilmot Road
Deerfield, IL 60015
800-621-2131

Grades K–12. Films and videos in many subject areas; for science, topics covered include life sciences, the environment, energy, physics, chemistry, space, biology, physical sciences, earth science. Distributors of Disney Educational Productions and Learning Corporation of America

Crabtree Publishing Company
350 Fifth Avenue, Suite 3308
New York, NY 10118
800-387-7560

Grades K–9. Books on animals and their environment; "The Primary Ecology Series," "Crabtree Environment Series"; books on the Arctic

Creative Publications
5040 West 11th Street
Oak Lawn, IL 60453
800-624-0822

Teacher's resource books, materials kits, posters. Topics include measurement and problem solving

Creative Teaching Press
P.O. Box 6017
Cypress, CA 90630-0017
800-444-4CTP

Investigating Science Series
Grades K–8. Blackline reproducible science books

Posters, discussion and reference charts

Cuisenaire Company of America, Inc.
P.O. Box 5026
White Plains, NY 10602-5026
800-237-3142

Grades K–9. Measurement materials, teacher's resource materials, environmental science, physical science, microscopes and magnifiers, life science, earth science, science equipment and supplies

Culver Company
Danvers House
130 Centre Street
Danvers, MA 01923
800-428-5837

Grades K–12. Activity booklets, films, videocassettes concerning energy and natural resources

Curriculum Associates, Inc.
5 Esquire Road
North Billerica, MA 01862-2589
800-225-0248
508-667-8000

Problem Solving in Science
Grades 5–8. Student book, teacher's guide, posters

Dandy Lion Publications
3563 Sueldo
San Luis Obispo, CA 93401
800-776-8032

Student workbooks, teacher's handbooks

Delmar Publishers, Inc.
2 Computer Drive, West
P.O. Box 15015
Albany, NY 12212-5015
800-347-7707

Exploring Technology Education Video Series
Grades 7–10. Videocassettes, orientation program, teacher's guide. Includes "Introduction to Technology," "Communication," "Construction," "Manufacturing," and "Energy, Power, and Transportation"

Interactions in Science and Society (series)
Grades 7–12. Videocassettes, instructor's guide. Student program includes "Waste Management," "Robots," "Superconductivity," "Acid Rain," "Energy," "Food," "The Auto," "Groundwater," "Genetic Engineering," "Climate," "Water," and "Wilderness." Teacher's program includes "Introduction," "Attitudes and Beliefs," "Economics," "Societal Needs," "Personal Needs," and "Politics."

Living with Technology
Grades 7–9. Text, Teacher's resource guide, computerized test bank

The Resources and Projects Book: A Student Guide to Design and Technology
Grades 5–7. Text

Space Simulation
Grades 7–9. Text, instructor's guide

Technology Activities (series)
Student activity guides. Includes "Communication," "Energy, Power, and Transportation," "Manufacturing," and "Construction"

Technology Activity Guides (series)
Student workbooks

Technology in Your World
Grades 7–9. Text, teacher's resource guide

You, Me, and Technology Video Programs (series)
Videocassettes, instructor's guides, workbooks. Includes "Living with Technology," "Decisions, Decisions, Decisions," "Energy for Societies," "Health and Technologies," "Feeding the World," "Communications," "China, Japan, and the West," "Population Patterns and Technology," "Exploring Space," and "Risk, Safety, and Technology"

Delta Education, Inc.
P.O. Box 950
Hudson, NH 03051
800-442-5444

Activity books, resource books, manipulative materials, kits, models, puzzles, study modules, laboratory supplies

T. S. Denison and Company, Inc.
9601 Newton Avenue South
Minneapolis, MN 55431
800-328-3831

Grades K–6. Kindergarten resource book for science; environmental resource book for grades 2–6; beginning science activity book

Didax, Inc.
One Centennial Drive
Peabody, MA 01960
800-458-0024

Preschool, elementary, special needs. Science kits, resource books, activity books

Edmund Scientific Company
101 E. Gloucester Pike
Barrington, NJ 08007-1380
609-573-6250

Supplier of optics, plus equipment for science experiments and projects

Education Development Center, Inc.
55 Chapel Street
Newton, MA 02160
800-225-4276

Grades K–6. "Insights," an inquiry-based, hands-on science curriculum: includes units on the environment, living things, the senses, habitats, sound, skeletons, the human body

Educational Activities, Inc.
P.O. Box 392
Freeport, NY 11520
880-645-3739

Grades K–9. Videocassettes, videodiscs, books, software

Educational Development Specialists
5505 East Carson Street, Suite 250
Lakewood, CA 90713-3093
213-420-6814

Think Earth
Grades K–3. Environmental education program. Instructional units, teacher's guides, posters, reproducible masters, videocassette

EME
41 Kenosia Avenue, P.O. Box 2805
Danbury, CT 06813-2805
800-848-2050

Software, video, microscopes, and overhead units for biology, chemistry, and physics classes

Encyclopaedia Britannica Educational Corp.
310 South Michigan Avenue
Chicago, IL 60604-9839
800-554-9862

Grades 3–6. The Full Option Science System (FOSS), a hands-on science program covering scientific reasoning and technology (measurement, ideas and inventions, variables, models and design), physical science (sound, magnetism, electricity, levers and pulleys, mixtures and solutions), earth science (earth materials, water, landforms, solar energy), life science (structures of life, human body, environments, food and nutrition)

Enterprise for Education
1320-A Third Street, Suite 302
Santa Monica, CA 90401
310-394-9864

Grades 5–12. Curriculum-based energy and environmental program. Student booklet, teacher's guide, teacher's resource books, year-book, workbooks

Fearon/Janus/Quercus
500 Harbor Boulevard
Belmont, CA 94002
800-877-4283

Special education/remedial programs. Textbooks, teacher's resource binders, lab books, teacher's guides for general science, biology, and life, earth, and physical science

First Byte
Davidson and Associates
P.O. Box 2961
Torrance, CA 90509
800-523-2983

Software programs on recycling and conservation, geometry, problem-solving skills

Forestry Suppliers, Inc.
205 W. Rankin Street, P.O. Box 8397
Jackson, MS 39284-8397
800-647-5368

Equipment, supplies, and accessories for teaching earth science, biology, and other sciences: compasses, dissecting equipment, mineral charts, microscopes, orienteering aids, soil test kits, timers, water test kits

Glencoe/Macmillan/McGraw-Hill
P.O. Box 543
Blacklick, OH 43004-0543
800-334-7344

Biology

Biology: The Dynamics of Life
Textbook, teacher's edition, teacher's resource package, supplementary materials including English/Spanish glossary, software, optical data videodiscs

Biology: An Everyday Experience
Textbook, teacher's edition, teacher's classroom resources, supplementary materials including computer test bank, Spanish resources, optical data videodisc

Biology: Living Systems
Textbook, teacher's edition, teacher's resource package, supplementary materials including computer test bank

Chemistry and Physics

Chemistry: A Modern Course
Textbook, teacher's edition, teacher's resource package, supplementary materials including software

Physics: Principles and Problems
Textbook, teacher's edition, teacher's classroom resources, supplementary materials including English/Spanish glossary, software, optical data videodiscs

Life, Earth, Physical Science

Focus on Science Series
Textbooks, teacher's editions, teacher's resource packages, supplementary materials including software. Includes "Focus on Life Science," "Focus on Earth Science," and "Focus on Physical Science"

Merrill Science Series
Textbooks, teacher's editions, teacher's classroom resources, supplementary materials including software, Spanish resources, optical data video-discs. Includes "Merrill Life Science," "Merrill Earth Science," and "Merrill Physical Science"

Science Connections (series)
Textbooks, teacher's editions, teacher's resource package, supplementary materials including software

Globe Book Company

Simon & Schuster
4350 Equity Drive
P.O. Box 2649
Columbus, Ohio 43216
800-848-9500

Concepts and Challenges in Science (series)
Textbooks, teacher's editions, teacher's resource books, laboratory program. Includes "Life Science," "Earth Science," and "Physical Science"

Exploring Science Series
Textbooks, teacher's resource manuals. Includes "Exploring Living Systems: Life Science," "Exploring Earth and Space: Earth Science," and "Exploring Matter and Energy: Physical Science"

Globe Biology
Textbook, teacher's edition, teacher's resource book, supplementary materials including laboratory program, Spanish foreign language supplement, software

Science Workshop Series
Softcover texts, teacher's editions. Topics include biology, earth science, physical science, chemistry

Softcover Science Series
Softcover texts, teacher's editions/manuals. Includes "The Globe Science Series," "The Science Work-a-Texts," and "Unlocking Science Skills"

Graphic Learning

61 Mattatuck Heights Road
Waterbury, CT 06705
800-874-0029

Steps in Science (series)
Grades K–5. Softcover texts, teacher's guides, supplementary materials

Harcourt Brace Jovanovich, Inc.

School Department
6277 Sea Harbor Drive
Orlando, FL 32821-9989
800-CALL-HBJ

HBJ Ciencias (series)
Levels 1–6. Spanish. Textbooks, teacher's editions, teacher's resource books, supplementary materials including English/Spanish learning systems, laboratory kits

HBJ Science (series)
Levels R–6. Textbooks, teacher's editions, teacher's resource banks, supplementary materials including English/Spanish learning systems, laboratory kits, software

Holt Science (series)
Grades 1–6. Textbooks, teacher's editions, teacher's resource binder, supplementary materials including software

Hawkhill Associates, Inc.

125 East Gilman Street
Madison, WI 53703
800-422-4295

Physical, life and earth science books, guides, filmstrips, videocassettes

D.C. Heath and Company

School Division
125 Spring Street
Lexington, MA 02173
800-235-3565

Biology

Biological Science: A Molecular Approach
High school. Textbook, teacher's edition, study guide, teacher's resource book, computer test bank

Advances in Genetic Technology
Student module, teacher's guide, computer test bank

Heath Biology
High school. Textbook, teacher's edition, teacher's resource package, supplementary materials including software, optical data videodisc series

Heath Biosolve Software (series)
Junior high/high school. Software, teacher's manual. Includes "Internal Medicine," "Infectious Diseases," and "Toxicology"

Chemistry

Chemistry
High school (advanced placement). Textbook,

instructor's guide, supplementary materials including software, videocassettes

General Chemistry
High school (advanced placement). Textbook, instructor's guide, supplementary materials including software

Heath Chemical Lecture Demonstrations
High school. Videocassettes

Heath Chemistry
High school. Textbook, teacher's edition, teacher's resource binder, supplementary materials including software

Introductory Chemistry
High school. Textbook, instructor's guide, supplementary materials including software, videocassettes

Introductory Chemistry: A Foundation
High school. Textbook, instructor's guide, supplementary materials including software, videocassettes

Earth Science

Earth Science
High school. Textbook, teacher's edition, teacher's resource binder, supplementary materials including software

Earth Science: The Challenge of Discovery
Textbook, teacher's edition, teacher's resource package, supplementary materials including software

Heath Earth Science Software (series)
Junior high/high school. Software, teacher's manual, worksheets. Includes "Mountains and Crystal Movement," and "Dating and Geologic Time"

Heath Elementary Science Software (series)
Includes "Climates of the World," "The Changing Earth," and "Traveling through the Solar System"

General Science

Explore-a-Science
Grades 1–6. Software, reader, teacher's guide. Includes "Animal Watch: Whales," "A Closer Look: The Desert," "The Dinosaur Construction Kit: Tyrannosaurus Rex," and "Earth Watch: Weather Forecasting"

Life Science

Heath Elementary Science Software (series)
Grades 4–8. Including "Classifying Animals with Backbones," "Classifying Animals without Backbones," "Life in the Ocean," and "The Insect World"

Heath Life Science Software (series)
Junior high/high school. Software, teacher's manual, worksheets. Includes "Blueprints for Green Plants," "The Simplest Living Things," "Genetics," and "Biomes"

Life Science: The Challenge of Discovery
Middle/junior high school. Textbook, teacher's edition, teacher's resource package, supplementary materials including software

Physical Science

Heath Elementary Science Software (series)
Includes "Electricity and Magnetism," "Heat Energy," and "Machines and Force"

Heath Physical Science Software (series)
Junior high/high school. Software, teacher's manual, activity sheets. Includes "Forces in Liquids and Gases," "Electric Circuits," "Combining the Elements," and "Nuclear Reactions"

An Introduction to Physical Science
High school (advanced placement). Textbook, instructor's guide, supplementary materials including software

Physical Science: The Challenge of Discovery
Middle/junior high school. Textbook, teacher's edition, teacher's resource package, supplementary materials including software

Physics

Cioffari's Experiments in College Physics
High school (advanced placement). Laboratory manual/workbook, instructor's guide

Fundamentals of Physics: A Senior Course
High school. Textbook, teacher's manual

Heath Physics
High school. Textbook, teacher's guide, supplementary materials including software

Physics Laboratory Experiments
High school. Student edition, instructor's resource manual

PSSC Physics
High school (advanced placement). Textbook,

teacher's resource book, supplementary materials including an advanced topic supplement

Holt, Rinehart, and Winston
6277 Sea Harbor Drive
Orlando, FL 32821-9989
800-225-5425

Biology

Modern Biology
High school. Student's edition, teacher's edition, teacher's resource binder, supplementary materials including Spanish glossary, software, videocassettes

Biology Today
High school. Textbook, teacher's edition, supplementary materials including Spanish glossary, audio programs, test generator software, video series

Chemistry

Modern Chemistry
High school. Textbook, teacher's edition, teacher's resource binder, supplementary materials including test generator software

Chemicals in Action
High school. Textbook, teacher's guide

Foundations of Chemistry
Textbook, teacher's guide, laboratory experiments

Earth Science

HBJ Earth Science
Middle school/junior high. Textbook, teacher's edition, teacher's resource bank, supplementary materials including computer test bank

Holt Earth Science
Middle school/junior high. Textbook, teacher's edition, teacher's resource book, supplementary materials including computer test bank

Modern Earth Science
High school. Textbook, teacher's edition, teacher's resource binder, supplementary materials including computer test bank

General Science

HBJ General Science
Textbook, teacher's edition, teacher's resource

bank, supplementary materials including computer test bank

Holt General Science
Textbook, teacher's edition, teacher's resource book, supplementary materials including computer test bank

Science Discovery
Middle school/junior high. Videodiscs, directory

Scienceplus: Technology and Society (series)
Middle school/junior high. Textbooks, teacher's editions, teacher's resource binders, supplementary materials including videodisc program

Life Science

HBJ Life Science
Middle school/junior high. Textbook, teacher's edition, teacher's resource bank, supplementary materials including computer test bank

Holt Life Science
Middle school/junior high. Textbook, teacher's edition, teacher's resource book, supplementary materials including computer test bank

Physical Science

HBJ Physical Science
Middle school/junior high. Textbook, teacher's edition, teacher's resource bank, supplementary materials including computer test bank

Holt Physical Science
Middle school/junior high. Textbook, teacher's edition, teacher's resource book, supplementary materials including computer test bank

Modern Physical Science
High school. Student's edition, teacher's edition, supplementary materials

Physics

Modern Physics
High school. Textbook, teacher's edition, teacher's resource binder, supplementary materials including computer problem and test generator

Physics in Action
High school. Student's edition, teacher's resource manual

Physiology

Modern Human Physiology
High school. Textbook, teacher's edition, supplementary materials

Houghton Mifflin
Department J
One Beacon Street
Boston, MA 02108-9971
800-323-5663

Basic Concepts of Chemistry
High school (advanced placement). Textbook

Computer Strategies for Chemistry Students
High school (advanced placement). Softcover textbook

General Chemistry
High school (advanced placement). Textbook

General Chemistry Study Guide
High school (advanced placement). Textbook

Investigating the Earth
Grades 10–12. Textbooks, teacher's edition, tests

The National Proficiency Survey (series)
Test booklets, easy-score answer sheets, technical manual with norms, administrator's survey

Organic Chemistry: A Short Course
High school (advanced placement). Textbook

Science Vision (series)
Grades 6–9. Interactive videodisc series for life science, earth science, and physical science. Videodiscs, software, guides

Hubbard Scientific, Inc.
P.O. Box 760
Chippewa Falls, WI 54729-0760
800-723-8021

Supplier of products for science education: maps, globes, slide sets, models, and investigation kits for astronomy, earth science, anatomy, physiology, life science, solar energy, environmental studies, botany, physical science, zoology, health science, meteorology, and oceanography

Interact
Box 997-H92
Lakeside, CA 92040
800-359-0961

Grades K–12. Simulation programs. Student guides, teacher's guides, supplementary materials including software. Topics include the solar system, space travel, earth science, genetic engineering, science fair projects

Kendall/Hunt Publishing Company
2460 Kerper Boulevard
P.O. Box 539
Dubuque, IA 52004-0539
800-258-5622

Basic Genetics: A Human Approach
Supplementary textbook, teacher's guide

Biological Science: An Ecological Approach
High school. Textbook, teacher's edition, supplementary materials including computer test bank

Biological Science: Patterns and Processes
Remedial. Softcover textbook, teacher's edition, supplementary materials

Biology: A personalized approach
High school. Textbook, teacher's guide, log book

Chemcom: Chemistry in the Community
High school. Textbook, teacher's guide

Geology Is
Remedial. Softcover textbooks, teacher's editions

Global Science: Energy, Resources, Environment
High school. Textbook, teacher's guide, supplementary materials

Middle School Life Science
Student text, teacher's guide, teacher's resource book

PSSC Physics
High school. Student edition, teacher's guide and resource book, supplementary materials including test bank software

Science for Life and Living: Integrating Science, Technology, and Health (series)
Grades K–6. Textbooks, teacher's editions, activity kits

Science, Technology, & Society Modules (series)
Softcover texts, teacher's guides. Includes "Genes and Surroundings," "Computers and Privacy,"

"Human Reproduction," "Biomedical Technology," "Television," and "Investigating the Human Environment"

Spice: Structured Pacing in Chemistry Education
High school. Textbook, teacher's resource manual

Lab-Aids, Inc.
249 Trade Zone Drive
Ronkonkoma, NY 11779
516-737-1133

Grades 4–12. Science kits for investigations in such topics as human genetics, mitosis, chromatography, pollutant effects, enzymes, plant tissue, DNA protein synthesis, and molecular structure. Also CEPUP kits and modules

Learning Spectrum
1390 Westridge Drive
Portola Valley, CA 94028
800-USE-SOS-2

"Science on a Shoestring": class sets of science materials.

LEGO Dacta
555 Taylor Road
Enfield, CT 06082
800-527-8339

Grades pre-K–2. Manipulatives, curriculum support materials. Scope and sequence includes cognitive development; transportation; animals and the environment; homes, family, and neighborhoods; problem solving and whole language; themes and project work
Grades 3–12. Technic sets for simple machines through technic control sets for robotics, physics, and artificial intelligence, integrating science, mathematics, social studies, and technology curriculum

Longman Publishing Group
10 Bank Street
White Plains, NY 10606
800-447-2226

An Introduction to the Human Body
Middle school/junior high. Student course manual, teacher's guide, tests

Problems in Biology
Student laboratory manual, teacher's guide

Understanding Ecology
High school. Textbook, teacher's guide

Lucent Books, Inc.
P.O. Box 28901
San Diego, CA 92198-00111
800-231-5163

Grades 4–12. "Nature Watch Series," "Creative Minds Biographies," "Opposing Viewpoints" series, "Encyclopedia of Discovery and Invention," "Overview Series" (includes science-related titles)

Macmillan/McGraw-Hill
School Division
220 East Danieldale Road
De Soto, Texas 75115-9990
800-442-9685

Science in Your World (series)
Grades K–6. Spanish/English bilingual edition available. Textbooks, teacher's editions, teacher's resource center, supplementary materials including audiocassettes and videocassettes, software, activity materials kits

Mr. Wizard's World Science Video Library (series)
Grades 3 and up. Videocassettes, teacher's guides

Helping Your Child at Home . . . with Science (series)
Grades K–6. Available in Spanish. Activity books, teacher's guides

McDonald Publishing Company
10667 Midwest Industrial Boulevard
St. Louis, MO 63132
800-722-8080

Grades 4–9. Teaching poster sets, activity sheets, teacher's guides, reproducible and duplicating books

Merrill
SRA School Group
P.O. Box 5380
Chicago, IL 60680-5380
800-621-0476

Laboratory Science Skills (series)
Grades 6–12. Student workbooks, teacher's guides
(See also under SRA School Group for supplementary programs; see under Glencoe/Macmillan/McGraw-Hill for grades 6–12 texts; see under Macmillan/McGraw-Hill for grades K–8 texts.)

Millbrook Press, Inc.
2 Old New Milford Road, Box 335
Brookfield, CT 06804
800-462-4703

Grades pre-K–12. Books on inventions, animals, ecosystem, disasters (oil spills, earthquakes, blizzards, tidal waves, etc.), Earth Day sourcebook

Milliken Publishing Company
1100 Research Boulevard
P.O. Box 21579
St. Louis, MO 63132-0579
800-643-0008

Pre-K–8. Duplicating masters, blackline reproducibles, transparency/duplicating books, diagrammatic study prints, poster books, videocassettes, filmstrips

Modern
5000 Park Street North
St. Petersburg, FL 33709
800-243-6877

Distributes films and videos, including titles on science; free loan program for selected titles

Modern Curriculum Press
13900 Prospect Road
Cleveland, OH 44136
800-321-3106

Concept Ecology (series)
Grades 1–6. Student books, teacher's guides. Series topics include habitats, endangered animals, environmental challenges

Concept Science (series)
Grades K–3. Available in Spanish. Student books, big books, teacher's guides. Special teacher's guides for ESL/LEP students. Set themes include matter, energy, the universe, animals, plants, our Earth

The MCP Science Series
Grades 1–6. Softcover texts, teacher's editions. Topics include life, health, earth, matter and energy, the universe

Science Workshop (series)
Grades 1–6. Activity books, teacher's editions

See How It Grows/See How It's Made
Grades K–1. Student books

Thinking about Science
Grades 2–6. Student readers, teacher's guides

Young Explorers in Science (series)
Grades K–4. Story books, big books, teaching companions

Mosby-Year Book
11830 Westline Industrial Drive
St. Louis, MO 63146
800-325-4177

High school. Textbooks, audio and videocassettes, laser discs, slides, for medicine, dentistry, nursing, allied health professions, veterinary medicine

National Science Teachers Association
Publication Sales
1742 Connecticut Avenue, N.W.
Washington, DC 20009
202-328-5800

Grades K–12. Curriculum guides and other publications for science teaching

Nightstar Company
1334 Brommer Street
Santa Cruz, CA 95062
408-462-1049

Astronomy activity materials: hands-on mini-planetarium, star and space posters

Orange Cherry/
Talking Schoolhouse Software
P.O. Box 390
Pound Ridge, NY 10576-0390
800-672-6002

Grades 3–12. Software for basic science concepts, life science, meteorology, oceanography, astronomy, and earth science. For Macintosh, Apple IIGS, and/or IBM; some software for Apple II, Commodore, and TRS-80

Pegasus Learning Company
16 North Chestnut Street
Colorado Springs, CO 80905
719-634-4969

Grades K–8. "Frontiers of Science: Our Environment," videodisc and resource manual with 60 activities on the environment, technology, energy, patterns, plants and animals; also "Insects: A Closer Look," videodisc for Grades 4–7

Peguis Publishers
520 Hargrave Street
Winnipeg, Manitoba
Canada R3A OX8
800-667-9673

Grades pre-K–4. Teacher's resource books, student reading and activity books

The Peoples Publishing Group, Inc.
P.O. Box 102
365 W. Passaic Street
Rochelle Park, NJ 07662
800-822-1080

Astronomy

Astronomy: A Self-Teaching Guide, 3E
High school. Textbook

Astronomy: The Cosmic Perspective
High school. Textbook, teacher's manual, transparencies, slides

Astronomy: The Evolving Universe, 6E
High school. Textbook, teacher's manual, teacher's resource manual including software

Discovering Astronomy
High school. Textbook, teacher's manual, supplementary materials including slides

Biology

Biology: Exploring Life
High school (advanced placement). Textbook, instructor's manual, supplementary materials including test bank software

Biology of Ourselves, 2E
High school. Textbook, teacher's manual

Chemistry

Basic Concepts of Chemistry, 3E
High school. Textbook, teacher's manual, supplementary materials

Chemistry: An Experimental Science
High school (advanced placement). Textbook, instructor's manual, supplementary materials including test bank software

Fundamentals of Chemistry
High school. Textbook, teacher's manual, supplementary materials including test bank software

General Chemistry: Principles and Structure, 5E
High school (advanced placement and honors students). Textbook, teacher's manual, supplementary materials including test bank software

Understanding Chemistry
High school. Textbook, laboratory manual, teacher's resource guide

General Science

The Hands-On Science Approach (series)
Middle school/junior high (remedial). Softcover textbooks, teacher's guides. Includes "Life Science," "Matter and Energy," and "Earth Below and Sky Above"

Integrated Science/STS

Science Directions 7, 8, & 9 (series)
Middle school/junior high school. Textbooks, teacher's resource packages

Science Probes 8, 9, & 10 (series)
High school. Textbooks, teacher's resource guides

Plexus Publishing, Inc.
143 Old Marlton Pike
Medford, NJ 08055
609-654-6500

Grades 10–12. "Working for Life: An Introduction to Careers in Biology": a video presentation for high school students

Prentice Hall
School Division of Simon & Schuster
Englewood Cliffs, NJ 07632-9940
800-848-9500

Biology

Biologia
Textbook in Spanish

Biology
Grades 9–10. Textbook, teacher's edition, teacher's resource book, supplementary materials including software, videocassettes, CNN VideoLink, videodisc

Biology and Human Progress
Grades 9–10. Textbook, teacher's resource handbook, supplementary materials

Biology Classroom Resources
Workbooks, posters, courseware, videocassettes, science fair manual, transparencies

Biology: The Study of Life
Grades 9–12. Textbook, teacher's edition, teacher's resource book, supplementary materials including software, videocassettes, CNN VideoLink, videodisc

Chemistry

Chemistry Critical Thinking Transparencies
Grades 6–12. Transparencies, teacher's guide

Chemistry: Experimental Foundations
Grades 10–12. Textbook, teacher's guide, laboratory manual and notebook

Chemistry Molecular Model Set
Complete teaching package

A Learning Program for Chemistry
Grades 9–12. Student workbook, teacher's edition

Prentice Hall Chemistry: The Study of Matter
Grades 9–12. Textbook, teacher's edition, teacher's resource book, supplementary materials including software, videocassettes

Solving Chemistry Problems: A Student's Illustrated Guide to Applying the Mole Concept
Grades 9–12. Softcover text

Earth Science

Earth Science Critical Thinking Skills Transparencies
Grades 6–12. Transparencies, teacher's guide

Learning Activities in Earth Science
Grades 7–12. Workbook, teacher's edition

Prentice Hall Earth Science
Grades 6–9. Textbook, teacher's edition, teacher's resource book, supplementary materials including software, videocassettes, CNN VideoLink

Elective/Advanced Placement

Basic Chemistry
Grades 11–12. Textbook, study guide, supplementary materials

Chemistry: The Central Science
Grades 11–12. Textbook, study guide, supplementary materials

Dynamic Astronomy
Grades 11–12. Textbook, laboratory manual

Environmental Science: The Way the World Works
Grades 10–12. Textbook, study guide, laboratory manual

Fundamentals of Anatomy and Physiology
Grades 11–12. Textbook, study guide

Oceanography: A View of the Earth
Grades 11–12. Textbook, study guide

Physical Geology
Grades 11–12. Textbook, study guide

Physics: Principles with Applications
Grades 11–12. Textbook, study guide, teacher's resource manual

General Science

Allyn and Bacon General Science
Grades 8–12. Textbook, teacher's edition, supplementary materials including software, videocassettes, CNN VideoLink

Prentice Hall General Science (series)
Grades 6–9. Student texts, teacher's editions, teacher's resource books, supplementary materials including software, videocassettes, CNN

VideoLink. Includes "A Voyage of Adventure," "A Voyage of Discovery," and "A Voyage of Exploration"

Prentice Hall General Science Transparencies
Grades 6–12. Transparencies, teacher's guide

Life Science

Learning Activities in Life Science
Grades 7–12. Workbook, teacher's edition

Life Science Critical Thinking Skills Transparencies
Grades 6–12. Transparencies, teacher's guide

Prentice Hall Life Science
Grades 6–9. Textbook, teacher's edition, teacher's resource book, supplementary materials including software, videocassettes, CNN VideoLink

Physical Science

Energy: A Sequel to IPS
Grades 9–11. Textbook, teacher's guide, supplementary materials

Introductory Physical Science
Grades 8–9. Textbook, teacher's guide and resource book, IPS/energy notebook

Learning Activities in Physical Science
Grades 7–12. Workbook, teacher's edition

Physical Science Critical Thinking Skills Transparencies

Prentice Hall Physical Science
Grades 6–9. Textbook, teacher's edition, teacher's resource book, supplementary materials including software, videocassettes, CNN VideoLink

Physics

Physics: Its Methods and Meanings
Textbook, laboratory manual, teacher's guide, teacher's resource book

Rainbow Educational Video
170 Keyland Court
Bohemia, NY 11716
800-331-4047

Grades K–8. Videos on botany, geology, machines, natural science, animals, astronomy, electricity, weather, energy

Redco Science
11 Robinson Lane
Oxford, CT 06483
203-881-2016

Grades 10–12. Supplies for physics experiments: scales, bench meters, measurement equipment, timers, magnets

Scholastic, Inc.
P.O. Box 7501
Jefferson City, MO 65105
800-325-6149

Interactive NOVA
Grades 5–12. Interactive videodisc library. Videodiscs, Macintosh software, user's guide, teaching guide, icon reference charts. Includes "Animal Pathfinders," "The Miracle of Life," and "Race to Save the Planet"

Operation: Frog
Grades 4–10. Software program

Science Explorers
Grades 1–6. Software program includes teaching guide, activity sheets, glossaries

Science Magazine
Includes "SuperScience," "ScienceWorld," and "BIG Science"

The Science Lab, Inc.
75 Todd Pond Road
Lincoln, MA 01773
617-259-8929

Grades K–6. Science activity and project books, videos, and magic kits. Sea Life software, Dinosaur Zoo software, gem collections, sand collections

Scott Resources
P.O. Box 2121K
Fort Collins, CO 80522
800-289-9299

Grades 6–12. Earth science materials: videocassettes, rock and mineral collections, fossils, equipment, charts. Materials cover environmental science, mineralogy, astronomy, meteorology, physical geography, earth history

Scott, Foresman
1900 East Lake Avenue
Glenview, IL 60025
800-554-4411

Biology: The Science of Life
High school (advanced placement, honors).
Textbook, laboratory manual, instructor's manual,
supplementary materials

Biosphere: The Realm of Life
Textbook, laboratory manual, instructor's manual,
supplementary materials

Chemistry
High school (advanced placement, honors).
Textbook, study guide, instructor's manual, lab
manual

Conceptual Physics
High school (advanced placement, honors).
Textbook, instructor's manual, workbook, user's
supplement

Discover Science (series)
Grades K–6. Textbooks, teacher's editions,
teacher's resource file, supplementary materials
including workbooks, software, videocassettes

Discover the Wonder (series)
Grades K–2. Big books, literature libraries,
activity books, teacher's guide, supplementary
materials including audio cassettes

The Environmental Detective Kit (series)
Grades 2–6. Textbooks, teacher's editions,
teacher's resource files, supplementary materials
including videocassettes

Introduction to the Human Body
High school (advanced placement, honors).
Textbook, instructor's manual, supplementary
materials including computerized testing

Marine Biology
High school (advanced placement, honors).
Softcover text, instructor's manual

Physics: A General Introduction
High school (advanced placement, honors).
Textbook, study guide

Principles of Anatomy and Physiology
High school (advanced placement, honors).
Textbook, instructor's manual, supplementary
materials including software

Scott, Foresman Biology
Grades 9–12. Textbook, teacher's edition,
teacher's resource book, supplementary materials

including software, teacher's resource book,
regional blackline masters

*Scott, Foresman Life, Earth, Physical Science
(series)*
Grades 7–9. Textbooks, teacher's editions,
teacher's resource files, supplementary materials

Dale Seymour Publications
P.O. Box 10888
Palo Alto, CA 94303-0879
800-USA-1100

Grades K–8. Resource kits, teacher's resource
guides, student readers, activity books, microscopes, posters, science kits

Silver Burdett & Ginn
4350 Equity Drive
P.O. Box 2649
Columbus, OH 43216
800-848-9500

Horizons Plus (series)
Grades 1–6. Science stories student books,
workbooks, teacher's editions, supplementary
materials

Horizontes en ciencias (series)
Grades 1–5. Textbooks, teacher's editions,
supplementary materials including videodiscs,
sound filmstrips, videocassettes, software, CNN
VideoLink

Science Courseware
Grades 3–9. Includes "Lunar Launch," "The
Great Freight Company: Simple Machines at
Work," "Food Chains and Webs," "Investigating
Chemical Reactions," "Investigating Plant
Growth," "Climatrolls: A Weather Simulation,"
and "The Human Body: Circulation and Respira-
tion"

Science Horizons (series)
Grades K–6. Textbooks, teacher's editions,
supplementary materials including videodiscs,
sound filmstrips, videocassettes, software, CNN
VideoLink

*Silver, Burdett and Ginn Life, Earth, Physical
Science, and General Science (series)*
Grades middle/junior high school. Textbooks,
teacher's editions, teacher's resource files, supplementary materials including sound filmstrips

Tom Snyder Productions
90 Sherman Street
Cambridge, MA 02140
800-342-0326

Grades 5–12. Software packages that promote critical thinking and problem-solving skills; "Decisions, Decisions: The Environment" looks at environmental problems

South-Western Publishing Co.
5101 Madison Road
Cincinnati, OH 45227
800-543-7972

Technology for Tomorrow
Textbook, teacher's manual, supplementary materials

Technology at Work
Textbook, teacher's manual, supplementary materials

SRA School Group
American School Publishers
Barnell Loft/Merrill/SRA
P.O. Box 5380
Chicago, IL 60680-5380
800-843-8855

Laboratory Science Series
Grades 6–10, older students with special needs. Workbooks, teacher's guides

Puzzlers—Software
Grades 4–8, high school (remedial). Software, user's manuals

Steck-Vaughn Company
P.O. Box 26015
Austin, TX 78755
800-531-5015

Basic Science for Living (series)
Grades 7–9. Student Texts. Includes "Earth and Life Science," and "Physical Science"

Science Today (series)
Grades 1–6, reading levels 1–4 (remedial and special education students). Student work-texts, teacher's editions

Supplemental Reading Series
Reading levels 2–3. Series include "World of Dinosaurs," "Animals in the Wild, "Look at Science," and "Save Our Species"

The Wonders of Science (series)
Grades 7–12, reading levels 2–3 (special- learning- needs students). Text-workbooks, teacher's editions. Includes "The Human Body," "Water Life," "The Earth and Beyond," "Land Animals," "Matter, Motion, and Machines," and "Plant Life"

Steel Can Recycling Institute
Foster Plaza 10
680 Anderson Drive
Pittsburgh, PA 15220
800-876-SCRI

Information on recycling and environmental concerns. Reproducible pages for instructional use

SWOOPE Program
Los Alamos National Laboratory
MS D447
Los Alamos, NM 87545
505-667-8950

Grades K–12. "Students Watching Over Our Planet Earth," a hands-on environmental science program

Teacher Ideas Press
Libraries Unlimited, Inc.
P.O. Box 3988
Englewood, CO 80155-3988
800-237-6124

Teacher's resource books for integrating science and literature, environmental activities, problem solving

The Teachers' Laboratory
P.O. Box 6480
Brattleboro, VT 05302-6480
802-254-3457

Grades K–12. Distributes books, equipment, and teaching units for study of the environment, measurement, magnets, electricity, design, and technology

United Learning, Inc.
6633 W. Howard Street
Niles, IL 60648-3305
800-424-0362

Grades K–12. Videos, videostrips, filmstrips, slides for physical science, chemistry, earth science, biology, and other subjects. Audiovisual games

U.S. Department of Energy
Office of Civilian Radioactive Waste Management
P.O. Box 44375
Washington, DC 20026
800-225-NWPA

Grades 8–12. Resource curriculum, "Science, Society, and America's Nuclear Waste," with teacher guide, videocassette, software, map, posters

Videodiscovery, Inc.
1700 Westlake Avenue North, Suite 600
Seattle, WA 98109
800-548-3472

Grades K–12. Videodiscs for life science, earth science, physical science, integrated science. "America 2000 School Science Package," a collection of science laserdiscs. Interactive science videos for middle school grades, "Science Sleuths" and "Image and Activity Bank," covering life science, earth science, and physical science

Wadsworth School Group
10 Davis Drive
Belmont, CA 94002-3098
800-831-6996

College textbooks and software appropriate for use by college-bound, honors, or advanced placement students in biology, environment, human physiology/anatomy, plant physiology, oceanography, astronomy, chemistry, photography, physics

Weekly Reader Corporation
3000 Cindel Drive
P.O. Box 8037
Delran, NJ 08075

Weekly Reader Skills Books (series)
Grades pre-K–9. Science reading stories, supplemental basic science books, science readiness books

Zaner-Bloser
1459 King Avenue
P.O. Box 16764
Columbus, OH 43216-6764
800-421-3018

Grades K–2. Kits, games, story books, and activity packets on environmental studies, conservation, waste management, electricity, energy, wildlife

Zephyr Press
3316 North Chapel Avenue
P.O. Box 13448-E
Tucson, AZ 85732-3448
800-350-0851

Grades K–12. Curriculum guides, activity books, resource books, building kits, self-directed learning packets

Zero Population Growth
ZPG Population Education Program
1400 16th Street, N.W., Suite 320
Washington, DC 20036
202-332-2200

"Earth Matters," an interdisciplinary teaching resource for studying how overpopulation contributes to climate change, air and water pollution, energy consumption, species extinction

STATEWIDE TEXTBOOK ADOPTION

THERE are twenty-two states that have statewide adoption of textbooks and other instructional materials: Alabama, Arizona, Arkansas, California, Florida, Georgia, Idaho, Indiana, Kentucky, Louisiana, Mississippi, Nevada, New Mexico, North Carolina, Oklahoma, Oregon, South Carolina, Tennessee, Texas, Utah, Virginia, and West Virginia.

The policies and procedures for textbook adoption are similar in all twenty-two states, with some minor variations.

Textbook Advisory Committee

In general, the state board of education is responsible for developing guidelines and criteria for the review and selection of textbooks and for appointing members to a textbook advisory committee. However, in a few states, the appointment of committee members is the responsibility of the governor or of the Commissioner of Education.

The textbook advisory committee is usually composed of educators, lay citizens, and parents, and can have from nine to twenty-seven appointees, depending upon the state. Membership is weighted, however, toward individuals who are educators: elementary and secondary teachers in the subject areas in which textbooks are to be adopted, instructors of teacher education and curriculum from local universities and colleges, school administrators, and school board members. Lay citizens, in order to sit on the committee, should be interested in and conversant with

educational issues. An effort is made to select appointees who reflect the diversity of their state's population, and therefore decisions about appointments are often made with the purpose of having a wide representation of ethnic backgrounds and geographical residence within the state.

Adoption Process

The textbook and instructional materials adoption process takes approximately twelve months.

Once the textbook advisory committee is formed, the members conduct an organizational meeting to formulate policy on such issues as adoption subjects and categories; standards for textbook evaluation, allocation of time for publisher presentations, and location of regional sites for such; sampling directions for publishers; and publisher contact. The committee may appoint subcommittees--made up of curriculum and/or subject specialists--to assist them in developing criteria for evaluating instructional materials.

After these procedural matters are agreed upon, the committee issues an official textbook call or "invitation to submit" to the textbook publishers. This document provides the publisher with adoption information and subject area criteria, which can either be the curriculum framework or essential skills list. Those publishers interested in having their materials considered for adoption submit their intention to bid, which shows the prices at which the publishers will agree to sell their material during the adoption period. Publishers usually bid current wholesale prices or lowest existing contract prices at which textbooks or other instructional materials are being sold elsewhere in the country.

If their bid has been accepted by the committee, the publishers submit sample copies of their textbooks for examination. The committee then hears presentations by the publishers. This meeting allows the publisher to present the texts submitted for adoption and to answer any questions the committee may have on the material. After publisher presentations, the textbooks are displayed in designated areas throughout the state for general public viewing. The committee then holds public hearings (usually two) which provide citizens with the opportunity to give an opinion on the textbooks offered for adoption. After much discussion and evaluation, the committee makes a recommendations for textbook adoption to the state board of education.

When the board of education approves the committee's recommendations, it negotiates the contract with the chosen publishers and disseminates the list of instructional materials to the school districts. The school districts will then make their textbook selections from this list. A few states also allow their school districts to use materials for the classroom that are not on the adoption list.

Textbook and Instructional Materials

There are two categories of instructional materials: basal and supplementary. Basal, or basic, materials address the goals, objectives, and content identified for a particular subject. Supplementary materials, used in conjunction with the basic text, enhance the teaching of the subject.

Instructional materials may include all or some of the following: hardcover books, softcover books, kits, workbooks, dictionaries, maps and atlases, electronic/computer programs, films, filmstrips, and other audiovisual materials.

The textbook adoption period generally runs from four to six years (California, the exception, has an eight-year contract period for K-8 only). The grade levels for adoption are usually K-12, with the following subject areas: English/language

arts, social studies, foreign languages, English as a second language (ESL), science, mathematics, fine arts, applied arts.

Textbooks and instructional materials are ultimately judged by how well they reflect the state curriculum framework and/or essential skills objectives. Materials are rated on the following criteria: organization, accuracy, and currency of subject content; correlation with grade level requirements for the subject; adaptability for students with different abilities, backgrounds, and experiences; types of teacher aids provided; author's background and training; physical features; and cost.

In addition, some states have social content requirements that textbooks have to meet. For instance, textbooks should be objective in content and impartial in interpretation of the subject, and should not include "offensive" language or illustrations. American values (e.g., democracy, the work ethic, free enterprise), culture, traditions, and government should be presented in a positive manner. Respect for the individual's rights, and for the cultural and racial diversity of American society, can also be addressed in the text. Finally, some states declare that textbooks should not condone civil disorder, lawlessness, or "deviance."

Kraus thanks the personnel we contacted at the state departments of education, for their help in providing the states' textbook adoption lists.

List of Textbooks

Following is a compilation of the textbooks and instructional materials approved by the twenty-two states that have statewide textbook adoption. This listing is based on the relevant publications submitted to Kraus by the textbook division of the respective departments of educations.

The list is alphabetized by state; under each state, the materials are organized by subject (e.g., English, handwriting, reading, literature, etc.). Note that the categories are those used by each state, and therefore they are not always consistent from state to state. In some cases, supplemental material is also noted. For each textbook (and supplemental publication), the title, grade level, publisher, and copyright date are provided, as well as the termination year of the textbook's adoption period.

Alabama

Elementary Science
Addison-Wesley Science: Grades 1–6
Addison-Wesley, 1989 (Termination Date: 1996)

Holt Science: Grades K–6
Harcourt Brace Jovanovich, 1989 (Termination Date: 1996)

Merrill Science: Grades K–6
Macmillan, 1989 (Termination Date: 1996)

Discover Science: Grades K–6
Scott, Foresman, 1989 (Termination Date: 1996)

Life Science
Addison-Wesley Life Science: Grade 7
Addison-Wesley, 1989 (Termination Date: 1996)

Focus on Life Science: Grade 7
Glencoe, 1989 (Termination Date: 1996)

Life Science: Grade 7
Holt, Rinehart & Winston, 1989 (Termination Date: 1996)

Macmillan Life Science: Grade 7
Macmillan, 1989 (Termination Date: 1996)

Prentice Hall Life Science: Grade 7
Prentice Hall, 1991 (Termination Date: 1996)

Scott, Foresman Life Science: Grade 7
Scott, Foresman, 1990 (Termination Date: 1996)

Silver Burdett & Ginn Life Science: Grade 7
Silver Burdett & Ginn, 1990 (Termination Date: 1996)

Understanding Life Science: Grades 7–10
Amsco, 1987 (Termination Date: 1996)

Life Science: Grade 7
Globe, 1986 (Termination Date: 1996)

Supplementary Materials, Life Science
Life Science: Grade 7
New Readers, 1988 (Termination Date: 1996)

Earth Science
Addison-Wesley Earth Science: Grade 8
Addison-Wesley, 1989 (Termination Date: 1996)

Focus on Earth Science: Grade 8
Glencoe, 1989 (Termination Date: 1996)

Earth Science: Grade 8
D. C. Heath, 1989 (Termination Date: 1996)

Earth Science: Grade 8
Holt, Rinehart & Winston, 1989 (Termination Date: 1996)

Modern Earth Science: Grade 8
Holt, Rinehart & Winston, 1989 (Termination Date: 1996)

Macmillan Earth Science: Grade 8
Macmillan, 1989 (Termination Date: 1996)

Prentice Hall Earth Science: Grade 8
Prentice Hall, 1991 (Termination Date: 1996)

Scott, Foresman Earth Science: Grade 8
Scott, Foresman, 1990 (Termination Date: 1996)

Silver Burdett & Ginn Earth Science: Grade 8
Silver Burdett & Ginn, 1990 (Termination Date: 1996)

Earth Science: Grade 8
Globe, 1986 (Termination Date: 1996)

Earth Science: Investigating Our World: Grade 8
Media, 1988 (Termination Date: 1996)

Supplementary Materials, Earth Science
Earth Below and Sky Above: Grade 8
New Readers, 1983 (Termination Date: 1996)

Physical Science
Addison-Wesley Physical Science: Grades 9–12
Addison-Wesley, 1988 (Termination Date: 1996)

Focus on Physical Science: Grades 9–12
Glencoe, 1989 (Termination Date: 1996)

Physical Science: Grades 9–12
Holt, Rinehart & Winston, 1989 (Termination Date: 1996)

Macmillan Physical Science: Grades 9–12
Macmillan, 1988 (Termination Date: 1996)

Prentice Hall Physical Science: Grades 9–12
Prentice Hall, 1991 (Termination Date: 1996)

Scott, Foresman Physical Science: Grades 9–12
Scott, Foresman, 1990 (Termination Date: 1996)

Silver Burdett & Ginn Physical Science: Grades 9–12
Silver Burdett, 1990 (Termination Date: 1996)

Addison-Wesley Introduction to Physical Science:
Grades 9–12
Addison-Wesley, 1988 (Termination Date: 1996)

Physical Science: Grade 9
Globe, 1986 (Termination Date: 1996)

Physical Science: Investigating Matter and Energy:
Grades 9–12
Media, 1986 (Termination Date: 1996)

Supplementary Materials, Physical Science
Matter and Energy: Grades 9–12
New Readers, 1983 (Termination Date: 1993)

General Science
*Environmental Science: How the World Works and
Your Place in It:* Grades 9–12
Le Bel, 1990 (Termination Date: 1996)

Science Connections: Grades 7–8
Glencoe, 1990 (Termination Date: 1996)

Merrill General Science: Grade 9
Glencoe, 1986 (Termination Date: 1996)

General Science: Grades 9–12
Holt, Rinehart & Winston, 1989 (Termination
Date: 1996)

Holt General Science: Grades 9–12
Holt, Rinehart & Winston, 1988 (Termination
Date: 1996)

Biology
Biology: Living Systems: Grades 9–12
Glencoe, 1989 (Termination Date: 1996)

Heath Biology: Grades 9–12
D. C. Heath, 1989 (Termination Date: 1996)

Biology: Grades 9–12
Holt, Rinehart & Winston, 1989 (Termination
Date: 1996)

Modern Biology: Grades 10–12
Holt, Rinehart & Winston, 1989 (Termination
Date: 1996)

Biology: A Personalized Approach: Grades 9–12
Kendall, 1989 (Termination Date: 1996)

Biology: The Living World: Grades 9–12
Prentice Hall, 1989 (Termination Date: 1996)

Prentice Hall Biology: Grades 9–12
Prentice Hall, 1990 (Termination Date: 1996)

Scott, Foresman Biology: Grades 9–12
Scott, Foresman, 1988 (Termination Date: 1996)

Biology: An Everyday Experience: Grades 9–12
Glencoe, 1988 (Termination Date: 1996)

Globe Biology: Grades 9–12
Globe, 1990 (Termination Date: 1996)

Basic Biology: The Science of Living Things:
Grades 9–12
Media, 1986 (Termination Date: 1996)

Supplementary Materials, Biology
Biological Science: An Ecological Approach:
Grades 9–12
Kendall, 1987 (Termination Date: 1996)

Chemistry
Addison-Wesley Chemistry: Grades 9–12
Addison-Wesley, 1990 (Termination Date: 1996)

Chemistry: A Modern Course: Grades 9–12
Glencoe, 1990 (Termination Date: 1996)

Heath Chemistry: Grades 9–12
D. C. Heath, 1987 (Termination Date: 1996)

Modern Chemistry: Grades 10–12
Holt, Rinehart & Winston, 1990 (Termination
Date: 1996)

Prentice Hall Chemistry: The Study of Matter:
Grades 9–12
Prentice Hall, 1989 (Termination Date: 1996)

Chemistry: Grades 9–12
D. C. Heath, 1989 (Termination Date: 1996)

Supplementary Materials, Chemistry
Chemcom: Chemistry in the Community: Grades
9–12
Kendall/Hunt, 1988 (Termination Date: 1996)

Spice: Structured Pacing in Chemistry Education:
Grades 9–12
Kendall/Hunt, 1987 (Termination Date: 1996)

Physics
Conceptual Physics: Grades 9–12
Addison-Wesley, 1987 (Termination Date: 1996)

Physics: Principles and Problems: Grades 9–12
Glencoe, 1990 (Termination Date: 1996)

Modern Physics: Grades 10–12
Holt, Rinehart & Winston, 1990 (Termination
Date: 1996)

Physic-Al: An Activity Approach to Physics: Grades
9–12
Le Bel, 1989 (Termination Date: 1996)

Human Anatomy and Physiology
Structure and Function of the Body: Grades 11–12
C. V. Mosby, 1988 (Termination Date: 1996)

Human Anatomy and Physiology: Grades 10–12
Addison-Wesley, 1989 (Termination Date: 1996)

Anatomy and Physiology: Grades 11–12
C. V. Mosby, 1989 (Termination Date: 1996)

Anthony's Textbook of Anatomy and Physiology:
Grades 11–12
C. V. Mosby, 1990 (Termination Date: 1996)

Botany/Marine Science/Zoology
Marine Biology: Grades 10–12
Addison-Wesley, 1986 (Termination Date: 1996)

The Botanical World: Grades 11–12
C. V. Mosby, 1984 (Termination Date: 1996)

Integrated Principles of Zoology: Grades 11–12
C. V. Mosby, 1988 (Termination Date: 1996)

Arizona

Science—Supplemental
Discover Science: Grades K–6
Scott, Foresman, 1989, 1991 (Termination Date:
1996)

Earth Science: Grades 7–8
Scott, Foresman, 1990 (Termination Date: 1996)

Physical Science: Grades 7–8
Scott, Foresman, 1990 (Termination Date: 1996)

Life Science: Grades 7–8
Scott, Foresman, 1990 (Termination Date: 1996)

Science Horizons: Grades K–6
Silver Burdett & Ginn, 1991 (Termination Date:
1996)

General Science: Grades 7–8
Silver Burdett & Ginn, 1989 (Termination Date:
1996)

Life Science: Grades 7–8
Silver Burdett & Ginn, 1990 (Termination Date:
1996)

Earth Science: Grades 7–8
Silver Burdett & Ginn, 1990 (Termination Date:
1996)

Physical Science: Grades 7–8
Silver Burdett & Ginn, 1990 (Termination Date:
1996)

Science in Your World: Grades K–6
Macmillan/McGraw-Hill, 1991 (Termination
Date: 1996)

Addison-Wesley Science: Grades K–6
Addison-Wesley, 1989 (Termination Date: 1996)

Life Science: Grades 7–8
Addison-Wesley, 1989 (Termination Date: 1996)

Physical Science: Grades 7–8
Addison-Wesley, 1989 (Termination Date: 1996)

Earth Science: Grades 7–8
Addison-Wesley, 1989 (Termination Date: 1996)

Science for Life and Living: Grades K–3
Kendall/Hunt, 1992 (Termination Date: 1996)

Middle School Life Science: Grades 7–8
Kendall/Hunt, 1991 (Termination Date: 1996)

MCP Science: Grades K–6
Modern Curriculum Press, 1987 (Termination Date: 1996)

Exploring Our World: Grades K–6
Modern Curriculum Press, 1990 (Termination Date: 1996)

Concept Science: Grades K–3
Modern Curriculum Press, 1990 (Termination Date: 1996)

Life Science: Grades 7–8
Prentice Hall, 1991 (Termination Date: 1996)

Earth Science: Grades 7–8
Prentice Hall, 1991 (Termination Date: 1996)

General Science: Grades 7–8
Prentice Hall, 1991 (Termination Date: 1996)

Science Connections: Grades 7–8
Glencoe/McGraw-Hill, 1990 (Termination Date: 1996)

Focus on Life Science: Grades 7–8
Glencoe/McGraw-Hill, 1989 (Termination Date: 1996)

Focus on Earth Science: Grades 7–8
Glencoe/McGraw-Hill, 1989 (Termination Date: 1996)

Focus on Physical Science: Grades 7–8
Glencoe/McGraw-Hill, 1989 (Termination Date: 1996)

HBJ Life Science: Grades 7–8
Holt, Rinehart & Winston, 1989 (Termination Date: 1996)

HBJ Earth Science: Grades 7–8
Holt, Rinehart & Winston, 1989 (Termination Date: 1996)

HBJ Physical Science: Grades 7–8
Holt, Rinehart & Winston, 1989 (Termination Date: 1996)

Concepts and Challenges in Science: Grades 7–8
Globe, 1991 (Termination Date: 1996)

Life Science: Grades 7–8
D. C. Heath, 1987 (Termination Date: 1996)

Physical Science: Grades 7–8
D. C. Heath, 1987 (Termination Date: 1996)

Earth Science: Grades 7–8
D. C. Heath, 1987 (Termination Date: 1996)

My World Books: Grades K–6
Steck-Vaughn, 1989–91 (Termination Date: 1996)

Counters and Seekers: Grades K–6
Steck-Vaughn, 1991 (Termination Date: 1996)

Science Today: Grades K–6
Steck-Vaughn, 1987 (Termination Date: 1996)

Wonders of Science: Grades 4–8
Steck-Vaughn, 1990 (Termination Date: 1996)

Basic Science for Living: Grades 4–8
Steck-Vaughn, 1990 (Termination Date: 1996)

Scholastic Science Collections: Grades K–3
Scholastic, n.d. (Termination Date: 1996)

Essentials of Life Science: Grades 7–8
Competency Press, 1990 (Termination Date: 1996)

Essentials of Earth Science: Grades 7–8
Competency Press, 1990 (Termination Date: 1996)

Essentials of Physical Science: Grades 7–8
Competency Press, 1990 (Termination Date: 1996)

Young Discovery Library: Grades K–6
Charlesbridge, 1989–92 (Termination Date: 1996)

Alphabet Books: Grades K–3
Charlesbridge, 1986–92 (Termination Date: 1996)

Chemicals, Health, Environment, and Me: Grades
4–6
Lawrence Hall of Science, 1990 (Termination
Date: 1996)

Arkansas

Basal Science
Addison-Wesley Science: Grades 1–6
Addison-Wesley, 1989 (Termination Date: 1995)

Holt Science: Grades 1–6
Harcourt Brace Jovanovich, 1989 (Termination
Date: 1995)

Merrill Science: Grades 1–6
Merrill, 1989 (Termination Date: 1995)

Discover Science: Grades 1–6
Scott, Foresman, 1989 (Termination Date: 1995)

Silver Burdett and Ginn Science: Grades 1–6
Silver Burdett & Ginn, 1989 (Termination Date:
1995)

Science All around Us Program: Grades 1–6
Nystrom, 1986 (Termination Date: 1995)

Anatomy and Physiology
Modern Human Physiology: Grades 7–12
Holt, Rinehart & Winston, 1987 (Termination
Date: 1995)

Anatomy and Physiology: Grades 11–12
C. V. Mosby, 1987 (Termination Date: 1995)

Structure and Function of the Body: Grades 11–12
C. V. Mosby, 1988 (Termination Date: 1995)

Anatomy and Physiology: Basic Principles: Grades
11–12
Prentice Hall, 1983 (Termination Date: 1995)

Astronomy
Dynamic Astronomy: Grades 11–12
Prentice Hall, 1989 (Termination Date: 1995)

Biology
Addison-Wesley Biology: Grades 9–12
Addison-Wesley, 1988 (Termination Date: 1995)

Pacemaker Biology: Grades 9–12
Fearon, 1990 (Termination Date: 1995)

Globe Biology: Grades 10–12
Globe, 1990 (Termination Date: 1995)

Biology Workshop: Grades 7–12
Globe, 1988 (Termination Date: 1995)

Biology: Grades 7–12
Harcourt Brace Jovanovich, 1989 (Termination
Date: 1995)

Heath Biology: Grades 9–12
D. C. Heath, 1989 (Termination Date: 1995)

Biological Science: A Molecular Approach: Grades
9–12
D. C. Heath, 1990 (Termination Date: 1995)

Modern Biology: Grades 9–12
Holt, Rinehart & Winston, 1989 (Termination
Date: 1995)

Biology: A Journey into Life: Grades 10–12
Holt, Rinehart & Winston, 1988 (Termination
Date: 1995)

Biological Science: An Ecological Approach:
Grades 9–12
Kendall/Hunt, 1987 (Termination Date: 1995)

Basic Biology: Grades 7–12
Media Materials, 1986 (Termination Date: 1995)

Biology: An Everyday Experience: Grades 9–12
Merrill, 1988 (Termination Date: 1995)

Biology: Living Systems: Grades 9–12
Merrill, 1989 (Termination Date: 1995)

Understanding Biology: Grades 11–12
C. V. Mosby, 1988 (Termination Date: 1995)

Biology: Grades 11–12
C. V. Mosby, 1989 (Termination Date: 1995)

Prentice Hall Biology: Grades 9–10
Prentice Hall, 1990 (Termination Date: 1995)

Biology: The Living World: Grades 9–12
Prentice Hall, 1989 (Termination Date: 1995)

Biology: The Study of Life: Grades 9–12
Prentice Hall, 1990 (Termination Date: 1995)

Scott, Foresman Biology: Grades 9–12
Scott, Foresman, 1988 (Termination Date: 1995)

Chemistry
Addison-Wesley Chemistry: Grades 9–12
Addison-Wesley, 1987 (Termination Date: 1995)

Chemistry Workshop: Grades 7–12
Globe, 1988 (Termination Date: 1995)

Heath Chemistry: Grades 9–12
D. C. Heath, 1987 (Termination Date: 1995)

Chemistry: Grades 10–12
D. C. Heath, 1989 (Termination Date: 1995)

Modern Chemistry: Grades 9–12
Holt, Rinehart & Winston, 1990 (Termination Date: 1995)

Chemcom: Chemistry in the Community: Grades 9–12
Kendall/Hunt, 1988 (Termination Date: 1995)

Chemistry: A Modern Course: Grades 9–12
Merrill, 1990 (Termination Date: 1995)

Prentice Hall Chemistry: The Study of Matter: Grades 9–12
Prentice Hall, 1989 (Termination Date: 1995)

Chemistry: The Central Science: Grades 11–12
Prentice Hall, 1988 (Termination Date: 1995)

Earth and Space Science
Addison-Wesley Earth Science: Grades 7–9
Addison-Wesley, 1989 (Termination Date: 1995)

Concepts and Challenges: Earth Science: Grades 7–12
Globe, 1986 (Termination Date: 1995)

Globe Earth Science: Grades 7–12
Globe, 1986 (Termination Date: 1995)

Work-A-Text in Earth Science: Grades 7–12
Globe, 1987 (Termination Date: 1995)

Earth Science Workshop: Grades 7–12
Globe, 1988 (Termination Date: 1995)

Earth Science: Grades 7–12
Harcourt Brace Jovanovich, 1989 (Termination Date: 1995)

Earth Science: Grades 9–12
D. C. Heath, 1989 (Termination Date: 1995)

Modern Earth Science: Grades 9–12
Holt, Rinehart & Winston, 1989 (Termination Date: 1995)

Investigating the Earth: Grades 10–12
Houghton Mifflin, 1990 (Termination Date: 1995)

Macmillan Earth Science: Grades 7–12
Macmillan, 1989 (Termination Date: 1995)

Earth Science: Grades 7–12
Media Materials, 1988 (Termination Date: 1995)

Focus on Earth Science: Grades 7–9
Merrill, 1989 (Termination Date: 1995)

Prentice Hall Earth Science: Grades 6–9
Prentice Hall, 1991 (Termination Date: 1995)

Arkansas Basic Skillbook: Earth Science: Grade 8
Rainbow Educational Concepts, 1989 (Termination Date: 1995)

Scott, Foresman Earth Science: Grades 7–9
Scott, Foresman, 1990 (Termination Date: 1995)

Environmental Science
Environmental Science: Grades 11–12
Addison-Wesley, 1989 (Termination Date: 1995)

Environmental Science: How the World Works and Your Place in It: Grades 9–12
Le Bel, 1989 (Termination Date: 1995)

Investigating Aquatic Ecosystems: Grades 9–12
Prentice Hall, 1987 (Termination Date: 1995)

General Science

Pacemaker General Science: Grades 9–12
Fearon, 1990 (Termination Date: 1995)

Introduction to General Science: Grades 7–12
Globe, 1987 (Termination Date: 1995)

General Science: Grades 7–12
Harcourt Brace Jovanovich, 1989 (Termination Date: 1995)

Holt General Science: Grades 7–12
Holt, Rinehart & Winston, 1988 (Termination Date: 1995)

Merrill General Science: Grades 9–12
Merrill, 1986 (Termination Date: 1995)

Science Connections: Grades 7–8
Merrill, 1990 (Termination Date: 1995)

Allyn and Bacon General Science: Grades 8–12
Prentice Hall, 1989 (Termination Date: 1995)

Life Science

Addison-Wesley Life Science: Grades 7–9
Addison-Wesley, 1989 (Termination Date: 1995)

Concepts and Challenges: Life Science: Grades 7–9
Globe, 1986 (Termination Date: 1995)

Life Science: Grades 7–12
Harcourt Brace Jovanovich, 1989 (Termination Date: 1995)

Macmillan Life Science: Grades 7–12
Macmillan, 1989 (Termination Date: 1995)

Focus on Life Science: Grades 7–9
Merrill, 1989 (Termination Date: 1995)

Prentice Hall Life Science: Grades 6–9
Prentice Hall, 1991 (Termination Date: 1995)

Arkansas Basic Skillbook: Life Science Review: Grade 8
Rainbow Educational Concepts, 1989 (Termination Date: 1995)

Scott Foresman Life Science: Grades 7–9
Scott, Foresman, 1990 (Termination Date: 1995)

Physical Science

Addison-Wesley Introduction to Physical Science: Grades 6–9
Addison-Wesley, 1988 (Termination Date: 1995)

Addison-Wesley Physical Science: Grades 7–9
Addison-Wesley, 1988 (Termination Date: 1995)

Concepts and Challenges: Physical Science: Grades 7–9
Globe, 1986 (Termination Date: 1995)

Physical Science: Grades 7–12
Harcourt Brace Jovanovich, 1989 (Termination Date: 1995)

Macmillan Physical Science: Grades 7–12
Macmillan, 1988 (Termination Date: 1995)

Physical Science: Grades 7–12
Media Materials, 1987 (Termination Date: 1995)

Focus on Physical Science: Grades 7–9
Merrill, 1989 (Termination Date: 1995)

Prentice Hall Physical Science: Grades 6–9
Prentice Hall, 1991 (Termination Date: 1995)

Introductory Physical Science: Grades 7–9
Prentice Hall, 1987 (Termination Date: 1995)

Scott, Foresman Physical Science: Grades 7–9
Scott, Foresman, 1990 (Termination Date: 1995)

Science in the Marketplace: Grades 9–12
Tiger, 1987 (Termination Date: 1995)

Physics

Conceptual Physics: Grades 9–12
Addison-Wesley, 1987 (Termination Date: 1995)

Physics Workshop: Grades 7–12
Globe, 1988 (Termination Date: 1995)

Modern Physics: Grades 9–12
Holt, Rinehart & Winston, 1990 (Termination Date: 1995)

Physic-Al: An Activity Approach to Physics: Grades 9–12
Le Bel, 1989 (Termination Date: 1995)

Physics: Principles and Problems: Grades 9–12
Merrill, 1990 (Termination Date: 1995)

Physics: Principles with Applications: Grades 11–12
Prentice Hall, 1985 (Termination Date: 1995)

Zoology
Biology of Animals: Grades 11–12
C. V. Mosby, 1986 (Termination Date: 1995)

The Earth's Crust: Grades 7–9
Nystrom, 1987 (Termination Date: 1995)

Jurica Biology Charts: Grades 9–12
Nystrom, 1985 (Termination Date: 1995)

The Four Seasons Filmstrips: Grades 7–9
Nystrom, 1989 (Termination Date: 1995)

California

Note: California did not have a science list.

Florida

General Science
HBJ Science Series: Grades K–6
Harcourt Brace Jovanovich, 1985 (Termination
Date: 1994)

Holt Science Series: Grades K–5
Holt, Rinehart & Winston, 1986 (Termination
Date: 1994)

Journeys in Science Series: Grades K–6
Macmillan/McGraw-Hill, 1988 (Termination
Year: 1994)

Silver Burdett & Ginn Science Series: Grades K–6
Silver Burdett & Ginn, 1987 (Termination Date:
1994)

Prentice Hall General Science Series: Grades 6–8
Prentice Hall, 1989 (Termination Date: 1995)

Merrill Science Connections: Blue Book: Grade 6;
Red Book: Grades 9–12
Glencoe/McGraw-Hill, 1990 (Termination Date:
1995)

HBJ General Science: Grades 9–12
Holt, Rinehart & Winston, 1989 (Termination
Date: 1995)

Allyn and Bacon General Science: Grades 9–12
Prentice Hall, 1989 (Termination Date: 1995)

Holt General Science: Grades 6–8
Holt, Rinehart & Winston, 1988 (Termination
Date: 1995)

Earth and Space Science
Globe Earth Science: Grades 6–8
Globe, 1987 (Termination Date: 1995)

Focus on Earth Science: Grades 6–8
Glencoe/McGraw-Hill, 1989 (Termination Date:
1995)

Heath Earth Science: The Challenge of Discovery:
Grades 6–8
D. C. Heath, 1991 (Termination Date: 1995)

HBJ Earth Science: Grades 6–8
Holt, Rinehart & Winston, 1989 (Termination
Date: 1995)

Prentice Hall Earth Science: Grade 8
Prentice Hall, 1991 (Termination Date: 1995)

Scott, Foresman Earth Science: Grades 6–8
Scott, Foresman, 1990 (Termination Date: 1995)

Concepts and Challenges in Earth Science: Grades
9–12
Globe, 1991 (Termination Date: 1995)

Addison-Wesley Earth Science: Grades 9–12
Addison-Wesley, 1989 (Termination Date: 1995)

Earth Science: Grades 9–12
D. C. Heath, 1989 (Termination Date: 1995)

Modern Earth Science: Grades 9–12
Holt, Rinehart & Winston, 1989 (Termination
Date: 1995)

Life Science
Addison-Wesley Life Science: Grades 6–8
Addison-Wesley, 1989 (Termination Date: 1994)

Focus on Life Science: Grades 6–8
Glencoe (Merrill), 1989 (Termination Date: 1994)

Life Science: Grades 6–8
Harcourt Brace Jovanovich, 1989 (Termination Date: 1994)

Prentice Hall Life Science: Grades 6–8
Prentice Hall, 1991 (Termination Date: 1994)

Silver Burdett & Ginn Life Science: Grades 6–8
Silver Burdett & Ginn, 1990 (Termination Date: 1994)

Physical Science

Concepts and Challenges in Physical Science: Grades 6–8
Globe, 1989 (Termination Date: 1994)

Heath Physical Science: Grades 6–8
D. C. Heath, 1987 (Termination Date: 1994)

Addison-Wesley Introduction to Physical Science: Grades 9–12
Addison-Wesley, 1988–89 (Termination Date: 1994)

Focus on Physical Science: Grades 6–8
Glencoe (Merrill), 1989 (Termination Date: 1994)

Physical Science: Grades 6–8
Harcourt Brace Jovanovich, 1989 (Termination Date: 1994)

Scott, Foresman Physical Science: Grades 6–8
Scott, Foresman, (n.d.) (Termination Date: 1994)

Silver Burdett & Ginn Physical Science: Grades 6–8
Silver Burdett & Ginn, 1988, 1990 (Termination Date:1994)

Addison-Wesley Physical Science: Grades 9–10
Addison-Wesley, 1988 (Termination Date: 1994)

Macmillan Physical Science: Grade 9
Macmillan, 1988 (Termination Date: 1994)

Prentice Hall Physical Science: Grade 9
Prentice Hall, 1988, 1991 (Termination Date: 1994)

Anatomy and Physiology

Structure and Function of the Body: Grades 11–12
C. V. Mosby, 1988 (Termination Date: 1994)

Anthony's Textbook of Anatomy and Physiology: Grades 11–12
C. V. Mosby, 1990 (Termination Date: 1994)

Human Anatomy and Physiology: Grades 11–12
Addison-Wesley, 1989 (Termination Date: 1994)

Anatomy and Physiology: Grades 11–12
C. V. Mosby, 1989 (Termination Date: 1994)

Biology

Biology: An Everyday Experience: Grades 9–12
Glencoe, 1988 (Termination Date: 1994)

Globe Biology: Grades 9–12
Globe, 1990 (Termination Date: 1994)

Biology: Living Systems: Grades 9–12
Glencoe, 1989 (Termination Date: 1994)

Biology: Grades 9–12
Harcourt Brace Jovanovich, 1989 (Termination Date: 1994)

Heath Biology: Grades 9–12
D. C. Heath, 1989 (Termination Date: 1994)

Modern Biology: Grades 9–12
Holt, Rinehart & Winston, 1989 (Termination Date: 1994)

Biology: The Living World: Grades 9–10
Prentice Hall, 1989 (Termination Date: 1994)

BSCS Blue Version, Biological Science, A Molecular Approach: Grades 9–12
D. C. Heath, 1990 (Termination Date: 1994)

BSCS Biological Science, An Ecological Approach: Grades 9–12
Kendall/Hunt, (n.d.) (Termination Date: 1994)

Biology: The Study of Life: Grades 9–10
Prentice Hall, 1990 (Termination Date: 1994)

The Nature of Life: Grades 9–12
Glencoe, 1989 (Termination Date: 1994)

Understanding Biology: Grades 11–12
C. V. Mosby, 1988 (Termination Date: 1994)

Biology: Grades 11–12
Addison-Wesley, 1987 (Termination Date: 1994)

Biology: Grade 12
Glencoe, 1988 (Termination Date: 1994)

Biology: Grades 11–12
C. V. Mosby, 1989 (Termination Date: 1994)

Chemistry

Addison-Wesley Chemistry: Grades 10–12
Addison-Wesley, 1990 (Termination Date: 1995)

Chemistry: A Modern Course: Grades 10–12
Glencoe/McGraw-Hill, 1990 (Termination Date: 1995)

Modern Chemistry: Grades 9–12
Holt, Rinehart & Winston, 1990 (Termination Date: 1995)

Chemcom: Chemistry in the Community: Grades 9–12
Kendall/Hunt, 1988 (Termination Date: 1995)

Prentice Hall Chemistry: The Study of Matter: Grades 9–12
Prentice Hall, 1991 (Termination Date: 1995)

General Chemistry: Grades 10–12
D. C. Heath, 1988 (Termination Date: 1995)

Chemistry: The Central Science: Grades 9–12
Prentice Hall, 1988 (Termination Date: 1988)

Chemistry: Grades 10–12
D. C. Heath, 1989 (Termination Date: 1995)

Chemistry: Principles and Reactions: Grades 10–12
Holt, Rinehart & Winston, 1989 (Termination Date: 1995)

Environmental Science

Environmental Science: A Framework for Decision Making: Grades 9–12
Addison-Wesley, 1989 (Termination Date: 1995)

Environmental Science: Grades 9–12
Holt, Rinehart & Winston, 1990 (Termination Date: 1995)

Global Science: Energy, Resources, Environment: Grades 9–12
Kendall/Hunt, 1991 (Termination Date: 1995)

Environmental Science: How the World Works and Your Place in It: Grades 9–12
Le Bel, n.d. (Termination Date: 1995)

Environmental Science: The Way the World Works: Grades 9–12
Prentice Hall, 1990 (Termination Date: 1995)

Marine Biology

Marine Biology: Grades 10–12
Addison-Wesley, 1986 (Termination Date: 1994)

Oceanography

Introduction to the World's Oceans: Grades 11–12
William C. Brown, 1991 (Termination Date: 1995)

Oceanography: A View of the Earth: Grades 9–12
Prentice Hall, 1990 (Termination Date: 1995)

Physics

Physics: Principles and Problems: Grades 11–12
Glencoe, 1990 (Termination Date: 1994)

PSSC Physics: Grades 11–12
D. C. Heath, 1986 (Termination Date: 1994)

Modern Physics: Grades 11–12
Holt, Rinehart & Winston, 1990 (Termination Date: 1994)

College Physics: Grades 11–12
Addison-Wesley, 1985 (Termination Date: 1994)

University Physics: Grades 11–12
Addison-Wesley, (n.d.) (Termination Date: 1994)

Zoology

Biology of Animals: Grades 11–12
C. V. Mosby, 1990 (Termination Date: 1994)

Georgia

Biology

Biology: Grades 11–12
Addison-Wesley, 1987 (Termination Date: 1993)

Addison-Wesley Biology: Grades 9–12
Addison-Wesley, 1988 (Termination Date: 1993)

Biology: An Everyday Experience: Grades 9–12
Glencoe/McGraw-Hill, 1988 (Termination Date: 1993)

Biology: Living Systems: Grades 9–12
Glencoe/McGraw-Hill, 1989 (Termination Date: 1993)

Biology for Living: Grades 10–12
Globe, 1987 (Termination Date: 1993)

Biology: Grades 9–12
Harcourt Brace Jovanovich, 1989 (Termination Date: 1993)

Heath Biology: Grades 9–12
D. C. Heath, 1989 (Termination Date: 1993)

Biology, A Journey into Life: Grades 10–12
Holt, Rinehart & Winston, 1988 (Termination Date: 1993)

Modern Biology: Grades 9–12
Holt, Rinehart & Winston, 1989 (Termination Date: 1993)

Biological Science: An Ecological Approach: Grades 9–12
Kendall/Hunt, 1987 (Termination Date: 1993)

Basic Biology: Grades 7–12
Media Materials, 1986 (Termination Date: 1993)

The Botanical World: Grades 11–12
C. V. Mosby, 1984 (Termination Date: 1993)

Biology, Second Edition: Grades 11–12
C. V. Mosby, 1989 (Termination Date: 1993)

Understanding Biology: Grades 11–12
C. V. Mosby, 1988 (Termination Date: 1993)

Biology: The Living World: Grades 9–12
Prentice Hall, 1989 (Termination Date: 1993)

Prentice Hall Biology: Grades 9–12
Prentice Hall, 1990 (Termination Date: 1993)

Biology: The Study of Life: Grades 9–12
Prentice Hall, 1990 (Termination Date: 1993)

Scott, Foresman Biology: Grades 9–12
Scott, Foresman, 1988 (Termination Date: 1993)

Chemistry

Chemistry: Grades 9–12
Addison-Wesley, 1987 (Termination Date: 1993)

Chemistry: A Modern Course: Grades 9–12
Glencoe/McGraw-Hill, 1987 (Termination Date: 1993)

Heath Chemistry: Grades 10–12
D. C. Heath, 1987 (Termination Date: 1993)

General Chemistry: Grades 11–12
D. C. Heath, 1988 (Termination Date: 1993)

Modern Chemistry: Grades 9–12
Holt, Rinehart & Winston, 1986 (Termination Date: 1993)

Chemcom: Chemistry in the Community: Grades 9–12
Kendall/Hunt, 1988 (Termination Date: 1993)

Alchem Chemistry: Grades 9–12
Le Bel, 1987 (Termination Date: 1993)

Chemistry: The Central Science: Grades 11–12
Prentice Hall, 1988 (Termination Date: 1993)

Chemistry: The Study of Matter: Grades 10–12
Prentice Hall, 1989 (Termination Date: 1993)

Chemistry: Experimental Foundations: Grades 11–12
Prentice Hall, 1987 (Termination Date: 1993)

Earth

Earth Science: Grade 8
Addison-Wesley, 1989 (Termination Date: 1993)

Macmillan Earth Science: Grade 8
Glencoe/McGraw-Hill, 1989 (Termination Date: 1993)

Focus on Science Series: Grades 6–9
Glencoe/McGraw-Hill, 1989 (Termination Date: 1993)

Concepts and Challenges in Earth Science: Grade 8
Globe, 1986 (Termination Date: 1993)

Earth Science: Grade 8
Harcourt Brace Jovanovich, 1989 (Termination Date: 1993)

Earth Science: Grades 7–12
D. C. Heath, 1989 (Termination Date: 1993)

Heath Earth Science: Grades 7–9
D. C. Heath, 1987 (Termination Date: 1993)

Holt Earth Science: Grades 7–9
Holt, Rinehart & Winston, 1986 (Termination Date: 1993)

Modern Earth Science: Grades 9–12
Holt, Rinehart & Winston, 1989 (Termination Date: 1993)

Investigating the Earth: Grades 9–12
Houghton Mifflin, 1987 (Termination Date: 1993)

Earth Science: Grades 7–12
Media Materials, 1988 (Termination Date: 1993)

Prentice Hall Earth Science: Grades 6–9
Prentice Hall, 1991 (Termination Date: 1993)

Scott, Foresman Earth Science: Grades 7–9
Scott, Foresman, 1990 (Termination Date: 1993)

Silver Burdett & Ginn Earth Science: Grade 8
Silver Burdett & Ginn, 1987 (Termination Date: 1993)

Global Science: Energy, Resources, Environment: Grades 9–12
Kendall/Hunt, 1984 (Termination Date: 1993)

Elementary Science

Addison-Wesley Science: Grades K–6
Addison-Wesley, 1989 (Termination Date: 1993)

HBJ Science, Nova Edition: Grades K–6
Harcourt Brace Jovanovich, 1989 (Termination Date: 1993)

Holt Science: Grades K–6
Holt, Rinehart & Winston, 1989 (Termination Date: 1993)

Journeys in Science: Grades K–6
Macmillan/McGraw-Hill, 1988 (Termination Date: 1993)

Merrill Science: Grades K–6
Macmillan/McGraw-Hill, 1989 (Termination Date: 1993)

Discover Science: Grades K–6
Scott, Foresman, 1989 (Termination Date: 1993)

Silver Burdett & Ginn Science: Grades K–6
Silver Burdett & Ginn, 1989 (Termination Date: 1993)

Life Science

Life Science: Grade 7
Addison-Wesley, 1989 (Termination Date: 1993)

Macmillan Life Science: Grade 7
Glencoe/McGraw-Hill, 1989 (Termination Date: 1993)

Focus on Science Series: Grades 6–9
Glencoe/McGraw-Hill, 1989 (Termination Date: 1993)

Concepts and Challenges in Life Science: Grade 7
Globe, 1986 (Termination Date: 1993)

Life Science: Grade 7
Harcourt Brace Jovanovich, 1989 (Termination Date: 1993)

Heath Life Science: Grades 7–9
D. C. Heath, 1987 (Termination Date: 1993)

Holt Life Science: Grades 7–9
Holt, Rinehart & Winston, 1986 (Termination Date: 1993)

Prentice Hall Life Science: Grades 6–9
Prentice Hall, 1991 (Termination Date: 1993)

Scott, Foresman Life Science: Grades 7–9
Scott, Foresman, 1990 (Termination Date: 1993)

Silver Burdett & Ginn Life Science: Grade 7
Silver Burdett, 1987 (Termination Date: 1993)

Physical Science

Physical Science: Grade 9
Addison-Wesley, 1988 (Termination Date: 1993)

Introduction to Physical Science: Grades 7–9
Addison-Wesley, 1988 (Termination Date: 1993)

Macmillan Physical Science: Grade 9
Glencoe/McGraw-Hill, 1989 (Termination Date: 1993)

Focus on Science Series: Grades 6–9
Glencoe/McGraw-Hill, 1989 (Termination Date: 1993)

Concepts and Challenges in Physical Science: Grade 9
Globe, 1986 (Termination Date: 1993)

Physical Science: Grade 9
Harcourt Brace Jovanovich, 1989 (Termination Date: 1993)

Heath Physical Science: Grades 7–9
D. C. Heath, 1987 (Termination Date: 1993)

Holt Physical Science: Grades 7–9
Holt, Rinehart & Winston, 1986 (Termination Date: 1993)

Physical Science: Grades 7–12
Media Materials, 1987 (Termination Date: 1993)

Prentice Hall Physical Science: Grades 6–9
Prentice Hall, 1991 (Termination Date: 1993)

Scott, Foresman Physical Science: Grades 7–9
Scott, Foresman, 1990 (Termination Date: 1993)

Silver Burdett & Ginn Physical Science: Grade 9
Silver Burdett & Ginn, 1988 (Termination Date: 1993)

Physics

Conceptual Physics: Grades 9–12
Addison-Wesley, 1987 (Termination Date: 1993)

Physics: Principles and Problems: Grades 11–12
Glencoe/McGraw-Hill, 1986 (Termination Date: 1993)

PSSC Physics: Grades 11–12
D. C. Heath, 1986 (Termination Date: 1993)

Modern Physics: Grades 9–12
Holt, Rinehart & Winston, 1984 (Termination Date: 1993)

Physiology

Textbook of Anatomy and Physiology: Grades 11–12
C. V. Mosby, 1987 (Termination Date: 1993)

Structure and Function of the Body: Grades 11–12
C. V. Mosby, 1988 (Termination Date: 1993)

Idaho

Elementary/Junior High—Basic Science

Addison-Wesley Science: Grades 4–6
Addison-Wesley, 1989 (Termination Date: 1994)

Merrill Science: Grades 4–6
Merrill, 1989 (Termination Date: 1994)

Focus on Earth Science: Grades 6–9
Merrill, 1989 (Termination Date: 1994)

Focus on Life Science: Grades 6–9
Merrill, 1989 (Termination Date: 1994)

Focus on Physical Science: Grades 6–9
Merrill, 1989 (Termination Date: 1994)

Holt Science: Grades 4–6
Holt, Rinehart & Winston/Harcourt Brace Jovanovich, 1989 (Termination Date: 1994)

Macmillan Earth Science: Grades 6–8
Macmillan, 1989 (Termination Date: 1994)

Macmillan Life Science: Grades 6–8
Macmillan, 1989 (Termination Date: 1994)

Macmillan Physical Science: Grades 6–8
Macmillan, 1989 (Termination Date: 1994)

Science in Your World: Grades 4–6
Macmillan/McGraw-Hill, 1991 (Termination Date: 1994)

Prentice Hall Earth Science: Grades 6–9
Prentice Hall, 1991 (Termination Date: 1994)

Prentice Hall Life Science: Grades 6–9
Prentice Hall, 1991 (Termination Date: 1994)

Silver Burdett & Ginn Science: Grades 4–6
Silver Burdett & Ginn, 1989, 1991 (Termination Date: 1994)

Discover Science: Grades 4–6
Scott, Foresman, 1989 (Termination Date: 1994)

Elementary/Junior High Science--Supplemental
Addison-Wesley Science: Grades K–3
Addison-Wesley, 1989 (Termination Date: 1994)

Merrill Science: Grades K–3
Merrill, 1989 (Termination Date: 1994)

Holt Science: Grades K–3
Holt, Rinehart & Winston/Harcourt Brace Jovanovich, 1989 (Termination Date: 1994)

Silver Burdett & Ginn Science: Grades K–3
Silver Burdett & Ginn, 1989 (Termination Date: 1994)

Scienceworks Computer Courseware: Grades 4–6
Silver Burdett & Ginn, 1986, 1987, 1989 (Termination Date: 1994)

Discover Science: Grades K–3
Scott, Foresman, 1989 (Termination Date: 1994)

Secondary Biology--Basic
Addison-Wesley Biology: Grades 10–12
Addison-Wesley, 1988 (Termination Date: 1994)

Biology: An Everyday Experience: Grades 9–12
Merrill, 1988 (Termination Date: 1994)

Biology: Living Systems: Grades 9–12
Merrill, 1989 (Termination Date: 1994)

Biology: The Dynamics of Life: Grades 9–12
Glencoe/Macmillan/McGraw-Hill, 1991 (Termination Date: 1994)

Globe Biology: Grades 10
Globe, 1990 (Termination Date: 1994)

Biology: Grades 9–12
Harcourt Brace Jovanovich, 1989 (Termination Date: 1994)

Heath Biology: Grades 9–12
D. C. Heath, 1989, 1991 (Termination Date: 1994)

Biological Science: A Molecular Approach, BSCS Blue Version: Grades 9–12
D. C. Heath, 1990 (Termination Date: 1994)

Modern Biology: Grades 9–12
Holt, Rinehart & Winston/Harcourt Brace Jovanovich, 1989, 1991 (Termination Date: 1994)

Biology: Journey into Life, School Ed.: Grades 10–12
Holt, Rinehart & Winston/Harcourt Brace Jovanovich, 1988 (Termination Date: 1994)

Biology Today: Grades 9–12
Holt, Rinehart & Winston/Harcourt Brace Jovanovich, 1991 (Termination Date: 1994)

Biological Science: An Ecological Approach: Grades 9–12
Kendall/Hunt, 1987 (Termination Date: 1994)

Biology: The Study of Life: Grades 9–12
Prentice Hall, 1990 (Termination Date: 1994)

Prentice Hall Biology: Grades 9–12
Prentice Hall, 1990 (Termination Date: 1994)

Biology: Grades 9–12
Prentice Hall, 1991 (Termination Date: 1994)

Secondary Biology--Supplemental
Action Biology—First Year: Grades 9–12
Clark, 1988 (Termination Date: 1994)

Action Biology–Advanced Placement: Grades 11–12
Clark, 1988 (Termination Date: 1994)

Secondary Chemistry--Basic
Addison-Wesley Chemistry: Grades 11–12
Addison-Wesley, 1990 (Termination Date: 1994)

Chemistry: A Modern Course: Grades 10–12
Merrill, 1990 (Termination Date: 1994)

Heath Chemistry: Grades 9–12
D. C. Heath, 1987 (Termination Date: 1994)

Modern Chemistry: Grades 9–12
Holt, Rinehart & Winston/Harcourt Brace Jovanovich, 1990 (Termination Date: 1994)

Chemcom: Chemistry in the Community: Grades 9–12
Kendall/Hunt, 1988 (Termination Date: 1994)

Prentice Hall Chemistry: The Study of Matter:
Grades 9–12
Prentice Hall, 1989 (Termination Date: 1994)

Chemistry: Experimental Foundations: Grades 10–12
Prentice Hall, 1987 (Termination Date: 1994)

Secondary Earth Science--Basic
Addison-Wesley Earth Science: Grades 7–10
Addison-Wesley, 1989 (Termination Date: 1994)

Focus on Earth Science: Grades 6–9
Merrill, 1989 (Termination Date: 1994)

Earth Science: Grades 7–12
Harcourt Brace Jovanovich, 1989 (Termination
Date: 1994)

Earth Science: Grades 9–12
D. C. Heath, 1989, 1991 (Termination Date: 1994)

Earth Science: The Challenge of Discovery: Grades
7–9
D. C. Heath, 1991 (Termination Date: 1994)

Investigating the Earth: Grades 9–12
Houghton Mifflin, 1987 (Termination Date: 1994)

Modern Earth Science: Grades 9–12
Holt, Rinehart & Winston/Harcourt Brace
Jovanovich, 1989 (Termination Date: 1994)

Macmillan Earth Science: Grades 6–8
Macmillan, 1989 (Termination Date: 1994)

Prentice Hall Earth Science: Grades 6–9
Prentice Hall, 1991 (Termination Date: 1994)

Silver Burdett & Ginn Earth Science: Grades 7–9
Silver Burdett & Ginn, 1987, 1990 (Termination
Date: 1994)

Scott, Foresman Earth Science: Grades 7–9
Scott, Foresman, 1990 (Termination Date: 1994)

Secondary Environmental Science--Basic
Environmental Science: Grades 11–12
Addison-Wesley, 1989 (Termination Date: 1994)

Environmental Science: Grades 10–12
Le Bel, 1990 (Termination Date: 1994)

*Global Science: Energy, Resources, Environment,
3rd Ed.:* Grades 9–12
Kendall/Hunt, 1991 (Termination Date: 1994)

Investigating Aquatic Ecosystems: Grades 9–12
Prentice Hall, 1987 (Termination Date: 1994)

Investigating Terrestrial Ecosystems: Grades 9–12
Prentice Hall, 1986 (Termination Date: 1994)

Environmental Science: The Way the World Works:
Grades 10–12
Prentice Hall, 1987 (Termination Date: 1994)

Secondary Life Science--Basic
Addison-Wesley Life Science: Grades 7–10
Addison-Wesley, 1989 (Termination Date: 1994)

Focus on Life Science: Grades 6–9
Merrill, 1989 (Termination Date: 1994)

Life Science: Grades 7–12
Harcourt Brace Jovanovich, 1989 (Termination
Date: 1994)

Life Science: The Challenge of Discovery: Grades
7–9
D. C. Heath, 1991 (Termination Date: 1994)

Macmillan Life Science: Grades 6–8
Macmillan, 1989 (Termination Date: 1994)

Prentice Hall Life Science: Grades 6–9
Prentice Hall, 1991 (Termination Date: 1994)

Scott Foresman Life Science: Grades 7–9
Scott, Foresman, 1990 (Termination Date: 1994)

Silver Burdett & Ginn Life Science: Grades 7–9
Silver Burdett & Ginn, 1987, 1990 (Termination
Date: 1994)

Secondary Physical Science--Basic
Addison-Wesley Introduction to Physical Science:
Grades 7–9
Addison-Wesley, 1988 (Termination Date: 1994)

Focus on Physical Science: Grades 6–9
Merrill, 1989 (Termination Date: 1994)

Physical Science: Grades 7–12
Harcourt Brace Jovanovich, 1989 (Termination Date: 1994)

Physical Science: The Challenge of Discovery: Grades 7–9
D. C. Heath, 1991 (Termination Date: 1994)

Macmillan Physical Science: Grades 6–8
Macmillan, 1988 (Termination Date: 1994)

Introductory Physical Science: Grades 7–9
Scott, Foresman, 1987 (Termination Date: 1994)

Prentice Hall Physical Science: Grades 10–12
Prentice Hall, 1991 (Termination Date: 1994)

Scott, Foresman Physical Science: Grades 7–9
Scott, Foresman, 1990 (Termination Date: 1994)

Silver Burdett & Ginn Physical Science: Grades 7–9
Silver Burdett & Ginn, 1988, 1990 (Termination Date: 1994)

Physics—Basic
Conceptual Physics: Grades 9–12
Addison-Wesley, 1987 (Termination Date: 1994)

Physics: Principles and Problems: Grades 11–12
Merrill, 1990 (Termination Date: 1994)

Modern Physics: Grades 9–12
Holt, Rinehart & Winston/Harcourt Brace Jovanovich, 1990 (Termination Date: 1994)

Physic-Al: An Activity Approach to Physics: Grades 10–12
Le Bel, 1989 (Termination Date: 1994)

Physiology--Secondary—Basic
Essentials of Human Anatomy and Physiology: Grades 11–12
Addison-Wesley, 1988 (Termination Date: 1994)

Indiana

General Science
Science and Technology: Grades 1–6
Coronado, 1985 (Termination Date: 1993)

HBJ Science: Grades 1–6
Harcourt Brace Jovanovich, 1985 (Termination Date: 1993)

Holt Science: Grades 1–8
Holt, Rinehart & Winston, 1986 (Termination Date: 1993)

Accent on Science: Grades 1–8
Merrill, 1985 (Termination Date: 1993)

Prentice Hall General Science: Grades 6–8
Prentice Hall, 1986 (Termination Date: 1993)

Scott, Foresman Science: Grades 1–6
Scott, Foresman, 1986 (Termination Date: 1993)

Silver Burdett Science: Grades 1–6
Silver Burdett, 1987 (Termination Date: 1993)

Middle School Life Science
Addison-Wesley Life Science: Grades 6–8
Addison-Wesley, 1986 (Termination Date: 1993)

Heath Life Science: Grades 6–8
D. C. Heath, 1987 (Termination Date: 1993)

Holt Life Science: Grades 6–8
Holt, Rinehart & Winston, 1986 (Termination Date: 1993)

Experiences in Life Sciences: Grades 6–8
Laidlaw, 1985 (Termination Date: 1993)

Life Science: Grades 6–8
Macmillan, 1986 (Termination Date: 1993)

Focus on Life Science: Grades 6–8
Merrill, 1987 (Termination Date: 1993)

Prentice Hall Life Science: Grades 6–8
Prentice Hall, 1986 (Termination Date: 1993)

Scott, Foresman Life Science: Grades 6–8
Scott, Foresman, 1987 (Termination Date: 1993)

Life Science: Grades 6–8
Silver Burdett, 1987 (Termination Date: 1993)

Earth/Space Science
Addison-Wesley Earth Science: Grades 6–12
Addison-Wesley, 1987 (Termination Date: 1993)

Earth Science: A Study of a Changing Planet:
Grades 9–12
Allyn & Bacon, 1986 (Termination Date: 1993)

Heath Earth Science: Grades 6–8
D. C. Heath, 1987 (Termination Date: 1993)

Earth Science: Grades 9–12
D. C. Heath, 1985 (Termination Date: 1993)

Holt Earth Science: Grades 6–8
Holt, Rinehart & Winston, 1986 (Termination
Date: 1993)

Modern Earth Science: Grades 9–12
Holt, Rinehart & Winston, 1983 (Termination
Date: 1993)

AGI: Investigating the Earth: Grades 9–12
Houghton Mifflin, 1987 (Termination Date: 1993)

Experiences in Earth–Space Science: Grades 6–8
Laidlaw, 1965 (Termination Date: 1993)

Earth Science: Grades 6–8
Macmillan, 1986 (Termination Date: 1993)

Focus on Earth Science: Grades 6–8
Merrill, 1987 (Termination Date: 1993)

Prentice Hall Earth Science: Grades 6–12
Prentice Hall, 1986 (Termination Date: 1993)

Scott, Foresman Earth Science: Grades 6–12
Scott, Foresman, 1986 (Termination Date: 1993)

Earth Science: Grades 6–8
Silver Burdett and Ginn, 1987 (Termination
Date: 1993)

Physical Science
Addison-Wesley Physical Science: Grades 6–12
Addison-Wesley, 1984 (Termination Date: 1993)

Heath Physical Science: Grades 6–12
D. C. Heath, 1987 (Termination Date: 1993)

Holt Physical Science: Grades 6–8
Holt, Rinehart & Winston, 1986 (Termination
Date: 1993)

Modern Physical Science: Grades 9–12
Holt, Rinehart & Winston, 1983 (Termination

Date: 1993)

Experiences in Physical Science: Grades 6–12
Laidlaw, 1985 (Termination Date: 1993)

Physical Science: Grades 6–12
Macmillan, 1986 (Termination Date: 1993)

Focus on Physical Science: Grades 9–12
Merrill, 1987 (Termination Date: 1993)

Prentice-Hall Physical Science: Grades 6–12
Prentice Hall, 1986 (Termination Date: 1993)

Introductory Physical Science: Grades 9–12
Prentice Hall, 1987 (Termination Date: 1993)

Scott, Foresman Physical Science: Grades 6–12
Scott, Foresman, 1986 (Termination Date: 1993)

Basic Science
Prentice Hall General Science: Grades 9–12
Prentice Hall, 1986 (Termination Date: 1993)

Introductory Science
Allyn & Bacon General Science: Grades 9–12
Allyn & Bacon, 1985 (Termination Date: 1993)

Holt General Science: Grades 9–12
Holt, Rinehart & Winston, 1983 (Termination
Date: 1993)

Merrill General Science: Grades 9–12
Merrill, 1986 (Termination Date: 1993)

Biology
Addison-Wesley Biology: Grades 9–12
Addison-Wesley, 1984 (Termination Date: 1993)

Biology: Grades 9–12
Addison-Wesley, 1983 (Termination Date: 1993)

Biology: Grades 9–12
Allyn & Bacon, 1987 (Termination Date: 1993)

Biology: Grades 9–12
Harcourt Brace Jovanovich, 1986 (Termination
Date: 1993)

Heath Biology: Grades 9–12
D. C. Heath, 1985 (Termination Date: 1993)

Biological Science, A Molecular Approach: Grades 9–12
D. C. Heath, 1985 (Termination Date: 1993)

Modern Biology: Grades 9–12
Holt, Rinehart & Winston, 1985 (Termination Date: 1993)

Biology: Grades 9–12
Holt, Rinehart & Winston, 1985, 1987 (Termination Date: 1993)

Experiences in Biology: Grades 9–12
Laidlaw, 1985 (Termination Date: 1993)

Biology: Living Systems: Grades 9–12
Merrill, 1986 (Termination Date: 1993)

Biology: Grades 9–12
C. V. Mosby, 1986 (Termination Date: 1993)

Prentice Hall Biology: Grades 9–12
Prentice Hall, 1987 (Termination Date: 1993)

Biology: Grades 9–12
Prentice Hall, 1986 (Termination Date: 1993)

Biological Science: Interaction of Experiments and Ideas: Grades 9–12
Prentice Hall, 1983 (Termination Date: 1993)

Scott, Foresman Biology: Grades 9–12
Scott, Foresman, 1985 (Termination Date: 1993)

Macmillan Biology: Grades 9–12
Scribner, 1985 (Termination Date: 1993)

Biology: Life on Earth: Grades 9–12
Scribner, 1985 (Termination Date: 1993)

Silver Burdett Biology: Grades 9–12
Silver Burdett and Ginn, 1986 (Termination Date: 1993)

Basic Biological Science
Heath Life Science: Grades 9–12
D. C. Heath, 1987 (Termination Date: 1993)

Living Things: Grades 9–12
Holt, Rinehart & Winston, 1985 (Termination Date: 1993)

Biology: An Everyday Experience: Grades 9–12
Merrill, 1985 (Termination Date: 1993)

Biology and Human Progress: Grades 9–12
Prentice Hall, 1986 (Termination Date: 1993)

Scott, Foresman Life Science: Grades 9–12
Scott, Foresman, 1987 (Termination Date: 1993)

Human Physiology
Essentials of Human Anatomy and Physiology: Grades 9–12
Addison-Wesley, 1984 (Termination Date: 1993)

Modern Human Physiology: Grades 9–12
Holt, Rinehart & Winston, 1987 (Termination Date: 1993)

Textbook of Anatomy and Physiology: Grades 9–12
C. V. Mosby, 1983 (Termination Date: 1993)

Structure and Function of the Body: Grades 9–12
C. V. Mosby, 1984 (Termination Date: 1993)

Anatomy and Physiology: The Basic Principles: Grades 9–12
Prentice Hall, 1983 (Termination Date: 1993)

Zoology
Biology of Animals: Grades 9–12
C. V. Mosby, 1986 (Termination Date: 1993)

Integrated Principles of Zoology: Grades 9–12
C. V. Mosby, 1984 (Termination Date: 1993)

Chemistry
Addison-Wesley Chemistry: Grades 9–12
Addison-Wesley, 1987 (Termination Date: 1993)

Chemical Principles, Properties and Reactions: Grades 9–12
Addison-Wesley, 1984 (Termination Date: 1993)

Chemistry: The Study of Matter: Grades 9–12
Allyn & Bacon, 1987 (Termination Date: 1993)

General Chemistry: Grades 9–12
W. H. Freeman, 1984 (Termination Date: 1993)

Heath Chemistry: Grades 9–12
D. C. Heath, 1987 (Termination Date: 1993)

Chemistry: Experiments and Principles: Grades 9–12
D. C. Heath, 1982 (Termination Date: 1993)

College Chemistry with Qualitative Analysis:
Grades 9–12
D. C. Heath, 1984 (Termination Date: 1993)

Chemistry: Grades 9–12
D. C. Heath, 1986 (Termination Date: 1993)

General Chemistry: Grades 9–12
D. C. Heath, 1984 (Termination Date: 1993)

Modern Chemistry: Grades 9–12
Holt, Rinehart & Winston, 1986 (Termination
Date: 1993)

Chemical Principles, Sixth Edition: Grades 9–12
Holt, Rinehart & Winston, 1985 (Termination
Date: 1993)

Chemistry: A Modern Course: Grades 9–12
Merrill, 1987 (Termination Date: 1993)

Chemistry: Experimental Foundations: Grades 9–12
Prentice Hall, 1987 (Termination Date: 1993)

Chemistry: The Central Science: Grades 9–12
Prentice Hall, 1985 (Termination Date: 1993)

*Introduction to Chemical Principles, Second
Edition:* Grades 9–12
Scribner, 1986 (Termination Date: 1993)

General Chemistry, Fourth Edition: Grades 9–12
Scribner, 1985 (Termination Date: 1993)

Physics
Conceptual Physics: Grades 9–12
Addison-Wesley, 1987 (Termination Date: 1993)

Physics: Its Methods and Meanings: Grades 9–12
Allyn & Bacon, 1986 (Termination Date: 1993)

PSSC Physics: Grades 9–12
D. C. Heath, 1986 (Termination Date: 1993)

Modern Physics: Grades 9–12
Holt, Rinehart & Winston, 1984 (Termination
Date: 1993)

Physics: Principles and Problems: Grades 9–12
Merrill, 1986 (Termination Date: 1993)

Physics: Principles with Applications: Grades 9–12
Prentice Hall, 1985 (Termination Date: 1993)

Kentucky

Elementary Science
Addison-Wesley Science: Grades 1–6
Addison-Wesley, 1989 (Termination Date: 1995)

Concepts and Challenges: Physical Science: Grade 6
Globe, 1986 (Termination Date: 1995)

HBJ Science: Grades K–6
Harcourt Brace Jovanovich, 1989 (Termination
Date: 1995)

Holt Science: Grades 1–6
Holt, Rinehart & Winston, 1989 (Termination
Date: 1995)

Journeys in Science: Grades K–6
Macmillan, 1988 (Termination Date: 1995)

Merrill Science: Grades K–6
Merrill, 1989 (Termination Date: 1995)

Discover Science: Grades 1–6
Scott, Foresman, 1989 (Termination Date: 1995)

Silver Burdett and Ginn Science: Grades 1–6
Silver Burdett and Ginn, 1989 (Termination
Date: 1995)

Introduction to Biological Science
Addison-Wesley Life Science: Grade 7
Addison-Wesley, 1989 (Termination Date: 1995)

Heath Life Science: Grade 7
D. C. Heath, 1987 (Termination Date: 1995)

Concepts and Challenges: Life Science: Grade 7
Globe, 1986 (Termination Date: 1995)

HBJ Life Science: Grade 7
Harcourt Brace Jovanovich, 1989 (Termination
Date: 1995)

Holt Life Science: Grade 7
Holt, Rinehart & Winston, 1986 (Termination
Date: 1995)

Macmillan Life Science: Grade 7
Macmillan, 1989 (Termination Date: 1995)

Focus on Life Science: Grade 7
Merrill, 1989 (Termination Date: 1995)

Prentice Hall Life Science: Grade 7
Prentice Hall, 1988 (Termination Date: 1995)

Scott, Foresman Life Science: Grade 7
Scott, Foresman, 1987 (Termination Date: 1995)

Silver Burdett and Ginn Life Science: Grade 7
Silver Burdett and Ginn, 1987 (Termination
Date: 1995)

Understanding Life Science: Grade 7
Amsco, 1987 (Termination Date: 1995)

Biology
Heath Biology: Grades 9–12
D. C. Heath, 1989 (Termination Date: 1995)

Biology for Living: Grades 9–12
Globe, 1987 (Termination Date: 1995)

Biology: Grades 9–12
Harcourt Brace Jovanovich, 1989 (Termination
Date: 1995)

Modern Biology: Grades 9–12
Holt, Rinehart & Winston, 1989 (Termination
Date: 1995)

Biology: Living Systems: Grades 9–12
Merrill, 1989 (Termination Date: 1995)

Biology: An Everyday Experience: Grades 9–12
Merrill, 1988 (Termination Date: 1995)

Biology: The Living World: Grades 9–12
Prentice Hall, 1989 (Termination Date: 1995)

Prentice Hall Biology: Grades 9–12
Prentice Hall, 1987 (Termination Date: 1995)

Biology: Study of Life: Grades 9–12
Prentice Hall, 1987 (Termination Date: 1995)

Scott, Foresman Biology: Grades 9–12
Scott, Foresman, 1988 (Termination Date: 1995)

Biological Science: An Ecological Approach:
Grades 9–12
Kendall/Hunt, 1987 (Termination Date: 1995)

Biology II
Biology: Journey into Life: Grades 11–12
Holt, Rinehart & Winston, 1988 (Termination
Date: 1995)

Understanding Biology: Grades 11–12
C. V. Mosby, 1988 (Termination Date: 1995)

AP General Biology
Biology: Grades 11–12
Prentice Hall, 1986 (Termination Date: 1995)

Biology: Grades 11–12
Random House, 1988 (Termination Date: 1995)

Biology: Grades 11–12
William C. Brown, 1987 (Termination Date:
1995)

Biology: Grades 11–12
C. V. Mosby, 1986 (Termination Date: 1995)

Special Topics in Biological Science
Environmental Science: The Way the World Works:
Grades 10–12
Prentice Hall, 1987 (Termination Date: 1995)

Environmental Science: Grades 11–12
William C. Brown, 1986 (Termination Date:
1995)

Integrated Science
General Science: Grade 9
Harcourt Brace Jovanovich, 1989 (Termination
Date: 1995)

Holt Science: Grades 7–8
Holt, Rinehart & Winston, 1986 (Termination
Date: 1995)

Holt General Science: Grade 9
Holt, Rinehart & Winston, 1988 (Termination
Date: 1995)

Principles of Science: Grades 7–8
Merrill, 1986 (Termination Date: 1995)

Merrill General Science: Grade 9
Merrill, 1986 (Termination Date: 1995)

Voyage of Adventure: Grade 6
Prentice Hall, 1989 (Termination Date: 1995)

Voyage of Discovery: Grade 7
Prentice Hall, 1989 (Termination Date: 1995)

Voyage of Exploration: Grade 8
Prentice Hall, 1989 (Termination Date: 1995)

Allyn & Bacon General Science: Grade 9
Prentice Hall, 1989 (Termination Date: 1995)

Silver Burdett and Ginn General Science: Grades 7–8
Silver Burdett and Ginn, 1989 (Termination Date: 1995)

Introduction to Earth/Space Science

Addison-Wesley Earth Science: Grade 8
Addison-Wesley, 1989 (Termination Date: 1995)

Heath Earth Science: Grade 8
D. C. Heath, 1987 (Termination Date: 1995)

Concepts and Challenges: Earth Science: Grade 8
Globe, 1986 (Termination Date: 1995)

HBJ Earth Science: Grade 8
Harcourt Brace Jovanovich, 1989 (Termination Date: 1995)

Holt Earth Science: Grade 8
Holt, Rinehart & Winston, 1986 (Termination Date: 1995)

Macmillan Earth Science: Grade 8
Macmillan, 1989 (Termination Date: 1995)

Focus on Earth Science: Grade 8
Merrill, 1989 (Termination Date: 1995)

Prentice Hall Earth Science: Grade 8
Prentice Hall, 1988 (Termination Date: 1995)

Scott, Foresman Earth Science: Grade 8
Scott, Foresman, 1986 (Termination Date: 1995)

Silver Burdett and Ginn Earth Science: Grade 8
Silver Burdett and Ginn, 1987 (Termination Date: 1995)

Earth Science

Heath Earth Science: Grades 10–12
D. C. Heath, 1989 (Termination Date: 1995)

Modern Earth Science: Grades 10–12
Holt, Rinehart & Winston, 1989 (Termination Date: 1995)

Physical Science

Introduction to Physical Science: Grades 9–12
Addison-Wesley, 1988 (Termination Date: 1995)

Physical Science: Grades 9–12
Addison-Wesley, 1988 (Termination Date: 1995)

Heath Physical Science: Grades 9–12
D. C. Heath, 1987 (Termination Date: 1995)

Physical Science: Grades 9–12
Harcourt Brace Jovanovich, 1989 (Termination Date: 1995)

Holt Physical Science: Grades 9–12
Holt, Rinehart & Winston, 1986 (Termination Date: 1995)

Macmillan Physical Science: Grades 10–12
Macmillan, 1988 (Termination Date: 1995)

Focus on Physical Science: Grades 9–12
Merrill, 1989 (Termination Date: 1995)

Prentice Hall Physical Science: Grades 9–12
Prentice Hall, 1988 (Termination Date: 1995)

Introductory Physical Science: Grades 9–12
Prentice Hall, 1987 (Termination Date: 1995)

Scott, Foresman Physical Science: Grades 9–12
Scott, Foresman, 1986 (Termination Date: 1995)

Silver Burdett & Ginn Physical Science: Grades 9–12
Silver Burdett and Ginn, 1988 (Termination Date: 1995)

Chemistry

Addison-Wesley Chemistry: Grades 10–12
Addison-Wesley, 1987 (Termination Date: 1995)

Heath Chemistry: Grades 10–12
D. C. Heath, 1987 (Termination Date: 1995)

Modern Chemistry: Grades 10–12
Holt, Rinehart & Winston, 1986 (Termination Date: 1995)

Chemistry: A Modern Course: Grades 10–12
Merrill, 1987 (Termination Date: 1995)

Chemistry: The Study of Matter: Grades 10–12
Prentice Hall, 1989 (Termination Date: 1995)

Chemistry: Experimental Foundations: Grades 10–12
Prentice Hall, 1987 (Termination Date: 1995)

Chemcom: Chemistry in the Community: Grades 10–12
Kendall/Hunt, 1988 (Termination Date: 1995)

Chemistry II
Heath Chemistry: Grades 11–12
D. C. Heath, 1986 (Termination Date: 1995)

AP General Chemistry
Chemistry: The Central Science: Grades 11–12
Prentice Hall, 1988 (Termination Date: 1995)

Chemistry: Grades 11–12
Random House, 1988 (Termination Date: 1995)

Physics
Conceptual Physics: Grades 10–12
Addison-Wesley, 1987 (Termination Date: 1995)

PSSC Physics: Grades 10–12
D. C. Heath, 1986 (Termination Date: 1995)

Modern Physics: Grades 10–12
Holt, Rinehart & Winston, 1984 (Termination Date: 1995)

Physics: Principles and Problems: Grades 10–12
Merrill, 1986 (Termination Date: 1995)

Anatomy and Physiology
Modern Human Physiology: Grades 10–12
Holt, Rinehart & Winston, 1987 (Termination Date: 1995)

Textbook of Anatomy and Physiology: Grades 10–12
C. V. Mosby, 1987 (Termination Date: 1995)

Functional Science I
Life Science: Grade 9
Janus, 1987 (Termination Date: 1995)

Earth Science: Grade 9
Janus, 1987 (Termination Date: 1995)

Physical Science: Grade 9
Janus, 1987 (Termination Date: 1995)

Louisiana

Note: Louisiana did not provide a list of science textbooks.

Mississippi

Science—Average to Accelerated
Addison-Wesley Science: Grades 1–6
Addison-Wesley, 1989 (Termination Date: 1995)

Holt Science: Grades 1–6
Holt, Rinehart & Winston, 1989 (Termination Date: 1995)

Journeys in Science: Grades 1–6
Macmillan, 1988 (Termination Date: 1995)

Merrill Science: Grades 1–6
Macmillan/McGraw-Hill, 1989 (Termination Date: 1995)

Discover Science: Grades 1–6
Scott, Foresman, 1989 (Termination Date: 1995)

Silver Burdett & Ginn Science: Grades 1–6
Silver Burdett & Ginn, 1989 (Termination Date: 1995)

Physical Science—Average to Accelerated
Earth Science: Grade 7
Harcourt Brace Jovanovich, 1989 (Termination Date: 1995)

Macmillan Earth Science: Grade 7
Macmillan, 1989 (Termination Date: 1995)

Focus on Earth Science: Grade 7
Glencoe/Merrill, 1989 (Termination Date: 1995)

Prentice Hall Earth Science: Grade 7
Prentice Hall, 1988 (Termination Date: 1995)

Scott, Foresman Earth Science: Grade 7
Scott, Foresman, 1990 (Termination Date: 1995)

Silver Burdett & Ginn Earth Science: Grade 7
Silver Burdett & Ginn, 1987 (Termination Date: 1995)

Addison-Wesley Physical Science: Grade 8
Addison-Wesley, 1988 (Termination Date: 1995)

Physical Science: Grade 8
Harcourt Brace Jovanovich, 1989 (Termination Date: 1995)

Macmillan Physical Science: Grade 8
Macmillan, 1988 (Termination Date: 1995)

Focus on Physical Science: Grade 8
Glencoe/Merrill, 1989 (Termination Date: 1995)

Prentice Hall Physical Science: Grade 8
Prentice Hall, 1988 (Termination Date: 1995)

Silver Burdett & Ginn Physical Science: Grade 8
Silver Burdett & Ginn, 1988 (Termination Date: 1995)

Physical Science—Basal Program for the Slow Learner

Concepts and Challenges in Earth Science: Grade 7
Globe, 1986 (Termination Date: 1995)

Concepts and Challenges in Physical Science:
Grade 8
Globe, 1986 (Termination Date: 1995)

Addison-Wesley Introduction to Physical Science:
Grade 8
Addison-Wesley, 1988 (Termination Date: 1995)

Chemistry

Addison-Wesley Chemistry: Grades 9–12
Addison-Wesley, 1987 (Termination Date: 1995)

Heath Chemistry: Grades 9–12
D. C. Heath, 1987 (Termination Date: 1995)

Modern Chemistry: Grades 9–12
Holt, Rinehart & Winston, 1986 (Termination Date: 1995)

Chemistry: A Modern Course: Grades 9–12
Glencoe/Merrill, 1987 (Termination Date: 1995)

Chemistry: The Study of Matter: Grades 9–12
Prentice Hall, 1989 (Termination Date: 1995)

Chemistry: Grades 9–12
D. C. Heath, 1986 (Termination Date: 1995)

Advanced Placement Chemistry
Chemical Principles: Grades 9–12
Holt, Rinehart & Winston, 1985 (Termination Date: 1995)

Chemistry: The Central Science: Grades 9–12
Prentice Hall, 1988 (Termination Date: 1995)

Consumer Science
General Science: Grades 9–12
Harcourt Brace Jovanovich, 1989 (Termination Date: 1995)

Holt General Science: Grades 9–12
Holt, Rinehart & Winston, 1988 (Termination Date: 1995)

Merrill General Science: Grades 9–12
Glencoe/Merrill, 1986 (Termination Date: 1995)

Allyn and Bacon General Science: Grades 9–12
Prentice Hall, 1989 (Termination Date: 1995)

Science in the Marketplace: Grades 9–12
Tiger, 1987 (Termination Date: 1995)

Geology
Modern Earth Science: Grades 9–12
Holt, Rinehart & Winston, 1989 (Termination Date: 1995)

Physical Geology: Grades 9–12
William C. Brown, 1991 (Termination Date: 1995)

Physics
Conceptual Physics: Grades 9–12
Addison-Wesley, 1987 (Termination Date: 1995)

Modern Physics: Grades 9–12
Holt, Rinehart & Winston, 1984 (Termination Date: 1995)

Physics: Principles and Problems: Grades 9–12
Glencoe/Merrill, 1986 (Termination Date: 1995)

Physics: Methods and Meanings: Grades 9–12
Prentice Hall, 1986 (Termination Date: 1995)

Applied Life Science

Addison-Wesley Life Science: Grades 9–12
Addison-Wesley, 1989 (Termination Date: 1995)

Macmillan Life Science: Grades 9–12
Macmillan, 1989 (Termination Date: 1995)

Focus on Life Science: Grades 9–12
Glencoe/Merrill, 1989 (Termination Date: 1995)

Prentice Hall Life Science: Grades 9–12
Prentice Hall, 1988 (Termination Date: 1995)

Silver Burdett & Ginn Life Science: Grades 9–12
Silver Burdett & Ginn, 1987 (Termination Date: 1995)

Biology

Heath Biology: Grades 9–12
D. C. Heath, 1989 (Termination Date: 1995)

Biology: Grades 9–12
Harcourt Brace Jovanovich, 1989 (Termination Date: 1995)

Modern Biology: Grades 9–12
Holt, Rinehart & Winston, 1989 (Termination Date: 1995)

Biology: Living Systems: Grades 9–12
Glencoe/Merrill, 1989 (Termination Date: 1995)

Biology: The Living World: Grades 9–12
Prentice Hall, 1989 (Termination Date: 1995)

Biology: Grades 9–12
Addison-Wesley/Bencum, 1987 (Termination Date: 1995)

Understanding Biology: Grades 9–12
C. V. Mosby, 1988 (Termination Date: 1995)

Biology: Evolution, Diversity and the Environment: Grades 9–12
William C. Brown, 1987 (Termination Date: 1995)

Inquiry into Life: Grades 9–12
William C. Brown, 1988 (Termination Date: 1995)

The Botanical World: Grades 9–12
C. V. Mosby, 1984 (Termination Date: 1995)

Environmental Science: Grades 9–12
Addison-Wesley, 1989 (Termination Date: 1995)

Introduction to Environmental Studies: Grades 9–12
Holt, Rinehart & Winston, 1985 (Termination Date: 1995)

Essentials of Human Anatomy and Physiology: Grades 9–12
Addison-Wesley, 1988 (Termination Date: 1995)

Modern Human Physiology: Grades 9–12
Holt, Rinehart & Winston, 1987 (Termination Date: 1995)

Anatomy and Physiology: Grades 9–12
Prentice Hall, 1983 (Termination Date: 1995)

Structure and Function of the Body: Grades 9–12
C. V. Mosby, 1988 (Termination Date: 1995)

Essentials of Human Anatomy and Physiology: Grades 9–12
William C. Brown, 1989 (Termination Date: 1995)

Marine Biology: Grades 9–12
Addison-Wesley, 1986 (Termination Date: 1995)

Marine Biology: Grades 9–12
Prentice Hall, 1988 (Termination Date: 1995)

Diversity of Marine Plants: Grades 9–12
University Press of Mississippi, 1984 (Termination Date: 1995)

Marine and Estuarine Ecology: Grades 9–12
University Press of Mississippi, 1984 (Termination Date: 1995)

Marine Habitats: Grades 9–12
University Press of Mississippi, 1984 (Termination Date: 1995)

Introduction to the Biology of Marine Life: Grades 9–12
William C. Brown, 1988 (Termination Date: 1995)

AP Biology
Biology: A Journey into Life: Grades 9–12
Holt, Rinehart & Winston, 1988 (Termination Date: 1995)

Biology: Grades 9–12
Prentice Hall, 1986 (Termination Date: 1995)

Biology: Grades 9–12
C. V. Mosby, 1989 (Termination Date: 1995)

Biology: Grades 9–12
William C. Brown, 1987 (Termination Date: 1995)

Nevada

General Science
Explorations in Science: Grades 1–2
Addison-Wesley, 1992 (Termination Date: 1996)

FOSS: Earth Materials: Grades 3–4
Britannica, 1992 (Termination Date: 1996)

FOSS: Human Body: Grades 3–4
Britannica, 1992 (Termination Date: 1996)

FOSS: Ideas and Inventions: Grades 3–4
Britannica, 1991 (Termination Date: 1996)

FOSS: Magnetism and Electricity: Grades 3–4
Britannica, 1991 (Termination Date: 1996)

FOSS: Measurement: Grades 3–4
Britannica, 1990 (Termination Date: 1996)

FOSS: Physics of Sound: Grades 3–4
Britannica, 1990 (Termination Date: 1996)

FOSS: Structures of Life: Grades 3–4
Britannica, 1991 (Termination Date: 1996)

FOSS: Water: Grades 3–4
Britannica, 1992 (Termination Date: 1996)

FOSS: Environment: Grades 5–6
Britannica, 1991 (Termination Date: 1996)

FOSS: Food and Nutrition: Grades 5–6
Britannica, 1992 (Termination Date: 1996)

FOSS: Landforms: Grades 5–6
Britannica, 1990 (Termination Date: 1996)

FOSS: Levers and Pulleys: Grades 5–6
Britannica, 1990 (Termination Date: 1996)

FOSS: Mixtures and Solutions: Grades 5–6
Britannica, 1991 (Termination Date: 1996)

FOSS: Models and Designs: Grades 5–6
Britannica, 1991 (Termination Date: 1996)

FOSS: Solar Energy: Grades 5–6
Britannica, 1992 (Termination Date: 1996)

FOSS: Variables: Grades 5–6
Britannica, 1990 (Termination Date: 1996)

Discover the Wonder: Grades K–2
Scott, Foresman, 1992 (Termination Date: 1996)

Merrill Science: Grades K–6
Merrill, 1989 (Termination Date: 1993)

Silver Burdett & Ginn Science: Grades K–6
Silver Burdett & Ginn, 1989 (Termination Date: 1993)

Merrill General Science: Grades 7–12
Merrill, 1986 (Termination Date: 1992)

General Science, Book 2: Grade 9
Silver Burdett & Ginn, 1989 (Termination Date: n.d.)

General Science: Grade 9
Harcourt Brace Jovanovich, 1989 (Termination Date: n.d.)

General Science: Grades 10–12
Prentice Hall, 1989 (Termination Date: n.d.)

The Way the World Works: Grades
Prentice Hall, 1987 (Termination Date: n.d.)

Biology
Biology: Grades 7–9
Harcourt Brace Jovanovich, 1989 (Termination Date: n.d.)

Biology and Human Progress: Grades 9–12
Prentice Hall, 1986 (Termination Date: n.d.)

Biology: The Study of Life: Grades 9–12
Prentice Hall, 1987 (Termination Date: n.d.)

Biology: Grades 9–12
Saunders, 1987 (Termination Date: n.d.)

Modern Biology: Grades 9–12
Holt, Rinehart & Winston, 1991 (Termination Date: n.d.)

Biology: Unity and Diversity of Life: Grades 10–12
Wadsworth, 1978, 1981 (Termination Date: n.d.)

Botany
Botany: An Introduction to Plant Biology: Grades 10–12
Saunders, 1991 (Termination Date: 1996)

Chemistry
Chemistry: The Study of Matter: Grades 10–12
Prentice Hall, 1989 (Termination Date: 1994)

Modern Chemistry: Grades 10–12
Holt, Rinehart & Winston, 1990 (Termination Date: 1993)

Anatomy and Physiology
Principles of Anatomy and Physiology: Grades 11–12
Harper & Row, 1987 (Termination Date: 1994)

Physics
Conceptual Physics: Grades 9–12
Addison-Wesley, 1987 (Termination Date: 1993)

Modern Physics: Grades 9–12
Holt, Rinehart & Winston, 1990 (Termination Date: 1993)

Addison-Wesley Physics: Grades 9–12
Addison-Wesley, 1988 (Termination Date: n.d.)

Physics: Its Methods and Meanings: Grades 9–12
Allyn & Bacon, 1986 (Termination Date: n.d.)

Physics for Scientists and Engineers (with Modern Physics): Grades 9–12
Holt, Rinehart & Winston, 1986 (Termination Date: n.d.)

Physics: Grades 9–12
Little, Brown, 1987 (Termination Date: n.d.)

Physics: Principles and Problems: Grades 9–12
Merrill, 1986 (Termination Date: n.d.)

Fundamentals of Physics: A Senior Course: Grades 9–12
D. C. Heath, 1986 (Termination Date: n.d.)

College Physics: Grades 9–12
McGraw-Hill, 1987 (Termination Date: n.d.)

Earth Science
Earth Science: Grade 8
Harcourt Brace Jovanovich, 1989 (Termination Date: n.d.)

Earth Science: Grade 8
Prentice Hall, 1988 (Termination Date: n.d.)

Addison-Wesley Earth Science: Grades 8–12
Addison-Wesley, 1987 (Termination Date: n.d.)

Earth Science: Grades 9–12
D. C. Heath, 1985 (Termination Date: n.d.)

Focus on Earth Science: Grades 9–12
Merrill, 1987 (Termination Date: n.d.)

Prentice Hall Earth Science: Grades 9–12
Prentice Hall, 1988 (Termination Date: n.d.)

Modern Earth Science: Grades 9–12
Holt, Rinehart & Winston, 1989 (Termination Date: n.d.)

Earth Science: Grades 7–8
Fearon/Janus/Quercus, 1987 (Termination Date: n.d.)

Life Science
Life Science: Grade 7
Harcourt Brace Jovanovich, 1989 (Termination Date: n.d.)

Life Science: Grade 7
Prentice Hall, 1988 (Termination Date: n.d.)

Prentice Hall Life Science: Grades 9–12
Prentice Hall, 1988 (Termination Date: n.d.)

Life Science: Grades 9–12
Silver Burdett & Ginn, 1987 (Termination Date: n.d.)

Life Science: Grades 7–8
Fearon/Janus/Quercus, 1987 (Termination Date: n.d.)

Physical Science

Physical Science: Grades
Prentice Hall, 1988 (Termination Date: n.d.)

Prentice Hall Physical Science: Grades 9–12
Prentice Hall, 1988 (Termination Date: n.d.)

Physical Science: Grades 7–8
Fearon/Janus/Quercus, 1987 (Termination Date:)

Environmental Science

Environmental Science: A Framework for Decision Making: Grades 9–12
Addison-Wesley, 1989 (Termination Date: n.d.)

Environmental Science: The Study of Interrelationships: Grades
William C. Brown, 1989 (Termination Date: n.d.)

Environmental Science: The Way the World Works: Grades
Prentice Hall, 1989 (Termination Date: n.d.)

Investigating the Earth: Grades 9–12
Houghton Mifflin, 1987 (Termination Date: n.d.)

What's Ecology?: Grades 9–12
Addison-Wesley, 1986 (Termination Date: n.d.)

Microbiology

Microbiology: Principles and Applications: Grades 10–12
Prentice Hall, 1990 (Termination Date: n.d.)

Consumerism—Science

Science in the Market Place: Grades 9-12
Tiger, 1987 (Termination Date: n.d.)

New Mexico

Advanced Physical Science

Modern Physical Science: Grades 9–12
Holt, Rinehart & Winston, 1983 (Termination Date: 1993)

Biology

Macmillan Biology: Grades 9–12
Glencoe, 1985 (Termination Date: 1993)

Experiences in Biology: Grades 10–12
Glencoe, 1985 (Termination Date: 1993)

Biology: An Everyday Experience: Grades 9–12
Glencoe, 1985 (Termination Date: 1993)

Biology: Living Systems: Grades 9–12
Glencoe, 1986 (Termination Date: 1993)

Biology: The Key Ideas: Grades 9–12
Globe, 1983 (Termination Date: 1993)

Biological Science: A Molecular Approach: Grades 10–12
D. C. Heath, 1985 (Termination Date: 1993)

Heath Biology: Grades 10–12
D. C. Heath, 1985 (Termination Date: 1993)

Biology: Grades 9–12
Holt, Rinehart & Winston, 1986 (Termination Date: 1993)

Modern Biology: Grades 9–12
Holt, Rinehart & Winston, 1986 (Termination Date: 1993)

Living Things: Grades 9–12
Holt, Rinehart & Winston, 1985 (Termination Date: 1993)

Biology: The Study of Life: Grades 9–12
Prentice Hall, 1990 (Termination Date: 1993)

Prentice Hall Biology: Grades 10–12
Prentice Hall, 1990 (Termination Date: 1993)

Anatomy and Physiology: The Basic Principles: Grades 10–12
Prentice Hall, 1983 (Termination Date: 1993)

Biology and Human Progress: Grades 9–12
Prentice Hall, 1986 (Termination Date: 1993)

Silver Burdett Biology: Grades 10–12
Prentice Hall, 1986 (Termination Date: 1993)

Biology: Grades 10–12
Prentice Hall, 1986 (Termination Date: 1993)

Scott, Foresman Biology: Grades 9–12
Scott, Foresman, 1985 (Termination Date: 1993)

Addison-Wesley Biology: Grades 9–12
Addison-Wesley, 1984 (Termination Date: 1993)

Biology: Grades 9–12
Addison-Wesley, 1984 (Termination Date: 1993)

Essentials of Biology: Grades 11–12
William C. Brown, 1986 (Termination Date: 1993)

Essentials of Human Anatomy and Physiology:
Grades 11–12
William C. Brown, 1989 (Termination Date: 1993)

Inquiry into Life: Grades 11–12
William C. Brown, 1988 (Termination Date: 1993)

Biology: Evolution, Diversity and Environment:
Grades 11–12
William C. Brown, 1990 (Termination Date: 1993)

Chemistry
Chemistry: A Modern Course: Grades 10–12
Glencoe, 1987 (Termination Date: 1993)

Chemistry II: Grades 10–12
D. C. Heath, 1986 (Termination Date: 1993)

Heath Chemistry I: Grades 10–12
D. C. Heath, 1987 (Termination Date: 1993)

Modern Chemistry: Grades 9–12
Holt, Rinehart & Winston, 1986 (Termination Date: 1993)

Chemical Principles: Grades 9–12
Holt, Rinehart & Winston, 1985 (Termination Date: 1993)

Chemistry: Experimental Foundations: Grades 10–12
Prentice Hall, 1987 (Termination Date: 1993)

Chemistry: The Study of Matter: Grades 9–12
Prentice Hall, 1987 (Termination Date: 1993)

Chemistry: The Central Science: Grades 10–12
Prentice Hall, 1985 (Termination Date: 1993)

Addison-Wesley Chemistry: Grades 10–12
Addison-Wesley, 1987 (Termination Date: 1993)

Elementary Science
MCP Science Series: Grades 1–6
Modern Curriculum, 1987 (Termination Date: 1993)

SB Ciencias: Grades K–6
Silver Burdett, 1985 (Termination Date: 1993)

Silver Burdett Science: Grades K–6
Silver Burdett, 1987 (Termination Date: 1993)

Ciencia de Holt: Grade 6
Holt, Rinehart & Winston, 1986 (Termination Date: 1993)

HBJ Science Readiness: Grades K–2
Holt, Rinehart & Winston, 1985 (Termination Date: 1993)

HBJ Science: Grades 2–6
Holt, Rinehart & Winston, 1985 (Termination Date: 1998)

HBJ Ciencias: Grades 1–6
Holt, Rinehart & Winston, 1985 (Termination Date: 1993)

Holt Elementary Science: Grades K–6
Holt, Rinehart & Winston, 1986 (Termination Date: 1993)

Science and Technology: Grades 1–6
Holt, Rinehart & Winston, 1985 (Termination Date: 1993)

Accent on Science: Grades K–6
Macmillan, 1985 (Termination Date: 1993)

Science: Grades 1–6
Scott, Foresman, 1986 (Termination Date: 1993)

Environment
Introduction to Environment Studies: Grades 9–12
Holt, Rinehart & Winston, 1985 (Termination Date: 1993)

Environmental Science: Grades 9–12
Holt, Rinehart & Winston, 1984 (Termination
Date: 1993)

What's Ecology?: Grades 9–12
Addison-Wesley, 1986 (Termination Date: 1993)

*Science, Technology, and Society: Investigating the
Human:* Grades 9–12
Kendall/Hunt, 1984 (Termination Date: 1993)

Global Science: Energy, Resource, Environment:
Grades 9–12
Kendall/Hunt, 1984 (Termination Date: 1993)

Environmental Science: Grades 11–12
William C. Brown, 1989 (Termination Date: 1993)

Earth Science
Experiences in Earth–Space Science: Grades 7–9
Glencoe, 1985 (Termination Date: 1993)

Focus on Earth Science: Grades 7–9
Glencoe, 1987 (Termination Date: 1993)

Silver Burdett Earth Science: Grades 7–9
Silver Burdett, 1987 (Termination Date: 1993)

Concepts and Challenges in Earth Science: Grades
7–9
Globe, 1986 (Termination Date: 1993)

Unlocking Science Skills: Earth Science: Grades 7–9
Globe, 1987 (Termination Date: 1993)

Globe Earth Science: Grades 7–9
Globe, 1986 (Termination Date: 1993)

Earth Science Workshop: Grades 7–12
Globe, 1983 (Termination Date: 1993)

Work-A-Text in Earth Science: Grades 9–12
Globe, 1987 (Termination Date: 1993)

Earth Science: Grades 7–9
D. C. Heath, 1985 (Termination Date: 1993)

Heath Earth Science: Grades 7–9
D. C. Heath, 1987 (Termination Date: 1993)

Holt Earth Science: Grades 7–8
Holt, Rinehart & Winston, 1986 (Termination
Date: 1993)

Modern Earth Science: Grades 9–12
Holt, Rinehart & Winston, 1983 (Termination
Date: 1993)

Macmillan Earth Science: Grades 7–9
Macmillan, 1989 (Termination Date: 1993)

Prentice Hall Earth Science: Grades 6–9
Prentice Hall, 1987 (Termination Date: 1993)

Investigating the Earth: Grades 10–12
Houghton Mifflin, 1987 (Termination Date: 1993)

Scott, Foresman Earth Science: Grades 7–9
Scott, Foresman, 1986 (Termination Date: 1993)

Addison-Wesley Earth Science: Grades 7–10
Addison-Wesley, 1987 (Termination Date: 1993)

General Science
Principles of Science, Books 1 & 2: Grades 7–9
Glencoe, 1986 (Termination Date: 1993)

Merrill General Science: Grades 10–12
Glencoe, 1986 (Termination Date: 1993)

Concepts and Challenges in Science, Books 1–3:
Grades 7–9
Globe, 1984 (Termination Date: 1993)

Holt Elementary Science: Grades 7–8
Holt, Rinehart & Winston, 1986 (Termination
Date: 1993)

Holt General Science: Grade 9
Holt, Rinehart & Winston, 1986 (Termination
Date: 1993)

Hammond-Barnhart Science Dictionary: Grades 7–
12
Holt, Rinehart & Winston, 1986 (Termination
Date: 1993)

Allyn & Bacon General Science: Grades 8–12
Prentice Hall, 1989 (Termination Date: 1993)

Prentice Hall General Science: Grades 6–9
Prentice Hall, 1986 (Termination Date: 1993)

Science, Technology, and Society: Grades 9–12
Kendall/Hunt, 1984 (Termination Date: 1993)

Encyclopedia of Science: Grades 4–12
World Book Childcraft, 1986 (Termination Date: 1993)

Geology
Physical Geology: Grades 11–12
William C. Brown, 1988 (Termination Date: 1993)

Life Science
Experiences in Life Science: Grades 7–9
Glencoe, 1985 (Termination Date: 1993)

Focus on Life Science: Grades 7–9
Glencoe, 1987 (Termination Date: 1993)

Silver Burdett & Ginn Life Science: Grades 7–9
Silver Burdett & Ginn, 1987 (Termination Date: 1993)

Concepts and Challenges in Life Science: Grades 7–9
Globe, 1986 (Termination Date: 1993)

Unlocking Science Skills: Life Science/Biology: Grades 7–12
Globe, 1987 (Termination Date: 1993)

Globe Life Science: Grades 7–9
Globe, 1986 (Termination Date: 1993)

Biology Workshop: Grades 7–12
Globe, 1983 (Termination Date: 1993)

Work-A-Text in Life Science: Grades 7–12
Globe, 1987 (Termination Date: 1993)

Heath Life Science: Grades 7–9
D. C. Heath, 1987 (Termination Date: 1993)

Holt Life Science: Grades 7–8
Holt, Rinehart & Winston, 1986 (Termination Date: 1993)

Macmillan Life Science: Grades 7–9
Macmillan, 1989 (Termination Date: 1993)

Prentice Hall Life Science: Grades 6–9
Prentice Hall, 1986 (Termination Date: 1993)

Scott, Foresman Life Science: Grades 7–9
Scott, Foresman, 1986 (Termination Date: 1993)

Addison-Wesley Life Science: Grades 7–10
Addison-Wesley, 1986 (Termination Date: 1993)

Genes and Surroundings: Grades 7–8
Kendall/Hunt, 1983 (Termination Date: 1993)

Biological Science: Patterns and Processes: Grades 9–10
Kendall/Hunt, 1986 (Termination Date: 1993)

Physics I and II
Physics: Principles and Problems: Grades 10–12
Glencoe, 1986 (Termination Date: 1993)

Modern Physics: Grades 10–12
Holt, Rinehart & Winston, 1984 (Termination Date: 1993)

Physics: Its Methods and Meanings: Grades 10–12
Prentice Hall, 1986 (Termination Date: 1993)

Physics: Principles with Applications: Grades 10–12
Prentice Hall 1985 (Termination Date: 1993)

Conceptual Physics: Grades 10–12
Addison-Wesley, 1987 (Termination Date: 1993)

Physical Science
Experiences in Physical Science: Grades 7–9
Glencoe, 1985 (Termination Date: 1993)

Focus on Physical Science: Grades 7–9
Glencoe, 1987 (Termination Date: 1993)

Silver Burdett & Ginn Physical Science: Grades 7–9
Silver Burdett & Ginn, 1988 (Termination Date: 1993)

Concepts and Challenges in Physical Science: Grades 7–9
Globe, 1986 (Termination Date: 1993)

Unlocking Science Skills: Physical Science: Grades 7–12
Globe, 1987 (Termination Date: 1993)

Globe Physical Science: Grades 7–9
Globe, 1986 (Termination Date: 1993)

Physical Science: The Key Ideas: Grades 9–12
Globe, 1984 (Termination Date: 1993)

Physics Workshop: Grades 7–12
Globe, 1983 (Termination Date: 1993)

Work-A-Text in Physical Science: Grades 7–12
Globe, 1987 (Termination Date: 1993)

Heath Physical Science: Grades 7–9
D. C. Heath, 1987 (Termination Date: 1993)

Holt Physical Science: Grade 9
Holt, Rinehart & Winston, 1986 (Termination Date: 1993)

Macmillan Physical Science: Grades 7–9
Macmillan, 1988 (Termination Date: 1993)

Introduction to Physical Science: Grades 9–10
Prentice Hall, 1987 (Termination Date: 1993)

Prentice Hall Physical Science: Grades 6–9
Prentice Hall, 1986 (Termination Date: 1993)

Scott, Foresman Physical Science: Grades 9–12
Scott, Foresman, 1986 (Termination Date: 1993)

Addison-Wesley Physical Science: Grades 7–10
Addison-Wesley, 1984 (Termination Date: 1993)

North Carolina

General Science
Addison-Wesley Science: Grades 1–6
Addison-Wesley, 1989 (Termination Date: 1995)

Merrill Science: Grades 1–6
Merrill, 1989 (Termination Date: 1995)

Discover Science: Grades 1–6
Scott, Foresman, 1989 (Termination Date: 1995)

Integrated Science: Grades 7–8
Carolina, 1990 (Termination Date: 1995)

General Science: Grades 7–8
Harcourt Brace Jovanovich, 1989 (Termination Date: 1995)

Science Connections: Grades 7–8
Glencoe, 1990 (Termination Date: 1995)

General Science: Grades 7–8
Silver Burdett, 1989 (Termination Date: 1995)

Biology
Biology: Grade 10
Harcourt Brace Jovanovich, 1989 (Termination Date: 1995)

Heath Biology: Grades 9–12
D. C. Heath, 1989 (Termination Date: 1995)

Modern Biology: Grades 9–12
Holt, Rinehart & Winston, 1989 (Termination Date: 1995)

Prentice Hall Biology: Grades 9–12
Prentice Hall, 1990 (Termination Date: 1995)

Addison-Wesley Biology: Grades 9–12
Addison-Wesley, 1987 (Termination Date: 1995)

Globe Biology: Grades 9–12
Globe, 1990 (Termination Date: 1995)

Biology: An Everyday Experience: Grades 9–12
Glencoe, 1988 (Termination Date: 1995)

Scott, Foresman Life Science: Grades 9–12
Scott, Foresman, 1990 (Termination Date: 1995)

Biology: A Journey into Life: Grades 9–12
Holt, Rinehart & Winston, 1988 (Termination Date: 1995)

Understanding Biology: Grades 9–12
C. V. Mosby, 1988 (Termination Date: 1995)

Chemistry
Addison-Wesley Chemistry: Grades 9–12
Addison-Wesley, 1990 (Termination Date: 1995)

Modern Chemistry: Grades 9–12
Holt, Rinehart & Winston, 1990 (Termination Date: 1995)

Chemcom: Chemistry in the Community: Grades 9–12
Kendall/Hunt, 1988 (Termination Date: 1995)

Chemistry: A Modern Course: Grades 9–12
Glencoe, n.d. (Termination Date: 1995)

Chemistry: Grades 9–12
D. C. Heath, 1989 (Termination Date: 1995)

General Chemistry: Grades 9–12
D. C. Heath, 1988 (Termination Date: 1995)

Chemistry: The Central Science: Grades 9–12
Prentice Hall, 1988 (Termination Date: 1995)

Physical Science
Physical Science: Grades 9–12
Harcourt Brace Jovanovich, 1989 (Termination Date: 1995)

Focus on Physical Science: Grades 9–12
Glencoe, 1989 (Termination Date: 1995)

Prentice Hall Physical Science: Grades 9–12
Prentice Hall, 1991 (Termination Date: 1995)

Scott, Foresman Physical Science: Grades 9–12
Scott, Foresman, 1990 (Termination Date: 1995)

Silver Burdett & Ginn Physical Science: Grades 9–12
Silver Burdett & Ginn, 1990 (Termination Date: 1995)

Addison-Wesley Introduction to Physical Science: Grades 9–12
Addison-Wesley, 1988 (Termination Date: 1995)

Concepts and Challenges in Physical Science: Grades 9–12
Globe, 1989 (Termination Date: 1995)

Physics
Conceptual Physics: Grades 9–12
Addison-Wesley, 1987 (Termination Date: 1995)

Modern Physics: Grades 9–12
Holt, Rinehart & Winston, 1990 (Termination Date: 1995)

An Activity Approach to Physics: Grades 9–12
Le Bel, 1989 (Termination Date: 1995)

Principles and Problems: Grades 9–12
Glencoe, 1990 (Termination Date: 1995)

Physics for Career Education: Grades 9–12
Prentice Hall, 1988 (Termination Date: 1995)

Principles with Applications: Grades 9–12
Prentice Hall, 1985 (Termination Date: 1995)

Anatomy and Physiology
Human Anatomy and Physiology: Grades 9–12
Addison-Wesley, 1989 (Termination Date: 1995)

Modern Human Physiology: Grades 9–12
Holt, Rinehart & Winston, 1987 (Termination Date: 1995)

Structure and Function of the Body: Grades 9–12
C. V. Mosby, 1988 (Termination Date: 1995)

Fundamentals of Anatomy and Physiology: Grades 9–12
Prentice Hall, 1989 (Termination Date: 1995)

Earth Science
Earth Science: Grades 9–12
Harcourt Brace Jovanovich, 1989 (Termination Date: 1995)

Modern Earth Science: Grades 9–12
Holt, Rinehart & Winston, 1989 (Termination Date: 1995)

Focus on Earth Science: Grades 9–12
Glencoe, 1989 (Termination Date: 1995)

Prentice Hall Earth Science: Grades 9–12
Prentice Hall, 1991 (Termination Date: 1995)

Scott, Foresman Earth Science: Grades 9–12
Scott, Foresman, 1990 (Termination Date: 1995)

Astronomy
Dynamic Astronomy: Grades 9–12
Prentice Hall, 1989 (Termination Date: 1995)

Environmental Science
How the World Works and Your Place in It: Grades 9–12
Le Bel, 1989 (Termination Date: 1995)

Environmental Science: Grades 9–12
Prentice Hall, 1990 (Termination Date: 1995)

Geology
Physical Geology: Grades 9–12
Prentice Hall, 1990 (Termination Date: 1995)

Marine Science

Marine Biology: Grades 9–12
Prentice Hall, 1988 (Termination Date: 1995)

Introduction to Oceanography: Grades 9–12
Prentice Hall, 1988 (Termination Date: 1995)

Oklahoma

Science

Merrill Science: Grades K–6
Merrill, 1989 (Termination Date: 1994)

MCP Science: Grades 1–6
Modern Curriculum, 1987 (Termination Date: 1994)

Holt Science: Grades K–8
Holt, Rinehart & Winston, 1989 (Termination Date: 1994)

Discover Science: Grades K–6
Scott, Foresman, 1989 (Termination Date: 1994)

HBJ Science Readiness, Nova Edition: Grades K–6
Harcourt Brace Jovanovich, 1989 (Termination Date: 1994)

Silver Burdett & Ginn Science: Grades K–6
Silver Burdett & Ginn, 1989 (Termination Date: 1994)

Journeys in Science: Grades K–6
Macmillan, 1988 (Termination Date: 1994)

Addison-Wesley Science: Grades K–6
Addison-Wesley, 1989 (Termination Date: 1994)

Principles of Science: Grades 7–8
Merrill, 1986 (Termination Date: 1994)

Silver Burdett & Ginn General Science: Grades 7–8
Silver Burdett & Ginn, 1989 (Termination Date: 1994)

A Voyage of Adventure: Grades 7–8
Prentice Hall, 1989 (Termination Date: 1994)

A Voyage of Discovery: Grades 7–8
Prentice Hall, 1989 (Termination Date: 1994)

A Voyage of Exploration: Grades 7–8
Prentice Hall, 1989 (Termination Date: 1994)

General Science

Merrill General Science: Grades 9–12
Merrill, 1986 (Termination Date: 1994)

Holt General Science: Grades 9–12
Holt, Rinehart & Winston, 1988 (Termination Date: 1994)

General Science: Grades 9–12
Harcourt Brace Jovanovich, 1989 (Termination Date: 1994)

Allyn & Bacon General Science: Grades 9–12
Prentice Hall, 1989 (Termination Date: 1994)

Earth Science

Focus on Earth Science: Grades 7–8
Merrill, 1989 (Termination Date: 1994)

Heath Earth Science: Grades 7–8
D. C. Heath, 1987 (Termination Date: 1994)

Holt Earth Science: Grades 7–8
Holt, Rinehart & Winston, 1986 (Termination Date: 1994)

Scott, Foresman Earth Science: Grades 7–8
Scott, Foresman, 1990 (Termination Date: 1994)

Earth Science: Grades 7–8
Harcourt Brace Jovanovich, 1989 (Termination Date: 1994)

Silver Burdett & Ginn Earth Science: Grades 7-8
Silver Burdett & Ginn, 1987 (Termination Date: 1994)

Prentice Hall Earth Science: Grades 7–8
Prentice Hall, 1988 (Termination Date: 1994)

Macmillan Earth Science: Grades 7–8
Macmillan, 1989 (Termination Date: 1994)

Addison-Wesley Earth Science: Grades 7–8
Addison-Wesley, 1989 (Termination Date: 1994)

Concepts and Challenges in Earth Science: Grades 7–8
Globe, 1991 (Termination Date: 1994)

Earth Science: Grades 9–12
Media Materials, 1988 (Termination Date: 1994)

Earth Science: Grades 9–12
D. C. Heath, 1989 (Termination Date: 1994)

Modern Earth Science: Grades 9–12
Holt, Rinehart & Winston, 1989 (Termination Date: 1994)

Life Science

Focus on Life Science: Grades 7–8
Merrill, 1989 (Termination Date: 1994)

Heath Life Science: Grades 7–8
D. C. Heath, 1987 (Termination Date: 1994)

Holt Life Science: Grades 7–8
Holt, Rinehart & Winston, 1986 (Termination Date: 1994)

Scott, Foresman Life Science: Grades 7–8
Scott, Foresman, 1990 (Termination Date: 1994)

Life Science: Grades 7–8
Harcourt Brace Jovanovich, 1989 (Termination Date: 1994)

Silver Burdett & Ginn Life Science: Grades 7–8
Silver Burdett & Ginn, 1987 (Termination Date: 1994)

Prentice Hall Life Science: Grades 7–8
Prentice Hall, 1988 (Termination Date: 1994)

Macmillan Life Science: Grades 7–8
Macmillan, 1989 (Termination Date: 1994)

Addison-Wesley Life Science: Grades 7–8
Addison-Wesley, 1989 (Termination Date: 1994)

Concepts and Challenges in Life Science: Grades 7–8
Globe, 1986–91 (Termination Date: 1994)

Biology: First Year

Biology: An Everyday Experience: Grades 9–12
Merrill, 1988 (Termination Date: 1994)

Heath Biology: Grades 9–12
D. C. Heath, 1989 (Termination Date: 1994)

Biological Science: An Ecological Approach:
Grades 9–12
Kendall/Hunt, 1987 (Termination Date: 1994)

Modern Biology: Grades 9–12
Holt, Rinehart & Winston, 1989 (Termination Date: 1994)

Scott, Foresman Biology: Grades 9–12
Scott, Foresman, 1988 (Termination Date: 1994)

Biology: Grades 9–12
Harcourt Brace Jovanovich, 1989 (Termination Date: 1994)

Prentice Hall Biology: Grades 9–12
Prentice Hall, 1990 (Termination Date: 1994)

Biology: The Living World: Grades 9–12
Prentice Hall, 1989 (Termination Date: 1994)

Biology: The Study of Life: Grades 9–12
Prentice Hall, 1990 (Termination Date: 1994)

Addison-Wesley Biology: Grades 9–12
Addison-Wesley, 1988 (Termination Date: 1994)

Biology: Second Year

Biology: Living Systems: Grades 9–12
Merrill, 1989 (Termination Date: 1994)

Understanding Biology: Grades 9–12
C. V. Mosby, 1988 (Termination Date: 1994)

Biology: A Journey into Life: Grades 9–12
Holt, Rinehart & Winston, 1988 (Termination Date: 1994)

Biological Science: Interaction of Experiments and Ideas: Grades 9–12
Prentice Hall, 1983 (Termination Date: 1994)

Biology: Grades 9–12
Prentice Hall, 1986 (Termination Date: 1994)

Biology: Grades 9–12
Addison-Wesley, 1987 (Termination Date: 1994)

Biological Science: A Molecular Approach: Grades 9–12
D. C. Heath, 1990 (Termination Date: 1994)

Understanding Biology: Grades 9–12
Mosby–Year Book, 1991 (Termination Date: 1994)

Chemistry: First Year

Chemistry: A Modern Course: Grades 9–12
Merrill, 1987 (Termination Date: 1994)

Heath Chemistry: Grades 9–12
D. C. Heath, 1987 (Termination Date: 1994)

Chemcom: Chemistry in the Community: Grades 9–12
Kendall/Hunt, 1988 (Termination Date: 1994)

Modern Chemistry: Grades 9–12
Holt, Rinehart & Winston, 1986 (Termination Date: 1994)

Chemistry: The Study of Matter: Grades 9–12
Prentice Hall, 1989 (Termination Date: 1994)

Chemistry: Experimental Foundations: Grades 9–12
Prentice Hall, 1987 (Termination Date: 1994)

Addison-Wesley Chemistry: Grades 9–12
Addison-Wesley, 1987 (Termination Date: 1994)

Modern Chemistry: Grades 9–12
Holt, Rinehart & Winston/Harcourt Brace Jovanovich, 1990 (Termination Date: 1994)

Chemistry: Second Year

Chemistry: Grades 9–12
D. C. Heath, 1986 (Termination Date: 1994)

Chemical Principles: Grades 9–12
Holt, Rinehart & Winston, 1985 (Termination Date: 1994)

Chemistry: The Central Science: Grades 9–12
Prentice Hall, 1988 (Termination Date: 1994)

Environmental Science

Global Science: Energy Resources, Environment: Grades 9–12
Kendall/Hunt, 1984 (Termination Date: 1994)

Introduction to Environmental Studies: Grades 9–12
Holt, Rinehart & Winston, 1986 (Termination Date: 1994)

Environmental Science: Grades 9–12
Addison-Wesley, 1989 (Termination Date: 1994)

Physical Science

Focus on Physical Science: Grades 7–8
Merrill, 1989 (Termination Date: 1994)

Heath Physical Science: Grades 7–8
D. C. Heath, 1987 (Termination Date: 1994)

Holt Physical Science: Grades 7–8
Holt, 1986 (Termination Date: 1994)

Scott, Foresman Physical Science: Grades 7–8
Scott, Foresman, 1990 (Termination Date: 1994)

Physical Science: Grades 7–8
Harcourt Brace Jovanovich, 1989 (Termination Date: 1994)

Silver Burdett & Ginn Physical Science: Grades 7–8
Silver Burdett & Ginn, 1988 (Termination Date: 1994)

Prentice Hall Physical Science: Grades 7–8
Prentice Hall, 1988 (Termination Date: 1994)

Macmillan Physical Science: Grades 7–8
Macmillan, 1988 (Termination Date: 1994)

Addison-Wesley Introduction to Physical Science: Grades 7–8
Addison-Wesley, 1988 (Termination Date: 1994)

Concepts and Challenges in Physical Science: Grades 7–8
Globe, 1991 (Termination Date: 1994)

Physical Science: Grades 9–12
Media Materials, 1987 (Termination Date: 1994)

The Physical Universe: Grades 9–12
McGraw-Hill, 1986 (Termination Date: 1994)

Addison-Wesley Physical Science: Grades 9–12
Addison-Wesley, 1988 (Termination Date: 1994)

Introductory Physical Science: Grades 9–12
Prentice Hall, 1987 (Termination Date: 1994)

Physics: First Year

Physics: Principles and Problems: Grades 9–12
Merrill, 1986 (Termination Date: 1994)

Modern Physics: Grades 9–12
Holt, 1984 (Termination Date: 1994)

Physics: Its Methods and Meanings: Grades 9–12
Prentice Hall, 1986 (Termination Date: 1994)

Addison-Wesley Conceptual Physics: Grades 9–12
Addison-Wesley, 1987 (Termination Date: 1994)

Modern Physics: Grades 9–12
Holt, Rinehart & Winston/Harcourt Brace
Jovanovich, 1990 (Termination Date: 1994)

Physiology
Textbook of Anatomy and Physiology: Grades 9–12
C. V. Mosby, 1987 (Termination Date: 1994)

Structure and Function of the Body: Grades 9–12
C. V. Mosby, 1988 (Termination Date: 1994)

Modern Human Physiology: Grades 9–12
Holt, Rinehart & Winston, 1987 (Termination
Date: 1994)

Anatomy and Physiology: Grades 9–12
Prentice Hall, 1983 (Termination Date: 1994)

Essentials of Anatomy and Physiology: Grades 9–12
Mosby–Year Book, 1991 (Termination Date: 1994)

Zoology
Biology of Animals: Grades 9–12
Mosby–Year Book, 1990 (Termination Date: 1994)

Integrated Principles of Zoology: Grades 9–12
Mosby–Year Book, 1988 (Termination Date: 1994)

Oregon

Elementary Science
Addison-Wesley Science: Grades K–6
Addison-Wesley, 1989 (Termination Date: 1995)

SCIIS, Science: Grades K–6
Delta Education, 1988 (Termination Date: 1995)

Merrill Science: Grades K–6
Merrill, 1989 (Termination Date: 1995)

Discover Science: Grades K–6
Scott, Foresman, 1989/1991 (Termination Date:
1995)

Silver Burdett & Ginn Science: Grades K–6
Silver Burdett & Ginn, 1989 (Termination Date:
1995)

Earth/Space Science
Addison-Wesley Earth Science: Grades 6–9
Addison-Wesley, 1989 (Termination Date: 1995)

Earth Science: Grades 6–9
Harcourt Brace Jovanovich, 1989 (Termination
Date: 1995)

Modern Earth Science: Grades 6–9
Holt, Rinehart & Winston/Harcourt Brace
Jovanovich, 1989 (Termination Date: 1995)

Macmillan Earth Science: Grades 6–9
Macmillan, 1989 (Termination Date: 1995)

Focus on Earth Science: Grades 6–9
Merrill, 1989 (Termination Date: 1995)

Prentice Hall Earth Science: Grades 6–9
Prentice Hall, 1988/1991 (Termination Date: 1995)

Scott, Foresman Earth Science: Grades 6–9
Scott, Foresman, 1990 (Termination Date: 1995)

Silver Burdett & Ginn Earth Science: Grades 6–9
Silver Burdett & Ginn, 1987 (Termination Date:
1995)

Life Science
Addison-Wesley Life Science: Grades 6–9
Addison-Wesley, 1989 (Termination Date: 1995)

Life Science: Grades 6–9
Harcourt Brace Jovanovich, 1989 (Termination
Date: 1995)

Macmillan Life Science: Grades 6–9
Macmillan, 1989 (Termination Date: 1995)

Focus on Life Science: Grades 6–9
Merrill, 1989 (Termination Date: 1995)

Prentice Hall Life Science: Grades 6–9
Prentice Hall, 1988/1991 (Termination Date:
1995)

Scott, Foresman Life Science: Grades 6–9
Scott, Foresman, 1990 (Termination Date: 1995)

Silver Burdett & Ginn Life Science: Grades 6–9
Silver Burdett & Ginn, 1987/1990 (Termination
Date: 1995)

Physical Science
Addison-Wesley Physical Science: Grades 6–9
Addison-Wesley, 1988 (Termination Date: 1995)

Addison-Wesley Introduction to Physical Science:
Grades 6–9
Addison-Wesley, 1988 (Termination Date: 1995)

Physical Science: Grades 6–9
Harcourt Brace Jovanovich, 1989 (Termination
Date: 1995)

Macmillan Physical Science: Grades 6–9
Macmillan, 1988 (Termination Date: 1995)

Focus on Physical Science: Grades 6–9
Merrill, 1989 (Termination Date: 1995)

Prentice Hall Physical Science: Grades 6–9
Prentice Hall, 1988/1991 (Termination Date: 1995)

Scott, Foresman Physical Science: Grades 6–9
Scott, Foresman, 1990 (Termination Date: 1995)

Silver Burdett & Ginn Physical Science: Grades 6–9
Silver Burdett & Ginn, 1988/1990 (Termination
Date: 1995)

General Science
General Science: Grades 6–9
Harcourt Brace Jovanovich, 1989 (Termination
Date: 1995)

Holt General Science: Grades 6–9
Holt, Rinehart & Winston/Harcourt Brace
Jovanovich, 1988 (Termination Date: 1995)

Merrill Science Connections: Grades 6–9
Merrill, 1990 (Termination Date: 1995)

Prentice Hall General Science Series: Grades 6–9
Prentice Hall, 1989 (Termination Date: 1995)

Silver Burdett & Ginn General Science: Grades 6–9
Silver Burdett & Ginn, 1989 (Termination Date:
1995)

Biology
Globe Biology: Grades 9–12
Allyn & Bacon/Prentice Hall, 1990 (Termination
Date: 1995)

Biology: Grades 9–12
Harcourt Brace Jovanovich, 1989 (Termination
Date: 1995)

Heath Biology: Grades 9–12
D. C. Heath, 1989 (Termination Date: 1995)

Modern Biology: Grades 9–12
Holt, Rinehart & Winston/Harcourt Brace
Jovanovich, 1989 (Termination Date: 1995)

Biology: A Journey into Life: Grades 9–12
Holt, Rinehart & Winston/Harcourt Brace
Jovanovich, 1988 (Termination Date: 1995)

BSCS, Biological Science: An Ecological Approach: Grades 9–12
Kendall/Hunt, 1987 (Termination Date: 1995)

Biology: Living Systems: Grades 9–12
Merrill, 1989 (Termination Date: 1995)

Biology: An Everyday Experience: Grades 9–12
Merrill, 1988 (Termination Date: 1995)

Prentice Hall Biology: Grades 9–12
Prentice Hall, 1987/1990 (Termination Date: 1995)

Biology: The Study of Life: Grades 9–12
Prentice Hall, 1987/1990 (Termination Date: 1995)

Biology: The Living World: Grades 9–12
Prentice Hall, 1989 (Termination Date: 1995)

Scott, Foresman Biology: Grades 9–12
Scott, Foresman, 1988 (Termination Date: 1995)

Scott, Foresman Biology Courseware Series: Grades
9–12
Scott, Foresman, 1985 (Termination Date: 1995)

Chemistry
Addison-Wesley Chemistry: Grades 9–12
Addison-Wesley, 1987/1990 (Termination Date:
1995)

Heath Chemistry: Grades 9–12
D. C. Heath, 1987 (Termination Date: 1995)

Modern Chemistry: Grades 9–12
Holt, Rinehart & Winston/Harcourt Brace
Jovanovich, 1990 (Termination Date: 1995)

Chemistry: A Modern Course: Grades 9–12
Merrill, 1987/1990 (Termination Date: 1995)

Chemistry: The Study of Matter: Grades 9–12
Prentice Hall, 1989 (Termination Date: 1995)

Physics
Conceptual Physics: Grades 9–12
Addison-Wesley, 1987 (Termination Date: 1995)

PSSC Physics: Grades 9–12
D. C. Heath, 1986 (Termination Date: 1995)

Modern Physics: Grades 9–12
Holt, Rinehart & Winston/Harcourt Brace
Jovanovich, 1990 (Termination Date: 1995)

Physics: Principles and Problems: Grades 9–12
Merrill, 1986 (Termination Date: 1995)

South Carolina

Science
HBJ Science: Grades 1–6
Harcourt Brace Jovanovich, 1985 (Termination
Date: 1992)

Holt Science: Grades 1–6
Holt, Rinehart & Winston, 1986 (Termination
Date: 1992)

Journeys in Science: Grades 1–6
Macmillan, 1988 (Termination Date: 1992)

Prentice Hall General Science: A Voyage of Adventure: Grade 6
Prentice Hall, 1986 (Termination Date: 1992)

Silver Burdett & Ginn Science: Grades 1–6
Silver Burdett & Ginn, 1987 (Termination Date:
1992)

Science Today: Grades 1–6
Steck–Vaughn, 1986 (Termination Date: 1992)

Life Science
Life Science: Grade 7
Harcourt Brace Jovanovich, 1989 (Termination
Date: 1994)

Life Science: Discovering Basic Concepts: Grade 7
Janus, 1987 (Termination Date: 1994)

Focus on Life Science: Grade 7
Merrill, 1989 (Termination Date: 1994)

Prentice Hall Life Science: Grade 7
Prentice Hall, 1991 (Termination Date: 1994)

Scott, Foresman Life Science: Grade 7
Scott, Foresman, 1990 (Termination Date: 1994)

Silver Burdett & Ginn Life Science: Grade 7
Silver Burdett & Ginn, 1990 (Termination Date:
1994)

Earth Science
Earth Science: Grade 8
Harcourt Brace Jovanovich, 1989 (Termination
Date: 1994)

Modern Earth Science: Grade 8
Holt, Rinehart & Winston, 1989 (Termination
Date: 1994)

Earth Science: Discovering Basic Concepts: Grade 8
Janus, 1987 (Termination Date: 1994)

Focus on Earth Science: Grade 8
Merrill, 1989 (Termination Date: 1994)

Scott, Foresman Earth Science: Grade 8
Scott, Foresman, 1990 (Termination Date: 1994)

Silver Burdett & Ginn Earth Science: Grade 8
Silver Burdett & Ginn, 1990 (Termination Date:
1994)

Astronomy
Contemporary Astronomy: Grades 11–12
Holt, Rinehart & Winston, 1987 (Termination
Date: 1994)

Realm of the Universe: Grades 11–12
Holt, Rinehart & Winston, 1988 (Termination
Date: 1994)

Dynamic Astronomy: Grades 11–12
Prentice Hall, 1989 (Termination Date: 1994)

Environmental Education
What's Ecology?: Grades 9–12
Addison-Wesley, 1986 (Termination Date: 1990)

An Introduction to the Biology of Marine Life:
Grades 10–12
William C. Brown, 1984 (Termination Date:
1990)

*Laboratory and Field Investigations in Marine
Biology:* Grades 11–12
William C. Brown, 1984 (Termination Date: 1990)

Concepts of Ecology: Grades 11–12
Prentice Hall, 1984 (Termination Date: 1990)

General Science
General Science: Grades 9–12
Harcourt Brace Jovanovich, 1989 (Termination
Date: 1994)

Holt General Science: Grades 9–12
Holt, Rinehart & Winston, 1988 (Termination
Date: 1994)

Silver Burdett & Ginn General Science: Grades 9–12
Silver Burdett & Ginn, 1989 (Termination Date:
1994)

Physical Science—Practical
Addison-Wesley Introduction to Physical Science:
Grades 9–12
Addison-Wesley, 1988 (Termination Date: 1994)

Concepts and Challenges in Physical Science:
Grades 9–12
Globe, 1989 (Termination Date: 1994)

Scott, Foresman Physical Science: Grades 9–12
Scott, Foresman, 1990 (Termination Date: 1994)

Physical Science—Regular
Physical Science: Grade 9
Harcourt Brace Jovanovich, 1989 (Termination
Date: 1994)

Macmillan Physical Science: Grade 9
Macmillan/McGraw-Hill, 1988 (Termination
Date: 1994)

Focus on Physical Science: Grade 9
Merrill, 1989 (Termination Date: 1994)

Silver Burdett & Ginn Physical Science: Grade 9
Silver Burdett & Ginn, 1990 (Termination Date:
1994)

Biology I—Practical
Globe Biology: Grades 10–12
Globe, 1990 (Termination Date: 1994)

Biology: An Everyday Experience: Grades 10–12
Merrill, 1988 (Termination Date: 1994)

Biology I—Regular
Biology: Grades 10–12
Harcourt Brace Jovanovich, 1989 (Termination
Date: 1994)

Heath Biology: Grades 10–12
D. C. Heath, 1989 (Termination Date: 1994)

Modern Biology: Grades 10–12
Holt, Rinehart & Winston, 1989 (Termination
Date: 1994)

Biological Science: An Ecological Approach:
Grades 10–12
Kendall/Hunt, 1987 (Termination Date: 1994)

Biology: The Living World: Grades 10–12
Prentice Hall, 1989 (Termination Date: 1994)

Biology II
Biology: A Journey into Life: Grades 11–12
Holt, Rinehart & Winston, 1988 (Termination
Date: 1994)

Understanding Biology: Grades 11–12
C. V. Mosby, 1988 (Termination Date: 1994)

Biology—Advanced Placement
Biology: Grades 11–12
Addison-Wesley, 1990 (Termination Date: 1994)

Biology: Grades 11–12
Worth, 1989 (Termination Date: 1994)

Chemistry I

Addison-Wesley Chemistry: Grades 10–12
Addison-Wesley, 1987 (Termination Date: 1993)

Heath Chemistry: Grades 10–12
D. C. Heath, 1987 (Termination Date: 1993)

Modern Chemistry: Grades 10–12
Holt, Rinehart & Winston, 1986 (Termination Date: 1993)

Chemcom: Chemistry in the Community: Grades 10–12
Kendall/Hunt, 1988 (Termination Date: 1993)

Chemistry: The Study of Matter: Grades 10–12
Prentice Hall, 1989 (Termination Date: 1993)

Chemistry II and Advanced Placement

General Chemistry: Grades 11–12
D. C. Heath, 1988 (Termination Date: 1993)

Chemistry: Grades 11–12
D. C. Heath, 1989 (Termination Date: 1993)

Chemistry: The Central Science: Grades 11–12
Prentice Hall, 1988 (Termination Date: 1993)

Chemistry: Grades 11–12
Random House, 1988 (Termination Date: 1993)

Physics I

Conceptual Physics: Grades 11–12
Addison-Wesley, 1987 (Termination Date: 1993)

Modern Physics: Grades 11–12
Holt, Rinehart & Winston, 1990 (Termination Date: 1993)

Physic-Al: An Activity Approach to Physics: Grades 11–12
Le Bel, 1989 (Termination Date: 1993)

Physics: Principles and Problems: Grades 11–12
Merrill, 1986 (Termination Date: 1993)

Tennessee

Science

Science in Your World: Grades 1–6
Macmillan/McGraw-Hill, 1991 (Termination Date: 1997)

Prentice Hall General Science: A Voyage of Adventure
Prentice Hall, 1992 (Termination Date: 1997)

Discover Science: Grades 1–6
Scott, Foresman, 1991 (Termination Date: 1997)

Science Horizons: Grades 1–6
Silver Burdett & Ginn, 1991 (Termination Date: 1997)

Fearon's General Science: Grades 7–8
Fearon, 1990 (Termination Date: 1997)

Science Connections/Blue Book and Red Book: Grades 7–8
Macmillan/McGraw-Hill, 1990 (Termination Date: 1997)

Prentice Hall General Science: A Voyage of Discovery: Grades 7–8
Prentice Hall, 1992 (Termination Date: 1997)

Prentice Hall Science: A Voyage of Exploration: Grades 7–8
Prentice Hall, 1992 (Termination Date: 1997)

General Science: Grades 7–8
Silver Burdett & Ginn, 1989 (Termination Date: 1997)

Biology

Biology: An Everyday Experience: Grades 9–12
Macmillan/McGraw-Hill, 1988 (Termination Date: 1997)

Biology: Living Systems: Grades 9–12
Macmillan/McGraw-Hill, 1989 (Termination Date: 1997)

Biology: Dynamic of Life: Grades 9–12
Macmillan/McGraw-Hill, 1991 (Termination Date: 1997)

Globe Biology: Grades 9–12
Globe, 1990 (Termination Date: 1997)

Heath Biology: Grades 10–12
D. C. Heath, 1991 (Termination Date: 1997)

Modern Biology: Grades 9–12
Holt, Rinehart & Winston/Harcourt Brace
Jovanovich, 1991 (Termination Date: 1997)

Biology Today: Grades 9–12
Holt, Rinehart & Winston/Harcourt Brace
Jovanovich, 1991 (Termination Date: 1997)

Basic Biology: Grades 9–12
Media Materials, 1986 (Termination Date: 1997)

Biology: Grades 9–12
Prentice Hall, 1991 (Termination Date: 1997)

Biology: The Study of Life: Grades 9–12
Prentice Hall, 1991 (Termination Date: 1997)

Biology II: Grades 9–12
Addison-Wesley, 1990 (Termination Date: 1997)

Biology: Grades 11–12
William C. Brown, 1990 (Termination Date:
1997)

BSCS Blue Version, Biological Science: A Molecular Approach: Grades 10–12
D. C. Heath, 1990 (Termination Date: 1997)

World of Biology: Grades 9–12
Holt, Rinehart & Winston/Harcourt Brace
Jovanovich, 1990 (Termination Date: 1997)

Understanding Biology: Grades 11–12
Mosby–Year Book, 1991 (Termination Date: 1997)

Biology: Grades 11–12
Mosby–Year Book, 1989 (Termination Date: 1997)

Chemistry

Addison-Wesley Chemistry: Grades 9–12
Addison-Wesley, 1990 (Termination Date: 1997)

Chemistry: A Modern Course: Grades 9–12
Macmillan/McGraw-Hill, n.d. (Termination Date:
1997)

Introductory Chemistry: A Foundation: Grades 11–12
D. C. Heath, 1990 (Termination Date: 1997)

Modern Chemistry: Grades 9–12
Holt, Rinehart & Winston/Harcourt Brace
Jovanovich, 1990 (Termination Date: 1997)

Prentice Hall Chemistry: The Study of Matter:
Grades 9–12
Prentice Hall, 1992 (Termination Date: 1997)

Chemistry: Grades 11–12
D. C. Heath, 1990 (Termination Date: 1997)

Chemistry: Principles and Reactions: Grades 9–12
Holt, Rinehart & Winston/Harcourt Brace
Jovanovich, 1989 (Termination Date: 1997)

Chemistry: The Central Science: Grades 9–12
Prentice Hall, 1991 (Termination Date: 1997)

Earth Science

Addison-Wesley Earth Science: Grades 9–12
Addison-Wesley, 1989 (Termination Date: 1996)

Quercus Earth Science: Grades 9–12
Fearon, 1989 (Termination Date: 1996)

Focus on Earth Science: Grades 9–12
Macmillan/McGraw-Hill, 1989 (Termination
Date: 1997)

Concepts and Challenges in Science: Earth Science:
Grades 9–12
Globe, 1991 (Termination Date: 1997)

Earth Science: The Challenge of Discovery: Grades
9–12
D. C. Heath, 1991 (Temination Year: 1997)

Earth Science: Grades 9–12
D. C. Heath, 1989 (Termination Date: 1997)

HBJ Earth Science: Grades 9–12
Holt, Rinehart & Winston/Harcourt Brace
Jovanovich, 1989 (Termination Date: 1997)

Modern Earth Science: Grades 9–12
Holt, Rinehart & Winston/Harcourt Brace
Jovanovich, 1989 (Termination Date: 1997)

Earth Science: Investigating Our World: Grades 9–12
Media Materials, 1988 (Termination Date: 1997)

Prentice Hall Earth Science: Grades 9–12
Prentice Hall, 1991 (Termination Date: 1997)

Earth Science: Grades 9–12
Scott, Foresman, 1990 (Termination Date: 1997)

Earth Science: Grades 9–12
Scott, Foresman, 1990 (Termination Date: 1997)

Earth Science: Grades 9–12
Silver Burdett & Ginn, 1990 (Termination Date: 1997)

General Science

Holt General Science: Grade 9
Holt, Rinehart & Winston/Harcourt Brace
Jovanovich, 1983 (Termination Date: 1992)

Principles of Science, Books 1 and 2: Grades 7–9
Glencoe, 1983 (Termination Date: 1992)

Allyn & Bacon General Science: Grades 7–9
Prentice Hall, 1989 (Termination Date: 1992)

Ecology

Environmental Science: The Way the World Works:
Grades 9–12
Prentice Hall, 1990 (Termination Date: 1997)

Life Science

Life Science: Grades 9–12
Addison-Wesley, 1989 (Termination Date: 1997)

Fearon's Biology: Grades 9–12
Fearon, 1990 (Termination Date: 1997)

Quercus Biology of Plants and Animals: Grades 9–12
Fearon, 1989 (Termination Date: 1997)

Quercus Human Biology: Grades 9–12
Fearon, 1989 (Termination Date: 1997)

Focus on Life Science: Grades 9–12
Macmillan/McGraw-Hill, 1989 (Termination Date: 1997)

Concepts and Challenges in Science-Life Science:
Grades 9–12
Globe, 1991 (Termination Date: 1997)

Life Science: The Challenge of Discovery: Grades 9–12
D. C. Heath, 1991 (Termination Date: 1997)

HBJ Life Science: Grades 9–12
Holt, Rinehart & Winston/Harcourt Brace
Jovanovich, 1989 (Termination Date: 1997)

Life Science: Grades 9–12
Prentice Hall, 1991 (Termination Date: 1997)

Life Science: Grades 9–12
Scott, Foresman, 1990 (Termination Date: 1997)

Life Science: Grades 9–12
Silver Burdett & Ginn, 1989 (Termination Date: 1997)

Physical Science

Addison-Wesley Introduction to Physical Science:
Grades 9–12
Addison-Wesley, 1988 (Termination Date: 1997)

Addison-Wesley Physical Science: Grades 9–12
Addison-Wesley, 1988 (Termination Date: 1997)

Quercus Chemistry: Grades 9–12
Fearon, 1989 (Termination Date: 1997)

Quercus Physical Science: Grades 9–12
Fearon, 1989 (Termination Date: 1997)

Focus on Physical Science: Grades 9–12
Macmillan/McGraw-Hill, 1989 (Termination Date: 1997)

Concepts and Challenges in Science: Physical Science: Grades 9–12
Globe, 1991 (Termination Date: 1997)

Physical Science: The Challenge of Discovery:
Grades 9–12
D. C. Heath, 1991 (Termination Date: 1997)

HBJ Physical Science: Grades 9–12
Holt, Rinehart & Winston/Harcourt Brace
Jovanovich, 1989 (Termination Date: 1997)

Modern Physical Science: Grades 9–12
Holt, Rinehart & Winston/Harcourt Brace
Jovanovich, 1991 (Termination Date: 1997)

Physical Science: Grades 9–12
Media Materials, 1987 (Termination Date: 1997)

Physical Science: Grades 9–12
Prentice Hall, 1991 (Termination Date: 1997)

Physical Science: Grades 9–12
Scott, Foresman, 1990 (Termination Date: 1997)

Physical Science: Grades 9–12
Silver Burdett & Ginn, 1990 (Termination Date: 1997)

Physics

Conceptual Physics: Grades 9–12
Addison-Wesley, 1987 (Termination Date: 1997)

Physics: Principles and Problems: Grades 9–12
Macmillan/McGraw-Hill, 1990 (Termination Date: 1997)

Modern Physics: Grades 9–12
Holt, Rinehart & Winston/Harcourt Brace Jovanovich, 1990 (Termination Date: 1997)

Physics: Principles with Applications: Grades 9–12
Prentice Hall, 1991 (Termination Date: 1997)

Physiology

Structure and Function of the Body: Grades 9–12
Mosby-Year Book, 1988 (Termination Date: 1997)

Anthony's Textbook of Anatomy and Physiology: Grades 9–12
Mosby–Year Book, 1990 (Termination Date: 1997)

Mosby's Anatomy and Physiology Laboratory Manual: Grades 9–12
Mosby–Year Book, n.d. (Termination Date: 1997)

Texas

Elementary Science

Discover Science: Grades 1–6
Scott, Foresman, 1991 (also in Spanish edition) (Termination Date: 1997)

Science Horizons: Grades 1–6 (also in Spanish ed.)
Silver Burdett, 1991 (Termination Date: 1997)

Elementary Science Electronic Instructional Media Systems

Windows on Science: Grades 2–6 (also in Spanish ed.)
Optical Data, 1990 (Termination Date: 1997)

Life Science

Life Science: Grade 7
Macmillan/McGraw-Hill, 1986 (Termination Date: 1992)

Holt Life Science: Grade 7
Holt, Rinehart & Winston, 1986 (Termination Date: 1992)

Heath Life Science: Grade 7
D. C. Heath, 1985 (Termination Date: 1992)

Addison-Wesley Life Science: Grade 7
Addison-Wesley, 1986 (Termination Date: 1992)

Focus on Life Science: Grade 7
Glencoe/McGraw-Hill, 1986 (Termination Date: 1992)

Earth Science

Macmillan Earth Science: Grades 7–8
Macmillan/McGraw-Hill, 1986 (Termination Date: 1993)

Silver Burdett Earth Science: Grades 7–8
Silver Burdett & Ginn, 1987 (Termination Date: 1993)

Addison-Wesley Earth Science: Grades 7–8
Addison-Wesley, 1987 (Termination Date: 1993)

Merrill Earth Science: Grades 7–8
Glencoe/McGraw-Hill, 1987 (Termination Date: 1993)

Prentice Hall Earth Science: Grades 7–8
Prentice Hall, 1987 (Termination Date: 1993)

Physiology and Anatomy

Human Anatomy and Physiology: Grades 9–12
Addison-Wesley, 1989 (Termination Date: 1996)

Physical Science
Physical Science: Grades 9–12
Addison-Wesley, 1988 (Termination Date: 1994)

Heath Physical Science: Grades 9–12
D. C. Heath, 1987 (Termination Date: 1994)

Holt Physical Science: Grades 9–12
Holt, Rinehart & Winston, 1988 (Termination Date: 1994)

Macmillan Physical Science: Grades 9–12
Glencoe/McGraw-Hill, 1988 (Termination Date: 1994)

Focus on Physical Science: Grades 9–12
Glencoe/McGraw-Hill, 1987 (Termination Date: 1994)

Prentice Hall Physical Science: Grades 9–12
Prentice Hall, 1988 (Termination Date: 1994)

Silver Burdett Physical Science: Grades 9–12
Silver Burdett & Ginn, 1988 (Termination Date: 1994)

Introduction to Physical Science: Grades 9–12
Addison-Wesley, 1988 (Termination Date: 1994)

Concepts and Challenges in Physical Science:
Grades 9–12
Globe, 1986 (Termination Date: 1994)

Scott, Foresman Physical Science: Grades 9–12
Scott, Foresman, 1986 (Termination Date: 1994)

Biology
Biology for Living: Grades 9–12
Globe, 1987 (Termination Date: 1992)

Biology and Human Progress: Grades 9–12
Prentice Hall, 1986 (Termination Date: 1992)

Introduction to Biology: Grades 9–12
Scott, Foresman, 1983 (Termination Date: 1992)

Living Things: An Introduction to Biology: Grades
9–12
Holt, Rinehart & Winston, 1985 (Termination Date: 1992)

Biology: An Everyday Experience: Grades 9–12
Glencoe, 1985 (Termination Date: 1992)

Biology: The Dynamics of Life: Grades 9–12
Glencoe/McGraw-Hill, 1991 (Termination Date: 1997)

Heath Biology: Grades 9–12
D. C. Heath, 1991 (Termination Date: 1997)

BSCS Blue Version, Biological Science: A Molecular Approach: Grades 9–12
D. C. Heath, 1991 (Termination Date: 1997)

Biology Today: Grades 9–12
Holt, Rinehart & Winston, 1991 (Termination Date: 1997)

Modern Biology: Grades 9–12
Holt, Rinehart & Winston, 1991 (Termination Date: 1997)

Biological Science: An Ecological Approach:
Grades 9–12
Kendall/Hunt, 1987 (Termination Date: 1997)

Biology: Grades 9–12
Prentice Hall, 1991 (Termination Date: 1997)

Biology: The Study of Life: Grades 9–12
Prentice Hall, 1991 (Termination Date: 1997)

Biology: Grades 9–12
Addison-Wesley, 1990 (Termination Date: 1997)

Essentials of Biology: Grades 9–12
Glencoe/McGraw-Hill, 1990 (Termination Date: 1997)

Biology: Grades 9–12
Mosby–Year Book, 1989 (Termination Date: 1997)

Chemistry
Modern Chemistry: Grades 9–12
Holt, Rinehart & Winston, 1986 (Termination Date: 1993)

Chemistry: Grades 9–12
Addison-Wesley, 1987 (Termination Date: 1993)

Merrill Chemistry: Grades 9–12
Glencoe/McGraw-Hill, 1987 (Termination Date: 1993)

Allyn & Bacon Chemistry: Grades 9–12
Prentice Hall, 1987 (Termination Date: 1993)

Heath Chemistry: Grades 9–12
D. C. Heath, 1987 (Termination Date: 1993)

Chemistry: Grades 9–12
D. C. Heath, 1986 (Termination Date: 1993)

Chemical Principles: Grades 9–12
Holt, Rinehart & Winston, 1985 (Termination
Date: 1993)

Chemistry: The Central Science: Grades 9–12
Prentice Hall, 1985 (Termination Date: 1993)

General Chemistry: Grades 9–12
Glencoe/McGraw-Hill, 1985 (Termination Date:
1993)

Physics
Modern Physics: Grades 9–12
Holt, Rinehart & Winston, 1984 (Termination
Date: 1992)

Physics: Principles and Problems: Grades 9–12
Glencoe/McGraw-Hill, 1986 (Termination Date:
1992)

Physics: Its Methods and Meanings: Grades 9–12
Prentice Hall, 1986 (Termination Date: 1992)

Marine Science
Marine Biology: Grades 9–12
Prentice Hall, 1988 (Termination Year 1993)

Introduction to Oceanography: Grades 9–12
Prentice Hall, 1988 (Termination Date: 1993)

Geology
Heath Earth Science: Grades 9–12
D. C. Heath, 1981 (Termination Date: 1992)

AGI Investigating the Earth: Grades 9–12
Houghton Mifflin, 1981 (Termination Date: 1992)

Environmental Science
Environmental Science: Grades 9–12
Addison-Wesley, 1989 (Termination Date: 1995)

Environmental Science: How the World Works:
Grades 9–12
Le Bel, 1989 (Termination Date: 1995)

Utah

Note: Utah did not provide list.

Virginia

Biology I
Heath Biology: Grade 10
D. C. Heath, 1989 (Termination Date: 1993)

Biology: An Everyday Experience: Grades 9–12
Glencoe, 1988 (Termination Date: 1993)

Biology: Living Systems: Grades 9–12
Glencoe, 1989 (Termination Date: 1993)

Biology: Grades 9–12
Harcourt Brace Jovanovich, 1989 (Termination
Date: 1993)

Modern Biolgy: Grades 10–12
Holt, Rinehart & Winston/Harcourt Brace
Jovanovich, 1989 (Termination Date: 1993)

Biological Science: An Ecological Approach:
Grades 9–12
Kendall/Hunt, 1987 (Termination Date: 1993)

Prentice Hall Biology, Rev. Ed.: Grade 10
Prentice Hall, 1990 (Termination Date: 1993)

Biology II
Biology: Grades 11–12
Addison-Wesley, 1987 (Termination Date: 1993)

Inquiry into Life: Grades 11–12
William C. Brown, 1991 (Termination Date:
1993)

Biology: Evolution, Diversity and the Environment:
Grades 11–12
William C. Brown, 1987 (Termination Date:
1993)

Biology: A Journey into Life, 3rd Ed.: Grades 10–12
Holt, Rinehart & Winston/Harcourt Brace
Jovanovich, 1988 (Termination Date: 1993)

Understanding Biology: Grades 11–12
Mosby–Year Book, 1988 (Termination Date: 1993)

Chemistry I

Addison-Wesley Chemistry: Grades 10–12
Addison-Wesley, 1987 (Termination Date: 1993)

Chemistry: The Study of Matter: Grade 11
Prentice Hall, 1989 (Termination Date: 1993)

Chemistry: Experimental Foundations: Grade 11
Prentice Hall, 1987 (Termination Date: 1993)

Chemistry II

Chemistry: Advanced: Grade 11
D. C. Heath, 1989 (Termination Date: 1993)

Chemistry: The Central Science: Grade 11
Prentice Hall, 1988 (Termination Date: 1993)

Earth/Space Science

Focus on Earth Science: Grade 9
Glencoe, 1989 (Termination Date: 1993)

Holt Earth Science: Grade 9
Holt, Rinehart & Winston/Harcourt Brace
Jovanovich, 1986 (Termination Date: 1993)

Modern Earth Science: Grade 9
Holt, Rinehart & Winston/Harcourt Brace
Jovanovich, 1988 (Termination Date: 1993)

Investigating the Earth: Grade 9
Houghton Mifflin, 1987 (Termination Date: 1993)

Macmillan Earth Science: Grade 9
Macmillan/McGraw-Hill, 1989 (Termination
Date: 1993)

Silver Burdett & Ginn Earth Science: Grade 9
Silver Burdett & Ginn, 1987 (Termination Date:
1993)

Elementary Science

Addison-Wesley Science: Grades 1–6
Addison-Wesley, 1989 (Termination Date: 1993)

Holt Science: Grades 1–7
Holt, Rinehart & Winston/Harcourt Brace
Jovanovich, 1989 (Termination Date: 1993)

Merrill Science: Grades K–6
Macmillan/McGraw-Hill, 1989 (Termination
Date: 1993)

Discover Science: Grades 1–6
Scott, Foresman, 1989 (Termination Date: 1993)

Silver Burdett & Ginn Science: Grades 1–6
Silver Burdett & Ginn, 1989 (Termination Date:
1993)

Life Science

Focus on Life Sciences: Grade 7
Glencoe, 1989 (Termination Date: 1993)

Holt Life Science: Grade 7
Holt, Rinehart & Winston/Harcourt Brace
Jovanovich, 1986 (Termination Date: 1993)

Macmillan Life Science: Grade 7
Macmillan/McGraw-Hill, 1989 (Termination
Date: 1993)

Prentice Hall Life Science: Grade 7
Prentice Hall, 1988 (Termination Date: 1993)

Silver Burdett & Ginn Life Science: Grade 7
Silver Burdett & Ginn, 1987 (Termination Date:
1993)

Physical Science

Addison-Wesley Physical Science: Grade 8
Addison-Wesley, 1989 (Termination Date: 1993)

Focus on Physical Science: Grade 8
Glencoe, 1989 (Termination Date: 1993)

Physical Science: Grade 8
Harcourt Brace Jovanovich, 1989 (Termination
Date: 1993)

Macmillan Physical Science: Grade 8
Macmillan/McGraw-Hill, 1988 (Termination
Date: 1993)

Prentice Hall Physical Science: Grade 8
Prentice Hall, 1988 (Termination Date: 1993)

Silver Burdett & Ginn Physical Science: Grade 8
Silver Burdett & Ginn, 1988 (Termination Date:
1993)

Physics

Conceptual Physics: Grades 9–12
Addison-Wesley, 1987 (Termination Date: 1993)

PSSC Physics: Grade 12
D. C. Heath, 1986 (Termination Date: 1993)

West Virginia

Science
Science and Technology: Grades K–6
Coronado, 1985/86 ((Termination Date: 1993)

HBJ Science: Grades K–6
Harcourt Brace Jovanovich, 1985 (Termination Date: 1993)

Holt Elementary Science: Grades K–6
Holt, Rinehart & Winston/Harcourt Brace Jovanovich, 1986 (Termination Date: 1993)

Accent on Science: Grades K–6
Merrill, 1985 (Termination Date: 1993)

Scott, Foresman Science: Grades K–6
Scott, Foresman, 1986 (Termination Date: 1993)

Silver Burdett Science: Grades K–6
Silver Burdett & Ginn, 1987 (Termination Date: 1993)

Life Science
Addison-Wesley Life Science: Grades 7–9
Addison-Wesley, 1986 (Termination Date: 1993)

Heath Life Science: Grades 7–9
D. C. Heath, 1987 (Termination Date: 1993)

Concepts and Challenges in Life Science: Grades 7–9
Globe, 1986 (Termination Date: 1993)

Holt Life Science: Grades 7–9
Holt, Rinehart & Winston/Harcourt Brace Jovanovich, 1986 (Termination Date: 1993)

Experiences in Life Science: Grades 7–9
Laidlaw, 1985 (Termination Date: 1993)

Macmillan Life Science: Grades 7–9
Macmillan, 1986 (Termination Date: 1993)

Focus on Life Science: Grades 7–9
Merrill, 1987 (Termination Date: 1993)

Prentice Hall Life Science: Grades 7–9
Prentice Hall, 1986 (Termination Date: 1993)

Scott, Foresman Life Science: Grades 7–9
Scott, Foresman, 1987 (Termination Date: 1993)

Silver Burdett & Ginn Life Science: Grades 7–9
Silver Burdett & Ginn, 1987 (Termination Date: 1993)

Earth Science
Addison-Wesley Earth Science: Grades 7–9
Addison-Wesley, 1987 (Termination Date: 1993)

Earth Science: Grades 7–9
D. C. Heath, 1985 (Termination Date: 1993)

Heath Earth Science: Grades 7–9
D. C. Heath, 1987 (Termination Date: 1993)

Concepts and Challenges in Earth Science: Grades 7–9 Globe, 1986 (Termination Date: 1993)

Globe Earth Science: Grades 7–9
Globe, 1986 (Termination Date: 1993)

Holt Earth Science: Grades 7–9
Holt, Rinehart & Winston/Harcourt Brace Jovanovich, 1986 (Termination Date: 1993)

Modern Earth Science: Grades 7–9
Holt, Rinehart & Winston/Harcourt Brace Jovanovich, 1983 (Termination Date: 1993)

Experiences in Earth-Space Science: Grades 7–9
Laidlaw, 1985 (Termination Date: 1993)

Macmillan Earth Science: Grades 7–9
Macmillan, 1986 (Termination Date: 1993)

Focus on Earth Science: Grades 7–9
Merrill, 1987 (Termination Date: 1993)

Prentice Hall Earth Science: Grades 7–9
Prentice Hall, 1986 (Termination Date: 1993)

Scott, Foresman Earth Science: Grades 7–9
Scott, Foresman, 1986 (Termination Date: 1993)

Silver Burdett Earth Science: Grades 7–9
Silver Burdett & Ginn, 1987 (Termination Date: 1993)

General/Physical Science

Addison-Wesley Physical Science: Grades 7–12
Addison-Wesley, 1984 (Termination Date: 1993)

Allyn & Bacon General Science: Grades 7–12
Allyn & Bacon, 1985 (Termination Date: 1993)

Heath Physical Science: Grades 7–12
D. C. Heath, 1987 (Termination Date: 1993)

Concepts and Challenges in Physical Science:
Grades 7–12
Globe, 1986 (Termination Date: 1993)

Holt Physical Science: Grades 7–12
Holt, Rinehart & Winston/Harcourt Brace
Jovanovich, 1983/1986 (Termination Date: 1993)

Modern Physical Science: Grades 7–12
Holt, Rinehart & Winston/Harcourt Brace
Jovanovich, 1983 (Termination Date: 1993)

Experiences in Physical Science: Grades 7–12
Laidlaw, 1985 (Termination Date: 1993)

Macmillan Physical Science: Grades 7–12
Macmillan, 1986 (Termination Date: 1993)

Focus on Physical Science: Grades 7–12
Merrill, 1987 (Termination Date: 1993)

Merrill General Science: Grades 7–12
Merrill, 1986 (Termination Date: 1993)

Scott, Foresman Physical Science: Grades 1–12
Scott, Foresman, 1986 (Termination Date: 1993)

Biological Science

Addison-Wesley Biology: A System Approach:
Grades 9–12
Addison-Wesley, 1988 (Termination Date: 1993)

Biology: The Study of Life: Grades 9–12
Allyn & Bacon/Prentice Hall, 1983/1987 (Termination Date: 1993)

Heath Biology: Grades 9–12
D. C. Heath, 1985 (Termination Date: 1992)

Biology: Grades 9–12
Harcourt Brace Jovanovich, 1986 (Termination
Date: 1993)

Modern Biology: Grades 9–12
Holt, Rinehart & Winston/Harcourt Brace
Jovanovich, 1985 (Termination Date: 1993)

Living Things: Grades 9–12
Holt, Rinehart & Winston/Harcourt Brace
Jovanovich, 1985 (Termination Date: 1993)

Experiences in Biology: Grades 9–12
Laidlaw, 1985 (Termination Date: 1993)

Basic Biology: Grades 9–12
Media Materials, 1986 (Termination Date: 1993)

Biology: An Everyday Experience: Grades 9–12
Merrill, 1985 (Termination Date: 1993)

Biology: Living Systems: Grades 9–12
Merrill, 1986 (Termination Date: 1993)

Prentice Hall Biology: Grades 9–12
Prentice Hall, 1987 (Termination Date: 1993)

Prentice Hall Biology: Grades 9–12
Prentice Hall, 1986 (Termination Date: 1993)

Silver Burdett Biology: Grades 9–12
Prentice Hall, 1986 (Termination Date: 1993)

Scott, Foresman Biology: Grades 1–12
Scott, Foresman, 1985 (Termination Date: 1993)

Macmillan Biology: Grades 9–12
Scribner, 1985 (Termination Date: 1993)

Chemistry

Addison-Wesley Chemistry: Grades 9–12
Addison-Wesley, 1987 (Termination Date: 1993)

General Organic and Biological Chemistry: Grades
9–12
Addison-Wesley, 1986 (Termination Date: 1993)

Chemistry: The Study of Matter: Grades 9–12
Allyn & Bacon/Prentice Hall, 1987 (Termination
Date: 1993)

Heath Chemistry: Grades 9–12
D. C. Heath, 1987 (Termination Date: 1993)

Modern Chemistry: Grades 9–12
Holt, Rinehart & Winston/Harcourt Brace
Jovanovich, 1986 (Termination Date: 1993)

Chemical Principles: Grades 9–12
Holt, Rinehart & Winston/Harcourt Brace
Jovanovich, 1985 (Termination Date: 1993)

Chemistry: A Modern Course: Grades 9–12
Merrill, 1987 (Termination Date: 1993)

Chemistry: Experimental Foundations: Grades 9–12
Prentice Hall, 1987 (Termination Date: 1993)

Physics
Physics: Its Methods and Meanings: Grades 9–12
Allyn & Bacon/Prentice Hall, 1986 (Termination
Date: 1993)

PSSC Physics: Grades 9–12
D. C. Heath, 1986 (Termination Date: 1993)

Modern Physics: Grades 9–12
Holt, Rinehart & Winston/Harcourt Brace
Jovanovich, 1984 (Termination Date: 1993)

Physics: Principles and Problems: Grades 9–12
Merrill, 1986 (Termination Date: 1993)

INDEX TO REVIEWS
OF EDUCATIONAL MATERIALS

THIS index cites reviews of recently published materials for use in social studies classes, including curriculum guides, lesson plans, project books, software programs, videos, and filmstrips. The citations cover reviews from the past two years (up to March 1992), and they reflect a search of educational journals, magazines, and newsletters that would include reviews of social studies materials. The journals chosen are those that are available in teacher college libraries, in other college and university collections, and in many public libraries. They also include the major publications sent to members of the appropriate educational organizations. The review for each item can be found under the following listings:

- the title of the item
- the author(s)
- the publisher or producer/distributor
- school level (elementary, middle school, or high school)
- subject (a broad subject arrangement is used)
- special medium (for "Software packages" and "Films/videos")

Activities/experiments

Activities for Teaching K–6 Math/Science Concepts, by Walter A. Farmer and Margaret A. Farrell (Bowling Green, OH: School Science and Mathematics, 1989). Reviewed in: *Science and Children* 28, no. 4 (Jan. 1991): 58

Adaptations, software (Galesburg, MI: MCE, n.d.). Reviewed in: *Science and Children* 29, no. 1 (Sept. 1992): 59

Bet You Didn't Know That, by Carol Iverson (Minneapolis: Lerner, 1990). Reviewed in: *Science and Children* 29, no. 6 (Mar. 1992): 55

Chemical Activities, by Christie L. Borgford and Lee R. Summerline (Washington, DC: American Chemical Society, 1988). Reviewed in: *Science Activities* 28, no. 3 (Fall 1991): 44

The Complete Science Fair Handbook, by Issac Asimov and Anthony D. Fredericks (Glenview, IL: Scott Foresman, 1990). Reviewed in: *Science and Children* 28, no. 2 (Oct. 1990): 41

Consider the Earth: Environmental Activities for Grades 4–8, by Julie M. Gates (Englewood, CO: Teacher Ideas Press, 1989). Reviewed in: *Science Activities* 28, no. 1 (Spring 1991): 44

Activities/experiments *(cont'd)*

Cosmic Chemistry, video (Warren, NJ: Optical Data, n.d.). Reviewed in: *Science Books and Films* 28, no. 2 (Mar. 1992): 59

Designasaurus II, software (San Francisco: Britannica Software, 1990). Reviewed in: *Science and Children* 29, no. 1 (Sept. 1991): 59

Developing Science in the Primary Classroom, by Wynne Harlen and Sheila Jelly (Portsmouth, NH: Heinemann Educational Books, 1990). Reviewed in: *Curriculum Review* 30, no. 7 (Mar. 1991): 31

Dinosaur Construction Kit—Tyrannosaurus Rex, software (Acton, MA: D.C. Heath & Co./ William K. Bradford, 1987). Reviewed in: *Teaching with Technology* (Nov./Dec. 1991): 83

Dive into Science: Hands-on Water-Related Experiments, by Peggy K. Perdue (Glenview, IL: Scott Foresman, n.d.). Reviewed in: *Science and Children* 28, no. 7 (Apr. 1991): 54

Dyno-Quest, software (Tucson: Mindplay/ Methods and Solutions, 1984). Reviewed in: *Science and Children* 28, no. 1 (Sept. 1990): 19

Earth Science for Every Kid: 101 Experiments That Really Work, by Janice VanCleave (New York: John Wiley and Sons, 1991). Reviewed in: *Journal of Geography* 91, no. 1 (Jan./Feb. 1992): 46

Earth Science Investigations, by Margaret A. Oosterman and Mark T. Schmidt (Alexandria, VA: American Geology Institute, 1990). Reviewed in: *The Science Teacher* 59, no. 2 (Feb. 1992): 84–85

The Environment, software (Boca Raton, FL: IBM, n.d.). Reviewed in: *Science and Children* 28, no. 6 (Mar. 1991): 47

Eyewitness Juniors, by Alexander Parsons (New York: Knopf, 1990). Reviewed in: *Science and Children* 29, no. 4 (Jan. 1992): 39

Famous Experiments You Can Do, by Robert Gardner (New York: Franklin Watts, 1990). Reviewed in: *The Science Teacher* 59, no. 2, (Feb. 1992): 76

Five Star Forecast, software (St. Paul: MECC, 1990). Reviewed in: *Science and Children* 28, no. 8 (May 1991): 30

Forecasting the Weather, software (Galesburg, MI: MCE, n.d.). Reviewed in: *Science and Children* 29, no. 4 (Jan. 1992): 35

Frog Dissection Lab Report, software (Uniondale, NY: Bergwall Educational Software, 1988). Reviewed in: *Science and Children* 27, no. 8 (May 1990): 38

Genetics and Heredity, software (Freeport, NY: Educational Activities, 1991). Reviewed in: *Science and Children* 29, no. 5 (Feb. 1992): 39

Hothouse Planet, software (Danbury, CT: EME, 1990). Reviewed in: *Science and Children* 28, no. 7 (Apr. 1991): 54

How to Make a Chemical Volcano and Other Mysterious Experiments, by Alan Kramer (New York: Franklin Watts, 1989). Reviewed in: *Curriculum Review* 31, no. 7 (Mar. 1992): 27

Insights into Science Data, software (Pleasantville, NY: Sunburst Communications, n.d.). Reviewed in: *Science and Children* 29, no. 6 (Mar. 1992): 51

Jungle Safari, software (Pound Ridge, NY: Orange Cherry/Talking School House Software, 1990). Reviewed in: *Science and Children* 29, no. 4 (Jan. 1992): 35

Junior Science, by Terry Jennings (Gloucester: n.p., 1990). Reviewed in: *Science and Children* 29, no. 1, (Sept. 1990) 64

Lake Study, software (Ypsilanti, MI: Eastern Michigan Univ., n.d.). Reviewed in: *School Science and Mathematics* 90, no. 8 (Dec. 1990): 741

Life Science Help Series, software (Garden City, NY: Focus Media, n.d.). Reviewed in: *Science and Children* 27, no. 7 (Apr. 1990): 44

Modern Genetics, software (Boca Raton, FL: IBM, n.d.). Reviewed in: *Science and Children* 28, no. 3 (Nov./Dec. 1990): 46

Activities/experiments *(cont'd)*
Murphy's Minerals, software (St. Paul: MECC, 1990). Reviewed in: *Science and Children* 28, no. 4 (Jan. 1991): 41

Oceanography for Landlocked Classrooms, ed. by Gerry M. Madrazo and Paul B. Hounshell (Reston, VA: National Association of Biology Teachers, 1990). Reviewed in: *The Science Teacher* 59, no. 2 (Feb. 1992): 76–77

100 Science Puzzles, by Colin McCarty and Jane Young (London: Unwin Hyman, 1989). Reviewed in: *Physics Education* 25, no. 5 (Sept. 1990): 293

The Oregon Trail, software (Minneapolis: MECC, n.d.). Reviewed in: *Science and Children* 29, no. 6 (Mar. 1992): 49

Paper Plane Pilot, software (Minneapolis: MECC, 1991). Reviewed in: *Science and Children* 29, no. 2 (Oct. 1991): 46

Physical Science Laboratory, software (Garden City, NY: Focus Media, 1990). Reviewed in: *Science and Children* 29, no. 6 (Mar. 1992): 50–51

Physics Explorer: One Body, software (Scotts Valley, CA: Wings for Learning, 1991). Reviewed in: *Technology & Learning* 12, no. 4 (Jan. 1992): 10, 11, 14

Physics 1.2, software (San Rafael, CA: Broderbund Software, n.d.). Reviewed in: *Journal of Geographical Education* 39, no. 1 (Jan. 1991): 71

Playing with Science: Motion, software (Pleasantville, NY: Sunburst Communications, n.d.). Reviewed in: *Science and Children* 28, no. 4 (Jan. 1991): 44–45

Pollution Control, software (Garden City, NY: Focus Media, 1989). Reviewed in: *Science and Children* 28, no. 7 (Apr. 1991): 52

Pollution Patrol, software (Victoria, B.C.: Entrex Software, 1987). Reviewed in: *Pollution Patrol* 27, no. 6 (Mar. 1990): 47

Raintree Science Adventures, by Helen H. Cary and Judith E. Greenberg (Milwaukee, WI:

Raintree, 1990). Reviewed in: *Science and Children* 29, no. 5 (Feb. 1992): 48

School Yard Science, by Peggy Perdue (Glenview IL: Scott Foresman, 1991). Reviewed in: *Curriculum Review* 30, no. 3 (Nov. 1990): 30

Science in Cinema: Teaching Science Fact Through Science Fiction Films, by Judith E. Boss, Leroy W. Dubeck, and Susan Moshier (New York: Teachers College Press, 1988). Reviewed in: *The Science Teacher* 59, no. 2 (Feb. 1992): 78-79

Science Fair Success, by R. Bombaugh (Hillside, NJ: Enslow, 1990). Reviewed in: *American Biology Teacher* 53, no. 3 (Mar. 1991): 192

SimEarth, software (Orinda, CA: Maxis, 1990). Reviewed in: *School Science and Mathematics* 92, no. 1 (Jan. 1992): 47; *Journal of Geography* 91, no. 1 (Jan./Feb. 1992): 47

Simple and Safe Experiments, by William R. Wellnitz (n.p., 1990). Reviewed in: *Science and Children* 29, no. 6 (Mar. 1992): 55

Storm, software, by Thomas Pesek (Houston, TX: Utopia Software, n.d.). Reviewed in: *Journal of Geography* 89, no. 2

Story Starters: Science, software (Farmington, CT: Pelica Software, 1989). Reviewed in: *Science and Children* 29, no. 2 (Oct. 1991): 47–48

Students and Research: Practical Strategies for Science Classrooms and Competitions, by Julia H. Cothron, Ronald H. Giese, and Richard J. Rezba (Dubuque: Kendall/Hunt, 1989). Reviewed in: *The Science Teacher* 59, no. 2 (Jan. 1992): 78–79

Time Table History, software (Los Angeles: Xiphias, 1987). Reviewed in: *Science and Children* 29, no. 2 (Oct. 1992): 47

Unique Science: Demonstrations and Laboratories for the Physics Instructor, by E. M. Kinsman and C. Waters (Syracuse: Kinsman Physics, 1991). Reviewed in: *Science Books and Films* 28, no. 1 (Jan./Feb. 1992): 15

Activities/experiments *(cont'd)*
The Water Cycle, software (Galesburg, MI: MCE, n.d.). Reviewed in: *Science and Children* 29, no. 4 (Jan. 1992): 35

Weather Academy, software (Garden City, NY: Focus Media, 1989). Reviewed in: *Science and Children* 28, no. 6 (Mar. 1991): 46

Weather in Action, software (Washington, DC: National Geographic Society, 1988). Reviewed in: *Science and Children* 28, no. 8 (May 1991): 29–30

The Weather Machine, software (Washington DC: National Geographic Society, 1988). Reviewed in: *School Science and Mathematics* 90, no. 4 (Apr. 1990): 346

Woolly Bounce, software (Minneapolis: MECC, 1991). Reviewed in: *Science and Children* 29, no. 4 (Jan. 1992): 34, *Technology & Learning* 12, no. 4 (Jan. 1992): 8-9

Activities for Teaching K–6 Math/Science Concepts by Walter A. Farmer and Margaret A. Farrell (Bowling Green, OH: School Science and Mathematics, 1989). Reviewed in: *Science and Children* 28, no. 4 (Jan. 1991): 58

Adaptations
software (Galesburg, MI: MCE, n.d.). Reviewed in: *Science and Children* 29, no. 1 (Sept. 1992): 59

Addison-Wesley Publishing
Animals in the Classroom, by David C. Kramer (Menlo Park, CA: Addison-Wesley Publishing, 1989). Reviewed in: *School Science and Mathematics* 90, no. 3 (Mar. 1990): 261

The Age of Dinosaurs
filmstrip (Washington, DC: National Geographic Society, 1990). Reviewed in: *American Biology Teacher* 53, no. 3 (Mar. 1991): 189

AIMS Media Film and Video
The Animal Life Series, film/video (Van Nuys, CA: AIMS Media Film and Video, 1991). Reviewed in: *Media and Methods* 28, no. 1 (Sept./Oct. 1991): 46

Aladdin (publishers)
Animals in Danger, by William McCay (New York: Aladdin, 1990). Reviewed in: *Science and Children* 29, no. 4 (Jan. 1992): 39

Albert Whitman (publishers)
Pet Gerbils, by Jerome Wexler (Morton Grove, IL: Albert Whitman, 1990). Reviewed in: *Science and Children* 29, no. 6 (Mar. 1992): 55

Alfred A. Knopf (publishers)
Eyewitness Juniors, by Alexander Parsons (New York: Knopf, 1990). Reviewed in: *Science and Children* 29, no. 4 (Jan. 1992): 39

American Chemical Society
Chemical Activities, by Christie L. Borgford and Lee R. Summerline (Washington, DC: American Chemical Society, 1988). Reviewed in: *Science Activities* 28, no. 3 (Fall 1991): 44

American Geology Institute
Earth Science Investigations, by Margaret A. Oosterman and Mark T. Schmidt (Alexandria, VA: American Geology Institute, 1990). Reviewed in: *The Science Teacher* 59, no. 2 (Feb. 1992): 84–85

Anatomy
The Brain and Nervous System, software (Mahwah, NJ: Troll Associates, 1991). Reviewed in: *Science and Children* 29, no. 4 (Jan. 1992): 34-35

Dissection and Anatomy of the Brain, video (Omaha: Nebraska Scientific, 1989). Reviewed in: *American Biology Teacher* 52, no. 4 (Apr. 1990): 309

The Skeletal and Muscular System, software (Mahwah, NJ: Troll Associates, 1991). Reviewed in: *Science and Children* 28, no. 1 (Sept. 1990): 50

Why Do Bodies Stop Growing?, by Philip Whitfield and Ruth Whitfield (New York: Viking Penguin, 1988). Reviewed in: *School Science and Mathematics* 90, no. 7 (Nov. 1988): 656

Animal dissection
Frog Dissection Lab Report, software (Uniondale, NY: Bergwall Educational Software, 1988). Reviewed in: *Science and Children* 27, no. 8 (May 1990): 38

The Animal Life Series
film/video (Van Nuys, CA: AIMS Media Film and Video, 1991). Reviewed in: *Media and Methods* 28, no. 1 (Sept./Oct. 1991): 46

Animals and Their World
by Judith E. Rinard, Gene S. Stuart, and Jennifer C. Urquhart (Washington, DC: National Geographic Society, 1990). Reviewed in: *Science and Children* 29, no. 5 (Feb. 1992): 48

Animals in Danger
by William McCay (New York: Aladdin, 1990). Reviewed in: *Science and Children* 29, no. 4 (Jan. 1992): 39

Animals in the Classroom
by David C. Kramer (Menlo Park, CA: Addison-Wesley Publishing, 1989). Reviewed in: *School Science and Mathematics* 90, no. 3 (Mar. 1990): 261

Antarctica
by Helen Cowcher (New York: Farrar, Straus & Giroux, 1990). Reviewed in: *Science and Children* 29, no. 4 (Jan. 1992): 39

Aquatic studies
Clearwater Detectives, software (Minneapolis: MECC, 1991). Reviewed in: *Science and Children* 29, no. 5 (Feb. 1992): 36–38

Dive into Science: Hands-on Water-Related Experiments, by Peggy K. Perdue (Glenview, IL: Scott Foresman, n.d.). Reviewed in: *Science and Children* 28, no. 7 (Apr. 1991): 54

Lake Study, software (Ypsilanti, MI: Eastern Michigan Univ., n.d.). Reviewed in: *School Science and Mathematics* 90, no. 8 (Dec. 1990): 741

The Water Cycle, software (Galesburg, MI: MCE, n.d.). Reviewed in: *Science and Children* 29, no. 4 (Jan. 1992): 35

The Art of Science Writing
by Bernadette Mayer and Dale Worsley (New York: Teachers and Writers Collaborative, 1989). Reviewed in: *American Biology Teacher* 52, no. 3 (Mar. 1990): 192

Asimov, Issac
The Complete Science Fair Handbook, by Issac Asimov and Anthony D. Fredericks (Glenview, IL: Scott Foresman, 1990). Reviewed in: *Science and Children* 28, no. 2 (Oct. 1990): 41

Astronomy
Sun and Seasons, software (St. Paul: MECC, 1990). Reviewed in: *Science and Children* 28, no. 7 (Apr. 1991): 52

Aviation
Paper Plane Pilot, software (Minneapolis: MECC, 1991). Reviewed in: *Science and Children* 29, no. 2 (Oct. 1991): 46

Aziz, Laurel
Exploring the World of Birds: An Equinox Guide to Avian Life, by Laurel Aziz and Adrian Forsyth (Charlotte, VT: Camden House, 1990). Reviewed in: *Science and Children* 29, no. 5 (Feb. 1992): 48

Barrett, Norman
Picture Library Series, by Norman Barrett (New York: Franklin Watts, 1989). Reviewed in: *Science and Children* 28, no. 1 (Sept. 1990): 79

Benchmark Films
Enzymes, video (Franklin Lakes, NJ: Benchmark Films, 1990). Reviewed in: *Science Books and Films* 28, no. 2 (Mar. 1992): 57

Bergwall Educational Software
Frog Dissection Lab Report, software (Uniondale, NY: Bergwall Educational Software, 1988). Reviewed in: *Science and Children* 27, no. 8 (May 1990): 38

Bet You Didn't Know That
by Carol Iverson (Minneapolis: Lerner, 1990). Reviewed in: *Science and Children* 29, no. 6 (Mar. 1992): 55

Biology
The Animal Life Series, film/video (Van Nuys, CA: AIMS Media Film and Video, 1991). Reviewed in: *Media and Methods* 28, no. 1 (Sept./Oct. 1991): 46

Biology *(cont'd)*

Animals and Their World, by Judith E. Rinard, Gene S. Stuart, and Jennifer C. Urquhart (Washington, DC: National Geographic Society, 1990). Reviewed in: *Science and Children* 29, no. 5 (Feb. 1992): 48

Animals in the Classroom, by David C. Kramer (Menlo Park, CA: Addison-Wesley Publishing, 1989). Reviewed in: *School Science and Mathematics* 90, no. 3 (Mar. 1990): 261

The Biology of Water, video (Niles, IL: United Learning, 1991). Reviewed in: *Media and Methods* 28, no. 1 (Sept./Oct. 1991): 46

The Brain and Nervous System, software (Mahwah, NJ: Troll Associates, 1991). Reviewed in: *Science and Children* 29, no. 4 (Jan. 1992): 34-35

Dissection and Anatomy of the Brain, video (Omaha: Nebraska Scientific, 1989). Reviewed in: *American Biology Teacher* 52, no. 4 (Apr. 1990): 309

Enzymes, video (Franklin Lakes, NJ: Benchmark Films, 1990). Reviewed in: *Science Books and Films* 28, no. 2 (Mar. 1992): 57

Evolutionary Biology, 2d ed. by Douglas J. Futuyma (Sunderland, MA: Sinauer Associates, 1986). Reviewed in: *American Biology Teacher* 52, no. 4 (Apr. 1990): 318

Frog Dissection Lab Report, software (Uniondale, NY: Bergwall Educational Software, 1988). Reviewed in: *Science and Children* 27, no. 8 (May 1990): 38

Genetics and Heredity, software (Freeport, NY: Educational Activities, 1991). Reviewed in: *Science and Children* 29, no. 5 (Feb. 1992): 39

The Immune System, software (Shawnee Mission, KS: Marshmedia, n.d.). Reviewed in: *Science and Children* 28, no. 8 (May 1991): 30

Immunity, film (New Hyde Park, NY: National Teaching Aids, 1989). Reviewed in: *American Biology Teacher* 52, no. 7 (Oct. 1989): 444

Life Cycles, software (Galesburg, MI: MCE, n.d.). Reviewed in: *Science and Children* 29, no. 1 (Sept. 1991): 58–59

Life Science, software (Ramsey, NJ: K–12 Micromedia, 1991). Reviewed in: *Methods and Media* 28 no. 4 (Mar./Apr. 1992): 60

Life Science Help Series, software (Garden City, NY: Focus Media, n.d.). Reviewed in: *Science and Children* 27, no. 7 (Apr. 1990): 44

Protozoa, software (Newbury Park, CA: Ventura Educational Systems, 1989). Reviewed in: *Science and Children,* 29, no. 5 (Feb. 1992): 36

Who Lives Here?, video (Washington, DC: National Geographic Society, 1990). Reviewed in: *American Biology Teacher* 52, no. 7 (Oct. 1990): 443

Why Do Bodies Stop Growing?, by Philip Whitfield and Ruth Whitfield (New York: Viking Penguin, 1988). Reviewed in: *School Science and Mathematics* 90, no. 7 (Nov. 1988): 656

Wild Wings, by Phyllis Emert (n.p.: Julian Messner, 1990). Reviewed in: *Science and Children* 29, no. 5 (Feb. 1992): 48

The World's Harvest Series, by Jaqueline Dineen (Hillsdale, NJ: Enslow, 1988). Reviewed in: *American Biology Teacher* 52, no. 4 (Apr. 1990): 317

The Biology of Water
video (Niles, IL: United Learning, 1991). Reviewed in: *Media and Methods* 28, no. 1 (Sept./Oct. 1991): 46

Birds
Exploring the World of Birds: An Equinox Guide to Avian Life, by Laurel Aziz and Adrian Forsyth (Charlotte, VT: Camden House, 1990). Reviewed in: *Science and Children* 29, no. 5 (Feb. 1992): 48

Bombaugh, R.
Science Fair Success, by R. Bombaugh (Hillside, NJ: Enslow, 1990). Reviewed in: *American Biology Teacher* 53, no. 3 (Mar. 1991): 192

Bookright (publishers)
Wildlife at Risk, by Malcom Penny (n.p.: Bookright, 1990). Reviewed in: *Science and Children* 29, no. 4 (Jan. 1992): 39

Books for Young Explorers—Set XVI
by National Geographic Society (Washington, DC: National Geographic Society, 1989). Reviewed in: *American Biology Teacher* 53, no. 5 (May 1991): 314–315

Borgford, Christie L.
Chemical Activities, by Christie L. Borgford and Lee R. Summerline (Washington, DC: American Chemical Society, 1988). Reviewed in: *Science Activities* 28, no. 3 (Fall 1991): 44

Boss, Judith E.
Science in Cinema: Teaching Science Fact Through Science Fiction Films, by Judith E. Boss, Leroy W. Dubeck, and Susan Moshier (New York: Teachers College Press, 1988). Reviewed in: *The Science Teacher* 59, no. 2 (Feb. 1992): 78-79

Botany
Life's Devices: The Physical World of Plants and Animals, by Steven Vogel (Princeton: Princeton University Press, 1989). Reviewed in: *American Biology Teacher* 52, no. 6 (Sept. 1990): 388

More Than Just a Garden, by Dwight Kuhn (Englewood Cliffs, NJ: Silver Burdett, 1990). Reviewed in: *Science and Children* 29, no. 2 (Oct. 1991): 53

The Brain and Nervous System
software (Mahwah, NJ: Troll Associates, 1991). Reviewed in: *Science and Children* 29, no. 4 (Jan. 1992): 34-35

Britannica Software
Designasaurus II, software (San Francisco: Britannica Software, 1990). Reviewed in: *Science and Children* 29, no. 1 (Sept. 1991): 59

Broderbund Software
Physics 1.2, software (San Rafael, CA: Broderbund Software, n.d.). Reviewed in: *Journal of Geographical Education* 39, no. 1 (Jan. 1991): 71

Camden House
Exploring the World of Birds: An Equinox Guide to Avian Life, by Laurel Aziz and Adrian Forsyth (Charlotte, VT: Camden House, 1990). Reviewed in: *Science and Children* 29, no. 5 (Feb. 1992): 48

Carey, Helen H.
Raintree Science Adventures, by Helen H. Cary and Judith E. Greenberg (Milwaukee, WI: Raintree, 1990). Reviewed in: *Science and Children* 29, no. 5 (Feb. 1992): 48

Chemaid
software (Newbury Park, CA: Ventura Educational Systems, 1990). Reviewed in: *Science and Children* 29, no. 5 (Feb. 1992): 36; *Journal of Chemical Education* 68, no. 4 (Apr. 1991): 157

Chemical Activities
by Christie L. Borgford and Lee R. Summerline (Washington, DC: American Chemical Society, 1988). Reviewed in: *Science Activities* 28, no. 3 (Fall 1991): 44

Chemistry
Chemaid, software (Newbury Park, CA: Ventura Educational Systems, 1990). Reviewed in: *Science and Children* 29, no. 5 (Feb. 1992): 36; *Journal of Chemical Education* 68, no. 4 (Apr. 1991): 157

Chemical Activities, by Christie L. Borgford and Lee R. Summerline (Washington, DC: American Chemical Society, 1988). Reviewed in: *Science Activities* 28, no. 3 (Fall 1991): 44

Chemistry at Work, video (Seattle: Videodiscovery, 1991). Reviewed in: *Science Books and Films* 28, no. 2 (Mar. 1992): 59

Cosmic Chemistry, video (Warren, NJ: Optical Data; n.d.). Reviewed in: *Science Books and Films* 28, no. 2 (Mar. 1992): 59

Chemistry at Work
video (Seattle: Videodiscovery, 1991). Reviewed in: *Science Books and Films* 28, no. 2 (Mar. 1992): 59

The Children's Television Workshop
3–2–1 Contact: Wild Things, software by The Children's Television Workshop (Scott's Valley, CA: Wings for Learning, 1991). Reviewed in: *Teaching with Technology* (Feb. 1992): 59

Clearwater Detectives
software (Minneapolis: MECC, 1991). Reviewed in: *Science and Children* 29, no. 5 (Feb. 1992): 36–38

Clip Art for Science Teachers
software (Newbury Park, CA: Ventura Education Systems, 1991). Reviewed in: *Science and Children* 29, no. 4 (Jan. 1992): 34

The Complete Science Fair Handbook
by Issac Asimov and Anthony D. Fredericks (Glenview, IL: Scott Foresman, 1990). Reviewed in: *Science and Children* 28, no. 2 (Oct. 1990): 41

Consider the Earth: Environmental Activities for Grades 4–8
by Julie M. Gates (Englewood, CO: Teacher Ideas Press, 1989). Reviewed in: *Science Activities* 28, no. 1 (Spring 1991): 44

Cosmic Chemistry
video (Warren, NJ: Optical Data, n.d.). Reviewed in: *Science Books and Films* 28, no. 2 (Mar. 1992): 59

Cothron, Julia H.
Students and Research: Practical Strategies for Science Classrooms and Competitions, by Julia H. Cothron, Ronald H. Giese, and Richard J. Rezba (Dubuque: Kendall/Hunt, 1989). Reviewed in: *The Science Teacher* 59, no. 2 (Jan. 1992): 78–79

Cowcher, Helen
Antarctica, by Helen Cowcher (New York: Farrar Straus & Giroux, 1990). Reviewed in: *Science and Children* 29, no. 4 (Jan. 1992): 39

Crown (publishers)
Dragons in the Trees, by James Martin (New York: Crown, 1991). Reviewed in: *Science and Children* 29, no. 6 (Mar. 1992): 55

D.C. Heath & Co./William K. Bradford
Dinosaur Construction Kit—Tyrannosaurus Rex, software (Acton, MA: D.C. Heath & Co./ William K. Bradford, 1987). Reviewed in: *Teaching with Technology* (Nov./Dec. 1991): 83

Data gathering
Insights into Science Data, softw[are] (Pleasantville, NY: Sunburst C[...] n.d.). Reviewed in: *Science an[d ...]* 6 (Mar. 1992): 51

Designasaurus II
software (San Francisco: Brit[annica,] 1990). Reviewed in: *Science a[nd Children 29,]* no. 1 (Sept. 1991): 59

Developing Science in the Prima[ry ...]
by Wynne Harlen and Sheila [...] mouth, NH: Heinemann Ed[ucational,] 1990). Reviewed in: *Curricul[um ...]* 7 (Mar. 1991): 31

Dineen, Jaqueline
The World's Harvest Series, [by Jacqueline] Dineen (Hillsdale, NJ: Enslow, 1988). Reviewed in: *American Biology Teacher* 52, no. 4 (Apr. 1990): 317

Dinosaur Construction Kit—Tyrannosaurus Rex
software (Acton, MA: D.C. Heath & Co./ William K. Bradford, 1987). Reviewed in: *Teaching with Technology* (Nov./Dec. 1991): 83

Dinosaurs
The Age of Dinosaurs, filmstrip (Washington, DC: National Geographic Society, 1990). Reviewed in: *American Biology Teacher* 53, no. 3 (Mar. 1991): 189

Designasaurus II, software (San Francisco: Britannica Software, 1990). Reviewed in: *Science and Children* 29, no. 1 (Sept. 1991): 59

Dinosaur Construction Kit—Tyrannosaurus Rex, software (Acton, MA: D.C. Heath & Co./ William K. Bradford, 1987). Reviewed in: *Teaching with Technology* (Nov./Dec. 1991): 83

Dyno-Quest, software (Tucson: Mindplay/ Methods and Solutions, 1984). Reviewed in: *Science and Children* 28, no. 1 (Sept. 1990): 19

Dissection
  Dissection and Anatomy of the Brain, video
  (Omaha: Nebraska Scientific, 1989). Reviewed
  in: *American Biology Teacher* 52, no. 4 (Apr.
  1990): 309

  Frog Dissection Lab Report, software
  (Uniondale, NY: Bergwall Educational Software, 1988). Reviewed in: *Science and Children*
  27, no. 8 (May 1990): 38

Dissection and Anatomy of the Brain
  video (Omaha: Nebraska Scientific, 1989).
  Reviewed in: *American Biology Teacher* 52, no.
  4 (Apr. 1990): 309

Dive into Science: Hands-on Water-Related
Experiments
  by Peggy K. Perdue (Glenview, IL: Scott
  Foresman, n.d.). Reviewed in: *Science and
  Children* 28, no. 7 (Apr. 1991): 54

Dragons in the Trees
  by James Martin (New York: Crown, 1991).
  Reviewed in: *Science and Children* 29, no. 6
  (Mar. 1992): 55

Dubeck, Leroy W.
  *Science in Cinema: Teaching Science Fact
  Through Science Fiction Films,* by Judith E.
  Boss, Leroy W. Dubeck, and Susan Moshier
  (New York: Teachers College Press, 1988).
  Reviewed in: *The Science Teacher* 59, no. 2
  (Feb. 1992): 78-79

Dyno-Quest
  software (Tucson: Mindplay/Methods and
  Solutions, 1984). Reviewed in: *Science and
  Children* 28, no. 1 (Sept. 1990): 19

Eames, Charles and Charles
  Powers of Ten, by Charles Eames and Ray
  Eames, video (San Francisco: Pyramid Video,
  1989). Reviewed in: *The Science Teacher* 59, no.
  1 (Jan. 1992): 87–89

Earth science
  Antarctica, by Helen Cowcher (New York:
  Farrar Straus & Giroux, 1990). Reviewed in:
  Science and Children 29, no. 4 (Jan. 1992): 39

  The Biology of Water, video (Niles, IL: United
  Learning, 1991). Reviewed in: *Media and
  Methods* 28, no. 1 (Sept./Oct. 1991): 46

Clearwater Detectives, software (Minneapolis:
MECC, 1991). Reviewed in: *Science and
Children* 29, no. 5 (Feb. 1992): 36–38

*Consider the Earth: Environmental Activities for
Grades 4–8,* by Julie M. Gates (Englewood, CO:
Teacher Ideas Press, 1989). Reviewed in:
Science Activities 28, no. 1 (Spring 1991): 44

*Dive into Science: Hands-on Water-Related
Experiments,* by Peggy K. Perdue (Glenview,
IL: Scott Foresman, n.d.). Reviewed in: *Science
and Children* 28, no. 7 (Apr. 1991): 54

Earth Science, software (Warren, NJ: Optical
Data, n.d.). Reviewed in: *Science and Children*
28, no. 3 (Nov./Dec. 1990): 45

*Earth Science for Every Kid: 101 Experiments
That Really Work,* by Janice VanCleave (New
York: John Wiley and Sons, 1991). Reviewed
in: *Journal of Geography* 91, no. 1 (Jan./Feb.
1992): 46

Earth Science Investigations, by Margaret A.
Oosterman and Mark T. Schmidt (Alexandria,
VA: American Geology Institute, 1990).
Reviewed in: *The Science Teacher* 59, no. 2
(Feb. 1992): 84–85

The Environment, software (Boca Raton, FL:
IBM, n.d.). Reviewed in: *Science and Children*
28, no. 6 (Mar. 1991): 47

Five Star Forecast, software (St. Paul: MECC,
1990). Reviewed in: *Science and Children* 28,
no. 8 (May 1991): 30

Forecasting the Weather, software (Galesburg,
MI: MCE, n.d.). Reviewed in: *Science and
Children* 29, no. 4 (Jan. 1992): 35

Hothouse Planet, software (Danbury, CT:
EME, 1990). Reviewed in: *Science and Children* 28, no. 7 (Apr. 1991): 54

*How to Make a Chemical Volcano and Other
Mysterious Experiments,* by Alan Kramer (New
York: Franklin Watts, 1989). Reviewed in:
Curriculum Review 31, no. 7 (Mar. 1992): 27

Earth science *(cont'd)*
Lake Study, software (Ypsilanti, MI: Eastern Michigan Univ., n.d.). Reviewed in: *School Science and Mathematics* 90, no. 8 (Dec. 1990): 741

More Than Just a Garden, by Dwight Kuhn (Englewood Cliffs, NJ: Silver Burdett, 1990). Reviewed in: *Science and Children* 29, no. 2 (Oct. 1991): 53

Murphy's Minerals, software (St. Paul: MECC, 1990). Reviewed in: *Science and Children* 28, no. 4 (Jan. 1991): 41

An Ocean of Air, software (Galesburg, MI: MCE, n.d.). Reviewed in: *Science and Children* 29, no. 2 (Oct. 1991): 47

Oceanography for Landlocked Classrooms, ed. by Gerry M. Madrazo and Paul B. Hounshell (Reston, VA: National Association of Biology Teachers, 1990). Reviewed in: *The Science Teacher* 59, no. 2 (Feb. 1992): 76–77

The Oregon Trail, software (Minneapolis: MECC, n.d.). Reviewed in: *Science and Children* 29, no. 6 (Mar. 1992): 49

SimEarth, software (Orinda, CA: Maxis, 1990). Reviewed in: *School Science and Mathematics* 92, no. 1 (Jan. 1992): 47; *Journal of Geography* 91, no. 1 (Jan./Feb. 1992): 47

Sun and Seasons, software (St. Paul: MECC, 1990). Reviewed in: *Science and Children* 28, no. 7 (Apr. 1991): 52

Volcano, by Christopher Lampton (Brookfield, CT: Millbrook Press, 1991). Reviewed in: *Science Books and Films* 28, no. 1 (Jan./Feb. 1992): 15–16

The Water Cycle, software (Galesburg, MI: MCE, n.d.). Reviewed in: *Science and Children* 29, no. 4 (Jan. 1992): 35

Weather Academy, software (Garden City, NY: Focus Media, 1989). Reviewed in: *Science and Children* 28, no. 6 (Mar. 1991): 46

Weather in Action, software (Washington, DC: National Geographic Society, 1988). Reviewed in: *Science and Children* 28, no. 8 (May 1991): 29–30

The Weather Machine, software (Washington DC: National Geographic Society, 1988). Reviewed in: *School Science and Mathematics* 90, no. 4 (Apr. 1990): 346

Earth Science
software (Warren, NJ: Optical Data, n.d.). Reviewed in: *Science and Children* 28, no. 3 (Nov./Dec. 1990): 45

Earth Science for Every Kid: 101 Experiments That Really Work
by Janice VanCleave (New York: John Wiley and Sons, 1991). Reviewed in: *Journal of Geography* 91, no. 1 (Jan./Feb. 1992): 46

Earth Science Investigations
by Margaret A. Oosterman and Mark T. Schmidt (Alexandria, VA: American Geology Institute, 1990). Reviewed in: *The Science Teacher* 59, no. 2 (Feb. 1992): 84–85

Eastern Michigan University (publishers)
Lake Study, software (Ypsilanti, MI: Eastern Michigan University, n.d.). Reviewed in: *School Science and Mathematics* 90, no. 8 (Dec. 1990): 741

Educational Activities
Genetics and Heredity, software (Freeport, NY: Educational Activities, 1991). Reviewed in: *Science and Children* 29, no. 5 (Feb. 1992): 39

Elementary materials
Activities for Teaching K–6 Math/Science Concepts, by Walter A. Farmer and Margaret A. Farrell (Bowling Green, OH: School Science and Mathematics, 1989). Reviewed in: *Science and Children* 28, no. 4 (Jan. 1991): 58

Adaptations, software (Galesburg, MI: MCE, n.d.). Reviewed in: *Science and Children* 29, no. 1 (Sept. 1992): 59

The Age of Dinosaurs, filmstrip (Washington, DC: National Geographic Society, 1990). Reviewed in: *American Biology Teacher* 53, no. 3 (Mar. 1991): 189

Elementary materials *(cont'd)*

The Animal Life Series, film/video (Van Nuys, CA: AIMS Media Film and Video, 1991). Reviewed in: *Media and Methods* 28, no. 1 (Sept./Oct. 1991): 46

Animals and Their World, by Judith E. Rinard, Gene S. Stuart, and Jennifer C. Urquhart (Washington, DC: National Geographic Society, 1990). Reviewed in: *Science and Children* 29, no. 5 (Feb. 1992): 48

Animals in the Classroom, by David C. Kramer (Menlo Park, CA: Addison-Wesley Publishing, 1989). Reviewed in: *School Science and Mathematics* 90, no. 3 (Mar. 1990): 261

Animals in Danger, by William McCay (New York: Aladdin, 1990). Reviewed in: *Science and Children* 29, no. 4 (Jan. 1992): 39

Antarctica, by Helen Cowcher (New York: Farrar Straus & Giroux, 1990). Reviewed in: *Science and Children* 29, no. 4 (Jan. 1992): 39

Bet You Didn't Know That, by Carol Iverson (Minneapolis: Lerner, 1990). Reviewed in: *Science and Children* 29, no. 6 (Mar. 1992): 55

The Biology of Water, video (Niles, IL: United Learning, 1991). Reviewed in: *Media and Methods* 28, no. 1 (Sept./Oct. 1991): 46

Books for Young Explorers—Set XVI, by National Geographic Society (Washington, DC: National Geographic Society, 1989). Reviewed in: *American Biology Teacher* 53, no. 5 (May 1991): 314–315

The Brain and Nervous System, software (Mahwah, NJ: Troll Associates, 1991). Reviewed in: *Science and Children* 29, no. 4 (Jan. 1992): 34-35

Clearwater Detectives, software (Minneapolis: MECC, 1991). Reviewed in: *Science and Children* 29, no. 5 (Feb. 1992): 36–38

Clip Art for Science Teachers, software (Newbury Park, CA: Ventura Education Systems, 1991). Reviewed in: *Science and Children* 29, no. 4 (Jan. 1992): 34

The Complete Science Fair Handbook, by Issac Asimov and Anthony D. Fredericks (Glenview, IL: Scott Foresman, 1990). Reviewed in: *Science and Children* 28, no. 2 (Oct. 1990): 41

Consider the Earth: Environmental Activities for Grades 4–8, by Julie M. Gates (Englewood, CO: Teacher Ideas Press, 1989). Reviewed in: *Science Activities* 28, no. 1 (Spring 1991): 44

Designasaurus II, software (San Francisco: Britannica Software, 1990). Reviewed in: *Science and Children* 29, no. 1 (Sept. 1991): 59

Developing Science in the Primary Classroom, by Wynne Harlen and Sheila Jelly (Portsmouth, NH: Heinemann Educational Books, 1990). Reviewed in: *Curriculum Review* 30, no. 7 (Mar. 1991): 31

Dinosaur Construction Kit—Tyrannosaurus Rex, software (Acton, MA: D.C. Heath & Co./ William K. Bradford, 1987). Reviewed in: *Teaching with Technology* (Nov./Dec. 1991): 83

Dive into Science: Hands-on Water-Related Experiments, by Peggy K. Perdue (Glenview, IL: Scott Foresman, n.d.). Reviewed in: *Science and Children* 28, no. 7 (Apr. 1991): 54

Dragons in the Trees, by James Martin (New York: Crown, 1991). Reviewed in: *Science and Children* 29, no. 6 (Mar. 1992): 55

Dyno-Quest, software (Tucson: Mindplay/ Methods and Solutions, 1984). Reviewed in: *Science and Children* 28, no. 1 (Sept. 1990): 19

Earth Science, software (Warren, NJ: Optical Data, n.d.). Reviewed in: *Science and Children* 28, no. 3 (Nov./Dec. 1990): 45

Earth Science for Every Kid: 101 Experiments That Really Work, by Janice VanCleave (New York: John Wiley and Sons, 1991). Reviewed in: *Journal of Geography* 91, no. 1 (Jan./Feb. 1992): 46

Eyewitness Juniors, by Alexander Parsons (New York: Knopf, 1990). Reviewed in: *Science and Children* 29, no. 4 (Jan. 1992): 39

Elementary materials *(cont'd)*

Five Star Forecast, software (St. Paul: MECC, 1990). Reviewed in: *Science and Children* 28, no. 8 (May 1991): 30

Food Chains, software (Galesburg, MI: MCE, n.d.). Reviewed in: *Science and Children* 29, no. 2 (Oct. 1991): 46

Genetics and Heredity, software (Freeport, NY: Educational Activities, 1991). Reviewed in: *Science and Children* 29, no. l5 (Feb. 1992): 39

How to Make a Chemical Volcano and Other Mysterious Experiments, by Alan Kramer (New York: Franklin Watts, 1989). Reviewed in:

1991): 30

Life Cycles, software (Galesburg, MI: MCE, n.d.). Reviewed in: *Science and Children* 29, no. 1 (Sept. 1991): 58–59

More Than Just a Garden, by Dwight Kuhn (Englewood Cliffs, NJ: Silver Burdett, 1990). Reviewed in: *Science and Children* 29, no. 2 (Oct. 1991): 53

An Ocean of Air, software (Galesburg, MI: MCE, n.d.). Reviewed in: *Science and Children* 29, no. 2 (Oct. 1991): 47

Paper Plane Pilot, software (Minneapolis: MECC, 1991). Reviewed in: *Science and Children* 29, no. 2 (Oct. 1991): 46

Pet Gerbils, by Jerome Wexler (Morton Grove, IL: Albert Whitman, 1990). Reviewed in: *Science and Children* 29, no. 6 (Mar. 1992): 55

Picture Library Series, by Norman Barrett (New York: Franklin Watts, 1989). Reviewed in: *Science and Children* 28, no. 1 (Sept. 1990): 79

Playing with Science: Motion, software (Pleasantville, NY: Sunburst Communications, n.d.). Reviewed in: *Science and Children* 28, no. 4 (Jan. 1991): 44–45

Project Zoo, software (Washington DC: National Geographic Society, 1987). Reviewed in: *School Science and Mathematics* l90, no. 6 (Nov. 1990): 652

Raintree Science Adventures, by Helen H. Cary and Judith E. Greenberg (Milwaukee, WI: Raintree, 1990). Reviewed in: *Science and Children* 29, no. 5 (Feb. 1992): 48

Random House Encyclopedia, software (Pittsford, NY: Microlytics, 1990). Reviewed in: *Science and Children* 29, no. 6 (Mar. 1992): 49–50

Ready Set Go: How Animals Move, filmstrip (Washington, DC: National Geographic Society, 1989). Reviewed in: *American Biology Teacher* 52, no. 8 (Nov./Dec. 1990): 514

Safe Science Teaching, software (Des Moines: Jakel, n.d.). Reviewed in: *Science and Children* 29, no. 1 (Sept. 1991): 58

School Yard Science, by Peggy Perdue (Glenview IL: Scott Foresman, 1991). Reviewed in: *Curriculum Review* 30, no. 3 (Nov. 1990): 30

The Secret Codes of C.Y.P.H.E.R., software (San Leandro, CA: Tanager Software, 1991). Reviewed in: *Technology & Learning* 12, no. 6 (Mar. 1992): 7

Simple and Safe Experiments, by William R. Wellnitz (n.p., 1990). Reviewed in: *Science and Children* 29, no. 6 (Mar. 1992): 55

Elementary materials *(cont'd)*

The Skeletal and Muscular System, software (Mahwah, NJ: Troll Associates, 1991). Reviewed in: *Science and Children* 28, no. 1 (Sept. 1990): 50

Story Starters: Science, software (Farmington, CT: Pelica Software, 1989). Reviewed in: *Science and Children* 29, no. 2 (Oct. 1991): 47–48

Sun and Seasons, software (St. Paul: MECC, 1990). Reviewed in: *Science and Children* 28, no. 7 (Apr. 1991): 52

3–2–1 Contact: Wild Things, software by The Children's Television Workshop (Scott's Valley, CA: Wings for Learning, 1991). Reviewed in: *Teaching with Technology* (Feb. 1992): 59

Volcano, by Christopher Lampton (Brookfield, CT: Millbrook Press, 1991). Reviewed in: *Science Books and Films* 28, no. 1 (Jan./Feb. 1992): 15–16

The Water Cycle, software (Galesburg, MI: MCE, n.d.). Reviewed in: *Science and Children* 29, no. 4 (Jan. 1992): 35

Weather in Action, software (Washington, DC: National Geographic Society, 1988). Reviewed in: *Science and Children* 28, no. 8 (May 1991): 29–30

Weather Academy, software (Garden City, NY: Focus Media, 1989). Reviewed in: *Science and Children* 28, no. 6 (Mar. 1991): 46

Who Lives Here?, video (Washington, DC: National Geographic Society, 1990). Reviewed in: *American Biology Teacher* 52, no. 7 (Oct. 1990): 443

Wild Wings, by Phyllis Emert (n.p.: Julian Messner, 1990). Reviewed in: *Science and Children* 29, no. 5 (Feb. 1992): 48

Wildlife at Risk, by Malcom Penny (n.p.: Bookright, 1990). Reviewed in: *Science and Children* 29, no. 4 (Jan. 1992): 39

Woolly Bounce, software (Minneapolis: MECC, 1991). Reviewed in: *Science and Children* 29,

no. 4 (Jan. 1992): 34; *Technology & Learning* 12, no. 4 (Jan. 1992): 8-9

The World's Harvest Series, by Jaqueline Dineen (Hillsdale, NJ: Enslow, 1988). Reviewed in: *American Biology Teacher* 52, no. 4 (Apr. 1990): 317

EME (publishers)

Hothouse Planet, software (Danbury, CT: EME, 1990). Reviewed in: *Science and Children* 28, no. 7 (Apr. 1991): 54

Emert, Phyllis

Wild Wings, by Phyllis Emert (n.p.: Julian Messner, 1990). Reviewed in: *Science and Children* 29, no. 5 (Feb. 1992): 48

England, Nick

Physics Matters, by Nick England (London: Hodder and Stoughton, 1989). Reviewed in: *Physics Matters* 25, no. 2 (Mar. 1990): 130

Enslow (publishers)

Science Fair Success, by R. Bombaugh (Hillside, NJ: Enslow, 1990). Reviewed in: *American Biology Teacher* 53, no. 3 (Mar. 1991): 192

The World's Harvest Series, by Jaqueline Dineen (Hillsdale, NJ: Enslow, 1988). Reviewed in: *American Biology Teacher* 52, no. 4 (Apr. 1990): 317

Entrex Software

Pollution Patrol, software (Victoria, B.C.: Entrex Software, 1987). Reviewed in: *Pollution Patrol* 27, no. 6 (Mar. 1990): 47

The Environment

software (Boca Raton, FL: IBM, n.d.). Reviewed in: *Science and Children* 28, no. 6 (Mar. 1991): 47

Environmental education

Animals in Danger, by William McCay (New York: Aladdin, 1990). Reviewed in: *Science and Children* 29, no. 4 (Jan. 1992): 39

Antarctica, by Helen Cowcher (New York: Farrar Straus & Giroux, 1990). Reviewed in: *Science and Children* 29, no. 4 (Jan. 1992): 39

Environmental education *(cont'd)*

The Biology of Water, video (Niles, IL: United Learning, 1991). Reviewed in: *Media and Methods* 28, no. 1 (Sept./Oct. 1991): 46

Clearwater Detectives, software (Minneapolis: MECC, 1991). Reviewed in: *Science and Children* 29, no. 5 (Feb. 1992): 36–38

Consider the Earth: Environmental Activities for Grades 4–8, by Julie M. Gates (Englewood, CO: Teacher Ideas Press, 1989). Reviewed in: *Science Activities* 28, no. 1 (Spring 1991): 44

Dive into Science: Hands-on Water-Related Experiments, by Peggy K. Perdue (Glenview, IL: Scott Foresman, n.d.). Reviewed in: *Science and Children* 28, no. 7 (Apr. 1991): 54

Earth Science, software (Warren, NJ: Optical Data, n.d.). Reviewed in: *Science and Children* 28, no. 3 (Nov./Dec. 1990): 45

Earth Science for Every Kid: 101 Experiments That Really Work, by Janice VanCleave (New York: John Wiley and Sons, 1991). Reviewed in: *Journal of Geography* 91, no. 1 (Jan./Feb. 1992): 46

Earth Science Investigations, by Margaret A. Oosterman and Mark T. Schmidt (Alexandria, VA: American Geology Institute, 1990). Reviewed in: *The Science Teacher* 59, no. 2 (Feb. 1992): 84–85

The Environment, software (Boca Raton, FL: IBM, n.d.). Reviewed in: *Science and Children* 28, no. 6 (Mar. 1991): 47

Exploring the World of Birds: An Equinox Guide to Avian Life, by Laurel Aziz and Adrian Forsyth (Charlotte, VT: Camden House, 1990). Reviewed in: *Science and Children* 29, no. 5 (Feb. 1992): 48

Five Star Forecast, software (St. Paul: MECC, 1990). Reviewed in: *Science and Children* 28, no. 8 (May 1991): 30

Food Chains, software (Galesburg, MI: MCE, n.d.). Reviewed in: *Science and Children* 29, no. 2 (Oct. 1991): 46

Forecasting the Weather, software (Galesburg, MI: MCE, n.d.). Reviewed in: *Science and Children* 29, no. 4 (Jan. 1992): 35

Hothouse Planet, software (Danbury, CT: EME, 1990). Reviewed in: *Science and Children* 28, no. 7 (Apr. 1991): 54

How to Make a Chemical Volcano and Other Mysterious Experiments, by Alan Kramer (New York: Franklin Watts, 1989). Reviewed in: *Curriculum Review* 31, no. 7 (Mar. 1992): 27

Jungle Safari, software (Pound Ridge, NY: Orange Cherry/Talking School House Software, 1990). Reviewed in: *Science and Children* 29, no. 4 (Jan. 1992): 35

Lake Study, software (Ypsilanti, MI: Eastern Michigan Univ., n.d.). Reviewed in: *School Science and Mathematics* 90, no. 8 (Dec. 1990): 741

Learn about Insects, software (Pleasantville, NY: Sunburst Communications, n.d.). Reviewed in: *Science and Children* 28, no. 8 (May 1991): 30

Life Science Help Series, software (Garden City, NY: Focus Media, n.d.). Reviewed in: *Science and Children* 27, no. 7 (Apr. 1990): 44

Life's Devices: The Physical World of Plants and Animals, by Steven Vogel (Princeton: Princeton University Press, 1989). Reviewed in: *American Biology Teacher* 52, no. 6 (Sept. 1990): 388

More Than Just a Garden, by Dwight Kuhn (Englewood Cliffs, NJ: Silver Burdett, 1990). Reviewed in: *Science and Children* 29, no. 2 (Oct. 1991): 53

An Ocean of Air, software (Galesburg, MI: MCE, n.d.). Reviewed in: *Science and Children* 29, no. 2 (Oct. 1991): 47

Oceanography for Landlocked Classrooms, ed. by Gerry M. Madrazo and Paul B. Hounshell (Reston, VA: National Association of Biology Teachers, 1990). Reviewed in: *The Science Teacher* 59, no. 2 (Feb. 1992): 76–77

Environmental education *(cont'd)*
The Oregon Trail, software (Minneapolis: MECC, n.d.). Reviewed in: *Science and Children* 29, no. 6 (Mar. 1992): 49

Pollution Control, software (Garden City, NY: Focus Media, 1989). Reviewed in: *Science and Children* 28, no. 7 (Apr. 1991): 52

Pollution Patrol, software (Victoria, B.C.: Entrex Software, 1987). Reviewed in: *Pollution Patrol* 27, no. 6 (Mar. 1990): 47

Raintree Science Adventures, by Helen H. Cary and Judith E. Greenberg (Milwaukee, WI: Raintree, 1990). Reviewed in: *Science and Children* 29, no. 5 (Feb. 1992): 48

SimEarth, software (Orinda, CA: Maxis, 1990). Reviewed in: *School Science and Mathematics* 92, no. 1 (Jan. 1992): 47; *Journal of Geography* 91, no. 1 (Jan./Feb. 1992): 47

Sun and Seasons, software (St. Paul: MECC, 1990). Reviewed in: *Science and Children* 28, no. 7 (Apr. 1991): 52

3–2–1 Contact: Wild Things, software by The Children's Television Workshop (Scott's Valley, CA: Wings for Learning, 1991). Reviewed in: *Teaching with Technology* (Feb. 1992): 59

Volcano, by Christopher Lampton (Brookfield, CT: Millbrook Press, 1991). Reviewed in: *Science Books and Films* 28, no. 1 (Jan./Feb. 1992): 15–16

The Water Cycle, software (Galesburg, MI: MCE, n.d.). Reviewed in: *Science and Children* 29, no. 4 (Jan. 1992): 35

Weather Academy, software (Garden City, NY: Focus Media, 1989). Reviewed in: *Science and Children* 28, no. 6 (Mar. 1991): 46

Weather in Action, software (Washington, DC: National Geographic Society, 1988). Reviewed in: *Science and Children* 28, no. 8 (May 1991): 29–30

The Weather Machine, software (Washington DC: National Geographic Society, 1988). Reviewed in: *School Science and Mathematics* 90, no. 4 (Apr. 1990): 346

Who Lives Here?, video (Washington, DC: National Geographic Society, 1990). Reviewed in: *American Biology Teacher* 52, no. 7 (Oct. 1990): 443

Wild Wings, by Phyllis Emert (n.p.: Julian Messner, 1990). Reviewed in: *Science and Children* 29, no. 5 (Feb. 1992): 48

Wildlife at Risk, by Malcom Penny (n.p.: Bookright, 1990). Reviewed in: *Science and Children* 29, no. 4 (Jan. 1992): 39

World Population, video (Washington, DC: ZPG Population Education Program, 1990). Reviewed in: *The American Biology Teacher* 53, no. 3 (Mar. 1991): 189

The World's Harvest Series, by Jaqueline Dineen (Hillsdale, NJ: Enslow, 1988). Reviewed in: *American Biology Teacher* 52, no. 4 (Apr. 1990): 317

Enzymes
video (Franklin Lakes, NJ: Benchmark Films, 1990). Reviewed in: *Science Books and Films* 28, no. 2 (Mar. 1992): 57

Evolutionary Biology
2d ed. by Douglas J. Futuyma (Sunderland, MA: Sinauer Associates, 1986). Reviewed in: *American Biology Teacher* 52, no. 4 (Apr. 1990): 318

Experiments. *See* Activities/experiments

Exploring the World of Birds: An Equinox Guide to Avian Life
by Laurel Aziz and Adrian Forsyth (Charlotte, VT: Camden House, 1990). Reviewed in: *Science and Children* 29, no. 5 (Feb. 1992): 48

Eyewitness Juniors
by Alexander Parsons (New York: Knopf, 1990). Reviewed in: *Science and Children* 29, no. 4 (Jan. 1992): 39

Famous Experiments You Can Do
by Robert Gardner (New York: Franklin Watts, 1990). Reviewed in: *The Science Teacher* 59, no. 2, (Feb. 1992): 76

Farmer, Walter A.
Activities for Teaching K–6 Math/Science Concepts, by Walter A. Farmer and Margaret A. Farrell (Bowling Green, OH: School Science and Mathematics, 1989). Reviewed in: *Science and Children* 28, no. 4 (Jan. 1991): 58

Farrar, Straus & Giroux
Antarctica, by Helen Cowcher (New York: Farrar Straus & Giroux, 1990). Reviewed in: *Science and Children* 29, no. 4 (Jan. 1992): 39

Farrell, Margaret A.
Activities for Teaching K–6 Math/Science Concepts, by Walter A. Farmer and Margaret A. Farrell (Bowling Green, OH: School Science and Mathematics, 1989). Reviewed in: *Science and Children* 28, no. 4 (Jan. 1991): 58

Films/videos
The Age of Dinosaurs, filmstrip (Washington, DC: National Geographic Society, 1990). Reviewed in: *American Biology Teacher* 53, no. 3 (Mar. 1991): 189

The Animal Life Series, film/video (Van Nuys, CA: AIMS Media Film and Video, 1991). Reviewed in: *Media and Methods* 28, no. 1 (Sept./Oct. 1991): 46

The Biology of Water, video (Niles, IL: United Learning, 1991). Reviewed in: *Media and Methods* 28, no. 1 (Sept./Oct. 1991): 46

Chemistry at Work, video (Seattle: Videodiscovery, 1991). Reviewed in: *Science Books and Films* 28, no. 2 (Mar. 1992): 59

Cosmic Chemistry, video (Warren, NJ: Optical Data, n.d.). Reviewed in: *Science Books and Films* 28, no. 2 (Mar. 1992): 59

Dissection and Anatomy of the Brain, video (Omaha: Nebraska Scientific, 1989). Reviewed in: *American Biology Teacher* 52, no. 4 (Apr. 1990): 309

Enzymes, video (Franklin Lakes, NJ: Benchmark Films, 1990). Reviewed in: *Science Books and Films* 28, no. 2 (Mar. 1992): 57

Immunity, film (New Hyde Park, NY: National Teaching Aids, 1989). Reviewed in: *American Biology Teacher* 52, no. 7 (Oct. 1989): 444

Powers of Ten, by Charles Eames and Ray Eames, video (San Francisco: Pyramid Video, 1989). Reviewed in: *The Science Teacher* 59, no. 1 (Jan. 1992): 87–89

Ready Set Go: How Animals Move, filmstrip (Washington, DC: National Geographic Society, 1989). Reviewed in: *American Biology Teacher* 52, no. 8 (Nov./Dec. 1990): 514

Who Lives Here?, video (Washington, DC: National Geographic Society, 1990). Reviewed in: *American Biology Teacher* 52, no. 7 (Oct. 1990): 443

World Population, video (Washington, DC: ZPG Population Education Program, 1990). Reviewed in: *The American Biology Teacher* 53, no. 3 (Mar. 1991): 189

Five Star Forecast
software (St. Paul: MECC, 1990). Reviewed in: *Science and Children* 28, no. 8 (May 1991): 30

Focus Media
Life Science Help Series, software (Garden City, NY: Focus Media, n.d.). Reviewed in: *Science and Children* 27, no. 7 (Apr. 1990): 44

Physical Science Laboratory, software (Garden City, NY: Focus Media, 1990). Reviewed in: *Science and Children* 29, no. 6 (Mar. 1992): 50–51

Pollution Control, software (Garden City, NY: Focus Media, 1989). Reviewed in: *Science and Children* 28, no. 7 (Apr. 1991): 52

Weather Academy, software (Garden City, NY: Focus Media, 1989). Reviewed in: *Science and Children* 28, no. 6 (Mar. 1991): 46

Food Chains
software (Galesburg, MI: MCE, n.d.). Reviewed in: *Science and Children* 29, no. 2 (Oct. 1991): 46

Forecasting the Weather
software (Galesburg, MI: MCE, n.d.). Reviewed in: *Science and Children* 29, no. 4 (Jan. 1992): 35

Forsyth, Adrian
Exploring the World of Birds: An Equinox Guide to Avian Life, by Laurel Aziz and Adrian Forsyth (Charlotte, VT: Camden House, 1990). Reviewed in: *Science and Children* 29, no. 5 (Feb. 1992): 48

Franklin Watts
Famous Experiments You Can Do, by Robert Gardner (New York: Franklin Watts, 1990). Reviewed in: *The Science Teacher* 59, no. 2, (Feb. 1992): 76

How to Make a Chemical Volcano and Other Mysterious Experiments, by Alan Kramer (New York: Franklin Watts, 1989). Reviewed in: *Curriculum Review* 31, no. 7 (Mar. 1992): 27

Picture Library Series, by Norman Barrett (New York: Franklin Watts, 1989). Reviewed in: *Science and Children* 28, no. 1 (Sept. 1990): 79

Fredericks, Anthony D.
The Complete Science Fair Handbook, by Issac Asimov and Anthony D. Fredericks (Glenview, IL: Scott Foresman, 1990). Reviewed in: *Science and Children* 28, no. 2 (Oct. 1990): 41

Frog Dissection Lab Report
software (Uniondale, NY: Bergwall Educational Software, 1988). Reviewed in: *Science and Children* 27, no. 8 (May 1990): 38

Fuller, Robert G.
What If?, by Robert G. Fuller (New York: Wilson Learning, 1989). Reviewed in: *Physics Teacher* 28, no. 5 (May 1990): 349

Futuyma, Douglas J.
Evolutionary Biology, 2d ed. by Douglas J. Futuyma (Sunderland, MA: Sinauer Associates, 1986). Reviewed in: *American Biology Teacher* 52, no. 4 (Apr. 1990): 318

Gardner, Robert
Famous Experiments You Can Do, by Robert Gardner (New York: Franklin Watts, 1990). Reviewed in: *The Science Teacher* 59, no. 2, (Feb. 1992): 76

Gates, Julie M.
Consider the Earth: Environmental Activities for Grades 4–8, by Julie M. Gates (Englewood, CO:

Teacher Ideas Press, 1989). Reviewed in: *Science Activities* 28, no. 1 (Spring 1991): 44

General science
Developing Science in the Primary Classroom, by Wynne Harlen and Sheila Jelly (Portsmouth, NH: Heinemann Educational Books, 1990). Reviewed in: *Curriculum Review* 30, no. 7 (Mar. 1991): 31

Junior Science, by Terry Jennings (Gloucester: n.p., 1990). Reviewed in: *Science and Children* 29, no. 1, (Sept. 1990) 64

Powers of Ten, by Charles Eames and Ray Eames, video (San Francisco: Pyramid Video, 1989). Reviewed in: *The Science Teacher* 59, no. 1 (Jan. 1992): 87–89

Genetics and Heredity
software (Freeport, NY: Educational Activities, 1991). Reviewed in: *Science and Children* 29, no. 5 (Feb. 1992): 39

Geography
Antarctica, by Helen Cowcher (New York: Farrar Straus & Giroux, 1990). Reviewed in: *Science and Children* 29, no. 4 (Jan. 1992): 39

Books for Young Explorers—Set XVI, by National Geographic Society (Washington, DC: National Geographic Society, 1989). Reviewed in: *American Biology Teacher* 53, no. 5 (May 1991): 314–315

Physics 1.2, software (San Rafael, CA: Broderbund Software, n.d.). Reviewed in: *Journal of Geographical Education* 39, no. 1 (Jan. 1991): 71

Geology
The Age of Dinosaurs, filmstrip (Washington, DC: National Geographic Society, 1990). Reviewed in: *American Biology Teacher* 53, no. 3 (Mar. 1991): 189

Designasaurus II, software (San Francisco: Britannica Software, 1990). Reviewed in: *Science and Children* 29, no. 1 (Sept. 1991): 59

Dyno-Quest, software (Tucson: Mindplay/ Methods and Solutions, 1984). Reviewed in: *Science and Children* 28, no. 1 (Sept. 1990): 19

Geology *(cont'd)*

How to Make a Chemical Volcano and Other Mysterious Experiments, by Alan Kramer (New York: Franklin Watts, 1989). Reviewed in: *Curriculum Review* 31, no. 7 (Mar. 1992): 27

Murphy's Minerals, software (St. Paul: MECC, 1990). Reviewed in: *Science and Children* 28, no. 4 (Jan. 1991): 41

Volcano, by Christopher Lampton (Brookfield, CT: Millbrook Press, 1991). Reviewed in: *Science Books and Films* 28, no. 1 (Jan./Feb. 1992): 15–16

Giese, Ronald H.
Students and Research: Practical Strategies for Science Classrooms and Competitions, by Julia H. Cothron, Ronald H. Giese, and Richard J. Rezba (Dubuque: Kendall/Hunt, 1989). Reviewed in: *The Science Teacher* 59, no. 2 (Jan. 1992): 78–79

Harlen, Wynne
Developing Science in the Primary Classroom, by Wynne Harlen and Sheila Jelly (Portsmouth, NH: Heinemann Educational Books, 1990). Reviewed in: *Curriculum Review* 30, no. 7 (Mar. 1991): 31

Heinemann Educational Books
Developing Science in the Primary Classroom, by Wynne Harlen and Sheila Jelly (Portsmouth, NH: Heinemann Educational Books, 1990). Reviewed in: *Curriculum Review* 30, no. 7 (Mar. 1991): 31

Heredity/genetics
Genetics and Heredity, software (Freeport, NY: Educational Activities, 1991). Reviewed in: *Science and Children* 29, no. 5 (Feb. 1992): 39

Modern Genetics, software (Boca Raton, FL: IBM, n.d.). Reviewed in: *Science and Children* 28, no. 3 (Nov./Dec. 1990): 46

High school materials
The Art of Science Writing, by Bernadette Mayer and Dale Worsley (New York: Teachers and Writers Collaborative, 1989). Reviewed in: *American Biology Teacher* 52, no. 3 (Mar. 1990): 192

Chemaid, software (Newbury Park, CA: Ventura Educational Systems, 1990). Reviewed in: *Science and Children* 29, no. 5 (Feb. 1992): 36; *Journal of Chemical Education* 68, no. 4 (Apr. 1991): 157

Chemical Activities, by Christie L. Borgford and Lee R. Summerline (Washington, DC: American Chemical Society, 1988). Reviewed in: *Science Activities* 28, no. 3 (Fall 1991): 44

Chemistry at Work, video (Seattle: Videodiscovery, 1991). Reviewed in: *Science Books and Films* 28, no. 2 (Mar. 1992): 59

Cosmic Chemistry, video (Warren, NJ: Optical Data, n.d.). Reviewed in: *Science Books and Films* 28, no. 2 (Mar. 1992): 59

Dissection and Anatomy of the Brain, video (Omaha: Nebraska Scientific, 1989). Reviewed in: *American Biology Teacher* 52, no. 4 (Apr. 1990): 309

Earth Science, software (Warren, NJ: Optical Data, n.d.). Reviewed in: *Science and Children* 28, no. 3 (Nov./Dec. 1990): 45

Earth Science Investigations, by Margaret A. Oosterman and Mark T. Schmidt (Alexandria, VA: American Geology Institute, 1990). Reviewed in: *The Science Teacher* 59, no. 2 (Feb. 1992): 84–85

The Environment, software (Boca Raton, FL: IBM, n.d.). Reviewed in: *Science and Children* 28, no. 6 (Mar. 1991): 47

Enzymes, video (Franklin Lakes, NJ: Benchmark Films, 1990). Reviewed in: *Science Books and Films* 28, no. 2 (Mar. 1992): 57

Evolutionary Biology, 2d ed. by Douglas J. Futuyma (Sunderland, MA: Sinauer Associates, 1986). Reviewed in: *American Biology Teacher* 52, no. 4 (Apr. 1990): 318

Famous Experiments You Can Do, by Robert Gardner (New York: Franklin Watts, 1990). Reviewed in: *The Science Teacher* 59, no. 2, (Feb. 1992): 76

High school materials *(cont'd)*

Frog Dissection Lab Report, software (Uniondale, NY: Bergwall Educational Software, 1988). Reviewed in: *Science and Children* 27, no. 8 (May 1990): 38

Hothouse Planet, software (Danbury, CT: EME, 1990). Reviewed in: *Science and Children* 28, no. 7 (Apr. 1991): 54

Immunity, film (New Hyde Park, NY: National Teaching Aids, 1989). Reviewed in: *American Biology Teacher* 52, no. 7 (Oct. 1989): 444

Insights into Science Data, software (Pleasantville, NY: Sunburst Communications, n.d.). Reviewed in: *Science and Children* 29, no. 6 (Mar. 1992): 51

Lake Study, software (Ypsilanti, MI: Eastern Michigan Univ., n.d.). Reviewed in: *School Science and Mathematics* 90, no. 8 (Dec. 1990): 741

Life Science, software (Ramsey, NJ: K–12 Micromedia, 1991). Reviewed in: *Methods and Media* 28 no. 4 (Mar./Apr. 1992): 60

Life Science Help Series, software (Garden City, NY: Focus Media, n.d.). Reviewed in: *Science and Children* 27, no. 7 (Apr. 1990): 44

Life's Devices: The Physical World of Plants and Animals, by Steven Vogel (Princeton: Princeton University Press, 1989). Reviewed in: *American Biology Teacher* 52, no. 6 (Sept. 1990): 388

Modern Genetics, software (Boca Raton, FL: IBM, n.d.). Reviewed in: *Science and Children* 28, no. 3 (Nov./Dec. 1990): 46

Oceanography for Landlocked Classrooms, ed. by Gerry M. Madrazo and Paul B. Hounshell (Reston, VA: National Association of Biology Teachers, 1990). Reviewed in: *The Science Teacher* 59, no. 2 (Feb. 1992): 76–77

100 Science Puzzles, by Colin McCarty and Jane Young (London: Unwin Hyman, 1989). Reviewed in: *Physics Education* 25, no. 5 (Sept. 1990): 293

Physical Science Laboratory, software (Garden City, NY: Focus Media, 1990). Reviewed in:

Science and Children 29, no. 6 (Mar. 1992): 50–51

Physics 1.2, software (San Rafael, CA: Broderbund Software, n.d.). Reviewed in: *Journal of Geographical Education* 39, no. 1 (Jan. 1991): 71

Physics Explorer: One Body, software (Scotts Valley, CA: Wings for Learning, 1991). Reviewed in: *Technology & Learning* 12, no. 4 (Jan. 1992): 10, 11, 14

Physics Matters, by Nick England (London: Hodder and Stoughton, 1989). Reviewed in: *Physics Matters* 25, no. 2 (Mar. 1990): 130

Pollution Control, software (Garden City, NY: Focus Media, 1989). Reviewed in: *Science and Children* 28, no. 7 (Apr. 1991): 52

Powers of Ten, by Charles Eames and Ray Eames, video (San Francisco: Pyramid Video, 1989). Reviewed in: *The Science Teacher* 59, no. 1 (Jan. 1992): 87–89

Protozoa, software (Newbury Park, CA: Ventura Educational Systems, 1989). Reviewed in: *Science and Children,* 29, no. 5 (Feb. 1992): 36

Random House Encyclopedia, software (Pittsford, NY: Microlytics, 1990). Reviewed in: *Science and Children* 29, no. 6 (Mar. 1992): 49–50

Science in Cinema: Teaching Science Fact Through Science Fiction Films, by Judith E. Boss, Leroy W. Dubeck, and Susan Moshier (New York: Teachers College Press, 1988). Reviewed in: *The Science Teacher* 59, no. 2 (Feb. 1992): 78-79

SimEarth, software (Orinda, CA: Maxis, 1990). Reviewed in: *School Science and Mathematics* 92, no. 1 (Jan. 1992): 47; *Journal of Geography* 91, no. 1 (Jan./Feb. 1992): 47

Storm, software, by Thomas Pesek (Houston, TX: Utopia Software, n.d.). Reviewed in: *Journal of Geography* 89, no. 2 (Mar./Apr. 1990): 194

High school materials *(cont'd)*
Students and Research: Practical Strategies for Science Classrooms and Competitions, by Julia H. Cothron, Ronald H. Giese, and Richard J. Rezba (Dubuque: Kendall/Hunt, 1989). Reviewed in: *The Science Teacher* 59, no. 2 (Jan. 1992): 78–79

Time Table History, software (Los Angeles: Xiphias, 1987). Reviewed in: *Science and Children* 29, no. 2 (Oct. 1992): 47

Unique Science: Demonstrations and Laboratories for the Physics Instructor, by E. M. Kinsman and C. Waters (Syracuse: Kinsman Physics, 1991). Reviewed in: *Science Books and Films* 28, no. 1 (Jan./Feb. 1992): 15

The Weather Machine, software (Washington DC: National Geographic Society, 1988). Reviewed in: *School Science and Mathematics* 90, no. 4 (Apr. 1990): 346

What If?, by Robert G. Fuller (New York: Wilson Learning, 1989). Reviewed in: *Physics Teacher* 28, no. 5 (May 1990): 349

Why Do Bodies Stop Growing?, by Philip Whitfield and Ruth Whitfield (New York: Viking Penguin, 1988). Reviewed in: *School Science and Mathematics* 90, no. 7 (Nov. 1988): 656

World Population, video (Washington, DC: ZPG Population Education Program, 1990). Reviewed in: *The American Biology Teacher* 53, no. 3 (Mar. 1991): 189

History of science
Famous Experiments You Can Do, by Robert Gardner (New York: Franklin Watts, 1990). Reviewed in: *The Science Teacher* 59, no. 2, (Feb. 1992): 76

Time Table History, software (Los Angeles: Xiphias, 1987). Reviewed in: *Science and Children* 29, no. 2 (Oct. 1992): 47

Hodder and Stoughton
Physics Matters, by Nick England (London: Hodder and Stoughton, 1989). Reviewed in: *Physics Matters* 25, no. 2 (Mar. 1990): 130

Hothouse Planet
software (Danbury, CT: EME, 1990). Reviewed in: *Science and Children* 28, no. 7 (Apr. 1991): 54

Hounshell, Paul B., ed.
Oceanography for Landlocked Classrooms, ed. by Gerry M. Madrazo and Paul B. Hounshell (Reston, VA: National Association of Biology Teachers, 1990). Reviewed in: *The Science Teacher* 59, no. 2 (Feb. 1992): 76–77

How to Make a Chemical Volcano and Other Mysterious Experiments
by Alan Kramer (New York: Franklin Watts, 1989). Reviewed in: *Curriculum Review* 31, no. 7 (Mar. 1992): 27

Human physiology
The Brain and Nervous System, software (Mahwah, NJ: Troll Associates, 1991). Reviewed in: *Science and Children* 29, no. 4 (Jan. 1992): 34-35

Enzymes, video (Franklin Lakes, NJ: Benchmark Films, 1990). Reviewed in: *Science Books and Films* 28, no. 2 (Mar. 1992): 57

The Immune System, software (Shawnee Mission, KS: Marshmedia, n.d.). Reviewed in: *Science and Children* 28, no. 8 (May 1991): 30

Immunity, film (New Hyde Park, NY: National Teaching Aids, 1989). Reviewed in: *American Biology Teacher* 52, no. 7 (Oct. 1989): 444

The Skeletal and Muscular System, software (Mahwah, NJ: Troll Associates, 1991). Reviewed in: *Science and Children* 28, no. 1 (Sept. 1990): 50

Why Do Bodies Stop Growing?, by Philip Whitfield and Ruth Whitfield (New York: Viking Penguin, 1988). Reviewed in: *School Science and Mathematics* 90, no. 7 (Nov. 1988): 656

IBM (publishers)
The Environment, software (Boca Raton, FL: IBM, n.d.). Reviewed in: *Science and Children* 28, no. 6 (Mar. 1991): 47

IBM (publishers) *(cont'd)*
Modern Genetics, software (Boca Raton, FL: IBM, n.d.). Reviewed in: *Science and Children* 28, no. 3 (Nov./Dec. 1990): 46

The Immune System
software (Shawnee Mission, KS: Marshmedia, n.d.). Reviewed in: *Science and Children* 28, no. 8 (May 1991): 30

Immunity
film (New Hyde Park, NY: National Teaching Aids, 1989). Reviewed in: *American Biology Teacher* 52, no. 7 (Oct. 1989): 444

Insects
Learn about Insects, software (Pleasantville, NY: Sunburst Communications, n.d.). Reviewed in: *Science and Children* 28, no. 8 (May 1991): 30

Insights into Science Data
software (Pleasantville, NY: Sunburst Communications, n.d.). Reviewed in: *Science and Children* 29, no. 6 (Mar. 1992): 51

Iverson, Carol
Bet You Didn't Know That, by Carol Iverson (Minneapolis: Lerner, 1990). Reviewed in: *Science and Children* 29, no. 6 (Mar. 1992): 55

Jakel (publishers)
Safe Science Teaching, software (Des Moines: Jakel, n.d.). Reviewed in: *Science and Children* 29, no. 1 (Sept. 1991): 58

Jelly, Sheila
Developing Science in the Primary Classroom, by Wynne Harlen and Sheila Jelly (Portsmouth, NH: Heinemann Educational Books, 1990). Reviewed in: *Curriculum Review* 30, no. 7 (Mar. 1991): 31

Jennings, Terry
Junior Science, by Terry Jennings (Gloucester: n.p., 1990). Reviewed in: *Science and Children* 29, no. 1, (Sept. 1990) 64

John Wiley and Sons
Earth Science for Every Kid: 101 Experiments That Really Work, by Janice VanCleave (New York: John Wiley and Sons, 1991). Reviewed in: *Journal of Geography* 91, no. 1 (Jan./Feb. 1992): 46

Julian Messner (publishers)
Wild Wings, by Phyllis Emert (n.p.: Julian Messner, 1990). Reviewed in: *Science and Children* 29, no. 5 (Feb. 1992): 48

Jungle Safari
software (Pound Ridge, NY: Orange Cherry/ Talking School House Software, 1990). Reviewed in: *Science and Children* 29, no. 4 (Jan. 1992): 35

Junior Science
by Terry Jennings (Gloucester: n.p., 1990). Reviewed in: *Science and Children* 29, no. 1, (Sept. 1990) 64

K–12 Micromedia (publishers)
Life Science, software (Ramsey, NJ: K–12 Micromedia, 1991). Reviewed in: *Methods and Media* 28 no. 4 (Mar./Apr. 1992): 60

Kendall/Hunt Publishing Co.
Students and Research: Practical Strategies for Science Classrooms and Competitions, by Julia H. Cothron, Ronald H. Giese, and Richard J. Rezba (Dubuque: Kendall/Hunt, 1989). Reviewed in: *The Science Teacher* 59, no. 2 (Jan. 1992): 78–79

Kinsman, E. M.
Unique Science: Demonstrations and Laboratories for the Physics Instructor, by E. M. Kinsman and C. Waters (Syracuse: Kinsman Physics, 1991). Reviewed in: *Science Books and Films* 28, no. 1 (Jan./Feb. 1992): 15

Kinsman Physics (publishers)
Unique Science: Demonstrations and Laboratories for the Physics Instructor, by E. M. Kinsman and C. Waters (Syracuse: Kinsman Physics, 1991). Reviewed in: *Science Books and Films* 28, no. 1 (Jan./Feb. 1992): 15

Kramer, Alan
How to Make a Chemical Volcano and Other Mysterious Experiments, by Alan Kramer (New York: Franklin Watts, 1989). Reviewed in: *Curriculum Review* 31, no. 7 (Mar. 1992): 27

Kramer, David C.
Animals in the Classroom, by David C. Kramer (Menlo Park, CA: Addison-Wesley Publishing, 1989). Reviewed in: *School Science and Mathematics* 90, no. 3 (Mar. 1990): 261

Kuhn, Dwight
More Than Just a Garden, by Dwight Kuhn (Englewood Cliffs, NJ: Silver Burdett, 1990). Reviewed in: *Science and Children* 29, no. 2 (Oct. 1991): 53

Lab safety
Safe Science Teaching, software (Des Moines: Jakel, n.d.). Reviewed in: *Science and Children* 29, no. 1 (Sept. 1991): 58

Lake Study
software (Ypsilanti, MI: Eastern Michigan Univ., n.d.). Reviewed in: *School Science and Mathematics* 90, no. 8 (Dec. 1990): 741

Lampton, Christopher
Volcano, by Christopher Lampton (Brookfield, CT: Millbrook Press, 1991). Reviewed in: *Science Books and Films* 28, no. 1 (Jan./Feb. 1992): 15–16

Language arts
The Art of Science Writing, by Bernadette Mayer and Dale Worsley (New York: Teachers and Writers Collaborative, 1989). Reviewed in: *American Biology Teacher* 52, no. 3 (Mar. 1990): 192

Learn about Insects
software (Pleasantville, NY: Sunburst Communications, n.d.). Reviewed in: *Science and Children* 28, no. 8 (May 1991): 30

Lerner (publishers)
Bet You Didn't Know That, by Carol Iverson (Minneapolis: Lerner, 1990). Reviewed in: *Science and Children* 29, no. 6 (Mar. 1992): 55

Life Cycles
software (Galesburg, MI: MCE, n.d.). Reviewed in: *Science and Children* 29, no. 1 (Sept. 1991): 58–59

Life Science
software (Ramsey, NJ: K–12 Micromedia, 1991). Reviewed in: *Methods and Media* 28 no. 4 (Mar./Apr. 1992): 60

Life Science Help Series
software (Garden City, NY: Focus Media, n.d.). Reviewed in: *Science and Children* 27, no. 7 (Apr. 1990): 44

Life's Devices: The Physical World of Plants and Animals
by Steven Vogel (Princeton: Princeton University Press, 1989). Reviewed in: *American Biology Teacher* 52, no. 6 (Sept. 1990): 388

Literature
Dragons in the Trees, by James Martin (New York: Crown, 1991). Reviewed in: *Science and Children* 29, no. 6 (Mar. 1992): 55

McCarty, Colin
100 Science Puzzles, by Colin McCarty and Jane Young (London: Unwin Hyman, 1989). Reviewed in: *Physics Education* 25, no. 5 (Sept. 1990): 293

McCay, William
Animals in Danger, by William McCay (New York: Aladdin, 1990). Reviewed in: *Science and Children* 29, no. 4 (Jan. 1992): 39

Madrazo, Gerry M., ed.
Oceanography for Landlocked Classrooms, ed. by Gerry M. Madrazo and Paul B. Hounshell (Reston, VA: National Association of Biology Teachers, 1990). Reviewed in: *The Science Teacher* 59, no. 2 (Feb. 1992): 76–77

Marine studies
The Biology of Water, video (Niles, IL: United Learning, 1991). Reviewed in: *Media and Methods* 28, no. 1 (Sept./Oct. 1991): 46

Oceanography for Landlocked Classrooms, ed. by Gerry M. Madrazo and Paul B. Hounshell (Reston, VA: National Association of Biology Teachers, 1990). Reviewed in: *The Science Teacher* 59, no. 2 (Feb. 1992): 76–77

Marshmedia (publishers)
The Immune System, software (Shawnee Mission, KS: Marshmedia, n.d.). Reviewed in: *Science and Children* 28, no. 8 (May 1991): 30

Martin, James
Dragons in the Trees, by James Martin (New York: Crown, 1991). Reviewed in: *Science and Children* 29, no. 6 (Mar. 1992): 55

Mathematics and science
Activities for Teaching K–6 Math/Science Concepts, by Walter A. Farmer and Margaret A. Farrell (Bowling Green, OH: School Science and Mathematics, 1989). Reviewed in: *Science and Children* 28, no. 4 (Jan. 1991): 58

Maxis (publishers)
SimEarth, software (Orinda, CA: Maxis, 1990). Reviewed in: *School Science and Mathematics* 92, no. 1 (Jan. 1992): 47; *Journal of Geography* 91, no. 1 (Jan./Feb. 1992): 47

Mayer, Bernadette
The Art of Science Writing, by Bernadette Mayer and Dale Worsley (New York: Teachers and Writers Collaborative, 1989). Reviewed in: *American Biology Teacher* 52, no. 3 (Mar. 1990): 192

MCE (publishers)
Adaptations, software (Galesburg, MI: MCE, n.d.). Reviewed in: *Science and Children* 29, no. 1 (Sept. 1992): 59

Food Chains, software (Galesburg, MI: MCE, n.d.). Reviewed in: *Science and Children* 29, no. 2 (Oct. 1991): 46

Forecasting the Weather, software (Galesburg, MI: MCE, n.d.). Reviewed in: *Science and Children* 29, no. 4 (Jan. 1992): 35

Life Cycles, software (Galesburg, MI: MCE, n.d.). Reviewed in: *Science and Children* 29, no. 1 (Sept. 1991): 58–59

An Ocean of Air, software (Galesburg, MI: MCE, n.d.). Reviewed in: *Science and Children* 29, no. 2 (Oct. 1991): 47

The Water Cycle, software (Galesburg, MI: MCE, n.d.). Reviewed in: *Science and Children* 29, no. 4 (Jan. 1992): 35

MECC (publishers)
Clearwater Detectives, software (Minneapolis: MECC, 1991). Reviewed in: *Science and Children* 29, no. 5 (Feb. 1992): 36–38

Five Star Forecast, software (St. Paul: MECC, 1990). Reviewed in: *Science and Children* 28, no. 8 (May 1991): 30

Murphy's Minerals, software (St. Paul: MECC, 1990). Reviewed in: *Science and Children* 28, no. 4 (Jan. 1991): 41

The Oregon Trail, software (Minneapolis: MECC, n.d.). Reviewed in: *Science and Children* 29, no. 6 (Mar. 1992): 49

Paper Plane Pilot, software (Minneapolis: MECC, 1991). Reviewed in: *Science and Children* 29, no. 2 (Oct. 1991): 46

Sun and Seasons, software (St. Paul: MECC, 1990). Reviewed in: *Science and Children* 28, no. 7 (Apr. 1991): 52

Woolly Bounce, software (Minneapolis: MECC, 1991). Reviewed in: *Science and Children* 29, no. 4 (Jan. 1992): 34; *Technology & Learning* 12, no. 4 (Jan. 1992): 8-9

Measurement
Insights into Science Data, software (Pleasantville, NY: Sunburst Communications, n.d.). Reviewed in: *Science and Children* 29, no. 6 (Mar. 1992): 51

Powers of Ten, by Charles Eames and Ray Eames, video (San Francisco: Pyramid Video, 1989). Reviewed in: *The Science Teacher* 59, no. 1 (Jan. 1992): 87–89

Medical topics
The Brain and Nervous System, software (Mahwah, NJ: Troll Associates, 1991). Reviewed in: *Science and Children* 29, no. 4 (Jan. 1992): 34-35

The Immune System, software (Shawnee Mission, KS: Marshmedia, n.d.). Reviewed in: *Science and Children* 28, no. 8 (May 1991): 30

Immunity, film (New Hyde Park, NY: National Teaching Aids, 1989). Reviewed in: *American Biology Teacher* 52, no. 7 (Oct. 1989): 444

The Skeletal and Muscular System, software (Mahwah, NJ: Troll Associates, 1991). Reviewed in: *Science and Children* 28, no. 1 (Sept. 1990): 50

Meteorology
Five Star Forecast, software (St. Paul: MECC, 1990). Reviewed in: *Science and Children* 28, no. 8 (May 1991): 30

Forecasting the Weather, software (Galesburg, MI: MCE, n.d.). Reviewed in: *Science and Children* 29, no. 4 (Jan. 1992): 35

An Ocean of Air, software (Galesburg, MI: MCE, n.d.). Reviewed in: *Science and Children* 29, no. 2 (Oct. 1991): 47

Storm, software, by Thomas Pesek (Houston, TX: Utopia Software, n.d.). Reviewed in: *Journal of Geography* 89, no. 2

Sun and Seasons, software (St. Paul: MECC, 1990). Reviewed in: *Science and Children* 28, no. 7 (Apr. 1991): 52

Weather Academy, software (Garden City, NY: Focus Media, 1989). Reviewed in: *Science and Children* 28, no. 6 (Mar. 1991): 46

Weather in Action, software (Washington, DC: National Geographic Society, 1988). Reviewed in: *Science and Children* 28, no. 8 (May 1991): 29–30

The Weather Machine, software (Washington DC: National Geographic Society, 1988). Reviewed in: *School Science and Mathematics* 90, no. 4 (Apr. 1990): 346

Microlytics (publishers)
Random House Encyclopedia, software (Pittsford, NY: Microlytics, 1990). Reviewed in: *Science and Children* 29, no. 6 (Mar. 1992): 49–50

Middle school materials
Activities for Teaching K–6 Math/Science Concepts, by Walter A. Farmer and Margaret A. Farrell (Bowling Green, OH: School Science and Mathematics, 1989). Reviewed in: *Science and Children* 28, no. 4 (Jan. 1991): 58

Adaptations, software (Galesburg, MI: MCE, n.d.). Reviewed in: *Science and Children* 29, no. 1 (Sept. 1992): 59

The Age of Dinosaurs, filmstrip (Washington, DC: National Geographic Society, 1990).

Reviewed in: *American Biology Teacher* 53, no. 3 (Mar. 1991): 189

The Animal Life Series, film/video (Van Nuys, CA: AIMS Media Film and Video, 1991). Reviewed in: *Media and Methods* 28, no. 1 (Sept./Oct. 1991): 46

Animals and Their World, by Judith E. Rinard, Gene S. Stuart, and Jennifer C. Urquhart (Washington, DC: National Geographic Society, 1990). Reviewed in: *Science and Children* 29, no. 5 (Feb. 1992): 48

The Brain and Nervous System, software (Mahwah, NJ: Troll Associates, 1991). Reviewed in: *Science and Children* 29, no. 4 (Jan. 1992): 34-35

Chemaid, software (Newbury Park, CA: Ventura Educational Systems, 1990). Reviewed in: *Science and Children* 29, no. 5 (Feb. 1992): 36; *Journal of Chemical Education* 68, no. 4 (Apr. 1991): 157

Chemical Activities, by Christie L. Borgford and Lee R. Summerline (Washington, DC: American Chemical Society, 1988). Reviewed in: *Science Activities* 28, no. 3 (Fall 1991): 44

Chemistry at Work, video (Seattle: Videodiscovery, 1991). Reviewed in: *Science Books and Films* 28, no. 2 (Mar. 1992): 59

Clearwater Detectives, software (Minneapolis: MECC, 1991). Reviewed in: *Science and Children* 29, no. 5 (Feb. 1992): 36–38

Clip Art for Science Teachers, software (Newbury Park, CA: Ventura Education Systems, 1991). Reviewed in: *Science and Children* 29, no. 4 (Jan. 1992): 34

The Complete Science Fair Handbook, by Issac Asimov and Anthony D. Fredericks (Glenview, IL: Scott Foresman, 1990). Reviewed in: *Science and Children* 28, no. 2 (Oct. 1990): 41

Consider the Earth: Environmental Activities for Grades 4–8, by Julie M. Gates (Englewood, CO: Teacher Ideas Press, 1989). Reviewed in: *Science Activities* 28, no. 1 (Spring 1991): 44

Middle school materials *(cont'd)*
Cosmic Chemistry, video (Warren, NJ: Optical Data, n.d.). Reviewed in: *Science Books and Films* 28, no. 2 (Mar. 1992): 59

Designasaurus II, software (San Francisco: Britannica Software, 1990). Reviewed in: *Science and Children* 29, no. 1 (Sept. 1991): 59

Dinosaur Construction Kit—Tyrannosaurus Rex, software (Acton, MA: D.C. Heath & Co./ William K. Bradford, 1987). Reviewed in: *Teaching with Technology* (Nov./Dec. 1991): 83

Dragons in the Trees, by James Martin (New York: Crown, 1991). Reviewed in: *Science and Children* 29, no. 6 (Mar. 1992): 55

Dyno-Quest, software (Tucson: Mindplay/ Methods and Solutions, 1984). Reviewed in: *Science and Children* 28, no. 1 (Sept. 1990): 19

Earth Science, software (Warren, NJ: Optical Data, n.d.). Reviewed in: *Science and Children* 28, no. 3 (Nov./Dec. 1990): 45

Earth Science for Every Kid: 101 Experiments That Really Work, by Janice VanCleave (New York: John Wiley and Sons, 1991). Reviewed in: *Journal of Geography* 91, no. 1 (Jan./Feb. 1992): 46

The Environment, software (Boca Raton, FL: IBM, n.d.). Reviewed in: *Science and Children* 28, no. 6 (Mar. 1991): 47

Exploring the World of Birds: An Equinox Guide to Avian Life, by Laurel Aziz and Adrian Forsyth (Charlotte, VT: Camden House, 1990). Reviewed in: *Science and Children* 29, no. 5 (Feb. 1992): 48

Eyewitness Juniors, by Alexander Parsons (New York: Knopf, 1990). Reviewed in: *Science and Children* 29, no. 4 (Jan. 1992): 39

Five Star Forecast, software (St. Paul: MECC, 1990). Reviewed in: *Science and Children* 28, no. 8 (May 1991): 30

Food Chains, software (Galesburg, MI: MCE, n.d.). Reviewed in: *Science and Children* 29, no. 2 (Oct. 1991): 46

Forecasting the Weather, software (Galesburg, MI: MCE, n.d.). Reviewed in: *Science and Children* 29, no. 4 (Jan. 1992): 35

Frog Dissection Lab Report, software (Uniondale, NY: Bergwall Educational Software, 1988). Reviewed in: *Science and Children* 27, no. 8 (May 1990): 38

Genetics and Heredity, software (Freeport, NY: Educational Activities, 1991). Reviewed in: *Science and Children* 29, no. 5 (Feb. 1992): 39

Hothouse Planet, software (Danbury, CT: EME, 1990). Reviewed in: *Science and Children* 28, no. 7 (Apr. 1991): 54

How to Make a Chemical Volcano and Other Mysterious Experiments, by Alan Kramer (New York: Franklin Watts, 1989). Reviewed in: *Curriculum Review* 31, no. 7 (Mar. 1992): 27

The Immune System, software (Shawnee Mission, KS: Marshmedia, n.d.). Reviewed in: *Science and Children* 28, no. 8 (May 1991): 30

Insights into Science Data, software (Pleasantville, NY: Sunburst Communications, n.d.). Reviewed in: *Science and Children* 29, no. 6 (Mar. 1992): 51

Life Cycles, software (Galesburg, MI: MCE, n.d.). Reviewed in: *Science and Children* 29, no. 1 (Sept. 1991): 58–59

Life Science Help Series, software (Garden City, NY: Focus Media, n.d.). Reviewed in: *Science and Children* 27, no. 7 (Apr. 1990): 44

Modern Genetics, software (Boca Raton, FL: IBM, n.d.). Reviewed in: *Science and Children* 28, no. 3 (Nov./Dec. 1990): 46

More Than Just a Garden, by Dwight Kuhn (Englewood Cliffs, NJ: Silver Burdett, 1990). Reviewed in: *Science and Children* 29, no. 2 (Oct. 1991): 53

Murphy's Minerals, software (St. Paul: MECC, 1990). Reviewed in: *Science and Children* 28, no. 4 (Jan. 1991): 41

Middle school materials *(cont'd)*

An Ocean of Air, software (Galesburg, MI: MCE, n.d.). Reviewed in: *Science and Children* 29, no. 2 (Oct. 1991): 47

The Oregon Trail, software (Minneapolis: MECC, n.d.). Reviewed in: *Science and Children* 29, no. 6 (Mar. 1992): 49

Paper Plane Pilot, software (Minneapolis: MECC, 1991). Reviewed in: *Science and Children* 29, no. 2 (Oct. 1991): 46

Physical Science Laboratory, software (Garden City, NY: Focus Media, 1990). Reviewed in: *Science and Children* 29, no. 6 (Mar. 1992): 50–51

Playing with Science: Motion, software (Pleasantville, NY: Sunburst Communications, n.d.). Reviewed in: *Science and Children* 28, no. 4 (Jan. 1991): 44–45

Pollution Control, software (Garden City, NY: Focus Media, 1989). Reviewed in: *Science and Children* 28, no. 7 (Apr. 1991): 52

Pollution Patrol, software (Victoria, B.C.: Entrex Software, 1987). Reviewed in: *Pollution Patrol* 27, no. 6 (Mar. 1990): 47

Powers of Ten, by Charles Eames and Ray Eames, video (San Francisco: Pyramid Video, 1989). Reviewed in: *The Science Teacher* 59, no. 1 (Jan. 1992): 87–89

Protozoa, software (Newbury Park, CA: Ventura Educational Systems, 1989). Reviewed in: *Science and Children,* 29, no. 5 (Feb. 1992): 36

Raintree Science Adventures, by Helen H. Cary and Judith E. Greenberg (Milwaukee, WI: Raintree, 1990). Reviewed in: *Science and Children* 29, no. 5 (Feb. 1992): 48

Random House Encyclopedia, software (Pittsford, NY: Microlytics, 1990). Reviewed in: *Science and Children* 29, no. 6 (Mar. 1992): 49–50

Safe Science Teaching, software (Des Moines: Jakel, n.d.). Reviewed in: *Science and Children* 29, no. 1 (Sept. 1991): 58

Science Fair Success, by R. Bombaugh (Hillside, NJ: Enslow, 1990). Reviewed in: *American Biology Teacher* 53, no. 3 (Mar. 1991): 192

The Secret Codes of C.Y.P.H.E.R., software (San Leandro, CA: Tanager Software, 1991). Reviewed in: *Technology & Learning* 12, no. 6 (Mar. 1992): 7

The Skeletal and Muscular System, software (Mahwah, NJ: Troll Associates, 1991). Reviewed in: *Science and Children* 28, no. 1 (Sept. 1990): 50

Storm, software, by Thomas Pesek (Houston, TX: Utopia Software, n.d.). Reviewed in: *Journal of Geography* 89, no. 2 (Mar./Apr. 1990): 194

Story Starters: Science, software (Farmington, CT: Pelica Software, 1989). Reviewed in: *Science and Children* 29, no. 2 (Oct. 1991): 47–48

Time Table History, software (Los Angeles: Xiphias, 1987). Reviewed in: *Science and Children* 29, no. 2 (Oct. 1992): 47

The Water Cycle, software (Galesburg, MI: MCE, n.d.). Reviewed in: *Science and Children* 29, no. 4 (Jan. 1992): 35

Weather in Action, software (Washington, DC: National Geographic Society, 1988). Reviewed in: *Science and Children* 28, no. 8 (May 1991): 29–30

Weather Academy, software (Garden City, NY: Focus Media, 1989). Reviewed in: *Science and Children* 28, no. 6 (Mar. 1991): 46

The Weather Machine, software (Washington DC: National Geographic Society, 1988). Reviewed in: *School Science and Mathematics* 90, no. 4 (Apr. 1990): 346

Who Lives Here?, video (Washington, DC: National Geographic Society, 1990). Reviewed in: *American Biology Teacher* 52, no. 7 (Oct. 1990): 443

Middle school materials *(cont'd)*
　The World's Harvest Series, by Jaqueline
　Dineen (Hillsdale, NJ: Enslow, 1988). Re-
　viewed in: *American Biology Teacher* 52, no. 4
　(Apr. 1990): 317

　Why Do Bodies Stop Growing?, by Philip
　Whitfield and Ruth Whitfield (New York:
　Viking Penguin, 1988). Reviewed in: *School
　Science and Mathematics* 90, no. 7 (Nov. 1988):
　656

　Wild Wings, by Phyllis Emert (n.p.: Julian
　Messner, 1990). Reviewed in: *Science and
　Children* 29, no. 5 (Feb. 1992): 48

Millbrook Press
　Volcano, by Christopher Lampton (Brookfield,
　CT: Millbrook Press, 1991). Reviewed in:
　Science Books and Films 28, no. 1 (Jan./Feb.
　1992): 15–16

Mindplay/Methods and Solutions
　Dyno-Quest, software (Tucson: Mindplay/
　Methods and Solutions, 1984). Reviewed in:
　Science and Children 28, no. 1 (Sept. 1990): 19

Modern Genetics
　software (Boca Raton, FL: IBM, n.d.). Re-
　viewed in: *Science and Children* 28, no. 3 (Nov./
　Dec. 1990): 46

More Than Just a Garden
　by Dwight Kuhn (Englewood Cliffs, NJ: Silver
　Burdett, 1990). Reviewed in: *Science and
　Children* 29, no. 2 (Oct. 1991): 53

Moshier, Susan
　*Science in Cinema: Teaching Science Fact
　Through Science Fiction Films,* by Judith E.
　Boss, Leroy W. Dubeck, and Susan Moshier
　(New York: Teachers College Press, 1988).
　Reviewed in: *The Science Teacher* 59, no. 2
　(Feb. 1992): 78-79

Murphy's Minerals
　software (St. Paul: MECC, 1990). Reviewed in:
　Science and Children 28, no. 4 (Jan. 1991): 41

National Association of Biology Teachers
　Oceanography for Landlocked Classrooms, ed.
　by Gerry M. Madrazo and Paul B. Hounshell

(Reston, VA: National Association of Biology
Teachers, 1990). Reviewed in: *The Science
Teacher* 59, no. 2 (Feb. 1992): 76–77

National Geographic Society
　The Age of Dinosaurs, filmstrip (Washington,
　DC: National Geographic Society, 1990).
　Reviewed in: *American Biology Teacher* 53, no.
　3 (Mar. 1991): 189

　Animals and Their World, by Judith E. Rinard,
　Gene S. Stuart, and Jennifer C. Urquhart
　(Washington, DC: National Geographic
　Society, 1990). Reviewed in: *Science and
　Children* 29, no. 5 (Feb. 1992): 48

　Books for Young Explorers—Set XVI, by Na-
　tional Geographic Society (Washington, DC:
　National Geographic Society, 1989). Reviewed
　in: *American Biology Teacher* 53, no. 5 (May
　1991): 314–315

　Project Zoo, software (Washington DC:
　National Geographic Society, 1987). Reviewed
　in: *School Science and Mathematics* 90, no. 6
　(Nov. 1990): 652

　Ready Set Go: How Animals Move, filmstrip
　(Washington, DC: National Geographic
　Society, 1989). Reviewed in: *American Biology
　Teacher* 52, no. 8 (Nov./Dec. 1990): 514

　The Weather Machine, software (Washington
　DC: National Geographic Society, 1988).
　Reviewed in: *School Science and Mathematics*
　90, no. 4 (Apr. 1990): 346

　Weather in Action, software (Washington, DC:
　National Geographic Society, 1988). Reviewed
　in: *Science and Children* 28, no. 8 (May 1991):
　29–30

　Who Lives Here?, video (Washington, DC:
　National Geographic Society, 1990). Reviewed
　in: *American Biology Teacher* 52, no. 7 (Oct.
　1990): 443

National Teaching Aids
　Immunity, film (New Hyde Park, NY: National
　Teaching Aids, 1989). Reviewed in: *American
　Biology Teacher* 52, no. 7 (Oct. 1989): 444

Natural science

The Animal Life Series, film/video (Van Nuys, CA: AIMS Media Film and Video, 1991). Reviewed in: *Media and Methods* 28, no. 1 (Sept./Oct. 1991): 46

Animals and Their World, by Judith E. Rinard, Gene S. Stuart, and Jennifer C. Urquhart (Washington, DC: National Geographic Society, 1990). Reviewed in: *Science and Children* 29, no. 5 (Feb. 1992): 48

Animals in Danger, by William McCay (New York: Aladdin, 1990). Reviewed in: *Science and Children* 29, no. 4 (Jan. 1992): 39

Animals in the Classroom, by David C. Kramer (Menlo Park, CA: Addison-Wesley Publishing, 1989). Reviewed in: *School Science and Mathematics* 90, no. 3 (Mar. 1990): 261

Jungle Safari, software (Pound Ridge, NY: Orange Cherry/Talking School House Software, 1990). Reviewed in: *Science and Children* 29, no. 4 (Jan. 1992): 35

Learn about Insects, software (Pleasantville, NY: Sunburst Communications, n.d.). Reviewed in: *Science and Children* 28, no. 8 (May 1991): 30

Life Cycles, software (Galesburg, MI: MCE, n.d.). Reviewed in: *Science and Children* 29, no. 1 (Sept. 1991): 58–59

Life Science, software (Ramsey, NJ: K–12 Micromedia, 1991). Reviewed in: *Methods and Media* 28 no. 4 (Mar./Apr. 1992): 60

Life Science Help Series, software (Garden City, NY: Focus Media, n.d.). Reviewed in: *Science and Children* 27, no. 7 (Apr. 1990): 44

Life's Devices: The Physical World of Plants and Animals, by Steven Vogel (Princeton: Princeton University Press, 1989). Reviewed in: *American Biology Teacher* 52, no. 6 (Sept. 1990): 388

Pet Gerbils, by Jerome Wexler (Morton Grove, IL: Albert Whitman, 1990). Reviewed in: *Science and Children* 29, no. 6 (Mar. 1992): 55

Project Zoo, software (Washington DC: National Geographic Society, 1987). Reviewed in: *School Science and Mathematics* 90, no. 6 (Nov. 1990): 652

Ready Set Go: How Animals Move, filmstrip (Washington, DC: National Geographic Society, 1989). Reviewed in: *American Biology Teacher* 52, no. 8 (Nov./Dec. 1990): 514

School Yard Science, by Peggy Perdue (Glenview IL: Scott Foresman, 1991). Reviewed in: *Curriculum Review* 30, no. 3 (Nov. 1990): 30

3–2–1 Contact: Wild Things, software by The Children's Television Workshop (Scott's Valley, CA: Wings for Learning, 1991). Reviewed in: *Teaching with Technology* (Feb. 1992): 59

Who Lives Here?, video (Washington, DC: National Geographic Society, 1990). Reviewed in: *American Biology Teacher* 52, no. 7 (Oct. 1990): 443

Wild Wings, by Phyllis Emert (n.p.: Julian Messner, 1990). Reviewed in: *Science and Children* 29, no. 5 (Feb. 1992): 48

Wildlife at Risk, by Malcom Penny (n.p.: Bookright, 1990). Reviewed in: *Science and Children* 29, no. 4 (Jan. 1992): 39

Woolly Bounce, software (Minneapolis: MECC, 1991). Reviewed in: *Science and Children* 29, no. 4 (Jan. 1992): 34, *Technology & Learning* 12, no. 4 (Jan. 1992): 8-9

Nebraska Scientific

Dissection and Anatomy of the Brain, video (Omaha: Nebraska Scientific, 1989). Reviewed in: *American Biology Teacher* 52, no. 4 (Apr. 1990): 309

An Ocean of Air

software (Galesburg, MI: MCE, n.d.). Reviewed in: *Science and Children* 29, no. 2 (Oct. 1991): 47

Oceanography for Landlocked Classrooms

ed. by Gerry M. Madrazo and Paul B. Hounshell (Reston, VA: National Association of Biology Teachers, 1990). Reviewed in: *The Science Teacher* 59, no. 2 (Feb. 1992): 76–77

100 Science Puzzles
by Colin McCarty and Jane Young (London: Unwin Hyman, 1989). Reviewed in: *Physics Education* 25, no. 5 (Sept. 1990): 293

Oosterman, Margaret A.
Earth Science Investigations, by Margaret A. Oosterman and Mark T. Schmidt (Alexandria, VA: American Geology Institute, 1990). Reviewed in: *The Science Teacher* 59, no. 2 (Feb. 1992): 84–85

Optical Data (publishers)
Cosmic Chemistry, video (Warren, NJ: Optical Data, n.d.). Reviewed in: *Science Books and Films* 28, no. 2 (Mar. 1992): 59

Earth Science, software (Warren, NJ: Optical Data, n.d.). Reviewed in: *Science and Children* 28, no. 3 (Nov./Dec. 1990): 45

Orange Cherry/Talking School House Software
Jungle Safari, software (Pound Ridge, NY: Orange Cherry/Talking School House Software, 1990). Reviewed in: *Science and Children* 29, no. 4 (Jan. 1992): 35

The Oregon Trail
software (Minneapolis: MECC, n.d.). Reviewed in: *Science and Children* 29, no. 6 (Mar. 1992): 49

Paper Plane Pilot
software (Minneapolis: MECC, 1991). Reviewed in: *Science and Children* 29, no. 2 (Oct. 1991): 46

Paleontology
The Age of Dinosaurs, filmstrip (Washington, DC: National Geographic Society, 1990). Reviewed in: *American Biology Teacher* 53, no. 3 (Mar. 1991): 189

Designasaurus II, software (San Francisco: Britannica Software, 1990). Reviewed in: *Science and Children* 29, no. 1 (Sept. 1991): 59

Dinosaur Construction Kit—Tyrannosaurus Rex, software (Acton, MA: D.C. Heath & Co./ William K. Bradford, 1987). Reviewed in: *Teaching with Technology* (Nov./Dec. 1991): 83

Dyno-Quest, software (Tucson: Mindplay/ Methods and Solutions, 1984). Reviewed in: *Science and Children* 28, no. 1 (Sept. 1990): 19

Parsons, Alexander
Eyewitness Juniors, by Alexander Parsons (New York: Knopf, 1990). Reviewed in: *Science and Children* 29, no. 4 (Jan. 1992): 39

Pelica Software
Story Starters: Science, software (Farmington, CT: Pelica Software, 1989). Reviewed in: *Science and Children* 29, no. 2 (Oct. 1991): 47–48

Penny, Malcom
Wildlife at Risk, by Malcom Penny (n.p.: Bookright, 1990). Reviewed in: *Science and Children* 29, no. 4 (Jan. 1992): 39

Perdue, Peggy K.
Dive into Science: Hands-on Water-Related Experiments, by Peggy K. Perdue (Glenview, IL: Scott Foresman, n.d.). Reviewed in: *Science and Children* 28, no. 7 (Apr. 1991): 54

School Yard Science, by Peggy Perdue (Glenview IL: Scott Foresman, 1991). Reviewed in: *Curriculum Review* 30, no. 3 (Nov. 1990): 30

Pesek, Thomas
Storm, software, by Thomas Pesek (Houston, TX: Utopia Software, n.d.). Reviewed in: *Journal of Geography* 89, no. 2 (Mar./Apr. 1990): 194

Pet Gerbils
by Jerome Wexler (Morton Grove, IL: Albert Whitman, 1990). Reviewed in: *Science and Children* 29, no. 6 (Mar. 1992): 55

Photography
Picture Library Series, by Norman Barrett (New York: Franklin Watts, 1989). Reviewed in: *Science and Children* 28, no. 1 (Sept. 1990): 79

Physical science
Physical Science Laboratory, software (Garden City, NY: Focus Media, 1990). Reviewed in: *Science and Children* 29, no. 6 (Mar. 1992): 50–51

Physical Science Laboratory
software (Garden City, NY: Focus Media, 1990). Reviewed in: Science and Children 29, no. 6 (Mar. 1992): 50–51

Physics
Physics Explorer: One Body, software (Scotts Valley, CA: Wings for Learning, 1991). Reviewed in: Technology & Learning 12, no. 4 (Jan. 1992): 10, 11, 14

Physics Matters, by Nick England (London: Hodder and Stoughton, 1989). Reviewed in: Physics Matters 25, no. 2 (Mar. 1990): 130

Physics 1.2, software (San Rafael, CA: Broderbund Software, n.d.). Reviewed in: Journal of Geographical Education 39, no. 1 (Jan. 1991): 71

Playing with Science: Motion, software (Pleasantville, NY: Sunburst Communications, n.d.). Reviewed in: Science and Children 28, no. 4 (Jan. 1991): 44–45

Unique Science: Demonstrations and Laboratories for the Physics Instructor, by E. M. Kinsman and C. Waters (Syracuse: Kinsman Physics, 1991). Reviewed in: Science Books and Films 28, no. 1 (Jan./Feb. 1992): 15

What If?, by Robert G. Fuller (New York: Wilson Learning, 1989). Reviewed in: Physics Teacher 28, no. 5 (May 1990): 349

Physics Explorer: One Body
software (Scotts Valley, CA: Wings for Learning, 1991). Reviewed in: Technology & Learning 12, no. 4 (Jan. 1992): 10, 11, 14

Physics Matters
by Nick England (London: Hodder and Stoughton, 1989). Reviewed in: Physics Matters 25, no. 2 (Mar. 1990): 130

Physics 1.2
software (San Rafael, CA: Broderbund Software, n.d.). Reviewed in: Journal of Geographical Education 39, no. 1 (Jan. 1991): 71

Picture Library Series
by Norman Barrett (New York: Franklin Watts, 1989). Reviewed in: Science and Children 28, no. 1 (Sept. 1990): 79

Playing with Science: Motion
software (Pleasantville, NY: Sunburst Communications, n.d.). Reviewed in: Science and Children 28, no. 4 (Jan. 1991): 44–45

Pollution Control
software (Garden City, NY: Focus Media, 1989). Reviewed in: Science and Children 28, no. 7 (Apr. 1991): 52

Pollution Patrol
software (Victoria, B.C.: Entrex Software, 1987). Reviewed in: Pollution Patrol 27, no. 6 (Mar. 1990): 47

Population
World Population, video (Washington, DC: ZPG Population Education Program, 1990). Reviewed in: The American Biology Teacher 53, no. 3 (Mar. 1991): 189

Powers of Ten
by Charles Eames and Ray Eames, video (San Francisco: Pyramid Video, 1989). Reviewed in: The Science Teacher 59, no. 1

Princeton University Press
Life's Devices: The Physical World of Plants and Animals, by Steven Vogel (Princeton: Princeton University Press, 1989). Reviewed in: American Biology Teacher 52, no. 6 (Sept. 1990): 388

Project Zoo
software (Washington DC: National Geographic Society, 1987). Reviewed in: School Science and Mathematics 90, no. 6 (Nov. 1990): 652 (Jan. 1992): 87–89

Protozoa
software (Newbury Park, CA: Ventura Educational Systems, 1989). Reviewed in: Science and Children, 29, no. 5 (Feb. 1992): 36

Pyramid Video
Powers of Ten, by Charles Eames and Ray Eames, video (San Francisco: Pyramid Video, 1989). Reviewed in: The Science Teacher 59, no. 1 (Jan. 1992): 87–89

Raintree Science Adventures
by Helen H. Cary and Judith E. Greenberg (Milwaukee, WI: Raintree, 1990). Reviewed in: Science and Children 29, no. 5 (Feb. 1992): 48

Random House Encyclopedia
software (Pittsford, NY: Microlytics, 1990).
Reviewed in: *Science and Children* 29, no. 6
(Mar. 1992): 49–50

Reading skills
Books for Young Explorers—Set XVI, by National Geographic Society (Washington, DC:
National Geographic Society, 1989). Reviewed
in: *American Biology Teacher* 53, no. 5 (May
1991): 314–315

Story Starters: Science, software (Farmington,
CT: Pelica Software, 1989). Reviewed in:
Science and Children 29, no. 2 (Oct. 1991): 47–48

Ready Set Go: How Animals Move
filmstrip (Washington, DC: National Geographic Society, 1989). Reviewed in: *American
Biology Teacher* 52, no. 8 (Nov./Dec. 1990): 514

Reference
Random House Encyclopedia, software
(Pittsford, NY: Microlytics, 1990). Reviewed
in: *Science and Children* 29, no. 6 (Mar. 1992):
49–50

Research
The Art of Science Writing, by Bernadette
Mayer and Dale Worsley (New York: Teachers
and Writers Collaborative, 1989). Reviewed in:
American Biology Teacher 52, no. 3 (Mar.
1990): 192

The Secret Codes of C.Y.P.H.E.R., software
(San Leandro, CA: Tanager Software, 1991).
Reviewed in: *Technology & Learning* 12, no. 6
(Mar. 1992): 7

*Students and Research: Practical Strategies for
Science Classrooms and Competitions,* by Julia
H. Cothron, Ronald H. Giese, and Richard J.
Rezba (Dubuque: Kendall/Hunt, 1989).
Reviewed in: *The Science Teacher* 59, no. 2
(Jan. 1992): 78–79

Rezba, Richard J.
*Students and Research: Practical Strategies for
Science Classrooms and Competitions,* by Julia
H. Cothron, Ronald H. Giese, and Richard J.
Rezba (Dubuque: Kendall/Hunt, 1989).
Reviewed in: *The Science Teacher* 59, no. 2
(Jan. 1992): 78–79

Rinard, Judith E.
Animals and Their World, by Judith E. Rinard,
Gene S. Stuart, and Jennifer C. Urquhart
(Washington, DC: National Geographic
Society, 1990). Reviewed in: *Science and
Children* 29, no. 5 (Feb. 1992): 48

Safe Science Teaching
software (Des Moines: Jakel, n.d.). Reviewed
in: *Science and Children* 29, no. 1 (Sept. 1991):
58

Schmidt, Mark T.
Earth Science Investigations, by Margaret A.
Oosterman and Mark T. Schmidt (Alexandria,
VA: American Geology Institute, 1990).
Reviewed in: *The Science Teacher* 59, no. 2
(Feb. 1992): 84–85

School Science and Mathematics Association
*Activities for Teaching K–6 Math/Science
Concepts,* by Walter A. Farmer and Margaret
A. Farrell (Bowling Green, OH: School Science
and Mathematics, 1989). Reviewed in: *Science
and Children* 28, no. 4 (Jan. 1991): 58

School Yard Science
by Peggy Perdue (Glenview IL: Scott
Foresman, 1991). Reviewed in: *Curriculum
Review* 30, no. 3 (Nov. 1990): 30

Science fairs
The Complete Science Fair Handbook, by Issac
Asimov and Anthony D. Fredericks (Glenview,
IL: Scott Foresman, 1990). Reviewed in:
Science and Children 28, no. 2 (Oct. 1990): 41

Science Fair Success, by R. Bombaugh (Hillside, NJ: Enslow, 1990). Reviewed in: *American
Biology Teacher* 53, no. 3 (Mar. 1991): 192

*Students and Research: Practical Strategies for
Science Classrooms and Competitions,* by Julia
H. Cothron, Ronald H. Giese, and Richard J.
Rezba (Dubuque: Kendall/Hunt, 1989).
Reviewed in: *The Science Teacher* 59, no. 2
(Jan. 1992): 78–79

Science Fair Success
by R. Bombaugh (Hillside, NJ: Enslow, 1990).
Reviewed in: *American Biology Teacher* 53, no.
3 (Mar. 1991): 192

Science fiction
  Science in Cinema: Teaching Science Fact Through Science Fiction Films, by Judith E. Boss, Leroy W. Dubeck, and Susan Moshier (New York: Teachers College Press, 1988). Reviewed in: *The Science Teacher* 59, no. 2 (Feb. 1992): 78-79

Science in Cinema: Teaching Science Fact through Science Fiction Films
  by Judith E. Boss, Leroy W. Dubeck, and Susan Moshier (New York: Teachers College Press, 1988). Reviewed in: *The Science Teacher* 59 no. 2 (Feb. 1992): 78-79

Scott Foresman
  Dive into Science: Hands-on Water-Related Experiments, by Peggy K. Perdue (Glenview, IL: Scott Foresman, n.d.). Reviewed in: *Science and Children* 28, no. 7 (Apr. 1991): 54

  The Complete Science Fair Handbook, by Issac Asimov and Anthony D. Fredericks (Glenview, IL: Scott Foresman, 1990). Reviewed in: *Science and Children* 28, no. 2 (Oct. 1990): 41

  School Yard Science, by Peggy Perdue (Glenview IL: Scott Foresman, 1991). Reviewed in: *Curriculum Review* 30, no. 3 (Nov. 1990): 30

The Secret Codes of C.Y.P.H.E.R.
  software (San Leandro, CA: Tanager Software, 1991). Reviewed in: *Technology & Learning* 12, no. 6 (Mar. 1992): 7

Silver Burdett
  More Than Just a Garden, by Dwight Kuhn (Englewood Cliffs, NJ: Silver Burdett, 1990). Reviewed in: *Science and Children* 29, no. 2 (Oct. 1991): 53

SimEarth
  software (Orinda, CA: Maxis, 1990). Reviewed in: *School Science and Mathematics* 92, no. 1 (Jan. 1992): 47; *Journal of Geography* 91, no. 1 (Jan./Feb. 1992): 47

Simple and Safe Experiments
  by William R. Wellnitz (n.p., 1990). Reviewed in: *Science and Children* 29, no. 6 (Mar. 1992): 55

Sinauer Associates
  Evolutionary Biology, 2d ed. by Douglas J. Futuyma (Sunderland, MA: Sinauer Associates, 1986). Reviewed in: *American Biology Teacher* 52, no. 4 (Apr. 1990): 318

The Skeletal and Muscular System
  software (Mahwah, NJ: Troll Associates, 1991). Reviewed in: *Science and Children* 28, no. 1 (Sept. 1990): 50

Software products
  Adaptations, software (Galesburg, MI: MCE, n.d.). Reviewed in: *Science and Children* 29, no. 1 (Sept. 1992): 59

  The Brain and Nervous System, software (Mahwah, NJ: Troll Associates, 1991). Reviewed in: *Science and Children* 29, no. 4 (Jan. 1992): 34-35

  Chemaid, software (Newbury Park, CA: Ventura Educational Systems, 1990). Reviewed in: *Science and Children* 29, no. 5 (Feb. 1992): 36; *Journal of Chemical Education* 68, no. 4 (Apr. 1991): 157

  Clearwater Detectives, software (Minneapolis: MECC, 1991). Reviewed in: *Science and Children* 29, no. 5 (Feb. 1992): 36–38

  Clip Art for Science Teachers, software (Newbury Park, CA: Ventura Education Systems, 1991). Reviewed in: *Science and Children* 29, no. 4 (Jan. 1992): 34

  Designasaurus II, software (San Francisco: Britannica Software, 1990). Reviewed in: *Science and Children* 29, no. 1 (Sept. 1991): 59

  Dinosaur Construction Kit—Tyrannosaurus Rex, software (Acton, MA: D.C. Heath & Co./William K. Bradford, 1987). Reviewed in: *Teaching with Technology* (Nov./Dec. 1991): 83

  Dyno-Quest, software (Tucson: Mindplay/Methods and Solutions, 1984). Reviewed in: *Science and Children* 28, no. 1 (Sept. 1990): 19

  Earth Science, software (Warren, NJ: Optical Data, n.d.). Reviewed in: *Science and Children* 28, no. 3 (Nov./Dec. 1990): 45

Software products *(cont'd)*

The Environment, software (Boca Raton, FL: IBM, n.d.). Reviewed in: *Science and Children* 28, no. 6 (Mar. 1991): 47

Five Star Forecast, software (St. Paul: MECC, 1990). Reviewed in: *Science and Children* 28, no. 8 (May 1991): 30

Food Chains, software (Galesburg, MI: MCE, n.d.). Reviewed in: *Science and Children* 29, no. 2 (Oct. 1991): 46

Forecasting the Weather, software (Galesburg, MI: MCE, n.d.). Reviewed in: *Science and Children* 29, no. 4 (Jan. 1992): 35

Frog Dissection Lab Report, software (Uniondale, NY: Bergwall Educational Software, 1988). Reviewed in: *Science and Children* 27, no. 8 (May 1990): 38

Genetics and Heredity, software (Freeport, NY: Educational Activities, 1991). Reviewed in: *Science and Children* 29, no. 5 (Feb. 1992): 39

Hothouse Planet, software (Danbury, CT: EME, 1990). Reviewed in: *Science and Children* 28, no. 7 (Apr. 1991): 54

The Immune System, software (Shawnee Mission, KS: Marshmedia, n.d.). Reviewed in: *Science and Children* 28, no. 8 (May 1991): 30

Insights into Science Data, software (Pleasantville, NY: Sunburst Communications, n.d.). Reviewed in: *Science and Children* 29, no. 6 (Mar. 1992): 51

Jungle Safari, software (Pound Ridge, NY: Orange Cherry/Talking School House Software, 1990). Reviewed in: *Science and Children* 29, no. 4 (Jan. 1992): 35

Lake Study, software (Ypsilanti, MI: Eastern Michigan Univ., n.d.). Reviewed in: *School Science and Mathematics* 90, no. 8 (Dec. 1990): 741

Learn about Insects, software (Pleasantville, NY: Sunburst Communications, n.d.). Reviewed in: *Science and Children* 28, no. 8 (May 1991): 30

Life Cycles, software (Galesburg, MI: MCE, n.d.). Reviewed in: *Science and Children* 29, no. 1 (Sept. 1991): 58–59

Life Science, software (Ramsey, NJ: K–12 Micromedia, 1991). Reviewed in: *Methods and Media* 28 no. 4 (Mar./Apr. 1992): 60

Life Science Help Series, software (Garden City, NY: Focus Media, n.d.). Reviewed in: *Science and Children* 27, no. 7 (Apr. 1990): 44

Modern Genetics, software (Boca Raton, FL: IBM, n.d.). Reviewed in: *Science and Children* 28, no. 3 (Nov./Dec. 1990): 46

Murphy's Minerals, software (St. Paul: MECC, 1990). Reviewed in: *Science and Children* 28, no. 4 (Jan. 1991): 41

An Ocean of Air, software (Galesburg, MI: MCE, n.d.). Reviewed in: *Science and Children* 29, no. 2 (Oct. 1991): 47

The Oregon Trail, software (Minneapolis: MECC, n.d.). Reviewed in: *Science and Children* 29, no. 6 (Mar. 1992): 49

Paper Plane Pilot, software (Minneapolis: MECC, 1991). Reviewed in: *Science and Children* 29, no. 2 (Oct. 1991): 46

Physical Science Laboratory, software (Garden City, NY: Focus Media, 1990). Reviewed in: *Science and Children* 29, no. 6 (Mar. 1992): 50–51

Physics Explorer: One Body, software (Scotts Valley, CA: Wings for Learning, 1991). Reviewed in: *Technology & Learning* 12, no. 4 (Jan. 1992): 10, 11, 14

Physics 1.2, software (San Rafael, CA: Broderbund Software, n.d.). Reviewed in: *Journal of Geographical Education* 39, no. 1 (Jan. 1991): 71

Playing with Science: Motion, software (Pleasantville, NY: Sunburst Communications, n.d.). Reviewed in: *Science and Children* 28, no. 4 (Jan. 1991): 44–45

Software products *(cont'd)*

Pollution Control, software (Garden City, NY: Focus Media, 1989). Reviewed in: *Science and Children* 28, no. 7 (Apr. 1991): 52

Pollution Patrol, software (Victoria, B.C.: Entrex Software, 1987). Reviewed in: *Pollution Patrol* 27, no. 6 (Mar. 1990): 47

Project Zoo, software (Washington DC: National Geographic Society, 1987). Reviewed in: *School Science and Mathematics* 90, no. 6 (Nov. 1990): 652

Protozoa, software (Newbury Park, CA: Ventura Educational Systems, 1989). Reviewed in: *Science and Children,* 29, no. 5 (Feb. 1992): 36

Random House Encyclopedia, software (Pittsford, NY: Microlytics, 1990). Reviewed in: *Science and Children* 29, no. 6 (Mar. 1992): 49–50

Safe Science Teaching, software (Des Moines: Jakel, n.d.). Reviewed in: *Science and Children* 29, no. 1 (Sept. 1991): 58

The Secret Codes of C.Y.P.H.E.R., software (San Leandro, CA: Tanager Software, 1991). Reviewed in: *Technology & Learning* 12, no. 6 (Mar. 1992): 7

SimEarth, software (Orinda, CA: Maxis, 1990). Reviewed in: *School Science and Mathematics* 92, no. 1 (Jan. 1992): 47; *Journal of Geography* 91, no. 1 (Jan./Feb. 1992): 47

The Skeletal and Muscular System, software (Mahwah, NJ: Troll Associates, 1991). Reviewed in: *Science and Children* 28, no. 1 (Sept. 1990): 50

Story Starters: Science, software (Farmington, CT: Pelica Software, 1989). Reviewed in: *Science and Children* 29, no. 2 (Oct. 1991): 47–48

Sun and Seasons, software (St. Paul: MECC, 1990). Reviewed in: *Science and Children* 28, no. 7 (Apr. 1991): 52

Time Table History, software (Los Angeles: Xiphias, 1987). Reviewed in: *Science and Children* 29, no. 2 (Oct. 1992): 47

The Water Cycle, software (Galesburg, MI: MCE, n.d.). Reviewed in: *Science and Children* 29, no. 4 (Jan. 1992): 35

Weather Academy, software (Garden City, NY: Focus Media, 1989). Reviewed in: *Science and Children* 28, no. 6 (Mar. 1991): 46

Weather in Action, software (Washington, DC: National Geographic Society, 1988). Reviewed in: *Science and Children* 28, no. 8 (May 1991): 29–30

The Weather Machine, software (Washington DC: National Geographic Society, 1988). Reviewed in: *School Science and Mathematics* 90, no. 4 (Apr. 1990): 346

Woolly Bounce, software (Minneapolis: MECC, 1991). Reviewed in: *Science and Children* 29, no. 4 (Jan. 1992): 34, *Technology & Learning* 12, no. 4 (Jan. 1992): 8-9

Storm
software, by Thomas Pesek (Houston, TX: Utopia Software, n.d.). Reviewed in: *Journal of Geography* 89, no. 2 (Mar./Apr. 1990): 194

Story Starters: Science
software (Farmington, CT: Pelica Software, 1989). Reviewed in: *Science and Children* 29, no. 2 (Oct. 1991): 47–481990): 194

Stuart, Gene S.
Animals and Their World, by Judith E. Rinard, Gene S. Stuart, and Jennifer C. Urquhart (Washington, DC: National Geographic Society, 1990). Reviewed in: *Science and Children* 29, no. 5 (Feb. 1992): 48

Students and Research: Practical Strategies for Science Classrooms and Competitions
by Julia H. Cothron, Ronald H. Giese, and Richard J. Rezba (Dubuque: Kendall/Hunt, 1989). Reviewed in: *The Science Teacher* 59, no. 2 (Jan. 1992): 78–79

Summerline, Lee R.
Chemical Activities, by Christie L. Borgford and Lee R. Summerline (Washington, DC: American Chemical Society, 1988). Reviewed in: *Science Activities* 28, no. 3 (Fall 1991): 44

Sun and Seasons
software (St. Paul: MECC, 1990). Reviewed in: *Science and Children* 28, no. 7 (Apr. 1991): 52

Sunburst Communications
Insights into Science Data, software (Pleasantville, NY: Sunburst Communications, n.d.). Reviewed in: *Science and Children* 29, no. 6 (Mar. 1992): 51

Learn about Insects, software (Pleasantville, NY: Sunburst Communications, n.d.). Reviewed in: *Science and Children* 28, no. 8 (May 1991): 30

Playing with Science: Motion, software (Pleasantville, NY: Sunburst Communications, n.d.). Reviewed in: *Science and Children* 28, no. 4 (Jan. 1991): 44–45

3–2–1 Contact: Wild Things
software by The Children's Television Workshop (Scott's Valley, CA: Wings for Learning, 1991). Reviewed in: *Teaching with Technology* (Feb. 1992): 59

Tanager Software
The Secret Codes of C. Y.P.H.E.R., software (San Leandro, CA: Tanager Software, 1991). Reviewed in: *Technology & Learning* 12, no. 6 (Mar. 1992): 7

Teacher Ideas Press
Consider the Earth: Environmental Activities for Grades 4–8, by Julie M. Gates (Englewood, CO: Teacher Ideas Press, 1989). Reviewed in: *Science Activities* 28, no. 1 (Spring 1991): 44

Teachers and Writers Collaborative
The Art of Science Writing, by Bernadette Mayer and Dale Worsley (New York: Teachers and Writers Collaborative, 1989). Reviewed in: *American Biology Teacher* 52, no. 3 (Mar. 1990): 192

Teachers College Press
Science in Cinema: Teaching Science Fact Through Science Fiction Films, by Judith E.

Boss, Leroy W. Dubeck, and Susan Moshier (New York: Teachers College Press, 1988). Reviewed in: *The Science Teacher* 59 no. 2 (Feb. 1992): 78-79

Teaching methods
Safe Science Teaching, software (Des Moines: Jakel, n.d.). Reviewed in: *Science and Children* 29, no. 1 (Sept. 1991): 58

Science in Cinema: Teaching Science Fact Through Science Fiction Films, by Judith E. Boss, Leroy W. Dubeck, and Susan Moshier (New York: Teachers College Press, 1988). Reviewed in: *The Science Teacher* 59, no. 2 (Feb. 1992): 78-79

Time Table History
software (Los Angeles: Xiphias, 1987). Reviewed in: *Science and Children* 29, no. 2 (Oct. 1992): 47

Troll Associates
The Brain and Nervous System, software (Mahwah, NJ: Troll Associates, 1991). Reviewed in: *Science and Children* 29, no. 4 (Jan. 1992): 34-35

The Skeletal and Muscular System, software (Mahwah, NJ: Troll Associates, 1991). Reviewed in: *Science and Children* 28, no. 1 (Sept. 1990): 50

Unique Science: Demonstrations and Laboratories for the Physics Instructor
by E. M. Kinsman and C. Waters (Syracuse: Kinsman Physics, 1991). Reviewed in: *Science Books and Films* 28, no. 1 (Jan./Feb. 1992): 15

United Learning
The Biology of Water, video (Niles, IL: United Learning, 1991). Reviewed in: *Media and Methods* 28, no. 1 (Sept./Oct. 1991): 46

Unwin Hyman
100 Science Puzzles, by Colin McCarty and Jane Young (London: Unwin Hyman, 1989). Reviewed in: *Physics Education* 25, no. 5 (Sept. 1990): 293

Urquhart, Jennifer C.
Animals and Their World, by Judith E. Rinard, Gene S. Stuart, and Jennifer C. Urquhart (Washington, DC: National Geographic Society, 1990). Reviewed in: *Science and Children* 29, no. 5 (Feb. 1992): 48

Utopia Software
Storm, software, by Thomas Pesek (Houston, TX: Utopia Software, n.d.). Reviewed in: *Journal of Geography* 89, no. 2 (Mar./Apr. 1990): 194

VanCleave, Janice
Earth Science for Every Kid: 101 Experiments That Really Work, by Janice VanCleave (New York: John Wiley and Sons, 1991). Reviewed in: *Journal of Geography* 91, no. 1 (Jan./Feb. 1992): 46

Ventura Educational Systems
Chemaid, software (Newbury Park, CA: Ventura Educational Systems, 1990). Reviewed in: *Science and Children* 29, no. 5 (Feb. 1992): 36; *Journal of Chemical Education* 68, no. 4 (Apr. 1991): 157

Clip Art for Science Teachers, software (Newbury Park, CA: Ventura Education Systems, 1991). Reviewed in: *Science and Children* 29, no. 4 (Jan. 1992): 34

Protozoa, software (Newbury Park, CA: Ventura Educational Systems, 1989). Reviewed in: *Science and Children,* 29, no. 5 (Feb. 1992): 36

Videodiscovery (publishers)
Chemistry at Work, video (Seattle: Videodiscovery, 1991). Reviewed in: *Science Books and Films* 28, no. 2 (Mar. 1992): 59

Viking Penguin
Why Do Bodies Stop Growing?, by Philip Whitfield and Ruth Whitfield (New York: Viking Penguin, 1988). Reviewed in: *School Science and Mathematics* 90, no. 7 (Nov. 1988): 656

Visual aids
Clip Art for Science Teachers, software (Newbury Park, CA: Ventura Education Systems, 1991). Reviewed in: *Science and Children* 29, no. 4 (Jan. 1992): 34

Picture Library Series, by Norman Barrett (New York: Franklin Watts, 1989). Reviewed in: *Science and Children* 28, no. 1 (Sept. 1990): 79

Vogel, Steven
Life's Devices: The Physical World of Plants and Animals, by Steven Vogel (Princeton: Princeton University Press, 1989). Reviewed in: *American Biology Teacher* 52, no. 6 (Sept. 1990): 388

Volcano
by Christopher Lampton (Brookfield, CT: Millbrook Press, 1991). Reviewed in: *Science Books and Films* 28, no. 1 (Jan./Feb. 1992): 15–16

The Water Cycle
software (Galesburg, MI: MCE, n.d.). Reviewed in: *Science and Children* 29, no. 4 (Jan. 1992): 35

Waters, C.
Unique Science: Demonstrations and Laboratories for the Physics Instructor, by E. M. Kinsman and C. Waters (Syracuse: Kinsman Physics, 1991). Reviewed in: *Science Books and Films* 28, no. 1 (Jan./Feb. 1992): 15

Weather. *See* Meteorology

Weather Academy
software (Garden City, NY: Focus Media, 1989). Reviewed in: *Science and Children* 28, no. 6 (Mar. 1991): 46

Weather in Action
software (Washington, DC: National Geographic Society, 1988). Reviewed in: *Science and Children* 28, no. 8 (May 1991): 29–30

The Weather Machine
software (Washington DC: National Geographic Society, 1988). Reviewed in: *School Science and Mathematics* 90, no. 4 (Apr. 1990): 346

Wellnitz, William R.
Simple and Safe Experiments, by William R. Wellnitz (n.p., 1990). Reviewed in: *Science and Children* 29, no. 6 (Mar. 1992): 55

Wexler, Jerome
   Pet Gerbils, by Jerome Wexler (Morton Grove, IL: Albert Whitman, 1990). Reviewed in: *Science and Children* 29, no. 6 (Mar. 1992): 55

What If?
   by Robert G. Fuller (New York: Wilson Learning, 1989). Reviewed in: *Physics Teacher* 28, no. 5 (May 1990): 349

Whitfield, Philip and Ruth
   Why Do Bodies Stop Growing?, by Philip Whitfield and Ruth Whitfield (New York: Viking Penguin, 1988). Reviewed in: *School Science and Mathematics* 90, no. 7 (Nov. 1988): 656

Who Lives Here?
   video (Washington, DC: National Geographic Society, 1990). Reviewed in: *American Biology Teacher* 52, no. 7 (Oct. 1990): 443

Why Do Bodies Stop Growing?
   by Philip Whitfield and Ruth Whitfield (New York: Viking Penguin, 1988). Reviewed in: *School Science and Mathematics* 90, no. 7 (Nov. 1988): 656

Wild Wings
   by Phyllis Emert (n.p.: Julian Messner, 1990). Reviewed in: *Science and Children* 29, no. 5 (Feb. 1992): 48

Wildlife at Risk
   by Malcom Penny (n.p.: Bookright, 1990). Reviewed in: *Science and Children* 29, no. 4 (Jan. 1992): 39 Mathematics 90, no. 7 (Nov. 1988): 656

Wilson Learning
   What If?, by Robert G. Fuller (New York: Wilson Learning, 1989). Reviewed in: *Physics Teacher* 28, no. 5 (May 1990): 349

Wings for Learning
   Physics Explorer: One Body, software (Scotts Valley, CA: Wings for Learning, 1991). Reviewed in: *Technology & Learning* 12, no. 4 (Jan. 1992): 10, 11, 14

   3–2–1 Contact: Wild Things, software by The Children's Television Workshop (Scott's Valley,

CA: Wings for Learning, 1991). Reviewed in: *Teaching with Technology* (Feb. 1992): 59

Woolly Bounce
   software (Minneapolis: MECC, 1991). Reviewed in: *Science and Children* 29, no. 4 (Jan. 1992): 34, *Technology & Learning* 12, no. 4 (Jan. 1992): 8-9

World Population
   video (Washington, DC: ZPG Population Education Program, 1990). Reviewed in: *The American Biology Teacher* 53, no. 3 (Mar. 1991): 189

The World's Harvest Series
   by Jaqueline Dineen (Hillsdale, NJ: Enslow, 1988). Reviewed in: *American Biology Teacher* 52, no. 4 (Apr. 1990): 317

Worsley, Dale
   The Art of Science Writing, by Bernadette Mayer and Dale Worsley (New York: Teachers and Writers Collaborative, 1989). Reviewed in: *American Biology Teacher* 52, no. 3 (Mar. 1990): 192

Xiphias (publishers)
   Time Table History, software (Los Angeles: Xiphias, 1987). Reviewed in: *Science and Children* 29, no. 2 (Oct. 1992): 47

Young, Jane
   100 Science Puzzles, by Colin McCarty and Jane Young (London: Unwin Hyman, 1989). Reviewed in: *Physics Education* 25, no. 5 (Sept. 1990): 293

Zoology
   The Animal Life Series, film/video (Van Nuys, CA: AIMS Media Film and Video, 1991). Reviewed in: *Media and Methods* 28, no. 1 (Sept./Oct. 1991): 46

   Animals and Their World, by Judith E. Rinard, Gene S. Stuart, and Jennifer C. Urquhart (Washington, DC: National Geographic Society, 1990). Reviewed in: *Science and Children* 29, no. 5 (Feb. 1992): 48

   Animals in Danger, by William McCay (New York: Aladdin, 1990). Reviewed in: *Science and Children* 29, no. 4 (Jan. 1992): 39

Zoology *(cont'd)*

Animals in the Classroom, by David C. Kramer (Menlo Park, CA: Addison-Wesley Publishing, 1989). Reviewed in: *School Science and Mathematics* 90, no. 3 (Mar. 1990): 261

Jungle Safari, software (Pound Ridge, NY: Orange Cherry/Talking School House Software, 1990). Reviewed in: *Science and Children* 29, no. 4 (Jan. 1992): 35

Life Cycles, software (Galesburg, MI: MCE, n.d.). Reviewed in: *Science and Children* 29, no. 1 (Sept. 1991): 58–59

Life Science, software (Ramsey, NJ: K–12 Micromedia, 1991). Reviewed in: *Methods and Media* 28 no. 4 (Mar./Apr. 1992): 60

Life Science Help Series, software (Garden City, NY: Focus Media, n.d.). Reviewed in: *Science and Children* 27, no. 7 (Apr. 1990): 44

Life's Devices: The Physical World of Plants and Animals, by Steven Vogel (Princeton: Princeton University Press, 1989). Reviewed in: *American Biology Teacher* 52, no. 6 (Sept. 1990): 388

Pet Gerbils, by Jerome Wexler (Morton Grove, IL: Albert Whitman, 1990). Reviewed in: *Science and Children* 29, no. 6 (Mar. 1992): 55

Project Zoo, software (Washington DC: National Geographic Society, 1987). Reviewed in: *School Science and Mathematics* 90, no. 6 (Nov. 1990): 652

Ready Set Go: How Animals Move, filmstrip (Washington, DC: National Geographic Society, 1989). Reviewed in: *American Biology Teacher* 52, no. 8 (Nov./Dec. 1990): 514

3–2–1 Contact: Wild Things, software by The Children's Television Workshop (Scott's Valley, CA: Wings for Learning, 1991). Reviewed in: *Teaching with Technology* (Feb. 1992): 59

Wildlife at Risk, by Malcom Penny (n.p.: Bookright, 1990). Reviewed in: *Science and Children* 29, no. 4 (Jan. 1992): 39

ZPG Population Education Program

World Population, video (Washington, DC: ZPG Population Education Program, 1990). Reviewed in: *The American Biology Teacher* 53, no. 3 (Mar. 1991): 189

KRAUS CURRICULUM DEVELOPMENT LIBRARY CUSTOMERS

T HE following list shows the current subscribers to the Kraus Curriculum Development Library (KCDL), Kraus's annual program of curriculum guides on microfiche. Customers marked with an asterisk (*) do not currently have standing orders to KCDL, but do have recent editions of the program. This information is provided for readers who want to use KCDL for models of curriculum in particular subject areas or grade levels.

Alabama

Auburn University
Ralph Brown Draughton Library/Serials
Mell Street
Auburn University, AL 36849

Jacksonville State University
Houston Cole Library/Serials
Jacksonville, AL 36265

University of Alabama at Birmingham
Mervyn H. Sterne Library
University Station
Birmingham, AL 35294

*University of Alabama at Tuscaloosa
University Libraries
204 Capstone Drive
Tuscaloosa, AL 35487-0266

Alaska

*University of Alaska—Anchorage
Library
3211 Providence Drive
Anchorage, AK 99508

Arizona

Arizona State University, Phoenix
Fletcher Library/Journals
West Campus
4701 West Thunderbird Road
Phoenix, AZ 85069-7100

Arizona State University, Tempe
Library/Serials
Tempe, AZ 85287-0106

Northern Arizona University
University Library
Flagstaff, AZ 86011

University of Arizona
Library/Serials
Tucson, AZ 85721

Arkansas

Arkansas State University
Dean B. Ellis Library
State University, AR 72467

Southern Arkansas University
The Curriculum Center
SAU Box 1389
Magnolia, AR 71753

University of Central Arkansas
The Center for Teaching & Human Development
Box H, Room 104
Conway, AR 72032

California

California Polytechnic State University
Library/Serials
San Luis Obispo, CA 93407

California State Polytechnic University
Library/Serials
3801 West Temple Avenue
Pomona, CA 91768

California State University at Chico
Meriam Library
Chico, CA 95929-0295

*California State University, Dominguez Hills
Library
800 East Victoria Street
Carson, CA 90747

California State University at Fresno
Henry Madden Library/Curriculum Department
Fresno, CA 93740

California State University at Fresno
College of the Sequoia Center
5241 North Maple, Mail Stop 106
Fresno, CA 93740

California State University at Fullerton
Library Serials BIC
Fullerton, CA 92634

California State University at Long Beach
Library/Serials Department
1250 Bellflower Boulevard
Long Beach, CA 90840

*California State University at Sacramento
Library
2000 Jed Smith Drive
Sacramento, CA 95819

California State University, Stanislaus
Library
801 West Monte Vista Avenue
Turlock, CA 95380

*La Sierra University
Library
Riverside, CA 92515

Los Angeles County Education Center
Professional Reference Center
9300 East Imperial Highway
Downey, CA 90242

National University
Library
4007 Camino del Rio South
San Diego, CA 92108

San Diego County Office of Education
Research and Reference Center
6401 Linda Vista Road
San Diego, CA 92111-7399

San Diego State University
Library/Serials
San Diego, CA 92182-0511

*San Francisco State University
J. Paul Leonard Library
1630 Holloway Avenue
San Francisco, CA 94132

San Jose State University
Clark Library, Media Department
San Jose, CA 95192-0028

*Stanford University
Cubberly Library
School of Education
Stanford, CA 94305

*University of California at Santa Cruz
Library
Santa Cruz, CA 95064

Colorado

Adams State College
Library
Alamosa, CO 81102

University of Northern Colorado
Michener Library
Greeley, CO 80639

Connecticut

*Central Connecticut State University
Burritt Library
1615 Stanley Street
New Britain, CT 06050

District of Columbia

The American University
Library
Washington, DC 20016-8046

*United States Department of Education/OERI
Room 101
555 New Jersey Avenue, N.W., C.P.
Washington, DC 20202-5731

*University of the District of Columbia
Learning Resource Center
11100 Harvard Street, N.W.
Washington, DC 20009

Florida

*Florida Atlantic University
Library/Serials
Boca Raton, FL 33431-0992

Florida International University
Library/Serials
Bay Vista Campus
North Miami, FL 33181

Florida International University
Library/Serials
University Park
Miami, FL 33199

Marion County School Board
Professional Library
406 S.E. Alvarez Avenue
Ocala, FL 32671-2285

*University of Central Florida
Library
Orlando, FL 32816-0666

University of Florida
Smathers Library/Serials
Gainesville, FL 32611-2047

*University of North Florida
Library
4567 St. John's Bluff Road South
Jacksonville, FL 32216

*University of South Florida
Library/University Media Center
4202 Fowler Avenue
Tampa, FL 33620

University of West Florida
John C. Pace Library/Serials
11000 University Parkway
Pensacola, FL 32514

Georgia

*Albany State College
Margaret Rood Hazard Library
Albany, GA 31705

Atlanta University Center in Georgia
Robert W. Woodruff Library
111 James P. Brawley Drive
Atlanta, GA 30314

*Columbus College
Library
Algonquin Drive
Columbus, GA 31993

Kennesaw College
TRAC
3455 Frey Drive
Kennesaw, GA 30144

University of Georgia
Main Library
Athens, GA 30602

Guam

*University of Guam
Curriculum Resources Center
College of Education
UOG Station
Mangilao, GU 96923

Idaho

*Boise State University
Curriculum Resource Center
1910 University Drive
Boise, ID 83725

Illinois

Community Consolidated School District 15
Educational Service Center
505 South Quentin Road
Palatine, IL 60067

Illinois State University
Milner Library/Periodicals
Normal, IL 61761

Loyola University
Instructional Materials Library
Lewis Towers Library
820 North Michigan Avenue
Chicago, Illinois 60611

National–Louis University
Library/Technical Services
2840 North Sheridan Road
Evanston, IL 60201

Northeastern Illinois University
Library/Serials
5500 North St. Louis Avenue
Chicago, IL 60625

*Northern Illinois University
Founders Memorial Library
DeKalb, IL 60115

Southern Illinois University
Lovejoy Library/Periodicals
Edwardsville, IL 62026

*University of Illinois at Chicago
Library/Serials
Box 8198
Chicago, IL 60680

University of Illinois at Urbana–Champaign
246 Library
1408 West Gregory Drive
Urbana, IL 61801

Indiana

Indiana State University
Cunningham Memorial Library
Terre Haute, IN 47809

Indiana University
Library/Serials
Bloomington, IN 47405-1801

Kentucky

Cumberland College
Instructional Media Library
Williamsburg, KY 40769

*Jefferson County Public Schools
The Greens Professional Development Academy
4425 Preston Highway
Louisville, KY 40213

Maine

University of Maine
Raymond H. Fogler Library/Serials
Orono, ME 04469

Maryland

*Bowie State University
Library
Jericho Park Road
Bowie, MD 20715

Western Maryland College
Hoover Library
2 College Hill
Westminster, MD 21157

Massachusetts

*Barnstable Public Schools
230 South Street
Hyannis, MA 02601

Boston College
Educational Resource Center
Campion Hall G13
Chestnut Hill, MA 02167

Framingham State College
Curriculum Library
Henry Whittemore Library
Box 2000
Framingham, MA 01701

Harvard University
School of Education
Monroe C. Gutman Library
6 Appian Way
Cambridge, MA 02138

*Lesley College
Library
30 Mellen Street
Cambridge, MA 02138

*Salem State College
Professional Studies Resource Center
Library
Lafayette Street
Salem, MA 01970

Tufts University
Wessell Library
Medford, MA 02155-5816

*University of Lowell
O'Leary Library
Wilder Street
Lowell, MA 01854

*Worcester State College
Learning Resource Center
486 Chandler Street
Worcester, MA 01602

Michigan

*Grand Valley State University
Library
Allendale, MI 49401

*Wayne County Regional Educational Services
    Agency
Technical Services
5454 Venoy
Wayne, MI 48184

Wayne State University
Purdy Library
Detroit, MI 48202

*Western Michigan University
Dwight B. Waldo Library
Kalamazoo, MI 49008

Minnesota

Mankato State University
Memorial Library
Educational Resource Center
Mankato, MN 56002-8400

Moorhead State University
Library
Moorhead, MN 56563

University of Minnesota
170 Wilson Library/Serials
309 19th Avenue South
Minneapolis, MN 55455

Winona State University
Maxwell Library/Curriculum Laboratory
Sanborn and Johnson Streets
Winona, MN 55987

Mississippi

Mississippi State University
Mitchell Memorial Library
Mississippi State, MS 39762

University of Southern Mississippi
Cook Memorial Library/Serials
Box 5053
Hattiesburg, MS 39406-5053

Missouri

Central Missouri State University
Ward Edwards Library
Warrensburg, MO 64093-5020

Missouri Southern State College
George A. Spiva Library
3950 Newman Road
Joplin, MO 64801-1595

Northeast Missouri State University
Pickler Library/Serials
Kirksville, MO 63501

Southwest Baptist University
ESTEP Library
Bolivar, MO 65613-2496

Southwest Missouri State University
#175 Library
Springfield, MO 65804-0095

*University of Missouri at Kansas City
Instructional Materials Center
School of Education
5100 Rockhill Road
Kansas City, MO 64110-2499

University of Missouri at St. Louis
Library
St. Louis, MO 63121

Webster University
Library
470 East Lockwood Avenue
St. Louis, MO 63119-3194

Nebraska

Chadron State College
Library
10th and Main Streets
Chadron, NE 69337

University of Nebraska
University Libraries
Lincoln, NE 68588

University of Nebraska at Kearney
Calvin T. Ryan Library/Serials
Kearney, NE 68849-0700

*University of Nebraska at Omaha
Education Technology Center/Instructional
 Material
Kayser Hall, Room 522
Omaha, NE 68182-0169

Nevada

*University of Nevada, Las Vegas
Materials Center—101 Education
Las Vegas, NV 89154

*University of Nevada, Reno
Library (322)
Reno, NV 89557-0044

New Hampshire

Plymouth State College
Herbert H. Lamson Library
Plymouth, NH 03264

New Jersey

Caldwell College
Library
9 Ryerson Avenue
Caldwell, NJ 07006

Georgian Court College
Farley Memorial Library
Lakewood, NJ 08701

Jersey City State College
Forrest A. Irwin Library
2039 Kennedy Boulevard
Jersey City, NJ 07305

*Kean College of New Jersey
Library
Union, NJ 07083

Paterson Board of Education
Media Center
823 East 28th Street
Paterson, NJ 07513

*Rutgers University
Alexander Library/Serials
New Brunswick, NJ 08903

St. Peter's College
George F. Johnson Library
Kennedy Boulevard
Jersey City, NJ 07306

Trenton State College
West Library
Pennington Road CN4700
Trenton, NJ 08650-4700

William Paterson College
Library
300 Pompton Road
Wayne, NJ 07470

New Mexico

University of New Mexico
General Library/Serials
Albuquerque, NM 87131

New York

*BOCES–REPIC
Carle Place Center Concourse
234 Glen Cove Road
Carle Place, NY 11514

*Canisius College
Curriculum Materials Center
Library
2001 Main Street
Buffalo, NY 14208

Fordham University
Duane Library
Bronx, NY 10458

Hofstra University
Library
1000 Hempstead Turnpike
Hempstead, NY 11550

*Hunter College
Library
695 Park Avenue
New York, NY 10021

*Lehman College
Library/Serials
Bedford Park Boulevard West
Bronx, NY 10468

*New York University
Bobst Library
70 Washington Square South
New York, NY 10012

*Niagara University
Library/Serials
Niagara, NY 14109

Queens College
Benjamin Rosenthal Library
Flushing, NY 11367

St. John's University
Library
Grand Central and Utopia Parkways
Jamaica, NY 11439

State University of New York at Albany
University Library/Serials
1400 Washington Avenue
Albany, NY 12222

State University of New York, College at Buffalo
E. H. Butler Library
1300 Elmwood Avenue
Buffalo, NY 14222

State University of New York, College at
    Cortland
Teaching Materials Center
Cortland, NY 13045

State University of New York, College at
    Oneonta
James M. Milne Library
Oneonta, NY 13820

Teachers College of Columbia University
Millbank Memorial Library/Serials
525 West 120th Street
New York, NY 10027

North Carolina

*Appalachian State University
Instructional Materials Center
Belk Library
Boone, NC 28608

Charlotte–Mecklenburg Schools
Curriculum Resource Center
Staff Development Center
428 West Boulevard
Charlotte, NC 28203

*East Carolina University
Joyner Library
Greenville, NC 27858-4353

North Carolina A&T State University
F. D. Bluford Library
Greeensboro, NC 27411

North Carolina State University
D. H. Hill Library
Box 7111
Raleigh, NC 27695-7111

University of North Carolina at Chapel Hill
Davis Library/Serials
Campus Box 3938
Chapel Hill, NC 27599-3938

University of North Carolina at Charlotte
Atkins Library
UNCC Station
Charlotte, NC 28223

University of North Carolina at Wilmington
William M. Randall Library
601 South College Road
Wilmington, NC 28403-3297

Ohio

Bowling Green State University
Curriculum Center
Jerome Library
Bowling Green, OH 43403-0177

Miami University
Library
Oxford, OH 45056

*Ohio State University
2009 Millikin Road
Columbus, OH 43210

University of Akron
Bierce Library/Serials
Akron, OH 44325

*University of Rio Grande
Davis Library
Rio Grande, OH 45674

*Wright State University
Educational Resource Center
Dayton, OH 45435

Oklahoma

Southwestern Oklahoma State University
Al Harris Library
809 North Custer Street
Weatherford, OK 73096

*University of Tulsa
McFarlin Library
600 South College
Tulsa, OK 74104

Oregon

Oregon State University
Kerr Library/Serials
Corvallis, OR 97331-4503

Portland State University
Library/Serials
Portland, OR 97207

University of Oregon
Knight Library/Serials
Eugene, OR 97403

Pennsylvania

*Bucks County Intermediate Unit #22
705 Shady Retreat Road
Doylestown, PA 18901

*Cheyney University
Library
Cheyney, PA 19319

East Stroudsburg University of Pennsylvania
Library
East Stroudsburg, PA 18301

Holy Family College
Grant and Frankford Avenues
Philadelphia, PA 19114

*Indiana University of Pennsylvania
Media Resource Department
Stapleton Library
Indiana, PA 15705

Kutztown University
Curriculum Materials Center
Rohrbach Library
Kutztown, PA 19530

La Salle College
Instructional Materials Center
The Connelly Library
Olney Avenue at 20th Street
Philadelphia, PA 19141

Lock Haven University of Pennsylvania
Library
Lock Haven, PA 17745

*Millersville University
Ganser Library
Millersville, PA 17551-0302

*Pennsylvania State University
Pattee Library/Serials
University Park, PA 16802

*Shippensburg University of Pennsylvania
Ezra Lehman Library
Shippensburg, PA 17257-2299

*Slippery Rock University
Bailey Library
Instructional Materials Center
Slippery Rock, PA 16057

University of Pittsburgh
Hillman Library/Serials
Pittsburgh, PA 15260

West Chester University
Francis H. Green Library
West Chester, PA 19383

Rhode Island

Rhode Island College
Curriculum Resources Center
600 Mt. Pleasant Avenue
Providence, RI 02908

South Dakota

Northern State University
Williams Library
Aberdeen, SD 57401

University of South Dakota
I. D. Weeks Library
414 East Clark
Vermillion, SD 57069

Tennessee

Tennessee Technological University
Library
Cookeville, TN 38505

Trevecca Nazarene College
Curriculum Library
Mackey Library
333 Murfreesboro Road
Nashville, TN 37210-2877

*University of Tennessee at Chattanooga
Library/Serials
Chattanooga, TN 37403

*University of Tennessee at Martin
Instructional Improvement
Gooch Hall—Room 217
Martin, TN 38238

*Vanderbilt University
Curriculum Laboratory
Peabody Library
Peabody Campus, Magnolia Circle
Nashville, TN 37203-5601

Texas

Baylor University
School of Education
Waco, TX 76798-7314

East Texas State University
Curriculum Library
Commerce, TX 75429

*East Texas State University
Library
Texarkana, TX 75501

*Houston Baptist University
Moody Library
7502 Fondren Road
Houston, TX 77074

*Incarnate Word College
Library
4301 Broadway
San Antonio, TX 78209

*Sam Houston State University
Library
Huntsville, TX 77341

*Southern Methodist University
Fondren Library
Dallas, TX 75275-0135

Stephen F. Austin State University
Library/Serials
Box 13055 SFA Station
Nacogdoches, TX 75962

Texas A&M University
Library/Serials
College Station, TX 77843-5000

*Texas Tech University
Library
Lubbock, TX 79409

Texas Woman's University
Library
Box 23715 TWU Station
Denton, TX 76204

University of Houston—University Park
University of Houston Library
Central Serial
4800 Calhoun
Houston, TX 77004

University of North Texas
Library
Denton, TX 76203

University of Texas at Austin
General Libraries/Serials
Austin, TX 78713-7330

University of Texas at El Paso
Library
El Paso, TX 79968-0582

Utah

Utah State University
Educational Resources Center
College of Education
Logan, UT 84322-2845

Vermont

University of Vermont
Guy W. Bailey Library/Serials
Burlington, VT 05405

Virginia

Longwood College
Dabney Lancaster Library
Farmville, VA 23909-1897

*Regent University
Library
Virginia Beach, VA 23464-9877

University of Virginia
Alderman Library
Serials/Periodicals
Charlottesville, VA 22901

*Virginia Beach City Public Schools
Instruction and Curriculum
School Administration Building
2512 George Mason Drive
Virginia Beach, VA 23456

Washington

Central Washington University
Library/Serials
Ellensburg, WA 98926

University of Puget Sound
Collins Library
Tacoma, WA 98416

University of Washington
Library/Serials
Seattle, WA 98195

Washington State University
Library
Pullman, WA 99164-5610

Western Washington University
Wilson Library
Bellingham, WA 98225

Wisconsin

University of Wisconsin—Eau Claire
Instructional Media Center
Eau Claire, WI 54702-4004

University of Wisconsin—Madison
Instructional Materials Center
225 North Mills
Madison, Wisconsin 53706

University of Wisconsin—Oshkosh
F. R. Polk Library
Oshkosh, WI 54901

University of Wisconsin—Platteville
Library
One University Plaza
Platteville, WI 53818-3099

University of Wisconsin—Whitewater
Learning Resources
Whitewater, WI 53190

Wyoming

*University of Wyoming
Coe Library
15th and Lewis
Laramie, WY 82071

AUSTRALIA

Griffith University
Library
Mount Gravatt Campus
Nathan, Queensland 4111

CANADA

The Ontario Institute for Studies in Education
Library
252 Bloor Street West
Toronto, Ontario M5S 1V6

*University of New Brunswick
Harriet Irving Library/Serials
Fredericton, New Brunswick E3B 5H5

University of Regina
Library/Serials
Regina, Saskatchewan S4S 0A2

University of Saskatchewan
Library
Saskatoon, Saskatchewan S7N 0W0

University of Windsor
Leddy Library/Serials
Windsor, Ontario N9B 3P4

*Vancouver School Board
Teachers' Professional Library
123 East 6th Avenue
Vancouver, British Columbia V5T 1J6

HONG KONG

*The Chinese University of Hong Kong
University Library
Shatin, N.T.

THE NETHERLANDS

National Institute for Curriculum Development
(Stichting voor de Leerplanontwikkeling)
7500 CA Enschede

INDEX

AAAS. *See* American Association for the Advancement of Science

Accomodation, strategy, 26

Achievement tests
as indicators of curriculum quality, 56
in math and science, 34-35

Active learning, 127

Activities, curriculum guide feature, 51

Activity-based instruction, defined, 127

Activity sourcebooks, 225-26, 228-30

Adler, Mortimer, 5-6, 9

Adoption
curriculum, 54-55
textbook. *See* Textbook adoption

African-American students, and science education, 34-36

Alabama
KCDL customers, 363
state curriculum guide, 92-93
bibliographic information, 116
State Department of Education, 116
textbook adoption, 276-78

Alaska
KCDL customers, 363
state curriculum guide, 93-94
bibliographic information, 116
State Department of Education, 116

Aldridge, Bill, 83

"Alphabet soup" curriculum projects, 74-76

Alport, Jennifer, 160

America 2000 plan, 91

American Association for the Advancement of Science, **22**, 47, 50, 127
Project 2061, 22, 23, 50, 91, 94, 145

American Chemical Society, 22

American Forest Council, resources from, 20

American Geological Institute, The, 19

American Library Association, resources from, 240

Anatomy, textbooks adopted for, 278, 280, 284, 297, 299, 300, 301, 302, 307, 318

Anthropology, trade books, 246-47

Apple, Michael, 7, 10

Application phase, of learning cycle, 19

"Applied" science, defined, 18

Applying, process skill, 74

Appraisal: Science Books for Young People, 240

Aquatic environments, curriculum guide reprint, 149-220

Archeology, trade books, 246-47

Arizona
KCDL customers, 363
state curriculum guide, 94-95
bibliographic information, 117
State Department of Education, 117
textbook adoption, 278-80

Arkansas
KCDL customers, 364
state curriculum guide, 95-96
bibliographic information, 117
State Department of Education, 117
textbook adoption, 280-83

ASCD. *See* Association for Supervision and Curriculum Development

Assessment reforms, in science education, 36

Assimilation, strategy, 26

Association for Supervision and Curriculum Development, 51

Astronomy
resources for teaching, 230
textbooks adopted for, 280, 307, 313-14
trade books, 251-53

"Attitudes," development of positive, 72

"Back to basics" movement, 76-77
Bailey, Liberty Hyde, 17
Banks, James, 8
Basal instructional materials, 275
    physical science program, 298
    textbooks adopted for, 280
Basic Principles of Curriculum and Instruction (Tyler), 4
Beane, DeAnna Banks, 160
Behaviorist view, of learning, 26
Bennett, Willliam J., 160
Best Science Books and AV Materials for Children, The, 240
Bilingual programs, for Hispanic students, 35, 36, 78-79
Bilingual Science: An Integrated Approach, 79
Biography, trade books, 253-54
Biological Science, An Ecological Approach, 82
Biological Sciences Curriculum Study, 20, 36, 75-76, 79-80, 82
Biology (*see also* Life science)
    curriculum, 20, 75-76, 89
    resources for teaching, 129-45 *passim,* 229-30
    teaching of, 17
    textbooks adopted for, 277, 280-81, 284-85, 286, 289, 292-93, 294-95, 299-300, 300-301, 302-3, 306, 309, 312, 314-15, 315-16, 319, 320, 323
        advanced placement, 295, 300, 314-15
    topics, 48, 49, 77, 89
Bioscience videodiscs, 34
"Black box," human mind as, 26
Bloom, Benjamin, 26
Blosser, Patricia E., 161
Bobbitt, Franklin, 3-4
Botany, textbooks adopted for, 278, 301
Boys, and science education, 35
Bredderman, Ted, 160
BSCS. *See* Biological Sciences Curriculum Study
Budgeting, for curriculum process, 45-46
Bulletin boards, electronic, 34

CAI. *See* Computer-assisted instruction
California
    integrated-subjects curriculum framework, 84
    KCDL customers, 364-65
    state curriculum guide, 96-97
        bibliographic information, 117
    State Department of Education, 117
    textbook adoption, 275
California State Environmental Education Guide, 78
Canada, KCDL customers, 372
Career, choosing a science, 18, 21
Categorizing, process skill, 73
CEPUP. *See* Chemical Education for Public Understanding Program
Challenge factor, in motivation, 30
ChemCom. See *Chemistry in the Community*
Chemical Education for Public Understanding Program, 22, 81, 231-32
Chemical Education Material Study, 20, 76
Chemistry
    curriculum, 20, 82, 89
    resources for teaching, 129-45 *passim,* 230, 231
    teaching of, 17
    textbooks adopted for, 277-78, 281, 285, 286, 289-90, 293-94, 296-97, 298, 301, 303, 306-7, 310, 312-13, 315, 316, 319-20, 321, 323-24
        advanced placement, 297, 298, 315
    topics, 48, 49, 77
Chemistry in the Community, 22, 82
CHEM Study. See *Chemical Education Material Study*
Chiappetta, E.L., 18
Children (*see also* Students)
    and gender inequities in science teaching, 35-36
    misconceptions about science, 29
    as natural scientists, 26
    stage of development and curriculum, 6, 9, 26
    study of interests, 31
trade books for, in science, 239-54
Classifying, process skill, 163, 168, 174, 208
CLASS Project, 20, 82
Classrooms, use of computers in, 9-10
Cognitive pluralism, 8-9, 11
    recommended reading on, 13
    and use of computers in classroom, 10
Cognitive psychologists, 23-24
Cognitive science, and constructivism, 26-31, 37
Cognitive style, defined, 35
Cognitive understanding, 10
Collette, A.T., 18
Colorado
    KCDL customers, 365
    State Department of Education, 117
    statewide curriculum (mentioned), 117
Columbia University
    Horace Mann Laboratory School, 17
    Teachers College, 3
Committee, forming a curriculum, 45
Committee of Fifteen, 3
Committee of Ten, 2, 3, 5, 17
Common sense, view of natural phenomena, 28
Communicating, process skill, 73, 163, 168, 184, 188, 192, 200, 204, 208, 216
Comparing, process skill, 73
Competencies, curriculum guide feature, 51
Competitions, sourcebooks on science, 235
Computer-assisted instruction, 33

Computers
    and science teaching, 33-34, 127
    use in classrooms, 9-10
Conceptually Oriented Program in Elementary Science,
        75
Conceptual Physics, 82-83
Connecticut
    KCDL customers, 365
    state curriculum guide, 97, 147
        bibliographic information, 117
    State Department of Education, 117
Constitution, U.S., state responsibility for education,
        46
Constructivism, 24
    and cognitive science, 26-31
    and curriculum, 78, 82
Consumer science, textbooks adopted for, 298
Content Core, The: A Guide for Curriculum Designers
        (NSTA), 23, 47-49, 83-84
Contract approaches, to organization, 31
Control factor, in motivation, 30-31
Cooperative learning, 31-33, 127
*COPES. See Conceptually Oriented Program in
        Elementary Science*
Cornell School Leaflets, 17
Council for Elementary Science International,
        resources from, 221 Craig, Gerald, 17
Critical theory, 7-8, 11
    recommended reading on, 12
    and use of computers in classrooms, 10
Cultural inequities, in science teaching, 34-36
Curiosity factor, in motivation, 31
Curricularist, 1
Curriculum (*see also* Science curriculum)
    committee, 45
    definition of, 1
    development. *See* Curriculum development
    funding for projects, 61-71
    glossary of common usages, 13
    ideologies, 5-11
        recommended reading, 12-13
    interdisciplinary, 52
    materials, 127-28
    nineteenth century, 2
    thematic, 52
Curriculum, The (Bobbitt), 3
*Curriculum and Evaluation Standards for School
        Mathematics,* 23
Curriculum development
    funding for projects, 61-71
    interdisciplinary school-based, 127
    local, 42-43
    philosophies and history of, 1-15
    resources, 128, 147-48, 221-38
"Curriculum discoverers," 3-4
Curriculum guides
    74-84 (*see also* State curriculum guides)
    defined, 128
    features, 50-52
    process and design of, 42-59

recommended, 126-48
Curriculum maps, curriculum feature, 51
Curriculum theorist, 1
Curriculum theory, origin of term, 3

Delaware
    state curriculum guide, 97-98
        bibliographic information, 117
    State Department of Public Information, 117
Delivered curriculum, defined, 13
Department of Education, U.S., 128, 129
Departments of education, state, 91
        addresses and phone numbers, 116-25
        (*see also under specific states*)
Designs, curriculum guide, 50-52
Developmentalism, 2, 6, 11
    recommended reading on, 12
    and use of computers in the classroom, 9
Dewey, John, 6
Directorate in Science Education, 18
Dissemination, of curriculum guide, 54
District of Columbia
    curriculum guide, 98
    KCDL customers, 365
Domains, of science education, 24-26, 36, 37
Duckworth, Eleanor, 6, 9

Earth Day, 20
Earth science
    resources for teaching, 129-45 *passim,* 230-31
    teaching of, 17, 91-92
    textbooks adopted for, 276, 278, 279, 281, 283, 286-
        87, 288, 290, 291-92, 296, 297, 297-98, 301,
        304, 307, 308-9, 311, 313, 316-17, 318, 321,
        322
    topics, 48-49, 76, 89
Earth Science Curriculum Project, 19, 76
Easley, J.A., 21
Ecology. *See* Environmental science
Editing, a curriculum guide, 53-54
Education
    mathematics, 23
    science
        assessment reforms, 36
        "back to basics" movement, 76-77
        critique, 21

eras, 16-24, 74-84
    gender and cultural inequities, 34-36
    reform movements, 18-24, 74-76, 77-84
    state responsibility for, 46
"Educational engineers," 3-4
Educational Resources Information Center (ERIC), 128-29
"Education for being," 7
"Education for having," 7
Eisner, Elliot, 5, 8, 10
Electronic bulletin boards, 34
Elementary science, textbooks adopted for, 276, 287, 294, 303, 311, 318, 321, 322
Elementary Science Study, 18-19, 75, 160, 226-27
Eliot, Charles W., 2, 5
Enacted curriculum, defined, 13
Environmental science
    curriculum, 82
    curriculum guide reprint, 149-220
    devlopment of, 20-21
    resources for teaching, 129-45 *passim,* 223-25
    textbooks adopted for, 277, 281, 285, 290, 299, 300, 302, 303-4, 307, 310, 314, 317, 320
    trade books, 243-46
ERIC. *See* Educational Resources Information Center
ESCP. *See Earth Science Curriculum Project*
ESS. *See Elementary Science Study*
"Essential Changes in Secondary School Science: Scope, Sequence and Coordination," 83
Ethnicity. *See* Minorities; Multiculturalism
Evaluation
    curriculum guide feature, 51
    of curriculum guides, 56
        sample, 57, 152
Experience, learning through, 6-7
Experience curriculum, defined, 13
Experimenting, process skill, 163, 168, 184, 192, 204, 208, 216
Explicit curriculum, defined, 13
Exploration phase, of learning cycle, 19
Extrinsic motivation, 30
Eyeopeners!, 240

Fairs, sourcebooks on science, 235
Fantasy, and constructivist learning, 31
FAST. See Foundational Approaches in Science Teaching
Federal government
    America 2000, 91
    funding programs for school projects, 62-63
"Field independent," versus "field dependent," 35

Field testing, of new curriculum guide, 53
Finding Out/Descubrimiento, 78
Five Domains of Science Education, 24-26, 36, 37
Florida
    KCDL customers, 365
    state curriculum guide, 98
        bibliographic information, 118
    State Department of Education, 118
    textbook adoption, 283-85
FOSS. See Full-Option Science System
Foundational Approaches in Science Teaching, 81-82, 134
Foundation Center Libraries, locations, 61
Foundations
    funding science education projects, 63-64
    providing funds for education projects, 64-71
Frameworks. *See* State curriculum guides
Frankfurt school. *See* Institute for Social Research
Fresno Unified School District, curriculum guide, 79, 86
Full-Option Science System, 78, 80, 130
Funding, for curriculum projects, 61-71

Gagné, Robert, 26
Gardner, Howard, 8-9
Gender, inequities in science teaching, 34-36
General science
    activity sourcebooks, 228-30
    resources for teaching, 221-23
    teaching of, 17
    textbooks adopted for, 277, 278, 279, 282, 283, 291, 292, 300, 304-5, 306, 308, 312, 314, 315, 323
Geology, textbooks adopted for, 298, 305, 307, 320
Georgia
    KCDL customers, 365-66
    state curriculum guide, 98-99
        bibliographic information, 118
    State Department of Education, 118
    textbook adoption, 286-88
Getting Started in Science: A Blueprint for Elementary School Science Education, 36
"G factor," 8
Girls, and science education, 35
Global Science, 79
Glossary, common types of curriculum, 13
Government. *See* Federal government
Grants. *See* Funding
Great Books of the Western World, The (Hutchins and Adler), 5
Greene, Maxine, 7
Grumet, Madeleine, 7, 9

Hall, G. Stanley, 2
"Hands-on" approach
    assessment, 228
    and informal texts, 239
    to science education, 17, 18, 160-62, 163
    testing, 36
Hawaii
    Department of Education, 118
    statewide curriculum (mentioned), 118
Health science, trade books, 247-48
Hidden curriculum, defined, 13
Hispanic students
    bilingual programs for, 78-79
    and science education, 34-36
Horace Mann Laboratory School (Columbia University), 17
Humanism. *See* Rational humanism
Human mind, and learning, 26-28
Hutchins, Robert Maynard, 5

Idaho
    KCDL customers, 366
    state curriculum guide, 99-100
        bibliographic information, 118
    State Department of Education, 118
    textbook adoption, 288-91
Ideologies
    curriculum, 5-11
        chart summary, 11
Illinois
    KCDL customers, 366
    State Board of Education, 118
    state curriculum guide, 100
        bibliographic information, 118
Implicit curriculum, defined, 13
Indiana
    KCDL customers, 366
    state curriculum guide, 100-101, 129, 137, 141
        bibliographic information, 119
    State Department of Education, 118
    textbook adoption, 291-94
Industrial efficiency, 17
Inert knowledge, problem of, 29
Inferring, process skill, 74, 163, 168, 184, 192, 200, 204, 208, 216
Inquiry, teaching science through, 127
Institute for Social Research, 7

Instructional materials, types, 275
Instructional strategies, curriculum guide feature, 51
Integrated science
    resources for teaching, 233
    textbooks adopted for, 295-96
Intelligence
    as changeable entity, 30
    single versus multiple, 8-9
    student views of, 29-30
Intended curriculum, defined, 13
Interaction Science Curriculum Project, 75
Interdisciplinary
    approach to science education, 78
    curriculum, 52, 127
    designs and school schedules, 52
Interests, of children, 31
Intermediate Science Curriculum Study, 75
Intrinsic motivation, 30
Introductory Physical Science, 19, 75
Invention phase, of learning cycle, 19
Inventors Workshop, 30
Investigating Gravitational Forces, 34
Iowa
    state curriculum guide, 101-2
        bibliographic information, 119
    State Department of Education, 119
IPS. See Introductory Physical Science
ISCS. See Intermediate Science Curriculum Study

Jackson, Philip, 3

Kansas
    State Department of Education, 119
    statewide curriculum (mentioned), 119
KCDL. *See* Kraus Curriculum Development Library
Kentucky
    KCDL customers, 366
    state curriculum guide, bibliographic information, 119
    State Department of Education, 119
    textbook adoption, 294-97
Key topics, in science, 47-50, 72-90
Kliebard, Herbert, 2-3
Knowledge
    inert, 29
    theories of, 26-29
Kobrin Letter, The, 240

Kraus Curriculum Development Library
curriculum models, 51
customers, 363-73
Kyle, William, Jr., 160

Laboratory work, 18
Lawrence Hall of Science, resources from, 78, 133, 226-27, 230, 231
"Layer cake" approach, to teaching science, 23
Learning
active, 127
cooperative, 31-33, 127
by discovery, 18
by experience, 6-7
by hands-on investigation, 18
by inquiry, 18, 23
and motivation, 29-31
Learning centers, 30-31
"Learning cycle," three phases of, 19
LEAs. *See* Local educational agencies
Lecture, value in science education, 17
Life science (*see also* Biology)
key topics, 49
resources for teaching, 129-45 *passim,* 223-25, 229-30
teaching of, 17, 91-92
textbooks adopted for, 276, 278, 279, 282, 283-84, 287, 288, 290, 291, 297, 299, 301-2, 305, 309, 311-12, 313, 317, 318, 321, 322
trade books, 240-43
Living in Water: An Aquatic Science Curriculum for Grades 4-6, 130-31
partial reprint, 149-220
Local educational agencies, 46
Locus of control, 35
Louisiana
state curriculum guide, 102-3
bibliographic information, 119
State Department of Education, 119

Macmillan/McGraw-Hill Science K-8, 80-81
Maieutic teaching, 5
Maine
KCDL customers, 366
State Department of Education, 119
statewide curriculum (mentioned), 119

Marine biology/marine science
curriculum guide reprint, 149-220
sample curriculum topics, 78
textbooks adopted for, 278, 285, 299, 308, 320
Marine Science Project: For Sea, 78
Maryland
KCDL customers, 366-67
state curriculum guide, 103-4
bibliographic information, 120
State Department of Education, 120
Massachusetts
KCDL customers, 367
State Department of Education, 120
statewide curriculum (mentioned), 120
Massachusetts Audubon Society, resources from, 223
Massachusetts Institute of Technology, 19
Materials, reviews of educational, 325-62
McCormack, A.J., 24, 30
Measuring, process skill, 163, 168, 184, 196, 200, 216
Mechling, Kenneth R., 161
Medical science, trade books, 247-48
Memorization
emphasis on, 16
and science teaching, 17
"Mental discipline," 2
Mesa, Arizona, science program, 81
Mexican-American students, in bilingual classrooms, 35, 36
Michigan
KCDL customers, 367
State Board of Education, 120
state curriculum guide, 104
bibliographic information, 120
Microbiology, textbooks adopted for, 302
Mind, human, and learning, 26-28
Minnesota
KCDL customers, 367
state curriculum guide, 104
bibliographic information, 120
State Department of Education, 120
Minorities, and inequities in science teaching, 34-36
(*see also* Multiculturalism)
Mission statement, defining the, 44
Mississippi
KCDL customers, 367
state curriculum guide, 104
bibliographic information, 120
State Department of Education, 120
textbook adoption, 297-300
Missouri
Department of Elementary and Secondary Education, 120
KCDL customers, 368
state curriculum guide, 104-5
bibliographic information, 120-21
Money. *See* Budgeting; Funding
Monitoring, curriculum implementation, 55-56
Montana
Office of Public Instruction, 121
state curriculum guide, bibliographic information, 121

Motivation, as impetus to learning, 29-31
Multiculturalism, 8, 11
    recommended reading on, 12
    and use of computers in the classroom, 10
Multiethnic ideology, 8
Multiple intelligence, 8-9
Museum of Science and Industry Basic List of Children's Science Books, The, 240
Mystery boxes, use of, 30

NAEP. *See* National Assessment of Educational Progress
National Academy of Sciences, 47, 84
National Aeronautics and Space Administration, resources from, 132, 133-34
National Aquarium in Baltimore, curriculum guide, 130, 149-220
National Assessment of Educational Progress, performance assessments, 36
National Center for Earth Science Education, program framework, 146
National Center for Improving Science Education, program frameworks, 146-47
National Commission on Excellence in Education, The, 21
National Committee on Science Education, Standards, and Assessment, 23, 47
National Council of Teachers of Mathematics, 23, 47, 84
National Council on Science and Technology Education, program framework, 145-46
National Education Association
    Committee of Fifteen, 3
    Committee of Ten, 2, 3, 5, 17
National Geographic Society, resources from, 134-35, 139, 140, 142
National Research Council, 23, 84
    resources from, 148
National Science Foundation
    curriculum projects, 74
funding for education projects, 62
    Directorate in Science Education, 18
    Project Synthesis, 21
National Science Resources Center, resources from, 148
National Science Teachers Association
    curriculum design (*The Content Core*), 23, 47-49, 83-84
    position statement, 22
    publications, 240
    resources from, 134, 135, 146, 222, 223, 224, 234, 236, 240

Scope, Sequence, and Coordination of Secondary Science project, 22-23, 37, 47, 83, 91
National standards, for curriculum, 47, 84
National Wildlife Federation, resources from, 20, 222, 230
Nation at Risk, A, 21
Nature-Study Movement, 17
NCISE Elementary Science Framework, 94
NCTM. *See* National Council of Teachers of Mathematics
NEA. *See* National Education Association
Nebraska
    KCDL customers, 368
    State Department of Education, 121
    statewide curriculum (mentioned), 121
Needs assessment, 56, 57
    performing, a, 44
Nevada
    KCDL customers, 368
    state curriculum guide, 105-6
        bibliographic information, 121
    State Department of Education, 121
    textbook adoption, 300-302
New Hampshire
    KCDL customers, 368
    state curriculum guide, bibliographic information, 121
    State Department of Education, 121
New Jersey
    Department of Education, 121
    KCDL customers, 368-69
    statewide curriculum (mentioned), 121
New Mexico
    KCDL customers, 369
    state curriculum guide, 106
        bibliographic information, 122
    State Department of Education, 122
    textbook adoption, 302-6
New York
    KCDL customers, 369
    state curriculum guide, 106-7
        bibliographic information, 122
    State Education Department, 122, 233-34
New York Zoological Society, resources from, 131, 135-36, 138
North Carolina
    Department of Public Instruction, 122
    KCDL customers, 370
    state curriculum guide, 107-8
        bibliographic information, 122
    textbook adoption, 306-8
North Dakota
    state curriculum guide, 108-10
        bibliographic information, 122
    State Department of Public Instruction, 122
NSF. *See* National Science Foundation
NSTA. *See* National Science Teachers Association
Null curriculum, defined, 13

Objectives, curriculum feature, 51
"Object teaching," 16-17
Observing, process skill, 73, 163, 168, 184, 188, 192, 196, 200, 204, 208
Oceanography
    resources for teaching, 231
    textbooks adopted for, 285
Official curriculum, defined, 13
Ohio
    KCDL customers, 370
    State Department of Education, 122
    statewide curriculum (mentioned), 123
Okey, James, 160-61
Oklahoma
    Department of Education, 123
    KCDL customers, 370
    state curriculum guide, 110
        bibliographic information, 123
    textbook adoption, 308-11
Oliver, Donna L., 161
Ontario Science Centre, resources from, 226
Operational curriculum, defined, 13
Ordering, process skill, 73
Oregon
    KCDL customers, 370
    state curriculum guide, 111
        bibliographic information, 123
    State Department of Education, 123
    textbook adoption, 311-13
Organizations
    funding science education projects, 63-64
    providing funds for education projects, 64-71
Organizing, process skill, 163, 168, 200, 216

Paideia Proposal, The (Adler), 5
    recommended reading on, 12
Paleontology, trade books, 246-47
PBO. *See* Planning by objectives
Pennsylvania
    Department of Education, 123
    KCDL customers, 370-71
    statewide curriculum (mentioned), 123
Pestalozzi, Johann, 16
Physical science
    resources for teaching, 129-45 *passim,* 230-31
    teaching of, 17, 91-92
    textbooks adopted for, 276-77, 278, 279, 282, 284,

288, 290-91, 292, 294, 296, 297, 297-98, 302, 305-6, 307, 310, 312, 314, 317-18, 319, 321, 323
    trade books, 248-51
Physical Science Study Committee, 19-20, 74, 76
Physics
    courses, 19-20, 82-83
    key topics, 49, 90
    resources for teaching, 129-45 *passim,* 231
    teaching of, 17
    textbooks adopted for, 278, 282-83, 285, 288, 291, 294, 297, 298-99, 301, 305, 307, 310-11, 313, 315, 318, 320, 321-22, 324
Physiology, textbooks adopted for, 278, 280, 284, 288, 291, 293, 297, 299, 301, 302, 307, 311, 318
Piaget, Jean, 6, 26
Pinar, William, 4-5, 7, 9
Plannng by objectives, 4
Predicting, process skill, 163, 168, 184, 188, 192, 208
Prereading, 7
Prior knowledge, of students, 26, 28-29, 30
Probes, coupled with computers, 34
Process skills, development of, 72, 73-74, 160, 163, 168-216 *passim*
Production, of curriculum guide, 54
Program frameworks, for curriculum guides, 128, 145-47
Project 2061, 22, 23, 50, 91, 94, 145
Project Learning Tree, 20, 141
Project Synthesis, 21
Project WET, 20
Project WILD, 20, 142
PSInet, 34
PSSC. *See* Physical Science Study Committee
Public input, and curriculum development, 53, 54
Publishers
    of curriculum materials and textbooks, 255-73
    and textbook adoption, 274-75
"Pure" science, defined, 18

Ratification, procedures for curriculum guide, 54
Rational humanism, 2, 5-6, 11
    recommended reading on, 12
    and use of computers in the classroom, 9
"Rational thinking processes," development of, 72
Rawls, John, 7
"Readiness for learning," 6
Received curriculum, defined, 13
Recommended reading, curriculum development, 12-13
Reconceptualism, 6-7
    recommended reading on, 12
    and use of computers in the classroom, 9-10

Reform movements, in science education, 18-24, 74-76, 77-84
Relating, process skill, 73
Renner, John W., 161
Resource books suppliers, 236-37
Resources
    curriculum guide feature, 51
    to enhance instruction, 221-38
Resources in Education, 129
Reviews, of educational materials, 325-62
Revision, of curriculum guides, 56-57
Revolutions, in science education, 18-24
Rhode Island
    Department of Education, 123
    KCDL customers, 371
    statewide curriculum (mentioned), 123
Rowe, Mary Budd, 160-61

SAPA. See *Science-A Process Approach*
Schools
    critique of American, 21, 22-23
    expressing curriculum ideologies, 10, 11
    as neutral institutions, 7
    schedules and interdisciplinary designs, 52
    and science leadership, 42
    use of computers, 9-10, 33
Schwab, Joseph, 9, 20
Science (*see also specific branches*)
    choosing a career in, 18, 21
    definition, 72
    interdependency of branches, 23
    key topics, 47-50, 72-90
    main areas of, 91-92
    trade books, 239-54
Science and Children, 240
Science and Technology for Children, 80
Science-A Process Approach, 18, 19, 74, 160
Science clubs, resources on, 235-36
Science curriculum
    "alphabet soup" projects, 74-76
    components of ideal, 72-74
    evolution of, 16-24
    guidelines, 116-25
        analysis, 91-115
    guides
        recommended, 126-48
        reprint, 149-220
    materials producers, 255-73
    and National Science Foundation, 18
    resources to support development, 221-38
    taxonomy blueprint, 24-26
    topics in, 47-50, 72-90
    trends and issues, 16-41

Science Curriculum Improvement Study, 18, 19, 74-75, 160, 161
Science events, resources on, 235-36
Science Fare; An Illustrated Guide and Catalog of Toys, Books, and Activities for Kids, 240
Science for All Americans, 22, 50
Science for Life and Living, 79-80
Science Report Card-Trends and Achievement, The, 49
Science Scope, 240
Science, Technology, and Society (STS), 21-22, 23, 79
Science/Technology/Society: Science Education for the 1980's, 22
Science through Children's Literature, 240
Science: Understanding Your Environment, 76
"Scientific knowledge," development of, 72-73
Scientific literacy, 19, 126-27
    dimensions of, 22
    improving, 42
    Project 2061 recommendations for, 50
Scientific management movement, 3
"Scientific process skills," development of, 72, 73-74, 160, 163, 168-216 *passim*
SCIS. See *Science Curriculum Improvement Study*
Scope, Sequence, and Coordination of Secondary Science (NSTA), 22-23, 37, 47, 83-84, 91
    models, 86-90
Shor, Ira, 7, 9
Shymansky, James, 160
Single intelligence, 8
Skills, curriculum guide feature, 51
Smithsonian Institution, resources from, 226
Socratic questioning, 5
Source Book Profiles, 61
South Carolina
    State Department of Education, 123
    statewide curriculum (mentioned), 123
    textbook adoption, 313-15
South Dakota
    Department of Education and Cultural Affairs, 123
    KCDL customers, 371
    state curriculum guide, 111
        bibliographic information, 123
Space science, 91-92
    key topics, 48-49
    SSC model curriculum, 89
    textbooks adopted for, 281, 283, 291-92, 296, 311, 321
    trade books, 251-53
Sputnik, 18
SS&C. See *Scope, Sequence, and Coordination of Secondary Science*
Staff development, for implementing curriculum, 55
Stake, R.E., 21
Standards
    for curriculum guides, 46-47
    national curriculum, 47, 84
    for science teaching, 23
State curriculum guides
    bibliographic information, 116-25
    guidelines analysis, 91-115

recommended, 126-48
reprint, 149-220
standards, 46-47
States (*see also under specific states*)
    control over education, 46, 91
    curriculum guides. *See* State curriculum guides
    departments of education (addresses and phone
        numbers), 116-25
    KCDL customers, 363-73
    textbook adoption, 274-324
Steiner, Rudolph, 9
Stockholm Declaration and Action Plan, 20
Story Stretchers, 240
STS. *See* Science, Technology, and Society
Student (*see also* Children)
    activities curriculum feature, 51
    bilingual programs, 78-79
    gender and cultural inequities in science teaching,
        34-36
    population analysis for curriculum guides, 52-53
    as questioners, 19
    textbook reading strategies, 29
    views of intelligence, 29-30
Subject information, curriculum guide feature, 51
Supervision, of curriculum implementation, 55-56
Supplemental science programs, 226-27
    resources for, 231-32
Supplementary materials
    for curriculum guides, 128, 140-45
    instructional, 275

"Taxonomy for Science Education," 24-26
Taylor, Frederick Winslow, 3
Teachers
    as cause for gender inequities in science teaching,
        35-36
    and cooperative learning, 32
    as curriculum designers, 42-43, 44
    and curriculum implementation, 55
    National Science Foundation training, 18
Teachers College (Columbia University), 3
Teaching
    as "associations" process, 26
    constructivist approach to science, 27-28
    gender and cultural inequities in science, 34-36
    "layer cake" approach to science, 23
    methods of science, 16-24, 31-34, 126-27
Technology
    resources on, 227-28
    and science teaching, 33-34
    sourcebooks, 233-35

trade books, 248-51
use to enhance instruction, 127
Tennessee
    KCDL customers, 371
    state curriculum guide, 111
        bibliographic information, 124
    State Department of Education, 124
    textbook adoption, 315-18
Testing
    curriculum guide feature, 51
    curriculum guide field, 53
Texas
    KCDL customers, 372
    state curriculum guide, 111-12
        bibliographic information, 124
    Texas Education Agency, 124
    textbook adoption, 318-20
Textbook adoption, 274-324
    adoption process, 274-75
    advisory committee, 274
    period of adoption, 275
Textbook period, in science education, 17-18
Textbooks
    authors as de facto curriculum specialists, 3
    domination of science curriculum, 76-77
    as force in curriculum development, 3, 42
    as inert knowledge, 29
    programs, 20
    social content requirements, 275
    use versus "hands-on" approach, 160
Thematic curriculum, 52, 77-78
    resources on, 227
Time, Space, and Matter, 75
Timetable, for curriculum process, 44-45
Trade books, recommended, 239-54
TSM. See Time, Space, and Matter
Tyler, Ralph, 4, 6

United Nations Conference on the Human Environ-
    ment, 20
University of California (Sacramento), guide collec-
    tion, 51
Urbanization, influence on schooling, 3
U.S. government. *See* Federal government
Utah
    KCDL customers, 372
    state curriculum guide, 112-13
        bibliographic information, 124
    State Office of Education, 124
Utilitarian period, in science education, 17-18

Vermont
    KCDL customers, 372
    state curriculum guide, 113-14
        bibliographic information, 124
    State Department of Education, 124
Videodisc technology, 34
Virginia
    Department of Education, 124
    KCDL customers, 372
    state curriculum guide, 114
        bibliographic information, 124
    textbook adoption, 320-22

Waldorf educators, 9
Walker, Decker, 4
Washington
    KCDL customers, 372
    state curriculum guide, 114
        bibliographic information, 124
    State Superintendent of Public Instruction, 124
Water, curriculum guide reprint, 149-220
Weather, resources for teaching, 231
Western Association of Fish and Wildlife Agencies, 20
Western Regional Environment Education Council, 20
Western Water Course, 20
West Virginia
    state curriculum guide, bibliographic information, 125
    State Department of Education, 124
    textbook adoption, 322-24

Williams, L.V., 31
Wisconsin
    KCDL customers, 372
    state curriculum guide, 114-15
        bibliographic information, 125
    State Department of Public Instruction, 125
Wise, Kevin C., 160
Wyoming
    KCDL customers, 372
    State Department of Education, 125
    statewide curriculum (mentioned), 125

Yager, R.E., 24
Young Astronaut Council, resources from, 236

Zoology, textbooks adopted for, 278, 283, 285, 293, 311